The
HUMAN ODYSSEY

The
HUMAN ODYSSEY

*Navigating
the Twelve Stages
of Life*

Thomas Armstrong, PhD

STERLING

New York / London
www.sterlingpublishing.com

STERLING and the distinctive Sterling logo are registered trademarks of
Sterling Publishing Co., Inc.

Published by Sterling Publishing Co., Inc.
387 Park Avenue South, New York, NY 10016

© 2007 by Thomas Armstrong

Distributed in Canada by Sterling Publishing
℅ Canadian Manda Group, 165 Dufferin Street
Toronto, Ontario, Canada M6K 3H6

Distributed in the United Kingdom by GMC Distribution Services
Castle Place, 166 High Street, Lewes, East Sussex, England BN7 1XU
Distributed in Australia by Capricorn Link (Australia) Pty. Ltd.
P.O. Box 704, Windsor, NSW 2756, Australia

Sterling ISBN-13: 978-1-4027-3996-5

Book design: Amy Henderson
Chapter illustrations: Scott McKowen

This book is dedicated to my mother,
Dorothy Beatrice Armstrong

Acknowledgments

I began conceiving of this project twenty-five years ago, in 1982, when I started to teach courses in childhood, adolescent, and adult development at several San Francisco Bay Area graduate schools of psychology. I'd like to thank the people at these institutions who gave me an opportunity to integrate a psychospiritual perspective into what might otherwise have been typical college courses on human development: David Surrenda and Bryan Wittine at John F. Kennedy University's School of Consciousness Studies, Ernest Pecci and Jon Klimo at Rosebridge Graduate School, and Arthur Hastings at the California Institute of Transpersonal Psychology (now the Institute of Transpersonal Psychology). I'd like to thank several administrators and faculty at the California Institute for Integral Studies (CIIS), where I received my PhD in East-West Psychology in 1986 (and also taught), for providing an inspiring, engaging, and encouraging learning atmosphere that was perfectly tailored to my needs as an independent learner and that helped lay some important foundations for this book: Bina Chadhuri, John Broomfield, Cathy Coleman, John Welwood, Tanya Wilkinson, Paul Herman, Ralph Metzner, DeLee Lantz, and Rowena Pattee Kryder. Thanks to the Kern Foundation for supporting research I did at CIIS that related to psychospiritual approaches to human development. Also thanks to Frank Barr, who gave me encouragement at this early stage.

I began work on the proposal for this book in the early 1990s and would like to thank Janice Gallagher, who had been my editor at Jeremy

Tarcher on a previous book (*In Their Own Way*), for her editing skills on some of my early efforts. I want to thank the Association for Supervision and Development (ASCD), for whom I wrote five books for educators between 1993 and 2006, which gave me enough financial support to spend the time it took to research and write this book. I especially want to thank Nancy Modrak, Scott Willis, Carolyn Pool, Deborah Siegel, and Julie Houtz.

Thanks to Maureen Wolf at the Association for Pre- & Perinatal Psychology and Health (APPPAH), who helped me locate hard-to-find sources for the prebirth chapter, and to the film critic Charles Champlain, who gave me suggestions and encouragement for the book's filmography while I was attending the Santa Barbara Writers Conference in the summers of 1996–98. Thanks to the staff of the Santa Rosa Memorial Hospice volunteer program, especially Nina Arbour, Cheri Plattner, and Mary DeLuca, for letting me go through their training program in 2004 and giving me two brief assignments that helped me immensely with the death and dying chapter and that I mark as among the most significant experiences of my life (everyone who can, should consider spending time as a hospice volunteer sometime during their lives).

There are several people I'd like to thank for reviewing a final draft of the book and providing specific feedback, corrections, and additions to the manuscript, including: Allan Chinen, Arthur Hastings, George Leonard, Jack Travis, Marian Diamond, Stanley Krippner, John Kotre, and Jaak Panksepp. Thanks also to those individuals who gave encouragement and support after reading all or portions of the manuscript, including Howard Gardner, Jan Hunt, Barbara Findeisen, Sonny and Sheri Saruk, Joseph Chilton Pearce, Thomas Verny, Laura Huxley, Michael Murphy, Ralph Metzner, and Stanislav Grof. Thanks to several other people whose direct or indirect help or inspiration over the years was instrumental in making this book a reality, including: R. S. Issac Gardner, Andrew Sears, Lonnie Barbach, Lenore Lefer, Jack Kornfield, and Stephen and Linda Hann.

I'd like to give an extra special thanks to my two literary "guardian angels" for believing in my vision and shepherding it into publication. First, thank you to my literary agent, Joëlle Delbourgo, who even if you were lucky and went straight to book heaven you wouldn't find an agent as wonderful as she is. Second, to my splendid editor at Sterling, Patty Gift, who is the person I have always wished and hoped would edit this book, but never thought in a million years I would get, given that the publishing industry generally seeks to play it safe with whatever has worked in the past. Thanks also to Patty's assistant, Jack Tycher, who was immensely helpful with all kinds of details related to the book. Thanks too to Becky Maines; to Melanie Gold, who did a wonderful job of copyediting the book; and to Amy Henderson and Chrissy Kwasnik, who were responsible for the great design of the book. Thanks also to Alex Lencicki, Sarah Ritter, and Marilyn Kretzer at Sterling.

Last, and most important, I'd like to thank my wife, Barbara Turner, sandplay psychotherapist and fiber artist extraordinaire, who read and edited the manuscript, put up with me, supported me, helped me through times of stagnation and doubt, and ultimately inspired me to complete this book.

Contents

Starting Your Incredible Odyssey

So gladly from the songs of modern speech
Men turn, and see the stars, and feel the free
Shrill wind beyond the close of heavy flowers,
And through the music of the languid hours
They hear like Ocean on a western beach
The surge and thunder of the Odyssey.

—ANDREW LANG, "THE ODYSSEY"[1]

Of all the journeys that have taken place in the history of the world, real or imagined, few can match that of Odysseus in Homer's epic poem *The Odyssey*. Here's a traveler who had more than his share of adventures. After fighting for ten years in Troy, he invented the Trojan horse, smuggled it into enemy territory, and helped to win the war for the Greeks. Then he spent another ten years trying to return home to Ithaca.

During his trip, he encountered lotus eaters whose flower food enchanted his shipmates. He did battle with a one-eyed giant whom he blinded with fire. Next, a group of cannibals destroyed his fleet of ships and a witch turned his shipmates into pigs. After that, he journeyed to Hades, where he received advice from a blind ghost about how to get back home. He lost more shipmates when a six-headed monster swooped down on them. A bolt of lightning shattered his last ship and he clung to the keel as the only survivor. After a long exile with a nymph named Calypso and a few more tempests and disasters, he returned home only to find his wife besieged by suitors. After slaughtering them all, he settled down and finally got some rest. Quite a journey, indeed.

But that was nothing compared to what you've been through.

As a tiny multicelled organism you traveled down a treacherous canal called a fallopian tube and made your way to a large underground uterine cavern. Here you encountered killer bacteria, disturbing hormones, and maybe even a menacing bug-eyed birth control device designed to destroy you. As you grew, the cavern walls started to collapse around you and the only way out was through a small opening that almost crushed you. On the other side, giants in white coats pulled you out of the tunnel and sprayed stinging chemicals in your eyes. Then you were sent off to live in an alien land as a slave to other giants who alternately threatened and enchanted you. There, you had to explore strange new territory and face creatures your own size that knocked you down, pulled your hair, and spit up on you. After a time you were sent off to a strange hall where you were required to unscramble mysterious codes and pass many tests set for you by a goddess with a bachelor's degree in education. As you continued to grow, you fell under the enchantment of beautiful creatures, battled rivals, came perilously close to whirlpools created out of your own passions and desires, and endured the rites and rituals of the marketplace as you sought to find your place in the mysterious world around you.

Already, you've gone through far more than Odysseus ever did in his legendary life. And your journey isn't even finished! Ahead of you lie many more adventures: encounters with hydra-headed bosses, tempests and seductions with spouses or lovers, battles and truces with growing children, periods of exile and times of reunion with family and friends, struggles and triumphs with aging, and ultimately perhaps, passage through another tunnel into other incredible worlds in other dimensions. Whether you happen to be just setting out on your adult voyage of discovery, hitting midstream, or winding up a long journey and heading back to harbor, you are going through your own odyssey right now, a journey that is as unique as your thumbprint and yet as universal as the age-old stories of heroes and heroines from world mythology.

Preparations for the Journey

I'd like you to think of this book as a kind of travelogue to your past, present, and future life. It seems incredible, but, apart from our sacred texts, our culture appears to lack any truly comprehensive road map to our own existence. The book critic Christopher Lehmann-Haupt once wrote: "... more than ever these days people seem to yearn for any extended form of narrative that might lend coherence to an existence that feels to them increasingly fragmentary."[2] I wrote this book because I wanted to provide readers with such a narrative; one that told the story of our journey through life in the broadest and most expansive way possible: from conception to death, or as a person at one of my lectures put it: "from sperm to worm." I realized that this was a monumental task that could never be fully achieved, given the innumerable uncertainties and complexities of life, and the tremendous variations in our own individual life histories. Nevertheless, I persisted, feeling that the contemporary narratives that already existed for telling the story of human development were incomplete. Erik Erikson's renowned "Eight Ages of Man" theory left out the most important parts of the story: the beginning and the end (birth and death). College textbooks on human development told the story in a pedantic and detached way. Most of the popular books that I'd read on the subject seemed to tell the story of our lives from a limited point of view (e.g., psychoanalytic, Jungian, Christian) or focused only on one stage of life (e.g., childhood, midlife, aging). It seemed to me that there needed to be a book about the life span that told as much of the story as possible.

Further, I wanted to write a book that responded to the increasing diversity of our population, and to the growing threat of rigid ideologies around the world, by describing our journey through life in a pluralistic and interdisciplinary way. Thus, I drew on a wide range of cultural, intellectual, philosophical, religious, and spiritual traditions. Having been fortunate in my education to study at schools that embraced an integral vision of human growth and transformation, I was inspired to tell the story of human development using material from anthropology, neuropsychology, evolutionary psychobiology, folklore, world literature, psychiatry, religion, physics, sociology, the arts, and a host of other fields. I passionately believe that in order to encompass the richness and complexity of our journey through life, we need to take advantage of as many tools at our disposal as possible.

In the course of this book, I will take you through each stage of life, chapter by chapter. Think of it as if you were settling into an ancient Greek sailing vessel at the beginning of the book, and then navigating your way through twelve different worlds as you read through the chapters. In fact, this is what I discovered: that each stage of life *is* a world unto itself, a veritable ecosystem with its own atmosphere, geography, fauna and flora, and other environmental features. I've also included an additional chapter on the possibilities of existence after physical death since most cultures from the beginning of recorded history have included this dimension as part of their stories about the journey of life.

Believing as I do that no stage of life is any better or worse than any other stage, I've described at the end of each chapter a special "gift" to humanity, which that particular stage of life provides. These twelve gifts include: potential, hope, vitality, playfulness, imagination, ingenuity, passion, enterprise, contemplation, benevolence, wisdom, and life. Near the end of each chapter, I've described the nature of each gift and made suggestions for how how we can use that gift to make our lives richer and more meaningful regardless of our age or stage.

Each chapter also includes a practical section at the end, where you can engage in activities to connect your new understandings about that particular stage of life to your personal growth, the well-being of your family and friends, and the health of your community. You may find, for example, that the material in this book helps you think about and perhaps resolve issues from your childhood, or assists you in coping with difficulties in your current adult life, or prepares you to meet future challenges, including concerns about aging and death. In addition, you may discover that this book provides you with insights that will assist you in taking better care of your children or aging parents, or in better understanding the developmental needs of coworkers or close friends. Finally, you might wish to apply your knowledge gained from this book to the healing of the broader community. So many of the problems that plague our society are developmental ones, from unwanted pregnancies and child abuse to adolescent violence and age discrimination. These end-of-chapter activities provide a number of ways in which readers can get immediately involved in making a difference in the lives of others.

The three appendices at the end of the book include a filmography, a reading list, and a list of organizations. Each appendix is organized so that the films, books, or organizations are categorized according to the stage of life that they most directly address. You may want to watch a movie or read a book on a specific stage of life with friends or loved ones, and then discuss the issues that come up regarding that stage. Or, after having been inspired by a particular stage of life, you might want to volunteer for, or contribute financially to, an organization that is fighting for the needs of individuals at that stage.

Finally, I've included a rather substantial notes section that includes source material for most of the quotations, research studies, and ideas in the book, as well as additional thoughts or material I couldn't bear to leave out. You'll have to forgive me, but I used to type dissertations to support myself in my early adulthood, and I really think that notes are amazingly cool. Moreover, they're the closest that a book can get to hyperlinks in today's high-tech world. Don't be intimidated by them. I put them in so that people who want to engage in further explorations will be able to do so. If this doesn't interest you, that's okay. Feel free to ignore them.

Traveling "Up from the Body" and "Down from the Spirit"

The major premise of this book is that there are two fundamental forces operating upon us as we journey through life: the biological and the spiritual. These influences are really two apparently distinct but intertwining developmental trajectories that interact to propel us through life. Their relationship represents the essential paradox of life itself: that each one of us is a material substance—a few pounds of clay, so to speak—enlivened by a mysterious nonmaterial entity that different traditions have referred to as soul, life force, mind, consciousness, essence, monad, or spirit. As French philosopher Blaise Pascal put it: "... man is to himself the greatest prodigy in nature, for he cannot conceive what body is, and still less what mind is, and least of all how a body can be joined to a mind. This is his supreme difficulty, and yet it is his very being."[3] How matter and spirit, or body and mind, came together to create living form is the great mystery of life.

World religions and mythologies have attempted to fathom this mystery by telling creation stories. Some stories declare that spirit created matter. Genesis 2:5;7–8, for example, says: "When the Lord God made earth and heaven, there was neither shrub nor plant growing wild upon the earth... Then the Lord God formed a man from the dust of the ground and breathed into his nostrils the breath of life. Thus the man became living creature." Other creation stories portray spirit as emerging *out* of matter. Certain Native American cultures, for example, believe that all things material and spiritual first emerged from deep within the heart of the earth. There are also creation stories that indicate how matter and spirit came together as coequals to produce life. In ancient Egyptian mythology, for example, Seb (a male earth god) and Nut (a female sky goddess) were said to form all creation from their sexual union.[4]

Contemporary scientists, theologians, and philosophers periodically update these ancient versions of life's biggest riddle with theories of their own. Most scientists, for example, believe that the brain (matter) creates consciousness. Many mystics take the opposite view and believe that the brain is simply a material manifestation of consciousness. Still other thinkers see brain and mind as equal partners interacting to create reality.[5] Regardless of specific views concerning this mind-boggling topic, I find it useful in this book simply to regard matter and spirit as two seemingly separate but interconnected journeys. I'd like to take you through these two journeys of matter and spirit to illustrate just what I mean.

Your biological journey began with your appearance on life's stage as a zygote or one-celled organism: a mere speck of matter not too much different from a bit of mud or dust. From that point on, you became a blastocyst or multicelled organism, then an embryo, a fetus, and finally a newborn babe. As an infant, you were still very much a biological organism focused on the physical comforts and discomforts of eating, elimination, and clinging to your mother's body. Eventually, you grew *up from the body* into more complex forms of thinking, feeling, and behaving. All along, however, you maintained this thread of connection to your biological origins. As human potential writer Joseph Chilton Pearce explains: "Throughout our lives, the earth remains the matrix of all matrices. No matter how abstract our explorations of pure thought and created reality, the mind draws its energy from the brain, which draws its energy from the body matrix, which draws its energy from the earth matrix."[6]

This biological line of human development is best symbolized by the umbilical cord. This cord is what linked you not only to your own mother but to her mother, and her mother's mother, and so forth all the way back to the beginnings of biological life. James Joyce expressed this connection lyrically when he wrote in his great novel *Ulysses*, which was a modern updating of Homer's Odyssey: "The cords of all link back, strandentwining cable of all flesh . . ."[7] In *body up* development, we trace the growth of our "root system" back through millions of years of evolution and genetics and experience ourselves ultimately as linked with the earliest forms of life, and even further back, as Joseph Chilton Pearce indicated above, to the very body of mother earth herself.

There is another journey you take, however, that has quite different origins from that of the earth. This is a hidden journey that only the poets and mystics seem to know much about. It represents the part of you that came *down from the spirit*, that descended from a higher or broader realm of being into a lower or narrower state of material existence. William Wordsworth referred to this *spirit down* journey in his poem "Ode: On Intimations of Immortality in Childhood" when he wrote: "Not in entire forgetfulness / And not in utter nakedness / But trailing clouds of Glory do we come / From God, who is our home: Heaven lies about us in our infancy!"[8] William Blake spoke of *spirit down* development when he observed: " . . . the source of life descends to be a weeping babe."[9] Religious traditions refer to the *spirit down* journey when they speak of the fall from grace, the exile from Paradise, the incarnation of the soul into the body, or the imprisonment of spirit in matter.

The key image for *spirit down* development is the angel, a celestial being that linked you as an unborn or newborn child to a higher power. Many world cultures have given a name to this perinatal being. Christianity refers to this power as a Guardian Angel; Judaism calls this angel Lailah; Buddhism calls her Avalokiteshwara, Kwan Yin, or Kannon; and Maori tradition refers to her as Hine-Titama. In the next chapter, we will discuss this imagery in detail. This spiritual guardian helps us on our journey. While we may forget our spiritual origins as we grow *up from the body*, this guardian periodically reminds us of our life's purpose. *Spirit down* development also manifests unexpectedly during our lives in such moments as poetic inspiration, archetypal dreams, peak experiences, mystical visions, or aesthetic awakenings, experiences that are particularly likely to emerge at transitional periods in our lives such as early childhood, adolescence, midlife, or old age.

The *body up* journey is the story told in just about all of the college textbooks and most of the popular books on human development available in bookstores. There is scant reference to *spirit down* development in any of these books. This is unfortunate since most cultures from the beginning of recorded history have included the spiritual journey as an integral part of their story, and still today, the spiritual life is a central focus of the majority of people's experience around the world. In my estimation, leaving the essence or soul out of the stages of life is like studying birds in the forest without considering their song or their flight.

Two Modes of Being: Adapting and Remembering

The process of coming *up from the body* is a story of *adaptation*. Along this line of development we evolved in true Darwinian fashion, struggling to survive in the jungles of life while striving to fit our own uniqueness into the game plan of the world around us. *Adaptation* looks to the past only for clues as to how to face the present and the future. *Adaptation* is about mastering the tools and skills necessary to survive and thrive in the existing social order. The thread of *adaptation* runs through such fields as politics, business, economics, science, and technology. All stage theories of human development—including those of Jean Piaget, Sigmund Freud, and Erik Erikson—are mainly stories about *adaptation*.[10] Each of these models describes how human beings grow *up from the body* in a series of graduated steps, becoming more facile over time in adapting to the surrounding environment. These theories, however, have little to say about *spirit down* development.

The story of coming *down from the spirit* is about *remembering*. It involves paying attention to who we are in our essence as nonmaterial beings. The process of *remembering* encompasses all those aspects of life that look back to our spiritual origins as individuals or as cultural groups. It includes explorations in folklore, mythology, consciousness studies, transpersonal psychology, anthropology, and also in religion, whose Latin root, *religare*, means literally "to link back." The arts are also an important part of *remembering*. After all, it was Mnemosyne or Memory who was the mother of the nine muses in Greek mythology, encompassing poetry, music, history, dance, comedy, and drama.

Everyone has some combination of the *adapter* and the *rememberer* in them. The *adapter* in us seeks to acquire skills that teach about how the world works, and seeks to develop competence in order to move up the ladder of success and face the challenges of the future. The *rememberer* in us reads poetry, views art that stirs the soul, grapples with philosophical questions, and struggles in therapy to recover a lost self. These two activities—*adapting* and *remembering*—seem to have been at the heart of human activity since the beginning of recorded time. For thousands of years societies engaged in *adaptive* tasks—hunting, gathering, building shelters, and crafting tools—to ensure their physical survival. But they also devoted a great deal of attention to activities designed to help them *remember* who they were as people, by engaging in dance, play, song, storytelling, religious rituals, and other "nonadaptive" activities.

While everybody possesses a mixture of the *adapter* and the *rememberer*, many people show more of one quality than of the other. Full-fledged *adapters* tend to be practical and sensible—sometimes even ruthless—in learning the game of life and leaving the competition behind. Classic examples of *adapters* include Napoleon, Margaret Thatcher, and Bill Gates. *Rememberers*, on the other hand, tend to be sensitive and aesthetic as they regard the depths of their own souls and those of others. Famous examples include Saint Francis, Marcel Proust, and Virginia Woolf. Our modern technological culture tends to honor the *adapters* more than the *rememberers*. After all, the superadapter CEOs of society make far more money than the rememberer poets. In other cultures, however, it's the *rememberers*—the shamans, healers, artists, storytellers, and mystics—who receive far more prestige and support from the community than the business and political leaders.

To illustrate some of the key differences between *adapters* and *rememberers*, I'd like to share the stories of two Americans who lived through the middle part of the nineteenth century: railroad magnate Leland Stanford and poet Emily Dickinson. Both were associated with important centers of learning in the United States. Stanford founded the university that bears his name. Dickinson's grandfather was the founder of Amherst College. But each had a radically different life course that distinctly marked them as *adapter* and *rememberer* respectively.

Leland Stanford studied law in New York and had a successful legal practice in Wisconsin until a fire wiped him out financially in 1852 at the age of twenty-eight. He responded to this crisis by joining his brothers in the California Gold Rush. After mining gold for a while, he began to assist them in selling merchandise to miners. He also served as a justice of the peace, and helped to organize what later became the Sacramento Public Library. Eventually he bought out the Stanford Brothers store, amassed some wealth, and became active in politics. In 1861 he was elected governor of California (he would later be a U.S. Senator). In the 1860s he joined a group of wealthy financiers to create the Central Pacific Railroad. In 1869 he drove in the stake that completed the transcontinental railroad. Stanford built a mansion on what later became known as Nob Hill in San Francisco, developed a horse breeding business that set nineteen world records, and owned two wineries, one with the largest vineyard in the world.

While traveling in Europe in 1884, Stanford's son, Leland Jr., contracted typhoid fever and died two months before his sixteenth birthday. Stanford fell into a troubled sleep the day the boy died, and when he awoke he turned to his wife and said: "The children of California shall be our children." Stanford put $20 million of his fortune ($400 million in 2007 dollars) into a new learning center on the site of his horse farm. This is how Stanford University (still affectionately referred to as "the farm") was born.

Stanford's life embodied the role of a true *adapter*. After financial ruin early in his career, instead of collapsing in despair he adapted by seeking his fortune in the California Gold Rush. When he saw that he would make no money mining gold, he joined his brothers in selling provisions to miners and became successful. He made his fortune and got involved in politics, the happy hunting ground of true *adapters*. He literally joined the country together with a golden stake in Promontory, Utah, by completing the transcontinental railway—a move that would help millions of people start new lives on the West Coast. In the horse breeding business, he developed his own theories of blood lines and training, and triumphed there too. At the peak of his power, his son died unexpectedly, and he adapted to this tragedy by channeling his grief into the development of a world-class center of learning that would help the sons and daughters of others prosper and flourish. Leland Stanford was a man of action who worked hard, consolidated his financial and political power, and met adversity with courage and determination.[11]

Emily Dickinson, on the other hand, was quite a different sort of person. After attending college for one year at Mount Holyoke Female Seminary (now Mount Holyoke College), she became homesick and returned to her childhood home in Amherst, where she lived for the rest of her life. Although she had a few strong intellectual relationships in her life, she was basically a loner who rarely left the house. She read a great deal, corresponded with many people, and wrote poems. Despite having written 1,775 poems in the course of her fifty-six years, many among the greatest in American literature, her brilliance never received public recognition while she was alive. Only eleven of her poems were even published during her lifetime. A true nonconformist, she renounced her Puritan Christian upbringing when she was twenty years old, and worked out her unique spiritual beliefs and disbeliefs through her iridescent poetry. Not content with standard writing methods, she punctuated her poems with dashlike marks of various sizes and directions (some are even vertical), capitalized words in the middle of sentences, and often used unconventional syntax. Her poems dealt with themes of love, death, time, nature, loneliness, ecstasy, religion, and the spirit.

Emily Dickinson showed few traits of the *adapter*. She didn't set out to conquer the world like Leland Stanford did. When she encountered difficulty in life, she retreated to her family home. Even in her most important work—her poetry—she didn't seek to become famous. Her poems, with their strange punctuation, looked nothing like what was being published at the time. To most people, she was a reclusive eccentric.

It was as a *rememberer*, however, that Emily Dickinson excelled beyond measure. The delicate fabric of the inner life was what transported her. A friend of Dickinson's wrote: "[Emily] once asked me, if it did not make me shiver to hear a great many people talk, [she said] they took all the clothes off their souls—and we discussed this matter."[12] It is interesting that after her father died, she wore only white for the rest of her life. Her poems quiver with a sensitivity to the deepest topics of existence, especially death. Her most famous poem begins: "Because I could not stop for Death / He kindly stopped for me / The Carriage held but just Ourselves / And Immortality."[13]

Although she renounced formal religion early in life, her poems continually tested her own personal faith. One poem declares: "I know that He exists. Somewhere—in Silence—He has hid his rare life / From our gross eyes."[14] While those around her went on with their ambitious *adapter* lives, Dickinson inhabited a hidden world woven of deep inner feeling, spiritual struggle, and an extraordinary receptivity to nature and to the inner lives of those around her. She spent a lifetime trying to *remember* the essence of what it means to exist. While she did not go out into the world and make the kind of impact that Leland Stanford did, in her own way she lived an inner life that was as rich and powerful as his outer life, and ultimately, perhaps even more influential.

Although you may not see yourself reflected in the life of either Leland Stanford or Emily Dickinson, their stories serve as two poles of the *adapter-rememberer* continuum. From them you can begin to understand where you might fit in between these two extremes. As you read through the chapters of this book, you'll probably get a better sense of whether you're more of an *adapter* or a *rememberer*. If you lean toward the *adapter* side of the spectrum you'll probably be more interested in the chapters of this book that relate to your present and future stages of life, so that you can figure out ways of meeting the challenges that lie ahead. On the other hand, if you see yourself better reflected in the *rememberer*, you'll more likely be drawn to the first half of this book (and the chapters on death and the afterlife), where you can explore your past stages and recover yourself in the earliest moments of life.

The truth is that you need to have the qualities of both the *adapter* and the *rememberer* in order to be fully human. A person who focuses too much time on *adapting* to whatever the present and the future may hold squanders away her energies on an endless pursuit of material gain and societal approval and loses sight of the richer dimensions of life. On the other hand, an individual who spends too much time *remembering* the deeper dimensions of life finds it hard to keep appointments, loses his car keys, and has an all-around difficult time fitting in with the world around him. Too much adapting and you might become obsessive-compulsive. Too much remembering and you could become schizophrenic. In either case, you're out of balance.

Homer's *Odyssey* suggests a way out of this dilemma. At one point in his journey, Odysseus had to sail his boat past the island of the Sirens.

These sylphs were known to sing a song so enchanting that anyone who heard it wanted to remain on the island forever. The Sirens' beaches were strewn with the skeletons of sailors who'd listened to the melody and died for it. Odysseus had heard of this legendary song and how beautiful it was, and he longed to hear it. This was the *rememberer* side of his personality speaking. But the *adapter* in him wanted to get the boat safely home to Ithaca. So, with the advice of Circe, the daughter of the sun, he worked out a compromise. He gave his crew members wax to put in their ears so they wouldn't hear the enchanting song and could thus focus all their energies on the adaptive task of sailing the boat back to Ithaca. Odysseus elected not to put the wax in his ears so he could hear the song, thus satisfying the *rememberer* side of his personality. But he also instructed his men to lash him to the mast so that he could direct them home to Ithaca without yielding to the Sirens' enchantment, thereby placating his *adapter* self.[15] In this way, he heard the enchanting music and still managed to get back home. This is what it means to be fully human: to find the balance between the demands of outer necessity and the call of the inner life; between what is yet to come and what has passed. The journey of life draws us onward to Ithaca, but it also invites us to take in all the rich scenery along the way. My hope is that after reading this book, you will feel a deepened appreciation for the miracle of life, and will be able to look at your own journey, as well as the journeys of those around you, with a renewed sense of compassion and wonder.

May you each have amazing stories to tell and powerful insights to gain as you journey through the twelve stages of your own personal Human Odyssey!

Prebirth: The Undiscovered Continent

Show me your original face before your parents were born.

—ZEN KOAN

There's a beautiful legend from the Jewish tradition about our life before birth. In this tale, the fetus in the womb has a light that shines above his head that sees from one end of the universe to the other. This light encompasses the unborn's own deep past and his ultimate destiny. Just before birth, however, the angel Lailah comes up to the unborn babe and lightly strikes her finger on his upper lip. This act extinguishes the light and causes the child to take birth in total forgetfulness of all he has known during his prebirth existence. The purpose of life is to recover this light. It's said that this is why we bear a little crease in our upper lip called the philtrum: This is the mark of the angel.[1] It's also said that this is why, when we suddenly recall a forgotten name or a misplaced object, we instinctively touch a finger to our upper lip and exclaim, "Ah yes, now I *remember!*" We've made contact with our angel of destiny once more.

This story hints at how our prenatal lives may not have been as unconscious as modern science suggests. Instead of a *body up* progression of purely biological steps leading to birth, prebirth might as well have been a whole universe of conscious experiences, now forgotten, but still perhaps alive at some deep level of our being. As the poet Samuel Taylor

Coleridge once wrote: "The history of man for nine months preceding his birth would, probably, be far more interesting and contain events of greater moment, than all the three score and ten years that follow it."[2]

The Countdown to Conception

The excitement all begins with conception. This is a kind of lunar docking operation that requires the precise coordination in time and space of two vehicles. The first vehicle is an ovum traveling down the fallopian tube and available for fertilization only for about a twenty-four-hour period. The second vehicle is one among hundreds of millions of sperm cells racing at a speed of three inches per hour toward this ovoid destination.

Imagine the entire population of the United States, Russia, and Japan leaving the starting block at the same time on a megamarathon sprint proportionately longer than a trip to the moon. In this contest only one robust runner makes it all the way to the finish line. You begin to get a picture of the challenges facing a sperm on his way to a link-up with his egg "cellmate." *Brave New World* author Aldous Huxley once expressed this event biblically when he wrote: "A million million spermatozoa / All of them alive / Out of their cataclysm but one poor Noah / Dare hope to survive."[3] Research suggests that the sperm may actually "sniff" its way to the egg.[4] That one lucky sperm succeeds essentially by using his lashing tail to outdrill the last couple of hundred survivors clamoring to break through the ovum wall. Once the victor gains entry, the ovum initiates chemical changes that essentially close the castle gates to any other competitor.

Then begins the single greatest event of all biological existence. The nucleus of the sperm cell travels deep into the ovum and fuses with the egg nucleus, mixing his rich genetic material with hers and bringing an entirely new life-form into being; a fertilized one-celled organism or zygote, the first "you."

It's amazing to think that each human body walking around on the planet today was only a little while ago a single cell buzzing around in a liquid environment. The bodies of the president of the United States, the Pope, the chairman of General Motors, your mother-in-law: They were all zygotes. And so were you. Look in a mirror at your adult self. As you do this, think about being a zygote just a few decades ago. You might even get a little bit dizzy trying to comprehend the mystery of it all.

Of course, this is only half of the story, the beginnings of the *body up* journey. There is also a *spirit down* side to this great mystery of creation. In fact, there may be more life in and around that little zygote than seems at first apparent from a purely physiological point of view. The medieval Christians referred to the male sperm as *numen* and viewed conception as a *numinous* process (a Latin word meaning "filled with divinity"). A twelfth-century miniature by Christian mystic Hildegard of Bingen shows this perspective graphically by depicting the descent of the soul directly into the fetus of the mother.[5] In many African creation myths, the first people are lowered to earth from the sky. Chinese Buddhist philosophy believes that the life force comes from the air above, down to and into the earth force of the fetus.

Perhaps the most remarkable map of prebirth as a *spirit down* journey is found in *The Tibetan Book of the Dead* (or *Bardo Thodöl*), an eighth-century Buddhist guide for helping departed souls achieve liberation from the wheel of rebirth.[6] Tibetan Buddhists believe that beings continually reincarnate until they come to realize the illusory nature of existence. Unfortunately, the "winds of karma" (a person's desires and past actions) usually push them back into rebirth. And so the last portion of the *Bardo Thodöl* contains explicit instructions on the art of choosing a womb site in which to be reborn. The text explains how the traveling soul will begin to see pairs of copulating couples. It counsels that the soul will start to feel attracted to the opposite-sex parent and angry toward the same-sex parent. The *Bardo Thodöl* thus anticipated the Oedipal complex a thousand years before Freud and suggested that it begins in the womb. Ultimately, the soul takes birth with parents who will provide the karmic lessons necessary for eventual liberation.

These crosscultural spiritual perspectives as noted above are mirrored in contemporary clinical accounts of individuals remembering their prenatal existence. In one account of a session of hypnotic regression, a patient reported: "I am a sphere, a ball, a balloon, I am hollow, I have no arms, no legs, no teeth, I don't feel myself to have a front or back, up or down. I float, I fly, I spin. Sensations come from everywhere. It is as though I am a spherical eye."[7] Canadian psychiatrist Thomas Verny comments, "I have heard dozens of similar accounts from my own and other psychiatrists' patients and, more to the point, I have found that if you examine them closely, these recollections often correspond to events in the early stages of pregnancy."[8]

In her book *The Child of Your Dreams*, author Laura Huxley, Aldous Huxley's wife, compared the moment of conception to the big bang theory of the universe: "Another explosion much closer in time and space to you was just as momentous: it took place when a sperm and an egg came together and created you. This event is usually not described in such terms in the average biology textbook. However, when regressed to the moment of their own conception, a number of individuals report this experience as a joyous burst of the exultant fireworks of life."[9]

The Great River Journey

After fertilization, you began the voyage down the remaining portion of the six-inch-long fallopian tube, headed toward implantation in the uterus, a journey that took about three days. This was probably the most treacherous journey that you've ever taken. You were lucky to have survived it at all. Only 50 percent of fertilized eggs make it all the way down the tube to implantation in the uterus. You could have died right after conception due to genetic defects. You might have been killed by white blood cells that mistook you for an intruder as you traveled down the fallopian tube (the equivalent, perhaps, of the one-eyed monster that tried to kill Odysseus on his journey back to Ithaca). You could have become entrapped among the various scars and adhesions in the fallopian tube left over from wear and tear to your mother's body tissues. But with time, you grew bigger and stronger.

About twenty-four hours after conception you began to divide into a multicelled clump called a *morula* (Latin for "mulberry"). Then, over the next three days, you grew in size to about one hundred cells and became a *blastocyst* (Greek for "sprouting pouch"). As you finished your trip through the fallopian tube, you had your first experience of "birth," not into the world of human beings, but into the world of your mother's own uterus. You actually had to squeeze through the last part of the fallopian tube at its narrowest point, and your mother helped you by going through mini-contractions of the fallopian tube. You could have gotten stuck right there in the tube and miscarried as an *ectopic* (Greek for "out of place") pregnancy. However, you made it!

Once inside the uterus you faced a whole new set of challenges. First, you had to break free of your *zona pellucida* (Latin for "transparent girdle"), a kind of suit of armor that protected you during your dangerous journey down the fallopian tube. Then, like a Greek sailing vessel, you had to search for a suitable landing site on the surface of your mother's uterus. For several days you floated along in the uterus until you found a soft, thick, warm surface that appeared hospitable, and expanding in mass, you attached yourself to this uterine lining or *endometrium* (Greek for "within the womb"). You were lucky to find such a site. If your mother had developed endometriosis or experienced other problems with the lining of her uterus, your attempts to attach to the uterine lining might have been like trying to land your boat on a rugged and rocky seacoast.

There were other dangers as well. The endometrium might have attempted to reject you as a foreign substance by flushing you out of the womb, or birth control measures might have thwarted your attempts to gain a foothold. However, nature provided just what you needed to survive. Your mother secreted chemicals to shut down the processes of rejection, and you found yourself set up in a brand-new home with a nine-month lease.

While you probably don't remember this incredibly dangerous journey, many cultures seem to have recorded the details of this trip in their heroic myths. There is a whole class of myths that reflect what mythologist Joseph Campbell in his book *The Mythic Image* termed "the infant exile motif": stories about the births of heroes who were threatened with death by evil authorities, hidden in a container by an ally, and sent up a body of water, only to be retrieved and nurtured by animals or people.[10] These stories narrate the origins of such legendary figures as Hercules, Krishna, and Romulus and Remus, the founders of Rome, who were raised by wolves. They might at some archetypal level also be telling the story of the journey of the human zygote on its way to implantation in the uterus.

The first tale of this kind in world mythology is from Babylonia around five thousand years ago and describes the birth of its founder, Sargon. As legend has it, after Sargon's mother gave birth to him in a hidden place, she put him into a vessel made of reeds, closed the opening with pitch, and dropped him into the Euphrates River. He floated down the river until Akki, a water carrier, discovered Sargon and raised him as his adopted son. Later Sargon would rule the kingdom of Akkad for fifty-five years.

Similarly, in the Bible, Moses was sent down a river in a basket of bulrushes as an infant. The pharaoh of Egypt had ordered all his people to throw every newborn Hebrew boy into the Nile. A Levite woman, however, hid her infant to avoid the pharaoh's plot. Exodus 2:3–4 reports: "...she got a rush basket for him, made it watertight with clay and tar, laid him in it, and put it among the reeds by the bank of the Nile." He was discovered by the pharaoh's daughter, who adopted him and raised him as her own in the royal household. Eventually, Moses escaped and led his people out of Egypt into the Promised Land.

R. D. Laing suggested that these scenarios parallel the uterine journey in many startling respects. The heroic leader is the zygote placed in a boat (zona pellucida), which floats down a river (the fallopian tube), lands on a shore (the endometrium), receives the care of people or animals (the nurturing forces of the mother's uterus), and grows into maturity (development of the fetus to full term). Laing saw these prenatal elements not only in mythology, but also in the dreams and struggles of his patients. One thirty-six-year-old businessman, for example, wrote: "I feel I'm hanging onto a cliff with my fingernails...if I let go, I'll float off down the river...I'll be washed away...I shall be completely mad."[11] Laing pointed out that many of life's deepest fears and most existential conflicts might be traced back to these earliest days of prenatal existence. Like Odysseus, each one of us encountered great dangers on the waters in our prenatal sailing craft.

Becoming a Fetus

Eight days after conception you were an embryo consisting of thousands of new stem cells governed by a genetic process that began assigning roles and job sites to areas that soon became your nervous system, digestive system, and other major physiological functions and anatomical structures. These embryonic stem cells were of the same type that are now being used in scientific research to generate specialized tissues for treating a wide range of diseases.[12] Over the next few weeks you went through more transformations than a contortionist in a traveling circus. Just fourteen days after implantation you looked a little like a plump frankfurter split at both ends.

Between weeks three and four, the split ends of the wiener closed to form a shrimplike brain and spine: the beginnings of your nervous system. Between weeks four and five, your eyes, nose, and mouth began to emerge, your spine curled around like a dragon's tail, and you resembled a strange prehistoric creature. In the nineteenth century it was believed that during these first few weeks of life, the human organism recapitulated all the stages of evolution from sea life to amphibian to mammal.[13] This isn't exactly what occurred. You didn't actually *become* a shrimp, a lizard, or a minuscule *Jurassic Park* monster. But, you did share some of the same genetic codes as primitive vertebrates, which in these early embryonic stages made you resemble them to some degree. By week six you looked like an alien from another planet, with a large head and beady eyes. In another couple of weeks the formation of your organs was complete and you had pretty much every physical structure found in a full-sized adult. At this point in your journey you became officially known as a *fetus* (Latin for "bringing forth"). Your *spirit down* soul may have been witnessing all these physical changes going on from its celestial realm, but it's around this time that the initial twinkling of a rudimentary *body up* consciousness may have begun. Your first neural reflexes occurred at eight weeks, when fetuses have been observed to withdraw their hands in response to stimu-lation of the lip region.[14]

During the next few months of intrauterine life you were like a scuba diver rolling around in a warm and comfy cushion of amniotic fluid at a temperature of about 99.5 degrees Fahrenheit. You were enveloped in water. It's interesting to note that many of humanity's creation myths begin in water. Genesis 1:1–2 says: "In the beginning of Creation, when God made heaven and earth, the earth was without form and void, with darkness over the face of the abyss, and a mighty wind that swept over the surface of the waters." In the Babylonian creation epic, Apsu (a freshwater god) and Tiamat (a saltwater god) represent the primeval waters at the beginning of time. Even the first Western philosopher, the Greek thinker Thales, suggested that the world originated from water, believing that the earth actually floated on the liquid stuff. Collective creation myths such as those found in the Bible and in other sacred and philosophical texts worldwide give us possibly the earliest chronicles of the actual collective memories of intrauterine existence as earthly *body up* awareness and celes-tial *spirit down* consciousness come together in a unified way.

Traditions differ in their accounts of when the spirit or soul actually enters the fetus. Buddhism generally regards *conception* as the time when the soul incarnates into matter. Judaism views the fetus as a "partial life" and only *at birth* is there a full human being. Aristotle wrote that the human fetus was animated or "ensouled" forty days after conception for males, and ninety days after conception for females. Some early Christian theologians regarded quickening (that time around the fourth or fifth month of pregnancy when the mother feels the life moving inside of her) as the central moment of the soul's entry into the fetus.[15] In Dante's *Divine Comedy* there is an account of the spiritualization of the fetus given by the deceased Roman poet Statius to Dante and Virgil as they travel through Purgatory. Statius says, "Know soon as in the embryo, to the brain, / Articulation is complete, then turns / The primal Mover with a smile of joy / On such great work of nature, and imbreathes / New spirit replete with virtue, that what here / Active it finds, to its own substance draws, /

And forms an individual soul, that lives, / And feels, and bends reflective on itself."[16] Here one may also think of the words in Genesis 1:3–4: "Let there be light. And there was light. And God saw that the light was good." From the time of quickening, the light of consciousness shines more brightly from within the womb. Even a purely *body up* perspective bears this out. Science tells us that myelin deposits, those substances that provide insulation to the nervous system's wiring and conduct nerve impulses, appear as early as the fourth month of pregnancy and that brain life as we know it may begin around the 28th week of pregnancy.[17]

Once your eyes opened during the seventh month of pregnancy, what images there were for you to see! Growing out of your belly was an enormous twisting vine—an umbilical cord—coiling upward into the branching treelike structure known as the *placenta* (Latin for "flat cake"), where you received all your nourishment from your mother. Perhaps here is where you encountered the archetypal Tree of Life that so many cultures have woven into the fabric of their mythic dreams: the Tree of Knowledge in the Garden of Eden, the Nordic tree of Yggdrasil, the sacred Hebrew pole called Asherah, or the Celtic sacred wood.[18] In some cultures, the umbilical and placental discharge after birth is saved, dried, and planted in the earth under a tree. These trees are thought to protect children and sometimes are referred to as the guardian angel of the child. Cinderella was actually saved by a magic tree and a few birds in the Grimm brothers' tale, not by a fairy godmother.[19]

Heaven and Hell Before Birth

On a physical level, you engaged in an intricate biological dance with your mother through the Tree of Life/placenta, which acted as a kind of referee or choreographer to keep the two of you in a biochemical balance. Though your mother's blood system was separate from yours, she still passed many hormones and chemical signals through the placenta to nourish you. And you also had a part to play as you interacted with these signals through your own chemical responses to keep your mother's immune system from rejecting you.

Being physically a part of your mother, you were involved in every action of her life. You were there when she had sex, got angry, cried, fought with your father, laughed, vomited, listened to music, and at every other moment besides. And she passed on her subjective moods not just through the physical experiences of jostling, bumping, singing, or rocking you, but through her hormonal responses to the positive or negative emotions in her own life. These hormones essentially set the thermostat on your "emotional climate control" and created intrauterine versions of sunny days and tropical breezes, or thunderstorms and hurricanes. I'd like you to consider the following "best-case" and "worst-case" scenarios of prenatal experiences.

A Best-Case Scenario: The Good Womb. Like aboriginal mothers in Australia, your mother began bonding with you even before conception by having dreams about you, and drawing images of those dreams. Once you were conceived, like Mbuti mothers in the Congo, she took you to a special place in nature, sung soothing lullabies to express her joy, talked with you about the world that you were about to enter, and gave assurances that life on earth was safe and full of blessings.[20] She ate a nutritious diet and avoided drugs, alcohol, and cigarettes. She also stayed away from any foods that might have had an adverse effect and received regular checkups to monitor the course of her pregnancy.[21] She enjoyed a loving relationship with your father, who was almost as involved in the pregnancy as she was, rubbing her belly, singing to you, and engaging in lots of hugging and love-making. She meditated and prayed, read stimulating literature, and engaged in her own highly creative life and professional study. She lived with you in a peaceful rural town that included both sides of your extended family, which provided a nurturing support system for the both of you.

A Worst-Case Scenario: The Bad Womb. Your mother was what some prenatal psychologists call a "catastrophic mother." She was a teenage dropout when she had you. She didn't expect to have you and she didn't want you when she realized you were there. She tried aborting you with different folk remedies and flooded you with "rejection" hormones. She smoked, drank, and used recreational drugs. She didn't eat regular meals but snacked erratically on fast food and candy. She was suffering from several different diseases when she carried you, including tuberculosis, gonorrhea, and chlamydia. She had a partner, not committed to the relationship, who physically beat her (you felt the punches), periodically left her (you felt the abandonment hormones), and screamed a lot (you felt the stress hormones). While she carried you, her own mother had a nervous breakdown, a war broke out in her native country, and her brother committed suicide.[22]

These scenarios represent two ends of a spectrum of womb experiences that could have made the difference between your being in heaven experiencing the bliss of angels or in hell undergoing the torments of demons. Leonardo da Vinci, who saw so much of the beauty and ugliness of life, recognized the importance of the pregnant mother's state almost five hundred years ago when he wrote: "And [the soul of the child] at first lies dormant and under the tutelage of the soul of the mother, who nourishes and vivifies it by the umbilical vein, with all its spiritual parts, and this happens because this umbilicus is joined to the placenta and the cotyledons, by which the child is attached to the mother. And these are the reason why a wish, a strong craving or a fright or any other mental suffering in the mother, has more influence on the child than on the mother; for there are many cases when the child loses its life from them. . . . "[23]

The surrealist painter Salvador Dalí claimed to remember his own intrauterine existence and wrote that it was hellish. Three years before Dalí was born, his parents had lost a son to meningitis. According to Dalí, they never recovered from it, and the anguish over the loss felt by his mother while pregnant with Salvador was transferred directly to the unborn artist-to-be. He wrote: "My fetus swam in an infernal placenta. . . . I have only to close my eyes, pressing on them with my two fists, to see again the colors of that intrauterine purgatory, the tints of Luciferian fire, red, orange, blue-glinting yellow; a goo of sperm and phosphorescent egg white in which I am suspended like an angel fallen from grace."[24]

Scientific studies now verify what Leonardo da Vinci and Salvador Dalí observed. We know, for example, that mothers who would have liked to abort the fetus but were prevented from doing so by legal restrictions have children with higher levels of delinquency, emotional disturbance, and physical illness than mothers who actively want their kids.[25] Mothers who are depressed during their pregnancies give birth to infants who are hard to console when upset, and mothers who are anxious have more cranky and colicky babies. According to one study, a woman trapped in a stormy marriage has a 236 percent greater chance of bearing a psychologically or physically damaged child than a woman in a safe and supportive relationship. Babies born during wartime—when a mother is worried about the well-being of her soldier husband—tend to also have more physical or emotional difficulties. Mothers who drink, smoke, or use drugs give birth to kids with more physical problems. In one study of pregnant mothers who smoked, fetal heart rates increased rapidly whenever the women even *thought* of having a cigarette.[26]

While mothers provide the all-important social, emotional, and physical nourishment for a positive prenatal experience, they also can create a spiritual climate of well-being that might compensate for whatever damage could be going on at the physical or emotional level. Along with the Jewish story of the angel Lailah that began this chapter, many cultures have mythic images of a protective spirit or guardian angel during pregnancy, which may be an archetypal representation of the mother's own spiritually nurturing influence. One of my favorite images is by a nineteenth-century Japanese artist showing the bodhisattva Kannon with an unborn child. In this image, Kannon is pouring the sweet dew of compassionate wisdom onto the smiling fetus, whose umbilical cord trails downward into the earthly realms below.[27] This image shows in a striking way how the fetus exists midway between the heavenly domain of the devas and angels above and the realms of biological development below described so well by modern science.

In Greek mythic tradition, this guardian spirit is represented by the *daemon* (Greek for "divinity").[28] Plato's classic book on education, *The Republic*, actually concludes with a description of how each soul about to be reborn chooses a daemon to serve as a guardian for the life it is about to embark on. The daemon leads the soul to the river of Lethe in the underworld, where it drinks from the waters of forgetfulness.[29] Just like the baby in the Jewish legend, the soul then takes birth without a memory of its origins. A similar deity existed in Roman mythology and was called a *genius* (Latin for "to beget"). The genius functioned much like the Christian guardian angel, helping the individual out of difficulties during his lifetime and inspiring him in moments of need. In that sense, it functioned much like the goddess Athena in Homer's *Odyssey*, who helped Odysseus (and his son, Telemachus) out of one disaster after another. These nurturing images may be, from a *body up* perspective, the positive hormones secreted by a mother in utero, but from a *spirit down* point of view they represent aspects of the spiritual universe that cradle the growing fetus.[30]

The Waters of Forgetfulness

As you entered the last weeks before birth, from a strictly physical perspective life inside the womb started to become a real squeeze. You were swallowing huge amounts of amniotic fluid comparable to a 120-pound adult drinking five gallons of Gatorade every day. You were developing enough independent skills to be able to live outside of the womb if you decided to make an early appearance. You also were spending time dreaming, since research shows that a fetus experiences the same kind of rapid eye movements (REMs) as children and adults do when they dream. Prenatal researcher Thomas Verny suggests that you may have even been able to tune into the thoughts or dreams of your mother so that her dreams became yours; possibly a precursor of extrasensory perception. Neurologist Dominick Purpura of the Albert Einstein Medical College in New York City speculates that "true brain life" (in the *body up* sense) begins in the weeks just before birth when the fetal brain actually has more nerve connections than the adult brain.[31]

Spirit down development, however, may bring in quite another dimension of consciousness during the time just before birth. Psychologist Helen Wambach analyzed 750 cases of individuals who remembered life before birth under hypnosis. Eighty-one percent of the subjects said that they remembered choosing to be born, and many of these reported having "counselors" available to them to help them make that decision. This serves as another echo of the presence of the spirit guardians described in this chapter.[32]

Given all of the incredible adventures that occur during prenatal existence, you may be wondering why you don't remember anything about this time of life. There may be a good biological explanation for this. What keeps most of us from remembering our prebirth experiences could be a set of chemical changes that occur just before birth. In the hours before birth, your mother (and possibly you as well) secreted a pituitary hormone called *oxytocin* (Greek for "quick birth") that stimulated contractions in your mother's uterus and started the delivery process. Doctors sometimes use a synthetic version of this hormone, called Pitocin, to induce or speed up labor. Oxytocin has a number of other important functions at birth including stopping postbirth bleeding and starting milk production in the mother's breasts. Controlled studies of oxytocin administration to healthy human subjects have documented its amnesic properties.[33] It causes people to forget things. Oxytocin, then, may be the biological equivalent of Lethe, the underworld river of Greek mythology that caused all who drank of its waters to forget their former lives. It could be the chemical correlate of the angel Lailah coming up to the fetus and striking its upper lip.

Perhaps those who receive an adequate supply of oxytocin at birth quickly forget their prebirth experiences, the better to attend to the demands of the life ahead. These individuals may grow up to become the *adapters* of society, content to let the past go and happy to move ahead into the challenges of the present and the future. Research indicates that early exposure to greater levels of oxytocin may be related to higher levels of interpersonal ability in later life, suggesting an improved ability to *adapt* to the social world.[34] On the other hand, it's also possible that those who didn't receive as large a dose of oxytocin at birth—those whom the angel of destiny didn't touch—grow up to become the *rememberers* of society. They are the children and adults who can't stop thinking about where they came from, and can't get it out of their minds that there is something deeper in them and in life that demands recognition.[35] This prenatal self may still be calling to them, echoing the sentiments of the American poet Walt Whitman who wrote: "Before I was born out of my mother generations guided me / My embryo has never been torpid, nothing could overlay it / For it the nebula cohered to an orb / The long slow strata piled to rest it on."[36]

cთთ

The Gift of Prebirth: Potential

If by some miracle we could conjure up the actual historical snapshots of the zygotes of Pope John Paul II, Adolf Hitler, Eleanor Roosevelt, Albert Einstein, Martin Luther King Jr., and Joseph Stalin, it is likely that they would all look more or less the same. Over time, life events, karma, DNA, and destiny formed these zygotes into vastly different individuals, each of whom had an immensely different influence on civilization. But at such an early stage of development, who could have said in advance what they would become? Similarly, the fetus in the womb has yet to emerge onto the earthly stage and make her mark upon the world. She exists, in that respect, in a state of pure potential. She could ultimately become a doctor who saves lives, a contractor who builds cities, a homeless schizophrenic who sleeps in a Dumpster, a young girl who dies of tuberculosis, or a gifted artist who creates masterpieces. These are only a few of the millions of possibilities that lie open for her. At this nascent point in the life cycle, however, we don't know what she will become. This is the gift that the unborn child symbolizes: the gift of potential.

As adults, the fetus carries the image of all the potential that exists within us. We may have the possibility to become a singer, a scientist, an attorney, or a teacher, but have never done anything to actualize this capacity. We may have the seed of a thought—to buy a house, to marry, to write a book—that lies fallow in our untilled garden of ideas. We may have grand dreams—for the betterment of humanity, the enrichment of our community, the saving of the environment—that remain dormant in our imaginations. Like the deeds of the unborn child, these are possibilities that continue to exist in an unrealized and unformed state. It is from these source waters that everything in life emerges. Because of this, we need to develop a state of reverence toward all that is unborn: in ourselves, our families, and our communities. For it is only through such a sense of the sacredness of *potential* that anything real and enduring can be born.

Ways to Explore and Support Prebirth

FOR YOURSELF

- Obtain a photo of a zygote (a single-celled human organism) and periodically look at it with the thought: "This is where I started… at least as a human body."
- Visualize or write a first-person account of what you imagine your life in the womb was like, given what you know about the circumstances of your mother's pregnancy.
- Soak in a warm bath, hot tub, or other body of water and imagine yourself in a safe, comfortable, and nurturing uterine environment.

FOR FRIENDS AND FAMILY

- Do household tasks or other chores for a pregnant family member or friend, to help make her daily life easier as she approaches birth.
- Encourage an expectant mother you know who is engaged in an unhealthy lifestyle habit (smoking, alcohol, drugs) or is under stress due to emotional or relationship difficulties to seek appropriate treatment with a trained mental health professional, go through a substance abuse program, or join a recovery group.
- Provide appropriate and accurate sex information for your own teenagers, and encourage family and friends to do the same with their own adolescents, to prevent unplanned pregnancies.

FOR THE COMMUNITY

- Give to the March of Dimes or similar organizations that fight against birth defects, low birth weight, and other problems in newborns.
- Volunteer at a community prenatal clinic.
- Encourage your community's schools to set up sex education programs, particularly at the middle school and high school levels, that provide comprehensive information about human sexuality, birth control, prenatal development, and the importance of personal responsibility in making good choices about sexual behavior.

∽∞∽

CHAPTER 2

Birth: Through the Tunnel

Our birth is but a sleep and a forgetting:
The Soul that rises with us, our life's Star,
Hath had elsewhere its setting,
And cometh from afar:
Not in entire forgetfulness,
And not in utter nakedness,
But trailing clouds of glory do we come
From God, who is our home:

—WILLIAM WORDSWORTH[1]

Thomas Hobbes always used to tell people that when he was born his mother gave birth to twins: himself and fear. The British philosopher was not yet due to be born when, on a fateful day in 1588, his mother received word that the Spanish armada was about to invade England. The jolt of anxiety she received upon hearing this news sent her into premature labor, and the result was a nervous babe who would grow up to create a political philosophy based largely upon fear. His literary masterpiece, *Leviathan*, would counsel that people are best governed by a monolithic government ruling through threat and intimidation. The fear that brought Hobbes into the world accompanied him throughout his life, and itself gave birth to a political philosophy based upon mistrust that would affect millions of people worldwide.[2]

This is the kind of impact that a traumatic birth can have upon a life and a culture. But that's just the beginning of the story. Two hundred and fifty years after Hobbes's ill-timed birth, the psychoanalyst Otto Rank caused a stir among his Viennese colleagues when he suggested that *every* birth is a trauma, that most people never recover from it, and that this deep-seated birth trauma colors an individual's entire attitude toward life as she grows to maturity. Rank's mentor, Sigmund Freud, at first approved of his pupil's theory, but then changed his mind. The newborn was too narcissistic and unaware of the outside world, according to Freud, to be bothered by the trauma of birth. Rank, however, refused to compromise on this matter, and the issue finally served to create a break in their relationship. Rank went on to elaborate upon his birth trauma theory, suggesting that all later psychological difficulties and all anxieties in life, whether of spiders, the dark, or death itself, are rooted in this one primordial fear.[3]

Was birth really that scary? For those of us who dread the feeling of being stuck in a train tunnel or being cooped up in an elevator, it may certainly seem frightening to think about being squeezed inside of a womb without a view. For those of us who have gone snorkeling or scuba diving and suddenly had our air supply threatened, the prospect of our major life support system—the umbilical cord—being shut off accidentally during birth may fill us with horror as well. There's certainly enough that can go wrong during birth to start a person worrying: being born before you are ready (a premature birth), being snapped at by surgical instruments (a forceps birth or cesarean section), coming out through the vaginal opening and getting stuck, losing blood, not getting enough air, being probed and prodded, slapped and squeezed. And to make matters even worse, newborns are not big, strong adults with plenty of physical cushion and psychic defenses, but totally vulnerable, highly sensitive organisms weighing only a few pounds.

On the other hand, the idea of being born certainly sounds like it *could* be quite interesting, a natural high, in fact. After all, birth brings with it feelings of freshness, renewal, spring, opening up to life, and blossoming.

Imagine the relief, after being cooped up in a tight closet for nine months, of finally getting a chance to break out of that tiny prison and experience the big beautiful world for the first time, to take a deep breath of air and drink in the dazzling array of new sensations, feelings, and energies. If the prospect of birth wasn't at least a little pleasant, then why do virtually all the major religions of the world create rituals that, in different ways, help their members try to achieve a second birth? I mean, if it's *that* painful the first time, don't ask me to go through it again!

Some people might argue along with Freud, however, that it doesn't matter whether birth was pleasant or painful, because we weren't really *there* during birth in a conscious way, and the best proof of this is by noticing that nobody shares their birth memories at office parties or family gatherings. As author William Saroyan put it in his book titled *Births*: "No man remembers his birth, although several liars have insisted they do, and that they also remember their nine months in the womb, but let us understand that such talk is surely solely to amuse and confuse us, and perhaps it is intended to make us feel like fools because we remember nothing of the sort."[4]

As we observed in the last chapter, however, the chemical oxytocin, the angel's touch on our upper lip, and the amnesic waters of the river of Lethe may have had a big role in making us forget our perinatal experiences. There is compelling evidence for the possibility that birth memories may still be active in our psyche and working out their magic or mischief in our lives, depending upon the kind of birth we each went through. To help you understand what you may have experienced during the beginning moments of life, I'd like to take you through some of the key events that could have happened to you during your birth.

The Journey to Be Born

Contrary to popular belief, you were anything but a passive subject during your own birth. In fact, there's growing support for the view that as a prenatal being, you actually helped your mother decide when it was time to be born. Researchers at Cornell University suggest that the original signal to initiate labor comes from a small region of the fetus's brain in the hypothalamus called the PVN or paraventricular nucleus. The sequence of events that start the birth process happens something like this: The PVN signal causes the hypothalamus of the baby to release a chemical message to the pituitary gland, which then stimulates the release of stress hormones from the fetus's adrenal glands. These hormones travel to the mother through the placenta, where they suppress the mother's production of progesterone, a chemical that inhibits contractions and helps keep a mother's body from expelling the baby during the nine months of pregnancy. The suppression of progesterone, in other words, starts the process of labor. Thus, in this indirect way, you signaled your mother's labor contractions.

The mother's body is also active in this process, opening and closing the chemical gates to this flow of hormones from the baby to create special windows of opportunity for birth to occur.[5] As with prebirth, there is a kind of biochemical conversation going on between mother and child that might sound something like this if it could be verbalized: Fetus: "I'm ready to be born now." Mother: "Not quite yet, wait a bit." Fetus: "But I want to be born!" Mother: "It isn't time." A few minutes or hours or days later. Fetus: "I'm waiting!" Mother: "Okay, now seems like a good time!"

Once labor starts, the birthing journey begins. Imagine you are inside of your mother's womb and her uterine muscles start to contract. You've got a cushion of water around you for protection (unless your mom's water broke already), so you're not going to be crushed to death, though it may feel like it. Up to a hundred pounds of pressure is being exerted upon your tiny form in its amniotic bubble. And of course, as you're being squeezed like a grapefruit, there's really nowhere to go except for this one place at the neck of your mother's womb. There you're pushed against an elastic wall, the cervix, that's taking its time dilating. This agony can go on for a long while as the tiny opening in the cervix expands centimeter by centimeter. First-time mothers spend an average of thirteen hours in this stage of labor.

But there's a problem. In fact, it's one of the biggest problems of human existence from a purely *body up* perspective. You've got a big head, and your mother has a tiny opening that you must get through. When we were less evolved as mammals our brains were smaller and it was no big deal to make it through the birth canal. But as our brains evolved and got larger, so did the problem of making it all the way through the tunnel. Finally, Nature said to the human brain something like: "I'm sorry, but if you get any bigger, you're never going to make it through the birth canal, and all that brilliance I've given you will be wasted! So here's what I'm doing to do for you. First, I'm going to delay some of that brain growth until after birth so that the problem doesn't get any worse. Second, I'm going to put into your big basketball of a brain the know-how to figure out what to do to help your own offspring give birth." So humans became the first species to organize others of its own kind—midwives—to assist mothers during the birth process.[6]

Meanwhile, you've got your head (or butt, if you're going to be a breech birth) pressed up against a tight little cervical window, and it's not giving you much slack. You may feel like that character in Edgar Allan Poe's short story "The Pit and the Pendulum," who had been placed unknowingly into a prison with walls that were closing in on him and the only way out was down a bottomless pit (Poe clearly must have had a traumatic birth himself). You're not exactly enduring this crushing experience in a dispassionate way. You start to feel the walls give way and you definitely want out. You may feel at this point like Odysseus and his men trying to escape from the Cyclops's cave (and, we should keep in mind that Cyclops was the son of Poseidon, the god of *water*).

But your mother may not be so cooperative. Birth pioneer Frederick Leboyer regarded this part of the mother-child dance as a struggle to the death. In his book *Birth Without Violence* he writes: "... this monstrous unremitting pressure that is crushing the baby, pushing it out toward the world—and this blind wall, which is holding it back, confining it—These things are all one: the mother! She is driving the baby out. At the same time she is holding it in, preventing its passage."[7]

Finally, the cervix reaches a diameter of ten centimeters—a little more than four inches—and your head "crowns," signaling that you are now ready to pass into the birth canal. I should mention at this point that if at any time during this whole process of birth or even before it begins something happens to go wrong, or your doctor's medical malpractice insurance premiums are about to go up, or your mother wants to avoid the mess of birth, or caretakers don't think you're up to making the trip on your own steam, then you might suddenly discover some mechanical gadgets coming down like whirligigs from the sky to surgically extract you from your mother's womb in a caesarian section.

Assuming that this hasn't happened, you're ready for the next stage of the birth process: expulsion. You may feel like a human cannonball as you ready yourself to explode out of your mother's body. But don't get too enthusiastic yet. This stage can take a few minutes, or it may last a few hours. You'll remember that head problem I mentioned earlier. There's also the business of the *rest* of your body coming through the birth canal. This can be a real challenge if you're leaving feet first, arm first, or have planned some other interesting exit strategy. You've still got this umbilical connection to your mother, and somehow you have to come out in such a way that you don't get strangled by your own cord, or push the cord into your mother's bony pelvis where it can cut off your oxygen and cause brain damage.

But assuming that everything is going along normally, your head is pressed against your own breastbone as you begin to move through the cervix on your way down the birth canal. Your head arches back as you move upward and outward into the light of day. Your neck twists to the left to assist the shoulders getting through. Then the "deliverer" gently guides your shoulders and chest out into the bright world. As soon as that's accomplished, the rest of you slips out like laundry from a chute. Tah-dah! You're born! Happy birthday!

During this whole process, you're a little bit like our hero, Odysseus, who was called "the man of twists and turns."

Etherized Upon a Table

Of course, this wasn't necessarily the way you were actually born. Each one of us had a unique birth with its own side trips, accidents, delays, surprises, annoyances, or other peculiarities. And in many ways, the idiosyncratic nature of this natal journey was fashioned by the kind of cultural sur-roundings that supported or restricted your mother. Consider the possi-bility, for example, that like most of us in contemporary Western culture, you were born in a modern hospital setting. Anthropologist Robbie Davis-Floyd has examined the alienating, life-negating messages a woman giving birth in a conventional American hospital all too often receives from the moment she enters the front door. First, she may be whisked away in a wheelchair, an act that implies the presence of a disability. Then she goes through the "prep," when her clothes are relinquished and replaced by a bland hospital gown. After this, she may be given an enema and have her pubic hair shaved, depersonalizing her in a way not unlike inmates in a prison or marines in boot camp.

Once in bed, she is attached to intravenous tubes and electronic mon-itors that further reinforce the image of her being sick and dependent. If her labor is not fast enough to conform to the hospital's time charts, then, as mentioned in the last chapter, she might be given a drug like Pitocin to speed up contractions. An internal fetal monitor may be inserted into her vagina, causing the rupture of placental membranes. Strangers—medical personnel, that is—may come around and periodically stick their gloved fingers into her vagina to check her cervical dilation, potentially intro-ducing bacteria into the birth canal She might be given epidural anes-thesia to numb out the lower portion of her body to kill the pain of birth.

Getting ready for the actual birth, she may be placed on a table in the lithotomy position, with feet up in the air and buttocks hanging over the table's edge—not exactly your high dignity position. Then, to create a bigger opening for the baby, she is likely to have her perineum cut in a procedure called an episiotomy, an intervention done in about a third of all hospital births.[8] If there are complications during delivery, the doctor may use forceps or do a C-section (cesarean birth) to pull you out. Even if there are no complications, the doctor may do a C-section anyway, as they are now performed during more than 30 percent of all births in the United States despite the fact that they put the mother at three times greater risk of death.[9, 10]

After the birth, the umbilical cord is usually cut quickly, any bloody remains washed away to maintain the hospital's sterile field, and the baby is snatched away from the mom at which time it is cleaned, given injections and eye drops, tested for certain diseases, and assigned an Apgar score to determine if it needs emergency care. While the baby may be given back to the mother for a brief "bonding period," the baby is usually then taken away for a four-hour separation period and put in a clean bassinet next to other babies who have gone through the same ritual.[11]

You can imagine the impact all of this has on your mother's physical and emotional state. Just the very fact of her being moved from familiar surroundings—home, friends, and family—into the impersonal space of a hospital could have had negative consequences. Animal studies suggest that being moved out of familiar surroundings during critical life cycle events like giving birth can cause a range of significant negative physiological and behavioral effects, from spontaneous abortions and stillbirths to impairment of mothering behaviors.[12] Administration of drugs to help your mother cope with the pain of birth, including tranquilizers, sleeping medications, painkillers, or anesthetics, could also have profoundly affected the birth process. These drugs may have dulled your mother's responses, affected the rhythm of her contractions, and kept her from fully participating in the process of giving birth to you.

What this means is that all the millions of years of evolutionary wisdom stored up in your mother's body telling her exactly what to do at each step of the way in giving birth to you was, at best, largely untapped or even seriously undermined. Psychologist Arthur Janov writes in his book *Imprints: The Lifelong Effects of the Birth Experience*, "After administration of drugs, the mother's uterine contractions grow fewer and weaker. Worse, drugs block important neural messages so that the sequence of contractions from back to front is also altered. This means that the baby is less apt to be propelled forward in a smooth way. Most often, it is squeezed and mashed by the out-of-synch contractions—a bit like going through a compacting machine."[13] Moreover, since anesthetics can pass through the placental barrier, then *you* might have been numbed out by the drugs as well and not been fully present for the most significant event in your life: your own birth.

Even if you *were* there for the birth, it wasn't likely to be a picnic if it was a typical hospital delivery. You probably had these strange feelers intruding upon you—monitors and probing fingers, or perhaps metal forceps and other surgical instruments—interfering with those biological rhythms of yours that were helping to propel you through the tunnel. You probably received fear hormones from your mother—biological reflections of her own state of disorientation, alienation, and anxiety— pouring through the umbilical cord and overloading your own stressed-out nervous system.

When you were born—before you'd had a chance to get your own respiratory system going—the doctor may have cut your umbilical cord too soon, severing your oxygen supply to your mother and leaving you to struggle in a death agony for the least little bit of air. And by snatching you away from your mother's body, the doctor was essentially destroying the only home you knew. Finally, the doctor may have dangled you briefly in midair and placed you on a cold metallic platform, where he probably put stinging drops in your eyes and injected you with needles while you stared up at artificial neon lights. It makes a person wonder whether all those stories of UFOs and alien abductions in the tabloids aren't just birth memories that have been suddenly and dramatically recalled.

Being "Sung" into the World

Compare the above experiences with the way your birth might have proceeded at any other time in human history except during the last hundred years, or even in many parts of the "undeveloped" world today. Chances are, your mother would have given birth at home surrounded by family and friends. She would have had help from others: women specially trained and gifted in the art of birth assistance. She would have been able to walk around during labor, and even been able to continue with her normal activities until close to the actual birth. She might have been given a birth stool to squat on, or backed up against a tree or wall for support, or had women holding her while she readied herself. Midwives might have massaged her in special ways to assist with the contractions.

Special rituals, charms, chants, or other symbolic activities could have helped to create a climate of confidence, warmth, and sacredness. At the moment of birth, you might simply have dropped out of your mother into a hole in the ground, where you would have been held by Mother Earth, or fallen into the arms of your family members or into a soft bundle of cloth. Or you might have been "sung" into the world with a grand-mother chanting in imitation of your birth cry.[14]

Finally birthed, you might have had a family member breathe into your nostrils to put the sacred spirit into you. A grandmother might have massaged your body with oil. Your umbilical cord might have been kept intact until the throbbing died away, and then cut with the teeth, or a shell, or piece of bamboo, which would have then been put around you or stored as a sacred necklace. Your placenta might have been regarded as sacred as well, perhaps planted under a tree (as we noted in the previous chapter) that then became your own "destiny tree." Your family might have welcomed you with rituals and ceremonies appropriate to their own vision of the cosmos.

Your birth would have had meaning and purpose, and a natural context within which every event leading up to and through it would have had deep cultural and spiritual significance. During such a birth, fear would be naturally present, but it would have been mediated through well-designed social support systems rather than through the culturally barren directives of scientific progress. Your own natural instincts to be born, and your mother's biological drive to give birth to you, would have been under-stood—not subdued, denied, or etherized—and would have been supported through a rich storehouse of indigenous knowledge and cultural lore.[15]

Natural Birth in Modern Times

To be fair, there *was* a darker side to being born before the advent of sci-ence, a side that still plays itself out in too many parts of the world today. Malnutrition on your mother's part could have devastated your prenatal development and left you or your mother too weak to survive. Without antibiotics, the risk of catastrophic infection for both you and your mother was an ever-present reality. If you didn't look strong and healthy at birth, or if you were a girl, there was a strong likelihood of your being snuffed out on the spot.[16] Even if you had survived all this, instead of being welcomed with open arms, you might have immediately had your ears pierced or air blown up your anus, or a family member might have whirled you around in a basket that was then let go of, sending you hurtling into the dust; a procedure intended to "shock" you out of the *spirit down* world that you came from, and into the *body up* world that you needed to adapt to.

Being born in most cultures around the world was and still is a hazardous undertaking. However, the essential principles of nontechnological birth—giving birth at home among family and friends within a coherent cultural and spiritual meaning-system—still has much to recommend it compared with being born among high-tech strangers in an alien hospital environment. The challenge for mothers in the modern era is to discover ways to link the best aspects of traditional birthing methods with the safety features of science and technology. This is exactly what has been happening in the alternative birthing movement over the past sixty years. Starting with the work of British obstetrician Grantly Dick-Read in 1933, a wide range of natural childbirth methods have been developed as a regular part of modern medical practice.[17]

You may have been born under such conditions, where your mother was allowed to go through labor and birth with minimal or no pain medication and the emotional support of a birth attendant to help her relax and trust the natural processes of birth. If your mother used the Bradley method of birth she would have been encouraged, with her husband's assistance, to accept the pain of birth without medications, to scream or cry loudly if she wished, and to treat each moment of labor as part of the total experience of birth.[18] Or if she prepared for birth through the Lamaze method, she would have been allowed to use pain medication as needed, discouraged from engaging in loud crying, and taught specific breathing exercises, again with the father's help, to perform in synchrony with con-

tractions and physical "pushing," to calm her and help her disassociate
from the pain of birth.[19]

If your mother had been influenced by the teachings of Frederick
Leboyer, your birth might have taken place in a quiet and dark environment—to remove disturbing stimuli—and been followed by a soothing
warm bath and lots of physical contact between you and mom.[20] You
might have been born in a birthing center—a facility within a hospital or
part of a health-care center—which would have provided a homelike
atmosphere for labor and birth with the ready availability of emergency
medical care if necessary. You might have been a water baby: born in a
swimming pool or other body of water to help ease the transition from
your watery womb. Or, you might have been born at home with the help
of a midwife or other nonmedical birth assistant.[21]

The most common argument given by those who feel reluctant to
explore alternative birthing options—especially those that involve being
away from a traditional hospital environment—is that they aren't safe for
either the mother or the baby. However, research suggests that planned
homebirths with certified professional midwives in North America are as
safe as hospital births for low-risk moms and are associated with lower
rates of medical intervention.[22] In the Netherlands, where midwife-
attended homebirth is practiced by up to one-third of all mothers, infant
mortality is 4.96 per 1,000 births compared with 6.43 per 1,000 in the
United States, where less than 1 percent of births occur at home.[23]

The Agony and the Ecstasy of Birth

Quite apart from the physical risks involved in a traditional hospital birth,
there are deep emotional wounds that can scar a child for the rest of her
life. Most hospital births take place under the assumption that the fetus
cannot feel or sense what is going on around her. A thousand-year-old
tradition contradicts this view. Eleventh-century Tibetan Buddhist monk
Milarepa, wrote: "I will explain the suffering of birth . . . In nine months it
emerges from the womb in pain excruciating, as if pulled out gripped by
pliers. When from the womb its head is squeezed, the pain is like being

thrown into a bramble pit . . . When from the baby's tender body the blood and filth are being cleansed, the pain is like being flayed alive. When the umbilical cord is cut, it feels as though the spine were severed."[24]

Contemporary research by pre- and perinatal scientists studying birth memories seems to demonstrate that many people actually *do* remember their birth when they go through hypnosis or some other method of accessing deeper states of consciousness. Obstetrician David Cheek, for example, in a study using hypnosis reported that subjects were able to demonstrate the exact movements of their head and shoulders during birth, knowledge that is usually known only to those with specialized obstetrical training.[25] Psychologist David Chamberlain studied mother-child pairs. The children ranged in age from nine to twenty-three and reported no previous conscious memories of their birth. The mothers indicated that they had shared no details of the birth with their children. Under hypnosis, mother and child reports showed remarkable similarities. Children accurately identified birth details such as the time of day, locale, people who were present, surgical instruments used, position of delivery, behavior of doctors and nurses, room layouts, and sequences of events.[26]

Especially intriguing is the research done by Stanislav Grof, a Czechoslovakian-born psychiatrist and former director of the Maryland Psychiatric Research Center. During the 1960s, when the use of drugs such as LSD and psilocybin was still legal and approved by the U.S. government for psychiatric research, Dr. Grof and his colleagues used psychedelic therapy to effectively treat mental disorders such as alcoholism and depression.[27] Grof noticed that individuals going through treatment sometimes had the sensation of being choked around the neck, experienced difficulty breathing, or felt stabbing pains in their navel or elsewhere in their body. These perceptions were often accompanied by images of tunnels, engulfment, torture, feelings of claustrophobia, excruciating pain, or alternatively, ecstatic rapture. Grof began to suspect that his patients were re-experiencing the trauma of birth, just as Otto Rank had predicted decades earlier. Out of hundreds of case histories of this kind, Grof formulated a conceptual model that helped make sense of the experience of being born.

According to Grof, the process of birth involves four primary stages or what he calls Basic Perinatal Matrices (BPMs).[28]

The first stage, or Basic Perinatal Matrix I (BPM I), is the period before labor has begun, when the fetus remains in a relatively undisturbed state within the mother. Grof's patients undergoing BPM I experienced the sensations of a "good womb" (e.g., cosmic unity, satisfaction of needs, feelings of fulfillment, a sense of harmony), and/or a "bad womb" (e.g., feelings of engulfment, threats of disease, emotional upheavals from the mother).

The second stage, Basic Perinatal Matrix II (BPM II), is the stage of birth when labor has begun but the cervix has not yet fully dilated. Grof's patients going through BPM II experiences often felt immense physical or emotional suffering, a sense of being trapped or confined without hope, and/or deep feelings of victimization and endless torture.

The third stage, or BPM III, is that point in the process where the cervix has fully dilated and the baby starts to move through the birth canal toward the outside world. Patients in this stage would often feel themselves going through a cosmic death-rebirth struggle that involved excruciating pain and pleasure, volcanic-like intensity, and/or a sense of imminent violence or danger.

The fourth and final stage, Basic Perinatal Matrix IV (BPM IV), is that point when the baby has emerged from the womb and the umbilical cord is cut. Patients going through BPM IV states would experience a feeling of enormous decompression or expansion of space, images of rebirth and redemption, as well as unpleasant sensations related to navel pain, loss of breath, or fear of death.

Grof's theory was that these patients were re-experiencing their own births, releasing the trauma and integrating the healing associated with each stage of the birth process. According to Grof, we all to some extent carry repressed birth experiences into life with us that can have significant negative consequences for our later physical and emotional health. Specific unresolved traumas or complications that occur at each stage of birth can pop up as physical, emotional, or mental difficulties in later life. The hellish intrauterine memories of artist Salvador Dalí that we discussed in the last chapter may represent a good example of a BPM I "bad womb" experience. Perhaps Dalí's strange surrealistic paintings are both a reflection of those horrors as well as an attempt to come to grips with his difficult birth through creative expression.

The French philosopher Jean-Paul Sartre may represent a good example of a BPM II baby. Like Thomas Hobbes, his negative experiences in his mother's womb could have been formative to his philosophy (existentialism), which is based on the need to take decisive action in a menacing and meaningless universe. In Sartre's play *No Exit*, a work that takes place in a small room representing hell, people torture each other without even trying. This sounds a lot like BPM II, where the fetus is being compacted by the mother's contractions but as yet has no way out due to the nondilated cervix. Interestingly, Sartre once took a psychedelic substance under the supervision of a psychiatrist but found the feeling of losing control disagreeable and he vowed never to touch the stuff again.

The trauma associated with BPM III, when the baby begins a bloody struggle out of the womb, may express itself in adulthood among those individuals who espouse or practice violence, including rapists, murderers, terrorists, and tyrants. Adolf Hitler may have been a BPM III baby. In his speech to the German people on June 22, 1941, Hitler refers to how the Allied forces "would have been ready to strangle and defeat the German Reich." He speaks of "preparing the rebirth of the Reich." His talk contains other telling references to fears that he had of Germany's "struggle," "encirclement," and potential "extermination." Over the course of his dictatorship, Hitler had many of his most hated enemies hanged, and one historian even argues that Hitler himself was strangled to death by a member of his inner circle in his Berlin bunker in 1945.[29] These clues lead me to wonder whether Hitler may have been threatened with strangulation from the umbilical cord during his own birth. As strange as it may seem, his path toward unparalleled violence could have been laid down as he was fighting his way out of his mother's womb.[30]

BPM IV experiences, those dealing with the actual expulsion from the mother, may be associated with religious leaders who have undergone a spiritual death-rebirth experience. These conversion or transformation experiences may in some sense have been a transcendent mirroring or even psychological completion of their physical birth. While psychoanalyst Erik Erikson's biography of Martin Luther, for example, focuses on the role of his overbearing father as a factor in Luther's religious conversion during a violent thunderstorm, it may be truer to look back to Luther's birth experience.[31] Similarly, the biblical Saul's vision on the road to Damascus, Blaise Pascal's "night of fire" religious conversion, and other dramatic religious conversion stories may represent the emergence, after a lifetime of repression, of the fireworks that took place at the end of the birth canal.[32]

These fireworks, buried as they are in most of us, represent an amazing and untold part of our life story. In retrospect, after looking back at all that we have surveyed in this chapter, it seems incredible to me that more individuals in our society have not recognized the psychological importance of the birth process in our later lives. The fact that the fetus at five months has about as many brain cells as the average adult should give us pause when we begin to doubt the impact of birth on our emotional well-being. Even Freud pointed out that a mother's uterus is the one place everybody in the world can definitively say they've lived. That means every person on the planet has had the experience of coming out of his mother's womb and seeing the world for the first time. And what a dramatic experience that must have been! As poet and historian William MacNeile Dixon put it: "Birth is the sudden opening of a window, through which you look out upon a stupendous prospect. For what has happened? A miracle. You have exchanged nothing for the possibility of everything."[33]

∽⊗∾

The Gift of Birth: Hope

During the first nine months of life, the unborn child gestates as pure potential. At birth, everything changes. Now the child comes out of the womb onto the world stage and anything can happen. We don't yet know *what* will happen, but we do know that our expectations are infused with *hope*. In the Bible, John 16:21 says: "A woman giving birth to a child has pain because her time has come; but when her baby is born she forgets the anguish because of her joy that a child is born into the world." The birth of a child is like the dawn, the spring, or the beginning of a new era, and in beginnings there is always hope. There is the hope that the child will thrive and prosper, the hope that the child will brighten the lives of those around him, and the hope that he will contribute in some way to making the world a better place in which to live.

The significance of birth as a symbol in our own adult lives, then, is the promise of new life; the hope that new and great things will be born in us from moment to moment. We can ask ourselves in each moment: "What is currently being born in me?" A new job? A new relationship? A new spiritual outlook? Whatever is emerging in our inner or outer lives, the gift of birth gives us the hope that it will lead to wonderful things. The job will lead us, perhaps, to the use of new abilities. The relationship will lead to us to new levels of intimacy. The spiritual outlook will expand our horizons beyond the daily grind of existence. When we treat new things in our lives with the same hopeful expectancy that a mother has for her newborn child, we immeasurably increase the probability that over time these events will flourish beyond our wildest dreams.

——————— *Ways to Explore and Support Birth* ———————

FOR YOURSELF
- Inquire about the circumstances of your birth from family, friends, archives, or other sources.
- Engage in psychotherapy with a trained mental health professional who has expertise in treating birth trauma and other perinatal issues (for more information, contact The Association for Pre- & Perinatal Psychology and Health, P.O. Box 1398, Forestville, CA 95436; apppah@aol.com; www.birthpsychology.com).

- Create an artwork that vividly depicts what you imagine to have been your personal experience of being born.

FOR FRIENDS AND FAMILY

- Help an expectant mom you know choose an appropriate birth method to meet her needs from among a range of alternatives (see, for example, the book *Gentle Birth Choices: A Guide to Making Informed Decisions About Birthing Centers, Birth Attendants, Water Birth, Home Birth, and Hospital Birth*, by Barbara Harper and Suzanne Arms).
- Serve as a birth coach to a close family member or friend who is expecting.
- Assist a pregnant family member or friend in creating a meaningful ritual to welcome her baby into the world.

FOR THE COMMUNITY

- Contribute financially to an organization that supports safe alternative birthing practices in technological societies, or that promotes safe medical births in undeveloped countries.
- Train as a midwife, doula, or other birthing paraprofessional to assist others in the birth process.
- Volunteer in the maternity wing of a hospital to assist with various tasks such as providing emotional support to expectant mothers, running errands, and providing child care.

⌒∞⌒

CHAPTER 3

Infancy: Legends of the Fall

Happy those early days! when I
Shined in my angel-infancy.
Before I understood this place
Appointed for my second race,
Or taught my soul to fancy ought
But a white, celestial thought;

—HENRY VAUGHAN[1]

The Sufi teacher Hazrat Inayat Khan once remarked that the infant is an exile from paradise and that is why her first expression on earth is a cry. Like so many poets, mystics, and other "rememberers," Inayat Khan believed that the infant comes *down from the spirit* before taking birth in a human body. He was aware that most people regard infancy as a time of ignorance, but believed that infants "can perceive or can receive impressions of human beings much more readily than grown-up people." He also observed that infants have an appreciation of music that goes far beyond that of most adults. "The infant is music itself," he wrote. "In the cradle it is moving its little arms and legs in a certain rhythm. And when our music falls on the ears of an infant it is of the lowest character compared with the music it is accustomed to."[2] The infant, in Inayat Khan's view, has descended from the stars and is still listening to the Music of the Spheres.

At birth, however, the infant's soul descends into matter and the memory of a celestial life diminishes. During the actual process of birth the newborn is usually positioned *head-downward* and falls away from the uterus into the world. In many cultures, where birthing takes place in a squatting position, the infant literally falls into a prepared hole in the ground.[3] This "fall" is one of the central themes of human culture. It is the story of Adam and Eve's fall from grace and their exile from the Garden of Eden. It is the story of humanity's falling away from the Golden Age as told in Greek, Persian, Sumerian, and Indian myths. It is the fall of the individual in Tibetan Buddhism away from the Clear Light of Primary Reality into the maelstrom of its own karmic deeds at rebirth. And, it is also the story of the fall of the soul of the infant into the constraints of material existence. The spirit, once so free to roam, now finds itself stuck in the muck, so to speak, having to contend with all manner of inner and outer forces that it has no control over. The process of *growing up from the body* consists in learning how to gain some degree of control over these material forces and in discovering how to find one's way in a world that has its own rhymes and reasons, and its own terrible gravity to conquer.

The Mother and Child Reunion

It takes a lot of time and care to accomplish this task of rising up from the rubble in the earliest stages of human development. Had you been born as an elephant you could have run with the herd shortly after birth. If you had been born as a baby seal you would have been able to swim the high seas at six weeks of age. But since you were born as a human being, you entered the world highly dependent upon others. In a sense, every human being is born prematurely. Psychoanalyst Adolph Portmann suggested that human beings were designed for a twenty-one-month gestation period, nine months of it taking place inside the womb, and another year of "extrauterine" development required to bring the infant to a minimal state of self-sufficiency (with, of course, many more years required for total independence).[4]

There are good evolutionary reasons for this arrangement. As we noted in the last chapter, the larger brain size of human beings served as an asset when it came to being smart enough to figure out how to adapt to a changing environment, but it posed a distinct problem at birth: how to get that large head through the birth canal. On average, the human skull at birth is 101.8 percent the size of the birth canal. Nature's solution was to delay some of that brain development until *after* birth. Not only did this keep the size of your head at birth from becoming watermelon-sized, but it also meant that your brain could keep on developing outside of the womb.

This meant that the structure of your brain could be tailored to a certain extent according to the specific environment in which you were born. Nature essentially worked it out so that a large portion of your brain, especially areas in your neocortex, could remain "uncommitted" in infancy, and thus could wait to see what was going to happen in the outer environment before being hardwired. Brain research over the past thirty years has demonstrated that environmental stimulation can strengthen connections between brain cells in human beings, especially in the early years, and conversely, that environmental deprivation can weaken or eliminate those connections.[5] Nature provided this convenient scenario in part so that depending upon what you needed in order to survive in your environment, your brain would be able to maintain those neural connections that promoted your survival and eliminate those linkages that weren't important to your thriving. This property of *plasticity*, as it's called, has distinct advantages over species that are hardwired at birth and thus can't adapt to changing circumstances in the outside world. To put it more bluntly, if we had been hardwired to respond at birth to the world in a fixed way like some of our primitive ancestors, we'd likely be fossils in some antediluvian lakebed!

Nowhere is this interaction between brain and environment more important than in the mother-child relationship in infancy. From the moment of birth, your mother—or primary caretaker—was the locus of mediation between your brain and the world. She was the one with the greatest responsibility for stimulating your brain, and thus the one best equipped to help strengthen those neural connections that would enable you to survive and thrive in the unique circumstances of your surroundings. Millions of years of evolution led up to this moment in time and endowed both you and your mother with an extraordinary ability to tune into each other to make the system work.

Your dreamy large eyes and cute bulging forehead were designed by Nature to elicit biologically based nurturing behaviors from your mother. Your near-sightedness at birth (20/150 vision) suited your relationship to your mother very well, since you could see only about six inches around you, a circumference that just took in your mother's face and body. As you gazed into your mother's face you optimally saw yourself, your moods, and your energies mirrored there in her frowns, her smiles, her *oohs* of sympathy and her *ahs* of understanding. The feel of her touch, the caress of her hands, the sound of her voice, and the taste of the milk from her nipples released hormones that comforted and calmed you. Your mother also produced chemicals that stimulated nurturing feelings in her. In fact, the same amnesia-producing neuropeptide (oxytocin) that may have caused you to forget your spiritual origins at birth served in the days and weeks after birth to stimulate your mother's own nurturing behaviors toward you. Research shows, for example, that mother rats given a drug blocking their natural production of oxytocin cease all nurturing behaviors.[6]

It's commonly observed that many mothers have an uncanny ability to sense the needs of their infants. Their hearing seems to be heightened and their ability to discriminate between different types of crying—angry, sad, hurt, scared—is legendary. Attuned mothers appear to be able to tell when infants are about to wet or soil themselves or are about to cry for food. One psychiatrist, Jan Ehrenwald, even suggested that the origins of Extrasensory Perception (ESP) go back to the earliest experiences of communication between mother and infant. He speculated that ESP evolved as a way for mother and infant to alert each other to urgent survival-related needs before the infant developed the ability to communicate using verbal language.[7]

The mother—and to a lesser extent, the father and other care providers—serves as a kind of psychic shock absorber for the infant against all of the unpredictabilities of the world: the bumps, thumps, flashes, and crashes of the outside environment, and the pain, wet, cold, heat, fear, and hunger of the world inside of the infant's body. Studies suggest that secure attachment between mother and infant during the first years of life provides a buffer or a kind of emotional vaccination against stressful events in later life. Older kids who are securely attached in infancy, for example, produce less cortisol (a stress hormone that can cause physical and psychological damage from chronic exposure) than kids who as infants were not as securely attached to their mothers. They also have higher self-esteem, lower rates of psychopathology, and enjoy more successful peer relationships and academic success.[8]

The Hand That Blocks the Cradle

Emotional attunement during the first years of life appears to be the social-emotional glue of the world, bonding the mother to the infant, and the growing child to all of his subsequent relationships in life, including his own future role as a parent A look at the world situation, however, reveals many tears and breaks in that social-emotional fabric. Divorce, estrangement, feuds, conflicts, crimes, wars, and looming catastrophes all threaten the harmony of our lives and even the continued existence of our species. The failure of attachment, or the breakdown of nature's exquisite plan for bonding an infant to its mother, may lie at the core of many of these social ills and deserves our very careful attention here for what it can teach us about healing early emotional scars before they grow into massive psychosocial wounds in later life.

Toward the end of World War II, scientists first became aware of the devastating consequences of the lack of emotional nurturing in infancy. Psychoanalyst René Spitz compared children institutionally reared in a war-time orphanage with those raised by their own mothers in a prison nursery. The orphanage infants—those who were fed and clothed but not held, played with, or talked to—had higher rates of physical illness, failure to gain weight, emotional disturbance, and infant mortality.[9] Years later, psychologist John Bowlby examined how the chronically abandoned infant responded to frequent experiences of separation. He observed that an infant goes through three distinct stages of separation anxiety: First the baby protests the separation by crying, screaming, and flailing about. If no help comes, he then goes through a stage of despair with diminished activity, monotone crying, and gradual withdrawal. Finally, with continued neglect there begins a detachment stage when he becomes passive, unresponsive, and "emotionally dead" even when care eventually does arrive.[10] He enters the realm of T. S. Eliot's *Waste Land*, "where . . . the dead tree gives no shelter, . . . "[11]

Initially, attachment disorders were examined in impersonal institutional settings like hospitals and orphanages. But in the last thirty years, there's been a great deal of clinical research showing how bonding problems show up in daily mother-child interactions. Child researcher and psychoanalyst Margaret Mahler observed mothers' behaviors with their infants and discovered many underlying pathologies. These included mothers who couldn't tolerate their babies' rejections of them because they reminded them of their own mothers' rejections when they were small; mothers who wouldn't let their infants explore the world because of their own fears of loss and abandonment, and mothers who narcissistically treated their infants as extensions of themselves rather than little beings with their own independent lives. Mahler wrote about one mother who "proudly breast-fed her babies, but only because it was convenient . . . it made her feel successful and efficient."[12] Regardless of how the mother-infant breakdown occurs, the consequences of impaired contact between mother and child during the first year of life can be devastating. Researchers have linked attachment disorders during infancy to a long list of problems in later life, including depression; anxiety disorders; eating disorders; and conduct disorders; violence; sex offenses; borderline personality disorder; physical illness; suicide; alcoholism; and drug abuse.

The link between attachment problems in infancy and violent behavior later on in life is particularly troublesome. Child advocate and neuropsychologist James W. Prescott has been particularly vocal in highlighting this connection. He has challenged the criminal justice system "to find one murderer, rapist, or drug addict in any correctional facility in America who has been breast-fed for 'two years and beyond' as recommended by the World Health Organization."[13] He suggests that if we spent more time, money, and attention on promoting healthy mother-child interactions during the first two years of life, then we might have considerably greater success in preventing crime in our communities. On a broader scale, the violence of war may be tracked back not only to a despotic leader's negative birth experiences, but to his abuse as an infant as well. A tyrant or dictator, after all, is in many respects just an infant who has been chronically roused into an emotional state of rage by overwhelming shame from a parent or caregiver, and now has the body, mind, and skills of an adult—plus a whole cadre of similarly raging infantile adults—to assist him in exacting revenge on others for his injuries.[14]

Through the Eyes of an Infant

The process of tracing the tyranny of some world leaders back to infancy raises broader questions about the inner world of the infant. What really *is* the subjective experience of an infant anyway? Can we ever really know for sure? These questions were rarely even asked historically because the young infant was regarded as having no real subjective experiences of its own. The British philosopher John Locke considered the newborn infant's mind a "blank slate" passively waiting to receive impressions from the outside world. American philosopher and psychologist William James called the newborn's experience "a bloomin' buzzin' confusion." As we saw in the last chapter, Freud thought of the newborn as a self-absorbed narcissist totally unaware of the outer world. And as recently as the 1980s, many physicians in the United States assumed that babies didn't have a nervous system sophisticated enough to feel pain.[15]

Over the past several years, however, researchers have developed a very different view of the infant's inner life, suggesting that from birth the infant is consciously seeking to make sense of the world. Through ingenious experiments that measure an infant's sucking, head turning, and gazing patterns (babies spend more time attending to things that interest them) scientists have been able to demonstrate a baby's preferences from the moment of birth. Studies suggest, for example, that the newborn has proclivities for looking at curved versus straight objects, patterns rather than plain fields, and human faces over inanimate objects.[16] Most of these preferences are highly adaptive in directing the infant's attention toward human beings who can provide nurturing behaviors. As infant researcher Daniel Stern points out: "Almost from the moment of birth, [the infant] has a capacity for perception, and a cognitive competence that enables it to initiate affective interactive exchanges with its mother."[17]

But what does this look like from the infant's point of view? This is certainly impossible to convey with words, since the infant lives in a preverbal world. The word *infant* literally means "unable to speak." Artists who work with nonverbal media come closest perhaps to conveying some of the subjective experiences of the infant. In writing about Mozart's *Piano Sonata in A Minor*, for example, biographer Maynard Solomon hears in the juxtaposition of calm and dissonant passages in the andante section representations of "an infancy-Eden of unsurpassable beauty but also a state completely vulnerable to terrors of separation, loss, and even fears of potential annihilation."[18] Similarly, pediatrician and child psychoanalyst D. W. Winnicott observed in the grotesque and misshapen portraits of contemporary British artist Francis Bacon an attempt to work out the infant's experience of seeing and being seen by his mother. He writes: "Bacon . . . is seeing himself in his mother's face, but with some twist in him or her that maddens both him and us."[19] Finally, there's the testimony of the Russian dancer Vaslav Nijinsky, whose barely coherent diaries mirror his own deeply fragmented state, yet whose frenzied dances may have expressed the shimmering vitality of an infant. Nijinsky wrote: "I work with my hands and feet and head and eyes and nose and tongue and hair and skin and stomach and guts. . . ."[20]

The best metaphor with which to characterize an infant's experience may be a creative fusion of some of the above elements that takes place through a combination of physical, visual, auditory, and emotional expression; a kind of pre-verbal Wagnerian opera or *Gesamkunstwerke* ("synthesis of the arts"). Recent infancy research suggests that infants do not separate their perceptions into seeing, hearing, smelling, tasting, and touching, but rather experience a unity of the senses. In one study, three-week-old infants were blindfolded and given either a smooth or a nubbed pacifier to suck on. After the pacifiers were taken away and the blindfolds removed, infants had an opportunity to look at both kinds of pacifiers. Results showed that babies looked longer at the pacifiers they had sucked on, indicating an underlying unity in their kinesthetic and visual-perceptual channels.

Babies also show the ability to associate musical experiences with visual ones. In a related study, babies looked at two balls bouncing at different rates and making no sounds. They then correctly matched a *boing, boing, boing* sound with the visual ball that was bouncing in synchrony with that particular musical pattern. Other research has shown that babies can watch a silent video of a face "expressing either the *ah* sound or the *ee* sound and match the correct audio recording to the appropriate face."[21]

This unity of the senses may occur because infants experience things as *energies* rather than as discrete objects bounded by Kantian time and space and clothed in discrete sensory packages.[22] Daniel Stern employs the term *vitality affects* in attempting to describe the subjective experience of the infant, suggesting that since we can't possibly know a baby's inner life, we must "invent" it as best we can. In his view, the infant experiences constant shifts of energy that can be described by such terms as "surging," "fading away," "fleeting," "explosive," "crescendo," "decrescendo," "bursting," and "drawing out."[23]

Most of us will recognize the experience of *vitality affects* after only a few minutes of playing with a baby. Your voice changes from a normal adult register to one that squeaks, modulates, trills, ascends, and descends, all according to instinct: "oooo!...lookit the cuuuutie bebeeee!" Your face comes alive in a mimelike display of grimaces, grins, pouts, frowns, and looks of surprise or astonishment. Your body moves differently, too, often conforming to your voice and face as you crescendo toward the infant with the two of you exploding together in laughter or surprise. You feel yourself tuning in to the emotions of the baby—frowning when he frowns, laughing when he laughs—and naturally mirroring your own actions to those of the infant. These multisensory performances of ours that seem to come out of nowhere provide direct evidence of how nature equips us with behaviors necessary to promote the positive well-being and the ultimate survival of the babies in our care.

You've probably also witnessed adults who *lack* these instinctive behaviors in their interactions with babies: individuals afflicted with what I like to call B.A.D.D.—"Baby Attunement Deficit Disorder," a potentially species-ending disorder. They're smiling brightly while the baby is crying his eyes out. They have an artificial quality to their voices when they talk to the infant like they're *trying* to do the right thing, but it all comes out forced and strange: "Does BAY-beee want a CRACK-er?" Or they make the infant conform to *their* moods rather than vice versa, as if they were saying something like: "Oh baby, I'm so sad today, can you comfort me?" Or they're like a really bad blind date, where the girl accidentally elbows the boy, and the boy drops his bouquet of flowers and steps on the girl's foot when he picks it up. The chemistry is all wrong. Perhaps most devastatingly, instead of trying to "dance" with infants' rhythms, B.A.D.D. adults often ignore, insult, or actively seek to suppress their symphony of vitality. Imagine this kind of dissonance going on for days, weeks, or months at a time, with the infant living in the midst of horribly unattuned parents or caregivers, and it's not hard to understand the kind of pain this must inflict—pain that gets passed on to the rest of the world when that baby reaches adulthood.

Babies in the Mythic World

As suggested earlier, the experiences of infants aren't blocked into neat categories of social, emotional, cognitive, perceptual, and moral development, and it grieves me to see textbooks on infant development organized around these lifeless categories. Your life as an infant wasn't marked out by the sequential passage of specific events taking place in Euclidean space.

There was no real autobiographical memory, which is why your earliest *ordinary* memories of life rarely extend back that far. You experienced the world almost as if you'd stumbled into a nonstop funhouse, tunnel of love, roller coaster, and house of horrors all wrapped up into one.

Imagine being swooped up suddenly by a face that gets bigger and bigger and smells all perfumey and feels all greasy, but you have a feeling of heart-love from it that hurts a little bit, too, and then being whooshed up in the air, and plopped back down on the ground, and left behind in the dust. And while all this "outside" stuff is going on, events are happening with as much fury "inside" of you, and you're not even really clear on the difference between the two. A swelling feeling starts to grow in your bottom, and feels good for a while, but then it starts to feel like a "bursting" and you cry, but no one comes and it explodes, and then "ahh-hhhh...," it feels so nice and warm and soft, but still no one comes, and it gets cooler and it starts to feel like "burning" and "sticky" and you cry, and still no one comes and you feel like a beached whale stuck in a carpet of wet cow dung, and no one comes and you're starting to feel hungry, like a gaping pit of gnawing leeches are in your stomach, and no one comes, and you feel like it's your Dark Night of the Soul, and still no one comes.

And when help finally does appear, it comes not in the form of individual persons as we know them in adulthood, but rather as larger-than-life entities that could perhaps best be compared to the gods, goddesses, and other supernatural beings of Homer's *Odyssey*. Enter Circe, who trains her seductive eyes on you and, instead of cleaning you and giving you her nurturing breast, poisons you and turns you into a squealing beast. Or enter the Lestrogynians, the cannibals that ate Odysseus's men, who threaten to annihilate you with one gulp. Or maybe it's your lucky day and the goddess Athena enters the room and lays you on white linen and cleans you and sanctifies you to the gods, while Demeter (the Greek goddess of the Earth) offers you nourishment from her fecund body. Possibly, too, father Zeus comes around to send off a thunderbolt of anger, while the music of the Sirens drifts through the air to remind you of where you came from before you got yourself into this mess called a physical body.[24]

Keep in mind that the various facets, qualities, traits, aspirations, and characteristics of mother and father have not yet been assimilated or coordinated by the baby's perceptions into anything like what we would call an individual human being in adulthood. Instead, the infant sees different aspects of mother or father fused together as holistic experiences. The polytheism of *The Odyssey* is actually a good comparison to the vivid diversity and kaleidoscopic changes that take place in the infant's experience of others. Remember, too, that the infant isn't watching these animated mythic creatures dance before his eyes like a Saturday morning TV cartoon. These early experiences of others are often referred to in psychoanalytic literature as "objects" or "images," but this can be misleading because they're not actually things or visual perceptions.[25] They're actually more like "kinesthetic-emotional-visual-musical-everything-comes-at-once" events. It makes a person wonder how the infant can possibly stand such an intense surging of experience, cope with such a rapidly changing succession of powerful emotional images, or fend off the impact of demons and deities that are particularly horrific or devastating.

The answer to this question lies in the existence of an integrating force that psychologists have referred to as the "ego" or "self." I'd like to suggest that this self may be closely related to the *spirit down* soul of the infant; a soul stuck in the mud of materiality, as it were, but one that seeks to shine its light out of the mire and climb its way up through the maelstrom of existence. Right from the very start of life this integrative principle appears and begins to make order out of the uncontrollable surge of life events that unfold in and around the baby's body.

Daniel Stern has studied the different phases of the development of self during the first two years of life.[26] According to Stern, from birth to two months of age the baby's self attempts to coordinate many of the different experiences of its life into unified wholes, a process observed earlier as the "unity of the senses." From about two months of age to seven to nine months, the infant develops a *core self* that recognizes she is the source of her own actions, and that she continues to exist even when others leave the scene. This may be one reason why infants at this age experience such great excitement while playing peek-a-boo games with other people. Starting at around nine months of age, according to Stern, baby starts to develop a subjective sense of self, where it dawns on her that she has her own world of experiences that are different from those of others. It's around this time that babies start looking back at their mothers after they've done something neat, wanting them to share the experience.

Finally, at around fifteen months, the infant develops a verbal self, and begins to understand that language can make the mutual interchange of wants, needs, feelings, and ideas far easier than the use of grunts, gestures, or even ESP. Baby discovers that there's a kind of magic and "muscle" in words. Simply by saying "Up!" for example, baby can effect miraculous changes in his outer environment, causing him to be brought up into the arms of a parent, and be fed, soothed, and loved.

At the same time, there's a distancing quality to the development of language that separates the infant from the vibrant perceptual immediacy of experience. Daniel Stern writes in his book *The Interpersonal World of the Infant*, "Suppose we are considering a child's perception of a patch of yellow sunlight on the wall. The infant will experience the intensity, warmth, shape, brightness, pleasure, and other amodal aspects of the patch. The fact that it is yellow light is not of primary or, for that matter, of any importance . . . [Then] Someone will enter the room and say, 'Oh, look at the *yellow* sun*light*!' Words in this case separate out precisely those properties that anchor the experience to a single modality of sensation. By binding it to words, they isolate the experience from the amodal flux in which it was originally experienced. Language can thus fracture amodal global experience. A discontinuity in experience is introduced."[27] The richness of the infant's perception, according to Stern, then begins to go underground, only to surface later on (if ever) as an artistic, contemplative, or emotional experience.[28]

The Journey of the Infant Hero
What I believe we're seeing in the unfolding of the self in infancy is the start—or perhaps the continuation from the prenatal stage—of the "hero's

journey" described so well by Joseph Campbell.[29] Against all odds, this tiny and vulnerable miniature-sized Odysseus marches through innumerable adventures only to (hopefully) become stronger and wiser for his deeds.[30] After emerging from the Cyclops's cave at birth, the hero-infant must now confront, integrate, and survive a pantheon of deities that are manifestations of the different emotions, drives, intentions, aspirations, and unconscious wishes of the baby, the mother, and the other significant members of the infant's universe.

At one moment our baby Odysseus is shrieking out for supernatural help—perhaps from his guardian angel, Athena—to rescue him from starvation. At another moment, he's busy appeasing with winsome smiles and gurgles (the amulets of his trade) the dark and angry god Poseidon, Cyclops's father, who threatens him with annihilation. As he develops the powers of locomotion, he begins arduous travels across carpet-lands and encounters cavernous closets, abysmal stair-drops, and furniture-mountains on his pilgrimage to the holy Mount Olympus. And finally, he rises up above the flat plane of the earth, like a priest climbing an ancient ziggurat, and walks for the first time. No modern-day hero—no Neil Armstrong or Sir Edmund Hillary—can compete with the exhilaration that an infant must feel in ascending into the rarefied atmosphere where the Giants dwell as he takes his first steps on Planet Earth.

Perhaps baby's most astonishing accomplishment, though, is his ability to find the thread of his own being through all these ramblings, and to be able to establish the foundations for a stable relationship with the world, and in particular with the emotional lives of other people. As mentioned earlier, right from the start of life there is an integrative principle within the infant that Daniel Stern calls the "emergent self." This self seeks to order experiences and stabilize images of others, particularly those of his mother since her stability is so vital to his continued existence. It is probably a breakdown in this early self during the first few months of life that gives rise to the most serious forms of mental illnesses: the psychoses. In some psychotic disorders the separate experiences of mother—as Circe, Demeter, Athena. Scylla, Thoosa (Cyclop's mother), and the rest—aren't integrated into a whole image of a nurturing person who also has imperfections. The infant does not have a unified experience of what D. W. Winnicott calls "the good enough mother." Instead, some of the particularly horrific images of a mother or of other significant people remain un-integrated because of their potentially destructive impact, and they continue to have a life of their own. Such images may lie dormant for years, only to emerge in later life as auditory hallucinations, sudden violent behaviors, multiple personalities, manic-depressive episodes, or other forms of psychic disintegration or "possession." In this type of scenario, the hero-infant rages away at the hydra-headed Scylla mother-monster and with each slash of his sword two more heads sprout up in their place. The child's own concept of self can fragment in a similar way.

The failure to integrate images of self and others, however, does not always predispose an infant to mental illness in later life. Episodes of fragmentation resulting from crises may have their own positive dimensions. Psychoanalyst Sandor Ferenczi observed in his clinical work the phenomenon of the "wise baby"—a healthy segment of the self that during trauma in early development disengages from the scene of the crime and attempts to heal the wounded part of the self. (It's interesting to note that the name "Odysseus" actually means "the son of pain.") Ferenczi writes in his *Selected Papers*: "It really seems as though, under the stress of imminent danger, part of the self splits off and becomes a psychic instance self-observing and desiring to help the self, and that possibly this happens in early—even the very earliest—childhood."[31] The early formation of an inner teacher self may be the basis in adult development for the "wounded healers" found in so many of the helping professions, and for the capacity of resilience that certain people possess in rising above extreme adversity in life.[32]

Such a phenomenon may be the psychic equivalent of the body's immune system coming to the rescue in dealing with danger. One theorist, psychologist Larry R. Vandervert, has suggested that the primitive image-schemas of infancy (those amodal "all-at-once" experiences described earlier) are actually sculpted from neural networks in the brain whose design evolved from circuits that enabled early vertebrates to survive in highly dynamic and dangerous environments.[33] It's possible, then, that the archetypes of infancy—the Athenas, Circes, Scyllas, Zeuses, Poseidons, and other transcendental beings—represent a kind of deep-structure mythological "world map" at a neurological level providing the infant-hero with a matrix of orientation and distinct markers to use in finding his way in the world. These markers allow the baby to recognize and avoid "predators" (e.g., aspects of the parents or others that are a threat to development) as well as to seek and join forces with the nurturers (e.g., healthy dimensions of parents or others) that are necessary for his survival.

Regardless of what Nature has provided in the way of help, the infant, like Odysseus, still must make critical choices in responding to life's events. The idea of a passive organism wired by evolution to respond to circumstances in a fixed way negates the precious spark of divinity that may be attempting to shine its way out of the gloom into greater freedom and liberty. Even as Odysseus receives help from heavenly forces above, there burns within him a strong desire to return home to Ithaca. It is the same with the infant. Theologian Martin Buber writes: "He has stepped out of the glowing darkness of chaos into the cool light of creation. But he does not possess it yet; he must first draw it truly out, he must make it into a reality for himself, he must find his own world by seeing and hearing and touching and shaping it."[34]

⚭

The Gift of Infancy: Vitality

The world's greatest energy source is not oil, gas, hydrogen, or nuclear power. It is infancy. Exhausted parents from around the world can testify to the fact that toddlers are greater bundles of power than any renewable energy source that science can deliver. The infant's ability to orchestrate an emotional crescendo from the darkest agony to a brilliant ecstasy in only a few seconds rivals the acceleration rate of most high-performance automobiles. The disproportionately huge brain of a newborn has more blood flow and oxygen consumption than an adult's brain. It's said that toddlers are stronger in their leg muscles, on a pound-for-pound basis, than oxen. Truly, an infant represents the greatest expression of vitality that ever crawled across the face of the earth.

The infant still glows within us to the extent that we are truly *alive* in adulthood. To find out if this is the case, we need to ask ourselves: "How do I show my vitality?" If a clear answer comes to us, then we may be sure that we are still connected to this precious energy source. Our vitality expresses itself through many avenues: sports, hobbies, work, child-rearing, relationships, lovemaking, social causes, and spiritual life, among others. At peak moments of involvement in any of these experiences, we feel invigorated by the world. If we aren't clear about what is personally enlivening to us, then we need to inquire: "How can I *nurture* my vitality?" We may need to exercise, eat better, pay attention to our dream life, take up art, or seek counseling. Or, we may simply need to get off the beaten track and do something radically different to put pizzazz back into our otherwise humdrum daily existence. However we decide to revitalize ourselves, we need to keep in mind that once long ago we were spirited two-year-old bundles of nonstop get-up-and-go, and deep within us there remains a spark of that infant vigor still yearning to dance ecstatically to the awesome rhythms of life.

———————— *Ways to Explore and Support Infancy* ————————

FOR YOURSELF
- Reconstruct what your relationship with your mother might have been like when you were an infant, using old photos, accounts from family and friends, recollections, and other sources. Then write a first-person narrative as if you were that infant living today.
- Give frequent hugs to family members and friends (with their permission, of course!) and schedule professional therapeutic massages to nourish your need to be touched.

- Listen to lullabies or other soothing music while rocking in a rocking chair or swinging in a hammock to simulate the feelings of being nurtured as an infant.

FOR FRIENDS AND FAMILY

- Provide information on the benefits and methods of breastfeeding for a family member or friend about to give birth whose preferences for postbirth feeding leans primarily toward infant formula.
- Volunteer to do out-of-the-house errands and chores for the mother of an infant to lighten her load.
- Encourage family members who have infants to restrict their access to computers, television, and other mass media (the American Academy of Pediatrics recommends no TV for kids under two years of age), and to use the time instead for free play with developmentally appropriate toys.

FOR YOUR COMMUNITY

- Financially support infant vaccination and oral rehydration programs in third world countries through organizations such as UNICEF or USAID.
- Volunteer at an infant learning program such as Early Head Start that provides home-based intervention for low-income families with infants.
- Adopt an infant or serve as a foster parent to an infant who has suffered from abuse and neglect, or physical and mental difficulties.

CHAPTER 4

Early Childhood: The Magical Mystery Years

*In Mira's family a young girl of two or three years sang a tune and
was saying to herself, "It is the tune I sang when I was a shepherdess
in Greece." The memory of it was evoked at such an early age
possibly by her fine psychic nature. It is not latent or precocious
genius here, but memory.*

—SRI AUROBINDO GHOSE[1]

The current Dalai Lama was only two years old in 1937 when followers of
the previous Dalai Lama, who had died two years before, were led by
dreams and visions to the boy's blue-roofed cottage in the small village of
Taktsher in eastern Tibet. These disciples believed that their master had
reincarnated somewhere in Tibet and they were looking for his successor.
The search party members, traveling in disguise, were given lodging by the
boy's family, who believed the travelers were simply itinerant pilgrims.
During their visit, the child, named Lhamo Dhondrub, acted with great
familiarity toward the head lama (priest) who was disguised as a servant.
He went up to the monk and touched his prayer beads, asking to have them.

"I shall give them to you if you tell me who I am," said the monk.

"You are a lama from Sera," said the boy correctly. Then he began to
chant, "Mani Mani," which was an abridged version of a mantra associated
with the late Dalai Lama.[2] Seeking to test the boy, the monks placed several

items that had belonged to the previous Dalai Lama in front of the child, including some prayer beads, a walking stick, and a miniature drum. Each item was accompanied by a cleverly duplicated fake. The child was then asked, successively, which of the two items he would like to have. In each case, he chose the previous lama's possession, and ultimately convinced the monks that he was the latest incarnation of the Dalai Lama in Tibet.

This cultural recognition of a young child's ability to remember his origins in another lifetime is not limited to the Dalai Lama, nor even to the Tibetan Buddhist tradition. In the United States, a professor of psychiatry at the University of Virginia, Ian Stevenson, has made it his life's work to interview children in localities as widespread as Sri Lanka, Lebanon, Europe, Burma, and Alaska who report having been some other personality during a previous lifetime. According to Dr. Stevenson: "A typical case of this type begins when a small child, usually between the ages of 2 and 4, starts to tell his parents, and anyone who will listen, that he remembers living another life before his birth . . . A child claiming to remember a previous life usually asks to be taken to the place where he says he lived during that life . . . If the child has furnished enough details . . . the search for the family of the person he has been talking about is nearly always successful . . . The child is then usually found to have been accurate in about 90 percent of the statements he has been making about the deceased person whose life he claims to remember."[3] Over the past forty years, Stevenson has investigated thousands of cases of this type and reported his findings in several scientific journals and in a number of meticulously researched books published by respected academic presses.[4]

In some cases, Dr. Stevenson traced unusual behavior patterns—such as a child's unexplained phobia—to events that occurred in the previous lifetime. Children who had a deep-seated fear of guns, for example, often reported having been killed in a past life by firearms. Even more remarkably, children who had birthmarks would frequently report having been killed in another lifetime in a manner consistent with the birthmark being a point of entry for the weapon. An Alaskan (Tlingit) child with a birthmark on his back, for example, said he had been killed during a fishing accident in a previous lifetime. When Dr. Stevenson investigated the individual reported to be that previous incarnation, it was discovered that he had been a fisherman who had in fact been speared and killed in that precise bodily location.[5] Stevenson indicates that children who remember past lives continue to make statements about their previous lives until about the age of six or seven, and then gradually cease referring to them. By the age of eight to ten, most of these children, as a result of adapting to the society around them, have completely forgotten their memories of other lives.[6]

Cases of this type represent a direct challenge to the rational scientific perspective of modern times, which regards the idea of reincarnation as a silly superstition or an exotic fantasy. If true, however, these cases reveal startling insights about the nature of early childhood. For here we see once again the child, like the infant, revealed as a deep *rememberer* of her origins. Unlike infants, however, by the age of two or three, children can now talk about their experiences. What seems remarkable about early childhood as a developmental period is that the child is still young enough to remember nonordinary states of consciousness, yet old enough to communicate with us about these memories through words or through other symbolic forms of representation such as drawing, singing, and playing. A few more years along, when the child has reached six or seven, the need to *adapt* to the social world around her (e.g., fitting in with peers, learning social norms, beginning to think rationally) will ultimately begin to crowd out these profound memories and experiences. For a few precious years, however, humanity seems to have a window onto a very magical and mystical part of its own deeper condition.

This capacity of young children to experience life at a fundamentally spiritual level has been recognized in most cultures, and in virtually every sacred tradition in recorded history.[7] Matthew 18:1–5, for example, says: "At that time the disciples came to Jesus and asked, 'Who is the greatest in the kingdom of Heaven?' He called a child, set him in front of them, and said, 'I tell you this: Unless you turn round and become like children, you will never enter the kingdom of Heaven. Let a man humble himself till he is like this child, and he will be the greatest in the kingdom of Heaven. Whoever receives one such child in my name receives me."[8]

In Islamic tradition, young children are said to understand the language of the angels, to hear the crying of the dead, to know remedies for sicknesses, and to confer *barakah* (blessing) on those they come into contact with.[9] In China during the Zhou dynasty (841–256 B.C.E.), young children often acted as mediums through which ancestral spirits could be channeled at sacrificial rituals. The Confucian scholar Mencius wrote: "The great man is he who does not lose his child's heart."[10] During the Middle Ages in the kabbalistic or mystical traditions of Judaism, adepts carried out prophecy and divination activities by asking small children to stare into a crystal or mirror and describe what they saw there with their imagination.[11] In shamanic cultures, young children's innocent words are taken seriously by holy men, as anthropologist Joan Halifax explains in *Shaman: The Wounded Healer*: " . . . he [Sila, a deity] has another means of (communication) by sunlight and calm of the sea, and little children innocently at play, themselves understanding nothing. Children hear a soft and gentle voice, almost like that of a woman. It comes to them in a mysterious way, but so gently that they are not afraid, they only hear that some danger threatens. And the children mention it (casually) when they come home, and it is then the business of the (shaman) to take such measures as shall guard against the danger."[12]

In mythology, the image of the child shows up time and again as a figure of both great power and deep understanding. The Greek god Apollo killed a dragon in his youth, and his half brother Hermes invented the lyre from the shell of a tortoise when he was a young child. In the Finnnish epic poem, *The Kalevala*, a child named Sampsa sows the land with trees, including an oak that rises to heaven and covers the moon and sun with its branches. Commenting on the archetype of the child, Carl Jung writes: "The 'child' is all that is abandoned and exposed and at the same time divinely powerful."[13]

Western developmental psychology, unfortunately, does not support this kind of deep regard for the power and wisdom of childhood. On the contrary, early childhood researchers tend to evaluate the child in terms of what he *lacks* rather than what he possesses. Jean Piaget, the Swiss child development researcher, used the term *preoperational* to describe children's thinking processes at this time of life, suggesting that the young child lacks the ability to use consistent logical operations in his musings about the world. Following Piaget, Harvard researcher Lawrence Kohlberg called young children's moral reasoning *preconventional* because it failed to take into consideration such factors as fair play, intentionality, and internal motivation. As we noted earlier, Freud and many of his followers tended to regard the young child as an egotist, continually projecting his selfish little fantasies onto the world around him.[14] In each of these cases, the life of the young child is measured against later stages of development and found to come up short. What these mainstream *adapter* models of early childhood fail to grasp is that this stage of development is not simply a "pre-" stage characterized by deficiency and immaturity, but a unique period of life with its own rich phenomenology of images, feelings, perceptions, and beliefs.

Varieties of Early Childhood Experience

The whole world is *alive* in early childhood. Dreams can be as real as waking experiences. One of the best ways, in fact, to recapture the feelings and perceptions of this time of life is to pay attention to your own dreams, which don't obey the rules of conventional waking reality. Young children experience so-called inanimate objects like stones, clouds, rivers, and toys as full of life, purpose, and meaning. I remember as a six-year-old, for example, seeing stones leaning awkwardly against a tree, and laying them down on the ground so that they could be more "comfortable." Young children don't separate feelings from perceptions and action: They all happen at the same time.

Pioneer developmental psychologist Heinz Werner referred to this sort of experience as *physiognomic perception*. In his book *Comparative Psychology of Mental Development*, he made a distinction between the normal perception of adulthood, where a landscape, for example, is viewed according to its geometrical technical matter-of-fact qualities, and the physiognomic perceptions of childhood, where the same landscape will be seen as expressing a certain kind of emotional quality: happy, sad, sinister, and so forth. Werner noted that this kind of perception could be found not only in young children, but also among creative individuals and members of indigenous cultures.

The experience of watching a dramatic film provides a good metaphor for what these kinds of perceptions in early childhood are like. For the young child, the entirety of life is an ongoing, highly gripping movie with an Oscar caliber soundtrack. Werner provides many delightful examples of this: One two-year-old boy, upon seeing a cup lying on its side, replied: "Poor, tired cup!" The parents later reported: "Today we found our boy in the twilight of the bedroom, sitting up in his bed, his eyes staring fixedly at the stove: 'Look, the stove is making *bah*... he's sticking out his tongue!' A four-year-old girl, seeing some cards on which angular figures were drawn cried, out: 'Ugh! What a lot of prickles and thorns!' And she hesitated to pick up the cards lest the thorns stick into her fingers. A five-and-a-half-year-old girl walking with her mother in the rain when light was fading said: 'I can't see a thing, it's so foggy. Everything is like whispering!'"[15]

This easy flow of perceptions into feelings and feelings into sensations seems to be a carry-over of the infant's unity of the senses described in the last chapter. When you were a young child, your senses were beginning to split off into touch, taste, smell, vision, and hearing, but they still frequently fused together in experiences of *synaesthesia*. You might have associated musical tones with different colors, tasted shapes, gotten tactile sensations from certain smells, or even seen sounds.[16] In addition, your experience of each particular sense was likely to have been far more vivid than it is in adulthood, undiluted as it was by the verbal mind chatter of maturity. Colors were deeper, sounds were richer, smells were more fragrant, and your imagination was very probably more highly developed. Research suggests that many young children possess a capacity known as *eidetic imagery*: They see images in their mind's eye that are as clear as outer perceptions are to the rest of us.[17] As one child told nineteenth-century writer Thomas De Quincey about the phantoms that he saw in the dark: "I can tell them to go, and they go; but sometimes they come, when I don't tell them to come."[18] I remember seeing people's faces looking down at me when I was in my crib as a young child, which didn't go away when I closed my eyes. For some reason, I called this phenomenon "the Leland" (my middle name is "Leigh," so perhaps that's why). I also remember making "imprints" of images in my mind (like an imaginary car or house) on the inside of my eyelids, These images were so clear that they would linger for a time with the clarity of an afterimage of something that I'd seen in the outer world.

The fact that children produce such clear imagery in early development is one of the reasons why their nightmares can be so terrifying. They literally can't tell the difference between what they've seen in their dream images and what they experience with their eyes open. Gary Larson humorously depicts this situation in one of his *Far Side* cartoons. A mother comes into her son's bedroom where the boy cowers under the covers showing only his terrified eyes. The mother exclaims: "Now Billy, how can you tell me there's a monster in this room when you can't even describe his *face* to me!" And in the corner, we can see a monster standing there with a bag over his head! From a strictly phenomenological point of view, monsters, fairies, elves, angels, and other fantastic creatures are quite real in early childhood, especially in these nighttime encounters, when the child might see visions of monsters that would stand Odysseus's hair on end.

As we noted earlier, these exceptional states of consciousness tend to gradually fade away as the child grows into middle childhood and is forced to adapt to the more rational world around him.[19] However, some people continue to hold on to these modes of perception into adulthood and use them in constructive ways. These are the artists, inventors, and visionaries who use such capacities to create works of art, make scientific discoveries, or develop other groundbreaking projects that transform the world around us. Nikola Tesla, the inventor of the Tesla coil and the alternating-current generator, used eidetic imagery to design many of his machines. He wrote in his autobiography: "When I get an idea, I start at once building it up in my imagination. I change the construction, make improvements and operate the device in my mind. It is absolutely immaterial to me whether I run my turbine in thought or test it in my shop."[20]

Composers like Alexander Scriabin and Olivier Messiaen used synaesthesia to create musical pieces that combined tone and color, as did Isaac Newton when he linked his theory of the color spectrum to the seven-toned intervals of the musical scale. Physiognomic or "feeling-toned" perceptions also interpenetrate the work of most painters and sculptors. The artist Marc Chagall once advised a young artist: "The older you grow, the less spontaneous you will be. A child paints with passionate intensity; that's the quality you must preserve."[21] After visiting an exhibition of children's art in 1956, Pablo Picasso was reported to have said: "When I was their age I could draw like Raphael, but it took me a lifetime to learn to draw like them."[22]

Young children not only perceive the world differently from the rest of us, they also *think* about the world in quite a distinct way. Their thoughts are somehow bigger, broader, more global and dynamic, and less systematic or rational than older kids or adults. This isn't to say that their ideas aren't rational, but they possess a different kind of logic than that used in adulthood; a rationality that as we noted earlier may be more akin to the logic of dreams and fantasies than waking life. Even though Jean Piaget characterized the years of early childhood in terms of what it lacked, in his earliest work, he seemed to be alive to the magic of the young child's thinking processes, and recorded his observations in rich detail.[23] For example, Piaget watched a three-year-old, after scratching herself on a wall, look at her hand and exclaim: "Who made that mark? . . . It hurts where the wall hit me."[24] In this instance, the child reversed adult cause and effect and viewed a so-called inert object as an active agent in her own fate. Similarly, Piaget wrote about a four-year-old who looked at the moon and said, "There's the moon; it's round," and then, when a cloud hid the moon, observed: "Look now, it's been killed."[25] Instead of thinking of the cloud as simply being superimposed over the moon, the child held a concept of the cloud as a destroyer.

This type of thinking seems very much like the mythological thinking of ancient peoples, who regarded solar eclipses, for example, as gods being destroyed by serpents or evil spirits. In the ancient Indian epic poem *The Mahabharata*, for example, there is a passage that illustrates this kind of effect regarding an eclipse:

"There is a cowherd who predicts that tonight the round silver moon will be swallowed up."

"Forever?" asked the king anxiously.

"No. Rahu the demon will swallow the Lord of the Lotus, but because Rahu has only a head and no body . . ."

"Ah! Of course, I remember," said the king. "The moon will come out his neck—I know. I am well educated. I studied all the natural sciences as a boy."[26]

It's interesting to consider how our own personal concepts of *moon*, *sun*, *tree*, *apple*, *chair*, and other objects and ideas that we take for granted in adulthood originally developed out of mythological or fanciful notions such as these. I remember as a child picking up the receiver of a telephone, hearing the ongoing hum of the signal, and thinking that I was listening to the voice of God. It scared me. I also used to think that there were little men in soda machines who dispensed the drinks. You may recall similarly fantastic notions that you held about how the world worked when you were a child. It's as if each concept that we hold in our mind as adults has its own unique autobiography that can be traced back through time into dimmer, hazier regions of our subconscious during early childhood when our thinking took on these mythic or archetypal forms. The young child's thinking processes also seem to link up in an undifferentiated way with moral concerns. Heinz Werner observed that young children appear to fuse ethical ideals with aesthetic judgments. A two-and-a-half-year-old, cited by Werner, for example, called a towel hook "a cruel thing," and at the age of three and a half thought that the number 5 looked "mean" while the number 4 looked "soft." These early judgments are not entirely unlike the aesthetics of those individuals and groups who view cultural forms, such as architecture, as reflections of a deeper moral order.[27]

The experiences of young children often include a deeply transpersonal dimension as well. Many of these, especially those that occur in the context of nature, have a *numinous* quality. In a study conducted at Manchester College in Oxford, England, a fifty-two-year-old woman remembering back to childhood reported: "The most profound experience of my life came to me when I was very young—between four and five years old... My mother and I were walking on a stretch of land... known locally as 'the moors.' As the sun declined and the slight chill of evening came on, a pearly mist formed over the ground... Suddenly I seemed to see the mist as a shimmering gossamer tissue and the harebells [flowers], appearing here and there, seemed to shine with a brilliant fire. Somehow I understood that this was the living tissue of life itself, in which that which we call consciousness was embedded. Appearing here and there was a shining focus of energy in that more diffused whole. In that moment I knew that I had my own special place, as had all other things, animate and so-called inanimate, and that we were all part of this universal tissue which was both fragile yet immensely strong and utterly good and beneficent. The vision has never left me. It is as clear today as fifty years ago, and with it the same intense feeling of love of the world and the certainty of ultimate good." [28]

Sometimes these deeper transpersonal intuitions come in the form of dreams. One young girl in psychoanalysis, for example, had a dream of being on the seashore: "I was on a beach with my nurse, only she wasn't there. A big wave came in and I ran away. When I came back, there were lots and lots of things on the beach and lots and lots of starfish, but one starfish was a *blue* starfish and he had an eye right in the middle of him, and he looked at me and he knew me, me-myself, I mean, and he was my starfish because he knew me-myself. So I took him home. And then I woke up." [29] The blue starfish, an embodiment of life's wholeness, saw not the small "me"—the *adapter* me of the girl, but rather, "me-myself," that is, her *rememberer* me, her real Self. The fact that she took the starfish home suggests that she had at least partially integrated this deeper aspect of herself into her daily life.

Young children's spiritual experiences sometimes serve as healing factors that help them cope with traumatic events. Surveys of adult women who have survived childhood violence reveal that many of them used spirituality or even out-of-body experiences to escape from the terror of physical abuse as children.[30] In one of my own child development classes, a fifty-year-old woman recorded in her class journal a spiritual experience that happened when she was five years old. Her mother had physically abused her since she was three, and one winter day she was thrown out of the house to fend for herself in the ice and snow. Just as she thought she might freeze to death, an angel appeared to her who told her she would not turn out to be evil as her mother had predicted but would grow up to become a kind, loving, gentle person with a pleasant voice and a soft touch, and that she would be able to help troubled people. As the angel left her, the girl remembered repeating to herself over and over again: "I'm five-years old and its 1939 and I will remember this forever... I'm five years old and it's 1939 and I will remember this forever... " And she did remember. In her adult life, she drew upon this image as she trained to be a psychotherapist to help to heal others. It seems that in cases of this kind, the *rememberer* side of an individual (embodied here in the guardian angel) comes to the fore when the *adapter* side is somehow blocked from advancing in life. This may be Sandor Ferenczi's "wise baby," who we referred to in the last chapter, growing up and helping to ward off attacks to the soul's integrity. It is also very much like the goddess Athena coming down from Mount Olympus to help Odysseus out of his difficulties during his quest to get back home to Ithaca.

Play Is the Thing

In the phenomena related above, the child appears to transgress the usual divisions made in adulthood between self and world, inside and outside, reality and fantasy, and subject and object. Western psychologists, as well as many of the rest of us, tend to regard this tendency of the child to fuse opposites as examples of "confused" thinking. And yet the child is not necessarily confused, and may be much more confused by an adult's attempts to impose a more rational perspective on him. On the contrary, the young child is quite often crystal clear in what he sees, feels, perceives, and otherwise experiences. What is unique about this stage of development is that the child lives life neither in the world of fantasy nor in the world of adult reality, but in the nexus between the two. Rational adults regard the so-called "magical thinking" of early childhood in terms of what it *isn't* (e.g., efficacy in the adult world), rather than looking at what it really *is*: the child's ability to create something new that is just coming into existence. And nowhere else is this seen more clearly than in the child's experience of play.

Nearly everybody agrees that play is good for young children. According to early childhood research, play develops social skills, increases cognitive functioning, stimulates creativity, and improves a host of other laudable and socially valued skills.[31] However, young children's play is something far more profound than an activity to help kids better adapt to the world around them. Play is as much about *remembering* as it is about *adapting*. Play is the critical factor not only in the development of individuals, but also in the creation of civilizations. When children play, they take what is merely *possible* from their inner worlds and make it *actual* by borrowing from the outer world, the materials, roles, and situations that they see around them.

During this transaction, as we've noted above, the young child exists in an "in-between" state that is neither fantasy nor reality. Child psychoanalyst D. W. Winnicott writes in his book *Playing and Reality* about the child's "play space" : "This area of playing is not inner psychic reality. It is outside the individual, but it is not the external world. Into this play area the child gathers objects or phenomena from external reality and uses these in the service of some sample derived from inner or personal reality. Without hallucinating the child puts out a sample of dream potential and lives with this sample in a chosen setting of fragments from external reality."[32] Within this space, the young child is totally focused upon the play experience and enters a state of absorption that psychologist Mihaly Csikszentmihalyi calls "flow": a type of concentration similar to meditation that he has also observed in brain surgeons at work in the operating room and in rock climbers moving up mountain walls.[33]

In the midst of this sacred space, the playing child serves as a kind of broker for innovation. In Ghana, groups of young children have gathered together and spontaneously created a new dance style called *Atikatika* that serves as a kind of political critique of their society. As one elder observed: "If you want to see our way of life, you will see it from the children."[34] In colonial Hawaii, young children playing together from different linguistic groups collectively created new Creole languages based upon the different dialects they heard around them. These languages, according to one linguist, exhibited "the complexity, nuance, and expressive power universally found in the more established languages of the world."[35]

In our early play experiences, we entered another universe, and either alone or with a group of others created a set of rules, scenarios, and realities that were unlike anything found in our interactions with adults. I remember living entire lifetimes with kids during play sessions that were spontaneous happenings extending through a whole day and into the early evening hours. I was married two or three times, divorced once, went through initiation ceremonies, took part in impromptu parades, concerts, and contests, dug for oil, explored the boundaries of the known world (a few blocks from my house), fought invisible enemies, and was rescued from danger by cats. And I was only five years old! When children enter the play space, they enter a magical zone of creation where spontaneous activities take on a life of their own, a life that vanishes like fairy dust at the sound of a parent's call in the distance: "Come home! It's time for dinner!" This cry signifies the end of play and the reentrance of the child into the conventional world of daily life. These play experiences are echoes of deeper creative forces working at the heart of culture. Johan Huizinga, author of *Homo Ludens* (Man, the Player), suggests that playfulness "as a social impulse [is] older than culture itself . . . Ritual grew up in sacred play; poetry was born in play and nourished on play; music and dancing were pure play . . . We have to conclude that civilization is, in its earliest phases, played."[36]

This deeper dimension of play also can be seen working in the lives of creative individuals who have given birth to their ideas and inventions. By their own admission, many of their creative activities are indistinguishable from the playful acts of young children. Isaac Newton once wrote: "I do not know what I may appear to the world; but to myself I seem to have been only like a boy playing on the sea shore and diverting himself and then finding a smoother pebble or a prettier shell than ordinary while the greater ocean of truth lay all undiscovered before me."[37] Nuclear physicist and father of the atomic bomb, J. Robert Oppenheimer, once said: "There are children playing on the streets who could solve some of my top physics problems, because they have modes of perception I lost long ago."[38] Frank Lloyd Wright traced his own architectural career back to his earliest play experiences with simple wooden blocks.[39] Alexander Fleming, the Scottish bacteriologist who discovered penicillin, said: "I play with microbes. It is very pleasant to break the rules."[40] It may be that most, if not all, of the greatest accomplishments of culture, though shaped and articulated through plenty of hard work and extraordinary skill, had their original spark from something playful in the mind, body, or spirit of these individuals.[41]

Given the monumental importance of young children's play, it is quite disturbing to realize that play is undergoing a profound deterioration in contemporary society. According to New Zealand play expert Brian Sutton-Smith, the typical image of a child at play in our time is of a solitary child in front of a television set (or perhaps now, a video game or Internet screen) playing with his action toys.[42] These toys leave little for the imagination. Some of these "play" figures come with their own manufacturer-devised personality profiles. Video games and computer time, sanctioned by child experts at earlier and earlier ages these days, threaten to overwhelm even these truncated play experiences. In addition, competitive games and sports, like soccer, hockey, and basketball, have largely replaced the kind of free unstructured play where kids create their own rules.

The danger in all of this is that these more organized, conventionalized, and prefabricated pastimes threaten to sever the crucial connection that real play makes between fantasy and reality, so that young children can no longer mix the rich contents of their own imagination—their dream potential—with self-selected components of the external world. Instead, the time normally devoted to play is now almost totally saturated with externally imposed fragments of the real world: images from market-driven toy and video game designers, scenarios from mediocre television and movie screenwriters, and game rules and regulations from high-stress coaches and achievement-driven parents.[43] In such an environment, civilization itself could be lost without our even noticing it.

The Sparkling Brain of a Three-Year-Old

The amazing work that young children do when they play—that is, when they create new realities—is mirrored in the awesome processes going on inside of their brains. Brain researcher Marian Diamond writes that: "... the energy use in a two-year-old [brain] is equal to an adult's. And then, *the levels keep right on rising* until, by age three, the child's brain is *twice* as active as an adult's. This metaphoric crackling, bristling, sparkling, and glowing of brain cells remains at double the adult rate until about age nine or ten; at that time, metabolism begins dropping and reaches adult levels by age eighteen."[44] During this time, the young child has an abundance of dendrites (connections between neurons) undergoing a process of "pruning," where neuronal connections are kept or discarded depending upon what kind of stimulation the child receives from the environment.[45] I'd like to suggest that this neurological richness in the young child represents a biological index of her "human potential." This neural symphony may be the biological manifestation of the kinds of experiences we've been looking at in this chapter: children's memories of other lifetimes, synaesthesia, eidetic imagery, physiognomic perception, spiritual and creative insight, spontaneity, curiosity, wonder, playfulness, humor, and other ordinary and nonordinary states of consciousness.

I believe Nature provides this high level of brain metabolism and wealth of brain connections during early childhood so that young children may offer to the culture an opportunity to transform, renew, and refresh itself out of this neurological fountain of possibilities.[46] As noted earlier, one of the most consistent findings in the neuropsychology of human development is that environmental stimulation creates new dendrites, which are those parts of a neuron or brain cell that receive information from surrounding cells. Culture is critical in determining which brain connections are retained throughout life and which are lost.

No culture can say yes to all of the young child's possibilities—at least no culture that we yet know about.[47] But cultures, just like mothers, make choices about which brain connections they wish to strengthen, stimulate, and maintain, and which they wish to weaken, ignore, and eliminate. This is how cultures essentially develop: by making choices in what to say yes to and what to say no to regarding their younger citizens' neurological possibilities. In the case of the Dalai Lama, the Tibetan culture around him said yes to that part of his brain that as a child enthusiastically responded to the possibility that he might be the previous Dalai Lama. The case of Wolfgang Amadeus Mozart is also instructive. His composer father, Leopold, said yes to Wolfgang's musical brain by giving up his own career as a musician to further his son's development as a composer and performer. In addition, eighteenth-century European culture said yes to Mozart's neurological possibilities in music by inviting him to play at its imperial courts. Had the Dalai Lama been born in B. F. Skinner's behaviorist household, or had Mozart been born to tone-deaf parents in Puritan England, where musical creativity was largely suppressed, then it is unlikely that their spiritual or musical potentials would have been integrated into their respective cultures.

These scenarios point out just how fragile the process is through which a young child's potentials come into being. A child can be born with the possibility to become a scientist, an artist, a musician, a business leader, an actor, a doctor, a humanitarian, or any of a thousand other life-enhancing roles, and all it takes is the heavy thud of one or more all-powerful adults to stamp those dreams into the dust. As Maria Montessori put it: "The child is like a soul in a dark dungeon striving to come out into the light . . . And, all the while, there is standing by a gigantic being of enormous power waiting to pounce upon it and crush it."[48]

Sometimes, the acts that destroy these creative possibilities are brutal and overt, as when children are physically beaten or sexually abused. In 2004, for example, the National Child Abuse and Neglect Data System reported that an estimated three million children were alleged to have been abused or neglected, and that almost a million of these children were determined to be the victims of childhood maltreatment.[49] As the Russian writer Fyodor Dostoyevsky pointed out in his masterwork novel *The Brothers Karamazov*, ". . . it is a peculiar characteristic of many people, this love of torturing children, and children only. To all other types of humanity these torturers behave mildly and benevolently, like cultivated and humane Europeans; but they are very fond of tormenting children, even fond of children themselves in that sense. It's just their defenseless-ness that tempts the tormentor, just the angelic confidence of the child who has no refuge and no appeal, that sets his vile blood on fire."[50]

More often children are tortured through subtler psychological means. Psychoanalyst Alice Miller describes how adults abuse children emotionally by demanding that they respond to the adults' own unre-solved feelings, rather than allowing kids to express freely their own authentic selves. She writes: "What child has never been laughed at for his fears [by an adult] and been told, 'You don't need to be afraid of a thing like that.' And what child will then not feel shamed and despised because he could not assess the danger correctly. . . . Such experiences come in all shades and varieties. Common to them all is the sense of strength that it gives the adult to face the weak and helpless child's fear and to have the possibility of controlling fear in another person, while he cannot control his own."[51]

There are perhaps an infinite variety of scenarios that play out this basic theme. Adults who shame children for being playful and dramatic at a social event because they show up the adults and make them feel inad-equate. Parents who won't let their kids express themselves musically or artistically because they, the parents, never could do those things. Parents who scorn their children for being lazy, when it is the parent who is a sloth. Parents who push their children into intellectual achievements before they're ready, so that they will look like "superparents" to their relatives and friends. These are only a few of the numberless "soul murders" that take place quietly, secretly, on a daily basis in some of our finest and most decent homes.

A Soap Opera World

Much of what young children see and experience in their daily lives is inaccessible to the average adult because it encompasses emotional, sub-verbal, and subconscious dimensions of awareness that most adults censored out of their awareness long ago. In her book *The Inner World of Childhood*, psychoanalyst Frances Wickes wrote: "Children gather from us the atmosphere of all that we most carefully ignore in ourselves."[52] This may help explain why so many child reports of adult abuse are deemed "false memories" in legal proceedings. The abuse may not be recorded in adult reality but it may truly exist inside of the child's own fragile and perceptive psyche. Young children see the sneer behind the adult smile. They hear the wounded cry within the adult laugh. They witness the pain behind the proud action. As one child psychiatrist told me: "Young children see not only who you are, but who you *could* have been." They perceive at an emotional level the unfulfilled expectations, the abandoned hopes, and the haunted aspirations of the adults around them.

This makes much of their experience growing up among family members and close friends and acquaintances quite similar to that of a soap opera. Freud was quite right to point out the importance of the "love romance" between the young child and his parents in his discussion of the Oedipus complex. But he, or at least many of his followers, oversimplified and stereotyped what is a far more complex phenomenon. Boys don't just want to kill their fathers and sleep with their mothers. They could also want to do the reverse, especially if they are gay.[53] They might even want to sleep with their sisters or their babysitters or their nursemaids. Freud himself suggested that his nurse had indoctrinated him into sexual matters at an early age.[54] Similarly, girls may wish to kill their fathers (especially if the fathers have been molesting them) and marry their mothers or grandmothers, or cuddle forever with their best friends. Out of this nest of intrigue there can emerge feelings of jealousy, anger, lust, and hurt to rival the greatest tragedies of Shakespearean and Greek drama. Freud shouldn't have limited himself to only one or two of these plays.

But Freud was correct when he declared that young children respond to the people around them with intense emotion. He is still far ahead of his time in declaring that children are highly sexual beings. His pronouncements shocked Victorian society, but he is still largely misunderstood by a modern culture that officially regards children as "cute" and "innocent" even as it mercilessly exploits their sexuality in advertisements, beauty contests, rock videos, and pornography. The natural and spontaneous sex play of children is an everyday occurrence in households across America. In one recent survey, parents reported that 48 percent of children between the ages of three and six were observed engaging in interactive sex play.[55] And as Freud even more provocatively pointed out, they obtain their sexual pleasure from all over their bodies, especially from the mouth, anus, and genital organs. This sexuality, like so much of the young child's world, is not cut off from the rest of his life, but fuses with spiritual feeling, aesthetic moods, creative aspirations, aggressive impulses, and passionate love.

Our first experiences of falling deeply in love with someone (a parent, a sibling, a playmate) most probably occurred during these years from two to seven. One study suggested that passionate love is as common in early childhood as it is in adolescence.[56] As some of the nation's leading child development researchers have pointed out, "Three-year-olds do act like lovers toward their parents. In fact, they act like lovers out of Italian opera, with passionate and sensual embraces and equally passionate despair at separation and jealousy of rivals."[57] These experiences of falling in love with a parent or another person during early childhood, and then being betrayed and feeling the loss of love and the anguish and heartache of rejection, represent some of the most deeply painful moments of our lives. Often these events leave emotional wounds that continue to plague our most intimate relationships in adulthood.

Moreover, because a young child is so incredibly sensitive to the moods and feelings of people in his personal world, he carries around the equivalent of a mood radar detection system, picking up on the emotions of those around him, amplifying those feelings to a screechingly high pitch, and all the while not knowing exactly where the signal is coming from.[58] Add to this the range of other phenomena described earlier in this chapter and you can begin to understand the emotional roller coaster nature of early childhood. As adults, we experience an event and immediately classify it into some convenient category to make it emotionally manageable. For the young child, however, each event is encountered in its raw immediacy. It might be a *Tristan and Isolde* throb of unrequited love, an archetypal image of a golden sun left over from a morning dream, or, more dangerously, a dagger of anger shot in his direction from an out-of-control caregiver.

Defending Their Young Lives

Such exquisite vulnerability requires some form of modulation and protection so that the child is not totally overwhelmed by a sea of subconscious material. In many cases, the efforts that the child goes through to accomplish this task serves only to cripple him in taking on the challenges of life. For here is the time of life when young children learn to stiffen their bodies, stifle their breathing, and develop what Wilhelm Reich called "body armor," a defensive shield that protects a person from painful feelings but also prevents them from experiencing any deep emotions whatsoever.[59] At this time, also, the child learns how to ward off unpleasantness through denial, a defense that will become a fine art later on in adulthood when practiced by politicians, sociopaths, and cheating spouses. Finally, and perhaps most devastatingly, it is at this time that children learn to give themselves away. They learn to sacrifice their own authentic selves in order to keep those they care about most from abandoning them. Feeling that there is no other way of averting psychic disaster, a child will adopt a mask or an "as-if personality" offered to him by a parent or guardian who demands conformity to a narrow set of behaviors even though it means the sacrifice of the child's very self.

At the same time, however, there is the hero ego, our little Odysseus, who very often rises to the challenge with a wide range of useful defensive strategies to make both the inner and the outer world more bearable (in the epic poem *The Iliad*, Homer often referred to Odysseus as "the great tactician" in his ability to strategically cope with the dangers of war). Of paramount importance is the child's emerging use of language to articulate the invisible, contain the inscrutable, and master the unknowable. It's at this time of life, for example, that we see the emergence of a wide range of bedtime rituals involving magical incantations to ward off the demons of the night. Heinz Werner reports how one four-year-old said every evening without exception the following phrase: "Goodnight, sleep well, sweet dreams, about a sour pickle again. Mother, you must buy me another sour pickle." In another case, two girls made up a complicated bedtime ritual that concluded with the word *bogosho*, which meant "good night." After this final word, the children allowed nothing more to be said, failing which the entire ceremony had to be totally repeated.[60]

Similarly, the child's ability to form mental images—and to represent these images in drawings, artwork, and symbolic play—serves as a tool to ward off inner beasts, deal with painful feelings, and gain a sense of control over life's tumults. Through creative expression, we could torment or kill off our enemies in early childhood and get relief from the feelings of humiliation we experienced as young children. We could create romantic fantasies or revenge fantasies about people we passionately loved who did not love us in return. We could represent through art and play the monsters we feared, the people we cared about, and the situations that made us angry or fearful, thus rendering them, if not harmless, then at least bearable. Some of my own drawings at five and six are representations of radios and electronic consoles with scores of buttons on them, as if I was trying to control the inner anxieties that afflicted me as I saw my father slipping into a clinical depression that would devastate my emotional life over the next decade.

These types of adaptive coping skills are probably the psychological equivalent of the maturation that is taking place inside the brain as nerve pathways develop myelin sheaths in early childhood. This biological process is, in fact, an apt metaphor for describing what goes on in the child's emotional life at this time. In myelination the raw nerves in the brain are insulated, thus allowing for the orderly passage of electrical impulses throughout the nervous system. In like manner, young children, with the help of trustworthy adults, learn how to insulate themselves from much of the *Sturm und Drang* of the psychic underworld so that they can adjust themselves to the broader social world of which they are becoming an increasingly integral part. In middle childhood, which is the topic of our next chapter, the growing child, even as she leaves a rich world of magical adventures and mysterious encounters behind, discovers a whole new set of powers and possibilities awaiting her.

⎯⎯⎯⎯⎯⎯⎯ *The Gift of Early Childhood: Playfulness* ⎯⎯⎯⎯⎯⎯⎯

Whenever you see children engaged in spontaneous open-ended play, you're seeing a miracle at work. Some scientists believe that the frontal lobes of the brain evolved as a result of millions of years of play behavior.[61] As we've noted in this chapter, when children play, they bring together fantasy and reality to create something that is neither of these things but is instead a fusion of possibility and practicality. In spontaneous play, children enter a sacred space where anything can happen. Play is the crucible out of which all vibrant new behaviors and understandings emerge. Play is the deep inner well of creativity that enlivens the calcified world of convention and routine.

There is much we can learn in adulthood from the playfulness of young children. We can learn, for example, not to take ourselves so seriously. When locked in a dispute with a spouse or colleague, play teaches us how to crack a smile, put on a funny voice, or make a strange face just to melt the tension away. Play can also help us avoid getting stuck in petrified ways of thinking and behaving. Dramatic improvisation around a

key problem can bring new ideas into a team meeting at work. A spontaneous game of "find the blue food" can turn a boring family dinner into a
happy and engaging meal. There is good reason why virtually every creative adult in history has shown some element of play in their work and
life. From Shakespeare's bawdy puns to Alexander Fleming's growing of
ballerina-shaped bacteria in petri dishes, creative individuals have all
known that life is just too amazing not to be fun. So they play in order to
keep that wonder alive. Let us take our cue from young children, and from
those adult geniuses who have held on to their wonder-filled child selves.
By allowing spontaneous play into our lives, who knows what incredible
things can happen!

──────── *Ways to Explore and Support Early Childhood* ────────

FOR YOURSELF

- Get out some crayons, finger paint, or clay and have fun drawing,
  painting, or modeling in a space where you can make a mess and
  feel like a creative child again.
- Keep a record of your dreams (especially those that take you back to
  early childhood experiences). Reflect on how the logic of dreams
  mirrors the logic of early childhood.
- Write down any experiences you remember from early childhood
  that were "nonordinary" (religious, spiritual, psychic, archetypal),
  and share them with friends who have gone through the same
  process.

FOR FRIENDS AND FAMILY

- Regularly engage in free play with your own children, or with
  children of friends or family who may not otherwise have many
  opportunities to play.
- Limit the amount of time your young children spend with mass
  media. Eliminate as much as possible your child's exposure to violent
  programming. Encourage other families to do the same.
- Provide toys for your own children or those of family and friends

that are developmentally appropriate (open-ended, creative, nonviolent).

For the Community

- Volunteer at a child protective day care center that provides shelter for children who have been abused or neglected at home.
- Support developmentally appropriate early childhood education programs in your community that emphasize play rather than academic achievement.
- Give financially to an organization that supports the healthy development of young children, such as the Association for Childhood Education International or the Alliance for Childhood.

᳇

CHAPTER 5

Middle Childhood: Entering the Civilized World

*In the summer of my sixth year a great expectation rose within me;
something overwhelming was pending. I was up each morning at
dawn, rushed to the top of Dorchester Hill, a treeless knoll of grass
and boulders, to await the sun, my heart pounding. A kind of
numinous expectancy loomed everywhere about and within me . . .
an awesome new dimension of life was ready to unfold. Instead,
I was put in school that fall . . . All year I sat at that desk, stunned,
wondering at such a fate, thinking over and over: something was
supposed to happen, and it wasn't this.*

—Joseph Chilton Pearce[1]

It all began quite by chance. The Reverend Patrick Brontë was visiting
Leeds, England, in June 1826 and brought back a gift of twelve wooden soldiers for his nine-year-old son, Branwell, to replace some older ones that
had been broken. The boy and his sisters, already used to making up little
plays, began to weave fanciful stories around the toy soldiers, inventing the
name "The Young Men" for them. The four children, led by the two oldest
siblings, Branwell and Charlotte, transformed the inert wooden figures
into a band of young adventurers. In their imagination, the children sent
the soldiers off to Africa to found a colony they named "Glass Town."
This community eventually grew into a completely self-contained world

peopled by descendants of the twelve soldiers. This miniature society in turn gave birth to the worlds of Angria, fashioned by Charlotte and Branwell, and Gondal, led by Emily and Anne. In the course of creating their worlds, the children wrote plays and stories, edited tiny magazines with jokes, puns, news, and gossip, drew maps and charts of the terrain, and developed systems of government and even a special language for the inhabitants.[2] Some of the verve and vitality of these worlds would later show up in the novels of the three girls, including Charlotte's *Jane Eyre*, Emily's *Wuthering Heights*, and Anne's *The Tenant of Wildfell Hall*.[3]

Inspired by the story of the Brontë children and by his own childhood fantasy of a world that he called the New Hentian States, BBC executive Robert Silvey asked readers of several British periodicals in 1977 to write about their own imaginary worlds in childhood. He received numerous replies and ultimately teamed up with a retired psychiatrist to write a study of sixty-four imaginary worlds or *paracosms*.[4] This term was coined by Silvey to describe meaningful private worlds of childhood that endure for some months or years, that are not confused with outer reality, and that matter a great deal to their creators. One paracosm in their study was a country called Branmail consisting totally of cats—except for its creator, a six-year-old girl named Holly who had access to the world by scaling a height called Bumpety Banks. Another paracosm was the island nation of Dobid created by a ten-year-old future artist who drew maps and wrote historic documents on vellum in an ancient Dobidian language. A third example was a shared world of two sisters aged five and nine that began as a continuous bedtime story and lasted for about three years. It was a matriarchal community called Mrs-es where all the husbands were "puppet figures."

Such imaginative worlds tell us a lot about life during the middle childhood years. They reveal, for example, the child's awareness of a more complex social world out there that is being internalized and acted out in fantasy play. They also tell us that children now *have* an imagination. In early childhood, as we saw in the last chapter, inner images and outer perceptions were often fused together in an undifferentiated whole. The entire waking world had a dreamlike quality to it and nighttime phantoms could assume daylike clarity. In middle childhood, however, this magical world is disappears as the child's own maturing cognition divides fantasy from reality. Over the course of middle childhood, the internal world of the imagination becomes a private space where children experiment with their understandings of how the world works, and where they explore the depths of their own increasingly sophisticated cognitive, emotional, social, and creative lives. Early childhood perceptions and experiences that are not considered to be objective reality by the culture (e.g., fairies, elves, witches, dragons, monsters, and angels) essentially "go underground" at this time and assume new identities, now as imaginative beings rather than as supernatural entities.[5] The external world gradually assumes for children in the middle years the geometric and logical proportions considered to be the "consensual reality" of most adult members of their culture.

The Five to Seven Shift

Cultures have long recognized that something special happens to children somewhere between the ages of five and seven. In Burma, starting at about age five, young boys are permitted to take part in the *ShinByu* initiation ceremony where they have their heads shaved and enter a Buddhist monastery. In Turkey, authorities don't circumcise boys until around age seven, believing that only at this age are they capable of comprehending its significance. Roman Catholics regard seven as the age when children start to become morally responsible for their acts and are capable of committing cardinal sins. The Jesuits are famous for saying: "Give me the child until he is seven and I will show you the man." In most nonliterate cultures around the world, children begin taking on adult responsibilities somewhere between five and seven years of age: They start to care for younger children, harvest grain, sew, spin, and hunt. Anthropologist Thomas Buckley, writing about a child in nineteenth-century Yurok culture in northwestern California, noted: "[He] learned very early to observe the men of his village carefully. After a while, using his toy bow, he killed a bird with valuable feathers. He made a small wooden storage box, as he'd seen done, put the feathers in this, and showed the men. One of them made him a real hunting bow, a small and light one, and from then on he was free to join hunting parties, with all of the rights and responsibilities of a hunter. He had done what a man does and, in this respect, was treated like a man. He was six at the time."[6]

This cultural recognition that children between the ages of five and seven are capable of greater responsibility and independence seems to have its roots in a new kind of thinking that takes place during this time. According to the pioneering work of Swiss epistemologist Jean Piaget, the child goes through a qualitative shift in her way of looking at and reflecting on the world around the age of six or seven.[7] In one of his classic experiments, researchers show a four-year-old child two identical drinking glasses each half filled with water. "Is there the same amount of water in both glasses?" the child is asked. "Yes," says the child. Then the researcher pours the water from one of the glasses into a tall, thin cylinder so that the water level is now much higher in the cylinder than it is in the remaining drinking glass. "Now is there the same amount of water?" "No," says the child, "that one [the tall cylinder] has more." Researchers then repeat the same experiment with a child two or three years older and discover a different result. The older child sees (as we do) that even though the second glass of water has been poured into a tall, thin cylinder, it still has the same amount of water as the first glass. It just *looks* like more. Piaget suggested that simple experiments like this one reveal a fundamental difference between the thinking structures of the four-year-old and the seven-year-old. Younger children are deceived by the outer appearances of things, Piaget wrote, while older children can execute *mental operations* on a situation like the one above. They can reverse in their mind the actions that were performed by *imaginatively* pouring the water from the cylinder back into the second drinking glass, understanding that the actual quantity of water never changed during the pouring.

This ability to implement what are simple mathematical operations, similar to addition and subtraction, has all sorts of ramifications for the world of the school-aged child according to Piaget and his followers.[8] It means that children can now begin to pull away from the purely sensory properties of concrete objects and think about the abstract traits that they possess: their blueness, squareness, heaviness, thinness, or wetness. They can start to classify, categorize, order, seriate, and in other ways mentally operate on the vast assemblage of things in their world. Piaget gives an example of the revelatory nature of such a newfound mental power in the life of a child in this recollection of a mathematician friend learning to count for the first time as a five-year-old: "He was seated on the ground in his garden and he was counting pebbles. Now to count these pebbles he put them in a row and he counted them one, two, three, up to ten. Then he finished counting them and started to count them in the other direction. He began by the end and once again found he had ten. He found this marvelous . . . So he put them in a circle and counted them that way and found ten once again."[9]

Concept Formation: The Good, the Bad, and the Ugly

Some of these cognitive revelations between the ages of five and seven have a quality of *remembering* about them. While we will see below that children at this age seem to be spending most of their time *adapting* to the social world around them, it appears that certain aspects of these new thinking abilities may be *coming down from the spirit* and reminding them about the deeper dimensions of life.[10] One adult, remembering back to a grammar lesson she had in school at the age of seven, reported: "I had an extraordinarily vivid insight, which is absolutely beyond description but which has remained with me ever since as an abiding spiritual experience. The teacher was explaining that in addition to common nouns and proper nouns there were also abstract nouns, which mostly ended in "-ness," such as goodness, badness, etc.; also a number of short but very important words such as love, hate, etc. It was at this point that I seemed to grow up mentally."[11] In another case, a seventy-five-year-old man remembered being seven years old and preparing to go out on a walk when he had the following thought: "'Here am I, a little boy of seven; I wonder where I was eight years ago.' At that tremendous thought I stood rooted to the carpet . . . with a wave of tremendous feeling sweeping over me. I suddenly felt old and aware of being somebody very ancient... Eight years ago, thought I, why not eighty or eight hundred?" The Norwegian composer Edvard Grieg reported having a spiritual experience with logical properties of music as a five-year-old: "Why not begin by remembering the wonderful, mystical satisfaction of stretching one's arms up to the piano and bringing forth—not a melody. Far from it! No, it had to be a chord. First a third, then a fifth, then a seventh. And finally, both hands helping—Oh joy!—a ninth, the dominant ninth chord. When I had discovered this my rapture knew no bounds. That was a success! Nothing since has been able to elate me so profoundly as this."[12] It almost seems as if a higher mind were incarnating in the child at this time, allowing him to step back from his immediate surroundings and see himself in the context of a greater whole.

Once children begin to engage in this sort of "transcendental thinking," they can also start to put themselves in the shoes of another person and imagine what the world might look like from their point of view, just as they are able to mentally project themselves onto both sides of the drinking glass experiment. This makes it possible for the child to engage in a mutual give-and-take with others, a process that underlies virtually all later social communication and engagement. You can see this process at work by watching a group of elementary school-aged kids playing a game of sandlot ball without adult supervision. Gone are the fuzzy parameters of early childhood where rules were made up on the spot and could be changed at the whim of any participant. These older kids seem to spend as much time arguing *about* the game as actually playing it. They squabble about whether a player touched second base, tagged the guy out at home, hit a ball within the foul line, or any of a thousand other scenarios. Questions of *fairness* predominate as the children use their new mental abilities to interpret formal rules that are designed to apply as much to one side as to the other.

Here we begin to see one of the most essential features of life in middle childhood. Kids are moving out of their family and neighborhood circle into a much broader and more complex social arena, and *they want to know what the rules are* in this larger world. So, society tells them. As we noted earlier, children at this age are capable of understanding categories and concepts like blueness, thinness, goodness, and badness. As a result, they are now also primed to learn the rules of societal prejudice. This is the age of stereotypes, the age of learning how to put people and things into little boxes: "ugly/cute," "stupid/smart," "nerdy/cool." Kids at this age are hungry to internalize the strictures of the surrounding community and take on the mores of their particular cultural context with a vengeance. They learn about patriotism and about the rightness of killing other human beings—"foreigners," "aliens" or "terrorists"—who threaten their country. They learn the dogma of their family's religion, and begin to understand that "nonbelievers" will burn in hell for eternity or suffer some comparable fate. They learn that the people down the block from them are "chinks," "spics," or "wackos," because of the way they look, the way they talk, or the beliefs they hold. In his classic book on prejudice, psychologist Gordon Allport recalled one child's need for a "refresher course" on what she had been taught in this regard by her parents: "Janet, six years of age, was trying hard to integrate her obedience to her mother with her daily social contacts. One day she came running home and asked, 'Mother, what is the name of the children I am supposed to hate?'"

Encountering Dysteachia

Besides the family, school is the primary formal institution for instilling social values and skills in middle childhood. It is the place where the older generation has the opportunity to set down large numbers of the younger generation all in one location and instruct them in those competencies that are believed to be most critical for the continued survival of the community. If the culture is a hunting society, then school will take place on the run. If the culture is an agrarian one, then the school will take place in the fields. If the culture is made up of artisans, then children will literally sit at the feet of master cobblers, weavers, and smiths and learn their craft by practicing it over and over again. And if the culture is a modern literate society such as our own, then school will take place in specially designed buildings set aside for the purpose of learning how to read, write, calculate, and compute. Instead of expert farmers, hunters, tailors, or other members of the living culture, our culture has designated a group of specially trained individuals whom we call "teachers" who are experts in using abstract symbol systems, and who attempt as best they can to instruct youngsters in skills that will promote their success in a complex technological society. The difficulty comes when most of this instruction takes place within the walls of an artificial learning environment called a *classroom* rather than out in the real world where this knowledge needs to be immediately applied to practical situations that have real meaning for children. This gap between the spuriousness of school culture and the authenticity of the real world has been a significant problem that continues to bedevil educators despite wave after wave of school reform.

And yet modern schooling does end up teaching kids quite a bit about how the world works. Kids learn how to sit still for long periods of time at small desks, just as they will have to sit at desks in corporate "cube farms" when they grow up. They learn how to submit to authority, follow bureaucratic rules, and compete against their peers for rewards and advantages, again, in preparation for what will come later on in adulthood. They also learn not to question too much, think too differently from their peers, or be too creative as they progress through the grades. Jules Henry, an anthropologist who did field research in American classrooms in the same way that his colleagues collected data from rain-forest cultures, once wrote: "The schools have never been places for the stimulation of young minds. If all through school the young were provoked to question the Ten Commandments, the sanctity of revealed religion, the foundations of patriotism, the profit motive, the two-party system, monogamy, the laws of incest and so on, we would have more creativity than we could handle. In teaching our children to accept fundamentals of social relationships and religious beliefs without question we follow the ancient highways of the human race, which extend backward into the dawn of the species, and indefinitely into the future."[13] It's probably true that schools are the most conservative of all cultural institutions, relentlessly seeking to pass on the rules of a damaged society to the next generation. As world philosopher and teacher J. Krishnamurti points out: "Of what value is it to be trained as lawyers if we perpetuate litigation? Of what value is knowledge if we continue in our confusion? What significance has technical and industrial capacity if we use it to destroy one another?"[14]

Brain connections continue to be "pruned" during this period of middle childhood, and schooling certainly has a lot to do with this process. While formal schooling *does* recognize certain kinds of abilities in its students and develops them into maturity—the ability to read, write, and solve logical problems being foremost among them—it also serves as a gatekeeper to prevent many other capacities, talents, and abilities from ever being recognized and nurtured. Many children enter kindergarten or first grade brimming with artistic, musical, physical, aesthetic, poetic, spiritual, philosophical, mechanical, practical, or other creative talents, only to have little or no attention given to these gifts by teachers or parents. As a result, these abilities—and the brain connections that sustain them—are literally starved out of existence from sheer neglect. Children at this age learn from countless standardized tests beginning in preschool and kindergarten that they are either "smart" or "dumb." Some jubilantly learn that they are "gifted," while others have the disappointment of discovering that they are "slow," or merely "average." Kids also learn that in order to survive, they need to master a number of tacit skills including currying favor with the teacher, cheating without getting caught, faking illness to get out of the classroom, and paying attention only to what is going to affect one's grade or test results.

On the positive side, there certainly are wonderful and passionate teachers out there who have retained a connection with the *rememberer* inside of themselves, and who have managed to create a refuge of sorts for children in school. One adult recalling his second-grade teacher said: "She knew I liked to write. One day I was really restless, walking around, not paying attention. Then she gave us an assignment. We had to write something, and I wrote about walking around. She pulled me aside and said, 'Why don't you learn the word meander?' I went home with a great new word and a great new attitude."[15] Talk show host Oprah Winfrey credits her fourth-grade teacher, Mrs. Duncan, at Wharton Elementary School in Nashville, Tennessee, with inspiring her to make something of herself in life. She commented: "For the first time, I wasn't afraid to be smart . . . It was in her class that I really came into myself."[16] Mrs. Duncan, without perhaps even knowing it, reminded Oprah of who she really is, and in this way affected millions of people worldwide who have been positively influenced by Oprah's inspirational work, thus proving what writer Henry Adams said a hundred years ago: "A teacher affects eternity; he can never tell where his influence stops."[17]

Montessori and Waldorf schools are good examples of entire school systems that were created by *rememberers* who recognized the *spirit down* dimensions of classroom learning. Maria Montessori wrote: "The child becoming incarnate is a spiritual embryo which needs its own special environment."[18] Her schools allow children to work at their own pace and honor the students' ability to become totally absorbed in a learning activity as if it were a meditation or sacred experience. Rudolf Steiner, the founder of Waldorf schools, believed that children didn't fully incarnate into their physical bodies until age seven (an event marked by the change of teeth), and only then could they begin to fully engage in abstract skills such as reading, writing, and mathematics. Referring to the boisterous nature of childhood, he wrote: "Suppose all you clever and well brought up people were suddenly condemned to remain always in a room having a temperature of 144° Fahrenheit. You couldn't do it! It is even harder for the spirit of the child, which has descended from the spiritual worlds, to accustom itself to earthly conditions. The spirit, suddenly transported into a completely different world, with the new experience of having a body to carry about, acts as we see the child act."[19] Waldorf classrooms have a gentle atmosphere, with pastel colors, natural wood furniture, nonlinear architecture, and an artistic focus. These two systems—Montessori and Waldorf—along with many other alternative school programs demonstrate that schools can be places for the nourishment of a child's soul. At the same time, the child's *body up* development is also worked with and nourished. Montessori schools provide a practical orientation to life skills such as cleaning, cooking, and gardening, and carefully plan out activities to help the child learn about how the world works using concrete manipulative materials. Waldorf schools also offer a balanced approach to learning that devotes a part of each day to activities that engage the body, the heart (emotions), and the head (intellect).

From Latency to Late Childhood

The child's process of coming *up from the body*, or emerging from her biological and physical origins, is particularly important at this time of life as she begins to gain greater control over her instincts. Children's energies at this age are like the winds that Aeolus stuffed into a bag for Odysseus as a gift on his journey, to be used only when he needed them to blow his ship back home to Ithaca. Freud called the time of middle childhood the "latency" years because of the child's ability to channel primitive emotional drives into socially acceptable—if at times barely acceptable—forms of expression. According to Freud, the powerful libidinal instincts of early childhood, as classically represented in the Oedipal urge of the young child to kill one parent and have sex with the other, become "latent" at this time; they essentially go underground during middle childhood only to emerge with renewed fury in the adolescent years.[20] There's some truth in what Freud said about this. One of the most comprehensive recent studies of sex and children indicated that observed sexual activity peaks at around age five, and then undergoes a steady decline until ages eleven or twelve.[21] What's missing from this account, of course, is the developmental fact that children at this age become more private with their sexuality, and engage in masturbation, exploratory activities with peers, and other sexual pursuits in secret where their activities can't be tabulated by sociologists or snoopy parents.

At the same time, however, it's also true to say that children at this age become better at doing constructive things with their instincts. They put their energies into engaging in sports, hanging out with friends, reading, exploring nature, playing with toys, and collecting things. It's almost as if much of the libidinal energy that was on the verge of boiling

over in early childhood is now bound up in each of the little action figures, dolls, trading cards, or other things that kids accumulate during
middle childhood. "What benefits come from collecting 376 rusty bottle
caps, 208 green marbles, 452 unmatched playing cards, and a string of
1,000 paper clips?" asks former school psychologist and author Dorothy
Corkille Briggs. "They are *symbols*—psychological tools—that nourish
self-esteem. They bring the joy of initiating, the excitement of the hunt,
the comfort of status, the fascination of management, and the pride of
ownership. The youngster gets experience in controlling, possessing, planning and trading."[22]

We observed in the last chapter how children in early childhood begin
to develop rituals, routines, and defenses that help to ward off painful
experiences that come from contact with the outside world. In middle
childhood, this ability becomes even more refined as the child develops
the capacity to handle feelings of rejected love, humiliation, embarrass-
ment, jealousy, anger, and fear through an increasingly sophisticated
arsenal of language tricks and social tools. I remember how I coped with
insults in the third grade. I had only to say to the insulter the words "A
skunk smells his own tracks first!" to remove the sting of hurt. My friends
at the time had a ritual for deflecting attention away from a potentially
embarrassing burp or fart. They would say the phrase: "Bulldog slugs, no
return, knock on wood," and then hurriedly knock on some nearby piece
of wood and proceed to slug the person nearest to them! In my capacity as
a teacher in elementary school decades later, I heard other choice "come-
back lines." For example, if a child had just insulted a peer and an
onlooker wanted to line himself up with the offender to protect himself
from future insult, he would say to the insulted party: "What a burn, what
a cut, stick a finger up your butt!" Phrases like this one give kids an opportunity to express sexual and aggressive feelings in a carefully structured
way. In my elementary school days, a good way to express anger and frustration toward a teacher was to sing "The Battle Hymn of the Republic"
with these words: "Glory, glory hallelujah, teacher hit me with a ruler,
bopped her in the bean with a rotten tangerine, and she won't be coming

round no more." There are literally thousands of songs, routines, pranks, and tricks that kids use in middle childhood to ward off unpleasantness and to help bolster their emerging egos. This kind of "child lore" was invented by kids, without adult involvement, and has been passed down from generation to generation for hundreds of years in one form or another.

Child lore includes a wide variety of tongue twisters, puns, riddles, and jokes that give kids a chance to show off their growing sophistication with language. There are also physical and emotional challenges with games such as "Truth, Dare, Double Dare, Promise, or Repeat" and "Captain, May I?" There are ghost stories, rumors, and gory tales like "The Dead Hitchhiker" and "The Golden Arm" to help channel anxiety and demonstrate mastery over the unknown. There are preteen games like "Kiss or Kill" and "Spin the Bottle," or jump-rope rhymes ("Mary Mack, dressed in black, silver buttons down her back. I love coffee. I love tea. I love the boys in the C.L.B.") to channel burgeoning sexual and aggressive drives. There are levitation tricks that involve pressing your arms against a door jamb to debunk the magic of early childhood, and devices like "cootie catchers" that serve as a way of shunning people perceived as having negative qualities. As folklorists Peter and Iona Opie, who devoted their lives to collecting child lore from the British Isles and America, explained: "The scraps of lore which children learn from each other are at once more real, more immediately serviceable, and more vastly entertaining to them than anything which they learn from grown-ups."[23]

While kids in middle childhood have an increasing number of defenses to help them cope with the emotional fallout around them, they also have the ability to express a growing variety of complex emotions in the course of daily life when compared with younger children. Rudolf Steiner believed that the key to understanding this time of life lay in acknowledging and nurturing the *feeling* nature of the child. He called this time "the *heart* of childhood" to emphasize the importance of addressing emotions and the imagination. He noted that kids especially need rhythmic experiences in middle childhood, observing how much they enjoy jump-rope rhymes and hopscotch out on the playground, and emphasizing rhythms as they read books or sing songs. This love of rhythm extends to the emotions as well. Steiner observed that children at this age move naturally between the poles of emotion. As British Waldorf educator A. C. Harwood pointed out: "How deeply children love to swing between the poles! What good lovers they are and what good haters! They must always have a favourite colour, a favourite flower, a favourite pudding. What they do not like is horrible and disgusting beyond expression. And how quickly they change. A little girl who has had a bosom friend for a week will make a face when her name is mentioned the week after: but a few days later they are arm in arm again."[24] As children advance to the age of nine or ten, their feelings change and become more subtle and nuanced. Their sense of subjectivity deepens and they develop a richer inner world to complement the busy social world of which they are becoming more and more an integral part. It is to this story of late childhood that we now turn in the next chapter.

~∞~

The Gift of Middle Childhood: Imagination

"Imagination is more important than knowledge," said Albert Einstein. If this is true, then children are smarter than college professors with encyclopedic minds. Middle childhood is a time when the vivid imagery of early childhood that combined inner and outer experiences transforms itself into a subjective imagination that is distinctly different from the objective world beyond the mind. This imagination may be all that links many children between the ages of five and ten to the spiritual worlds they inhabited more fully and freely during infancy and early childhood. Through imagination, children can bring entire worlds and civilizations into being. Many kids find their subjective daydreams far more interesting than anything they experience in school or around the house. Sadly, most adults consider the daydreams of children unimportant and a waste of time. The truth is that many of the greatest discoveries made in the twentieth century—Einstein's theory of relativity, Darwin's theory of evolution, and Freud's theory of the unconscious—have their roots in imaginative thinking. Images are like seeds that over time sprout into marvelous ideas with practical significance.

Most of us are too busy with our hectic lives to be concerned about imagination. We may occasionally remember a dream after waking, fantasize playing golf during a boring meeting at work, or see images in our mind as we try to describe a recent movie to a friend. Modern society downplays the importance of imagination in favor of clear, logical thinking. Yet imagination has many potential benefits to those who are willing to nurture it and keep it alive. Imagination serves as a powerful method of stress reduction by taking the mind away from situations that create anxiety or frustration, and by activating more pleasurable and healthy images. Visualizing a favorite place in nature, for example, may soothe and relax better than pain-killing medications. Imagination provides a rich source of creative ideas for the home and the workplace. Strategic problems are often best solved with a spouse at home or a group at work by imagining a wide range of possible solutions and then combining the best parts of each one. Imagination prevents us from getting stuck in a rut. It is the soil in which the creative life thrives. Just by allowing ourselves to imagine new possibilities in the way we work, play, relate, and think we can change our fortunes and create new realities that exceed anything we've previously known. This wonderful gift of middle childhood is always available to us if we periodically close our eyes and explore the marvelous wonderland of images that exist in our mind's eye.

————— *Ways to Explore and Support Middle Childhood* —————

FOR YOURSELF
- Write down any memories you have of imaginative experiences between the ages of five and ten. If you have artwork from this period stored away, take it out and look at the themes you were concerned with in middle childhood. What do they tell you about

your fears, loves, hates, and hopes during this time of life?

- Write down any memories you might have about sexual experiences (with others or alone) between the ages of five and ten. Reflect on the impact that these experiences had on your later life.
- Write down any thoughts that occur to you about your early school experiences. If you have old school records (report cards, photos, samples of schoolwork), take them out and notice what they have to tell you about your early experiences with formal education.

FOR FRIENDS AND FAMILY

- Tutor a five- to ten-year-old child (your own or a friend's) who has been labeled as having "attention deficit hyperactivity disorder," "learning disabilities," or "autistic spectrum disorder." Spend some time helping the child identify his particular strengths and talents, and then seek ways to develop them.
- Share examples of "child lore" from your middle childhood with a group of friends. Put together a scrapbook of these memories. Do you observe that today's children have their own child lore, or has today's mass media largely replaced it?

FOR THE COMMUNITY

- Help to preserve children's imaginations by supporting storytelling, creative writing, and the expressive arts at your community center, library, or local elementary school.
- Support Montessori schools, Waldorf schools, or other alternative school programs in your community that address the *spirit down* as well as the *body up* developmental needs of children. Investigate the possibility of integrating one of these approaches into the public school system of your community.
- Get involved in a school program that helps teach kids about prejudice, racism, and the need for tolerance (e.g., the Teaching Tolerance program of the Southern Poverty Law Center). If no such program exists, help to create one in your community.

∞

CHAPTER 6

Late Childhood: Becoming a Part of the Crowd

When I was a little girl in the fourth grade I used, after not too happy
days, to look forward with eagerness to the time when I went to bed,
when I could lie unmolested by other people and weave fantasies. . . .
I dreamed that I was a lovely young woman in Holland, with a
beautifully kept house and gardens and dairy, and spotless clothes
and a pretty crisp cap.

FROM FRANCES G. WICKES, THE INNER WORLD OF CHILDHOOD [1]

Almost everyone is familiar with the fairy tale where the girl kisses the
frog and he turns into a prince. Most people don't know, however, that the
original Brothers Grimm tale was not quite so romantic. It actually went
something like this: Once upon a time, a princess was playing alone under
an old lime tree near a well. She was throwing a golden ball high up in the
air and catching it with great delight, but one time she missed and the ball
rolled into the well. The princess cried deeply for the loss of her favorite
plaything. Suddenly, she heard a voice from the well say: "I can get that
ball back for you, but what will you give me in return?" It was a frog with
a big ugly head. The princess was so happy that she said, "Whatever you
want, frog!" He replied: "Will you let me sit at your dinner table, and eat
from your plate, and sleep in your little bed?" She was so desperate to get
the ball back that she immediately said, "Yes, of course!" The frog

retrieved the ball for her, and the princess ran back to her castle, completely forgetting about him and the promise she'd made. The next day she was eating a meal with her family when the frog came to the castle and reminded her of her vow. She was appalled at the suggestion, but her father the king said that she had to keep her promise. So she let the frog sit at her table and eat from her plate, even though she found it totally repulsive. Then the frog reminded her that she had promised to let him sleep in her little bed. This she adamantly refused to do, until her father again told her that she had to fulfill her obligations. Quite upset, she took the frog into her bedroom and put him into a corner saying: "There! Now keep quiet, frog!" But he insisted on sleeping in her bed. This enraged the princess so much that she took the frog in her hands and threw him violently against the wall. As he fell to the floor, he turned into a handsome prince. That night they went to bed, and the next day they sped off in a royal carriage to the prince's kingdom where they lived happily ever after.[2]

This fairy tale, turns out to be a rather remarkable description of late childhood as a transitional stage of human development. The princess who happily plays with her golden ball represents the magic of middle childhood, where the youngster is still engaged in a relatively carefree lifestyle and is immersed in playful scenarios, imaginary worlds, animated games, and high-spirited antics. But the princess loses the ball (curiously, there is an episode in Homer's *Odyssey* when a young princess is playing outdoors and loses her ball).[3] The golden age of childhood, full of youthful spirituality and creativity, is coming to a close. As William Wordsworth put it (with amendation for the twenty-first century): "Shades of the prison-house begin to close / Upon the growing [Child]." Something else emerges: a new kind of energy represented by the slimy frog. This is perhaps the dawning of sexuality, initially regarded by the preadolescent with loathing and disgust ("Boys, Ugh!"), but having an irresistable pull to it. Or possibly the frog is simply the harbinger of growing up in all of its alien glory. In any case, the child wants to stay in her carefree world and ignore this amphibious herald of things to come. But society, as represented here by the king, reminds the child that there are obligations and duties that must be kept. Late childhood is a time when the child must assume more responsibility in society; when household chores, homework, first jobs, tight schedules, higher parental expectations, and social pressures from one's own peer group impose greater burdens on daily life than ever before. As one parenting expert put it: "A preteen's social calendar can fill up tighter than an executive's Palm Pilot."[4] There is probably no other stage of life (except perhaps young adulthood) when the pressures to *adapt* to the surrounding world are so great, and when the voices to *remember* one's spiritual origins are so faintly heard.[5]

As our fairy tale progresses, a palpable tension can be felt building up inside of the princess as she confronts the frog's insistent demands. This mirrors the growing sense that preadolescents have of becoming separate individuals set apart from the environment and no longer Mommy's or Daddy's little boy or girl. Events in our fairy tale ultimately crescendo to a violent conclusion, pointing to the hormonal upsurges of puberty in adolescence, and the story concludes with a royal union that could be either an actual marriage, or a state of psychological integration where the child is transformed, like the frog, into a mature person in her own right. At heart, then, this classic story, which is widely celebrated and spoofed in contemporary media, seems to be a coming-of-age tale containing an acutely perceptive account of the sensitive dynamics that are involved as a child makes her way through the triumphs and struggles of late childhood and then moves on.

The Magic Age of Ten

A key event at the beginning of late childhood—which just might be the biochemical equivalent of the slimy frog in our fairy tale—is *adrenarche*. Often confused with puberty (which will be explored in the next chapter), *adrenarche* marks a critical stage in the maturation of the cortex of the adrenal glands, the two triangle-shaped endocrine organs that sit above the kidneys. According to biopsychologist Martha K. McClintock, "Our culture regards . . . childhood as a time of hormonal quiescence . . . But actually a great deal of activity is going on."[6] McClintock and her colleague, anthropologist Gilbert Herdt, point out that the adrenal glands begin increasing their production of a hormone associated with sexual attraction, dihydroepiandrosterone (DHEA), around the age of six and this production reaches a critical level in the endocrine system at about age ten, precipitating the occurrence of *adrenarche*. The most evident signs that occur as a result of this biological event are the first appearance of pubic hair (*pubarche*) and the beginning of adultlike body odor as a result of chemical changes in the composition of sweat. From a psychological perspective, several studies indicate that children begin to feel a sexual chemistry for others around this time, and that this is true of both straight and gay populations. McClintock and Herdt, for example, share the story of a gay eighteen-year-old male from Chicago who remembered watching the television program *Star Trek* with his family: " He reports that he was ten years old and had not yet developed any obvious signs of puberty. When Captain Kirk suddenly peeled off his shirt, the boy was titillated. At ten years of age, this was his first experience of sexual attraction."[7]

It's around this age—fourth grade—that one can begin to observe the presence of a palpable sexual tension between boys and girls, with teasing, chasing, gossip, and kissing starting to replace the staunchly militant same-sex groups that were so characteristic of life in the lower grades. Blogger Ryan MacMichael writes, "I remember my first kiss quite fondly . . . I'm talking about the time in fourth grade when my friend Josh had a boy/girl party and we decided to break out a bottle and do a little spinning . . . I remember one girl getting especially grossed out when my friend Pat tried to slip her the tongue. In any event, my first kiss was with Josh's super-shy cousin. All I remember is that she had red hair and barely said a word the whole party. Ah . . . but I made her smile after my spin landed on her."[8] Sometimes, there is a quality of *remembering* in these first encounters with the opposite sex. The Italian poet Dante Alighieri reported that he was almost ten years old when he saw eight-year-old Beatrice Portinari at a May Day party at the Portinaris' family home in Florence. He wrote, "The moment I saw her I say in all truth that the vital spirit, which dwells in the inmost depths of the heart, began to tremble so violently that I felt the vibration alarmingly in all my pulses, even the weakest of them . . . Love ruled over my soul."[9] Dante would later immortalize Beatrice by making her his spiritual guide through Paradise in *The Divine Comedy*.

Late childhood also marks important changes in the development of the brain. As we noted in the chapter on early childhood, metabolic rates in the brain of a three-year-old are double that of an adult's and continue at that level from about the age of four to ten. Around age ten, however, metabolic rates begin to decline until they reach normal adult levels by ages sixteen to eighteen.[10] Brain researcher Marian Diamond notes that "a child below the age of ten can lose part of the cerebral cortex near the language area—even the entire right hemisphere . . . and have no permanent difficulties speaking or interpreting language."[11] A more recent brain study shows that there is an actual *spike* in the growth of gray matter in the frontal and parietal lobes of the neocortex between the ages of ten and twelve.[12] "We were quite surprised," said psychiatrist and brain researcher Jay Giedd, the principal author of the study, "to see this unexpected increase in gray matter in the front part of the brain right before puberty. . . ."[13] Giedd speculates that the production of extra brain connections (if this, indeed, is the cause of the spike) may "herald a critical stage of development when the environment or activities of the teenager may guide selective synapse elimination during adolescence."[14] In other words, it may be that nature provides a brief abundance of gray matter in late childhood, just as it did for very young children, so that the environment can strengthen those connections necessary for survival (in this case, perhaps for mate seeking, care of young, or building a home), and eliminate synapses (brain connections) that are not needed, just at a time when kids are on the verge of procreating and thus able to pass their genes on to the next generation.

Something that is particularly noteworthy at this age is how ingenious kids can be in coming up with strategies for avoiding homework, improvising special tricks for solving math or science problems, or creating inventions for saving time and energy (recently, for example, a ten-year-old girl invented and trademarked Wristies, which are protective winter gear (long, fingerless gloves) designed to prevent snow, wind, and cold from entering the gaps in sleeves). Preteens are a little like "the great tactician" Odysseus tricking the Cyclops, inventing the Trojan Horse, or coming up with a solution for hearing the song of the Sirens while steering his men back home to Ithaca. Like Odysseus, they use their "street smarts" to help them make it through the ups and downs of their journey through the "tween years."

The biochemical changes of late childhood also appear to herald a shift in the sense of identity. As Annie Dillard writes in her memoir *An American Childhood*: "Children ten years old wake up and find themselves here, discover themselves to have been here all along . . . They wake like sleepwalkers, in full stride . . . equipped with a hundred skills. They know the neighborhood, they can read and write English, they are old hands at the commonplace mysteries, and yet they feel themselves to have just stepped off the boat . . . just flown down from a trance, to lodge in an eerily familiar life already well under way."[15]

An incident in the life of Benjamin Franklin as a ten-year-old humorously illustrates this new sense of being squarely planted on the earth. Franklin lived near the water and one day convinced his friends to help him turn a nearby salt marsh into something with a sounder foundation. As he recalls in his well-known autobiography, ". . . by much trampling, we had [turned the marsh into] a mere quagmire. My proposal was to build a wharf there fit for us to stand upon, and I showed my comrades a large heap of stones, which were intended for a new house near the marsh, and which would very well suit our purpose."[16] In the evening, when the workmen had gone, they built their wharf and the next day got into trouble for stealing the stones. Carl Jung wrote about a powerful experience of identity that occurred to him at the age of twelve: "I was taking the long road to school . . . when suddenly for a single moment I had the overwhelming impression of having just emeged from a dense cloud. I knew all at once: now I am myself! It was as if a wall of mist were at my back, and behind that wall there was not yet an 'I.' But at this moment I came upon myself."[17]

The experience of becoming a "self" is, however, a mixed blessing. As the child's sense of "I" becomes stronger, so too does the feeling of separation from the world. One adolescent remembered: " I used to have this recurring dream until I was about ten ... There was no story ... it was more of an image, a sensation; it was unpleasant. I could see waves, not necessarily sea waves, but they were often like that. They created a horrible, distressing distance between myself and the object of the dream I was having."[18] Children between the ages of ten and twelve start spending more time alone, thinking, reflecting, and brooding. I remember devoting a great deal of time at that age to listening to music on a small transistor radio alone in our basement. I listened to songs like Del Shannon's "Runaway," and "Raindrops" by Dee Clark, while feeling a new kind of emptiness or loneliness that hadn't been there before. British psychiatrist Harry Stack Sullivan wrote: "Loneliness reaches its full significance in the preadolescent era, and goes on relatively unchanged from thenceforth throughout life. Anyone who has experienced loneliness is glad to discuss some vague abstract of this previous experience of loneliness. But it is a very difficult therapeutic performance to get anyone to remember clearly how he felt and what he did when he was horribly lonely."[19]

The Big Learning Slump

School can help alleviate some of that loneliness. But it also represents a new kind of obstacle to navigate in late childhood. For many, school gets a lot harder around this time, leaving the fun and games of the lower grades behind. Philosopher Jean-Paul Sartre, who had been happily writing whole novels at home as an eight- to ten-year-old, suddenly found things quite changed as an eleven-year-old when the academic pressures of his schoolwork became more severe: "I had even stopped writing. The 'novel notebooks' had been thrown out, mislaid, or burned and had made way for grammar, arithmetic, and dictation notebooks. If someone had crept into my head, which was open to all the winds, he would have come upon a few busts, a stray multiplication table and the rule of three, thirty-two counties with the chief town of each but not the sub-prefecture, a rose called *rosarosarosamrosaerosaerose*, some historical and literary monuments, a few polite maxims engraved on stiles, and sometimes, like a scar of mist hovering over this sad garden, a sadistic reverie."[20] These new demands on kids sometimes elicit cries of rebellion. Filmmaker Orson Welles, who in adulthood would shock millions of Americans with his *War of the Worlds* radio program simulating an invasion of Earth by Martians, created a furor as a fourth grader when he gave a lecture on art to the student body and began lambasting the school's teachers for their lack of creativity. "'You mustn't criticize the public school system, Orson,' one teacher called out, to which the fourth grader responded, 'If the public school system needs criticizing, I will criticize it!'"[21]

More often, these new school pressures give rise to what some elementary school teachers have referred to despairingly as "the fourth-grade slump." Originally coined by reading expert Jeanne Chall to describe the drop-off in test scores of low-income children from third to fourth grade, the term is now used more generically to describe the difficulties that students in fourth grade begin to experience as the reading load starts to pile up.[22] According to educator Anne Grosso de León, "The slightly larger desks waiting for fourth graders when they return to school in the fall are designed, after all, to accommodate more than their growing bodies. Piled high on their new desks are a variety of new academic subject texts as well as samples of what is now called 'literature.' Their storybooks a fond memory, the children will be expected to read these new texts, laden with content and new vocabularies, not merely to demonstrate that they can sound out the words, but to demonstrate that they understand what they read."[23] The added pressure of schoolwork (smaller print, computer screens, detailed writing) often creates eyestrain. It's a fact that simple myopia (near-sightedness) is often called "school myopia," and generally starts between the ages of ten to twelve, just as these academic demands are beginning to mount.

The heavy emphasis that schools place on reading, writing, and reasoning, especially in these later grades, has come under criticism from some prominent educators. Howard Gardner, professor of education at Harvard

University, for example, suggests that schools primarily educate only two of the eight intelligences described in his book *Frames of Mind*: linguistic intelligence (reading, writing, and speaking) and logical-mathematical intelligence (reasoning, calculating, and experimenting). There are six other intelligences, however, that educators typically neglect in most classroom instruction: spatial (imagining, drawing, designing), bodily-kinesthetic (crafting, acting, displaying physical abilities), musical (listening, composing, performing on instruments), interpersonal (empathizing, negotiating, cooperating), intrapersonal (self-understanding, reflecting, feeling), and naturalist intelligences (discriminating, classifying, and nurturing living things).[24] Students who speak well, write well, and reason well are usually the ones who get the most praise, the best grades, and the highest test scores in school. On the other hand, students who learn best through one or more of the other intelligences—through pictures, physical experiences, music, social interactions, personal reflection, or experiences in nature—are put at a distinct disadvantage since teachers generally don't stray beyond the traditional lecture, textbook, and worksheet approach from the fourth grade on. Because of this, many talented students end up being put into remedial and special education programs.[25]

Children who are *rememberers* have a particularly difficult time in school in late childhood. These are usually the kids in late childhood who have somehow managed to hold on to the creative and spiritual perceptions of infancy and early and middle childhood despite all sorts of social pressures to give up their "immaturity" and fit in with the rest of the crowd. These *spirit down* kids have special trouble *adapting* to the academic demands imposed on them from a school system steeped in social convention. In many cases, these kids are given negative school labels such as "learning disabled," "attention deficit hyperactivity disorder," or "autistic spectrum disorder."[26] I taught a number of kids like these in special education programs in Canada and the United States during the 1970s and early 1980s. Many of these kids were artists, writers, actors, philosophers, poets, and rebels who did not fit in with the normal routine of traditional classrooms. In the course of my teaching, I discovered that these students do not think in the linear, one-step-at-a-time manner that is valued most in school ("now class, say b-a-t, bat") nor do they excel in the memorization abilities that are the hallmark of a good test taker.[27] Instead, they tend to be holistic learners with active imaginations, novel perceptions, artistic creativity, spiritual charisma, diffuse attention, and a love of nature.[28] They prefer living in the here-and-now to preparing for the future and are not enticed by a parent's or teacher's exhortations that they hand in their homework or study hard to get into a good college. In many cases, their school days in regular classrooms are punctuated by a series of "paralyzing experiences" where they are yelled at, laughed at, or in other ways humiliated because of the fact that they are not in step with the inexorable march toward mediocrity of those around them.

I was not surprised when I discovered that a study of four hundred eminent individuals of the twentieth century revealed that 60 *percent* of them had serious school problems, including "dull, irrational, or cruel teachers . . . other students who bullied, ignored, or bored them . . . [and] school failure."[29] Norwegian composer Edvard Grieg made the mistake of bringing his first piano composition to school and performing it, after which the teacher said, "Next time, bring to school your German homework, and leave this stupid stuff at home."[30] Ignacy Jan Paderewski was told by his teacher that he could never expect to be a good pianist because his third fingers were too short. Albert Einstein was reported by his teachers to be "mentally slow, unsociable, and adrift forever in his foolish dreams."[31]

Other turned-off students shift the focus of their attention away from the teacher's lessons and toward things that are more interesting. This is sometimes referred to as "the hidden curriculum." Johnny is whispering to Suzie about how Billy is going to get beat up after school because he let his dog pee on Eddie's homework assignment the day before. Mrs. Jones's false teeth are making a funny noise, which elicits tittering from the class. A note is being passed around from student to student with the declaration, "The principal sucks!" This is where the excitement and vitality in a school is often located: everywhere except where it actually *should* be happening, that is, in the formal curriculum. The presence of these kinds of subterranean activities suggests the existence of another layer of life in late childhood paralleling the official school program: a *peer culture* or social milieu that has virtually nothing to do with the adults in their midst. Research suggests that peer relationships in preadolescence may have more importance as a socializing influence than either teachers or parents.[32]

The Powers and Perils of Peers

Peer culture represents a whole new phenomenon for kids between the ages of nine and twelve. The cliques of late childhood start to replace the clubs of middle childhood. Mall shopping replaces jump-rope hopping for girls. Violent interactive video games replace superhero action figures as a source of entertainment for boys. Rumors and gossip replace the overt insults and accusations of earlier grades. Cell phones and Internet chat rooms replace, or at least supplement, neighborhoods and playgrounds as significant centers of social intercourse. Late childhood is when kids begin to worry big time about what others, especially their peers, think about them. Popularity becomes an important part of self-identity. Kids start to be more self-conscious about what they wear, what they weigh, what they smell like, who they hang out with, and whether or not they're in step with the latest trends.

Exposure to mass media, along with the pressures of living in a consumer-based society, fuel these concerns to a fever high pitch for some preadolescents. Surveys suggest that the more kids are exposed to media, the greater their concern about weight. Fifty-seven percent of kids above the age of eight have a television in their room. Exposed to images of thin models, glamorous movie stars, and elegant cosmetic queens, girls as young as ten years old begin a serious regimen of dieting. One mother, speaking about preadolescent peer culture in Sarasota, Florida, writes, "It's a world where taunts of 'fatty' follow the chubby 10-year-old onto school buses, and even slender 12-year-olds try to live on Diet Coke and salads because they're desperate to look like Jennifer Aniston."[33] Such a climate can set the stage for major physical and emotional problems in adolescence. University of Minnesota public health expert Nancy E. Sherwood notes, "Weight preoccupation in prepubertal girls is a concern because dieting at this age can impact growth and may increase risk for fatigue, irritability, low self-esteem, depression and eating disorders."[34]

Preteen boys, on the other hand, fed on raucous movies, violent television programs, and brutal video games, regard aggression, acting out, and being "cool" as the most prized behaviors within their peer group. Nine- to twelve-year-old boys constitute the greatest percentage of any group in the life span taking medication for attention deficit hyperactivity disorder (ADHD).[35] Studies suggest that tough, antisocial boys are often the most popular kids in school as judged not only by their peers but, amazingly, by their teachers as well.[36] Also important to this age group is athletic prowess and muscular strength. I remember being physically threatened by a fellow student on a field near school in sixth grade and, feeling humiliated by the encounter, responded by going home and trying to persuade my parents to get me some George Jowett weight-lifting equipment.[37] Nowadays, kids may go even further. A recent news report suggests that boys as young as ten are bulking up on steroids or legal derivatives like androstenedione—known as steroid precursors—simply so that they can look good.[38] At the same time, many boys and girls at this age, seeking to emulate popular sports figures, movie stars, and other media icons, are beginning to develop drug, alcohol, and/or cigarette habits that may turn out to be a regular part of their adult lifestyle. Twenty-nine percent of kids have had an alcoholic drink before the age of thirteen. In one study of adolescents in a juvenile detention facility, the average age for starting to experiment with inhalants was 9.7 years old, for marijuana 11.9 years old, and for cigarettes 11.2 years old.[39] According to the Carnegie Council on Adolescence, the preteen years are especially crucial in prevention efforts because preteens are often affected by shifting and inconsistent expectations, personal contradictions, and an increased sense of isolation.[40]

One thing that can help counteract some of these negative influences is a close friendship. As writer Mary Shelley put it, "The companions of our childhood always possess a certain power over our minds which hardly any later friend can obtain."[41] Friendships that bloom in late childhood often are our first mature relationships, containing plenty of give and take and emotional highs and lows. In these friendships we could trade secrets, gossip, comics or cards, learn about sex and other mysteries, copy each other's homework, find out how other people's families live, get into trouble, compete at sports or games, argue, fight, and sever relations, only to make up all over again, and all this without adult interference. British psychiatrist Harry Stack Sullivan placed a particular importance on the finding of a best friend or a "chum" around the age of nine or ten. He suggested that these primarily same-sex relationships represented the beginnings of "something very like full-blown, psychiatrically defined love."[42] If and when you developed such a friendship in late childhood, it was very probably the first time that you extended to another person the same quality of caring that you felt for yourself.

This kind of relationship, according to Sullivan, provides a buffer against the stresses and strains of living on the threshold of adolescence. Psychologist Michael Thompson, in his book *Best Friends, Worst Friends: Understanding the Social Lives of Children*, illustrates such a relationship with his story of Kate and Ann, two girls who became best friends early in the seventh grade. Kate was a newcomer to the school, uninitiated in the mysteries of boy-girl relationships, and still very much involved in the playfulness of middle childhood. Ann was one of the most popular kids in her class, socially adept and a bit rebellious, but was going through a difficult time with her parents' recent divorce. Ann gave Kate credibility with her peer group. As Thompson writes, "Ann loans Kate confidence, clothes, and status in the group. During the school day, Kate is able to say, 'Ann and I bought a bunch of magazines this weekend,' or 'Ann and I went swimming.' The other girls in their class remain a bit mystified by the whole thing. But those precious words 'Ann and I' render Kate worthy of their attention."[43] On the other hand, Kate keeps Ann in touch with the magic of childhood. On Saturday afternoons, they play at being horses, canter down hills, and make loud whinnying noises. Thompson observes, "...Kate offers Ann an important perspective on life. Playing imaginary horse games with Kate gives Ann a break. It's as if she has turned her speeding car off the superhighway of seventh grade for a quiet amble down two-lane roads familiar to her from earlier in her life."[44] In a sense, Ann introduces Kate to the green frog while Kate gives Ann a chance to keep on throwing the golden ball.

Friendships aside, as children begin to move into early adolescence, it seems as if something quite serious begins to kick in. Kids appear to lose some of their exuberance and zip. Girls in particular seem to be at risk for slipping into the doldrums. According to developmental researchers Carol Gilligan and Lyn Mikel Brown, "For over a century, the edge of adolescence has been identified as a time of heightened psychological risk for girls. Girls at this time have been observed to lose their vitality, their resilience, their immunity to depression, their sense of themselves, and their character."[45] At the age of eleven, Gloria Steinem fell into a depression after her parents divorced and her mother became ill: Her biographer reports, "She slept in the upper bunk, and her bed became her nest and retreat. 'Why am I not happy?' she would ask herself, wondering simultaneously if she were not being a bit melodramatic. She also found that if she lay on her back and concentrated very hard, she could reduce her field of vision until it encompassed only one small square of white plasterboard ceiling about a foot above her head. Then she would soothe herself. 'This is clean,' she would tell herself. 'This is neat. I'm just not going to look at any other place.'"[46]

Typical childhood vitality seems to go into hiding as children near adolescence. It often comes out only in dreams and daytime fantasies tinged with a range of vague and sometimes troubling emotional themes covering self, other, and the increasingly expanding world. One twelve-year-old girl remembered the following dream: "I am on a giant web and there is a giant spider coming towards me. She is smiling but as she gets nearer she lets out a horrible scream, so high it hurts my ears. She becomes scarey [sic] and ugly. She gets really close to me and I am stuck on the web unable to move. She looks like she is going to kill me and then she scuttles back to the beginning, puts on a smile, and it begins again. It goes on for ages."[47] While representing a full-blown nightmare, this dream is, in another sense, a presentiment of sorts. For it appears that the green frog and the handsome prince of our fairy tale are now giving way to something even darker that lurks just around the corner. It's to the topic of adolescence that we turn in the next chapter.

∞

The Gift of Late Childhood: Ingenuity

As a preadolescent, Frederick Douglass desperately wanted to learn how to read and write but was forbidden to do so by his slave masters. His solution was to trade bread for reading lessons from hungry little white boys as he pursued his master's errands on the streets of Baltimore. In this way he became literate, and as an adult, used his knowledge to lead the antislavery movement in the United States. Frederick Douglass's story illustrates how much ingenuity kids possess between the ages of nine and twelve. Having become familiar with the rules and responsibilities of society, preteens are able to use their savvy to come up with novel solutions to difficult problems. This is an age when many kids are fascinated with inventions and gadgets. Few people know, for example, that an eleven-year-old, Frank Epperson, invented the Popsicle in 1905. Recently, Taylor Hernandez, age ten, invented "Magic Sponge Blocks," which are large building blocks made from sponge that a child can safely stack without worrying that they could fall and hurt someone. Sometimes this ingenuity shows up in the way that kids are able to manipulate their way out of household chores or school assignments, or convince us to give them what they want for holidays or birthdays. At other times, kids put on their thinking caps and try to solve the big problems of poverty, disease, and war.

We need to treasure and cultivate this kind of ingenuity in our adult lives. Every day we encounter problems that require creative solutions from fixing a leak in the kitchen sink to placating the boss at work. All too often we put the problem out of our minds or defer to an "expert" to take care of the matter. But each little difficulty we find ourselves in offers an opportunity to generate some kind of ingenious response. Perhaps all that's needed is for us to "MacGyver" a leak with a rubber band, or sweeten up the boss with a box of candy. At other times, the situation demands that we go beyond easy answers and generate a number of truly innovative possibilities in order to come up with just the right solution. Ingenuity can help a burned-out employee, for example, brainstorm ideas for a self-run business that is badly needed but that no one has ever thought of before. After all, it was this kind of ingenuity that led Steve Jobs and Steve Wozniak to create the first home computer, inspired Wally Amos to establish a gourmet line of chocolate chip cookies, and directed Martha Stewart to turn household chores into a multimillion-dollar business. Developing or reclaiming ingenuity in our lives also helps to keep the mind active so that it doesn't become rigid from lack of use. By taking time each day to consider novel ways of responding to life's daily challenges, we can ensure that our lives will never be boring, and that the zest for problem-solving and creative thinking will remain vigorous and vibrant within us for as long as we live.

Ways to Explore and Support Late Childhood

FOR YOURSELF

- Recall your academic experiences from late childhood. Look at old report cards or other school-related documents from that time and notice what they tell you about your school experience. Did you go through anything like "fourth-grade slump" when you were in school? (Perhaps it started in an earlier or later grade.) Write about the attitudes you had about yourself as a learner and as a preteen.
- Bring to mind your friends between the ages of nine and twelve. What kinds of things did you do together? Do you still keep in touch with them? If not, consider contacting one or more of them and reminiscing about old times.

- Write down any memories you have concerning intimate relationships between the ages of nine and twelve. Do you remember feeling a "sexual chemistry" with any particular person during this time in your life? If so, write about this experience and how it affected your later life.

FOR FRIENDS AND FAMILY

- Tutor the child of a family member or friend who is having academic difficulties with her homework assignments or other school-related tasks.
- Counsel a preteen you know who has been experimenting with drugs, alcohol, or cigarettes. In a nonjudgmental way, let them know about the dangers of developing life-threatening habits with these substances. If possible, engage peers or older role models who don't smoke, or use drugs or alcohol, to talk with them about why staying away from these substances is a good idea.
- Volunteer to take a group of neighborhood kids, aged nine to twelve, on an overnight camping adventure or to a nearby cultural or historical attraction.

FOR THE COMMUNITY

- Get involved in a community program that seeks to prevent substance abuse (drugs, alcohol, smoking) among children in late childhood.
- Encourage your child's school or school district to use innovative learning methods that employ art, music, nature, physical activity, social interaction, and personal reflection to teach basic academic subjects. Volunteer to come into class and provide some of these alternative learning strategies to individuals or small groups.
- Be a Big Brother or Big Sister to a needy youngster, or sign up to be a leader for a scouting or recreational organization for kids.

⁓∞⁓

CHAPTER 7

Adolescence: Adventures in the Twilight Zone

At the age of fifteen or sixteen . . . we live through great storms of feeling . . . love and anger, joy and scorn . . . go jolting through us like electric impulses, now engulfing the whole world, then again shriveling into nothing; sadness, tenderness, nobility, and generosity of spirit form the vaulting empty skies above us.

—Robert Musil [1]

One of the greatest dramatic plays in the Western world—Shakespeare's *Hamlet*—is a literary work that has puzzled and fascinated critics for centuries. And yet this play seems somehow more accessible to us when we keep in mind that its principal characters, Hamlet and Ophelia, were both *teenagers*. In that respect, they were very much like today's adolescents in their fascination with the supernatural, their rebellion against authority figures, their emotional instability, their cynicism, and their retreat into solitude. In the course of the play, Hamlet communes with the occult when he sees his father's ghost, vents his anger at his mother and stepfather, goes through periods of depression, and even considers suicide in his famous "to be or not to be" speech. In addition, he scorns the hypocrisy of the adults around him, feels called upon to take up his father's mantle but is wracked with self-doubt, and has continual troubles in translating his seemingly haphazard intentions into a clear plan of action. For her own part, Ophelia tries to put on a happy face as she is alternately loved and scorned by Hamlet, but eventually retreats into a poetic fantasy world that looks a little bit like schizophrenia, and ultimately drowns herself in a lake. These behaviors seem strangely familiar to us because they remind us of experiences that have played themselves out in some form during our own, or a friend or relative's, adolescence. That both Hamlet and Ophelia failed at their respective developmental tasks in the play—Hamlet dying by homicide and Ophelia by suicide—serves only to underline the hazardous nature of this dramatic passage from childhood to adulthood. We all made it through these years to be reading this book right now, but there were times when it seemed like the world would end, and in some ways it actually did.

The Perils of Puberty

There we were in late childhood, cruising along in prepubescent bodies that were constantly growing but doing so rather nicely and smoothly, thank you very much, when all of a sudden it seemed as if someone had pulled a string on our body suit without our permission and started all sorts of uncontrollable events spiraling into action. Arms and legs shot off in all directions. Zits came out of nowhere. Armpit sweat poured down shirts and dresses like Niagara Falls. Hair sprouted like crabgrass in secret places. New odors began to attract the attention of dogs and offend family members. For both boys and girls, new aches and pains, new physical sensations, and powerful and strange new emotions began to course through their bodies. At times, it seemed like all we could do was to hang on tight and ride it out.

In a biological sense, it was almost literally a rebirth. The biochemical triple play that initiates puberty—hypothalamus to pituitary gland to sex organs—was first set into motion during fetal life and early infancy. Instead of turning us into teenagers at six months of age, however, these processes went into hiding for nearly a decade before being reactivated just before adolescence. Then, guided by genetics, nutrition, and factors like stress and family dynamics, complex changes in the brain's neurochemistry initiated a renewal of that process. Triggered by a gene ironically named KiSS-1 and the neurotransmitter it encodes (kisspeptin), the hypothalamus secreted a substance called gonadotropin-releasing hormone (GRH), which stimulated the pituitary gland to release two forms of gonadotropin: luteinizing hormone and follicle-stimulating hormone. These chemicals in turn activated the ovaries and testes to produce androgens and estrogens (sex hormones), as well as the sperm and ova that make reproduction possible. Puberty had arrived!

Whether there were fanfares or Bronx cheers accompanying this new phase of development depended not on genetics, but on the surrounding culture.[2] A young girl having her *menarche* (first menstruation) in Navajo culture, for example, would likely be treated to general rejoicing from its members at this sign of moving into womanhood. In other cultures, however, reactions might have been more muted. Anne Frank, writing in her diary during the Nazi occupation of Holland, expressed ambivalent feelings about menstruation: "Each time I have a period . . . I have the feeling that in spite of all the pain, unpleasantness, nastiness, I have a sweet secret. . . . "[3] And for many girls, the arrival of menarche was accompanied by confusion and even scorn. In Paula Weidegger's book *Menstruation and Menopause*, one woman interviewed about her experience of menarche reported, "I had no information whatsoever, no hint that anything was going to happen to me . . . [when it started] I thought I was on the point of death from internal hemorrhage . . . What did my highly educated mother do? She read me a furious lecture about what a bad, evil, immoral thing I was to start menstruating at the age of eleven!"[4]

The situation for boys is even more problematic. There is very little precedent in modern American culture for discussing a boy's *semenarche* (first ejaculation) with him. In the few studies that have been done on the subject, boys have typically been reluctant to discuss their experiences with parents or peers.[5] British psychoanalyst Janet Sayers shares one man's befuddled recollection of the event: "I was eleven . . . it may have been later than eleven . . . probably in the spring . . . it might have been the winter . . . it could have been in the autumn, I don't remember . . . I danced very close to a very attractive girl. I was a child. Nobody had ever told me about wet dreams. I don't know anything about anything. And that night I had my first wet dream . . . I think I put two and two together. But it is very disconcerting not to know quite what's happening . . . it was kissing, sexual stimulation, and then just falling apart."[6] The man compared the sense of shame he felt at that time to an experience he had when he was four years old and had been "caught" by a relative messing his pants. Boys usually don't have a social context for communicating this kind of information to others. As one researcher commented, "Imagine an American boy coming to the breakfast table exclaiming, 'Mom, guess what? I had my first wet dream last night. Now I'm a man.'" In contrast, a study of semenarche in Nigeria indicated the majority of boys interviewed reported telling someone (father or friends) about their first ejaculation.

As if these first experiences of puberty weren't enough to deal with, most people have their first experience of sexual intercourse during the years of adolescence (in the United States, the average age is 15.8).[7] Such events rarely measure up to teenagers' expectations. More commonly, the experience of first sex with another person involves awkwardness, vulnerability, confusion, and sometimes even coercion. This is especially true for women. In one study, nearly one in twenty women reported being forced into their first sexual intercourse in adolescence, and almost one-third of the respondents reported that they didn't want it to happen when it did.[8] One high school sophomore described her own troubled first experience of sexual intercourse with her boyfriend: "I felt as though I had to conform to everything he said that, you know, things that a girl and a guy were supposed to do, so like, when the sex came, like, I did it without thinking . . . I just did it because, maybe because he wanted it, and I was always like tryin' to please him and like, he was real mean, mean to me, now that I think about it. I was like kind of stupid, cause like I did everything for him and he just treated me like I was nothing."[9]

While glorified by the media as an event that is "cool," "hot," or "awesome," the experience of sex for many adolescents is more often a mixture of complex and conflicting emotions, as is much of the rest of their life. This is largely because the emotional centers deep inside the brain—collectively termed the *limbic system*—click into high action at puberty, while the frontal lobes, those areas of the neocortex behind our forehead that govern reserve, reflection, and restraint, don't mature until nineteen or twenty years old or later.[10] This means that from at least the age of twelve to twenty, the average teenager's brain has its emotional gas pedal pressed to the floor while its brakes haven't yet been completely installed![11] This helps to explain the quickly shifting moods of adolescence. In some ways, the emotional volatility of early childhood reasserts itself during the teenage years. This can be quite a problem because it's one thing for a toddler to throw a tantrum and quite another for that same quality of rage to be expressed through the physical frame of a two-hundred-pound sixteen-year-old boy. People can get hurt, and they do, in fact. By age group, adolescents have the highest rates of violent crime, auto accidents, homicide, and suicide. They are also at high risk for assault, rape, panic attacks, eating disorders, substance abuse, serious depression, and schizophrenia—a disorder that was originally called *dementia praecox* (precocious dementia) because it started so often in adolescence and early adulthood.

Diving into the Unconscious

One Jungian analyst even suggested that the entire experience of adolescence might itself represent a mild form of transient schizophrenia.[12] Moving out of the happy-go-lucky world of the pony lover and stamp collector, the ex-child starts to slip into the simmering, moody darkness of the subconscious. As we've noted, there is a kind of regression to earlier states of development going on here. It almost seems as if the adolescent is stopping for a period on his journey toward adulthood to see if there is anything that he has left behind before venturing forth into the unknown. And so he begins to drop some of the tasks that he had been doing so diligently during late childhood. He goes back—some would say he's pushed—into early childhood and infancy in an attempt to heal unresolved emotional conflicts, face powerful instinctual drives, and search for and gather up those long hidden seeds of a deeper authentic self to carry forward into adult life.

This is not, as a rule, a pretty process.[13] It is comparable to a descent into the belly of the whale, a trek into the dragon's lair, or a flight into the eye of the hurricane. It's a dangerous journey where the adolescent can be maimed or destroyed by his own uncontrolled instincts, or by his encounters with the archetypal fragments of his early childhood and infancy. Once again he has to face up to, and this time finally triumph over, the monsters and deities of his own personal odyssey, including Circe, the lustful seductress; Scylla, the devouring sea monster; Poseidon, the god of earthquakes; and a pantheon of other monumental images from his first few years of life. Like Odysseus, the adolescent has to descend into Hades and encounter the ghosts of the past in order to return home as a hero.

There's a magical, almost magnetic, allure to these larger-than-life images for the adolescent. That's one of the reasons why adolescents get so caught up in the occult, sorcery games, myth and legend, mystical philosophies, religious cults, and psychedelic or mood drugs that create altered states of consciousness. Adolescents are hungry for "merger states"; for feelings of "at-one-ment" where they can directly experience these early emotions and fantasies on a grand scale. One can see the earmarks of this archetypal longing in many aspects of adolescent culture, from the names of rock groups (Black Sabbath, Nirvana), to the terms used for street drugs (Angel Dust, Superman), to the fantasy role-playing games teens like to engage in (Dungeons & Dragons, Tunnels & Trolls). These names hint at the images that have been unconsciously controlling them throughout their childhood, that threaten to keep them in a state of infantile dependence, and from which they wish ultimately to break free.

In some cases, these threats stem directly from the nuclear family. Parents who themselves have not grown up or who have not moved ahead to create their own uniquely individual and interesting lives are among the worst instances of the kinds of internalized forces that seek to restrain the adolescent from emotionally advancing into adulthood. In Arthur Miller's classic American play *Death of a Salesman*, a frustrated middle-aged Willy Loman cheats on his wife in a Boston hotel room only to receive a surprise visit from his adolescent son Biff. The son is so shaken up by his father's infidelity and hypocrisy that he refuses to take a make-up summer school course that would insure a college athletic scholarship. This pivotal decision, born of his feelings about his father's bad faith, keeps Biff from going to college and having a successful young adulthood. As psychoanalyst Frances Wickes once pointed out, "The father who is still a child looking to his wife for motherly care, or who has never thought for himself nor acted from individual conviction, or who treats his children, especially his daughters, as emotional toys, can be of no real help when the child is reaching out for greater psychological maturity. There is also that eternally adolescent type of mother who not only keeps young for her children but who tries to keep her children young for herself . . . The daughter is still kept the little girl; the son perhaps begins to assume the place of the youthful lover."[14] In each case, something unresolved in the parent serves as a kind of reverse wind tunnel, sucking the adolescent back into a state of unconscious dependence and immaturity. One of the central projects of adolescence is to achieve liberation from these regressive forces by standing up to their full force and fury, while at the same time maintaining a sense of individual identity in the face of these dangers. It's at such times that the adolescent can pluck the treasure of selfhood from beneath the dragon's lair.

Finding the Rite Passage into Adulthood

Becoming liberated by the past, however, is no easy task and the adolescent needs to have help in stepping across the chasm. For that reason, cultures have evolved rituals of initiation, or "rites of passage" where adults who themselves had been initiated come together to help the younger generation across the threshold. In Homer's *Odyssey*, Telemachus, the adolescent son of Odysseus, goes through his own turbulent rite of passage when he fights alongside of his father to kill the suitors beseiging his home. Traditional rites of passage, while sometimes terribly brutal and politically incorrect by today's standards, are at least to be appreciated for their ingenuity and their sheer diversity of ways to promote "adult making." Of particular interest are those early rites of prehistoric origin from aboriginal Australia and certain parts of Africa that are still in evidence today despite modernization.

At the beginning of such rites, initiates are often separated from their mothers. The mother is sometimes told that a son or daughter is dying or being devoured by a divine monster. This signifies the end of childhood and the leaving behind of the old mother-child relationship. Then the adolescents are often put into some form of seclusion. Females who have just started to menstruate may be secluded in cabins or huts for a significant period of time. Males are often taken to open spaces where they may lie down in a pit representing a coffin and symbolically die to their old life. The pit also represents the womb where they are to be born into a new life as an adult. Sometimes the youths are smeared with red, white, blue, or black substances symbolizing blood, semen, or feces to indicate that they really have died to this life and gone back to the state of the newborn. Females may be placed in womblike cages, made fat and pale, and massaged like babies. Males may hear horrible sounds, or be shown masked figures said to be their ancestors who have come to "kill" them.

Both males and females are often subject to painful mutilations during these rituals. Teeth may be knocked out, subincisions made in the body, hair torn out, poisonous itching plants rubbed in the skin, or stinging ants released over their bodies. The boys may be circumcised and the girls may have their clitoris or labia removed, all without anesthetic. In some cases, there may be a ritual defloration of the girls by a priest or outsider. Sometimes feats of endurance are also required, including fasting, not sleeping for long periods of time, killing animals or human enemies, or being thrown into the sea and told to swim back to shore. Toward the end of these rituals, novices are usually taught the spiritual heritage of the tribe, shown the secret mysteries of the culture accessible only to male or female initiates (the two kinds of rituals are always kept separate), and given something tangible by the elders such as a piece of jewelry, a belt, or a new name to signify their newfound status as full-fledged members of the culture. The rites may conclude with a collective feast or celebration to welcome the initiated youth back into the community.

Such rites of passage, seen in terms of modern psychology, capitalize on the regressive tendencies of adolescents and their vulnerability to life-and-death scenarios by taking initiates directly back to early developmental states where they undergo a psychic death and rebirth only to reemerge as transfigured humans in a transformed world. In the course of this process, which encompasses both *adapting* and *remembering*, the initiates regress back to the instinctual and spiritual worlds of prebirth, birth, and infancy, and retrieve from these primitive and transpersonal realms the sacred treasures that hold the secret to their very identity.

Of particular importance in many of these rites of passage is the *collective* journey back to the beginnings of time and to the primordial source of all existence. Initiates frequently engage in rituals that reenact the origin myths of their culture. During these cosmic dramas they encounter the Ancestors who gave birth to the universe. They themselves take part directly in the spiritual renewal of their culture and of the cosmos itself. Referring to male Australian aboriginal rites, religious historian Mircea Eliade, observed, "Initiation recapitulates the sacred history of the world. And through this recapitulation, the whole world is sanctified anew. The boys die to their profane condition and are resuscitated in a new world; for, through the revelation they have received during their initiation, they can perceive the world as a sacred work, a creation of the Gods."[15] Hence, the passage from childhood to adulthood in these ancient societies is seen as a spiritual journey, and to cross the threshold, contact must first be made with the cosmic ground of all being that defines that culture's very existence.

Adolescents Without Guides

The types of conditions intended to help children reach adulthood described above are almost entirely unavailable to adolescents growing up in contemporary culture. One could argue that this is a good thing because modern teenagers avoid the harsh suffering inherent in many of these rites. After all, not everybody made it through these rituals to the other side. There were many deaths from starvation, infection, exposure, and trauma for those not fit enough to join the club.[16] The problem, however, is that today's adolescents for the most part lack *any* meaningful contact with adults who can show them the way to maturity. According to psychologist and adolescent researcher Mihaly Csikszentmihalyi, "Most of the time, adolescents are either alone (26%) or with friends (34%) and classmates (19%). Very little time is spent in the company of adults. The typical American adolescent spends only about five minutes a day alone with his or her father—not nearly enough to transmit the wisdom and values that are necessary for the continuation of a civil society. Less time is spent in a one-on-one interaction with a teacher or other adult."[17]

Even when adults *are* present, the adolescent may be emotionally and mentally removed from the scene, as Csikszentmihalyi himself found out when, in an experiment, he equipped high school students with beepers that would go off randomly throughout the school day. Students were instructed, whenever they heard the beeper go off, to write down whatever they were thinking at that precise moment. Twenty-seven students were beeped who were attending a high school lecture on Genghis Khan's invasion of China in the thirteenth century. Only two students were thinking about China. One student was thinking about what he'd eaten at a Chinese restaurant a few weeks before, and the other student wondered why men in old China wore their hair in ponytails. No one was paying attention to what the teacher was saying.[18]

Granted, it can be argued that there *are* fragments of the old rites of passage still available to some adolescents in contemporary society. A few examples include the school prom, high school graduation, religious coming-of-age ceremonies such as the Jewish bar mitzvah or bat mitzvah, and community events like the *quinceañera* or fifteenth birthday celebration of a Hispanic female. But because most adolescents, by and large, no longer have adults helping them make it through wholly integrated culturally sponsored rituals of initiation, they often have to make up their own rites of passage. And the results are often disastrous. This unconscious need to be initiated can help explain some of the more dangerous activities of adolescents that grab headlines and puzzle and disturb adults. These include binge drinking, drug use, gang-related violence, hate crimes, and high-speed auto chases. Girls may engage in unsafe sex rituals, including a variation on the Russian roulette theme where the initiate must have sex with multiple partners known to be infected with HIV. Boys may have to earn their way into a gang through injuring or even killing a rival gang member.[19]

Each of these destructive behaviors separates adolescents from their childhood life of innocence and regresses them back into the swirling maelstrom of infantile thrills and chills. Unfortunately, however, they don't bring teens back up from these earlier developmental levels as newly transformed individuals who are then incorporated into a community of mature adults. If these rite of passage victims aren't destroyed by illness, accident, murder, or suicide from these makeshift rituals, they often remain isolated as incomplete individuals or less-than-whole members of their group, gang, or cult, and stagnate, perhaps in prison, slums, or mental health facilities, for the rest of their lives.

I was one of the lucky ones. When I was eighteen I took LSD and had a nightmarish encounter with my unconscious that culminated in my incarceration in a psychiatric ward. I remember being put in a half nelson by a white-clad attendant as I was separated from my parents in a hospital corridor, and isolated in a bare room with bars on the windows (a good thing, too, for I believed at the time that I could have floated safely down from the seventh-story window). My do-it-yourself rite of passage included a *separation* from childhood (I literally felt ripped away from my parents), and a period of *isolation* in a locked room where I existed in a kind of nether state. But it lacked any sort of *incorporation* ritual where I was ceremonially welcomed into society as a mature adult. Instead, I was knocked out with Thorazine, asked where I got the LSD from by a strange-looking psychiatrist when I woke up, and discharged after three days without any follow-up.[20]

Without the benefit of traditional rites of passage, adolescents face incredible challenges in making their way safely and securely into adulthood. That so many are able to do so in spite of the obstacles suggests that there are protective and guiding factors available to adolescents in today's fragmented society. Much of the impetus for growth into early adulthood comes from meaningful contact with adults who have in one way or another made their own successful journey across the great divide from childhood to adulthood. It seems as if adolescents in the post-rites-of-passage world are able to grow (the Latin word *adolescere* means just that, "to grow up") essentially by patching together images of positive adulthood from wherever they can find them: from inspiring teachers, healthy relatives, vital neighbors, caring friends of the family, trustworthy clergy, and a host of other positive role models gathered from contemporary society, as well as from past history.[21]

Adolescents usually create this mosaic of maturity quite haphazardly and casually, for example, in weekly conversations with a school counselor, or via an informal apprenticeship with a local community artist or mechanic, or through travel with a favorite adult relative. Janet Sayers recorded the recollections of a man in his twenties thinking back to his troubled teens and the positive impact made by two older men: "They were near enough to gods . . . Nat is a formidable character in everything—he seems to be inscrutable, ineffable. He's traveled the world once or twice. He's got an extraordinary IQ, and a near photographic memory. And he's an artist . . . And when I met them I thought they saw me to be young and aspiring, but in somewhat of a quagmire, with various indoctrinated views of what was good, and what was bad . . . And slowly but surely they tended to lift [me] out of it . . ."[22]

In one way or another, older mature individuals provide stepping stones to adulthood by offering adolescents trust, special tools and skills, or simply by providing them with the gift of believing in themselves. As psychotherapist Mary Pipher writes, "I often use the North Star as a metaphor [with my adolescent girl clients]. I tell clients: "You are in a boat that is being tossed around by the winds of this world. The voices of your parents, your teachers, your friends and the media can blow you east, then west, then back again. To stay on course you must follow your own North Star, your sense of who you truly are. Only by orienting north can you chart a course and maintain it, only by orienting north can you keep from being blown all over the sea."[23]

A New Kind of Thinking

There's something else going on within the adolescent that helps her into the adult world. It's a newfound capacity to think in an entirely new way. Starting at about age eleven, kids move into what cognitive researcher Jean Piaget called the stage of formal operational thinking.[24] Now they're able to engage in purely abstract thinking. They can create whole sets of mental operations and manipulate them in their mind without reference to the real world. For example, they're now capable of doing algebraic operations ($x = y + z$) without having to worry about how these variables relate to some particular group of things like "ice cream cones" or "television sets." They're also able to create hypotheses like mature scientists and test them systematically. Give a nine-year-old child several different lengths of string and different weights to attach to them, and ask her to create a pendulum. Then ask her to tell you which of the following variables affects the pendulum's rate of swing: length of string, weight of ball, or force of push. The child will likely engage in a trial-and-error search for the right answer. Do the same experiment with a fourteen-year-old and you'll likely find her systematically testing each variable, for example, by varying each weight while keeping the other conditions constant, trying different lengths of string, and so on, until discovering the influential factor (answer: the string's the thing).

This ability to think logically, systematically, and abstractly can be taken to a *very* high level of sophistication in adolescence. A review of some of the greatest mathematical and scientific ideas in history reveals that teenagers made many of these discoveries. Mathematicians who did original work during their teen years include Blaise Pascal, Evariste Galois, Carl Friedrich Gauss, and John von Neumann, one of the pioneers of the computer revolution. Einstein got some of his original insights in physics as a high school student in Prussia and Switzerland. He would visualize what it would be like to race alongside a beam of light, or freefall in a sealed room in empty space, and through these "thought experiments" came up with the first inklings for his special and general theories of relativity. These kinds of logical-mathematical explorations show up to a lesser degree in the daily musings of adolescents. Many kids in their teen years show an avid interest in computer languages and abstract logical games like chess and Go. Some also become quite excited about science fiction because this new kind of mind revels in an exploration of not merely what *is*, but what is *purely possible*.[25] Consequently, their minds take off into explorations of alternate realities, space and time warps, parallel universes, and alien mutations.

This capacity to envision what is possible can also open them up to utopian visions and attract them to political and social movements that reflect their newly formed ideals. It was as a thirteen-year-old that Frederick Douglass began to feel deeply the moral yoke of slavery and to seek the means of escaping it. It was at eighteen years of age that Vladimir Ilyich Lenin responded to the czar's hanging of his brother by becoming involved in radical politics. For millennia, governments have infamously relied upon the idealism of adolescents to stoke the fires of its war machines, even as this same transcendent function has motivated youth to put those fires out through peace activities such as those that occurred in the United States during the 1960s Vietnam protests. At the same time, the maturation of the higher brain functions that occurs in the teen years empowers adolescents with the capacity to engage in metathinking, or "thinking *about* thinking." This means they can begin to reflect on their own actions in a more dispassionate way. This is a faculty that proves to be extremely useful in helping them to modulate their turbulent emotional lives. Adolescents also start to entertain competing points of view as equally valid, which adds fuel to their arguments with peers and adults as they embrace unpopular opinions, relish controversial positions, and detach themselves from many of the conformist beliefs of their childhood years in religion and politics.

One of the most significant contributions of adolescence to the human life cycle, I believe, is their ability, like Hamlet, to sniff out the hypocrisy of the adults around them. The critical consciousness that accompanies this new kind of mind is often devastatingly accurate and quite passionate in pinpointing the weak points, inconsistencies, and lapses that characterize "business as usual" in the adult world. It's during adolescence that we often begin to employ satire, cynicism, skepticism, and irony in our assault upon the shortcomings of the status quo. This type of criticism, of course, is rarely welcomed by the surrounding adult community. It was while attending the Blessed Sacrament Convent School in New York City, for example, that satirist Dorothy Parker was expelled for insisting that the immaculate conception was a form of "spontaneous combustion."

The Spiritual World of Adolescence

It's as if the adolescent moves helicopter-like out of the world of fixed ideas and beliefs of childhood, and can now look down at the big picture and see all sorts of inconsistencies and incongruities in the scenery below. This wider and more complex view of existence sometimes brings with it a sense of disillusionment, and can even plunge the teen into a "dark night of the soul" where identity, significant goals, and the meaning of life are all put seriously in doubt. During such times, philosophical musings, existential angst, and a deep brooding like Hamlet's may precipitate a real crisis out of which a new creative, philosophical, religious, or spiritual out-look may ultimately emerge. American psychologist G. Stanley Hall, the originator of the modern conception of adolescence, even went so far as to suggest that to complete adolescence successfully, a person must undergo a transformation in which "the older, lower selfish self is molted and a new and higher life of love and service emerges." He suggested that "religious conversion is the most effective and natural vehicle of this transformation."[26] Sometimes this experience happens very quietly. In his autobiography, evangelist Billy Graham shares his story of his own conver-sion at the age of sixteen, which occurred during an invitation to accept Christ at a revival meeting. He wrote, "No bells went off inside me. I simply felt at peace."[27]

At other times, this process of *remembering* is shocking and disorienting. Such was the case with Joan of Arc, the French peasant girl who was inspired by God to lead the battle against the English in the Hundred Years War in the fifteenth century. According to the most famous version,

"... when she was thirteen years of age, she had a voice from God to help her to know what to do. And on the first occasion she was much afraid. And this voice came about the hour of midday, in the summertime, in her father's garden ... She heard the voice upon the right side, towards the church, and she rarely heard it without an accompanying brightness ... And, after she had heard this voice upon three occasions, she understood that it was the voice of an angel."[28]

Contemporary Indian sage Ramana Maharshi provides an eastern version of adolescent spiritual awakening in his account of what happened to him when he was seventeen years old: "It was about six weeks before I left Madura [his home town] for good that the great change in my life took place. It was quite sudden. I seldom had any sickness, and on that day there was nothing wrong with my health, but a sudden violent fear of death overtook me. There was nothing in my state of health to account for it ... The shock of the fear of death drove my mind inwards and I said to myself mentally ... 'Now death has come; what does it mean? What is it that is dying?'" Maharshi proceeded to lie down on the ground as if dead, and continued this inquiry until finally realizing: "So I am Spirit transcending the body ... it flashed through me vividly as living truth which I perceived directly. Absorption in the Self continued unbroken from that time on."[29] Two months after this incident, he moved to a sacred mountain north of his home and began to teach his method of "self-inquiry" to spiritual seekers, continuing his work there until his physical death more than fifty years later.

Edna St. Vincent Millay's classic poem "Renascence" provides a stunning lyrical account of spiritual transformation in late adolescence. Written when she was nineteen, this initially quiet pastoral poem quickly crescendos to a climactic revelation: "And reaching up my hand to try / I screamed to feel it touch the sky / I screamed, and—lo!—Infinity / Came down and settled over me." In Millay's poem, after this cosmic epiphany the young narrator is buried "full six feet under ground" and then blasted into rebirth by a torrential downpour of rain, where she emerges finally able to see the world with newly transformed eyes: "The world stands out on either side / No wider than the heart is wide / Above the world is stretched the sky,— / No higher than the soul is high."[30] Standing at the bridge between the limiting world of childhood and the scary expansiveness of adulthood, the adolescent, finally revitalized by such a revelation, moves forward into a new life where the boundaries seem to be set only by her own boundless energies. It's to this new adventure, the story of young adulthood, that we now turn in the next chapter.

∞

The Gift of Adolescence: Passion

If there's one thing you can say about teenagers, it's that they're *passionate*. They're passionate about their clothes, their music, their love interests, their friends, and their ideals. The biochemical tide that surges through their brains and bodies during puberty virtually ensures that ardor and zeal will express themselves in some tangible way between the ages of thirteen and twenty. We often view the passionate intensity of adolescence with worry and even alarm. We remember what happened to Romeo and Juliet when they got carried away by their emotions. We know that strong feelings like envy, fear, anger, and jealousy can wreak havoc on the lives of teens and those around them. We heave a sigh of relief when the brain's frontal lobes finally mature and rein in unruly passions at the end of adolescence.

But we need to remember that passions have their beneficial side as well. The dancer Martha Graham was fourteen years old when she saw her first ballet performance in Los Angeles and was seized with a great passion to dance for the rest of her life. As an adolescent, Richard Wagner was transformed when he heard a female singer during a performance of the opera *Fidelio*. He wrote a letter to her wherein he dedicated his entire life to music, delivered it to her hotel room, and ran out into the street in a mad delirium. In the teen years, adolescents regress back to the kind of passionate intensity they experienced in infancy and early childhood, but now they've acquired a number of skills and abilities which they can use to direct these passions into positive social goals. Thus, it's now possible for them to pour their fiery feelings into music, dance, science, art, sports, journalism, and a host of other productive channels.

In adulthood, we tend to lose this fervor as we get drawn into the practical contingencies of daily living. Too often, we become detached and passive in our attitude toward life. To balance this tendency, we need to recapture some of our old adolescent passion. This renewed fire can spark our close relationships to new heights of intimacy. It can revitalize our work by motivating us to put energy into projects that we feel strongly about. Or, alternatively, our passions can heighten the need to find a new career that engages our resources in a more dynamic way. The passions of adolescence can also stir greater involvement in the community, prodding us to fight for political, moral, or ethical causes that lead to the betterment of society. Ultimately, this vibrant energy of adolescence can shake us to the core and provide the creative fuel for a new and better way of life. In order to fan the dying embers of our forgotten teenage passions, however, we need to view adolescence, and the adolescents in our lives, with a new attitude. We need to acknowledge the important contribution of their youthful zeal to the collective well-being of humanity. We also need to remember what filled us with passion during our own teen years and integrate some of that zest into our current lives. Recognizing and nurturing our own hidden passions helps ensure that this vital gift from adolescence will reawaken our untapped creative potentials and rouse the sleeping centers of our soul.

―――――― *Ways to Explore and Support Adolescence* ――――――

FOR YOURSELF
- Put together a collection of favorite songs from your adolescent years (e.g., download them from the Internet) and, after listening to them, write down the feelings, moods, and thoughts that come to you about that period in your life.

- Create a time line of your adolescence (thirteen to nineteen), putting in key events that affected you in a significant way (romances, rites of passage, traumatic and ecstatic events, travels, special projects).
- Pick out a creative activity that you used to do as an adolescent but stopped doing in adulthood, and begin doing it again (e.g., acting in musicals, painting, reading Russian novels, writing poetry, playing tennis).

For Friends and Family

- Along with other adults, help create meaningful rites of passage ceremonies with your own adolescents or the adolescent sons or daughters of friends or family members.
- Spend quality time with an adolescent who is going through a difficult time (your own or a friend's or family member's). Suggestions include taking walks, going to public events, engaging in projects of special interest to the teenager and, most importantly, listening carefully to what she has to say.
- Provide an unmotivated adolescent with resources, materials, or experiences to engage his expanding mind. Examples might include a computer, software, books, music, games, or travel opportunities.

For the Community

- Contribute financially to a local community teen center.
- Volunteer to help tutor or counsel a troubled teen in your community.
- Pick a specific social problem related to adolescence and work in your community to help eradicate it. Examples include gang violence, teenage pregnancy, HIV/AIDS, school drop-outs, school violence, eating disorders, substance abuse, or suicide prevention.

CHAPTER 8

Early Adulthood: Building an Independent Life

*It is a very strange sensation to inexperienced youth to feel itself quite
alone in the world, cut adrift from every connection, uncertain
whether the port to which it is bound can be reached, and prevented
by many impediments from returning to that it has quitted. The charm
of adventure sweetens that sensation, the glow of pride warms it;
but then the throb of fear disturbs it.*

—CHARLOTTE BRONTË, JANE EYRE [1]

The story is a familiar one. Starry-eyed young person leaves home to win
fame, fortune, and romance in the wide world. Life does not cooperate with
her plans. On the way, she encounters much unanticipated difficulty.
Finally, after a long series of adventures and misadventures, nsqow older and
wiser, she concludes that life is not the bowl of cherries she had imagined it
to be in her youth and settles down to a more sober and practical existence.

World literature teems with variations on this basic scenario of early
adult life. Charlotte Brontë's Jane Eyre leaves an abusive boarding school
in search of a better life and finds it as a governess when she falls in love
with her employer, Mr. Rochester. But then everything goes up in flames
and she has to settle for far less as a nurse-wife to her crippled ex-lover.
Goethe's Wilhelm Meister travels through Germany, supposedly to discharge family business, but actually spends most of his time with a troupe

of traveling actors. He struggles with conflicts about whether to live passionately as an artist or reasonably as a businessman. Finally, someone he trusts tells him that he has no talent as an actor and he reluctantly agrees and settles down with his long-lost son, his apprenticeship complete. Ralph Ellison's unnamed protagonist in the novel *Invisible Man* innocently leaves a black college in the South to develop himself in New York City, only to encounter such savage discrimination, violence, and betrayal that by the end of the book he is living underground as a fugitive in the city's sewer system. Each of these narratives is an example of a *bildungsroman*—a novel of character formation chronicling the growth of an individual from childhood to maturity.[2] These plots highlight what is the essential task of early adult development: to leave the familiar world of family, parents, community, and school—the chrysalis of the first eighteen to twenty years of life—and go off and try to make something of oneself in a world that puts all sorts of constraints on this urge to take wing and fly.

The Lost Generation

Researchers have devoted less attention to this stage of life (ages twenty to thirty-five) than to just about any other period of human development. This is rather surprising, given the fact that early adulthood is the time when most people marry and have children, and when lifelong habits and attitudes toward work and career are formed. Perhaps this neglect occurs because young adults don't require the intensive nurturing of the earlier stages of development, and they aren't plagued by the aging processes of the later stages. In fact, this is the healthiest time of life.[3] People in this age group have fewer colds, accidents, and allergies than they did in childhood. Visits to the doctor are lower than in later stages of life. Young adults are at their peak of muscular strength from ages twenty-five to thirty. Their manual dexterity is the most efficient, and their senses are the sharpest that they will ever be.[4]

But this is definitely a stage of life with unique problems of its own. Developmental psychologist Robert Havighurst characterized this time as the loneliest, most disorganized period of the life span.[5] In one study, more than half of the changes made by young adults up to age twenty-five from school to job, or job to job, involved floundering and unplanned decision making.[6] There is an emotional toll to this uncertainty. This age group has the highest rate of alcohol and drug abuse. Here you are in your twenties, thrown out into the big world with lots of demands put upon you. You may feel impelled to set up a household, find a mate, get a job, create a family, or find a niche for yourself. But there's not much support or direction from the world on how to actually go about doing any of these things, nor a great backlog of personal experience, judgment, or wisdom to fall back on in making just the right choices. Add to this the fact that you are probably still grappling with unresolved problems and conflicts from earlier stages of development, and you see how becoming an adult might turn out to be quite a struggle![7] Even the tremendous physical health of early adulthood can turn out to be a drawback of sorts. Because young adults are so physically healthy and don't get immediate feedback from poor health habits, they may push the envelope and eat poorly, smoke, drink, and work long hours without much sleep, only to pay for these infractions later on in their lives.[8]

Part of the difficulty is that no one has adequately defined what it means to be an adult, or when this is actually supposed to begin. In world mythology, heroes attain maturity after they have slain dragons, married princes, or deposed imposters to the throne. In the real world, it's a little more complicated. There *are* legal definitions for when a person is allowed to drink, drive, vote, and marry, but these requirements vary from place to place. There's also a great deal of diversity in the ways that people become adult. Some people leave home at fifteen or sixteen and get a job, a wife, and kids before they're twenty. Others stay in school until their early thirties and only then start to think about these sorts of commitments. As one sociologist put it: "A twenty-three-year-old may have a partner but no job, a child but no partner, be a student and living with parents, be a student and married, have a job but be living with parents; they may have no job, no partner, no child and be living with parents, but still feel adult."[9]

Perhaps the most internally satisfying response to the question of when adulthood starts is to recall the moment when you started to *feel like an adult* for the first time. Yale psychologist Daniel J. Levinson expressed it this way: "Once you can say in a meaningful way, 'it's my life, not my parents', you have reached psychological adulthood."[10] This moment can occur during even the most banal events of daily life. One woman observed, "I remember the moment when I felt like I wasn't a kid anymore. When I was twenty-three, I moved into my own apartment. The first time I listened to my refrigerator hum, I got this fleeting thing in my stomach. This was my refrigerator in my apartment. Sometime that first week, I remember getting up in the middle of the night to go to the bathroom and I got really excited because it was my own bathroom."[11] A twenty-six-year-old man living in Chicago wrote in his blog about his move from Texas to Illinois four years earlier: "I packed everything into a U-Haul trailer and was sad to know that every one of my possessions fit into that little thing. I drove north with the theme from 'Perfect Strangers' playing in my head, and I felt like an adult for the first time in my life. There'd be no family to help me, no comfortable job, no spacious apartment, and no safety net of any kind in Chicago. I'd also have to find all new friends."[12]

Because modern society doesn't have carefully worked out rites of passage for young people, the line between childhood and adulthood is a lot fuzzier than it used to be. Psychiatrist Kenneth Kenniston has suggested an intermediate stage between adolescence and adulthood called *youth*, where an individual attempts to work out a resolution between his own ideals and the demands of the world. Finding this balance is difficult because there's always the pressure to become a cog in society's machine, or on the other hand to refuse to compromise at all and retreat into isolation as a social misfit.[13] For many people, it simply takes more time to become an adult. This is especially true for highly creative individuals who discover that their own gifts and abilities may be in conflict with the values of the *adapter* culture around them. It is also true for *rememberers* who reconnected to their spiritual depths in late adolescence, and who are struggling to discover ways to integrate those experiences into the complexities of modern life in early adulthood.

When I was nineteen, after having hitchhiked around Europe the previous six months, I went through a kind of Dark Night of the Soul when I returned to my studies at Carleton College. Over the course of four months—from January to April 1971—I experienced a kind of cosmic terror, where I felt like I'd lost all my moorings to anything I'd previously known to be true. Gradually, I found myself transformed from a gloomy and insecure agnostic into a political activist and inspired mystic who embraced the unity of all religions. During the next couple of years, after having dropped out of Carleton, I struggled with how to bring my new intuitions about life into some sort of career focus. In my early twenties, I discovered that working with children allowed me to stay connected with my desire for social change and to my longings for the spiritual life. It was Maria Montessori's work that gave me the spark to go back to school and study education—not as a Montessori teacher, but as an alternative school teacher embracing a wide range of innovative educational philosophies and strategies. After finishing my bachelor's and master's degrees in my mid-twenties, I ended up teaching in two very traditional school systems in Canada and the United States. Just as with the characters in the novels that opened this chapter, I ultimately came to my own sobering conclusions about the hard facts of life, observing how education as a whole did not promote social change or spiritual expansion, but rather served to maintain the social sickness of the status quo, and suppress children's radiant vitality.

Psychoanalyst Erik Erikson used the term *moratorium* to describe the tentative, uncertain nature of this age, employing the word to describe a period of time when a young person may not commit directly to life, yet be inwardly working out the conditions that will make it possible for him eventually to do so. Erikson's concept came out of his own personal experience as a young adult. Never a good student, Erikson graduated from high school in Germany at eighteen and didn't know what to do with his life. He wandered through the Black Forest and walked along the shores of Lake Constance where for many months he spent time reading, sketching, and putting his thoughts down in a notebook. Eventually he enrolled in art school, became restless and left, studied at another art school, exhibited a few of his etchings and woodcuts, and then gave up art entirely and moved to Florence where he wandered through the streets and hills of Tuscany. Finally, when he was twenty-five, he received a letter from a friend inviting him to come to Vienna to teach the children of a mother who was being analyzed by Sigmund Freud. He went to Vienna, trained as a Montessori teacher, began work with Anna Freud, and eventually became the world's leading child psychoanalyst, and the creator of the most popular and highly regarded theory of the life span in the Western world.[14]

In Erikson's case the culture served as an important support during his wanderings. The Germans have a folk tradition that allows young people to wander as artists without committing to a fixed lifestyle (a period called the *Wanderjahr*), and even have a word for a young creative student who has his doubts about things (*Künstler* or "artist"). Had Erikson gone through his restless early twenties in today's more medicalized and pragmatic society, one wonders whether he might not have been given a diagnosis, some Prozac, and a job employment application.

Launching into Life

For most people, the process of quitting home is not so romantic, and is characterized by a slower process of moving out into the world—or *launching*—in a series of more predictable steps. Women leave home earlier than men, usually to marry, but men are more likely to return home after a "false start" at independence. Roughly half of all individuals return home after their initial leaving, a phenomenon that's been called by sociologists "boomerang children" and by comics "umbilical whiplash." The reasons for coming back home may include the inability to earn an income sufficient to establish a household, the failure of a "starter marriage" (a marriage of short duration usually begun during the twenties that has serious flaws from the start), or simply feeling psychologically unready to live on one's own. As one twenty-three-year-old man still living at home explained, "Where else can I get free rent, home cooking, cable TV, and free laundry? I'd be a fool to live anywhere else."[15]

The typical pattern is to leave home for a year or two, return home for two or three years, and then leave for the final time. Thus, launching into adulthood takes on average four and a half years.[16] But it's perfectly normal for many young adults—especially those in African-American or Latin-American cultures—to stay at home until their mid-twenties or later. As one thirty-year-old Latina put it "... both my parents are Peruvian. It's common to move out when you are married, but before then it doesn't really make any sense and really isn't accepted. My parents live close to the city and I have always worked in or around the city, so financially it didn't seem like it made sense to move out until I was married. ... I feel like I am making a wise and responsible decision. ... My parents have always respected the fact that I've decided to stay and save money and that I honor our culture and their wishes."[17]

On the path to self-sufficiency many young adults seek transitional ways to help them complete the split with parents: joining the military, going away for school, entering the Peace Corps, doing missionary work for a religious organization, or working as a tutor or domestic for a family. But by the mid-thirties, only around 10 percent of children are still living with their parents, often as individuals with disabilities.

As they strive to break with the past and move into a hopeful future, young adults during the time of launching are often driven by a desire to achieve great things. They often carry an inner image of themselves as successful adults, a phenomenon that Daniel Levinson calls "the Dream."[18] This Dream may be a vague feeling of living in the future as an active homemaker, a loving mother, a caring father, a wealthy businessperson, or a pillar of the community. Or it may involve very specific and ambitious plans to become a rock star by one's mid-twenties or to conquer the literary world by age thirty-five. Sometimes this image of oneself comes in the form of a "call" (the word *vocation* comes from the Latin word *vocare*, which means "to call"). The protagonist in Goethe's novel wonders: "What man in the whole world would not find his situation intolerable if he chooses a craft, an art, indeed any form of life, without experiencing an inner calling?"[19] I remember my own "call" to become a teacher of children while walking past the Smithsonian Astrophysical Laboratory on Garden Street in Cambridge, Massachusetts, in 1972. It was like a physical feeling of warmth that glided down from the heavens and lodged itself in my chest. Another celestial call was reported by a woman who was quoted in the book *Quarterlife Crisis: The Unique Challenges of Life in Your Twenties*, by Alexandra Robbins and Abby Wilner: "It was this huge flash of light, like a message in the sky. I had a cold, and I was totally stressed because I was trying to look for a new job in computers, and I went home to take a quick nap. When I woke up, the thought that was in my head was that if I were independently wealthy, I would sit around and decorate houses all the time. And that's when it hit me that decorating is actually a career. I just knew that was my passion. I'm just now having a dream for the first time in my life, so I'm not about to give it up now."[20]

The call to a career, however, is not something that happens to everyone, and the situation for women is particularly problematic. As researchers Judy Levinson and Daniel Levinson observed, "A person cannot afford the luxury of a Dream if she is totally occupied with survival in a barren environment or with conformity to a life scenario that leaves no room for personal choice—a widespread experience of young women."[21] Many women feel pulled into marriage and family responsibilities at an early age while at the same time experiencing a desire to explore career options that have opened up for females in the past few decades. Yet they are frustrated by a lack of support in a still largely male-driven world. At the same time, both men and women find their personal dreams of adult achievement contaminated to some degree by the voices of their parents ("My son is going to be a lawyer.") or by society at large ("Show me the money."). As one of the Levinsons' research subjects reported, "I had no image of a successful single woman who had happily made her career the center of her life. My image was that she had to be cold-hearted, she had to be grasping, she had to be cruel, she had to be embittered, frustrated, wishing she had done anything just to be sitting by the fireside knitting in the evening with children."[22]

Still, the Dream serves to propel many young adults into the world to seek their fame, happiness, or fortune. And it is often in the world of *work* where these expectations are initially hammered out for better or worse. In work, a young adult can begin to experience a sense of *achievement*, a sense of being somebody that makes a real difference and who plays a significant role in adult life. One man described his job working for a political party starting at the age of nineteen: "I was paid $600 a month. I felt like the richest guy in the world. I woke up each day so excited because I got to work for something I believed in so strongly. I pushed myself as hard as I could to get up as early as possible and leave work as late as I could. I loved my job and my life. I remember getting my paychecks and wanting to frame them because I was so proud that someone found me valuable enough to pay me."[23]

Too often, however, the initial work experiences of young adults hardly merit any real sense of accomplishment. In the first place, no one has usually helped these individuals discover what their innate talents are, nor what sort of career direction would best match their abilities. Consequently, many young adults begin their work life (and also sadly end it) in jobs totally out of synch with their natural proclivities. To add to the disappointment, most initial work experiences for young adults are low-paying part-time and entry-level jobs that involve routine work for bosses that care little about shepherding young talent toward greatness. It seems as if this stage of early adulthood does most of the *grunt work* of the world: computing, filing, hauling, lifting, schlepping, and whatever else anyone more senior than themselves can avoid doing and pawn off on these hapless young lackeys. As a twenty-four-year-old researcher at an economic consulting firm described it: "We're like the kids downstairs. We don't get many responsibilities because we're all thought of as lesser people rather than equal coworkers."[24]

One key to surviving in this kind of environment involves taking advantage of training or education opportunities. This is a time for learning new skills, for jumping through hoops, for acquiring new competencies, and for achieving advanced degrees or certifications that will qualify one for more highly respected and better paid positions. The nation's post-secondary schools and training centers act as an important broker in this movement toward greater stability and satisfaction in the workplace. Higher education—that is, beyond high school—in early adulthood correlates to higher income, better job satisfaction, and less risk of getting Alzheimer's disease later in life.[25]

Yet at the same time, young adults tend to abandon the formalisms of school once they get out into the nitty-gritty world of the workplace. Workers taking inventory of goods in warehouses abandon schoolhouse algorithms in favor of quick approximations based on physical features. Merchants do error-free arithmetic using informal rules of thumb as guides. Even expert radiologists interpret X-rays in rough-and-ready ways never taught in medical school.[26] There seems to be a shift in the thinking processes of young adults, from the right/wrong, we/they, good/bad polarities of adolescence to a "whatever works" type of philosophy. Young adults begin to see that there are multiple viewpoints, and ultimately no one right answer to a problem, that it all depends upon the context in which the problem is embedded. Hence, there's a new kind of pragmatism that rules the field in early adulthood. It's even a bit amusing to observe how quickly the youthful idealism and cynicism of adolescence gives way to hard-edged realism once you've got to survive on your own steam. As Mark Twain observed: "When I was a boy of fourteen, my father was so ignorant I could hardly stand to have the old man around. But when I got to be twenty-one, I was astonished at how much he had learned in seven years."[27]

Finding Someone to Love

Then there is the matter of mate selection. Erik Erikson considered this the single most important task of early adulthood: finding intimacy with another person, or losing out and living in isolation. Erikson's concept of intimacy, however, was somewhat limited. As he put it, intimacy meant "mutuality of orgasm, with a loved partner of the opposite sex with whom one is able and willing to share mutual trust, regulate cycles of work, procreation, and recreation so as to secure to the offspring their satisfactory development."[28] Unfortunately, this definition leaves out gay, lesbian, bisexual, and transgender people, as well as heterosexual couples who practice nonsexual ways of being intimate, or who don't plan on having children.[29] In actuality, this stage is concerned with finding somebody to love. Young adults look for romance or friendship in singles bars, through online dating services, by partying, through personal ads, at chess clubs, science classes, political rallies, charity auctions, or just about anywhere else.[30]

Early adulthood is about looking for someone who is like us, who turns us on, or who completes us. And it's a hazardous project. If things don't go well, we could wind up with someone who infects us, projects onto us, or defects on us. If, on the other hand, we play our cards right (and with a little luck thrown in), we'll find the soul mate of our dreams. Most people end up with someone in between these two extremes and marry sometime during their early adulthood. In the United States, by the age of thirty-five, 72 percent of men and 83 percent of women have been married at least once (mean age for first marriages—women 25.0; men 26.7).[31] The marriage ceremony becomes a new rite of passage. For some, it's the first real marker event of full adulthood. Many of the rituals of marriage unconsciously practiced in modern society reveal deeper developmental messages rooted in traditional customs and beliefs. The wedding veil was initially placed on the bride to ward off malevolent spirits that might attack during this important spiritual event. The throwing of rice at the end of the ceremony symbolized fertility or good fortune and dates back to the agrarian Middle Ages when seed, corn, or grain was used instead of rice. The crossing of the threshold, where the groom lifts the bride off her feet on entering their new home, was an important symbol of passage into a new life; the threshold is the liminal space, neither in the old life, nor the new. As ethnographer Arnold van Gennep wrote, "... to cross the threshold is to unite oneself with a new world ..."[32]

The Promises and Pitfalls of Parenting

This new life brings with it all sorts of possibilities, and none are more important or more amazing than having children. Parenthood completes the life cycle. Once kids have been brought into this world, they start the whole process of growth and development all over again. And this can be a real shocker for parents, because now *they* are the larger-than-life forces that they once beheld as infants and young children. *They* are now Scylla, Circe, or Poseidon in the eyes of the awe-stricken child. And it can be scary to be an archetype. Knowing that your three-year-old may see you on one of your bad days as a six-headed monster slurping her way through the house can be just too much responsibility to bear. Usually, however, parents don't even have time to think about such mythological possibilities. Their activities are generally directed toward more pedestrian concerns such as getting up in the middle of the night to feed the baby, changing messy diapers, and kissing away tears. Later on, these responsibilities become more complex as parents seek the best ways of disciplining, schooling, and nurturing their kids. It's an awesome task, and Nature probably assigned this job primarily to young people because they don't yet have a really good grip on how difficult it is to be a good parent. They flock uncritically to their roles as mothers and fathers, thus keeping the species evolving.

It's been pointed out before, but deserves repeating, that here we have what is probably the most important role that anyone could ever play in life—being a parent—and there is no training, education, certificate, or degree required. As one expert noted, "biological parenthood may be achieved by stuporous drug addicts or disorganized psychotics who are out of contact with reality."[33] Anyone can apply. And yet, as we've seen in earlier chapters, the negative consequences of poor parenting ripple throughout the life cycle both backward in time and forward into the future. It must be remembered that becoming a parent brings up one's own old childhood traumas, which in turn get visited upon the next generation. Seeing your helpless or angry baby may trigger your own early fears or rages. Observing traits in baby that remind you of family members can provoke unconscious aggression or ambivalence. Giving your children what you never got from your own parents can help defuse some of this, but it also can play into your pathologies by saddling your child with an agenda she might not really want or need.

And yet Nature also seems to have provided some built-in protective mechanisms that endow most parents with a newfound sense of selflessness, which causes them to surrender many of their own personal goals in the interest of their kids.[34] We've already seen some of the biological processes that take place in mothers, helping to bond them to their children. Something on a smaller scale may also happen in fathers. In one study, a majority of men regarded fatherhood as the single greatest shaper of their lives. Some saw it as a positive "jolt" to their life course, while others considered it more of a gentle evoker of some of their own latent personality traits of caring and giving.[35] One father looked back on his own violent adolescence and remarked on the change that fatherhood had made in his life: "Before, I was really rough and tumble on the street. My reputation is still known on the Westside. When I got around her [his newly born daughter] I would mellow. There's a lot of things I would have done if it wasn't for her. . . . I would've been in jail for murder, there's no doubt. I would have been dead, there's no doubt. . . . the reason that I wouldn't put in to effect the things I wanted to do was because I would think of her."[36]

Navigating the Age Thirty Shift

The end of the twenties brings with it a definite shift in perspective for many young adults. You've been going along for several years on your own, laboriously cobbling together a life structure made up of work experiences, social relationships, perhaps a marriage and some children. Suddenly the big 3-0 looms up ahead of you. Now the pressure of time begins to kick in. What have I done so far in my adult life? Has it been any good? Where do I go from here? Many individuals in their late twenties experience a crisis of sorts at this point. Daniel Levinson calls this the "Age 30 Transition." He says that most people at this time look back and see that the life they put together in their twenties is significantly flawed, and they become dissatisfied. His observations are borne out by the data. Fifty-seven percent of the males in his research study reported their lives as oppressive, incomplete, not going anywhere, or going in the wrong direction in their late twenties.[37] Ninety percent of the career women in his sample had moderate to severe crises around this time.[38] Similarly, an AFL-CIO poll revealed that young workers start their careers in their early twenties with great hope but are quickly disillusioned and by the time they reach thirty feel that they're getting a raw deal from the economy.[39] According to another survey, half of all high school graduates still have not found a steady job by age thirty.[40] There is also an increase in the number of divorces in the late twenties.[41]

On looking back at what they've done thus far, many young adults become frustrated that they haven't put more of *themselves* (their deeper authentic selves) into their lives.[42] In my own case, I went through an emotional crisis between twenty-eight and thirty, when I became disillusioned with the cult-like aspects of the spiritual group I had spent my entire twenties engaged with (followers of the Indian mystic Meher Baba). I had lost touch with the vital spiritual passion I had experienced during my early twenties, and saw how I'd used Meher Baba (a Persian word for "Compassionate Father") and certain leaders of the group as substitute parents who were now stifling me and who needed to be left behind.[43] Also, I was frustrated with my life as a school special education teacher because I wasn't developing children's creativity, as I'd hoped, but was forced by the school bureaucracy to focus on discipline and instruction based on kids' deficits rather than their abilities. By the age of thirty, I had quit both the spiritual group and my teaching job, moved to Berkeley, California, and begun anew as a writer and a teacher of college courses in human development.

Daniel Levinson suggests that biology may be behind the Age 30 Transition as the physical health and well-being that has been at its peak during the twenties begins its gradual decline around this time. It may also be a reaction to the trial and error nature of the previous ten years that causes many people in their late twenties to start getting serious about life. It was at age twenty-eight when Vincent van Gogh decided that trying to develop a career in the ministry wasn't the best use of his talents and he became a painter. William Faulkner wrote his first novel at age twenty-nine. Pulitzer Prize–winning poet Anne Sexton was a depressed housewife at twenty-eight who thought that her only talent might be for prostitution. She began to work with a psychiatrist who suggested that she start writing, after diagnostic tests revealed that she had a great deal of untapped creative potential.[44] This is probably the first time in life when people start to hear the clock ticking and realize that there isn't an unlimited amount of time in which to accomplish their goals. The Age 30 Transition may also be the time when the *rememberer* resurfaces after several years of *adapting* to the conventional world. It was at the age of twenty-eight when William Wordsworth penned his famous lines in "Tintern Abbey," mourning the loss of youth but affirming a new spiritual outlook: "For I have learned / To look on nature, not as in the hour / Of thoughtless youth; but hearing oftentimes / The still, sad music of humanity / . . . And I have felt / A presence that disturbs me with the joy / Of elevated thoughts; a sense sublime / Of something far more deeply interfused."[45] It was at the age of twenty-nine when legend has it that the Buddha left his palace and royal privileges to seek spiritual enlightenment for the first time. At the age of thirty, according to the New Testament, Jesus began his ministry (Luke 3:23).

For most young adults in today's modern world, religious or spiritual interest, which tends to decline during the twenties (except for families concerned with providing church instruction for their kids), may increase in the late twenties, as people start looking within for clues about their purpose in life. At age twenty-eight, the highly rational Bertrand Russell, already famous for his scholarly contributions to the fields of philosophy and mathematics, had a deep spiritual experience triggered by the illness of a friend: "She [the friend] seemed cut off from everyone and everything by walls of agony and the sense of the solitude of each human soul suddenly overwhelmed me . . . the ground seemed to give way beneath me . . . Within five minutes, I went through some such reflections as the following: the loneliness of the human soul is unendurable; nothing can penetrate it except the highest intensity of the sort of love that religious teachers have preached . . . At the end of those five minutes, I had become a completely different person . . . Having for years cared for exactness and analysis, I found myself filled with semi-mystical feelings about beauty, and with an intense interest in children, and with a desire almost as profound as that of the Buddha to find some philosophy which should make human life endurable."[46] Although Russell eventually returned to his analytical stance toward life, he said that from that moment on he became interested in humanitarian issues and in living life at a deeper level.

As young adults move out of the Age 30 Transition, there's often a newfound sense of direction and purpose that helps to guide them through the next few years. Confucius said that at age thirty he "stood firm." You're no longer a novice or underling taking abuse from higher-ups, or at the very least, you're definitely fed up with this sort of treatment by now. You want to be taken seriously as a person in your own right and find your place as a full-fledged member of the adult community.

Having a mentor—someone who knows the ropes—can be a great help in navigating your way through this labyrinth. The word *mentor* actually comes from Homer's *Odyssey*. When Odysseus left to fight in the Trojan War, he left his good friend Mentor in charge of guiding his son, Telemachus. When Odysseus returned to Ithaca to fight the suitors in his home, he received help from Athena, who took the form of Mentor and protected him from the suitor's arrows. In the eighteenth century, the word began to be used for any person who served as a trusted friend, counselor, or guide. In the context of early adulthood, mentors are usually from eight to fifteen years older than their protégées and function in the role of a teacher, a sponsor, and/or a role model to be admired and emulated. They're able to open doors, offer encouragement in times of despair, and provide valuable advice not usually found in the "official" guidebooks to success. A woman reported her own experience at age twenty-three: "Lou was a good mentor. He took a 'push people off cliffs, and they'll learn to fly' approach. . . . He took risks in promoting me in the first place; he sponsored me, went to bat on salary and job level, sent me on business trips overseas.[47] Daniel Levinson says that a mentor's most crucial role is to support the realization of the Dream of their charges. He suggests that the mentor role is comparable to that of the "good enough" parent during childhood. The mentor believes in the young adult, shares in her vision for herself, and helps to create a space for working out a life structure that can contain that image.[48]

Early adulthood comes to an end as individuals complete their apprenticeships, find a niche in society, and begin to achieve their dreams or at least reconfigure them. Or alternatively, it ends when they settle for a watered-down version of their youthful aspirations, as did the characters from the novels cited at the beginning of this chapter. These developments seem to herald the true beginnings of maturity. Sadly, though, there are many people in their thirties, dogged by dysfunction from earlier stages of life, who are still searching for a place in society; individuals who have difficulty finding steady work, who struggle with substance abuse, who live in isolation or crawl from one failed relationship to another, or who are bedeviled by emotional or physical illnesses that keep them from functioning in the world. These are the Biff Lomans of the world. In the play *Death of a Salesman*, after Biff had sabotaged his own chances for success by refusing to take a summer school class in order to graduate from high school, he proceeded to drift around the country with no stable job or relationship, even going to jail once for stealing a suit. After returning home to try to face his unresolved issues with his father, at one point he turns to his mother and says, "I just can't take hold, Mom. I can't take hold of some kind of a life." Biff speaks for many young adults in their mid-thirties who face poverty, illness, unemployment, and despair. And the bad news for them is, with age forty looming just around the corner, it may not get any easier. We'll turn to the story of midlife in the next chapter.

❧

The Gift of Early Adulthood: Enterprise

It takes a lot of work to navigate one's way through early adulthood. This project involves leaving home, setting up a new residence, looking for work, finding friends, perhaps searching for a mate, maybe getting married, and then possibly having children who need to be brought up. Whew! One needs an enterprising spirit to make these sorts of things happen. Thus, the gift of early adulthood is best described by the quality of *enterprise*. Young people setting out at the beginning of adulthood are establishing a new business: the business of becoming themselves. This business requires a lot of initiative and ambition. It necessitates a willingness to try new things, make mistakes, and learn from one's errors. Young adults have to learn how to sell themselves to the world without selling out. For the first time in their lives, they possess enough combined physical, emotional, and cognitive maturity to make a significant impact upon their surroundings. If the spirit of enterprise did not flow through their veins, society would likely suffer a sizeable loss of productivity in the work force, lack enough healthy individuals to take on the intensive job of raising children, and be without the youthful energies that infuse new life into rigid social structures

Enterprise is a quality that we need to hold on to into our forties, fifties, and beyond. As we age, we continue to encounter new problems that require an enterprising spirit. In midlife, the need for a new career or a new life focus may force us to reach out into the world in a venturesome way. Even in retirement, our charitable work or other projects still require hustle and punch in order to have a major impact. In old age, we might be seeking to sum up our lives, establish a legacy, or create a meaningful work of art. Each of these tasks involves the necessity of picking ourselves up and marshalling enough diligent energy to make good things happen. To maintain this youthful quality of enterprise as older adults, we need to recall the ambition and persistence we had in early adulthood: Remember the gumption it took to try to find a mate, get a job, create a family, or establish ourselves in some other way during this formidable time of person building. By recollecting and honoring our exuberance in early adulthood, we increase the odds of growth and expansion as we encounter new developmental challenges in each subsequent stage of life.

———— *Ways to Explore and Support Early Adulthood* ————

FOR YOURSELF

- Gather a group of friends together and talk about incidents in your lives when you realized that you were no longer children or adolescents but full-fledged adults.
- Write down what you felt was the "Dream"—your image of future adult achievement or accomplishment—that you set for yourself in early adulthood. Ask yourself whether you have (or currently are) realizing that Dream in adulthood.
- Make a list of adults who served as mentors or significant influences in your young adulthood. If possible, look one or more of them up and talk about old times and about where you are now in your life.

FOR FRIENDS AND FAMILY

- Informally serve as a mentor for a young adult who is in a "moratorium" period, that is, who is not yet situated in a suitable job or relationship but who is still searching to find a place for her own unique gifts in the world around her.
- Offer support and advice to a young couple struggling with their relationship. If necessary, refer them for appropriate relationship counseling, parent training, or other relevant services.
- Provide transitional housing or other support for a young adult who is seeking to "launch" himself away from his family home and forward into a life of his own.

FOR THE COMMUNITY

- Contribute to a scholarship fund that helps young adults receive training or certification to qualify for suitable careers in life.
- Help create a mentoring program for young adults at your place of work, house of worship, community center, or other organization (and if one already exists, serve as a volunteer).
- Support organizations that offer meaningful job experiences for young adults during their moratorium years, including the Peace Corps, Job Corps, and AmeriCorps.

CHAPTER 9

Midlife: Moving Through Muddy Waters

Midway upon the journey of our life
I found myself within a forest dark,
For the straightforward pathway had been lost.

DANTE ALIGHIERI[1]

During the time of Confucius (500 B.C.E.), when the parent of a member of the Chinese ruling elite died, the son was obliged to suspend his everyday activities, abandon his normal residence, and build a hut next to his parent's grave where he would live for the next three years in quiet mourning. This custom had the effect of freeing up members of the scholarly class from their busy governmental and political duties in midcareer. It allowed them time to engage in philosophical, artistic, literary, and spiritual pursuits, a practice that continued throughout the history of the imperial court and served ultimately to enrich the cultural life of China.[2]

In contemporary Japan, when women reach the age of thirty-three and men celebrate their forty-second birthdays, they are said to have entered their *yakudoshi* or "calamity year" when they are advised to take special precautions to avoid accidents, illnesses, or other misfortunes believed to be caused by evil spirits. During this year (and the year before and after it as well), a person is encouraged to visit Shinto shrines, acquire amulets for spiritual protection, engage in special rituals to ward off evil, and avoid starting new business ventures.[3]

Each of these Asian traditions requires its members to take a break from the hustle and bustle that had characterized early adulthood up to that point, and encourages them to create a quiet space in their lives for a few years within which to reflect upon the deeper meaning of their place in the cosmos. As such, these two cultural traditions were among the first to recognize the developmental significance of midlife as a time for temporarily getting off the treadmill of daily routine in order to assess the big picture of one's life.

The need for such a midlife break, however, has a far longer and more ominous history behind it. For most of humanity's existence, this "break," occurring in what we now call the *middle* of our human life span, was known as *death*. Few people in prehistoric times even made it into their thirties or forties.⁴ Once human beings had discharged their evolutionary responsibilities for reproducing children and raising them to the point where the children could take care of themselves, they were no longer biologically necessary, and so evolution made few genetic provisions for extending life beyond that point.⁵ Thus, for more than a hundred thousand years of human development, what we consider *midlife* was in fact *end of life* for most people. Although history and culture have intervened very recently to change that formula and add extra decades to our lives (as recently as 1900 in the United States the life span of the average adult was only forty-seven), there is still something inside of us that remembers our original ancestral date with destiny when we reach our thirties or forties. This recollection reverberates as a kind of atavistic death knell, demanding some new type of creative adaptation from those of us who are graced by modern sanitation methods and antibiotics to live into our fifties, sixties, seventies, and beyond.

Alone in a Dark Wood

The experience of going through midlife varies widely, extending from being totally bowled over by its repercussions—the so-called "midlife crisis"—to remaining relatively untouched by its impact. Among the *rememberers* in society, including artists, poets, and others who are most likely to tremble when the tympanum of humanity is struck at its deepest levels, the results are apt to be quite dramatic. Psychoanalyst Eliot Jacques, the man credited with "inventing" the concept of midlife crisis in a paper written in 1965, originally conceived of this developmental event when he noticed a tendency toward crisis in the lives of creative men during their middle and late thirties.[6] He discovered that many of them either died at midlife (including Mozart, Frédéric Chopin, Arthur Rimbaud, Henry Purcell, Charles Baudelaire, and van Gogh) or went through powerful transformations in their work during their mid- to late thirties when they embraced a more serious and hard-won creativity. Dante was thirty-seven when he began *The Divine Comedy*. Michelangelo was thirty-seven when he started to paint the Sistine Chapel. Shakespeare was in his late thirties when he wrote his great tragedies *Othello*, *Macbeth*, and *King Lear*. Jacques suggested that midlife is a signal that youth and childhood are gone, that maturity is now the chief developmental task in life, and that death is something that looms up ahead as an inevitable prospect.

For many creative individuals, midlife actually *feels* like death. The philosopher Friedrich Nietzsche wrote to a friend, "I am at the end of the 35th year of my life . . . for 1,500 years they called this period the 'mid-point of life' . . . But I, at the mid-point of life, am so 'in the midst of death' that it may take me hourly . . . "[7] The main character in Dostoyevsky's *Notes from the Underground* declares, "I am forty years old now, and you know forty years is a whole lifetime; you know it is extreme old age. To live longer than forty years is bad manners, is vulgar, immoral."[8] Jungian psychologist Maria von Franz suggested that the *puer aeternus* (eternal youth) who has refused to grow up as an adult, may be at risk for an early death at this time if he has not made a firm commitment to adult responsibilities.[9] I remember being terrified by this pronouncement when I read von Franz's book in my early thirties. Somewhat of a man-child myself, unmarried, and conflicted about whether I wanted to continue to work with children or not, I did, in fact, go through a depression at the age of thirty-seven when I had trouble eating, sleeping, and functioning at work due to an obsession with the fear of death.

While man's prehistory may tell him at midlife that his time is just about up, his history and culture whisper something else: that new and vastly different things are on the horizon and about to be born within him. As it turns out, my own midlife crisis at thirty-seven presaged my marriage at thirty-nine, my first-time status as a homeowner at forty, and the beginning of a successful writing and speaking career in my early forties. While struggling with my own midlife demons, I found the example of psychoanalyst Carl Jung inspirational in helping me to see that there was light at the end of the midlife tunnel. When Jung was in his late thirties, he went through a depression after he had made a decisive split with his mentor, Sigmund Freud, because of a number of personal and professional conflicts.[10] One night Jung had a dream that recalled to him the days that he had spent as a child playing on the shores of Lake Zurich where he had spent his childhood. He remembered that as a youngster he had created little towns from the sticks and stones that littered the beach (this childhood preoccupation was similar in some ways to the miniature worlds of the Brontë children). Always one to take the cue from his dream life, Jung began to play once again at the age of thirty-seven like the child he had been. After a morning of sessions with his psychiatric patients, Jung would go off on his lunch break to the beach—he still lived on the lake—and play with the sand, stones, and water to recreate his make-believe worlds of childhood.

The process of playing like a child at midlife initiated a period for Jung of vivid dreams, fantasies, and visions. Between the ages of thirty-seven and forty-two Jung went through an intense psychological-some would even say partially psychotic-process that almost destroyed him, but from which he eventually emerged as a stronger and more creative person. He wrote in *Memories, Dreams, and Reflections,* "The years when I was pursuing my inner images were the most important in my life—in them everything essential was decided. It all began then; the later details are only supplements and clarifications of the material that burst forth from the unconscious, and at first swamped me. It was the *prima materia* for a lifetime's work."[11] Jung visually documented this process in his famous

"Red Book," a folio volume bound in red leather vividly illustrated with mythic images that emerged during his dreams and his waking meditations at that time.[12] In his dreams and visions, Jung encountered biblical figures, Germanic heroes, Hindu deities, and images of fire, darkness, and blood among many other phenomena. Of particular importance was the discovery in his unconscious of a wise old man, Philomel, a gurulike figure that spoke to him and helped orient him to his new life. "It was he who taught me psychic objectivity, the reality of the psyche,"[13] wrote Jung.

Here at midlife, Jung seemed to be going through a transformative event that mirrored in many ways the journey of Odysseus into Hades. In Chapter 11 of the *Odyssey* (called the *Nekyia*, which is Greek for "journey into the night"), Odysseus descended into the world of the dead to consult with the soul of the old wise man Tereseias about how to get home to Ithaca. He had to confront his dead mother, his fellow Greek warriors who had fallen in the Trojan War, and a host of other figures, and had to give them blood to drink so that they could communicate with him from the other world. Similarly, Jung had to dive into his own psychic underworld, confront archetypal figures, and consult with his own wise old man, Philomel, in order to find his way home, that is, achieve greater psychological integration. Jung's journey mirrored in many ways the adolescent's rite of passage to maturity. Like the adolescent, Jung descended into the subconscious world to encounter once again the archetypes of early childhood and to retrieve his deeper self, the better to advance into the next stage of life. The profound difference between these two transitions, however, is the fact that the adolescent needs to be assisted through the passage by a mature adult, while Jung as a fully mature adult himself, found his mentor from within. Also, and more importantly, the adolescent's rite of passage was a movement *outward* into active involvement with the world, while Jung's journey was directed *inward* toward the source of his own creative becoming.

Approaching the Noon of Life

Jung's personal experience of midlife tumult was instrumental in advancing his revolutionary proposal that adulthood, and in particular life after the age of thirty-five, was a valuable area of study for psychologists. Up until that point, virtually all attention in developmental psychology had been focused on childhood and adolescence. Frequently in his writings Jung used the metaphor of the sun sweeping through the sky to describe midlife (noon) as a significant marker between the first and the second halves of life: "In the morning [the sun] rises from the nocturnal sea of unconsciousness and looks upon the wide, bright world which lies before it in an expanse that steadily widens the higher it climbs in the firmament . . . At the stroke of noon the descent begins. And the descent means the reversal of all the ideals and values that were cherished in the morning."[14]

Jung suggested that midlife marks the time to begin cultivating whatever was neglected during the first half of life. This means that if you spent the first half of your life seeking social prestige, material wealth, or other external trappings of a successful life, then during the second half of life you need to balance these outer achievements with a move toward the cultivation of less material pursuits, such as family and spirituality. The Nobel Prize–winning author Octavio Paz also regarded high noon as a critical stage in human development. He writes: "Noon and midnight are the hours of ritual suicide. At noonday everything stops for a moment, vacillating; life, like the sun, asks itself whether it is worth the effort to go on."[15] Perhaps, then, what is required turns out to be not physical death for most, but a death in outlook; the death of what is most valued during youth, and the subsequent birth of new possibilities for living in the years ahead.

Admittedly, few people go through the kind of massive psychological transformation that Jung went through in his thirties and forties. These existential midlife upheavals may happen mainly to the *rememberers* of society, or to emotionally disturbed individuals who failed to master the tasks of earlier stages, or to individuals possessing some combination of these two elements. In fact, many current studies of midlife development suggest that for most people midlife may not be a crisis at all but rather a series of more gentle incremental changes that occur physiologically, emotionally, and socially over the course of several years. "Almost everyone over 40 claims to have it, or knows someone who surely has it, but I do not think more than one person in ten is experiencing a genuine midlife crisis," says Orville Gilbert Brim, director of the MacArthur Foundation Research Network on Successful Midlife Development (also known as MIDMAC), a multiyear interdisciplinary research effort that carried out the most comprehensive scientific study of middle adulthood ever attempted.[16] While nearly one quarter of respondents indicated they had experienced a crisis during midlife, only 10 percent, according to Brim, seemed to fit the image of a person undergoing an existential upheaval or a crisis in meaning. For many others, midlife actually represented an improvement of their sense of well-being. We will look at these developments in the next chapter on mature adulthood. However, the basic issues that Jung and others like him have articulated concerning midlife crisis still seem highly germane to the lives of anyone who is traveling through their thirties and forties.

Noticing the Creases

Of particular importance to many people at midlife are the physical changes of aging that begin to occur around this time. A Shakespeare sonnet warns: "When forty winters shall besiege thy brow / And dig deep trenches in thy beauty's field, / Thy youth's proud livery, so gazed on now, / Will be a tottered weed of small worth held . . . "[17] As noted earlier, Nature seems to lose interest in us when we move out of the main childbearing and child-rearing years, and the body, no longer so necessary for that strenuous work of creating and raising children, begins to break down. As one man taking part in a research study on aging described it, "It was the sudden heart attack in a friend that made the difference. I realized that I could no longer count on my body as I used to do."[18] For many others, the changes are more subtle. You may notice that your eyes no longer focus like they used to and that you need to start using reading glasses. The name for this condition is *presbyopia*, meaning "old eyes," and is due to the loss of elasticity in the eye lens. Your joints may start to creak and hurt because of degeneration in the cartilage protecting the bone, a process that begins in the twenties and thirties. Men may notice changes in their hair. It's gone gray, or thinned out, or disappeared completely in some areas, while sprouting anew in ears, noses, and eyebrows. For women, eyebrows may thin, and hair may disappear on the arms and legs but reappear with a vengeance on the upper lip or chin. For both sexes, skin starts to wrinkle, the chin doubles, varicose veins pop out on legs, bags and crow's-feet surround eyes, and gigantic freckles appear on hands and the rest of the body that aren't freckles at all but rather *lentigo sinilis* (age spots).

Starting at about age forty, you get more easily winded due to reductions in the ability of your heart and lungs to keep up with the anaerobic load placed on them, and as a result you're not as able to keep up with your kids or young adults at strenuous sports. You may even start coming down with a plethora of sports-related injuries or develop back problems at work. Your height starts to go down due to the loss of thickness in the inter-vertebral discs, which decreases the space between the vertebrae and shortens the overall length of the spine. Your weight starts to go up, particularly in the nether regions. There seems to be a general loss of vitality compared to those early adult years, although exercise and a good diet can keep you from noticing this for many more years. Eventually, the time comes when you take a look in the mirror and startle for a moment when you see yourself. One female participant in a midlife study registered her own alarm: "The first time I saw myself as getting older...I picked up a mirror and...I went 'Oh, that's me!' It was really weird; it was funny because I saw my mother."[19]

Although your brain continues to grow new synapses, and even new neurons throughout mature and late adulthood, beginning in your mid-forties to early fifties there are gradual losses in neuron growth in certain areas of the brain that can contribute to age-associated memory loss, or the infamous "senior moments" of life. These losses also tend to slow down the quick mental reflexes that you had in early adulthood. You may find that you're not quite as "sharp" or quick-witted as you used to be, although you may make up for this by being more worldlywise and cagey in your judgments. You may take longer to think something through, but when you do, it is often more insightful than a younger person's thinking capacity. As an illustration, the mean age for world chess champions—who have three minutes to make a move—is thirty, while the mean age for "chess by mail" world champions—who have three days to deliberate—is forty-six.[20] Some research suggests that after leveling off in the twenties, brain myelination (the insulation of brain cells allowing for more efficient transmission of neural messages) takes off again in the forties and continues into the mid-fifties, accumulating on average a 50 percent increase before leveling off.[21] I'll have more to say about this brain growth in the next chapter.

Navigating "the Pause"

For women in midlife, a key biological change is the waning of reproductive capacity. You may start to notice fluctuations in your menstrual cycle as early as your thirties, but more often in the forties when the number of active follicles containing eggs in your ovaries begins to decline. Sometimes it may feel like menarche all over again but in reverse, as one woman noted: "All these physical changes are happening. At first, you're unsure of your body and what it's going to do each month. Your body is unfamiliar again, like when you were 14 and just starting your period."[22] This decline in the number of active follicles during the thirties and forties triggers hormones in the pituitary gland that start "screaming" at the ovaries to resume their early adulthood levels, which they're unable to do, causing wide fluctuations in the levels of estrogen and FSH (follicle-stimulating hormone). These hormonal ups and downs can result in mood swings, vasomotor or "hot" flashes, insomnia, and headaches that can be frequent and severe in ten to twenty percent of American women. Sometimes these symptoms produce anxiety, nausea, weakness, or feelings of claustrophobia or suffocation, but more often they are a minor nuisance, as indicated in this woman's account: "At times you do feel terribly warm. I would sit and feel the water on my head, and wonder how red I looked. But I wouldn't worry about it, because it is a natural thing, and why get worried about it? I remember one time, in the kitchen, I had a terrific hot flash . . . I went to look at myself in the mirror. I didn't even look red, so I thought, 'All right . . . the next time I'll just sit there, and who will notice? And if someone notices, I won't even care.'"[23]

It appears that at least some of the symptoms of menopause may be culturally conditioned. Japanese women, for example, are far less likely to report hot flashes than American women.[24] The Western medical tradition has probably fueled a negative image of menopausal women as a result of its male-biased disease-based view of this transition. As recently as 1963, physician Robert A. Wilson wrote about the psychological condition of women going through menopause in the following way: ". . . a large percentage of women . . . acquire a vapid cow-like feeling called a 'negative state' . . . it is a strange endogenous misery . . . the world appears as though through a gray veil and they live as docile, harmless creatures, missing most of life's values."[25] In actuality, depression is rare during *perimenopause* (the multiyear transition leading up to true menopause that occurs on the day when there is the actual cessation of a woman's menstrual cycle). It is mostly a problem in women who have already experienced depression earlier in their lives.[26]

Far more important than the physiological changes that accompany approaching menopause are the actual role transitions that women go through during this "change of life"; a euphemism that turns out to be far more accurate in many ways than the medical terminology used to describe it. Children may be starting to leave home to lead independent lives. Aging parents may require closer attention as their health begins to decline. Many women may be reassessing the roles they played during early adulthood, and possibly experience regrets over some of the choices they made ten or twenty years earlier. A study of women reviewing their lives in their thirties and forties indicated that most of their regrets were about having chosen a traditionally feminine role with a focus on marriage, mothering, and the home. The majority of those feeling these kinds of regrets desired to make changes in the future involving developing career goals or pursuing educational opportunities. Those who made changes in subsequent years experienced far more well-being than those who failed to take positive action.[27]

The life of author and Nobel Prize winner Toni Morrison provides a good example of a women's midlife individuation. In her twenties, Morrison had earned a master's degree in English and began teaching at the university level. Married at twenty-six, she continued teaching after having two sons. Unhappy in her marriage, she attended a small writers' group at age thirty. One day, having forgotten to bring something to read to the group, she sat down and wrote a short story loosely based on a girl she had known in childhood who had prayed to God to be given blue eyes like the white girls she envied. The writers' group loved the story, but Morrison put it away for several years. After her divorce at age thirty-three, she obtained a job as an associate editor with a textbook subsidiary at Random House. In the next couple of years, Morrison began turning the short story into a novel, drawing on her memories of childhood to create characters that began to have lives of their own. While working all day as a textbook editor, a housekeeper took care of her sons. In the evening, Morrison cooked dinner, played with the boys until bedtime, and then worked on her novel into the late hours. At thirty-six, she began working as a senior editor at Random House and started sending her novel out to various publishers. Finally, at age thirty-nine, her first novel, *The Bluest Eye*, was published to critical acclaim, beginning a literary career that would culminate in her winning the Nobel Prize for Literature in 1993 at the age of sixty-two. Like Jung, Morrison turned to her childhood at midlife to retrieve a storehouse of images that she then used as a foundation for her creative work in the second half of life. But as an African-American woman, Morrison had accomplished something even more remarkable: forging an identity as a novelist (a difficult proposition for anybody) in the shadow of centuries of racism, and in the midst of her heavy responsibilities as a single working mom.[28]

Beyond Male Midlife Myths

The real story of *men* at midlife has been in many ways obscured by the onslaught of media stereotypes concerning men who reach thirty-five or forty. These so-called *middlescents* (the midlife version of an adolescent)

are said to crave sports cars, women half their age, and life on exotic tropical islands. Or, alternatively, these "sad victims" of *andropause* (male
menopause) are depicted as unable to maintain the frantic lovemaking of
their early adult years without the benefit of Viagra, Cialis, or some other
drug designed to treat male erectile dysfunction. However, there appears
to be little empirical support for the view that men go through an actual
physiological "climacteric" that parallels in any significant way what
women experience in menopause.[29] Levels of the male hormone testosterone *do* decline in men as they age, but the decrease is so gradual (about
1 percent per year after age forty) that it is unlikely to account for the dramatic decrease in libido or loss of erectile function that some men may
experience during midlife. These events may be due instead to other
causes, including the stress of having greater responsibilities in middle
adulthood and changes in adrenal androgenic steroids, which decline by
50 percent from age twenty to age fifty.

On the other hand, like women, men may be going through significant personal and professional changes in their lives that give some cre-
dence to the idea that the male midlife crisis may have some basis in
fact. In particular, many men go through a process of reassessment when
it comes to their *work* life, where much of their identity has been
invested during the previous twenty years. Actually it is here, rather
than in a man's physiology, where the concept of a male climacteric
(from the Greek word *klimacter* meaning "rung of a ladder") may have
most relevance, The metaphor of a ladder is an apt image to use in
describing a man's ascent toward higher levels of achievement in the
workplace. Some men find their climb up the ladder of success in midlife
suddenly stopped by the logic of the business they are in, as they get
shunted aside into middle manager positions or other "dead-end" jobs.
After all, only a few men are allowed to occupy the top regions of the
corporate pyramid. One midlife businessman expressed his personal feelings of dread by saying, "Every once in a while, I just think, my God, the
whole goddamn roof is going to fall in. This is sort of what scares me at
45. I'm about halfway through and what is the second half going to be

like because the first half has been pretty good, business-wise. I sometimes think about what will the long downhill slope be like. Will I end
up at 65 making $15,000 or $10,000 a year? I think one of these days the
whole goddamn roof is going to fall in. I just can't keep going like this."[30]

Other men find to their horror that they have been climbing up the
wrong ladder. They long to reconnect with the Dream they may have formulated in their early twenties, yet worry that it might be too late to do
so. The Germans have a word for this fear: *Torschlusspanik*, meaning literally, "the panic of closing doors." This sort of tragic awakening is well
dramatized in Henrik Ibsen's play *Rosmersholm* by the figure of Ulrik
Brendel, a middle-aged tutor who had been bragging to acquaintances
about all the creative literary works that he had inside of him just waiting
to get out. One day, however, he came to a disturbing conclusion: "For five
and twenty years I have been like a miser sitting on his locked money-
chest. And then today, when I opened it to take out my treasure-there was
nothing there! The mills of time had ground it into dust."[31]

In a similar way, some men at midlife look back wistfully to the novel
they wanted to write, the business they wished they had started, or the
travels they desired to take, and they feel the pain and the distance of the
lost years of their youth, wondering if there is any time left for them to
redeem themselves.

Still other men reach the top of the ladder and may briefly exult at
their accomplishments. But after that, they wonder, "What now?" And
their very successes may precipitate a crisis in meaning. Such was the case
with nineteenth-century Russian novelist Leo Tolstoy. At midlife, Tolstoy
was a success by any outward measure. He was married with a large family,
was financially secure as a landowner, and had penned one of the greatest
novels ever written, *War and Peace*, among his other highly regarded literary works. But in his mid-forties, Tolstoy began to be plagued with misgivings about the meaning of all these achievements. These doubts were
at first transient, but they began to recur more and more often, always
with the same theme. Tolstoy writes: "Amid the thoughts of estate management which greatly occupied me at that time, the question would

suddenly occur: Well, you will have 6,000 desyatinas [approx. 2.75 acres) of land in Samara Government and 300 horses, and what then? . . . And I was quite disconcerted and did not know what to think. Or when considering plans for the education of my children, I would say to myself: What for? Or when considering how the peasants might become prosperous, I would suddenly say to myself: But what does it matter to me? Or when thinking of the fame my works would bring me, I would say to myself, Very well; you will be more famous than Gogol or Pushkin or Shakespeare or Molière, or than all the writers in the world—and what of it? And I could find no reply at all."[32] Tolstoy was plunged into a crisis that led to a religious conversion experience at age fifty and a life of piety until his death at the age of eighty-two. His developmental history serves as an excellent example of Jung's idea about how the second half of life should seek to develop qualities neglected in the first half of life. His youth was dedicated to hedonism, military exploits, carving out a literary career, and raising a family. His later years were devoted to pacifism, asceticism, philanthropy, and spiritual growth.

Interestingly, research has indicated that when men are asked to draw a picture of themselves, they draw bigger and bigger images throughout early adulthood, mirroring their burgeoning self-confidence, but then in midlife these images start to become smaller, as if revealing a greater sense of vulnerability or humility in the face of life's mysteries.[33] One can see a similar process going on in the self-portraits of Rembrandt van Rijn, who in his twenties showed himself as a dashing young blade with gold armor and a fashionable beret, but by his forties and beyond portrayed himself in simple peasant's clothing with a somber expression on his face.[34]

In midlife, whether he has reached his goals or not, a man often finds himself required to modify those goals that he set for himself in early adulthood by drawing back from the traditional "slash and burn" masculine attitude of youth, and adopting a softer, even feminine, outlook on life. Psychiatrist Allan B. Chinen observes that many myths and legends of midlife involve a man being rescued by a woman. In Homer's Odyssey, the Greek goddess Athena comes down from Mount Olympus and helps Odysseus through many difficulties in his quest to return to Ithaca and resume his rightful place at the helm of his household. In *The Divine Comedy*, Beatrice leads Dante out of the uncertainty of Purgatory and into the bliss of Paradise. In Egyptian mythology, Osiris is taken down from the tree of crucifixion and made whole again by his wife, Isis.[35] In a similar fashion, modern man may find himself incorporating more feminine qualities to balance the masculinity of his early adulthood by turning to the arts or by spending more time as a caregiver to his family or community.

The word *care* becomes particularly important as a watchword in midlife for both men and women as they begin to reach maturity and assume responsibility for the society that once took care of them. Now it is their turn to be the nurturers. Erik Erikson said that middle adulthood (from ages thirty-four to sixty) is a time when *generativity* becomes the chief developmental task, and *stagnation*, or failure to generate, is the main obstacle to further psychological growth. In early adulthood this meant literally giving birth to and raising children as well as contributing to society through one's productivity at work. In middle adulthood this broadens out to include other forms of generativity, including teaching, doing scientific research, or enriching the culture in other ways. In the next chapter, we will see how this concept of generativity ultimately flowers in the lives of the fully mature adult.

∽∞∾

————————— *The Gift of Midlife: Contemplation* —————————

Most people are familiar with Auguste Rodin's sculpture *The Thinker*, which shows a middle-aged man deep in thought. Few individuals, however, know that Rodin originally modeled this image on that of Dante Aligheri, the Italian poet who began his monumental work *The Divine Comedy* with the sober evaluation of his midlife crisis that began this chapter: If there is anything unique to midlife as a stage of human development, it seems to be *contemplation*. By the time a person reaches thirty-five or forty, she has accumulated enough adult life experience to deserve a good mulling over. She also has achieved enough brain maturity to be able to engage in a process of deeper reflection and evaluation. Many things happen in midlife that merit contemplation: the body is getting older, children are growing up, work roles may be changing, relationships may be going through a transition. We've already seen in this chapter how some societies have traditionally set aside time for people in midlife to engage in a period of reflection, during which they can probe into their psyches to find potentials that will help them move successfully into subsequent stages of life and enrich the quality of their culture.

This gift of contemplation in midlife is valuable at any time during adulthood. Even in early adulthood, when the focus tends to be on *adapting* to society, there is still a need for taking time out to reflect on where one is going in life, and on what the ultimate meaning of life may be. But especially as we age in midlife and beyond, we often find ourselves becoming increasingly inner-directed and need time to contemplate life's mysteries and our place in the universe. We may discover that we're paying more attention to nighttime dreams and daytime intuitions. We may find that deep reflection turns into prayer or meditation, and opens up new philosophical, religious, or spiritual horizons (traditionally, mystics such as Saint Teresa of Avila, Jakob Böhme, Jalalu'l-Din Rumi, and Isaac Luria were often referred to as "contemplatives"). We may decide to turn our contemplations into an integral part of our lifestyle through meditation, periodic retreats, or by staying mindful in the midst of everyday life. However we choose to gaze inwardly, we can be sure that our contemplations will enrich us by bringing insight, tranquillity, or even a new sense of identity into our lives.

——————— *Ways to Explore and Support Midlife* ———————

FOR YOURSELF

- Keep a journal of your dreams, visions, reflections, and feelings as you begin to experience the sense of becoming an older person.
- Make a list of all the things you want to do in your life before you die. Then start doing them.
- Go over the goals you've had for your life as an adult, and see if they are still relevant to your current life. If not, then modify them accordingly.

FOR FRIENDS AND FAMILY

- Gather friends into a "midlife" support group that meets regularly to discuss social, emotional, mental, physical, and spiritual changes going on in your lives.
- Support a friend or family member who may be going through a "midlife crisis" by offering counsel, friendship, and/or referral to an appropriate mental health professional or program.
- Help a midlife friend or family member who has been "downsized" find another job or career.

FOR THE COMMUNITY

- Start a women's or men's group for middle-aged adults in your community to help them cope with major life transitions in relationships, jobs, and/or illness.
- Contribute financially to a woman's midlife health center that serves the poor and indigent.
- Volunteer at an organization that provides midlife career advice or job placement services.

CHAPTER 10

Mature Adulthood: Scaling the Peaks

Youth is a silly, vapid state
Old age with fears and ills is rife
This simple boon I beg of Fate
A thousand years of Middle Life!

—CAROLYN WELLS[1]

In medieval times the Catholic worldview of the human life span was often depicted as a circle. In the center was the image of Christ. Around this divine hub, like a Wheel of Fortune, were illustrations of the different ages of life from infancy to the grave. Each age, like a spoke, was equidistant from the hub. This suggested that every point in human life existed in the same sacred relationship to the divine. During the Protestant Reformation in the sixteenth century, however, this symbolism underwent a profound and lasting change. Instead of a circle, the image of an ascending and descending staircase became prevalent. This image seemed better suited to the new importance of work, ambition, and changing social roles in the emerging market economy of Protestant Europe. Theater productions would be put on showing a tableau of five ascending and five descending steps. On each step was an actor representing that particular stage of life. This is where we may have originally developed our notion of the "stages of life." Each stage or step usually represented one decade. At the top of the tableau, on the highest step, stood a man or woman (or sometimes both) representing the age of fifty. To be fifty meant to be at the peak of life.[2]

In many ways, this valuation of middle age still holds true. While it may be granted that we live in a youth-oriented society, it is still the old-sters—especially those in their fifties through seventies—who control the financial and leadership positions that underwrite it. Behind every twenty-year-old singing star is a sixty-year-old stockholder who capitalizes on her fame. Shakespeare's image of this time of life was of the prosperous and portly judge in *As You Like It*: ". . . in fair round belly with good capon lined / With eyes severe, and beard of formal cut / Full of wise saws and modern instances . . ."[3] Late middle age, or mature adulthood as we're calling it here, is a time of culmination for many significant social roles. This is the time of life when Odysseus returned home after twenty years of fighting, scheming, and journeying, to assume his rightful place as the king of Ithaca. The pillars of the community come from this stage of life: justices, presidents, eminent professors, ambassadors, senators, CEOs, religious figures, philanthropists, Nobel Prize winners, and others who have capped a lifetime of achievement with positions of authority. As for the rest of us, mature adulthood is a time when, after years of everybody picking on us, telling us what to do, bossing us around, instructing us, and in other ways ruling over our lives, we're finally free of all that: We're on top! And yet, at the same time, the top step of life's staircase has a precarious quality to it because the next step, and all subsequent steps, at least in terms of *body up* development, head in one direction and one direction only: down toward the grave.

A Whole New Stage of Life

This staircase model of human development, which views the fifties as the beginning of decline, seems to be undergoing a major transformation. Nowadays experts are more likely to conceptualize the life span tableau as five ascending stairs, with a wide platform at the top for those in their fifties and sixties (and even for many in their seventies and eighties), before a rather precipitous drop into illness and death. At age fifty, Americans can look forward to another thirty years of life.[4] Advances in medicine and education mean that people in their fifties, sixties, and seventies are healthier, better educated, and have the prospect of far more *able* years ahead of them than was the case for their parents or grandparents.

Just to show how far this can go, journalist and author Dudley Clendinen related an incident that happened on a plane ride to Florida: "... I sat with a woman of 60, on her way to her winter home. Her latest boyfriend, a businessman of almost 70, had acquired a certain cachet in his peer group when sued by a young woman for sexual harassment. That did not bother my planemate so much because she believed him when he said the woman came after him, and so did the jury at the trial. But it troubled her mother, who is 85, and who found out about it when her fifth husband, who is 91, saw notice of it in a business journal he gets at his office."[5] This scenario makes us wonder when middle age actually ends. It recalls baseball great Satchel Paige's words when a reporter asked him how old he was. Paige reputedly replied: "How old would you be if you didn't know how old you was?"

The truth is that for many people, mature adulthood represents the time of greatest life satisfaction. You've passed beyond the insecurities of early adulthood ("Will anyone love me?" "Will I find a place for myself in the world of work?"). You've reconciled with many of the anxieties of midlife ("Oh my God! I'm growing older!" "Will I achieve my ambitions?"). But you haven't yet reached old age when chronic illness and concerns about approaching death can take center stage. You've raised a family perhaps, and seen your young ones leave the nest and live independent lives, freeing you up to enjoy your own life more fully. After years of work, you've hopefully accumulated at least some degree of financial security. You've perhaps begun to take on satisfying new roles as a grandparent, a mentor, and/or a community leader. You're possibly engaged in nurturing activities that involve less struggle and angst than earlier adult roles, where you might have had to discipline a cranky two-year-old or compete with a coworker for a better paying job.

Contrary to popular opinion and all those humorous "over-the-hill" greeting cards—which seem to take their cue from the sixteenth-century staircase motif noted earlier—life in the fifties, sixties, and beyond is in many cases *better* than what went before. Research from the MacArthur Foundation Study of Successful Midlife Development (MIDMAC) seems to bear this out. It suggests that as adults move into their fifties and beyond, negative emotions decrease and positive emotions increase steadily until very late in the life span when the physical decline associated with a final illness and death occurs.[6] The sense of control over work, finances, and marriage increases with age beginning in the late forties to the early fifties. Women in particular report higher levels of positive relations with others as they age.[7] Dancer and teacher Ruth Zaporah expresses this sentiment in her own reflections on life in mature adulthood: "In my fifties I feel ripely quiet. Life seems much simpler; I am more appreciative. More of life seems funny to me, humorous and light. I consistently have a good time. It hasn't always been like that. I'm worming my way out of the darkness. I can say that now I feel pretty comfortable in just about every situation, whereas I used to be nonverbal, never able to express myself. I could never go to parties. I haven't done much therapy; I think it's been my work that's done the healing."[8]

A Time to Be Generative

A vital key to successful aging appears to involve the capacity to give back to the community in some meaningful way. As Harvard psychiatrist and human development researcher George Vaillant has said, "Biology flows downhill." This means that the older generation is put on earth to take care of the younger generation, and not vice versa. Erik Erikson used the word *generativity* to describe this impulse and indicated that the term could be applied to roles as disparate as the birthing and parenting of a child, the creation of an artistic work, the teaching of students in a classroom, or the development of a community service project to feed the hungry. Being generative in one's fifties and beyond has less to do with giving birth to, raising, or educating individual children and more to do with nurturing and caring for future generations on a more collective basis. A person can do this through teaching, refereeing, coaching, mentoring, or engaging in other service-oriented pursuits. Generativity expert John Kotre explains, "Japanese colleagues have translated 'generativity' as 'sedai-keisho-sei.' 'Sedai' means 'the generations,' 'keisho' means something like 'receiving and putting your stamp on,' and 'sei' means 'the sense of.' Generativity, from this point of view, is the sense of receiving something from the past, putting your unique contribution into it, and passing it on to the future. It's what you do when you stand 'between the generations.'"[9]

MIDMAC research suggests that meaningful engagement in generative activities with schools, communities, the extended family, and other groups and organizations is linked to psychological well-being in middle age.[10] Drew Leder, an expert on the aging process, agrees: "Maybe we feel moved to cuddle abandoned crack babies warehoused in a local hospital. This gift of love is a simple kind of mentoring. Perhaps we might teach a business class in a local penitentiary. The inmates may be desperate to acquire usable skills, not to mention some self-esteem. Or maybe we will decide to volunteer time assisting a young AIDS patient. In helping him work through his fear of death, we might begin to process our own."[11] Such involvement with social institutions supplies an incredible human resource at little or no cost in dealing with the pressing needs of the world. As former counterculture expert and now generative senior Theodore Roszak writes: ". . . somebody who no longer has to worry about raising a family, pleasing a boss or earning more money [has] the chance to join with others in building a compassionate society. . ."[12]

Mature adulthood is often the time of life when seeds planted at earlier stages of development come to fruition. Former vice president Al Gore, for example, traced his own deep concern for the issue of global warming back to an inspiring teacher he had as an undergraduate at Harvard in 1968. Oceanographer Roger Revelle was one of the first scientists to measure the growing levels of carbon dioxide in the atmosphere and warn of its potentially toxic "greenhouse effect" on the earth's ecology. Gore writes in his book *An Inconvenient Truth*, "I will never forget the graph that he drew on the blackboard, nor the dramatic message it conveyed; that something profoundly new was happening to the atmosphere of the entire planet, and that this transformation was being caused by human beings."[13] Now in his late fifties, Gore is reaching a peak in his dedication to environmental issues, starring in a documentary film with the same name as his book, and founding an investment firm—Generation Investment Management—that seeks out companies taking a responsible view on big global issues like climate change.[14]

When primatologist Jane Goodall was four years old, she spent four hours sitting quietly in a henhouse because she wanted to know how there could be an opening on a hen big enough for an egg to come out. Eventually her patience paid off and she saw a round object protruding beneath the feathers of a hen who clucked with pride and left the coop. Goodall writes: "Filled with excitement I squeezed out after her and ran home."[15] In her mid-forties, after a renowned career studying the behavior of chimpanzees in Africa, Goodall founded the Jane Goodall Institute, and has spent her fifties, sixties, and now seventies, traveling the world and teaching people about the need to preserve endangered wildlife and support healthy ecosystems for all living species.[16]

Another way to assist future generations is by working to preserve cultural traditions. George Vaillant refers to individuals who do this as "Keepers of the Meaning." According to Vaillant, a person who is a Keeper of the Meaning "speaks for past cultural achievements and guides groups, organizations, and bodies of people toward the preservation of past traditions . . . Matriarchs, genealogy mavens, and antiques refinishers are all exemplars of what is involved in becoming a keeper of the meaning."[17] Individuals who are generative in this way create bridges between the past, present, and future. One thinks of people like Gutzon Borglund, who sought to preserve our nation's heritage by creating Mount Rushmore, a project he didn't even start until age sixty, or Alex Haley, whose book on his African heritage, Roots, came out when he was fifty-five, or Maggie Kuhn, who founded the Gray Panthers at age sixty-five. One participant in Vaillant's study of Harvard men from the 1930s (a study

that is still going on today), put it this way: "There is a certain peaceful-
ness about becoming interested in genealogy, conservation, and history
rather than meeting payrolls, running church rummage sales, and reining
in teenagers." [18]

Coping with the Aging Body

As bright as the above picture seems to be, life in the fifty to seventy-five
age bracket is not always a bed of roses. There is, for example, the matter
of physical decline to consider. As we noted in the last chapter, major
physical functions begin to deteriorate during midlife, and in mature
adulthood things don't get any better. For many people this will be the
time when they suffer their first major illness or chronic condition. Only
7 percent of those in their forties report having a disability. By the early
fifties 16 percent do, and by the early sixties almost a third are disabled. [19]
As we age into our fifties, the walls of the left ventricle of the heart
become thicker and less compliant during each contraction while arteries
are less able to accommodate the flow of blood. There is a progressive loss
of muscle mass (referred to as *sarcopenia*) beginning in the forties and
fifties that amounts to a 12 to 15 percent decline per decade. One study
suggests, in fact, that muscular weakness measured by one's *handgrip* in
midlife predicts functional limitations and physical disability in old age. [20]
In postmenopausal women (and in many men as well), bone density
decreases, leading to microfractures in response to stress, as well as to
the increased likelihood of developing osteoporosis. For some men, a
decline in blood levels of testosterone after age sixty leads to erectile
failures and loss of sexual appetite, while for others the prostate grows
in size, squeezing the urethra and causing numerous visits to the bathroom
at night. As one fifty-two-year-old Pennsylvania male observed, "At 40,
you know you're not as young as you used to be. At 50, you realize it
almost every day." [21]

Fortunately, there is a great deal we can do to ward off, delay, or minimize the impact of such physiological assaults. Research points strongly
to a number of practical measures that promote physical health in mature

adulthood, including not smoking, not drinking to excess, exercising regularly, and eating a diet moderate in saturated fats. What many people bemoan as the effects of aging, including being overweight or chronically ill, is often due instead to the impact of an unhealthy lifestyle and years of hard living. That's why I like to call this stage of life "the chickens come home to roost" stage. It represents a unique period in human development when genetic vulnerabilities are revealed for the first time in a big way while at the same time a person may receive a gigantic environmental wallop from years of overeating, poor nutrition, smoking, excessive use of alcohol, and/or lack of exercise. Studies suggests that these factors determine 70 percent of the physical attributes of people from sixty-five to seventy-five.[22] One startling finding from the MIDMAC study reveals that many middle-aged people at risk for major illness are remarkably naive about their personal contribution to their own destiny. For example, while 30 percent of forty-five to fifty-four-year-olds smoke regularly, 70 percent of them claim they have no higher risk of heart attack, and 60 percent say they have no higher risk of cancer, despite overwhelming evidence to the contrary from decades of highly publicized scientific research.[23] As French moralist Jean de la Bruyere believed, "Most men spend the first half of their lives making the last half miserable."

Another danger of this time is more psychological in nature: the risk of becoming mentally and emotionally rigid with the years. This may cause a person to turn away from others while retreating into the glories of the past. Such was the case with the mythical Greek scientist Daedelus, inventor of the labyrinth, the flying machine, and other ingenious devices, who became jealous of his talented inventor/nephew Perdix, and pushed him off a high tower.[24] Or, alternatively, an individual may become rigid with the years by falling into a pool of self-preoccupation and self-pity, like Oedipus the king of Thebes, who, after killing his father and marrying his mother as a young adult, curses his son in his old age, bewailing his fate, and denying any responsibility for his tragic life. Erik Erikson used the term *stagnation* to describe this potential peril during middle adulthood, saying that someone who becomes afflicted in this way is likely to retreat into invalidism or selfish obsessions. Shakespeare's portrayal of the hypocritical elder Polonius in *Hamlet* is a good example of this kind of "mature" stagnation. Polonius pretentiously offers his son "wise sayings" about life (including the famous line "To thine own self be true"), but then proceeds to violate them by spying on his son's youthful adventures. Carl Jung referred to middle-age stagnation when he wrote: "Anyone who fails to go along with life remains suspended, stiff and rigid in midair. That is why so many people get wooden in old age; they look back and cling to the past with a secret fear of death in their hearts. They withdraw from the life-process, at least psychologically, and consequently remain fixed like nostalgic pillars of salt, with vivid recollections of youth but no living relation to the present."[25] They are like Odysseus stranded in a becalmed Aegean Sea, without any wind to blow them home.

Instead of rolling with the years, stagnant middle-agers may seek to arrest the march of time by getting plastic surgery, taking "anti-aging" drugs, and retreating into "age ghettos" (retirement communities restricted to those over fifty or fifty-five), which shield them from contact with other stages of life. This static view of living one's "golden years" in a kind of sealed-off "haven of bliss," while golfing, shopping, and cruising the years away, has a hollow ring to it.[26] According to psychotherapist Irving Yalom, there is a danger that those who have lived through their productive years immersed in a materialistic culture will enter late middle age with a deep sense of existential emptiness. In the broader context of this book, these individuals have not used their time on earth to *remember* who they really are, nor to ponder life's deepest mysteries, but instead have squandered their years in a mindless *adaptation* to the superficial world around them. He writes, "I see patients in their 60's coming in and looking at their whole lives and feeling lots of sadness. They look back and say, 'I wasted my life. I filled it with worthless, trivial things, with rubbish.'"[27] One of the more dispiriting findings of the MIDMAC study is that for both men and women, there are steady declines in both personal growth and purpose in life as they move from midlife to old age.[28]

Enjoying Postmenopausal Zest

The above findings suggest that there is an absence of significant social structures in our culture to help middle-aged adults make meaningful transitions into full maturity and later life. While other stages of life have rites of passage to mark the movement from one stage to another, such transition rituals, at least in modern societies, don't show up very often during mature adulthood. And yet, mature adults undergo a number of important changes as they move into their fifties and sixties. Perhaps the most important biological change for women is the cessation of their menstrual cycle. This occurs on average at around age fifty or fifty-one but can occur at any time from forty to fifty-eight. Despite the discomforts of peri-menopause that were cited in the previous chapter, there is a definite upside. At menopause women are liberated from the biological constraints that Nature (and often society as well) placed upon them during their childbearing years. This frees them to explore other aspects of their being, including cultural, creative, and spiritual potentials. Perhaps this is why anthropologist Margaret Mead is reputed to have said, "The most creative force in the world is the woman with postmenopausal zest."

In many cultures around the world, menopause signals an important and positive shift in the social status of women. Some traditional societies believe that menstrual blood is the creative force of life and that when it no longer flows out of a woman it remains inside of her as a source of great creative power and wisdom. Because of this belief, postmenopausal women in indigenous cultures are often honored as *rememberers* and allowed to perform socially significant activities that were denied to them during their years of menstruation. Postmenopausal Iroquois women can hold religious and political office. Yoruba women become ritual specialists. The oldest clan member of the St. Lawrence Island Eskimos, if she is a woman, leads the group and makes the most important decisions.[29] In many societies, postmenopausal women are believed to possess magical or curative powers, which can lead to persecution as witches (as happened in Europe in the late middle ages), but may also lead to feelings of respect, admiration, and awe among members of the community. The image of the old women or *crone* is a powerful one in the mythologies and histories of indigenous cultures around the world, and includes the Slavic hag Baba Yaga, the Greek goddess Hecate, and the Nordic crone Urd.

Scientists now suspect that postmenopausal women may also have played a major adaptive role in the survival of our species. In one study of the Hadza people of northern Tanzania, the positive food-gathering behaviors of women in their fifties, sixties, and seventies were seen to be correlated with the nutritional welfare of the young children in the society. These Hadza "grandmothers" spent seven to eight hours a day foraging for food out in the woods, and gathered more food than any other segment of the population. Giving the mothers help in gathering food not only produced healthier babies, but also allowed mothers to have more children in a shorter space of time, thus increasing overall odds for survival.[30] This may help explain why women live for so many years beyond the cessation of their reproductive capacity, a feature that other primates do not have. In what has been called "the grandmother hypothesis," postmenopausal women are seen as critical supporters of our species' evolution, not only by foraging for food, but in assisting with prenatal care, helping with the birth event itself, and providing early childhood care and education. As anthropologist Dr. Kristen Hawkes of the University of Utah, explains: "Only with the ascent of the grandmother . . . were human ancestors freed to exploit new habitats, to go where no other hominid or primate had gone before."[31]

In today's modern world, this deeper evaluation of the gifts of older women may have a broader meaning, encouraging them to break free from feminine roles that no longer serve them. At the same time, this realization spurs them on to create new cultural, creative, and spiritual roles that support a changing society. Margaret Mead based her notion of postmenopausal zest on her own life experiences in her late forties and early fifties. As midlife expert Gail Sheehy relates it in her book *The Silent Passage,* "Her adored husband had left the marriage, her closest colleague died, and she spent several years improvising a life as a divorced professional mother of a small child. But between the ages of forty-five and fifty-five, as [her daughter Mary Catherine] Bateson pieces together the famous anthropologist's history, 'She seemed to become prettier, she bought a couple of designer dresses from Fabiani for the first time, and I think she started a new romantic relationship.' Boldly Dr. Mead returned to the field at the age of fifty-one: She boned up on languages and went back to New Guinea, forging a major intellectual new start with ground-breaking research on social change published in the book *New Lives for Old*."[32] Feminist Gloria Steinem suggests that this new burst of energy bears a resemblance to the life energy as it was originally expressed in a girl's childhood : "There is a great unexplored land after 60," she writes. "It may be best indicated by who you were when you were 9 or 10 and a little girl. Climbing trees and saying: 'I know who I am. I know what I want.' That's before the feminine role has come down upon you."[33]

Increasingly, women are beginning to celebrate their postmenopausal lives in contemporary culture with croning rituals that draw upon arche-typal symbols from mythology and religion. Author and teacher Savina Teubal originally created a ritual she called Simchat Hochmah (Joy of Wisdom) to mark her sixtieth birthday. Drawing on many elements from her Jewish faith, she writes: " . . . the reason I was drawn to assume my new status with a ceremony was inspired by the Genesis narratives I have been so involved with for the past decade. I came to realize that the biblical stories that dealt with Sarah, Hagar, and Abraham were, in most cases, rit-uals. Each time a ritual was performed, the life of the protagonist changed radically. . . " In her own ritual, Teubal wore an ancient Macedonian robe which she discarded in the middle of the ceremony for a simple white linen garment, and at the end of the ritual she planted a tree.[34] Women from many faiths have been inspired by Teubal's example and have created their own unique rituals to celebrate their cronehood. These ceremonies have included elements such as chanting, singing, feasting, drumming, or being crowned by a wreath. They incorporate Jewish, Greek, Native American, Celtic, Egyptian, Indian, and/or Christian imagery. Author Edna Ward says, "Since the patriarchy isn't going to value old women, we celebrate ourselves."[35]

From the Rocking Chair to Rembrandt

Another important transition faced by most people as they move into the fifties, sixties, and beyond is retirement. This change, at least for men, has its own traditional ritual of sorts in American life: the awarding of a gold watch in a ceremony witnessed by one's colleagues at work. At the beginning of the movie *About Schmidt* the aging Jack Nicholson character receives his watch at a hotel banquet, delivers a confused and meandering thank-you speech, and then abruptly walks out of the room and into an uncertain life in retirement. For many people, the prospect of retiring is a similarly daunting one. Typically in America, the time for retirement has been put at sixty-five, partly due to the customs of individual businesses, but also because Social Security benefits traditionally began at that age.[36] However, during the past two or three decades this pattern has become much fuzzier. Rather than living by labor leader Walter Reuther's dictum—"retire and then wait to die"—many people are deciding to retire early, or alternatively, to continue working full time or part time after official retirement age. At the same time, one study suggests that while 80 percent of people queried said they planned to keep on working at least part time past retirement age, fewer than 30 percent actually did so.[37]

A dramatic drop in employment occurs for the great majority of people during the sixties, according to midlife researcher Larry Bumpass.[38] Yet few people are prepared for it. Surveys show that most people welcome the idea of retirement if it's accompanied by adequate income. But studies show that more than 40 percent of households headed by someone aged forty-seven to sixty-four are not able to replace even *half* their preretirement income with savings and Social Security.[39] As television and movie personality Ben Stein observed, "I've seen so many friends whose lives were ruined by not planning for retirement. We have this obsession with spending and instant gratification and not saving or thrift."[40]

Graceful retirement is particularly problematic for cultures like the United States and Japan where the work ethic is so strong. In Japan, retired men are called *neureochiba* or "wet dead leaves" because of the way they seem to stick to their wives when they go out of the house. Still, retirement promises to bring years of satisfaction for those who plan adequate postretirement income, develop nurturing social networks, and cultivate their own personal development. Anthropologist Joel Savishinsky studied twenty-six people in upstate New York as they entered retirement. He followed his subjects for a number of years after retirement and discovered several amazing personal transformations during that time, including a banker who found Buddhism, a marine who became head of the school board, a social worker who fell in love with Rembrandt, an engineer who learned to sculpt water, a doctor who turned into a moral historian, and a technician who became a teacher of tai chi. Savishinsky wrote, "There is no age limit to enthusiasm, and retirement is a period in which individuals can discover or rediscover their passionate interests. These can take many forms, including creative production, public service, travel, or spiritual and personal growth—the kinds of involvements that many people once consigned to weekends, but which can now become the focus for a new way of being and a reason for living."[41]

The Sandwiched Generation

Another transition that affects most people in middle age is the final exit of children from the home. The average age of a parent when the last child leaves home for the last time ranges from fifty-five to fifty-nine.[42] The MIDMAC study suggests that the so-called "empty nest" is not really the crisis it has been portrayed to be by the media. Instead, most parents feel liberated from their roles as caregivers and free to explore their own personal goals, sometimes for the first time in their lives. In particular, those parents who maintain a positive relationship with their grown children often experience this time as a second honeymoon after the children leave.[43] Things can get a bit strained, however, when children who have left home return, and then return again, and yet again. As one mother explains, "I didn't expect that I would have to provide room and board once my son was past 18–20 years old. My son's multiple returning [three times] put a strain on my marriage. It is very expensive and we can't alter the rooms in the house to create more privacy."[44]

At the same time that parents are dealing with the problems of their still-maturing offspring, they may also be confronting the challenges of aging parents and feel squeezed between the two generations. "It is as if there are two mirrors before me, each held at a partial angle," says one woman. "I see part of myself in my mother who is growing old, and part of her in me. In the other mirror, I see part of myself in my daughter. I have had some dramatic insights, just from looking into those mirrors . . . It is a set of revelations that I suppose can only come when you are in the middle of three generations."[45] This can become a real problem for those parents who have postponed having children into the thirties and forties. One midlife mother with a seven-year-old child explained, "My husband's mother lives in Cape Town. He's traveled to her deathbed three times. She's had three heart operations—each time, she just sat up afterwards and carried on. People who don't have small children can't appreciate the split loyalties. But these days, if you've got younger children, [and] you've got an ailing parent—it goes with the territory."[46]

Middle-aged daughters (and daughters-in-law), provide up to 90 percent of the medical and personal care for their functionally impaired parents in the United States.[47] Theodore Roszak reports: "Women have become the default caregivers of our society; they have been thrown into that role and forced to make the best of it. Theirs has been called the 'sandwiched' life. No sooner do they finish raising their children than their ailing parents move in for care." This phenomenon of role reversal, where the children become the parents and the parents become the children, can be draining for some. As one woman put it: "I was always around older people. I like helping them. I have a knack for it, dealing with older people, older *nice* people [unlike her own father] . . . But now I've learned my lesson: That you don't mess with other people's illnesses. They want you to do more and more and more."[48] On the other hand, the process of caring for one's parents can bring certain rewards. A women whose mother-in-law had Alzheimer's disease and required considerable care explained how, ". . . even though she still gets in her 'moods,' . . . she loves to cook big old dinners . . ."[49] Another caregiver explained: "Sometimes you even feel like, well, you're exhausted emotionally after one conversation. But then the next one, they'll have some insight for you about dealing with your kids or something. So it's still, you know, it's still a really dynamic and giving-both-ways relationship."[50]

At some point during middle adulthood for most people, this relationship with parents, whether harmonious or strained, ends when a parent dies. Only 10 percent of twenty-five-year-olds have experienced the death of a parent, but by age fifty-five, 50 percent of us have lost both parents, and by age sixty-two this figure goes up to 75 percent.[51] In one survey of midlife adults who had experienced the death of a parent, most reported that the death changed their outlook on life.[52] As Linda Waite, director of the Center on Aging at the University of Chicago describes it, "There's the feeling that you're the next in line, and there's nothing between you and the abyss."[53] Seeing parents die can bring up all kinds of issues from the past, including positive memories of being cared for and loved as well as negative memories of a parent's abuse or lack of availability. When my own father died two years ago at the age of eighty-seven, here were only a few of the emotions I experienced: the sadness of a little boy losing his father, relief at the fact that he no longer walked the earth to terrify me (he had frequently exploded in rage at me during my childhood), forgiveness for his defects, fondness for his love of music, respect for his spiritual love of perfection, tension for that same love of perfection, regret for not having had a normal father-son relationship.

In a certain sense, parents were our gods and goddesses in early childhood and it can be very hard to watch a god die. According to author and psychologist Alexander Levy, "Parents provide a unique spot on this planet, which is called 'home,' where we can return, if we need to, to be loved and to feel that we belong . . . After parents die, it's gone." The unfathomable loss of that "spot called home," regardless of its location or the quality of what actually occurred there when parents were living, is a recurrent theme in many parental bereavement stories. Levy cites the example of Jason, a fifty-eight-year-old one-time battlefield medic who worked with soldiers who had had an arm or leg amputated yet who continued to experience a "phantom limb" after it had been cut off, feeling an itch or sensation where there was no limb. Jason noted that after his parents died, he would begin to call them on the phone to share an anecdote, only to discover that their number was disconnected. "Like the amputees...he often reaches to scratch what's missing, and is surprised, each time, to discover nothing there."[54]

The Dawning of Elder Wisdom

One crucial factor in successfully navigating through these life changes is having a healthy and active mind. Alzheimer's disease begins to take its toll at this stage of life, with 0.6 percent of people aged sixty-five to sixty-nine, and 1 percent of people aged seventy to seventy-four developing the disorder each year (this figure goes up to 8.4 percent after eighty-five). Others develop mild cognitive impairment (MCI), a nondementia memory-related condition (not related to the "senior moments" common to this age) that may precede the development of full-blown Alzheimer's disease.[55] A key to battling these conditions involves keeping the mind active throughout one's life. Columbia University neuropsychologist Yaakov Stern writes, "Some people—who are better educated, more active in work and leisure activities—seem to hold off developing the symptoms of Alzheimer's disease longer, despite having the same brain pathology as those who show symptoms earlier."[56] As noted in the chapter on early childhood, learning experiences create new dendrites, which in turn multiplies the number of synapses or connections available for transmitting information throughout the brain. Individuals who pursue a course of life-long learning maximize their synaptic connections. All other things being equal, if and when Alzheimer's disease or similar dementias related to aging occur, a more highly educated person will likely have a surplus of brain connections or neural networks to take over from damaged areas.[57]

New and surprising research suggests that from our early fifties to our late seventies there is an *increase* both in the *density* of dendrites, and in the *length* of individual dendrites in certain parts of the neocortex.[58] In addition, scientists have recently discovered that the brain continues to make new brain cells well into old age.[59] NYU neuropsychologist Elkhonon Goldberg points out that exposure to novel learning experiences creates neural networks that form the basis for expertise and intuition in life. These networks accumulate with life experience and may form the basis for what we call wisdom in old age.[60] This is the wisdom that comes from having banked a lot of life experience over the years, and thus being able to see through illusions and grasp the truer nature of things. The German philosopher Arthur Schopenhauer once noted that in youth we see the dazzling embroidery of life from the front, while in old age we see the stitchwork from behind.[61] A middle-aged research subject put it this way: "You feel you have lived long enough to have learned a few things that nobody can learn earlier. That's the reward . . . and also the excitement. I now see things in books, in people, in music, that I couldn't see when I was younger . . . It's a form of ripening that I attribute largely to my present age."[62]

Part of what characterizes cognitive growth in mature adulthood is the way in which heart and head become more balanced. Along with greater insight comes a more positive feeling toward others and a warmer attitude about life in general. One longitudinal study of aging noted that as members grew older, they were more forgiving, more able to meet adversity with cheerfulness, and less likely to take offense from others. This may be an important reason why people in middle age are particularly well suited to serve as judges, referees, and political leaders.[63] Another study comparing the facial expressions of people under fifty and over fifty as they recounted emotionally charged experiences in their lives revealed that older individuals were in general more emotionally expressive, and displayed more instances of complex feelings, exhibiting contrasting emotions—such as sadness and joy, or bitterness and sweetness—with single look.[64]

Middle age may be the first stage of life when a dysfunctional upbringing in childhood no longer has such a devastating impact on our lives. " . . . unhappy childhoods become less important with time . . . " says life span researcher George Vaillant.[65] Practically speaking, people in mature adulthood increasingly choose to use their time constructively. In contrast to younger adults who may seek to advance their lives with a wide range of social contacts and then experience the conflict that generally accompanies these choices, older adults prefer to spend more time with just a few good friends in situations that minimize conflict and maximize the number of emotionally meaningful experiences they can have.[66] Time is of the essence to middle-agers since they feel it literally whizzing by compared to younger adults. There is a good mathematical reason for this: One year in the life of a two-year old is 50 percent of her total existence on earth, while one year for a fifty-year-old is only 2 percent of her life span. Time goes by especially quickly for individuals who have created mental cubbyholes for every single aspect of existence, and no longer see, or *remember*, the richness of human experience.

Opening to Later Life Spirituality

Perhaps in reaction to this, people in mature adulthood increasingly seek to turn inward in search of timeless truths. Gerontologist Bernice Neugarten referred to this quality of later life as "interiority" or the growing sense of a deep inner life, a life of *substance*. If we haven't already made an inward spiritual or existential journey in midlife, by mature adulthood we realize that there are fewer things that we can control as individuals. We become more aware of our small place in the vast cosmos, and with this realization comes the emergence of a larger sense of self that has a vital relationship with the personal and collective unconscious. As Jungian analysts Jeffrey Satinover and Lenore Thomson Bentz have pointed out, "The enlargement of personality that can occur in the second half of life is almost universally experienced as a diminishment of one's own egotistical sense of importance and a growing awareness of the presence of God."[67]

Sometimes this growing into spirituality in mature adulthood can be sudden and dramatic. Emanuel Swedenborg was a Swedish scientist, inventor, and philosopher who underwent a powerful spiritual crisis and transpersonal opening when he was in his mid-fifties. He began seeing visions of a spiritual world where he talked with angels and experienced the delights of heaven and the agonies of hell. He believed that he was being directed by Jesus Christ to reveal the doctrine of his second coming. In his journals he wrote, "I saw... in vision that fine bread on a plate was presented to me; which was a sign that the Lord Himself will instruct me since I have now come first into the condition that I know nothing, and all preconceived judgments are taken away from me; which is where learning commences; namely, first to be a child and thus be nursed into knowledge...."[68] Swedenborg spent the next twenty-seven years writing and teaching about his mystical beliefs.

Carl Jung, who was influenced by Swedenborg's work, had his own powerful spiritual awakening in mature adulthood. At the age of sixty-nine, Jung broke his foot and subsequently suffered a heart attack. As he was being given oxygen and injections, he had a vision of the globe of the earth bathed in a blue light and saw incredible vistas stretching from Europe to India. During what appeared to be a near-death experience, he entered a Hindu temple hovering in empty space and received a visit from his doctor who appeared as an archetypal Greek chieftain telling him that he had to return to earth. In the weeks following these visions, Jung began experiencing feelings of ecstasy and had nighttime archetypal visions. In his autobiography Jung wrote: "I felt as though I were floating in space, as though I were safe in the womb of the universe—in a tremendous void, but filled with the highest possible feelings of happiness. 'This is eternal bliss,' I thought, 'This cannot be described; it is far too wonderful!"[69] Both Jung and Swedenborg had previously thought about and written a great deal about spiritual and existential issues, but these mature adult experiences provided them with a sense of clarity and certainty about the spiritual world, a feeling that remained with them for the rest of their lives.[70]

For many other people, mature adulthood represents a time when they are just starting to get an inkling that there are deeper truths waiting to be discovered. After having perhaps experienced illness, the death of loved ones, the culmination of one's career, or upheavals in the lives of sons and daughters, the space has been cleared for the beginnings of a new life based on something other than one's individual ego. Psychotherapist Doree Lynn quotes a sixty-three-year-old female client who said, "Although I entered therapy to try to come to terms with so many possibilities I never considered before, such as my failing health, my dislike of my body which no longer holds its shape, my fear of being alone should my husband Sam die before me, and, of course, my own potential death, the truth is that I never really expected to feel so peaceful and serene as I aged. I think it has to do with my new interest in spirituality and what meaning it holds for me. I have found myself going to church again after a lapse of many years. I'm still not sure I believe in God, but I do seem to believe in something greater than myself."[71] Whether this new shift in perspective emerges as a dramatic change in lifestyle, or as a vague but growing presence of some new dimension one's life, it presages an even greater transformation in the years ahead. In the next chapter, we'll examine how the physical limitations of late adulthood and the realities of approaching death compel us to reckon with these larger forces of existence in a more conclusive way than ever before.

∽∾

———— *The Gift of Mature Adulthood: Benevolence* ————

In June of 2006, the greatest act of philanthropy in history occurred when Warren Buffett, the second richest individual in the world, agreed to give away most of his $44 billion fortune to a foundation started by Bill Gates, the richest person in the world. This event has significance for the field of human development because it illustrates the level of *benevolence* that is possible for people in mature adulthood. Fifty-year-old Bill Gates and seventy-six-year-old Warren Buffett span the entire length of this stage of life. Were it not for the generosity of people in this age group, the world would endure much more poverty, disease, and ignorance than it does today. And it is not just rich philanthropists who show their benevolence. Most people become grandparents during mature adulthood, and their reputation is well known for showering gifts, privileges, encouragement, and guidance on their grandkids. Other people in this age bracket volunteer their time on grand juries and school boards, or devote countless hours to community organizations that support the needs of individuals at all stages of life. During this time period it simply becomes *easier* to be benevolent since this is the peak age for the accumulation of wealth, and because it is a period in life when one generally has both the good health and the time to devote to worthy causes.

Benevolence is a quality that can be expressed at any age. Examples include: an eight-year-old showing a six-year-old how to ride a bike, a young adult taking time out on weekends to mentor a troubled adolescent, and an eighty-five-year-old slipping a ten-dollar bill into a birthday card for a great-granddaughter. You don't need to be a billionaire to be benevolent. You don't need oodles of spare time to demonstrate your giving nature. Five minutes calling a sick friend or relative can bring a smile to a face. Everyone has some expertise that they can share with the world, whether it's baking pies, framing houses, packing boxes, teaching English, or any of a thousand other skills. The only thing that is absolutely required is a willingness to open your heart to the possibilities that exist around you every day for helping others. Essentially, we all need to find our "inner mature adult," regardless of age, so that those around us will be able to benefit from whatever benevolence we have to give. In this way, we can make the world a better place for our having been in it.

──────── *Ways to Explore and Support Mature Adulthood* ────────

FOR YOURSELF
- Exercise regularly, don't smoke, drink in moderation, eat well, and keep your mind active to help ensure that your later adult years are as healthy as possible.
- Plan in detail how you'd like to spend your retirement years (including information about work, travel, study, leisure, or other preferences).

- Organize your financial affairs (if you haven't already done so) to ensure that you have sufficient financial security during your mature and late adulthood.

FOR FRIENDS AND FAMILY

- Help put together a retirement celebration, "croning" ritual, or celebration of elderhood for a friend or relative who is going through an important transition in his or her middle adulthood years.
- Seek out the advice of a wise older individual whom you know for help with personal difficulties you might be going through that would benefit from the wisdom of experience.
- Encourage an older friend or family member who is stagnating after retirement to engage in study and travel (through Elderhostel or similar organizations), or to participate in volunteer activities or other generative experiences.

FOR THE COMMUNITY

- Contribute financially to organizations (hospitals, medical centers, research associations) that are working toward finding cures for diseases that typically strike in middle adulthood and later, such as the American Heart Association, the American Cancer Society, and/or the American Lung Association.
- Support businesses and organizations that hire adults aged fifty and older.
- Foster the development of programs in your community that encourage volunteerism among older adults in schools, clinics, courts, and other public institutions (e.g., Experience Corps, SERVE, etc.).

∞

CHAPTER 11

Late Adulthood: Approaching the Horizon

*To be seventy is like climbing the Alps. You reach a snow-covered
summit and see beyond you the deep valley stretching miles and miles
away, and before you other summits higher and whiter which you
may have the strength to climb or you may not. Then you sit down
and meditate and wonder which it will be.*

—HENRY WADSWORTH LONGFELLOW [1]

In ancient Hindu society when a man reached an age when his hair began
to turn white, his skin started to wrinkle, and his sons and daughters gave
birth to their own children, this was a signal to begin a new stage of life.
He was instructed by the laws of Manu to leave his household responsibilities and enter the forest, where he was to build a fire and perform rituals
to the gods as part of a growing preoccupation with a spiritual life. After
a time, even this stage was to be abandoned, and the old man was
instructed to renounce all worldly goods and activities and travel naked or
dressed only in a robe as a beggar in search of liberation.

Such a sanctified prescription for living was impractical for most
Hindus. They sought instead a modified approach to these ancient laws.
Many Hindus of both sexes discovered that a more realistic way to follow
the spirit of these laws was to begin gradually withdrawing from an active
worldly life and start devoting more time to contemplation, meditation,

and the study of sacred texts as they got older. Today, this tradition still lives on in many parts of India. One study of aging in a northern Indian Bengali village, for example, reported that old age there is characterized by a preoccupation with ways to cut the strings of *Maya*, those attachments to people, places, and things that bind us to this illusory world and to the endless cycle of birth and rebirth. Elder Bengali villagers take up celibacy, give away belongings, and make pilgrimages to holy sites in an attempt to loosen the bindings of Maya and prepare for death.[2]

This sacred approach to late adulthood is very different from the one generally supported by contemporary Western culture. Rather than entering into a stage of life that acknowledges one's own insignificance in the cosmos, many aging people in the West look for ways to extend their worldly lives into an indefinite future. Instead of beginning a process of disengagement with the world, Westerners tend to want to put off being old for as long as possible.

The idea that we can live healthy lives far past the biblical three score and ten years has been at least partially supported by medical science, which has made it possible for more and more people to live healthy lives into their eighties, nineties, and beyond. In fact, the pool of those who live past 100— the centenarians of society—has been increasing by leaps and bounds. Currently, there are about seventy thousand centenarians in the United States. The U.S. Census Department predicts that this number will increase almost thirty-fold to 834,000 by the year 2050.[3] And among the dozen or so projects that are currently studying people over 100, several suggest that if you can make it past the diseases of middle age, then the eighties and beyond can be a time of relatively robust health. Medical expenses, which peak for those sixty to sixty-nine, in fact, actually drop for those 85 to 105.[4] "The centenarians I have met have, with few exceptions, reported that their 90s were essentially problem-free," said Thomas Perls, a Harvard geriatrician who heads the New England Centenarian Study. "Many were employed, sexually active, and enjoyed the outdoors and the arts. They basically carried on as if age were not an issue."[5] Demographers are now starting to count the numbers of "supercentenarians"—people over the age of 110.

Do We Really Have to Die?

This expansion of the life cycle has led some to wonder whether we need to die at all. The quest for eternal life in the body is certainly not a new project. For thousands of years, Chinese Taoists have searched for the secrets of immortality in the control of breathing and diet, and the use of reputedly magical substances such as cinnabar and ginseng.[6] The ancient Greek poet Hesiod spoke of a golden age in humanity's past when mortals never aged. We've also grown up with legends of Shangri-la and the Fountain of Youth filling our imaginations with the possibility of living forever. This has led a few respectable scientists and thinkers, as well as a horde of savvy entrepreneurs, to suggest that the right combination of exercise, diet, meditation, rejuvenation formulas, and genetic engineering may be able to indefinitely prolong life. Biogerontologist Aubrey de Grey, for example, believes it is possible for humans to live thousands of years, and has initiated a project called "Engineered Neglible Senescence" to find ways to permanently reverse the aging process.[7] Inventor and futurist Ray Kurzweil suggests that if you can just stay alive for another fifty years, technology will have advanced to the point where you can live forever.[8]

Such claims, however, have met with sharp criticism from the main-stream scientific community. In one strongly worded manifesto published in the *Scientific American*, three scientists wrote: "No currently marketed intervention—none—has yet proved to slow, stop or reverse human aging, and some can be downright dangerous . . . anyone purporting to offer an anti-aging product today is either mistaken or lying."[9] Most sci-entists now believe that there are biological constraints that limit the human life span to a maximum of around 120 years. There are a number of theories for why we age and eventually have to die. One theory pro-poses that human DNA and other components of life in human cells are exposed to an accumulation of random damage that eventually exceeds the body's own self-repair capabilities. Highly reactive molecules called free radicals, which contain unpaired electrons frantically seeking their mates, damage human cells and are often pointed to as a particular culprit in this wear-and-tear theory. It may be that individuals who live to ripe old ages have genes that limit the activity of these free radicals. Another theory suggests that human cells can only divide a finite number of times. Genetic research indicates that each time a cell divides, the end section of each chromosome—called the telomere—becomes a little shorter. Like the burning of a candle, when the telomere eventually runs out of wick, so to speak, the cell no longer can divide and it dies. While the human body produces a chemical called telomerase that can lengthen the telomere (it keeps the length of chromosomes constant in egg and sperm cells throughout life), it is also responsible for the growth of cells in cancer. Though it has been used to extend the life span of fruit flies, its use as a way to prolong the human life span is still problematic.

Facing Our Fragility in Late Adulthood

Even if we *were* able to extend human life to 150, or even 1,500 years of age, eventually the life clock must run down and the human body must die. In late adulthood we have to face this fact more immediately and intimately than at any other stage of life. Most people in old age see the evidence of their body crumbling before their very eyes on a daily basis. Visual difficulties that are not corrected by eyeglasses increase sharply in the late seventies and eighties. By the age of eighty, 40 percent of all women have had at least one spinal fracture.[10] One out of four men past eighty require treatment of urinary complications caused by an enlarged prostate.[11] By age eighty-five, only one person in twenty is fully mobile.[12] For the majority of the very old, things that younger people take for granted, like taking a bath, opening a jar of pickles, or walking to the neighborhood store, are fraught with difficulty and risk due to failing eyesight and hearing loss, loss of muscle mass, stiffening of joints through osteoarthritis, and brittleness of bones through osteoporosis. As one elderly woman put it: "Every morning I wake up in pain. I wiggle my toes. Good. They still obey. I open my eyes. Good. I can still see. Everything hurts but I get dressed. I walk down to the ocean. Good. It's still there. Now my day can start. About tomorrow I never know. After all, I'm eighty-nine. I can't live forever."[13]

The mind, too, is at risk, the older you get. By age eighty-five, 16 to 35 percent of Americans suffer severe cognitive impairment, half of it due to Alzheimer's disease.[14] First identified in 1906 by German psychiatrists Emil Kraepelin and Alois Alzheimer, Alzheimer's disease is a neurodegenerative disease that causes a progressive loss of cognitive function and results in significant impairment of daily living. It is characterized by abnormal clumps and tangled bundles of fibers in areas of the brain responsible for memory and other mental abilities. People with Alzheimer's disease in its earliest stages have trouble remembering names, activities, and events, and may also experience difficulty solving simple math problems. In the middle stages of the disease, individuals forget how to do simple tasks like comb their hair or brush their teeth, and have problems speaking, reading, or understanding others. In its later stages, people with Alzheimer's disease may become anxious or aggressive, wander away from home, and need around-the-clock care and supervision. People live on average about eight to ten years after diagnosis. Although there is no cure for Alzheimer's disease, a number of interventions have been studied that might delay or minimize its symptoms, including a low calorie diet, a regimen of lifelong learning, certain vitamins and herbs (e.g., vitamin E and ginkgo biloba), and a range of prescription medicines. While there are debates about whether Alzheimer's disease is really a disease or just another feature of aging (half of all individuals by the age of ninety have it), it seems clear that people who are diagnosed with it experience a significant loss in their ability to experience life. According to one rehabilitation specialist, "[W]hat seems lost in the mind of the Alzheimer patient is that very detail—the bitter aftertaste of coffee, a fork laid on a plate, the sound of the kitchen door latch falling into place, that accumulation of concrete experience by which we know life ... [W]hat seems to be lost to the Alzheimer victim, piece by piece, is sense experience, the concrete particulars of the past, until there is only the present, blurred, incomprehensible."[15] This recalls Shakespeare's evocation of late adulthood: "Last scene of all, / That ends this strange eventful history, / Is second childishness and mere oblivion, / Sans teeth, sans eyes, sans taste, sans everything."[16]

One of the greatest fears among the elderly is that serious illness or disability will make it impossible to do everyday tasks like climb stairs, dress without help, or go to the bathroom unassisted. A survey of women seventy-five years of age and older revealed that nearly all were willing to trade off almost their entire life expectancy to avoid a hip fracture that would result in being admitted to a nursing facility.[17] In other words, they'd rather die than go into a nursing home. If and when that fateful day comes, total dependency on others looms as a frightening prospect. One physician writing in the *Journal of the American Medical Association* expresses things from the caregivers' point of view, noting that a day finally comes for many adult children of aging parents when they are confronted with behaviors that require some kind of immediate response: "We simply have to do something. . . . He's always knocking things over and falling . . . she thinks I'm her dead sister."[18]

As a result, many elderly people are sent to nursing homes, continuing-care facilities, or other assisted-living settings.[19] Almost a quarter of those eighty-five and older and about half of those ninety-five and older are in nursing homes. Anthropologist Barbara Meyerhoff has noted that unlike at birth or adolescence, we have few rites of passages for the elderly as they move into this new phase of dependency on others.[20] There are no "coming-of-age" ceremonies that mark the day when they finally give up the family home, or transfer property and privilege to their children, or relinquish their driver's license, or enter into an institution. Instead, these things just happen to them without their being able to grieve the losses and without their being able to acknowledge the changes that are happening to them. Once in a nursing home, the elderly may be treated with little dignity or even abuse. According to a congressional study, one nursing home in three has severe deficiencies that endanger people's health or their lives. Its author, U.S. Representative Henry Waxman, said: "We found examples of residents being punched, choked or kicked by staff members or other residents."[21]

Even if they are lucky and instead "age in place" (e.g., live in their own homes and apartments), many elderly risk entering a twilight zone of invisibility and experiencing derision in a society that values productivity and youth, qualities that are in short supply among the aged. We have a ready-made set of pejorative terms to describe people in late adulthood who block our way walking down the street, keep us waiting impatiently at checkout counters in supermarkets, or veer into our lane on a freeway: gaffer, old fogey, codger, geezer, galoot, old fart, curmudgeon, fuddy-duddy. In Australia, the elderly are called "wrinklies." In Japan, the young call an old man an *umeboshi baba:* a dried old plum. Very old people are significantly devalued in market-based economies like ours. They're not going to be buying luxury homes, fancy cars, or other status symbols since their priorities have changed from impressing their neighbors to appreciating or coping with the little time they have left on earth. They're not up on the latest trends of fashion and culture since they think more about the past than of what will be trendy long after they're dead. As noted earlier, the very old even use fewer health care services than middle agers who are more likely to get expensive heart bypass operations and plastic surgery. So from a marketing point of view, what good are they? Add to this litany of social negatives the fact that old people remind us of death, something most people don't even want to think about. As Shakespeare observed: "... men shut their doors against a setting sun."[22]

It's no wonder, then, that rates of depression are higher in late adulthood than at any other stage of life except adolescence. Although community surveys reveal only 3 percent of elderly people qualify for a diagnosis of major depression, almost 20 percent are found to have significant depressive symptoms, and as many as half of the elderly in long-term care suffer from depression at some time.[23] Old people who take care of spouses suffering from dementia are at especially high risk for depression, as are those who have lost a spouse during the previous year (the mean age for becoming a widow is sixty-six, and for becoming a widower is sixty-nine). Suicide rates are higher among the elderly than for any other age group. Those most at risk, older white men, have six times the national average suicide rate. Tragically, depression remains untreated in up to 90 percent of depressed elders.[24] Studies suggest that 20 percent of old people who kill themselves have visited their doctors *that very day*, 40 percent in the same week, and 70 percent within a month of their suicide. Even among those elderly who do not commit suicide, untreated depression increases the death rate by more than 50 percent independent of their physical health, and raises the risk of dying after a heart attack by a factor of five.[25] It appears that physical illness and depression interact in a downward spiral reinforcing each other: Persistent or severe illness raises the risk of depression, which increases the risk for further illness, more depression, and so on.[26] The sense of hopelessness and futility experienced by many older people has been articulated by French philosopher Jean Amery, who writes, "[Old people] look into their space to see what it will be like after them: a house where children and their children's children will be active and will work; a tombstone, gray and powerful will testify for them . . . but the house will deteriorate and the grandchildren will be scattered to all the winds . . . House and home . . . and tomb, everything will be like the nights of love and pain of the deceased: as good as if they had never existed."[27]

Honoring the Historical Mind

That the elderly should despair as they do and be denigrated by the society they have supported for much of their lives is a tragedy of King Lear proportions. After having spent their lives acquiring experiences, storing up knowledge, and gaining wisdom, they look up from their hard-won collection of inner riches to discover that nobody around them seems to give a damn. Yet, here in these time-ripened personalities lies a treasure of incomparable value: the historical mind. Old people have direct and immediate access to memories of long past events that sophisticated historians can only guess at with their theories, books, and lectures. When the oldest documented person in the world, the Frenchwoman Jeanne Calment, died in 1997 at the age of 122, it was revealed that she had met Vincent van Gogh as a child. What a marvel to contemplate that someone in our own time should have touched history in such an intimate way! Many of our own elders have had experiences, though perhaps less dramatic or distant in time, that are nevertheless significant connections with the atmosphere of other times, inaccessible to the rest of us: experiences of past wars, revolutions, depressions, cultural upheavals, and contact with great individuals of the past.

Consider, for example, your own grandparents or great-grandparents who attended lectures or concerts as children where they saw and heard famous actors, politicians, musicians, orators, or writers who are now long dead. Eighty-five-year-olds living today were entering their twenties at a time when the Japanese bombed Pearl Harbor, Orson Welles's film *Citizen Kane* was released, and the word *antibiotic* was first coined. More compellingly, they lived through times that had quite a distinctly different feel in contrast to today's world: times where everything from outdoor lighting and telephone communication to cultural values and intellectual trends were qualitatively different from current experience. Here, for example, are some reminiscences of Carolyn Peery, a ninety-nine-year-old African American, who shared her memories and some old photographs with cultural historian Studs Terkel: ". . . Here's a picture of my mother-in-law. She was born into slavery. She was six years old when freedom was declared. . . . My mother-in-law remembered seeing the slaves get behind the door, jumping up and down, saying 'God bless Mr. Lincoln. God bless Mr. Lincoln.'"[28]

Individuals in late adulthood have historical access not just to one era, but to a succession of eras and the events and trends that accompanied them, which gives them a sense of the big picture. Younger people are awed and shaken up as they go through events for the first time, whereas older people have seen them come and seen them go, and then seen them come once again. They have a longer view of history and a broader scope on current events. They hold the memory of a culture, its mores, its values, its treasures, and its misfortunes better than anyone else. There is no way to replicate this kind of expertise at an earlier age. You can't manufacture experience out of nothing. You've got to do the time. And people in late adulthood have done the time. That's one of the reasons why traditional cultures and their mythic heroes have so often consulted the very old for advice on important matters; why, for example, Agamemnon turned to the aged Nestor for advice on winning the Trojan War, or why Odysseus followed the advice of the ageless blind seer Teresias for getting back home to Ithaca.

Significantly, studies in cognitive science suggest that while the short-term memories of the elderly may deteriorate as they age, particularly when dementias are present, their long-term memories, especially for far distant events in their past, actually become more acute in some cases.[29] Though they may have difficulty remembering what they had for breakfast that morning, they can vividly recall the color of the leaves the autumn when they went off to college as a youth. Arthur Freeman was an eighty-six-year-old former civil service employee who suffered from severe dementia, experiencing delusions, violent outbursts, and short-term memory problems. But when asked about his childhood, he began to share how he played by the river when he was a child: "Yes we had both sides of the river itself . . . there was one part there were . . . er . . . trees, we played in there, and there was stones between the trees and the grass. There was stones running with the water. Oh many times we plunged across the . . . water . . . the bricks, stones piled like this. Plenty of bricks like that. We were running across those, across the river."[30] Although riddled with syntactic and semantic errors, Freeman's narrative shows a detailed memory for long passed events.

Researchers refer to this capacity of older adults to remember events early in their lives as the "reminiscence bump" and report that these memories often tend to cluster around events in childhood, adolescence, and early adulthood. These were the stages of life when the individual was forming a personal identity and represent those times when they essentially became themselves as contributing members of society. It could be that this renewed memory among elders for seminal events in their youth confers advantages to cultures or even to the species as a whole. Those who possess this trait can pass on vital information to younger people before they die about how they created themselves in youth, and in the process share how they learned to maintain the coherence of their culture.

Interestingly, recent studies suggest that the memories of individuals in late adulthood are actually sharper in countries where the elderly are highly valued, such as China, compared to those cultures where the old are neglected or denigrated.[31] At the same time, vocabulary skills continue to stay robust until the early eighties. In one study, people at age eighty-one performed at a higher level on vocabulary tests than people at age twenty-five.[32] Hence, both memory for distant events and the ability to communicate these memories verbally are optimal in late adulthood for many individuals. This may explain why very old people are so often the storytellers and cultural guardians of society. As Simone de Beauvoir writes about the people of Bali: "The elderly men work little: they talk and chew betel. But they have many duties—they direct the village assembly, practice medicine, tell tales, and teach the young poetry and art . . . Their opinion is asked on every subject."[33]

The Spiritual Lives of Elders

Liberated from the workaday roles of conventional society, people in late adulthood are free to stand apart from the society and serve as the feisty Socrates, the stormy Jeremiah, or the healer-crone Mother Teresa of their culture. As one eighty-six-year-old woman stated: "Now I don't care a bit about what people think . . . I dare to go out biking or walking in [X-town] wearing torn stockings, I couldn't do that before. . . . Sometimes I think, but I really can't do this, you know . . . but I do it anyway."[34] New avenues of creativity are opened up as elders begin to realize latent potentials and remember forgotten abilities. Perhaps it is here, almost at life's end, when the light of destiny originally silenced by the angel of forgetfulness in pre-birth finally begins to shine once again. Jungian analyst Florida Scott-Maxwell writes of this newly born power discovered late in life: "[a] secret we carry is that though drab outside-wreckage to the eye . . . inside we flame with a wild life that is almost incommunicable."[35] It may have been this fire that prompted Grandma Moses to begin painting at seventy-eight, Kin Narita and Gin Kanie to launch a singing career in Japan at age 100, and Su Juxian to publish his first book of poetry in China at age

104. As author Joan M. Erikson, the wife of Erik Erikson, put it: "I am profoundly moved, for I am growing old and feel shabby, and suddenly great riches present themselves and enlighten every part of my body and reach out to beauty everywhere."[36]

Approaching the end of life, people in late adulthood have an unparalleled view of life's horizon as they peer into the mysteries beyond. Old age brings with it access to a wider scope of being; to the collective unconscious of the psyche; to the transpersonal realms of human existence. Among the Fon of Benin in West Africa the oldest living man is said to be "between the two worlds of the living and the dead."[37] In a study of western China completed in the 1930s, the aged of both sexes were found to be intensely interested in their afterlives, cultivating spiritual knowledge in preparation for ancestorhood.[38] The myths and stories of many cultures speak of this opening to spirituality late in life. Psychiatrist Allan B. Chinen has examined fairy tales from world literature that depict older persons living in great outer poverty who by chance stumble upon something supernatural. He shares, for example, the Japanese tale of Princess Moonlight, a story about an old couple who find a child embedded in a stalk while they are cutting bamboo. They raise her as their own and she grows up to become the most beautiful and radiant lady in the land. Men come from all over to woo her, including the emperor himself, but she refuses them and finally reveals to the couple that she is really a celestial being and must return to heaven. They spend the rest of their days looking up at her shining among the stars.[39] This enchanting tale reminds me of the life of renowned author Iris Murdoch, who after developing Alzheimer's disease, used to enjoy watching the British children's TV show *Teletubbies*. At the end of each episode, a joyful baby's face appears in the sky as the sun. Her husband, John Bayley, reported: "Iris always returned its beaming smile."[40]

Young children and the very old share the experience of living at life's borders where the transpersonal life is more active than at any other time. As a result, people in late adulthood often recover a spiritual outlook on life by going back to remembrances of experiences in childhood. As an eighty-six-year-old woman related to a gerontology researcher, "You go back to childhood almost daily. It comes without reflection. I talked to a good friend about this . . . We both go back to the town where we grew up [in our thoughts] . . . Childhood means much more than one thinks. I go back to it all the time."[41] Jungian analyst Frances Wickes wrote about a dream she had when she was just a three-year-old that continued to influence her into her nineties: "I am in a high meadow, unknown yet strangely familiar. In its center is Behemoth: huge, terrifying, evil. By his side, unafraid and rooted in its own serenity, is a single bluet, that smallest flower of meadow or woodland, tiny, fragile, perfect in its four-petaled innocence." This dream, she wrote, "lived on in the psyche of an old, old woman until it blossomed into a faith by which, in her old age she lived; a faith in life itself, to which she sought to give testimony."[42]

Unfortunately, caregivers usually ignore these transpersonal experiences in late adulthood, just as parents and teachers dismiss transpersonal experiences in early childhood. In fact, most of the strengths that we've enumerated above as part of late adulthood—the historical mind, the broad sweep of perspective, the active storytelling abilities, the cultural guardianship, and the spiritual or transpersonal vision—in other words, the truly vital functions that old people have traditionally carried out in many cultures, are viewed as insignificant in the modern Western world. With more and more people reaching older ages in our culture, the singular wisdom that was the prerogative of those rare individuals who made it into old age in earlier times has lost its cachet, just as a precious metal or gem loses much of its value when it becomes possible to synthesize mass quantities of it. Moreover, the historical or cultural mind of the elderly has less value in a culture that turns increasingly to video, the Internet, or other media for high-impact reporting of historical and cultural events. Also, we live in a culture that is always changing, so the need to have elders around to maintain the sense of continuity in a long cultural tradition has largely disappeared. Finally, because we live in a materialistic culture—one where greed rules even where the churches are strong—there is little interest in the spiritual experiences of old people that may transcend conventional religious traditions and beliefs. Reflecting on the ways in which the wisdom of our elders have been marginalized, we have to ask ourselves, may it not be our *culture* that is deteriorating more than our elders? And if this is the case, then what great treasures are being lost because we ignore what they have to tell us?

Summing Up a Life

The greatest gift we can give to our elders is our attention: We simply must learn to *listen* to them once again. More than thirty years ago, psychiatrist Robert Butler coined the term *life review* to describe what he believed was a naturally occurring and universal mental process among the elderly to revive past experiences. He regarded the life review as the attempt of the very old to reintegrate memories, especially those involving conflict, into their current lives.[43] When I was a teacher in my mid-twenties, I used to visit an elderly French-Canadian woman named Bella who lived alone in her apartment in Montreal. She would cook me dinner, offer Cinzano to drink afterward (I declined, being a nondrinker), and then proceed to tell me about her life. Much of it had been difficult: Her son had died young, her husband had been much older and distant, she had regretfully left her spiritual teacher. And yet, through the telling of her story, she seemed to be working toward some kind of reconciliation and acceptance of her conflicted life.

Unfortunately, most of us regard the seemingly endless reminiscing of old people as a nuisance. We'd like to cut our visits to parents or grandparents short so that we can tend to our busy lives. Nevertheless, they persist in their ruminations about a moment of triumph or terror in a foreign war, or the time they missed a promotion with General Electric, or the day they received an award for their prize petunias at the state fair. Sometimes we even mistake their going on about the past with the symptoms of Alzheimer's disease. And yet the gift of attention that we give to our elders can be very healing. Having reached the end of their lives, people in late adulthood ask themselves: Did my life have any meaning? According to Erik Erikson, the answers they receive from this question will help determine whether they feel a sense of *integrity* about their lives, or instead, fall into *despair*. If a person can accept his life as something that *had to be*, says Erikson, then it becomes possible to face death without fear.[44]

Sometimes this acceptance is given visible form in a significant way at the very end of life as a kind of "swan song." This expression arises out of the Greek legend that the swan, which doesn't actually sing, is capable of giving voice to something like a song near the end of its life. Socrates believed that the song was a joyful one because it signaled that the swan was soon to join Apollo, the god of poetry and music that it served. At the end of Homer's epic, the father of Odysseus, Laertes, who is now an old man, dons the armor of his youth and joins his son and grandson in a swan song of last battle. The expression *swan song* has now come to be associated with the last work, or nearly final work, of a poet, composer, artist, or other creative person. It is generally seen as an attempt to sum up their creative lives in works that may be infused with great power or tinged with resignation, serenity, triumph, or acceptance. The Finnish composer Jean Sibelius, for example, had a successful career writing symphonies and other works, but apparently produced no new compositions during the last three decades of his life until it was discovered that in his ninety-second year he took up his composer's pen one final time to orchestrate a song from Shakespeare's *Twelfth Night* entitled, "Come Away, Death."[45] Another example can be seen in the life of African-American dancer and actor Josephine Baker, whose performances captivated Parisian audiences in the 1920s but whose career went into decline in the following decades. In 1975, however, at the age of sixty-eight, she returned to Paris to star in a retrospective show celebrating her fifty years in the theater. The show opened to rave reviews. A week later, she died in bed from a cerebral hemorrhage with glowing newspaper reviews spread around her.

Swan songs also show up in the lives of so-called ordinary people. One beautiful example appears in Akira Kurosawa's magnificent film *Ikiru*. The protagonist is a lifeless bureaucrat who has toiled away in a meaningless existence at the Tokyo City Hall for several decades, only to discover late in life that he has terminal stomach cancer. This realization ultimately shocks him into one final redemptive act to make up for his years of shallowness and self-absorption: He helps to create a children's playground on what was once a stagnant pond. Similarly, in the lives of our elderly relatives or friends, a swan song might be a last effort to support a worthy cause, a gift given in one's last days, or a small act of kindness before dying. It may be that in late adulthood such simple acts serve as a way of signaling that a human being has finally achieved some sort of rapprochement with life and with death. With the great adventure of life behind them, and the mystery of the unknown before them, such swan songs may be among the most poignant and precious manifestations of the human condition. We turn to that final mystery now in the next chapter, and examine the human encounter with death.

◦∞◦

The Gift of Late Adulthood: Wisdom

When I was thirteen and lived for a year with my grandmother, I used to mercilessly tease one of my cousins, who would get angry, cry, and stomp around the room in a fury. Instead of scolding me, Nana would give me a compassionate look and say in a kindly way, "Don't make her look *ugly!*" To this day, I can still hear the precise way in which she pronounced that word, and in that sound I hear the wisdom of my elders speaking. Sadly, it seems that much of the news about the elderly in today's world is negative, focusing on Alzheimer's disease, depression, abuse, poverty, and neglect. We seem to have forgotten that in past times, older people were regarded as the repositories of cultural wisdom. By late adulthood, people have done a lot of living. They've had successes and failures, made mistakes and discovered solutions, undergone a wide range of life events, and met up with many different types of people along the way. This rich tapestry of experience is mirrored in the aging brain, which holds a wealth of neural networks forged from innumerable interactions with life. These ancient minds see beyond the fads, trends, and moods that captivate the young.

They cut through to the deeper moral, aesthetic, and spiritual truths of life. Such wisdom is very much needed in a society that values quick sound bites and snappy one-liners. Instead of dismissing our elders by fitting them into convenient stereotypes of decrepitude, we ought instead to listen to what they have to say to us. Perhaps we will discover that their wisdom slows us down a bit and makes us think about what is really important in life in the long run.

The gift of wisdom is available to us at any time in our lives. We see this wisdom in the young child who asks timeless questions. We see it in the adolescent who desires to penetrate through adult hypocrisy and get to the essential truth of things. We see it in the midlife adult who gains new insight from having reevaluated his past in midcareer. In a sense, we all possess an "inner elder" that helps direct our lives. It's that part of ourselves that resides above our daily actions and calmly observes what we're doing against the backdrop of a larger perspective. If we're inwardly quiet, we can hear wisdom's voice speaking to us even in moments of turmoil or despair. To help develop our inner wisdom, we can meditate, pray, read texts from sacred traditions, keep a journal of our deepest thoughts, or spend time in nature or other sacred settings. But one of the best ways to discover wisdom in ourselves is to spend time with people who are themselves wise. And in many cases, it is among the very old that we will find the wisest among us. By paying attention to their words, their glances, and even the most trivial of their actions, we can begin to see what a full life really looks like and use this image of sagacity to help direct the course of our own journey through life.

Ways to Explore and Support Late Adulthood

FOR YOURSELF
- Look at yourself in a mirror and imagine what you will look like when you are very old.
- Determine what specific risk factors you must eliminate (e.g., smoking, drinking), and what positive life style choices you need

to initiate (e.g., exercise, diet) in order to have good health in late adulthood. Then, initiate a consistent plan.

- Make concrete plans to help ensure that you will be well cared for in your final years of life, by considering long term care insurance, making sound financial investments, and investigating the range of living options available to you as you grow old.

For Friends and Family

- Help an elderly family member or friend record her life story in some way through audio or videotape, writings, photos, or a scrapbook of memorabilia.
- Pay visits to elderly friends or relations who are physically, emotionally, or mentally ailing and provide them with cheer, conversation, or silent support.
- Regularly write, call, or send flowers or other tokens of affection to elderly friends or family members who are not living in your area and have few social contacts.

For the Community

- Volunteer to visit the elderly in a nursing home or other assisted living facility, and listen to their stories, sing songs, help with hobbies, or provide other forms of encouragement and support.
- Contribute to organizations that are dedicated to fighting ageism and that support the rights of the elderly.
- Report instances of elder abuse that you may learn about in your community to the appropriate authorities.

～∞～

CHAPTER 12

Death and Dying: Crossing the Bridge

Remember me as you draw nigh
As you are now, so once was I.
As I am now, so must you be,
Prepare for death and follow me.

—Epitaph found on Connecticut gravestone (1830)[1]

Once upon a time there was a powerful king named Gilgamesh who ruled over Uruk, a city set between the Tigris and the Euphrates rivers in ancient Babylonia. He was very lonely in his greatness until he met Enkidu, an uncivilized man about his own age. With Enkidu in his life, Gilgamesh was very happy, and together they went on a heroic quest to kill Humbaba the Evil One and slay the Bull of Heaven. During their adventures Enkidu was injured and eventually died. Gilgamesh was devastated by the death of his friend. At great peril to himself he crossed over to the far side of the waters of death in search of eternal life so that his friend Enkidu might be resurrected. Arriving at his destination, he was greeted by his ancestor Utnapishtim, who told him about a plant lying at the bottom of a river whose name means "as an old man, man becomes young again." Utnapishtim told him that this plant would bring his friend back to life. In great anticipation, Gilgamesh rushed to put weights on his feet and descended to the bottom of the river, where he joyously retrieved the magical rose-colored herb. On his journey back home to Uruk, Gilgamesh happened to stop for a rest and took a brief dip in a nearby river. While he was soaking in the pool, a snake came along and ate the plant that he had left unguarded on the riverbank. Gilgamesh went home with no solution to the problem of death and only the pain of loss for his best friend Enkidu.[2]

Thus ends the tale of Gilgamesh, the oldest major literary work in Western civilization. This story, inscribed on clay tablets, was deciphered by British archeologists in the late 1800s and dates back four thousand years. The story of Gilgamesh strikes a deep chord for those of us who read it so many years later, because Gilgamesh's pain mirrors our own anguish, confusion, and fear about death. The story ultimately offers no salvation, no miracle cure, and no happy ending. Death is defined in this tale as a termination that we must all accept as a part of being human. It is this great fact that ultimately unites every living being. Death, as cultural historian Studs Terkel points out, is the one experience that none of us have had, that all of us *will* have. Thus, we all share a collective uncertainty of what this experience will be, and a universal assurance—covered over as it might be by layers of denial—that it will indeed happen at some point in our lives.

Here's an obvious fact that becomes quite startling if you think about it long enough: Barring a major technological advance or a divine miracle, all six and a half billion people now living on the planet will be dead in one hundred and twenty-five years, if not sooner. And each death will be a personal drama with its own emotions, its own web of social connections (or lack thereof), and its own unique story. Yet all these six and a half billion deaths will come down to the same thing, at least in biological terms. The physical body will stop functioning. It will die, decay, and be disposed of. For each of us, this will occur at a very specific moment sometime in the next several decades. If you wish, you may consult Internet sites that will tabulate your vital statistics—age, gender, health status, and lifestyle—and then proceed to tell you how many years you have left.[3] One site will even provide you with a personalized "death clock" that will show your time slipping away.[4] Even taxes don't hold this level of certainty, although humorist Max Beerbohm suggested that many people won't admit it. He mused, "Even you, unassuming reader, go about with a vague notion that in your case, somehow, the ultimate demand of nature will be waived."[5]

Why We Die

Probably all of us during our lifetimes have experienced some variation of the thought Gilgamesh had: "Wouldn't it be great if death didn't exist and we could live forever!" In the last chapter we explored the biological or *body up* reasons for why this is improbable, if not impossible. We'll explore some existential or *spirit down* reasons for why this *may* be possible in the next chapter. But, for the moment, consider this question: Would it *really* be better never to die? The ancient Greeks answered this question in their mythology by telling the story of Tithonus, who was the brother of Priam, the future king of Troy. Eos, the goddess of the Dawn, fell in love with the human Tithonus and asked Zeus to grant him immortality, which Zeus proceeded to do. But she forgot to ask for eternal youth for him, and so Tithonus got older and grayer and more withered with every passing year until finally, out of mercy or desperation, Eos turned him into a grasshopper, forever begging to die.[6]

The message seems to be: It just isn't *natural* to live forever. After all, what are you going to do with all that time on your hands? It's part of the mystery of existence for things to be born, to grow, to wither, and then to die, only to be replaced by new life. Take a walk out in nature during springtime. Watch the tender young green plants shoot up around the old stiff and rotting stalks from last season. The death of the old makes way for the birth of the new in an endless cycle in the natural world. Human beings, to the extent that they are a part of the natural world (e.g., part of the *body up* line of development), must likewise grow old and die to make a place for new life. As Tennyson put it: "Old men must die; or the world would grow mouldy, would only breed the past again."[7] This is the ultimate form of generativity according to Michel de Montaigne: "to give place to others, as others have given place to you."

To be sure, the world's populations have never accepted death as a natural event, especially when it occurs in youth. In many myths around the world, death is treated as an unnatural occurrence in the *cosmic* order of things, and we will also examine this side of the story in the next chapter. However, for most of humanity's history, and still in many places around the world, death has been experienced as a part of the natural flow of life. In Bali, entire towns turn out for daylong cremation ceremonies. In Mexico, people remember the dead with skeletons, candles, and flowers during the annual Día de los Muertos ("Day of the Dead") festival. In some Arctic cultures, frail elders in times past willingly offered themselves to be euthanized at public gatherings.

The History of Death in America

Even in western Europe and America, death was considered a natural and public event for centuries. After the bubonic plague or Black Death of the fourteenth century in Europe, death became a cultural obsession. People wrote books on the art of dying, and a Christian tradition established itself that aspired toward a "noble death." In this ideal, the dying person would make his last glorious confession on his deathbed in the presence of the priest, family, friends, neighbors, and even strangers who happened along. According to social historian Philippe Aires, "The dying man's bed-chamber became a public place to be entered freely. At the end of the eighteenth century, doctors who were discovering the first principles of hygiene complained about the overcrowded bedrooms of the dying. In the early nineteenth century, passers-by who met the priest bearing the last sacrament still formed a little procession and accompanied him into the sickroom."[8] These strangers hoped to witness a victory of the Soul over the Devil that might boost their own chances for salvation.

Until the end of the nineteenth century in the United States, virtually everyone died at home, and it was common for groups of women to come into the house after a death and lay out the body for viewing in the family parlor. People wore black armbands, put wreaths on doors, made regular graveside visits, and displayed deathbed pictures and paintings.

When someone died in a community, everything stopped for a while so that this experience could be assimilated and integrated. With the beginning of the twentieth century, however, death began to disappear from public view. As methods of combating disease became more technologically proficient, people went to hospitals to die alone. By 1949, half of all U.S. deaths took place in hospitals. Philippe Aires observed, "In the course of the twentieth century, an absolutely new type of dying has made an appearance in some of the most industrialized, urbanized, and technologically advanced areas of the Western world ... Except for the death of statesmen, society has banished death. In the towns, there is no way of knowing that something has happened ... Society no longer observes a pause; the disappearance of an individual no longer affects its continuity. Everything in town goes on as if nobody died anymore."[9]

Although 90 percent of people currently report that they wish to die at home, this seems unlikely for most, since 80 percent of deaths in the U.S. now take place in hospitals.[10] Of this 80 percent, according to surgeon Sherwin Nuland, author of *How We Die*, almost all of them are hidden from the people who were closest to them in their lives.[11] This means that when you die there is a very good chance that you will die in a hospital room surrounded by life-saving machinery with tubes and needles stuck into you and all the expertise of modern science available to you, but without the contact of family members or other loved ones at the moment of your death. "Patients and families often feel abandoned at the end of life," says David Weissman, M.D., director of the palliative medicine program at the Medical College of Wisconsin. "Doctors tell patients there is nothing more they can do for them, but there is."[12]

Chances are good, as well, that you will spend your last days in some pain or in a coma with little opportunity to reflect on the meaning of your life and its passing. In the largest study of dying patients in American hospitals, it was reported that half died with moderate to severe pain that was not relieved by medications, and 40 percent spent at least ten days in a coma attached to a mechanical ventilator or in an intensive care unit separated for the most part from their families.[13] The availability (for those who can afford them) of life-prolonging surgery, chemotherapy, radiation treatments, respirators, CPR, feeding tubes, painkillers, antibiotics, and other miracles of modern science means that many chronically ill people in late adulthood can be kept alive indefinitely regardless of what this may do to the quality of their final days, weeks, or months of life. Doctors are trained to keep treating the illness and never to give up, even when this means that an old person will have to endure pain from surgeries, suffer debilitating side effects from drugs and treatments, and undergo other insults to their body and dignity to the very end of their days.

Preparing for the Final Exit

Thus, we have a major dilemma. On the one hand, modern medicine has evolved a huge arsenal of technological devices, drugs, and procedures to prolong human life. And a large part of the ethos of a physician is to cure disease and save lives. On the other hand, as we've already noted, growing old and dying is a natural process. When does it become appropriate to say that an elderly patient is no longer fighting illness, but instead, is involved in the process of dying? Unfortunately, it appears that most medical personnel lack an appropriate framework for answering this question. A 1999 survey by the Liaison Committee on Medical Education revealed that only 4 out of 125 medical schools had a required course on death and dying.[14] Another study indicated that leading medical textbooks failed to treat the subject of death and dying in a frank and honest manner.[15] Further studies have shown that doctors and nurses are reluctant to discuss death with seriously ill patients.[16]

In many cases, medical personnel resort to euphemisms when discussing death. One oncologist expressed his own amazement at this level of denial among his fellow doctors: "The most common metaphor I hear clinicians use when speaking to non-medical personnel and families is 'lost.' 'We lost the patient,' or 'We attempted resuscitation, but lost him anyway.' When I first came to this country, this struck me as rather odd. I wanted to say, 'Well, we didn't really lose your husband. We know where he is, it's just . . . he's not breathing there anymore.'"[17] Terminally ill patients and their families seem similarly reluctant to bring up the subject of dying and death. In one survey, only 14 percent of patients had prepared advance directives indicating when they would prefer to stop receiving life-saving measures and listing the person who would make the decision to terminate life support.[18]

On the other hand, if you've planned ahead, you might be fortunate enough to enter a hospice program and die at home or in some other natural setting surrounded by loved ones. The modern hospice movement was initiated in 1967 at St. Christopher's Hospice in London by Dame Cicely Saunders. There are currently about eight thousand hospices around the world. The hospice philosophy is based upon the belief that dying people should be in a supportive environment, usually at home, and be as free from pain as possible. Dame Saunders's innovation was to provide patients with painkillers *before* they had pain, rather than after the pain starts, or an hour before visiting hours. This palliative care, as it came to be known, was combined with help to the family to provide support for their dying relative, assistance in planning funeral arrangements, and grief therapy for family members of the deceased. Research suggests that hospice patients are more likely than nonhospice patients to receive more adequate pain relief and that both patients and caregivers are more likely to experience satisfaction from services, especially regarding home care.[19]

In a hospice program counselors will work with you and help you articulate your concerns, needs, and wishes for the last part of your life and its aftermath. They'll assist you in taking care of legal and financial matters, in drawing up living wills specifying how long you'd want to be on life support, what you'd like done with your body, and other postmortem issues. They'll provide emotional and spiritual support, helping you deal with feelings that come up at each stage of the dying process, including making sense out of your life and your death. They'll help you communicate with and even reconcile with loved ones, and assist you in saying good-bye to them when the time is appropriate. They'll also guide you and your family in making funeral arrangements, and attend to other matters after you are dead. Asked how she herself would want to die, Dame

Saunders responded, "Everybody else says they want to die suddenly, but I say I'd like to die of cancer, because it gives me time to say I'm sorry, and thank you, and goodbye."[20] She got her wish, dying of cancer at the age of eighty-seven in 2005, at the hospice she herself had founded.

Learning About the Facts of Death

Saying good-bye to life may be easier for those who possess a sound knowledge about the realities of physical death. In earlier times people kept reminders of death, or *memento mori*, to help them remember that death comes to everyone. In ancient Rome miniature coffins were sometimes passed among guests at a dinner party as a stimulus to enjoy the present fleeting moment before it slipped away forever. During the death-obsessed Middle Ages, prostitutes and priests alike wore death-head rings, while monks slept in their coffins each night as a constant reminder of their coming fate. Public clocks would be adorned with mottos such as *ultima forsan* ("perhaps the last [hour]") or *vulnerant omnes, ultima necat* ("they all wound, and the last kills"). In modern times we needn't be quite so morbid in our focus on death, but getting to know some of the details about dying and death can help make it less mysterious and frightening. As Carl Jung pointed out in his book *Modern Man in Search of a Soul*, ". . . shrinking away from [death] is something unhealthy and abnormal which robs the second half of life of its purpose."[21]

According to Sherwin Nuland, there is an 85 percent chance that you will die of one or more of the following conditions if you live into late adulthood: cancer, obesity, atherosclerosis, hypertension, adult-onset diabetes, mental deterioration such as Alzheimer's or other dementias, or decreased resistance to infection. The biggest cause of them all is coronary artery disease, which currently kills at least half of all people in the United States. Nuland points out that every life-ending disease or accident, whether it be a heart attack, suicide, brain tumor, stroke, or murder, relies upon one or more of five basic physiological processes: the stoppage of circulation, the inadequate transportation of oxygen to tissues, the flickering out of brain function, the failure of organs, or the destruction of vital centers. "These are the weapons of every horseman of death," says Nuland.[22] The bottom line is air. "Man is an obligate aerobe," according to the ancient Greek physician Hippocrates. Without oxygen delivered directly to the brain, each one of us would die within two to four minutes.

Knowing exactly *when* you are dying may be more difficult to pin down. As one dramatist noted, "Death hath ten thousand doors for men to take their exits."[23] Joanne Lynn, director of the Center to Improve Care of the Dying at the George Washington School of Medicine and Health Sciences in Washington, D.C., indicates that only 20 percent of us will die in a phase that is clearly "dying."[24] More likely, there will be a series of chronic diseases, hospitalizations, recoveries, and relapses before the end draws near. Another 20 to 25 percent of Americans will die suddenly, that is within a few hours of onset of symptoms, usually from a heart attack. Toward the very end, you may go through what clinicians call an "agonal phase," otherwise known as "death agonies" or the "death rattle" caused by relaxation of the muscles of the throat. According to Sherwin Nuland, "In the ultimate agonal moments, the rapid onset of final oblivion is accompanied either by the cessation of breathing or by a short series of great heaving gasps; on rare occasions . . . violent tightening of . . . laryngeal muscles into a terrifying bark. Simultaneously, the chest or shoulders will sometimes heave once or twice and there may be a brief agonal convulsion."[25]

The agonal phase is followed by what scientists call "clinical death," which is the interval after the heart has stopped beating, and where there is no breathing or measurable brain function, but when it's still possible to rescue the person. Finally, if no resuscitation occurs within a handful of minutes, the eyes become dulled, the pupils dilate, the eyeballs flatten out, and you die. Traditionally, the criteria for death was an absence of a heartbeat or the cessation of breathing, but in 1968 this changed to "brain death," defined as: "signs of loss of all reflexes, lack of response to vigorous external stimuli, and absence of electrical activity as shown by a flat electroencephalogram for a sufficient number of hours."[26] It is then that the miracle of physiological life, which started with a single cell and blossomed into 100,000 billion cells by late adulthood, ceases to be.

The Brighter Side of Dying

While the above description is sobering, there are indications that the act of dying isn't all about pain, distress, and coma, but that it has a positive, and even transcendent dimension. Stephen J. Levine, founder of the Hanuman Foundation Dying Center, a group that assists individuals in their dying process, has witnessed hundreds of deaths and reports, "From our experience with many patients at the time they are dying, we have come to see that the moment of death is often a moment of great quietude and peace. That often even those who have approached death with trepidation, in the moments before death, have an opening . . . It seems that the process of dying is like a melting, a dissolving . . . "[27] There have been a number of studies that support this more positive view of death and dying. Psychologists Karlis Osis and Erlendur Haraldsson, for example, conducted studies of "deathbed visions," where in the hours, days, or weeks before death the dying person witnessed and conversed with dead relatives, saw visions of other worlds, and experienced feelings of peace and serenity. They wrote about one sixty-five-year-old man with cancer of the stomach who "would look up to the wall and his eyes and face would brighten up as if he saw a person. He'd speak of the light, brightness, saw people who seemed real to him. He would say, 'Hello,' and 'There's my mother.' After it was over he closed his eyes and seemed very peaceful . . . Before the hallucinations he was very ill and nauseous; afterwards he was serene and peaceful."[28] In another account, an American woman dying of heart disease in her seventies "hallucinated about people who had recently expired. As time progressed she hallucinated about people who had been dead a long time. She regressed in age with each hallucination until finally she was in her baby stage . . . and expired curled up in a uterine position."[29]

Further indications that dying may have its resplendent side are drawn from accounts of people who have come close to death from accidents or illness but then have been brought back to life through chance or medical intervention. These "near-death experiences" (NDEs) vary from person to person, but often include one or more of the following features:

seeing other worlds, meeting guardian angels, experiencing tremendous peace, meeting friends or relatives who have died, going through a tunnel and encountering light, and having one's whole life pass by in a life review. One of the earliest published reports of an NDE is from Albert Heim, a Swiss geology professor who wrote at the end of the nineteenth century about his own close shave with death when he fell off a glacial sheet while climbing in the Swiss Alps. He dropped about sixty-five feet before landing on a border of snow. Heim writes: "I saw my whole past life take place in many images, as though on a stage at some distance from me . . . Everything was transfigured as though by a heavenly light and everything was beautiful without grief, without anxiety, and without pain . . . conflict had been transmuted into love. Elevated and harmonious thoughts dominated and united the individual images, and like magnificent music a divine calm swept through my soul . . . Then I heard a dull thud and my fall was over."[30] A more recent study in the British medical journal *Lancet* examined 344 cardiac patients in the Netherlands who had been resuscitated by CPR from clinical death, and reported that 18 percent of the subjects had near-death experiences. Many of these individuals were profoundly affected by their experiences even years later, becoming more empathic and intuitive, less afraid of death, and showing a strong belief in an afterlife.[31]

While NDEs have been used to support a belief in an afterlife—a topic we will take up in our next chapter—many skeptics regard near-death experiences as the brain's normal response to trauma. An article in the scientific journal *Nature* suggested that out-of-body experiences occurring during a NDE might be due to the misfiring under great stress of a part of our brain called the angular gyrus,which analyzes sensory data to give us a perception of our own bodies.[32] Other researchers have suggested that near-death experiences occur as brain cells die from lack of oxygen, or when the brain releases pain-reducing chemicals called endorphins. Interestingly, former magician and professional debunker of the supernatural James Randi (The Amazing Randi) has had two near-death experiences himself. He comments, "I've been through it twice and I recall quite distinctly seeing the tunnel and the light . . . It's what happens when the nervous system begins to relax."[33] Regardless of whether one is a skeptic or believer, there seems to be ample evidence that the act of dying itself, at least for some, may not be the fearful event it is set up to be in popular Western consciousness.[34]

What Happens to Dead Bodies

After you die, life still goes on for others and preparations must be made for disposing of your dead body. Once someone dies in the United States a physician must declare him dead using the criteria of death described earlier, and sign a death certificate, which is then filed with the appropriate governmental authorities. Beyond these civic formalities and a few other requirements, what happens to your body after you die has a lot to do with the kinds of directives that you gave your relatives, friends, or legal authorities before death. Did you elect to donate your organs to help others undergoing transplant surgery? Did you choose to be cremated, or embalmed, or buried quickly in a simple coffin? Did you decide to have a funeral? In some cases, your religious background may provide a context for these and other decisions. Most Western religions, including Christianity, Judaism, and Islam, provide for earth burials, since earth is regarded as the original source of mankind for people of these faiths. As Genesis 3:19 states: "Dust you are, to dust you shall return." In Judaism and Islam, the body must be buried as quickly as possible in a simple, unadorned coffin after having been washed, blessed, and covered with a white shroud. Among Hindus, the body is cremated after having been given a bath, dressed in elegant clothes, perfumed, decorated with flowers and garlands, blessed with prayers and rituals, and placed on a funeral pyre. Some cultures, such as the Yanomamo of Venzuela, may cremate the body, but then add some of the ashes to their plantain soup in a practice known in America as "endocannibalism."

In other cultures, a corpse must await an appropriate time for cremation or burial. The Torajans of Sulawesi (an island in Indonesian), for example, bundle the corpse in vast amounts of absorbent cloth to soak up the juices of putrefaction and then keep it around the house until it is ready for the next stage of the funeral. In some cases, such as in certain Mediterranean cultures, the body is buried until it reaches the skeleton stage, and then is dug up and reburied in another location in a more formal ceremony.[35] Zoroastrians do not bury or cremate the human body, since they regard the corpse as a source of pollution and do not wish to pollute either the earth or fire. Consequently, they leave the body in a Tower of Silence and let the vultures eat the remains. In Tibet, a person known as a "body breaker" dismembers the corpse before it is exposed to birds of prey and wild animals. Traditionally and still today, Buddhist monks meditated on these decomposing bodies, or images of them, as they reflected on the impermanence of all living things.[36]

A corpse left out in nature to rot will go through a number of changes as it decomposes. Within a minute after expiration, the face takes on the gray-white pallor of death. The body's musculature relaxes but soon begins to stiffen beginning with the eyelids, neck, and jaw, and then spreading to other muscles and internal organs within a few hours. This process, known as *rigor mortis* (literally, "stiffness of death"), results from the cessation of the production of adenosine triphosphate (ATP), which provides muscle cells with the energy needed to make a muscle relax after it has contracted. The body's temperature at death begins to fall two degrees Fahrenheit per hour until it reaches the surrounding temperature in a process called *algor mortis* ("coolness of death"). Also shortly after death, the skin begins to show purple-red blotches as red blood cells break down in what is referred to as *livor mortis* ("discoloration of death"). Within several hours after death, the skin loses its elasticity, obtaining the consistency of butcher's meat. Contrary to popular opinion, the teeth and hair do not continue growing after death. By seven days after death, most of the body is discolored and giant blood-tinged blisters begin to appear. Skin loosens and any pressure can cause the top layer to come off in larger sheets in a process known as "skin slip."

In warm to hot weather, a body completely exposed to the elements takes only two to four weeks to be reduced to a skeleton. Insects and small

234 THE HUMAN ODYSSEY

animals do most of the damage. If buried one to two feet deep, a body will turn into a skeleton within a few months. An unembalmed adult body buried six feet deep in ordinary soil within a wooden coffin normally takes about ten to twelve years to decompose down to bony skeleton.[37] Ultimately, given a long enough time interval, and exposure to the appropriate elements in nature, even the skeleton itself decomposes, leaving only dust behind. Jane Hollister Wheelwright, an eighty-year-old Jungian psychotherapist, shared her own thoughts about returning to nature as she contemplated her own death: "... my fantasy... is to melt into nature when I die; to become part of the trees, part of all vegetation; part of earth and rocks, also animals, even the reptiles and insects or anything else that moves—in short become part of the goddess nature ... "[38] To die in this way, at least in terms of *body up* development, is literally to be reintegrated back into the primal stuff of nature. In the next chapter, we will explore death and dying from the perspective of *spirit down* development, and look at how this final stage of life may represent only the beginning of a whole new stage of existence.

∞

---------------------- *The Gift of Death: Life* ----------------------

The gift of death is life. At first glance, this may seem quite absurd: life and death are diametrically opposing forces; death represents the absence of life. And yet, upon reflection, we can begin to see the intimate relationship that they have to one another. From a naturalist's point of view, death makes it possible for new biological life to come into being. From a Christian point of view, Jesus said, "I tell you the truth, whoever hears my word and believes him who sent me has eternal life and will not be condemned; he has crossed over from death to life" (John 5:24). Sufi mystics counsel that we must die to self to live in God. Thus death means life. Even many agnostics or atheists regard the human encounter with death as a stimulus to live one's life more fully. If there were no death, it would be easy to slip into an ongoing state of semi-conscious stupor. The fact of death rouses in us an impulse to discover what it really means to live. We have all heard stories of people who have faced death and survived, saying afterward: "I never felt so alive!" By making us aware of our potential nonexistence, death forces us to come to grips with *who we really are* beneath the surface of things. It cracks open our complacency and shocks us into facing the facts of our Being in all its rawness and immediacy.

To live consciously with the knowledge of death may be the supreme gift of the human life cycle. This doesn't mean that we should become morbidly obsessed with death like people did in the Middle Ages. Quite the opposite. Our understanding of death ought to serve as a trigger for the celebration of life. For some, this might mean simply having a greater appreciation for the brief time that we have here on earth. For others, it might mean dying to the petty squabbles and selfish pursuits that spoil our days so that we can live a more expansive life. For still others, it could mean facing physical death with the expectation of a more glorious existence in the afterlife. Regardless of what our personal understanding of death may be, we can strive to discover in it something that renovates and heals. By seeing death as a gift instead of something to be avoided, we can go beyond the superficial details of our existence and experience the mystery of life in all of its creative splendor.

———— *Ways to Explore and Support Death and Dying* ————

FOR YOURSELF
- Write an obituary for yourself as you would like to be remembered.
- Plan your own funeral, including setting, rituals, people, music, readings, events, food, and other appropriate details.
- Make out a legal will with the help of legal counsel or appropriate software. Also, create a living will that will stipulate how you wish to spend your last days, who you would like to make medical decisions if you are unable to do so, what kind of funeral you would

like, how you would like your remains to be disposed of, and other relevant matters.

FOR FRIENDS AND FAMILY

- Visit a friend or family member who is dying, and offer your presence in any way that would be helpful.
- Stay in touch with a friend or family member who has recently experienced the death of a close one, providing support, comfort, and possible referral to appropriate mental health services if necessary.
- Donate money to charity in the name of a loved one who has passed away.

FOR THE COMMUNITY

- Volunteer to train at a hospice in your community to provide respite care for caregivers, personal assistance for hospice patients, bereavement counseling for loved ones, or other appropriate services.
- Contribute financially to programs that make information about death and dying more readily available to the public (e.g., Americans for Better Care of the Dying, Hospice Foundation of America, your local hospice, etc.).
- Get involved with—or help put together—a forum, panel, or discussion group in your religious organization, workplace, or community center that focuses on raising awareness about issues related to death and dying.

∞

CHAPTER 13

Beyond Death: Travel to Other Lands

*Either death is a state of nothingness and utter unconsciousness,
or, as men say, there is a change and migration of the soul from this
world to another.*

—SOCRATES[1]

Among the Lakota Indians there exists a belief that each individual possesses not one, but four souls. Each soul is associated with a different stage of life: childhood, adolescence, maturity, and old age. When a person dies, parts of these four souls interpenetrate unborn fetuses and infuse them with life. At the same time, one of these souls travels southward along the *wanagi tacanker*, or "spirit path" of the Milky Way, and meets up with an old woman who proceeds to judge the soul according to its deeds during life. Depending upon the outcome, the soul is directed either to the spirit world, where it rejoins its deceased kin and enjoys a never-ending supply of buffalo meat, or is sent back to earth to exist in a marginal state as a ghost haunting the living.[2]

This vision of the afterlife, though not well known, has elements that connect with each of the world's major religions. It contains reincarnation, a feature of many Eastern religions such as Hinduism and Buddhism. It includes a heavenly paradise of abundance comparable to those found in Islam and Christianity. It also speaks of a marginal or "ghostly" state of existence similar to those of ancient Judaism or the classical worlds of Greece and Rome. In addition, like so many of the world's religions (including that of ancient Egypt), there is a "last judgment" to determine the soul's fate in the world to come. It is quite amazing to consider that an indigenous American culture, which developed quite apart from mainstream Western and Eastern cultures, developed a conception of the afterlife that mirrors and even synthesizes in many striking respects ideas from each of the world's main religions.

What should we make of this attempt to describe the world beyond death? Wishful thinking? Great storytelling? Or should we instead regard this effort as a sincere project to describe an authentic afterlife that exists beyond words and reason? In modern times, it has become standard practice for rational people to regard the prospect of life after death as an absurdity. In the past several decades, modern science has generated a great deal of research to support its claim that the human brain "creates" consciousness. If this is true, then it follows rationally that awareness of oneself and the world ceases to exist with the death of the brain. Our lives, in this view, are movies that have a final shot on the screen with the words *The End, Fin,* or *Thee-ah . . . thee-ah . . . thee-ah . . . that's all, folks!* emblazoned across it before fading into black. The predominance of this perspective in modern Western thought helps to explain why textbooks on human development never include a stage on the afterlife. From the standpoint of modern science, such a stage simply doesn't exist.

The Afterlife: An Ignored Stage of Human Development?

A review of crosscultural traditions, however, suggests that it is equally absurd to omit an afterlife from any comprehensive map of human development. For when one looks back at the history of civilization, virtually every culture has included an afterlife in its panoramic vision of existence. For thousands of years, cultures have had intimate contact with every aspect of death and out of these profound experiences have developed sophisticated models of postdeath existence. In contrast, modern society has had very little of this visceral connection to death, since much of it is hidden away in hospital intensive care units and mortuaries. Yet, experts in contemporary culture seem very confident of their assertions that there is nothing after death but oblivion. This contrasts starkly with traditional cultures such as those in China and Japan, which regard continued existence beyond death as an integral part of their existing social order, and where ancestorhood is ritualized along with other stages of life, including birth, marriage, and death. In some religions, including Islam, Buddhism, and certain versions of Christianity, the afterlife is considered far more important than life on earth. Several cultures have even developed elaborate "guide books" of postdeath existence. Ancient Egyptian priests, for example, created texts now known as the *Egyptian Book of the Dead*, which contain spells, incantations, rites, and prayers to assist the dead person in living successfully in the next world. Tibetan Buddhists wrote *The Tibetan Book of the Dead*, a manual read to a dead person over a period of forty-nine days, teaching them the ropes, so to speak, of traveling through the afterlife so as to attain freedom from rebirth. Medieval Catholic priests created the *Ars Moriendi* (The Art of Dying), a collection of texts showing the dying person how best to achieve salvation through Christ.

Many cultures around the world believe that the dead have power over the living. These cultures have developed elaborate rituals and strategies to make sure that deceased souls will favor the living rather than harm them or otherwise interfere in their lives. When my wife and I visited Bali several years ago, we attended a cremation ceremony that began with a procession to the cremation grounds. Scores of men carried an elaborately decorated funeral float with the body of the deceased person inside. Before they left the point of origin in downtown Ubud, I noticed that they rotated the float 360 degrees a number of times before they began their journey. Later on I discovered that this was done to "confuse" the dead soul and prevent it from finding its way back to its earthly home where it might bother the living. In contemporary China, family members of the deceased purchase miniature paper houses, cars, food items, television sets, and other worldly goods at specialty shops, and then ritually burn them to help placate their ancestors so that they might live comfortably in the afterworld. Even in our modern rationalistic American culture, belief in the afterlife runs high. Recent polls suggest that nearly three-quarters of the U.S. population believe that there is a heaven or hell, or at least *something* waiting for them on the other side of death.[3] The afterlife, for whatever modern science may think about it, is a universal feature of the human condition and needs to be represented in any full account of the journey of life.

Types of Immortality

One thing is absolutely certain: There will be an afterlife. The big question is whether or not we'll be a part of it. On one level we can be confident about our continued existence after death. No matter what happens to our physical bodies—whether they are cremated, buried, mummified, or shot into outer space—the atoms that make up our physical form will continue to exist, at least until they are converted to some other form such as energy. Something of us will always be there in the universe, even if, as some scientists predict, the universe eventually expands to the point where it reaches a condition of eternal stasis and nothing much ever happens again.[4] The nineteenth-century philosopher Friedrich Nietzsche suggested that if time is infinite and the number of atoms in the universe is finite, it will only be a matter of time before the exact combination of atoms now in place at this moment all over the universe—including those that sustain your and my consciousness—will recur, and then recur again and again an infinite number of times. He used this amazing intimation of immortality to suggest that each person must live each moment of life to its fullest, since everyone will have to live that moment over and over again for eternity.[5]

There are other ways to view existence after physical death without necessarily believing in a traditional religious afterlife. Biologist Lewis Thomas, for example, wrote, "There are some creatures that do not seem to die at all; they simply vanish totally into their own progeny. Single cells do this. The cell becomes two, then four, and so on, and after awhile the last trace is gone. It cannot be seen as death; barring mutation, the descendants are simply the first cell, living all over again."[6] At a far more complex level, something like this also occurs in humans as parents seek immortality by continuing to exist after death in their own children. Sociobiologists tell us that whenever we support our children, grandchildren, and even—if we are childless—our nephews, nieces, and cousins, we are shepherding our genes beyond our own physical demise into countless future generations.[7] Some have even suggested that it is we ourselves who are undergoing this continual transformation from the simplest elements to larger and larger units of life. Jalalu'l-Din Rumi, the Persian Sufi poet and mystic, for example, wrote: "I died as inanimate matter and arose a plant / I died as a plant and rose again an animal / I died as an animal and arose a man / Why then should I fear to become less by dying?"[8]

On the other hand, we may seek immortality through our own creative achievements. Shakespeare wrote in one of his sonnets: ". . . do thy worst, old Time: despite thy wrong / My love shall in my verse ever live young."[9] By creating literary, artistic, social, or scientific works, we pass on to new generations ideas that will have a life of their own and stir the lives of others to renewed vitality.

For the most part, however, people throughout the world have viewed the afterlife as a spiritual journey, whether illusory or real, to a place or to a series of places where the deceased is judged or tested. Based upon the final judgment, the traveler is then rewarded or punished for the life he has lived on earth, or alternatively, he is held back or promoted as a result of the lessons he has learned or failed to learn from his earthly experiences. While this pattern serves as a matrix for most world religions and world cultures, there is an incredible diversity in the ways that the details of an afterlife have been worked out. The Pangwe of southern Cameroon, for example, believe that after death a person lives on for a long time in heaven, but then he eventually dies and his "corpse" is thrown out with no chance of any further existence.[10] Norse legends speak of Vikings fallen in battle who journey on to Vallhalla, a place where they can continue to fight, drink, and sport as they did on earth. Taoist philosophers in China believe that when the breath or "life force" [ch'i] leaves the body at death it is redispersed as energy freely flowing between heaven and earth, like drops of a liquid poured back into water.[11] Most cultures view the afterlife as a solitary journey. However, certain Islamic traditions have it that on the day of resurrection entire communities will assemble, each at its own pond, and await judgment as a group.[12] Some views of the afterlife hold that if we are lucky we will disappear entirely at death into nirvana or the void, while others say that after death the actual physical body of the deceased will be resurrected and look and function exactly as it did during earthly life.

The Moment of Death

Strictly speaking, if there is total extinction of consciousness at the moment of death, then there is absolutely no way of verifying this, since there will be no one "there" to report back that "there is nothing there." The French mathematician and philosopher Blaise Pascal used this kind of logic to proffer a wager to doubters that a person was always better off betting on life after death than on extinction. He reasoned that if you bet on God and you won (e.g. God exists), then you gained everything. If you bet on God and you lost (e.g. God doesn't exist), then you lost nothing. On the other hand, if you didn't bet on God and God doesn't exist, you lost nothing, but if you didn't bet on God and He *does* exist, then you lost everything (e.g. God's presence in the afterlife). Thus, you were better off from a strictly mathematical point of view living with the expectation of being with God after death.[13] With this in mind, we can begin to explore in some depth the experiences that may subjectively happen to us in the moments just before, during, and after physical death.[14]

If there *is* some form of consciousness that survives physical death, then what happens at the moment of death if not extinction? Many answers have been given to this question. My own personal favorite comes from a spiritual advisor who once told me: "You take the last breath and God takes the very next breath." Traditions that believe in reincarnation frequently hold that *the last thought* one has at the moment of death will determine one's afterlife and ultimately one's next birth. According to the Tibetan Buddhist tradition, the moment of death is the single best opportunity in all of existence to achieve liberation from the wheel of rebirth. At that moment, one encounters the Dharma-Kaya or The Primary Clear Light of Absolute Being. *The Tibetan Book of the Dead* counsels the person who has just died: "O nobly-born (so-and-so), listen. Now thou art experiencing the Radiance of the Clear Light of Pure Reality. Recognize it. O nobly-born, thy present intellect, in real nature void, not formed into anything as regards characteristics or colour, naturally void, is the very Reality..."[15] If the deceased can recognize this Light as its own true nature, then he merges with it and attains liberation. On the other hand, if this encounter with Absolute Reality proves too overwhelming, the deceased may shrink back from it in terror, only to be given a second chance to recognize the Light as oneself. Failing this second encounter, the soul is driven by the "winds of karma" into contact with its own past deeds, which appear in the form of peaceful and wrathful deities, and eventually it takes birth in a new physical body.

Other accounts of the moment of death suggest that some people, especially those who expected nothingness, may not even recognize that they've died. Former psychologist and spiritual teacher Ram Dass explains that if an individual has been deeply identified with the physical body during life they may experience a type of confused "sleep" at death, while those who harbor strong connections to specific people, places, or things might continue to hover around these attachments without realizing that death has taken place.[16] American author E. J. Gold has written a book called the *The American Book of the Dead*, which seeks to translate the exotic symbolism of the *Tibetan Book of the Dead* into terms more easily understood by members of contemporary American culture. He suggests that the moment of death may feel like "a deep, incessant sensation of... being inexorably drawn downward into a pool of mercury or lead, of melting into the earth... [or] a sensation of clammy coldness as though one has been immersed in ice water... [or] a sensation of being just on the verge of explosion... [or] a feeling of being utterly at peace, utterly alone, completely outside space and time, free of all necessity."[17] Some of these descriptions match those given in ancient accounts. For example, the Pre-Columbian

Maya believed that the moment of death felt something like the downward plunge of a canoe. The ancient Vedic philosophers in India wrote, "When a person departs from this world, he goes to the air. It opens out there for him like the hole of a chariot wheel. Through that he goes upwards."[18] Other ancient myths have described the beginning of the journey after death in terms of descending into the bowels of the earth, crawling through a tunnel, entering a whirlpool, crossing a bridge, going through a door, being swallowed by a gigantic monster, or flying away into space.[19]

Journey of the Dead

If there is a conscious afterlife, then it's likely that you'll have a guide to help you navigate your way from this world to the land of the dead. In Norse mythology, the Valkyries or female warrior spirits who were servants of the Nordic god Odin appeared to warriors killed in battle and led them to a new life in Vallhalla. In Greek mythology, the god Hermes delivered the souls of the dead to Charon who ferried them across the rivers of the underworld to the gates of Hades. Among the Goldi people of Siberia, psychologist and afterlife researcher Sukie Miller writes, " . . . a shaman . . . takes a soul across to the other side. He traps the soul of a deceased person in a sacred pillow and then mounts a notched tree to see into the distance to preview his journey. Two spirits come to assist him, and the shaman, the assistants, and the soul set off on a special dogsled supplied with nourishing food. As soon as the travelers reach the afterworld . . . he leaves the soul with relatives and returns to the living, carrying gifts and greetings."[20] Spirit guides are reputed to have expert knowledge of the geography of the afterlife, and can help the soul avoid pitfalls, delays, or other interruptions in the journey, almost in the same way that a maitre d' can get you a good table at a fine restaurant without a long wait.

The guide who appears at death to take you into the afterlife may turn out to be the same guardian spirit who was present at your birth. Ancient Egyptians believed that after death, the *ba*, or personal soul of the deceased, became fully realized by joining up with its counterpart, the *ka*, which acted as a kind of guardian angel during life. The Maori goddess Hine-titama (Goddess of the Dawn), which protects pregnant mothers and newborns, is the same deity who becomes Hine-nui-te-po, Goddess of the Darkness, at the end of life, and helps souls across the threshold of death.[21] Elisabeth Kubler-Ross writes about guardian angels in childhood that sometimes reappear as one nears death in old age: "What the church tells little children about guardian angels is based on fact . . . Everyone has such a spirit guide, whether you believe it or not . . . A dying old lady conveys to me, 'Here he is again.' Since I do not know what she is referring to, I ask this lady if she could share with me what she has just seen. She tells me, 'You must know, when I was a little kid he used to always be around me. But I have totally forgotten that he existed.' A day later she dies, full of joy, knowing that someone who loves her dearly is waiting for her."[22] Here we see a case where the angel of destiny described in the chapter on prebirth, at the beginning of this book, comes back to the soul at the end of its life, to remind it of its divine nature and help it into the next stage of existence.

After being led to the afterworld by a guide, many accounts from cultures around the world suggest that you will face some type of judgment where your deeds on earth are reviewed and evaluated according to an eternal moral or spiritual standard. In Christianity, Jesus tells the parable of the last judgment when the Son of Man is to come and sit on his throne and all nations will gather before him while he separates them into two groups "as a shepherd separates the sheep from the goats" (Matthew 25:32). Those who have loved their neighbors will receive eternal life while those who did not will go to the eternal fire. In the Islamic afterlife, the two angels Munker and Nakir interrogate the dead, and depending upon the outcome, they are either ushered into paradise or cast into hell. Every soul must walk across the bridge of Sirat, a bridge that is "finer than a hair and sharper than a sword." Those who are righteous believers manage to keep their balance, while nonbelievers slip and plummet into the hellish abyss. In ancient Egyptian culture, the judgment scene occurs in the Hall of the Two Truths (the Hall of Maat). There, the heart of the deceased is placed on one pan of a scale, while on the other is put the feather of the Goddess Maat, symbolizing truth and justice. An ibis-headed God named Thoth impartially records the results, following which the righteous are wel-comed into heaven by the resurrected god Osiris while the unjust are devoured by a monster called Amemet who resembles a combined version of a crocodile, a lion, and a hippopotamus.[23]

Once you have been judged or tested, then it's likely that you will enter into a postdeath existence that has its own unique ecology. Although usually existing beyond space and time, cultures have generally employed metaphors based upon the geography of the earth and its nat-ural features to describe these otherworldly states. As such, afterworlds can be situated below the earth, on the earth, or above the earth. Those that are found under the earth—the "underworlds"—are usually dark, sometimes fiery, sometimes icy, and full of geological features like volcanic craters, chasms, jagged cliffs, pits, deep valleys, labyrinths, or swamps. Some of these are actual "hells" or places of punishment, as noted earlier, while others are simply "netherworlds" where the dead live an eternally shadowy existence as bodiless phantoms. These include Hades in ancient Greece, where Odysseus spoke with the phantom shapes of his fellow war-riors, and Sheol in ancient Judaism, which Job described as "a land of deep darkness . . . of gathering shadows, of deepening shadow, lit by no way of light, dark upon dark" (Job 10:21–22).

A number of indigenous cultures situate the afterlife directly on the surface of the earth. In many cases this place is represented as a mystical island. Australian aborigines called it Braklu, the Celts referred to it as Tirnanog, while many South Sea islanders speak of a mythic island of the dead they called Java (not the Indonesian island of the same name). Greek settlers in southern Italy considered certain wild and eerie regions in their vicinity as parts of the underworld existing on the surface of the earth. The Dusun of Borneo believe the abode of the dead exists on a high mountain. The Admiralty Islanders on Manus near New Guinea believed that the dead persist in the exact same spot as the living as a kind of double image, with the same profession, house, and other belongings: "The living and the dead coexist in space, having only different modes of being."[24]

Finally, there are those afterworlds located above the earth: in the sky, among the clouds, in the sun or other celestial bodies, or even beyond these orbs in higher spiritual realms. We've already noted how the Lakota Indians located at least part of their journey of the afterlife in the Milky Way. Alaska Native cultures often link the world of the dead closely with the aurora borealis (northern lights). The ancient Egyptians believed that the dead traveled in a barge to join the sun god. In the Judeo-Christian tradition, the concept of paradise (a word derived from the Persian *pairi-daeza*, meaning "walled garden") begins in the Old Testament or Hebrew Bible, when the prophet Daniel writes: "Many of those who sleep in the dust of the earth shall awake, some to everlasting life, and some to shame and everlasting contempt... Those who are wise shall shine like the brightness of the sky, and those who lead many to righteousness, like the stars forever and ever" (Daniel 12:1–3).

The New Testament speaks most explicitly about heaven in Revelations, authored by the apostle John. It is here where popular Christian culture received its images of a heaven filled with pearly gates, jeweled walls, and streets paved with gold. In Islam, paradise is described as a place where there are two kinds of every fruit, upholstered couches, palm trees and pomegranates, green pastures, and virgins with white skin and dark eyes.[25] Some Buddhist sects believe in a celestial "pure land" in the western part of the universe where the deceased blissfully contemplate the Amita Buddha or the Bodhisattva of Compassion, Kuan-Yin. In some cases, especially in Western religions, the journey of life concludes with eternal residence in one of these heavenly or hellish worlds. In other belief systems, such as in Hinduism and Buddhism, the soul's presence in the afterlife is but a temporary way station on the journey, as it travels from lifetime to lifetime in search of liberation from continual rebirth.

The Denial of Life After Death

If you are a rationalist, you may be thinking at this point that what's been described above is pure conjecture at best and mad delusion at worst. Your point of view is not strictly a modern one. A contemporary of the Buddha named Ajita Kesakambalin (who lived around 400–500 B.C.E.), taught that human beings do not survive physical death: "When he dies . . . his senses vanish into space . . . those who maintain the existence [of immaterial categories] speak vain and lying nonsense. When the body dies both fool and wise alike are cut off and perish. They do not survive after death."[26] Similarly in the Western cultural tradition, the denial of life after death extends back at least as far as the Hellenistic philosopher Epicurus (341–271 B.C.E.) and his Roman disciple Lucretius (95–55 B.C.E.), who believed that since death is final, humanity need not fear everlasting torture and punishment. It seems, however that the denial of life after death became a widely held perspective in Western civilization only in the seventeenth and eighteenth centuries with the flowering of the scientific method and modern rational discourse.

As noted earlier, the most commonly reasoned argument against life after death is that since the human brain causes consciousness, it follows that when the brain dies, consciousness vanishes along with it. When I questioned a leading brain surgeon about the possibility of consciousness continuing without the brain, he replied: "I have a pocket knife in my jacket in case you'd like to test this hypothesis." I politely declined his invitation and instead took the point I think he was trying to make: that when the brain is radically altered by surgery, crime, or accident, the effects on human consciousness are usually immediate, dramatic, and castastrophic. This intimate link between what is done to the brain and what directly ensues as a change or cessation of consciousness—something as basic as a knock on the head—is perhaps the best causal argument for the impossibility of life after death. Some rationalists suggest that a belief in life after death emerged as a way for humans, suddenly aware of mortality in a way that other animals were not, to avoid crippling anxiety. Others point out that systems of the afterlife are merely reflections of the social and moral prejudices of the specific cultures that developed them. After all, women and people from lower social classes have often been excluded from paradise in religions around the world.

Those who attempt to demonstrate the idea of life after death against the claims of scientific skepticism usually employ the tools and rules of conventional science to try to beat it at its own game. Thomas Edison wrote an article in a 1920 issue of *Scientific American* describing his own efforts to develop a machine that would be able to detect souls who had died. He reasoned, "If our personality survives, then it is strictly logical or scientific to assume that it retains memory, intellect, other faculties and knowledge that we acquire on this Earth. Therefore, if personality exists after what we call death, it is reasonable to conclude that those who leave the Earth would like to communicate with those they have left here. I am inclined to believe that our personality hereafter will be able to affect matter. If this reasoning be correct, then, if we can evolve an instrument so delicate as to be affected by our personality as it survives in the next life, such an instrument, when made available, ought to record something."[27] Although it was claimed that Edison worked on a prototype until his death in 1931, models or plans for the invention have never been found.

The escape artist Harry Houdini, a longtime skeptic who nevertheless was always curious about the possibility of life after death, devised a coded message with his wife, Bess, which he planned to relay back to her through a spiritualistic séance after he died as proof of his continued existence. After his death, his wife conducted ten séances over a period of ten years attempting to recover the message but gave up after there was no word from Harry.[28] One current project going on at the University of Arizona is attempting to do very much the same kind of thing by having psychic mediums transmit information from deceased discarnate entities to living people using strict scientific research methods and protocols.[29] Contemporary researchers of near-death experiences (NDEs) also use rational standards and scientific measures in arguing for an afterlife. Cases are pointed to, for example, of individuals blind from birth who are able to see visions during NDEs, or of people declared dead on the operating table who recover and report seeing instrument measurements and other features of the room not perceivable from the position of someone lying in a supine position.[30]

Science, Consciousness, and Survival

One difficulty with using scientific research methods and rational standards to defend a belief in life after death, however, is that there are always rational arguments and scientific research methods that can be used to refute these claims.[31] It is more useful, in my estimation, to critique the shortcomings of conventional science *itself* at its origins to explain why the scientific method may be inadequate to the task of either affirming or denying the existence of life after death. To be blunt about it, for all of its great accomplishments in describing the objective world, science has never been able to explain what consciousness really *is*. Science can describe how a lesion in the primary visual area of the brain can create a distortion in the visual world, but it can't account for what that unique visual distortion actually is *in itself*—let us say, a fuzzy sunflower with specks of light surrounding it.[32]

Science inevitably dismisses what it cannot explain as "subjective" and distrusts it for its lack of empirical validity. However, this so-called subjectivity, or consciousness, is really the basis for any type of inquiry, scientific or otherwise. When René Descartes, the French philosopher and pioneer of modern rationalism, wrote, "I think, therefore I am," he was attempting to create a stable footing for all rational inquiry to follow. However, he neglected to inquire, "Who is this 'I' that thinks in the first place?" In other words, he assumed this first "I" as a given, without proving it rationally. The problem that Descartes had in defining the nature of this "inquiring I" at the beginning of the history of modern science continues to bedevil the scientific enterprise.[33] Conventional science can explain to us what we see when we look outward into the world, but it too often forgets that there is always someone present doing the looking with a unique state of consciousness.[34] And who is that someone? Who is this "I" that Descartes unthinkingly posited at the start of the scientific era?

This may be the critical part of the puzzle that will enable us to move beyond mere scientific "proofs" or "refutations of whether there is life after death. Perhaps the question we should be asking is one that death and dying expert Stephen Levine suggests we all ask ourselves about this great mystery: "Who dies?"[35] In other words, when we die, *who* is it that actually dies? We observe from the objective exterior that the physical body of another person dies. But what dies *inwardly*? You might think: "I do." But who is this "I" that dies? The Scottish philosopher David Hume speculated that this "I" may not even really exist. Instead, he suggested that human beings experience individual moments of consciousness, one right after the other, and that these separate events somehow get spliced together and called an "I."[36] In this respect, he was in agreement with the Buddha, who said very much the same thing. According to Buddhism, the "I" is like an onion. Peel off the various layers, the emotions, sensations, perceptions, intuitions, and the rest, and at the very center you find nothing. Absolutely nothing. Ironically, there is corroboration of this conclusion from modern brain research.[37] Psychobiologist Michael Gazzaniga, for example, suggests that that the brain consists of multiple "selves," each designed to spring into action whenever a particular occasion demands it. One dramatic example of these multiple selves at work exists in the lives of those with severe "multiple personality disorder" (now called "dissociative disorder"), where as many as ten or twenty selves can erupt periodically over the course of a person's lifetime.[38]

More recent brain research suggests that there is an area in the posterior superior parietal lobe of the neocortex called the orientation association area (OAA), which among other things helps distinguish between the individual person and everything else, or in other words, marks out the you from the infinite not-you that makes up the rest of the universe. Scientists have intravenously injected radioactive tracers into the brains of Tibetan monks to track what goes on in the OAA as the meditators slip into altered states of consciousness. It turns out that this area of the brain, which sharpens the distinction between the "I" and the "not-I," actually slows down as the monks deepen their meditation.[39] In other words, the sense of "I-ness" or separateness from the world begins to disappear. This leads me to the following thought experiment: If the sense of "I" disappears during meditation, and let's say for the sake of argument, that the physical brain dies while the subject still happens to be in this state of I-lessness, then from a subjective point of view, what is it that actually changes? The sense of "I" was erased before the physical brain died in our experiment. What is it, then, in terms of consciousness, that actually dies here?

This brings us back to the difficulty that conventional science has always had in pinning down exactly what consciousness *is*. Since it really hasn't provided a satisfactory description, let alone a good explanation, for the nature of consciousness, science stumbles at this point. When the Buddha was asked where he would go when he died he is reported to have said, "Where does the fire go when the fuel is used up?"

The metaphor he used of consciousness as fire or light is a powerful one. When we turn off the lights in the bedroom, there is still light elsewhere in an otherwise fully lit house. Is that existing light the same as or different from the light we turned off? Where does the light from one bulb begin and another leave off? Dutch researcher Pim van Lommel, whose work on near-death experiences was cited in the last chapter, puts the metaphor into a telecommunications context: "Compare [consciousness] with a TV program. If you open the TV set, you will not find the program. The TV set is a receiver. When you turn off your TV set, the program is still there but you can't see it. When you put off your brain, your consciousness is there but you can't feel it in your body."[40]

Dying: A Question of Time

Because conventional science is unable to enter into the actual inner conscious states of its subjects, it is unable to say for sure what happens to that consciousness when the brain is "turned off" (e.g., dies). Moreover, its attempts to rationally interpret near-death experiences as merely the final pyrotechnics of dying neurons says nothing about the inner state of the dying person as this is going on. This issue becomes particularly important when we consider the nature of time. Science has become very adept at recording intervals of time with astonishing accuracy, down to 3.3×10^{-44}. Yet, as the French philosopher Henri Bergson observed, science is unable to measure *inner* time or what he called *real* time, as opposed to mathematical time.[41] Inner time, or the felt sense of duration, can differ dramatically from mathematical or "scientific" time. People often speak of important moments in their lives that seemed to last for hours, yet which turned out to be only a few seconds of "clock time." Some of these accounts include near-death experiences. People have reported at such times that "my whole life flashed in front of me." At other times, it's just been a feeling of time slowing down. When two cars collided in front of her as she drove on the freeway in Southern California, for example, psychologist Jean Houston reported that she was suddenly yanked into another time zone: "The two cars [crashing ahead of me] moved with ponderous slowness but with great grace up into the air. I marveled for the longest time at their balletic grace—they hovered up there like two elephantine Nijinskys executing a pas de deux in the Los Angeles air."[42]

Accounts of time slowing down near a moment of potential death remind me of a short story from one of my favorite authors, the Argentine Jorge Luis Borges, who was himself fascinated with the question of time. In "The Secret Miracle," a man is about to be executed by a firing squad during World War II, but just as the triggers are pulled he makes a wish to God to have one more year of life to compose the novel he has always been yearning to write. In the story, he is granted his wish—the bullets are retarded in their flight and he stands immobile in front of the soldiers, mentally constructing the book of his dreams. When he is done with his project after the designated year, the bullets come rushing toward him and finish him off.[43] If Bergsonian real time slows down as we approach death, then what is to prevent the possibility of an individual, within a few seconds of dying from an outside observer's point of view, going through hours, days, weeks, months, years, or even longer periods of subjective time before that final moment comes?[44]

We know that as we approach the limits of the objective universe at both ends, the very large and the very small, the conventional laws of traditional physics begin to break down. At the most cosmic levels, concepts like dark matter, black holes, and multiple dimensions distort the space and time of everyday life. At the tiniest levels, the indeterminacy of quantum mechanics interferes with the precise mathematical laws of both

Newton and Einstein. Who's to say that equivalent things might not occur in the subjective universe of each individual person as he reaches the limiting factor of physical death? We know that the length of a synaptic cleft in the brain is astonishingly short—200 to 300 angstroms (an angstrom equals one hundred-millionth of a centimeter)—a length approaching an atomic scale of dimensions when quantum indeterminacy starts to become important. Why then couldn't the decaying neurons of the dying brain lead human consciousness into similar conditions of indeterminacy?[45]

At a cosmic level, death may function very much like a "black hole" into which a person might descend but not be able to "report back" its light or consciousness to an outside observer. Similarly, the inner experience of time to the dying person may stretch on along a trajectory approaching infinity. While we're objectively watching a person going through their last few seconds of life, he or she may be subjectively experiencing, in a radically slowed down time frame, entire lifetimes, paradises, judgments, hells, eternities, or any of the other possible experiences of the afterlife that we've surveyed in this chapter. At this point, reality ceases to be what outside observers agree upon—the small-case reality of science. Now it becomes the inward Reality of a consciousness that stretches out beyond the limitations of conventional time and space into unlimited possibilities that human cultures may have only caught a glimpse of in their richly diverse descriptions of the afterlife.

Planting Your Oar in the Sand

Every phase [of life] exists for the benefit of the whole and for the benefit of every other phase; if it is damaged, both the whole and every individual phase suffers.

—FATHER ROMANO GUARDINI[1]

Congratulations, you made it! To the end of this book, that is. Making your way through the journey of life is another matter. Odysseus made it through his own incredible adventure and back to Ithaca. But even after all he went through, he still had one more important task to accomplish. During his journey he visited the underworld of Hades and received important advice from the blind seer Teiresias. Teiresias told Odysseus that after he returned to Ithaca and settled his accounts with the suitors who were pestering his wife, Penelope, he needed to embark on one last journey. He was to take an oar and travel inland until he came to a country where no man had ever known the sea, or seen ships, or tasted salt in their food. Teiresias told him that he would know that he had come to such a place when a passerby would look at him carrying the oar and remark: "What is that winnowing fan you have on your shoulder?" The man, having never seen an oar, would think it was an agricultural imple-ment. At that point Odysseus was instructed to plant his oar in the sand and make a *temenos*, or sacred place, at that spot to worship and sacrifice to Poseidon, who was the god that had caused him so much trouble in getting back to Ithaca. When this was successfully completed, Odysseus could return home and get some rest. Then, according to Teiresias, "death shall come to you from the sea, and your life shall ebb away very gently when you are full of years and peace of mind, and your people shall bless you."[2]

This final task for Odysseus—planting an oar in the sand—has special significance for those of us who have completed our journey through this book. After all that he went through, his struggles, temptations, stagnations, and salvations, Odysseus finally had acquired some wisdom about the human condition. This knowledge was not to be wasted. Odysseus traveled deep inland to a place where the inhabitants had never seen the sea; where the native population had never experienced the tumult, the turbulence, the richness, or the grandeur of the journey of life. It was, after all, a *desert* that Odysseus had come to. He was instructed to plant an oar—that is, to pierce the parched ground with a rich symbol of his sea journey—and by doing this sacred act to fructify the earth and bring new wisdom into barren regions. In this same way, after your own journey through the twelve stages life, you owe the gods a final sacred act. You must plant your own oar of understanding and wisdom concerning the human journey into the arid and undeveloped lands that lay scattered around you.

There are at least three ways for you to do this. Using the practical activities at the end of each chapter, you can use your newly acquired wisdom about the stages of life to transform yourself, nurture your family and friends, and/or support your community. First, you can plunge the oar of wisdom into the deserts of your own life by seeking to heal past traumas, address present trials and tribulations, and plan for the uncertainties of the future. Second, you may wish to focus your efforts on helping family and friends through the challenges of their own individual life stages by nurturing the growth of your children, mentoring your adolescents and young adults, and honoring the wisdom of your aging relatives. Third, you may want to sink your oar of understanding into the deserts of your own community, by, for example, contributing money to prevent birth defects, volunteering at a school, or advocating for the needs of the elderly. The appendices that follow provide resources (films, books, and organizations) that will help get you started on this next stage of your journey.

As we've seen in the course of this book, each stage of life has its own unique gift. These gifts represent the inner resources of the human life cycle that sustain it and keep it moving. It is my wish that after navigating your way through the twelve stages of life, you will feel inspired to draw upon these gifts and transform yourself and the world around you. Do as Odysseus did. Plant your oar in the sand. Make a difference in the world by doing what you can to improve the ecology of each stage of life. I was reminded, while watching the film *An Inconvenient Truth,* of how people started taking better care of the environment after seeing a photo of Earth taken from outer space in the early 1970s. I'd like to think that in my own imperfect way, I've provided a snapshot of the human life span, and that by seeing it in relief like this, you will begin to care for the stages of life in a new way. I hope that as a result of reading this book you'll be kinder to your elders, more understanding of your teenagers, more protective of your youngsters, more forgiving of yourself, and more sensitive to the developmental needs of all human beings as they travel through time on this miracle journey called life.

Films to Illuminate
the Times of Your Life

A movie can change your life. One changed mine. Twenty years ago I quit years of being in psychotherapy, after despairing of ever finding a mate to fill the gap in my lonely thirty-five-year-old bachelor existence. "You can't change the past," I thought to myself. "Better to accept my lot and prepare to endure another forty or fifty years of empty beds and solo dinners." Then I saw the Robert Zemeckis film *Back to the Future*. In that movie, Michael J. Fox plays Marty McFly, a 1980s teenager who goes back to the 1950s in a souped-up DeLorean time machine to literally change his destiny by altering his past. I burst out of the movie theater, rushed to a phone booth, and called my therapist to reestablish contact. Shortly thereafter, I started to work with her again on the self-defeating patterns in my own life. Within three months, on the first day of spring, I met my wife-to-be. Of course it was my own work, or perhaps destiny, that made it all happen, but I'll never forget that it was a film that served as a catalyst for change.

The list of 137 movies that follows may include one or more films that can change your own life. I call these "stages of life movies" because each one of them attempts to come to grips with the essential predicament of life—that we are physical beings trapped in the inexorable flow of time, are aware of this fact, and find our lives shaped by the tension between these two forces. The films are organized by the twelve stages of life that make up the structure of this book: prebirth, birth, infancy, early childhood, middle childhood, late childhood, adolescence, early adulthood, midlife, mature adulthood, late adulthood, and death and dying (with an additional section on postdeath existence). I've included an introductory category of movies that span many, if not most, of the stages of life. These include *Citizen Kane*, which seeks to find the underlying theme of a newspaper tycoon's life by following him from early childhood through early adulthood and midlife into late adulthood and death, and *Wild Strawberries*, which tracks an old professor as he goes on a journey to accept an award that brings him into contact with characters at several different stages of life—stages that mirror his own life history. (Erik Erikson used this film in his human development classes at Harvard to illustrate his "Eight Ages of Man" theory.) One could, of course, argue for the inclusion of many more movies on this list, for it seems that the most excellent films in the history of cinema have always had themes that revolve around life cycle issues: growth, stagnation, initiation, disintegration, death, rebirth, remembrance, and more.

Great films rivet us because they move us into the dramatic contours of our lives and the lives of those who are significant to us. They help us look back at who we were, mirror our present state of existence, and point beyond our current life toward a set of possibilities that we might yet achieve. Ultimately, movies—good movies—are about *becoming*; they move us to a new place in ourselves, and by moving us, they re-create the development that takes place (or fails to take place) in our own lives.

I hope you will find that the movies on this list provide you with opportunities to reflect on the stages of your life that you have already lived, the stage you are in now, and the stages that are yet to come. Watch them with friends or relations, and use the films as starting points to talk about your memories, reflections, dreams, and aspirations. These "stages of life movies" may be the closest that modern technology will ever come to the construction of an actual time machine. Enjoy your travels, and remember: These movies can change your life, if you're lucky enough, but in any event, they definitely will cause you to think about your life in a totally new way.

MULTISTAGE FILMS

49 Up Director Michael Apted began videotaping the lives of several British schoolchildren in 1964 when they were seven years old, and he has continued recording their lives every seven years since then. They are forty-nine years old in this latest documentary that includes spliced cuts from previous versions. See also his previous versions, including *28-Up*, *35-Up*, and *42-Up*. (2005) 180 min.

Antonia's Line This Oscar winner for Best Foreign Film chronicles the lives of five generations of women from postwar times to the present and beautifully illustrates all twelve stages of life. In Dutch with English subtitles (1995) 102 min.

The Autobiography of Miss Jane Pittman Cicely Tyson's Emmy Award–winning portrayal of a 110-year-old former slave reminiscing about her life from the Civil War to the start of the civil rights movement in the 1960s. (1974) 110 min. TV movie.

Cinema Paradiso A famous film director in midlife reminisces about his childhood and adolescence and the village projectionist who had such a major influence on his life. In Italian with English subtitles. (1988) 123 min.

Citizen Kane Called by many critics the best film ever made, this Orson Welles gem depicts a newspaper magnate as he moves through the innocence of childhood, the idealism of early adulthood, the disappointments of midlife, and the decrepitude of old age. (1941) 119 min.

Goodbye, Mr. Chips Follows the life of a British schoolteacher from the mistakes of his early career in the classroom, through a warm but tragic marriage, to his maturity and final deathbed scene where he affirms the integrity of his life. (1939) 115 min.

It's a Wonderful Life This Christmas favorite is also one of the best stages of life films around. We experience George Bailey's childhood, adolescence, young adulthood, midlife, and even a sort of "postdeath" experience in a parallel universe via Clarence, "the angel who never grew up." (1946) 125 min.

The Last Emperor Follows the life of Pu Yi, the last emperor of China, as he becomes a buoy in the waves of history, finally ending up as a common gardener during the Cultural Revolution of the 1960s. (1987) 140 min.

Our Town Paul Newman stars in this staging of Thornton Wilder's Pulitzer Prize–winning play, which portrays people at different stages of the life cycle reflecting upon life's deeper meanings in a small New Hampshire town in the 1930s. (2003) 120 min. TV movie

Same Time, Next Year A couple meets to have an affair at a seaside resort for a week every summer over a period of twenty years. The story device provides an opportunity to examine how life span changes (and social-historical events) profoundly affect relationships. (1978) 119 min.

Scrooge A musical version of Charles Dickens's *A Christmas Carol*, where Ebenezer Scrooge visits his past, present, and future on the way to a personal and spiritual transformation of his character. (1970) 86 min.

Seasons of Life A PBS five-part documentary series covering infancy and early childhood, childhood and adolescence, early adulthood, middle adulthood, and late adulthood, produced by WQED/Pittsburgh and the University of Michigan. (1990) five 60 min. videos. Available for free viewing as video stream at http://www.learner.org/resources/series54.html.

Wild Strawberries An old professor travels to his alma mater to accept an honorary degree and on the way there revisits his life. The psychoanalyst Erik Erikson used this Ingmar Bergman film in his course on human development at Harvard to illustrate each of his eight stages of man. In Swedish with English subtitles. (1957) 90 min.

Yi Yi This story of an extended family's daily life in Taiwan manages to illustrate all twelve stages of life in an intimate yet panoramic view of the human condition. In Mandarin Chinese with English subtitles. (2000) 173 min.

Prebirth, Birth, and Infancy Films

Journey to be Born: An Introduction to Pre- and Perinatal Psychology (1986) 28 min. VHS (Available from STAR Foundation, PO Box 516, Geyserville, CA 95441). (Also available: *The Psychology of Birth*).

Life's Greatest Miracle PBS sequel to *The Miracle of Life*, with new footage and state-of-the-art animation techniques. (2001) 60 min. Watch online for free at http://www.pbs.org/wgbh/nova/miracle/program.html#.

Look Who's Talking Depicts life from an infant's point of view, using the voice of actor Bruce Willis. (1989) (PG-13) 90 min.

The Miracle of Life This award-winning PBS documentary shows the development of human life from conception to birth, using stunning photography. (1983) 60 min.

Early Childhood Films

The Children Are Watching Us Before Vittorio de Sica began making neorealist films, he made this little-known studio gem about the life of an unhappily married couple seen from the perspective of their young son. In Italian with English subtitles. (1944) 92 min.

The Curse of the Cat People Fascinating mood piece about a girl who has an imaginary playmate that figures into a supernatural murder mystery. Amazingly, at one point, a reference is made to a classic book in Jungian child psychology, Frances Wickes's *The Inner World of Childhood*. (1944) 70 min.

Forbidden Games A young girl and boy seek to ritualize the horrors of war by creating their own cemetery. In French with English subtitles. (1952) 90 min.

The Fallen Idol A little boy's sheltered world is threatened when he gets caught up in the secrets and lies of the adults around him. (1949) 92 min.

Ponette A four-year-old tries to come to grips with the loss of her mother in an automobile accident through play, fantasy, peer interactions, and perhaps even through a supernatural encounter. In French with English subtitles. (1995) 92 min.

The Red Balloon Academy Award–winning short that depicts a day in the life of a lonely boy who befriends a red balloon that takes him on an adventure. (1956) 34 min.

MIDDLE CHILDHOOD FILMS

Amarcord Director Federico Fellini's growing-up memoir. In Italian with English subtitles. (1974) 124 min.

Avalon The world through the eyes of a boy growing up in 1940s Baltimore. (1990) 126 min.

Big A boy wishes he could be an adult, and it happens—with all sorts of complications. (1988) 98 min.

A Christmas Story Absolutely delightful holiday film that reveals the inner world of a nine-year-old boy growing up in the 1940s in Middle America. (1983) 95 min.

Fanny and Alexander A brother and sister see the varied worlds of adults—magical, austere, festive, raucous—mirrored around them in turn-of-the-century Sweden. In Swedish with English subtitles. (1983) 197 min.

Pather Panchali (The Song of the Road) The first of Indian director Satyajit Ray's Apu trilogy tells of Apu's childhood days. In Hindi with English subtitles. (1954) 112 min.

Small Change Francois Truffaut's postcard of childhood is an innocent yet poignant look at the inner worlds of children from two to puberty growing up in a small French village. In French with English subtitles. (1976) 104 min.

LATE CHILDHOOD FILMS

The 400 Blows François Truffaut's magnificent story about the making of a delinquent still stands out as one of the best films ever made about late childhood/ early adolescence. In French with English subtitles. (1959) 97 min.

Au Revoir Les Enfants (Good-bye, Children) Louis Malle's memoir of being an eleven-year-old forming a heartbreaking friendship with a Jewish boy who was eventually sent to Auschwitz. In French with English subtitles. (1987) 104 min.

Léolo A twelve-year-old boy growing up in a seedy part of Montreal tries to hold on to his dignity while undergoing "soul murder" at the hands of a super-dysfunctional family. (1992) 107 min.

Lord of the Flies Stranded on a desert island, a group of British schoolboys reveal a savage nature that could be their instincts coming out or a mirror of the cruel society in which they were raised. (1963) 91 min.

The Member of the Wedding A twelve-year-old girl living in a small Georgia town experiences the intensity and confusion of living in between childhood and adolescence on the eve of her brother's wedding. (1952) 90 min.

My Life as a Dog A wonderful, funny, and sad look at the world inside the mind of a twelve-year-old boy growing up in rural Sweden in the 1950s. In Swedish with English subtitles. (1985) 101 min.

Stand by Me Four boys go in search of a dead body. (1986) 87 min.

Sundays and Cybele A thirty-year-old man whose nerves have been shattered by combat finds the possibility of redemption in a relationship with an eleven-year-old girl abandoned by her father. In French with English subtitles. (1962) 110 min.

Zero for Conduct This early French classic of kids rebelling at a French boarding school illustrates the vitality of childhood better than perhaps any other film ever made. In French with English subtitles. (1933) 49 min.

Adolescence Films

American Graffiti Events that happen to a group of Modesto, California, teenagers the day after high school graduation. (1973) 112 min.

Aparajito (The Unvanquished) The second of Indian director Satyajit Ray's Apu trilogy follows Apu through his university days. In Hindi with English subtitles. (1958) 108 min.

The Apprenticeship of Duddy Kravitz An eighteen-year-old (played by Richard Dreyfuss in one of his earliest performances) struggles to make it big in the Jewish neighborhoods of 1948 Montreal. (1974) 121 min.

Back to the Future Teenager (Michael J. Fox) travels back to the 1950s and meets his parents as adolescents. (1985) 116 min.

Boyz N the Hood This coming of age story set in South Central L.A. depicts the negative impact of neighborhood violence as well as the positive influence of strong parenting with an African-American teen played by Cuba Gooding Jr. (1991) 112 min.

Breaking Away A Midwestern youth seeks to break away from his parents and working-class background as he moves toward adulthood. (1979) 100 min.

Closely Watched Trains Sensitive Czech film about a young man who seeks his identity as a man, both sexually and politically. In Czech with English subtitles. (1966) 89 min.

Dead Poets Society A prep school teacher (played by Robin Williams) inspires several young men to "seize the day" and follow their passions, in one case with catastrophic results. (1989) 128 min.

Gregory's Girl A young boy in Scotland falls for the new girl in school who is also an expert soccer player. This enchanting film captures the awkwardness of adolescence as well as its capriciousness, self-consciousness, and improvisational quality. (1980) 91 min.

If . . . Students at a British boarding school revolt in this violent remake of Jean Vigo's *Zero de Conduit* (Zero for Conduct). (1969) 111 min.

The Last Picture Show A young man living in a small Texas town graduates from high school and learns about adulthood from an aging cowboy and a lonely middle-aged woman. (1971) 118 min.

Peggy Sue Got Married A woman at midlife collapses at her high school reunion and travels back in time to re-experience her turbulent adolescent days with plenty of hindsight to guide her this time around. (1986) 103 min.

Peppermint Soda Teenage sisters in 1960s Paris encounter love, menstruation rites, leftist politics, incompetent teachers, and changing friendships in this auto-biographical debut film by director Diane Kurys. In French with English subtitles. (1977) 97 min.

Rebel Without a Cause Still relevant James Dean debut film illustrates several key issues of adolescence, including separation from parents, inner emotional turmoil, peer initiation rites, and preoccupation with existential questions. (1955) 111 min.

Salaam Bombay Portrays the lives of young adolescents living on the streets of Bombay amid drugs, prostitution, and poverty. In Hindi with English subtitles. (1988) 113 min.

Sixteen Candles A day in the life of a socially inhibited girl whose family forgets her sixteenth birthday. (1984) 93 min.

Splendor in the Grass A study of teenage sexuality and what happens when a young girl (played by Natalie Wood) is frustrated by restrictive parental/societal forces. (1961) 124 min.

Stand and Deliver Tells the story of a group of Hispanic high school students who find their world transformed by a charismatic teacher. Several excellent scenes show the positive impact a mentor can have on the lives of impressionable teens. (1988) 105 min.

The Sterile Cuckoo An odd but strangely satisfying movie about an unstable girl (played by Liza Minnelli) who forces her way into the life of a naive but clear-headed college freshman. (1969) 108 min.

Streetwise A frank and heartbreaking documentary about runaways struggling to survive on the streets of Seattle. (1984) 92 min.

Summer of '42 Poignant coming-of-age story of two fifteen-year-old boys who lose their virginity in very different ways. (1971) 102 min.

Walkabout An aboriginal youth interrupts his own rite of passage in the wilderness to help two children reach safety in the Australian outback. (1971) 100 min.

Welcome to the Dollhouse Junior high school as Dante's *Inferno*. A seventh-grade girl endures insults and abuse from classmates, siblings, and parents, while somehow managing to keep going in spite of it all. (1995) 87 min.

West Side Story Musical re-creation of Shakespeare's *Romeo and Juliet* is also a superb textbook on gangs, the bloom of young love, and the death wish in adolescence. (1961) 151 min.

Y Tu Mamá También Two brash adolescent males are initiated into the emotional and sexual complexities of adulthood by an older woman on a trip through rural Mexico. In Spanish with English subtitles. (2001) 105 min.

Early Adulthood Films

Bed and Board A twenty-six-year-old assistant florist marries, has a child, and then an affair, struggling all the while with his own immaturity. The fourth film in Francois Truffaut's Antoine Doinel cycle. In French with English subtitles. (1970) 100 min.

The Big Chill College friends gather in their thirties to reconnect and reignite old developmental wounds as they begin to wonder about what comes next in their lives. (1983) 108 min.

Billy Liar Painful story of a young working class man in England who cannot face the demands of moving into life as a full-fledged adult and continually escapes into fantasies as a defense. (1963) 94 min.

The Brothers McMullen Traces the lives of three brothers in their twenties and thirties as they struggle with issues of intimacy, their Catholic faith, and individuation. (1994) 98 min.

Crossing Delancey A Jewish woman in her early thirties confronts the challenges of making it in the publishing world, the delights and hurts of courtship with a pickle merchant, and the constraints of her Old World relatives. (1988) 97 min.

Diner Several men in their early twenties hang out at a diner in 1959 Baltimore and cope with the realities of tenuous relationships with women, old childhood dependencies, and financial difficulties. (1982) 110 min.

The Graduate A recent college graduate who has focused only on academic achievement and pleasing his parents faces the materialism and sexuality of the adult world as he struggles for intimacy and a sense of self. (1967) 106 min.

Groundhog Day Phil Connors (Bill Murray) has an eternity of February 2nds to try out different strategies for snaring Rita (Andie MacDowell), the love of his life, before discovering the secrets of true intimacy. (1993) 103 min.

High Fidelity A thirtysomething owner of a retro vinyl record store (John Cusack) looks back at his past relationship failures and struggles toward a new sense of commitment and intimacy with his current partner. (2000) 113 min.

How to Succeed in Business without Really Trying Bright and satiric musical about a young businessman learning to do whatever it takes to advance up the corporate ladder of success. (1967) 121 min.

The Loneliness of the Long Distance Runner A young man does time in a British reformatory, and while training for a long distance competition, reflects on his life and the society that seems to conspire against him. (1962) 104 min.

Love on the Run A man divorces his wife and has entanglements with other women from his past and present. The fifth and final installment of Francois Truffaut's Antoine Doinel series (which also includes *The 400 Blows*, *Antoine & Colette*, *Stolen Kisses*, and *Bed and Board*). In French with English subtitles. (1978) 95 min.

Marty Lonely working man in his twenties who lives with his mother struggles for intimacy and finds it. (1955) 91 min.

Now Voyager A young woman (Bette Davis) has difficulty breaking away from her critical mother and making her way in life, until she works with a psychiatrist (Paul Henreid) and goes on a South American cruise. (1942) 117 min.

A Portrait of the Artist as a Young Man Film treatment of James Joyce's novel depicts the emotional, moral, and intellectual struggles of a sensitive young Irish writer as he attempts to form an identity apart from his roots. (1979) 93 min.

Stolen Kisses A man in his early twenties is discharged from the military as unfit for service, and bounces from one job to another seeking to find his place in the world. The third installment of Francois Truffaut's Antoine Doinel series. In French with English subtitles. (1968) 90 min.

Stranger Than Paradise Oddball documentary-style film that reveals the hilariously empty lives of three Hungarians who beautifully illustrate the tentativeness of life in early adulthood. (1984) 90 min.

The Sweet Smell of Success Tony Curtis plays a manipulative young newspaper reporter trying to make it big in New York City. (1957) 96 min.

Ticket to Heaven Documentary-style film shows the vulnerability of a young man going through the turmoil of a broken relationship, who falls into the clutches of a religious cult and the equally manipulative influence of a cult deprogrammer. (1981) 109 min.

Why Shoot the Teacher An innocent young man starts his first teaching job in a rural Canadian one-room schoolhouse. (1979) 101 min.

The World of Apu The last of Indian director Satyaji Ray's trilogy of films about a young man named Apu. In this film, Apu struggles in early adulthood to make a living, marries and fathers a child, and confronts tragedy. In Hindi with English subtitles. (1959) 103 min.

Zorba the Greek A young English writer has his quiet cerebral existence upset and positively transformed by a lusty Greek peasant. (1964) 142 min.

Midlife Films

8½ Protagonist filmmaker faces midlife crisis after mega success (patterned after director Federico Fellini's own life history). In Italian with English subtitles. (1963) 135 min.

All About Eve Bette Davis plays a forty-year-old Broadway actor who faces competition from a younger protégée. (1950) 138 min.

Come Back, Little Sheba Shirley Booth's Academy Award–winning performance mourns the loss of youth, love, and her little dog, Sheba. (1952) 99 min.

Come Back to the Five and Dime, Jimmy Dean, Jimmy Dean This Robert Altman film based on a Broadway play chronicles the twenty-year reunion of four women who reveal the pain and emptiness of their growing-up years. (1982) 109 min.

La Dolce Vita Director Federico Fellini follows the circuitous journey of a jaded journalist trying to find meaning in the tempests of modern life in Rome. In Italian with English subtitles. (1960) 174 min.

My Dinner with Andre Two men discuss their midlife perspectives and adventures (which in the case of one of them become progressively bizarre) during a 110-minute dinner conversation. (1981) 110 min.

The Swimmer This neglected gem of a film tells the story of a man (played by Burt Lancaster) swimming from pool to pool in a wealthy Connecticut neighborhood, who conjures up idealized memories and confronts past failures as he attempts to make it all the way home. (1968) 94 min.

An Unmarried Woman A woman undergoes a major transformation when her husband of many years walks out on her. (1978) 124 min.

Vanya on 42nd Street A forty-seven-year-old Russian property manager (portrayed by Wallace Shawn) rails in bitterness over having wasted his life supporting a hypocritical father-in-law. David Mamet adapted the Anton Chekhov play *Uncle Vanya* in Louis Malle's last feature film. (1994) 119 min.

Who's Afraid of Virginia Woolf? A washed-up fortyish college professor (played by Richard Burton) and his abusive wife (played by a middle-aged Elizabeth Taylor) spend a wild night with a younger married couple just getting started in the world of academia. (1966) 127 min.

MATURE ADULTHOOD FILMS

About Schmidt Newly retired insurance executive (Jack Nicholson) goes on the road in a giant RV in order to deal with his deep sense of purposelessness and his perceived failures as a husband and father. (2002) 124 min.

Atlantic City Burt Lancaster is superb as an over-the-hill mobster who has the chance to commit an act of great moral courage. (1981) 104 min.

Central Station A lonely and frustrated older woman befriends a young boy whose mother has just been killed, and together they embark on a long journey from Rio de Janeiro to the northernmost part of Brazil on a quest for the boy's father. In Portuguese with English subtitles. (1998) 110 min.

Death of a Salesman Dustin Hoffman puts fury and pathos into the role of Willy Loman, a sixty-something over-the-hill traveling salesman who hangs on to the illusions of the past while being confronted with the realities of his failures over the years. (1985) TV movie, 135 min.

The Iceman Cometh Middle-aged men in a New York saloon are disabused of their illusions about "making it" in this remake of Eugene O'Neill's classic play. (1973) 259 min.

The Remains of the Day The story of a middle-aged English butler whose emotional blocks stunt his ability to develop intimacy, express generativity, or achieve integrity. (1993) 135 min.

Seconds A failed middle-aged businessman gets a second chance at life by living in the robust body of a young man (played by Rock Hudson). (1966) 107 min.

That's Life! Middle-aged man (Jack Lemmon) frets about aging and imaginary illnesses while his wife (Julie Andrews) secretly faces a real threat to her own life. (1986) 102 min.

Late Adulthood Films

Cocoon Don Ameche leads a group of seniors to the fountain of youth in a nearby swimming pool in this tale about finding vitality in elderhood. (1985) 117 min.

Driving Miss Daisy An aging white Southern lady forges a deep bond with her black chauffeur as they move together through the years. (1989) 99 min.

The Entertainer Follows the decline of an aging British music hall entertainer (played by Sir Laurence Olivier) as it touches all aspects of his life. (1960) 104 min.

Fried Green Tomatoes A woman in a retirement home gives new life to an overweight and sexually frustrated younger woman by telling her the story of her life. (1991) 130 min.

Harold and Maude A suicidal young man falls in love with an old woman with a zest for life in this black comedy directed by Hal Ashby. (1971) 92 min.

Harry and Tonto A tale of a seventy-two-year-old man's Odyssey around the country after being evicted from his New York apartment. (1974) 115 min.

I Never Sang for My Father Powerful drama of a writer facing unresolved feelings toward his newly widowed eighty-year-old father. Contains excellent segments illustrating the life review process in late adulthood. (1970) 90 min.

On Golden Pond Henry Fonda and Katharine Hepburn play an aged couple struggling with family conflicts, physical decline, and impending death at a summer lake cottage. (1981) 109 min.

A Sunday in the Country A widowed grandfather in his seventies who has etched a name for himself in the world of pre–World War I French art is visited by his family, during which we see his failures as a father and an artist. In French with English subtitles. (1984) 94 min.

Sunset Boulevard An aging movie star (played by aging movie star Gloria Swanson) seeks youth through romance with a struggling young writer. (1950) 100 min.

The Sunshine Boys George Burns and Walter Matthau play two retired vaudeville actors who try to team up again for one last show but find that the past is a formidable obstacle to the show's success. (1975) 111 min.

Tokyo Story An elderly couple leaves their rural home to visit their children in the big city, only to be treated as an inconvenience in the midst of their children's (and grandchildren's) busy urban lives. Voted as one of the top ten films of all time by *Sight and Sound* magazine. (1953) 134 min

The Trip to Bountiful An old woman caught in the crossfire between her troubled son and daughter-in-law flees to Bountiful, the town of her birth. (1985) 102 min.

Umberto D An elderly Italian man is evicted from his apartment and has only his dog as a companion. Unlike *Harry and Tonto*, the ending is not a happy one. In Italian with English subtitles. (1955) 89 min.

The Whales of August Two sisters (Lillian Gish in her last screen role and Bette Davis still recovering from a stroke in real life) cope with the problems of aging and their incompatible personalities in this charmer of a film set on the seacoast of Maine. (1987) 91 min.

DEATH AND DYING FILMS

All That Jazz This musical fantasy illustrates the five stages of dying and shows a death experience (with Jessica Lange as the angel of death). (1979) 120 min.

The Barbarian Invasions A hedonistic history professor suffering from advanced cancer struggles to come to grips with his past as he is joined by family and friends from all over the world who have gathered in Quebec to help him die. In French with English subtitles. (2003) 99 min. (112 min in Canadian version).

Cries and Whispers A woman's painful death from cancer is the impetus for her sisters to explore their own decaying lives and the possibilities of intimacy and passion. In Swedish with English subtitles. (1972) 91 min.

Dark Victory Bette Davis portrays a wealthy heiress with a terminal illness who confronts the denial of death in herself and in her close friends. (1939) 106 min.

Ikiru A petty bureaucrat learns he has terminal stomach cancer and attempts to salvage his meaningless life in this classic by Japanese film by director Akira Kurosawa. In Japanese with English subtitles. (1952) 134 min.

Last Holiday A confirmed bachelor and bank clerk (played by Alec Guinness) is told he has only six weeks to live and goes to a luxury resort to play out his last days on earth. (1950) 89 min.

The Loved One Mordant satire on the funeral industry (and many other things American, besides) based on Evelyn Waugh's trenchant novel. (1965) 118 min.

Resurrection Ellen Burstyn plays a young woman who has a near-death experience in a car accident and receives healing powers as a result. (1980) 103 min.

The Shootist An infamous and aged gunslinger returns to his old haunts in Carson City, Nevada, to die in this poignant film starring legendary cowboy hero John Wayne in his last screen appearance; Wayne himself was dying of lung cancer at the time. (1976) 100 min.

Six Feet Under This HBO television series portrays a family in Pasadena, California who owns a funeral home. The series explores the complexities and ambiguities of death and dying, along with the meanings and mysteries of living. (63 episodes, 55 min. each)

Beyond Death Films

After Life People who have died spend a week at a social service agency where they must select one memory from their lives to spend eternity with. In Japanese with English subtitles. (1998) 118 min.

Angel on My Shoulder A murdered convict, played by Paul Muni, is sent back to earth as a judge to make things right. (1946) 101 min.

Black Orpheus A streetcar conductor follows his dead love into the underworld in this cinematic treatment of the Greek myth of Orpheus and Eurydice set in modern-day Rio de Janeiro during Carnival. In Portuguese with English subtitles, (1958) 103 min.

Defending Your Life A man dies in a car crash and ends up in a courtroom-like waiting station called Judgment City where he must justify the actions of his self-absorbed life. (1991) 112 min.

Heaven Can Wait A character played by Don Ameche dies and tells the story of his life to the devil and finds his life wasn't as bad as he thought. (1943) 112 min.

Heaven Can Wait A pro football player (Warren Beatty) dies and returns to Earth as a multimillionaire/philanthropist in this remake of *Here Comes Mr. Jordan*. (1978) 101 min.

Here Comes Mr. Jordan A boxer is snatched up to heaven fifty years before his appointed time and has to go back to Earth and inhabit the body of a murdered millionaire. (1941) 94 min.

Books to Help
Throughout the Life Span

As research and knowledge has expanded over the past four decades concerning the human life span, a wide range of popular books have been
published that provide practical advice for readers who are seeking information to help them cope with the problems of daily living at each stage
of life. Expectant mothers look for up-to-date information on nurturing
their unborn babies and preparing for childbirth. Parents want solid
advice on raising their children and adolescents, and strategies for helping
them in school and preparing them for life. Young adults need guidance in
finding jobs, mates, and housing. Midlifers and those in mature and late
adulthood seek books that provide information about staying healthy,
revitalizing relationships, and finding new meaning and purpose in the
second half of life. With the increased awareness of death and dying, and
the growth of hospice programs nationwide, people are also looking for
books to help them prepare for this final stage of life and what may lie
beyond. This bibliography contains a small sample of the many books currently available to guide readers through the twelve stages of life. All are
currently in print. Where alternative versions of a title are available, the
least expensive version (usually paperback) is the one listed. Virtually all
of these titles can be ordered through any local independent or chain
bookstore, or purchased through online bookstores.

PREBIRTH BOOKS

Luminare-Rosen, Carista. *Parenting Begins Before Conception: A Guide to Preparing Your Body, Mind, and Spirit for You and Your Future Child.* Rochester, VT: Healing Arts Press, 2000. A practical guide to preparing mothers for pregnancy and birth using tools from both Eastern and Western psychologies.

Nathanielcz, Peter W., with Christopher Vaughn. *The Prenatal Prescription.* New York: HarperCollins, 2001. Advice for parents-to-be on proper nutrition, stress reduction, and avoidance of toxins, and how these factors help to create a positive prenatal environment that will set the stage for a healthy life for the child after birth, and even protect her against heart disease, stroke, and other diseases when she reaches adulthood.

Tsiaras, Alexander, and Barry Werth. *From Conception to Birth: A Life Unfolds.* New York: Doubleday, 2002. A visual diary of fetal development through computer imaging.

Verny, Thomas, and Pamela Weintraub. *Pre-Parenting: Nurturing Your Child from Conception.* New York: Simon & Schuster, 2003. Offers practical advice for expectant parents on nurturing their preborn child based upon recent findings from neuroscience and developmental psychology.

Wirth, Frederick. *Prenatal Parenting: The Complete Psychological and Spiritual Guide to Loving Your Unborn Child.* New York: Regan Books, 2001. Provides the expectant mother with guidelines on how to handle stress that might interfere with the fetus's emotional development, how to communicate with the fetus, and how to foster a spiritual environment between mother and child.

BIRTH BOOKS

Arms, Suzanne. *Immaculate Deception II.* Revised edition. Berkeley, CA: Celestial Arts, 2000. Critiques the disease-based medical model approach to birthing, and describes a wide range of positive alternative birthing practices that ease the fear of childbirth and provide an atmosphere of love, trust, and comfort for the child about to be born.

England, Pam, and Rob Horowitz. *Birthing from Within: An Extraordinary Guide to Childbirth Preparation.* Albuquerque, NM: Partera Press, 1998. Includes meditations, writing exercises, and other activities for expectant mothers to help them learn to trust their own innate knowledge of the birth process, and to become savvy about the world of modern hospital culture before they give birth.

Harper, Barbara, with Suzanne Arms. *Gentle Birth Choices: A Guide to Making Informed Decisions About Birthing Centers, Birth Attendants, Water Birth, Home Birth, Hospital Birth.* New York: Inner Traditions, 1994. A sensible guide that dispels myths about conventional hospital birth, offers birthing alternatives, gives practical tools for communicating with doctors and midwives, and provides guidance in constructing a plan for giving birth in a gentle and nurturing way.

Leboyer, Frederick. *Birth Without Violence: Revised Edition of the Classic*. Rochester, VT: Inner Traditions, 2002. Shows how to create an atmosphere of tranquillity during the birth process using relaxation, a quiet and soothing environment, and other techniques to reduce the trauma of birth.

McCutcheon, Susan. *Natural Childbirth the Bradley Way*. New York: Plume, 1996. A step-by-step introduction to the Bradley method of natural childbirth, which was the first major alternative birthing method to emphasize the role of the father in the birth process and the avoidance of drugs for the mother during birth.

Savage, Beverly. *Preparation for Birth: The Complete Guide to the Lamaze Method*. New York: Ballantine, 1987. A comprehensive guide to the Lamaze method of birth, which emphasizes breathing and relaxation techniques to ease pain.

INFANCY BOOKS

Gotsch, Gwen, Anwar Fazal, and Judy Torgus. *The Womanly Art of Breastfeeding*. New York: Plume, 1997. The La Leche League International's classic guide to breastfeeding includes a comprehensive rationale for breastfeeding as well as lots of practical support for mothers in dealing with the logistics of breastfeeding.

Leach, Penelope. *Your Baby and Child: From Birth to Age Five*. New York: Alfred A. Knopf, 1997. From diaper rash and teething to language development and play, this comprehensive guide to the first five years of life is one of the most popular and practical guides for parents of young children. (See also Early Childhood.)

Liedloff, Jean. *The Continuum Concept: In Search of Happiness Lost*. Boulder, CO: Perseus Publishing, 1986. Based upon her experiences with indigenous cultures in South America, Liedloff constructs a modern rationale for maintaining an environment of emotional and physical closeness between mother and child during the first years of life. (See also Early Childhood.)

Sears, William, and Martha Sears. *The Baby Book: Everything You Need to Know About Your Baby from Birth to Age Two*. Revised and updated edition. Boston: Little, Brown, & Co., 2003. Nuts-and-bolts guide to raising baby, covering such topics as teething, toilet training, feeding, carrying baby, breastfeeding, dealing with bothersome behaviors, baby proofing the house, and much more.

Small, Meredith. *Our Babies, Ourselves: How Biology and Culture Shape the Way We Parent*. New York: Anchor Books. 1999. A fascinating look into the anthropological and evolutionary basis for using appropriate methods to nurture babies.

EARLY CHILDHOOD BOOKS

Auerbach, Stevanne. *Dr. Toy's Smart Play: How to Raise a Child with a High PQ (Play Quotient)*. New York: St. Martin's Press, 1998. Practical guide to selecting toys for children from infancy to preteen includes information on toy safety, gender issues, and the importance of play to a child's development.

Elkind, David. *Miseducation: Preschoolers at Risk*. New York: Alfred A. Knopf, 1988. Criticizes the tendency in educational circles to make preschool environments less play-oriented and more academic, arguing that such developmentally inappropriate practices create stress for young children and fail to nurture their young minds.

Hunt, Jan, and Peggy O'Mara. *The Natural Child: Parenting from the Heart*. Gabriola Island, BC: New Society Publishers, 2001. Takes a loving child-centered perspective toward parenting and education in speaking out against spanking, labeling (as ADHD, LD, etc.), and other forms of child coercion, while offering tips for raising a happy child. (See also Birth, Infancy, Middle Childhood, and Late Childhood.)

Olfman, Sharna (ed.). *All Work and No Play: How Educational Reforms Are Harming Our Preschoolers*. Westport, CT: Praeger, 2003. A series of chapters that raise alarm at the demise of natural play among children, and the rise of stress-producing technologies such as computers, video games, and standardized testing.

Pearce, Joseph Chilton. *Magical Child*. New York: Plume, 1992. A celebration of the child's intrinsic wisdom and imagination, and a critique of modern methods of birthing, child rearing, and education that eliminate the magic from childhood. (See also Prebirth, Birth, Infancy, Middle Childhood, and Late Childhood.)

MIDDLE CHILDHOOD BOOKS

Armstrong, Thomas. *In Their Own Way: Discovering and Encouraging Your Child's Multiple Intelligences*. Revised and updated edition. New York: Tarcher, 2000. An introduction for parents and educators to Harvard psychologist Howard Gardner's theory of multiple intelligences, and how to use a knowledge of the different intelligences to help children succeed in school and in life. (See also Early Childhood, Late Childhood, and Adolescence.)

Elkind, David. *The Hurried Child: Growing Up Too Fast, Too Soon*. Third edition. Boulder, CO: Perseus Publishing, 2001. Examines how pressures in our culture to push kids too quickly into adulthood are causing an epidemic of stress-related problems. (See also Early Childhood and Late Childhood.)

Healy, Jane. *Endangered Minds: Why Children Don't Think and What We Can Do About It*. New York: Touchstone, 1999. Examines the dangers of modern media, including television, computers, and the Internet, in short-circuiting the natural brain development and thinking processes of children. (See also Early Childhood, Late Childhood, and Adolescence.)

Llewellyn, Grace, and Amy Silver. *Guerrilla Learning: How to Give Your Kids a Real Education With or Without School.* New York: John Wiley, 2001. Shows parents how to utilize everyday resources to give their children a brilliant education based on direct experience instead of artificial classroom tasks. (See also Early Childhood, Late Childhood, and Adolescence.)

Holt, John Caldwell. *How Children Fail.* Revised edition. Boulder, CO: Perseus Publishing, 1995. This classic text on alternative education reveals how schools are designed to produce students who have less concern with learning and more concern with trying to figure out the rules of a fundamentally incoherent educational system. (See also Late Childhood and Adolescence.)

LATE CHILDHOOD BOOKS

Gianetti, Charlene C., and Margaret Sagarese. *The Roller-Coaster Years: Raising Your Child Through the Maddening Yet Magical Middle School Years.* New York: Broadway, 1997. Guidance for parents on helping your "middler" (ten- to fifteen-year-old) with issues such as sibling rivalry, getting organized, handling conflict, school difficulties, and dealing with emotions.

Hartley-Brewer, Elizabeth. *Talking to Tweens: Getting It Right Before It Gets Rocky with Your 8- to 12-Year Old.* New York: Da Capo Books, 2005. Provides advice for parents on creating a balance between staying close to your children and, at the same time, letting them become themselves.

Mosatche, Harriet, and Karen Under. *Too Old For This, Too Young for That! Your Survival Guide for the Middle School Years.* Minneapolis, MN: Free Spirit Publishing, 2000. This book is designed for kids in grades five through eight to help them deal with their changing bodies, self-esteem, family relationships, school, and extracurricular activities.

Rimm, Sylvia. *Growing Up Too Fast: The Rimm Report on the Secret World of America's Middle Schoolers.* New York: Rodale Press, 2005. A child psychologist shares the results of a survey of more than 5,400 middle school kids, revealing that children at this age face pressures (e.g., sex, drugs, body image) that used to begin in high school. Provides advice for parents on how to help their kids cope in an increasingly complicated world.

Rosenberg, Ellen. *Get a Clue! What's Really Going on with Pre-Teens and How Parents Can Help.* New York: Owl Books/Henry Holt, 1999. Offers guidelines for parents on how to talk to their preteens on topics such as peer pressure, sexuality, teasing, and drugs.

ADOLESCENCE BOOKS

Elkind, David. *All Grown Up and No Place to Go: Teenagers in Crisis*. Revised edition. Boulder, CO: Perseus Publishing, 1997. One of America's leading developmental psychologists looks at how today's fast-paced culture makes the transition from childhood into adulthood exceedingly difficult, and even dangerous for many teenagers, and provides practical advice to parents for helping adolescents cope with the changes going on inside and outside of them.

Hersch, Patricia. *A Tribe Apart: A Journey into the Heart of American Adolescence*. New York: Ballantine Books, 1999. The author spent three years following eight "regular" teenagers in a "typical" American town, recording their concerns, rituals, and needs from the inside out, and coming to some disturbing conclusions about how American adults abandon their adolescents, leaving them to find their own way in a confusing world.

Kindlon, Daniel J., and Michael Thompson. *Raising Cain: Protecting the Emotional Life of Boys*. New York: Ballantine Books, 2000. The authors describe how boys in contemporary life are coerced into a culture of cruelty and a too-narrow definition of masculinity that stunts their emotional growth. The book provides seven tips for what boys really need to develop into mature men. (See also Middle Childhood and Late Childhood.)

Pipher, Mary. *Reviving Ophelia: Saving the Selves of Adolescent Girls*. New York: Ballantine Books, 2002. Despite decades of women's liberation, this adolescent psychotherapist argues that today's girls are caught in a "girl-poisoning culture" that emphasizes looks and other media stereotypes for feminine behavior, while squelching the inner spirit. (See also Middle Childhood and Late Childhood.)

Strauch, Barbara. *The Primal Teen: What the New Discoveries About the Teenage Brain Tell Us About Our Kids*. New York: Doubleday, 2003. Reviews recent research on the adolescent's changing brain to help explain to parents some of the reasons for their teenagers' erratic behaviors, roller-coaster moods, and "in-your-face" attitudes.

EARLY ADULTHOOD BOOKS

Bourland, Julia. *The Go-Girl Guide: Surviving Your 20s with Savvy, Soul, and Style*. New York: McGraw-Hill, 2000. A practical and humorous guide to help young female adults cope with everything from dating and relationships to job hunting and avoiding credit debt.

Furman, Elina, and Leah Furman. *The Everything After College Book: Real-World Advice for Surviving and Thriving on Your Own*. Avon, MA: Adams Media, 1998. Help for the recent college graduate on practical life skills such as finding an apartment, dealing with your family, cooking for one person, and making new friends.

Jedding, Kenneth. *Real Life Notes: Reflections and Strategies for Life After Graduation.* New York, NY: Double Rose Books, 2002. A self-help book for young adults that includes advice on how to figure out what you really want to do with your life, how to survive entry-level jobs, and how to relate to your parents in a new way.

Kobliner, Beth. *Get a Financial Life: Personal Finance in Your Twenties and Thirties.* New York: Fireside, 2000. Covers such topics as planning financial goals, understanding how the world of money works, saving up for a home, and paying taxes.

Robbins, Alexandra, and Abby Wilner. *Quarterlife Crisis: The Unique Challenges of Life in Your Twenties.* New York: Tarcher, 2001. Using personal accounts from the lives of twentysomethings, this book argues that there is a "quarterlife crisis" that precedes the more famous "midlife crisis" of the thirties and forties.

MIDLIFE BOOKS

Brehony, Kathleen A. *Awakening at Midlife: A Guide to Reviving Your Spirits, Recreating Your Life, and Returning to Your Truest Self.* New York: Riverhead, 1997. This book, written by a Jungian psychotherapist, provides activities for retrieving childhood memories , understanding the unconscious, caring for the body, and reconnecting with one's deepest spiritual beliefs as a way of navigating through the midlife passage. (See also Mature Adulthood.)

Chinen, Allan. *Once Upon a Midlife.* Philadelphia: Xlibris Corporation, 2003. A psychiatrist examines fairy tales from around the world that deal with midlife issues including mortality, gender attitudes, spirituality, and creative renewal. (See also Mature Adulthood.)

Edelstein, Linda N. *The Art of Midlife: Courage and Creative Living for Women.* Bergin & Garvey, 1999. This book celebrates the voices of women at midlife reflecting on issues such as letting go of the old, reconnecting with a deeper place, and realizing creative potentials. (See also Mature Adulthood.)

Gerzon, Mark. *Listening to Midlife: Turning Your Crisis into a Quest.* Boston: Shambhala, 1996. Using stories from his own life and those of others, the author encourages readers to craft their own unique way through the midlife passage by encountering family, work, and self with courage and creativity. (See also Mature Adulthood.)

Travis, John W., and Regina Sara Ryan. *Wellness Workbook: How to Achieve Enduring Health and Vitality.* Third edition. Berkeley, CA: Celestial Arts, 2004. Provides a holistic approach to taking better care of yourself, including information on diet, emotions, sex, spirituality, breath, communications, and more. (See also Early Adulthood, Mature Adulthood, and Late Adulthood.)

Sheehy, Gail. *Passages: Predictable Crises of Adult Life*. New York: Bantam, 1977. This is the classic book that launched "midlife crisis" as a term used in popular culture. Sheehy has written several follow-up books on midlife and mature adulthood, including *New Passages*, *Understanding Men's Passages*, and *The Silent Passage* (a book about menopause). (See also Mature Adulthood.)

Mature Adulthood Books

Cohen, Gene. *The Creative Age: Awakening Human Potential in the Second Half of Life*. New York: Perennial Currents, 2001. This book provides a positive perspective on aging by examining recent brain research and by providing numerous examples of individuals who reached their peak of creativity in the second half of life. Also available is Cohen's *The Mature Mind: The Positive Power of the Aging Brain*. New York: Basic Books, 2005. (See also Midlife and Late Adulthood.)

Kotre, John. *Make it Count: How to Generate a Legacy that Gives Meaning to Your Life*. New York: Free Press, 1999. Provides a step-by-step program for anyone in their thirties, forties, fifties, or beyond, to help overcome obstacles in midlife through the creation of meaningful generative projects that endure beyond one's own individual existence.

Schacter-Shalomi, Zalman. *From Age-ing to Sage-ing: A Profound New Vision of Growing*. New York: Warner, 1997. A rabbi describes how people in the second half of life can practice the art of "eldering" by engaging in spiritual practices, creating meaningful rituals, and giving to others. (See also Midlife and Late Adulthood.)

Roszak, Theodore. *Longevity Revolution: As Boomers Become Elders*. Albany, CA: Berkeley Hills Books, 2001. A cultural historian explores how the phenomenon of people living longer can serve as a positive social force. (See also Midlife and Late Adulthood.)

Snowden, David. *Aging with Grace: What the Nun Study Teaches Us About Leading Longer, Healthier, and More Meaningful Lives*. New York: Bantam, 2002. The author has studied a group of aging nuns who have followed a tradition of lifelong learning and good health habits, and in the process has made some interesting discoveries about the art of healthy aging. (See also Midlife and Late Adulthood.)

Vaillant, George. *Aging Well: Surprising Guideposts to a Happier Life from the Landmark Harvard Study of Adult Development*. Boston: Little, Brown, & Co., 2003. A Harvard psychiatrist uses several long-term studies of human development to come to important conclusions about what factors contribute to happiness in old age. (See also Midlife and Late Adulthood.)

LATE ADULTHOOD BOOKS

Cassel, Christine K., ed. *The Practical Guide to Aging: What Everyone Needs to Know*. New York: New York University Press, 1999. Provides advice on late life issues such as managing multiple medications, finding housing, dealing with legal issues, and handling finances. (See also Mature Adulthood.)

Enkelis, Liane. *On Being 100: Centenarians Share Their Extraordinary Lives and Wisdom*. Roseville, CA: Prima, 2000. An intimate collection of photos and interviews with thirty men and women who reached the age of one hundred.

Friedan, Betty. *The Fountain of Age*. New York: Touchstone, 1994. The author of the *Feminine Mystique* turns her critical gaze on modern culture's depreciation of the elderly, challenging elders to not buy into ageist myths but instead to create new and positive roles for themselves. (See also Mature Adulthood.)

Olshansky, S. Jay, and Bruce A. Carnes. *The Quest for Immortality: Science at the Frontiers of Aging*. New York: W. W. Norton, 2001. Debunks the claims of those who believe that herbs, potions, vitamins, diets, or hormones can indefinitely prolong life. Explores the science of aging in light of recent medical discoveries. (See also Mature Adulthood.)

Perls, Thomas T., and Margery Hutter Silver, with John F. Lauerman. *Living to 100: Lessons to Living to Your Maximum Potential at Any Age*. New York: Basic Books, 2000. Offers some startling revelations about the good health of many centenarians and examines factors that improve one's odds of reaching an advanced age (the book includes a life expectancy calculator).

DEATH AND DYING BOOKS

Duda, Deborah. *Coming Home: A Guide to Dying at Home With Dignity*. New York: NY: Aurora Press, 1987. A practical guide that relates the author's very personal experiences of attending to two home deaths, while offering sage advice for deciding when a home death is the best choice, plus hundreds of tips on day-to-day concerns including medical issues, legal help, creating a comfortable environment, and planning a burial and service.

Kubler-Ross, Elisabeth, and David Kessler. *Life's Lessons: Two Experts on Death and Dying Teach Us About the Mysteries of Life and Living*. New York: Scribner's, 2001. Personal accounts of how encountering death in ourselves and others helps us complete unfinished business, live life to its fullest, and open ourselves up to love.

Lattanzi-Licht, Marcia, with John J. Mahoney and Galen W. Miller. *The Hospice Choice: In Pursuit of a Peaceful Death*. New York: Fireside, 1998. An excellent introduction to the hospice movement, offering information on hospice services, and giving a wide range of scenarios to show how hospice adapts to individual needs. Provides personal accounts of families, professionals, and volunteers going through the hospice experience as a team.

Levine, Stephen, and Ondrea Levine. *Who Dies? An Investigation of Conscious Living and Conscious Dying*. New York: Anchor Press, 1989. An investigation into the process of dying using the author's own personal experiences gleaned from Buddhist, Hindu, and other mystical traditions. Includes a number of meditation exercises designed to help heal the fear of death and life.

Lynn, Joanne, and Joan Harrold. *Handbook for Mortals: Guidance for People Facing Serious Illness*. New York: Oxford University Press, 2001. A comprehensive practical guide to issues related to death and dying, including pain management, resolving old business, how to talk to doctors, finding meaning in loss, decision making as a family, and methods of foregoing medical treatment to avoid a long drawn-out dying process.

BEYOND DEATH BOOKS

Johnson, Christopher Jay, and Marsha G. McGee. *How Different Religions View Death and Afterlife*. Second edition. Philadelphia: The Charles Press, 1998. Provides straightforward descriptions of how twenty religious traditions view death and the afterlife, written by experts in each faith. Includes a chapter of special questions that are answered from the perspective of each tradition (e.g., "What happens to people who commit suicide?" etc.).

Miller, Sukie. *After Life: How People Around the World Map the Journey after We Die*. New York: Simon & Schuster, 1998. Drawing on her own experience as a psycho-therapist as well as on research-based interviews with shamans, priests, and holy men in India, Brazil, Indonesia, West Africa, and the United States, the author identifies and describes four distinct stages that appear to underlie many, if not most, of the world's cultural traditions: waiting, judgment, possibilities, and return.

Moody, Raymond. *Life After Life: The Investigation of a Phenomenon—Survival of Bodily Death*. San Francisco: HarperSan Francisco, 2001. An investigation into the cases of more than a hundred individuals who were declared clinically dead and then, on being revived, told stories about encountering tunnels, light, guardians, and ineffable joy "on the other side" of death.

Schwartz, Gary E. *The Afterlife Experiments: Breakthrough Scientific Evidence of Life After Death*. New York: Fireside, 2003. Using scientific research methods, this University of Arizona psychologist attempts to provide rational evidence of life after death by correlating information gathered from "psychics" communicating with dead relatives and friends with that of "sitters" who are blocked off from any contact with the mediums.

Sogyal Rinpoche. *The Tibetan Book of Living and Dying*. San Francisco: HarperSanFrancisco, 1994. A Tibetan monk shares his own modern insights and practical advice about encountering death and the afterlife experience, using as a guide the classic eighth-century C.E. text on death and dying, *The Tibetan Book of the Dead*.

Organizations That Support Human Development

It takes a community of concerned and involved citizens to guide the growth of human beings from conception to the final moments of death and beyond. The following list of organizations and Web sites is a preliminary attempt at pulling together a "stages of life yellow pages" to assist individuals who wish to pool their energies with others working to support people at each stage of the life cycle, or who themselves wish to benefit from the services that these groups offer. Listed here are organizations that fund scientific research into birth defects and Alzheimer's disease; telephone hotlines providing instant access for those wishing to report child abuse or elder abuse; Web sites offering comprehensive information about adolescence, job training, and death and dying; volunteer groups mentoring at-risk children or young adults; and much more. Many of the organizations provide seminars, conferences, specialized training, periodicals or journals, books and pamphlets, video programs, or other materials that offer useful information on a specific stage of life. To help the reader contact each organization, I've listed multiple sources of contact, including (when available): mailing address, regular phone number (and, if available, toll-free phone number), fax number, e-mail address, and Web site URL.

PREBIRTH ORGANIZATIONS

The Association for Pre- & Perinatal Psychology and Health, P.O. Box 1398, Forestville, CA 95436. E-mail: apppah@aol.com; Web site: www.birthpsychology.com. Holds yearly conferences and publishes a journal and newsletter on recent research in the psychological dimensions of prenatal care.

March of Dimes, 1275 Mamaroneck Avenue, White Plains, NY 10605. Phone: 888-MODIMES; Web site: www.marchofdimes.com. Funds research and educational programs that fight the problems of prematurity, birth defects, and low birth weight.

National Perinatal Association, 3500 E. Fletcher Avenue, Suite 205, Tampa, FL 33613-4712. Phone: 813-971-1008; toll-free 888-971-3295; fax: 813-971-9306; e-mail: npa@nationalperinatal.org. Coalition of health-care professionals seeking to improve social, cultural, and economic conditions for expectant mothers (See also Birth.)

Planned Parenthood Federation of America, 434 W. 33rd Street New York, NY 10001. Phone: 212-541-7800; fax: 212-245-1845; Web site: www.plannedparenthood.org Provides support in reproductive health care, sexuality, methods of contraception, abortion, and other areas to help ensure that every baby born is a wanted and cared-for baby.

Visible Embryo, Web site: www.visembryo.com. This Web site sponsored by the University of California Medical Center offers clickable images and accompanying information representing each of the twenty-three stages of the first trimester— and every two weeks of the second and third trimesters—of pregnancy.

BIRTH ORGANIZATIONS

American College of Nurse-Midwives (ACNM), 818 Connecticut Avenue NW, Suite 900, Washington, DC 20006. Phone: 202-728-9860; fax: 202-728-9897; Web site: www.midwife.org. The oldest woman's health-care organization in the United States, ACNM provides certification of nurse-midwives and midwives, establishes clinical practice standards, offers continuing education programs, and creates liaisons with state and federal agencies and members of Congress. (See also Prebirth.)

Birthing the Future, P.O. Box 1040, Bayfield, CO 81122; Phone: 970-884-4005; Web site: www.birthingthefuture.com. The Web site of birth activist Suzanne Arms includes information critical of conventional medical-institutional birthing practices, as well as a wide range of alternative resources for birth and infant care based upon a wellness paradigm. (See also Prebirth, Infancy.)

Coalition for Improving Maternity Services, P.O. Box 2346, Ponte Vedra Beach, FL 32004. Phone: 904-285-1613; toll-free 888-282-CIMS; fax 904-285-2120; e-mail: info@motherfriendly.org; Web site: www.motherfriendly.org. A coalition of more than fifty organizations that seeks to promote a wellness model of birth to improve birth outcomes and reduce health-care costs.

Lamaze International, 2025 M Street, Suite 800, Washington, DC 20036-3309. Phone: 800-368-4404; fax: 202-367-2128; Web site: www.lamaze.org. Promotes educational programs and advocacy to support the normal birth process in women. Encourages caregivers to "respect the birth process and not intervene without compelling medical indications." (See also Prebirth.)

National Association of Childbearing Centers, 3123 Gottschall Road, Perkiomenville, PA 18074. Phone: 215-234-8068; fax: 215-234-8829; e-mail: ReachNACC@BirthCenters.org; Web site: www.birthcenters.org. Supports a wellness model of pregnancy and birth by promoting the concept of birth centers, which are homelike care facilities operating within a health-care system designed for healthy women before, during, and after normal pregnancy, labor, and birth. (See also Prebirth.)

INFANCY ORGANIZATIONS

Alliance for Transforming the Lives of Children, 901 Preston Avenue, Suite 400, Charlottesville, VA 22903. Phone 206-666-4301, toll-free 888-574-7580, e-mail: info@atlc.org; Web site: http://atlc.org. An alliance of organizations that promote a comprehensive blueprint for evidence-based human development principles and practices that nurture the lives of children from conception through adolescence.

The American Academy of Pediatrics (AAP), 141 Northwest Point Boulevard, Elk Grove Village, IL 60007-1098. Phone: 847-434-4000; fax: 847-434-8000; Web site: www.aap.org. Organization of 57,000 pediatricians dedicated to the health, safety, and well-being of all infants, children, adolescents, and young adults. While the AAP is unable to respond to specific inquiries (it states: "your pediatrician is the best source for child and adolescent health information), the Web site contains general information for parents. (See also Early Childhood, Middle and Late Childhood, Adolescence, Young Adulthood.)

Children: Our Ultimate Investment, P.O. Box 1868, Los Angeles, CA 90078. Phone: 323-461-8248; fax: 323-461-8470; e-mail: childrenOUI@aol.com; Web site: www.children-ourinvestment.org. Founded in 1977 by Laura Huxley, this organization focuses on two projects, Project Caressing, which brings together toddlers and elders, and Teens and Toddlers, a high school curriculum designed to prepare adolescents for the important responsibilities of parenting. (See also Prebirth, Early Childhood, Adolescence, Late Adulthood.)

La Leche League International, 1400 N. Meacham Road, Schaumburg, IL 60173-4808. Phone: 847-519-7730; Web site: www.lalecheleague.org. Supports breastfeeding as a highly significant component of the mother-child relationship, and breast milk as a superior nutritional food for the infant.

National Clearinghouse on Child Abuse and Neglect, 330 C Street SW, Washington, DC 20447. Phone: 703-385-7565; toll-free: 800-394-3366; fax: 703-385-3206; e-mail: nccanch@caliber.com; Web site: www.childwelfare.gov. Federal agency (United States Department of Health and Human Services) established to collect, organize, and disseminate information on all aspects of child maltreatment. Provides guidelines on how to report suspected child maltreatment. For reports of suspected child abuse or neglect, or for crisis counseling, call the National Child Abuse Hotline 800-422-4453 (800-4-A-CHILD), 24 hours a day. (See also Early Childhood, Late Childhood, Adolescence.)

Prevent Child Abuse America (NCPCA), 500 N. Michigan Avenue, Suite 200, Chicago, IL 60611. Phone: 312-663-3520; fax: 312-939-8962; e-mail: mailbox@preventchildabuse.org; Web site: www.preventchildabuse.org; Volunteer-based coalition providing advocacy, and supporting the development of child abuse prevention programs. (See also Early Childhood, Late Childhood, Adolescence.)

United Nations Children's Fund (UNICEF), UNICEF House, 3 United Nations Plaza, New York, NY 10017. Phone: 212-326-7000; fax: 212-887-7465; Web site: www.unicef.org or www.unicefusa.org. World organization that provides support to a wide range of grass-roots partners, and influences decisionmakers regarding the safety, health, economic security, and basic human rights of children around the world. (See also Early Childhood, Late Childhood, Adolescence.)

Zero to Three: National Center for Infants, Toddlers and Families, 2000 M Street NW, Suite 200, Washington, DC 20036. Phone: 202-638-1144; Web site: www.zerotothree.org. Promotes the healthy development of the nation's infants and toddlers through advocacy, publications, training, and technical assistance.

Early Childhood Organizations

Alliance for Childhood, P.O. Box 444, College Park, MD 20741. Phone/fax: 301-779-1033; e-mail: info@allianceforchildhood.net; Web site: www.allianceforchildhood.net. A partnership of individuals and organizations committed to fostering the natural and unhurried development of children through advocacy in areas such as education, health, and the media.

National Head Start Association, 1651 Prince Street, Alexandria, VA 22314. Phone: 703-739-0875; fax: 703-739-0878; Web site: www.nhsa.org. Umbrella organization for the 2,500 Head Start programs in the United States.

Parents as Teachers National Center, Inc., 2228 Ball Drive, St. Louis, MO 63146. Phone: 314-432-4330; toll-free: 866-PAT4YOU (866-728-4968); fax: 314-432-8963; e-mail: info@patnc.org; Web site: www.patnc.org. International early childhood parent education and family support program serves families throughout pregnancy until their child enters kindergarten. (See also Prebirth, Birth, Infancy.)

Parents' Action for Children, 1875 Connecticut Avenue NW, Suite 650, Washington, DC 20009. Phone: 202-238-4878; fax: 202.986-2539; e-mail: info@parentsaction.org; Web site: www.iamyourchild.org. Formerly the I Am Your Child Foundation, this organization promotes the physical well-being and the social, emotional, and cognitive abilities of young children so that they have the capacities they need to succeed when entering school for the first time.

MIDDLE CHILDHOOD ORGANIZATIONS

Association for Childhood Education International, 17904 Georgia Avenue, Suite 215, Olney, MD 20832. Phone: 301-570-2111; toll-free: 800-423-3563; fax: 301-570-2212; e-mail: headquarters@acei.org; Web site: www.acei.org. Supports the optimal education and development of children from birth through early adolescence. (See also Birth, Infancy, Early Childhood, Adolescence.)

Association Montessori Internationale/USA, 410 Alexander Street, Rochester, NY 14607-1028. Phone: 585-461-5920; toll-free: 800-872-2643; fax: 585-461-0075; e-mail: ami-usa@montessori-ami.org; Web site: www.montessori-ami.org. Promotes the growth and dissemination of the teachings of Italian educator Maria Montessori in both private and public schools across the country. (See also Infancy, Early Childhood, Adolescence.)

Association of Waldorf Schools of North America, 337 Oak Grove Street, Minneapolis, MN 55403. Phone: 612-870-8310; Web site: www.awsna.org. Supports the development of Waldorf Education (based upon the work of artist/philosopher/educator Rudolf Steiner) in public and private schools from preschool through twelfth grade. (See also Early Childhood, Adolescence.)

FairTest—The National Center for Fair & Open Testing, 342 Broadway, Cambridge, MA 02139. Phone: 617-864-4810; fax: 617-497-2224; Web site: www.fairtest.org. Critiques the overuse of standardized testing, and advocates the establishment of fair, open, and educationally sound methods for the evaluation of schoolchildren and working adults. (See also Early Childhood, Adolescence, Young Adulthood, Midlife, Mature Adulthood.)

National Parent Teachers Association (PTA), 541 N. Fairbanks Court, Suite 1300, Chicago, IL 60611-3396. Phone: 312-670-6782; toll free: 800-307-4PTA (800-307-4782); fax: 312-670-6783; e-mail: info@pta.org; Web site: www.pta.org. The largest volunteer child advocacy organization in the United States, the PTA facilitates parental involvement in the schools, provides parent training, and advocates for the needs of school-aged children and youth in the community and through governmental organizations. (See also Early Childhood, Adolescence.)

Teaching Tolerance, Southern Poverty Law Center, 400 Washington Avenue, Montgomery, AL 36104. Phone: 334-956-8200; fax: 334-956-8488; Web site: www.teachingtolerance.org or www.tolerance.org. Advocates for the dismantling of bigotry and the creation, as an alternative to hate and hate groups, of communities that value diversity. Provides materials to parents, classroom teachers, and children and adolescents.

TV-Turnoff Network, 1200 29th Street NW, Lower Level #1, Washington, DC 20007. Phone: 202-518-5556; fax: 202-518-5560; e-mail: email@tvturnoff.org; Web site: www.tvturnoff.org. National nonprofit organization encourages children and adults to watch much less television to promote healthier lives and communities. (See also Infancy, Early Childhood, Adolescence, Young Adulthood, Midlife, Mature Adulthood.)

Late Childhood Organizations

Big Brothers Big Sisters of America. 230 N. 13th Street, Philadelphia, PA 19107. Phone: 215-567-7000; fax: 215-567-0394; Web site: www.bbbsa.org. Matches mentors with children who need consistent role models. Web site provides listings of local agencies across the country.

Boys & Girls Clubs of America, 1275 Peachtree Street NE, Atlanta, GA 30309-3506. Phone: 404-487-5700; e-mail: info@bgca.org; Web site: www.bgca.org. Supports the establishment of neighborhood-based locations where children and youth can engage in recreational activities and have contact with positive role models as an alternative to hanging out on the streets or staying at home alone.

National Middle School Association. 4151 Executive Parkway, Suite 300 Westerville, OH 43081. Phone: 614-895-4730; toll-free: (800)-528-NMSA (800-528-6672); fax: (614)-895-4750; e-mail: info@NMSA.org; Web site: http://www.nmsa.org/ Supports the educational and developmental needs of kids in late childhood and early adolescence.

Verb Yellowball for Community Organizations: Materials for Tweens, Youth Media Campaign, Centers for Disease Control and Prevention. Phone: 800-CDC-INFO (800-232-4636); e-mail: info@cdc.gov. Promotional program for getting youth more physically active on a regular basis. Web site provides downloadable materials. http://www.cdc.gov/youthcampaign/materials/tweens/yellowball_CBO/index.htm

ADOLESCENCE ORGANIZATIONS

Adolescence: Change and Continuity. E-mail: nxd10@psu.edu; Web site: www.oberlin.edu/faculty/ndarling/adolesce.htm. This Web site provides information about some of the developmental issues that are unique to the period between puberty and the end of college, including autobiographies of adolescents' own experiences.

Center for Adolescent and Family Studies (CAFS), 401 N. Union Street, Ashton Complex, Adyelotte Hall, Room 157, Bloomington, IN 47406. Phone: 812-855-2355; fax: 812-855-1847; e-mail: cafs@indiana.edu; Web site: www.indiana.edu/%7Ecafs/index.html. A research center based at the School of Education at Indiana University that disseminates information regarding effective strategies for helping at-risk adolescents and their families. Their Adolescence Directory On-line (ADOL) provides a comprehensive guide to information on adolescence for parents, teens, and professionals: http://www.education.indiana.edu/cas/adol/adol.html.

National Dropout Prevention Center, Clemson University, 209 Martin Street, Clemson, SC 29631-1555. Phone: 864-656-2599; fax: 864-656-0136; e-mail: ndpc@clemson.edu; Web site: www.dropoutprevention.org. Provides resources, technical assistance, training, and research on all aspects of dropout prevention programs and educational strategies to help youth succeed academically and graduate from high school.

EARLY ADULTHOOD ORGANIZATIONS

Alternatives to Marriage Project (ATMP), P.O. Box 320151, Brooklyn NY 11232. Phone: 718-788-1911; fax: 718-832-7098; Web site: www.unmarried.org. Provides resources, advocacy, and support for people who are unmarried, cohabit, are domestic partners, are living together, or are thinking aboutgetting married.

Association of Non-traditional Students in Higher Education (ANTSHE), 315 Grand View Park Drive, Grand Junction, CO 81503. Phone: 970-210-3159; fax: 866-887-9940; e-mail: gabe@wic.net; Web site: www.antshe.org. Supports the improvement of services to adult learners who are going to school, working, and raising children. (See also Midlife, Mature Adulthood.)

Coalition for Marriage, Family and Couples Education, LLC, 5310 Belt Road NW Washington, DC 20015-1961. Phone: 202-362-3332; fax: 202-362-0973; e-mail: Diane@smartmarriages.com; Web site: www.smartmarriages.com. Clearinghouse for marriage and relationship programs. Includes articles, directory, conferences, and seminars.

Office of Vocational and Adult Education, U.S. Department of Education, 400 Maryland Avenue SW, Washington, DC 20202. Phone: 202-245-7700; fax: 202-245-7838; e-mail: ovae@ed.gov; Web site: www.ed.gov/about/offices/list/ovae/index.html. Web site offers information, research, and resources to help prepare young people and adults for postsecondary education, successful careers, and productive lives. (See also Midlife, Mature Adulthood.)

MIDLIFE ORGANIZATIONS

National Action Forum for Midlife and Older Women, c/o Dr. Jane Porcino, P.O. Box 816, Stony Brook, NY 11790-0609. Publishes *Hot Flash: A Newsletter for Midlife and Older Women*. (See also Mature Adulthood.)

North American Menopause Society (NAMS), P.O. Box 94527, Cleveland, OH 44101. Phone: 440-442-7550; fax: 440-442-2660; e-mail: info@menopause.org; Web site: www.menopause.org. Promotes women's health during midlife and beyond by providing information on perimenopause, early menopause, menopause symptoms, long-term health effects of estrogen loss, and therapies that promote health and fitness. (See also Mature Adulthood.)

Older Women's League (OWL), The Voice of Midlife and Older Women, 3300 N. Fairfax Drive, Suite 218, Arlington, VA 22201. Phone: 703-812-7990; toll-free: 800-825-3695; fax: 703-812-0687; e-mail: owlinfo@owl-national.org; Web site: www.owl-national.org. Provides research, education, and advocacy for the 58 million women age forty and over in America in areas such as domestic violence, housing, caregiving, long-term care, and health-care issues. (See also Mature Adulthood, Late Adulthood.)

MATURE ADULTHOOD ORGANIZATIONS

Administration on Aging. One Massachusetts Avenue, Washington, DC 20201. Phone: 202-619-0724. Web site: www.aoa.gov and www.aoa.gov/eldfam/eldfam.asp. As part of the Department of Health and Human Services, AoA provides a wide range of services for older Americans, including home-delivered meals, transportation, adult day care, legal assistance, health information, and other services. (See also Late Adulthood.)

AgeWorks. Leonard Davis School of Gerontology, University of Southern California, Los Angeles, CA 90089-0191. Phone: 213-740-1364; fax: 213-740-7069; Web site: www.ageworks.com. Information on all aspects of aging from nutrition to Alzheimer's disease. (See also Late Adulthood.)

American Association of Retired Persons (AARP), 601 E Street NW, Washington, DC 20049. Phone (toll-free): 888-OUR-AARP (888-687-2277); Web site: www.aarp.com. The nation's largest organization of persons age fifty and over, with more than 30 million members, provides in-depth research, resources, and advocacy for older Americans. (See also Late Adulthood.)

Elderhostel, 11 Avenue de Lafayette, Boston, MA 02111-1746. Phone (toll free): 800-454-5768; e-mail: registration@elderhostel.org; Web site: www.elderhostel.org. Provides travel and learning experiences in more than ninety countries for adults fifty-five and older. (See also Late Adulthood.)

Experience Works, Inc., 2200 Clarendon Boulevard, Suite 1000, Arlington, VA 22201. Phone: 703-522-7272; toll-free: 866-EXP-WRKS (866-397-9757); fax: 703-522-0141; Web site: www.experienceworks.org. Helps mature individuals enter the workforce, secure more challenging positions, move into new career areas, or supplement their income. (See also Late Adulthood.)

SeniorNet, 900 Lafayette Street, Suite 604, Santa Clara, CA 95050. Phone: 408-615-0699; fax: 408-615-0928; Web site: www.seniornet.org. Nonprofit organization providing older adults with access to computer technologies to enhance their lives and enable them to share their knowledge and wisdom with others. (See also Late Adulthood.)

Late Adulthood Organizations

Gray Panthers, 1612 K Street, NW, Suite 300, Washington, DC 20006. Phone: 202-737-6637; toll-free: 800-280-5362; fax: 202-737-1160; e-mail: info@graypanthers.org; Web site: www.graypanthers.org. Founded in 1970 by social activist Maggie Kuhn, Gray Panthers is a national organization of intergenerational activists dedicated to taking on and solving the problems of peace, health care, jobs, and housing.

National Center on Elder Abuse (NCEA), 1201 15th Street, NW, Suite 350, Washington, DC 20005-2842. Phone: 202-898-2586; fax: 202-898-2583; e-mail: ncea@nasua.org; Web site: www.elderabusecenter.org. Promotes understanding, knowledge sharing, and action on elder abuse, neglect, and exploitation. (See also Mature Adulthood.)

National Citizens' Coalition for Nursing Home Reform. 1828 L Street, NW, Suite 801, Washington, DC 20036. Phone: 202-332-2275; fax: 202-332-2949; Web site: www.nccnhr.org. Advocates working to improve living conditions and the quality of care at nursing homes across the country.

National Council on Aging (NCOA), 300 D Street, SW, Suite 801, Washington, DC 20024. Phone: 202-479-1200; fax: 202-479-0735; TDD: 202-479-6674; e-mail: info@ncoa.org; Web site: www.ncoa.org. Private nonprofit association of 3,500 organizations and individuals, including senior centers, adult day service centers, senior housing, and meal sites, to promote the dignity, self-determination, well-being, and contributions of older persons. (See also Mature Adulthood.)

National Institute on Aging, Building 31, Room 5C27, 31 Center Drive, MSC 2292, Bethesda, MD 20892. Phone: 301-496-1752; fax: 301-496-1072; TTY: 800-222-4225; Web site: www.nia.nih.gov. Part of the National Institutes of Health, NIA is the primary federal agency engaged in Alzheimer's disease research and other diseases and problems related to aging. (See also Mature Adulthood.)

Death and Dying Organizations

Americans for Better Care of the Dying (ABCD), 1700 Diagonal Road, Suite 635, Alexandria, VA 22314. Phone: 703-647-8505; fax: 703-837-1233; e-mail: info@abcd-caring.org; Web site: www.abcd-caring.org. Dedicated to reforming health-care systems so that every person can experience comfort, dignity, and meaning at the end of life.

Compassion & Choices, P.O. Box 101810, Denver, CO 80250-1810. Phone: 800-247-7421; fax: 303-639-1224; Web site: www.compassionandchoices.org. National nonprofit organization working to improve care and expand choice at the end of life. "We also aggressively pursue legal reform to promote pain care, put teeth in advance directives and legalize physician aid in dying."

Hospice Foundation of America (HFA), 1621 Connecticut Avenue, NW, Suite 300, Washington DC 20009. Phone: 800-854-3402; fax: 202-638-5312; e-mail: hfaoffice@hospicefoundation.org; Web site: www.hospicefoundation.org. HFA is a not-for-profit organization that provides leadership in the development and application of hospice and its philosophy of care. The foundation produces an annual National Bereavement Teleconference and publishes the *Living with Grief* book series in conjunction with the teleconference.

International Association Hospice and Palliative Care (IAHPC), 5535 Memorial Drive, Suite F—PMB 509, Houston TX 77007. Phone: 936-321-9846; toll-free: 866-374-2472; fax: 713-880-2948; Web site: www.hospicecare.com. Provides information, resources, education, and advocacy to increase availability and access to high-quality hospice and palliative care for patients and families throughout the world.

National Hospice and Palliative Care Organization, 1700 Diagonal Road, Suite 625, Alexandria, VA 22314. Phone: 703-837-1500; fax: 703-837-1233; toll-free hotline: 800-658-8898, or in Spanish 877-658-8896; e-mail: caringinfo@nhpco.org; Web site: www.caringinfo.org. Provides state-specific living wills and offers other services to improve the way people die in our society. Caring Connections is the only national crisis and information hotline dealing with end-of-life issues

BEYOND DEATH ORGANIZATIONS

Association for Transpersonal Psychology (ATP), P.O. Box 50187, Palo Alto, CA 94303. Phone: 650-424-8764; fax: 650-618-1851; e-mail: info@atpweb.org; Web site: www.atpweb.org. ATP provides education, conferences, and publications that integrate insights from modern psychology with those drawn from traditional Eastern and Western spiritual practices.

Family Search, Web site: www.familysearch.org. Research your ancestors through the Church of Jesus Christ of Latter-Day Saints' online database, the world's largest family-history library.

Institute of Noetic Sciences (IONS), 101 San Antonio Road, Petaluma, CA 94952. Phone: 707-775-3500; fax: 707-781-7420; e-mail: membership@noetic.org; Web site: www.noetic.org. Founded by Willis Harman, Ph.D. and astronaut Edgar Mitchell in 1973, IONS conducts and sponsors research and education into phenomena that do not fit the conventional scientific model, such as out-of-body experiences and near-death experiences, while maintaining a commitment to scientific rigor.

International Association for Near-Death Studies, Inc. (IANDS), P.O. Box 502, East Windsor Hill, CT 06028-0502. Phone: 860-882-1211; fax: 860-882-1212; Web site: www.iands.org. Organization devoted to the study of near-death and similar experiences and their relationship to human consciousness.

Notes

INTRODUCTION

1 Andrew Lang, "The Odyssey," in Sir Arthur Thomas Quiller-Couch (ed.),
   The Oxford Book of English Verse. Oxford: Clarendon, 1919 [c. 1901];
   Bartleby.com, 1999. www.bartleby.com/101/. [November 15, 2006].

2 Christoper Lehman-Haupt, "Why 'To Be Continued' Is Continued," *The
   New York Times*, April 7, 1996, section 2, page 2, column 1.

3 Blaise Pascal, *Pensées* (New York: Penguin, 1995), p. 65.

4 For a sample of the wide range of crosscultural perspectives on the role of
   matter and spirit in the origins of the cosmos, see David Maclagan, *Creation
   Myths: Man's Introduction to the World* (London: Thames and Hudson, 1977).

5 For contemporary disputes in psychology, philosophy, and science regarding
   spirit and matter, or mind and brain, see Susan Blackmore, *Consciousness:
   An Introduction* (New York: Oxford University Press, 2004).

6 Joseph Chilton Pearce, *Magical Child* (New York: Bantam, 1980), p. 25.

7 James Joyce, *Ulysses* (New York: Modern Library, 1992), p. 38.

8 William Wordsworth, "Ode: Intimations of Immortality from Recollections
   of Early Childhood," in *The Norton Anthology of Poetry* (New York: W. W.
   Norton, 1975), p. 602.

9 Quoted in G. E. Bentley Jr., *The Stranger from Paradise: A Biography of
   William Blake* (New Haven, CT: Yale University Press, 2001), p. 199.

10 Piaget actually constructed his developmental theory in part from an
   examination of how biological organisms adapt to their surroundings. His
   first papers, written in adolescence, were studies of adaptation in mollusks.
   See F. Vidal, *Piaget Before Piaget* (Cambridge, MA: Harvard University Press,

1994). Similarly, Erik Erikson modeled his own epigenetic theory of development (known more widely as "The Eight Ages of Man") on organic developmental processes. He writes: ". . . it is well to remember the epigenetic principle which is derived from the growth of organisms in utero." Erik Erikson, *Identity and the Life Cycle* (New York: Norton, 1994), p. 53. While Freud's developmental theory has certain *rememberer* characteristics (see, for example, William B. Parsons, *The Enigma of Oceanic Feeling: Revisioning the Psychoanalytic Theory of Mysticism* [Oxford, UK: Oxford University Press, 1999], his use of physiological terms to describe his developmental phases (oral, anal, phallic, and genital) clearly reveals his *body up* bias.

11 For more information about the life and times of Leland Stanford, see Norman E. Tutorow, *The Governor: The Life and Legacy of Leland Stanford*, 2 vols. (Spokane, WA: Arthur H. Clark Co., 2004).

12 Quoted in Cynthia Griffin Wolff, *Emily Dickinson* (New York: Knopf, 1986).

13 Emily Dickinson, Poems by Emily Dickinson, Three Series, Complete, Project Gutenberg, http://www.gutenberg.org/etext/12242.

14 Ibid.

15 I am indebted to Ernest Schachtel for this metaphor. See Ernest G. Schachtel, "On Memory and Childhood Amnesia," in *Metamorphosis: On the Development of Affect, Perception, Attention and Memory* (New York, Basic Books, 1959), pp. 279–322.

CHAPTER 1
PREBIRTH: THE UNDISCOVERED CONTINENT

1 The story of the angel Lailah is taken from Howard Schwartz, *Gabriel's Palace: Jewish Mystical Tales* (New York: Oxford University Press, 1993), pp. 57–58. Consciousness researcher Ralph Metzner has pointed out to me that in Chinese medicine a point just above the middle of the philtrum is the locus of the acupuncture point TU 26 (Jen-Chung), which is to be treated in cases of coma (i.e., to bring back consciousness). See Stephen Thomas Chang, *The Complete Book of Acupuncture* (Millbrae, CA: Celestial Arts, 1976), p. 145.

2 Quoted in Martin Herbert, *Typical and Atypical Development: From Conception to Adolescence* (London: Blackwell, 2002), p. 17.

3 Aldous Huxley, "The Fifth Philosopher's Song," in *Leda* (New York: George H. Doran, 1920), p. 33.

4 M. Spehr et al. "Identification of a Testicular Odorant Receptor Mediating Human Sperm Chemotaxis," *Science* 299 (March 28, 2003): 2054–58.

5 Hildegard of Bingen, "Descent of the Soul"; miniature, about 1150 C.E., reproduced in Alvin H. Lawson, "Perinatal Imagery in UFO Abduction Reports," in Thomas Verny, ed., *Pre- and Perinatal Psychology: An Introduction* (New York: Human Sciences Press, 1987), p. 271.

6 W. Y. Evans-Wentz, trans. *The Tibetan Book of the Dead* (London: Oxford University Press, 1960).

7 Thomas Verny, *The Secret Life of the Unborn Child* (New York: Delta, 1981), p. 190.

8 Ibid.

9 Laura Huxley, *The Child of Your Dreams* (Rochester, VT: Destiny Books, 1992), p. 29.

10 Joseph Campbell, *The Mythic Image* (Princeton, NJ: Princeton University Press, 1981), pp. 43–49.

11 R. D. Laing, "Life Before Birth," in *The Facts of Life* (New York: Pantheon, 1976), p. 46.

12 See National Institutes of Health, *Stem Cells: Scientific Progress and Future Research Directions*, Honolulu, HI: University Press of the Pacific, 2004. It should be noted for those who prize human potential that stem cells represent the ultimate building blocks in this project from a *body up* point of view.

13 See Stephen Jay Gould, *Ontogeny and Phylogeny* (Cambridge, MA: Belknap Press, 1985).

14 See Stuart Campbell, *Watch Me Grow: A Unique 3-Dimensional Week-by-Week Look at Your Baby's Behavior and Development in the Womb* (New York: St. Martin's Griffin, 2004). Again, it's interesting to note that it is the lip region (the area that received the touch of the angel), that is the locus of a fetus's first neural responses.

15 Information on when different religious traditions consider personhood to begin is available online at: http://www.religioustolerance.org/abortion2.htm.

16 Dante Aligieri, *The Divine Comedy: Purgatory*, Canto XXV, Henry Francis Cary (trans.). Project Gutenberg: http://www.gutenberg.org/etext/8795.

17 See H. Eswaran et al., "Magnetoencephalographic Recordings of Visual Evoked Brain Activity in the Human Fetus," *The Lancet* 360, no. 9335 (September 7, 2002): 779–80.

18 See Roger Cook, *The Tree of Life: Image for the Cosmos* (London: Thames and Hudson, 1988).

19 See "Cinderella" in *The Complete Fairy Tales of the Brothers Grimm* (New York: Bantam, 2003), pp. 79–83.

20 For an account of the aboriginal mother-fetus bond, see David Abram, *The Spell of the Sensuous* (New York: Pantheon, 1996), p. 167. For an account of the Mbuti mother-fetus bond, see Colin M. Turnbull, *The Human Cycle* (New York: Simon and Schuster, 1983), pp. 33–34.

21 For an evolutionary look at how a mother's "pregnancy sickness" during the first trimester may help guard the fetus against toxic substances, see Margie Profet, *Protecting Your Baby-to-Be* (New York: Perseus, 1995).

22 It bears mentioning at this point that there is evidence in this chapter that can be cited by either side of the abortion question. On the one hand, prolife advocates can be heartened by ample evidence of the existence of consciousness in the womb. On the other hand, prochoice advocates can cite the wealth of material in this chapter indicating that unwanted children can often look forward to a life of misery, both for themselves and for other people. Some researchers have even suggested that abortion may be related to a drop in the nation's crime rate. See, for example, Steven D. Levitt and Stephen J. Dubner, *Freakonomics: A Rogue Economist Explores the Hidden Side of Everything* (New York: William Morrow, 2005), pp. 117–44.

23 Jean Paul Richter (trans.), The Notebooks of Leonardo da Vinci, #837— Project Gutenburg: http://www.gutenberg.org/etext/5000.

24 Salvador Dalí, *The Unspeakable Confessions of Salvador Dalí as told to André Parinaud*, Harold J. Salemsom, trans. (New York: Morrow, 1976), pp. 12–13.

25 See, for example, Henry P. David, Zdenek Dytrych, and Zdenek Matejcek, "Born Unwanted: Observations from the Prague Study," *American Psychologist* 58, no. 3 (March 2003): 224–29; and John J. Sigal, "Studies of Unwanted Babies," *American Psychologist* 59, no. 3 (April 2004): 183–84.

26 For studies of the negative impact of the mother's emotional, social, and physical life on the fetus, see, A. M. Jernberg, "Promoting Prenatal and Perinatal Mother-Child Bonding: A Psychotherapeutic Assessment of Parental Attitudes," in *Prenatal and Perinatal Psychology and Medicine* (New York: Parthenon Publishing Group, 1988), p. 254; David B. Chamberlain, "The Sentient Prenate: What Every Parent Should Know," *Pre- and Perinatal Psychology Journal* 9, no. 1 (Fall, 1994): 20–21; and Thomas Verny, *The Secret Life of the Unborn Child*, pp. 73–95.

27 This image is shown and described in George Elder, *The Body: An Encyclopedia of Archetypal Symbolism* (Boston: Shambhala, 1996), pp. 10–11.

28 Later Christian writers used the term to refer to the gods of pagans (e.g., Greek and Roman deities), which is where we got the pejorative term *demon*.

29 Allan Bloom, ed. *The Republic of Plato* (New York: Basic Books, 1991), p. 303.

30 See Thomas Armstrong, "The Genius Within Us: Psychospiritual Guidance During Prenatal and Perinatal Development and Its Connection to Human Potential After Birth," *Journal of Prenatal and Perinatal Psychology and Health* 14, nos. 3–4 (Spring & Summer, 2000): 291–97.

31 Cited in Verny, *The Secret Life of the Unborn Child*, p. 41.

32 Helen Wambach, *Life Before Life* (New York: Bantam, 1984), p. 42.

33 Markus Heinrichs et al., "Selective Amnesic Effects of Oxytocin on Human Memory," *Physiology and Behavior* 83 (2004): 31–38.

34 Michael Kosfeld et al., "Oxytocin Increases Trust in Humans," *Nature*, 435 (June 2, 2005): 673–76.

35 Writer and photographer Jane English suggests that cesarean-born individuals tend be more spiritually minded than those who undergo a normal labor birth. Perhaps this is because they weren't exposed to the amnesiac oxytocin (or were exposed to less of it during an emergency cesarean birth), and thus remember more from their prebirth existence. See Jane English, *A Different Doorway: Adventures of a Caesarean Born* (Mt. Shasta, CA: Earth Heart, 1985).

36 Walt Whitman, "Song of Myself #44," in *Walt Whitman* (New York: Modern Library, 1921), p. 70.

CHAPTER 2
BIRTH: THROUGH THE TUNNEL

1 From "Ode: Intimations of Immortality from Recollections of Early Childhood," in William Wordsworth, *The Complete Poetical Works*. London: Macmillan and Co., 1888; Bartleby.com, 1999. www.bartleby.com/145/. [November 15, 2006].

2 For the story of Thomas Hobbes's birth, see Richard S. Peters's introduction to Thomas Hobbes, *Leviathan: Or the Matter, Forme and Power of a Commonwealth Ecclesiasticall and Civil* (New York: Simon & Schuster/ Touchstone, 1997), p. 7.

3 Otto Rank, *The Trauma of Birth* (New York: Dover, 1994).

4 William Saroyan, *Births* (Berkeley, CA: Creative Arts Book Co., 1985), p. 6.

5 This discussion of the physiology of birth owes much to Christopher Vaughan's book *How Life Begins: The Science of Life in the Womb* (New York: Times Books), 1996.

6 For information on the evolutionary dimensions of the birth process, see Wenda Trevathan, *Human Birth: An Evolutionary Perspective* (New York: Aldine de Gruyter, 1987).

7 Frederick Leboyer, *Birth Without Violence*, Revised Edition of the Classic (Rochester, VT: 2002) Healing Arts Press.

8 "Episiotomy Rates Decreasing, But Procedure Still Overused," *Science Blog*, May 2002. http://www.scienceblog.com/community/older/2002/B/20026493.html.

9 J. A. Martin et al., *Preliminary Births for 2004: Infant and Maternal Health* (Hyattsville, MD: National Center for Health Statistics, November 15, 2005); Catherine Deneux-Tharaux et al., "Postpartum Maternal Mortality and Cesarean Delivery," *Obstetrics & Gynecology* 108(2006): 541–48.

10 Robbie Davis-Floyd, "Hospital Birth Routines as Rituals: Society's Messages to American Women," *Journal of Prenatal and Perinatal Psychology and Health* 1, no. 4 (1987): 276–96. See also Robbie Davis-Floyd, *Birth as an American Rite of Passage* (Berkeley, CA: University of California Press, 1992); and Suzanne Arms, *Immaculate Deception II: Myth, Magic & Birth* (Berkeley, CA: Celestial Arts, 1994).

11 Wenda Trevathan, *Human Birth: An Evolutionary Perspective*, p. 68.

12 Arthur Janov, *Imprints: The Lifelong Effects of the Birth Experience* (New York: Coward-McCann, 1983), p. 35.

13 Margaret Mead, *New Lives for Old: Cultural Transformation—Manus, 1928–1953* (New York: William Morrow, 1956), p. 345.

14 See, for example, David Meltzer, *Birth: An Anthology of Texts, Songs, Prayers, and Stories* (Berkeley, CA: North Point Press, 1981).

15 See, for example, Lloyd de Mause, "On Writing Childhood History," *The Journal of Psychohistory*, 16, no. 2 (Fall 1988): 135–71. Rather than abandoning female babies on hillsides or killing them in other direct ways as was done in the past, many parents in contemporary China and India are using cheap ultrasound technologies to determine the sex of the fetus, and if they are female, aborting them. This has resulted in a kind of "gendercide" with troubling consequences. See "China Grapples with the Legacy of Its 'Missing Girls'," *China Daily*, September 15, 2004; and "Number of Girl Children Declines Sharply in India," *China Daily*, October 21, 2003.

16 Michel Odent and Grantly Dick-Read, *Childbirth Without Fear: The Principles and Practices of Natural Childbirth* (London: Pinter & Martin Ltd., 2005).

17 See Robert A. Bradley, *Husband-Coached Childbirth: The Bradley Method of Natural Childbirth* (New York: Bantam, 1996); and Susan McCutcheon, *Natural Childbirth the Bradley Way* (New York: Plume, 1996).

18 See Beverly Savage and Diana Simkin, *Preparation for Birth: The Complete Guide to the Lamaze Method* (New York: Ballantine, 1987).

19 See Frederick Leboyer, *Birth Without Violence: Revised Edition of the Classic.*

20 See, for example, Barbara Harper with Suzanne Arms, *Gentle Birth Choices: A Guide to Making Informed Decisions About Birthing Centers, Birth Attendants, Water Birth, Home Birth, Hospital Birth* (New York: Inner Traditions, 1994).

21 See, for example, Kenneth C. Johnson and Betty Anne Daviss, "Outcomes of Planned Home Births with Certified Professional Midwives: Large Prospective Study in North America," *British Medical Journal* 330 (June 18, 2005): 1416.

22 Central Intelligence Agency, *The World Fact Book*, updated March 29, 2006. http://www.cia.gov/cia/publications/factbook/rankorder/2091rank.html.

23 From "The Hundred Thousand Songs of Milarepa," quoted in David Melzer, *Birth: An Anthology of Texts, Songs, Prayers, and Stories* (Berkeley, CA: North Point Press, 1981), pp. 91–92.

24 D. B. Cheek, "Sequential Head and Shoulder Movements Appearing with Age Regression in Hypnosis to Birth," *American Journal of Clinical Hypnosis* 16 (1974): 261–66.

25 David Chamberlain, "Reliability of Birth Memories: Evidence from Mother and Child Pairs in Hypnosis, *Journal of the American Academy of Medical Hypnoanalysis* 1 (1986): 89–98.

26 See, for example, Walter N. Pahnke et al., "The Experimental Use of Psychedelic (LSD) Psychotherapy," *Journal of the American Medical Association* 212 (1970): 1856–63.

27 On Stanislav Grof's work with Basic Perinatal Matrices using psychedelic therapy, see his book, *Realms of the Human Unconscious: Observations from LSD Research* (London: Souvenir Press, 1994). On his work with Basic Perinatal Matrices using a drug-free method known as Holotropic Therapy (a combination of breathing, music, and other nondrug techniques) see Stanislav Grof, *The Adventure of Self-Discovery: Dimensions of Consciousness and New Perspectives in Psychotherapy and Inner Exploration* (Albany, NY: State University of New York Press, 1988).

28 See David Drake, *Sartre (Life and Times)* (London: Haus Publishing Limited, 2005), p. 36.

29 See Hugh Thomas, *The Murder of Adolf Hitler: The Truth About the Bodies in the Berlin Bunker* (New York: St. Martin's Press, 1996).

30 For more on the connections between war and birth trauma, see Lloyd DeMause, *The Foundations of Psychohistory* (New York: Creative Roots Publications, 1982). The text is available in its entirety online at http://www.psychohistory.com.

31 Erik Erikson, *Young Man Luther* (New York: W. W. Norton, 1993).

32 For an account of Saul's conversion experience, see Acts 9:1–17. Pascal's religious conversion experience is recorded in Blaise Pascal, *Pensées* (New York: Penguin, 1995), p. 285.

33 William MacNeile Dixon, *The Human Situation* (London: Edward Arnold, 1964).

CHAPTER 3
INFANCY: LEGENDS OF THE FALL

1 From Henry Vaughan "The Retreate," in Grierson, Herbert J. C., ed. *Metaphysical Lyrics & Poems of the 17th c.* Oxford: The Clarendon Press, 1921; Bartleby.com, 1999. www.bartleby.com/105/ [November 8, 2006].

2 Inayat Khan, Hazrat. *The Sufi Message of Hazrat Inayat Khan*, Volume 3, (London: Barrie and Jenkins, 1971), p. 27.

3 In Bali, however, the infant is not even allowed to touch the ground for some months after birth. Since the Balinese believe that the infant has descended from the home of the gods, he is treated like a god for the first few months of life. But around six months of age, the baby starts to lose its godlike status and thus must come down to the earth to join the human race. See Fred B. Eiseman, Jr. Bali: *Sekala & Niskala: Volume I: Essays on Religion, Ritual, and Art.* (Hong Kong: Periplus Editions, 1990), p. 94.

4 Cited in Erich Neumann, *The Child* (New York: Harper, 1973), p. 7.

5 See Marian Diamond and Janet Hopson, *Magic Trees of the Mind* (New York: Dutton), 1998.

6 Natalie Angier, "Illuminating How Bodies Are Built for Sociability," *The New York Times*, April 30, 1996.

7 Jan Ehrenwald, *The ESP Experience: A Psychiatric Validation* (New York: Basic Books), 1978.

8 See Beth Azar, "The Bond Between Mother and Child," *American Psychological Association Monitor*, September, 1985, p. 28; A. H. Schore, "The Effects of a Secure Attachment Relationship on Right Brain

Development, Affect Regulation, and Infant Mental Health," *Infant Mental Health Journal*, 2001, vol. 22, pp. 7–66; and Jaak Panksepp, "The Long-Term Psychobiological Consequences of Infant Emotions: Prescriptions for the Twenty-First Century," *Infant Mental Health Journal*, 2001, vol. 22, nos. 1–2, pp. 132–173.

9 R. A. Spitz, 1945. "Hospitalism: An inquiry into the genesis of psychiatric conditions in early childhood." *Psychoanalytic Studies of the Child* 1: 53–74; 2: 113–117.

10 See John Bowlby's three-volume series *Attachment and Loss: Vol. 1: Attachment*, 1969; *Vol. 2: Separation: Anxiety and Anger*, 1973; and *Vol. 3. Loss: Sadness and Depression*, 1980. All are published by Basic Books.

11 From "The Waste Land," in *T. S. Eliot, Collected Poems 1909–1962* (New York: Harcourt Brace and Company, 1991), p. 53.

12 Margaret Mahler, Fred Pine, and Anni Bergman, *The Psychological Birth of the Human Infant: Symbiosis and Individuation*. (New York: Basic Books, 2000), p. 49.

13 Jim Prescott, "Essential Brain Nutrients: Breastfeeding for the Development of Human Peace and Love," in *Touch the Future*, Spring, 1997, p. 14. See also his article, "The Origins of Love and Violence: An Overview," at http://ttfuture.org/services/bonding/main.htm.

14 For a look at the connections between disruptions in parent-child interactions and war, see: Alice Miller, *For Your Own Good: Hidden Cruelty in Child-Rearing and the Roots of Violence* (New York: Noonday Press, 1990); and Samir Qouta, Raija-Leena Punamaki, and Eyad al Sarraj, "Mother-Child Expression of Distress in War Trauma," *Clinical Child Psychology and Psychiatry*, 2005, vol. 10, no. 2, pp. 135–156.

15 Beth Azar, "Research Seeks to Soothe Infant Pain," *American Psychological Association Monitor*, December, 1996, p. 21.

16 Alison Gopnik, Andrew N. Meltzoff, and Patricia K. Kuhl, *The Scientist in the Crib: What Early Learning Tells us About the Mind* (New York: Perennial, 2001).

17 Daniel Stern, "The Infant's Subjective Experience of Its Objects," *Zeitschrift fur psychoanalytische Theorie und Praxis*, 1997, vol. 12, no. 1, pp. 8–21.

18 Maynard Solomon, *Mozart: A Life* (New York: HarperCollins, 1995), p. 191. I believe that one can hear very much the same kind of ecstasy/anxiety crescendo in Chopin's well-known "Etude in E Major," op. 10, no. 4.

19 D. W. Winnicott, *Playing and Reality* (London: Routledge, 1991), p. 114.

20 Joan Acocella (ed.). *The Diary of Vaslav Nijinsky* (New York: Farrar, Straus and Giroux, 1999), p. 44.

21 Alison Gopnik et al., *The Scientist in the Crib*, p. 69.

22 Daniel Stern uses the term *amodal perception*, rather than unity of the senses, to describe the infant's ability to take information in one sensory modality and translate it into another sensory modality. He writes: "We do not know how they accomplish this task. The information is probably not experienced as belonging to any one particular sensory mode. More likely it transcends mode or channel and exists in some unknown supra-modal form." Daniel Stern, *The Interpersonal World of the Infant: A View from Psychoanalysis and Developmental Psychology* (New York: Basic Books, 2000), p. 51.

23 Daniel Stern, *The Interpersonal World of the Infant*, p. 54.

24 Circe was a sorceress in Homer's Odyssey who could turn men into beasts. Athena was the Greek goddess of wisdom, the arts, war, justice, and skill. Demeter was the Greek goddess of the harvest.

25 Much of the psychoanalytic literature of early childhood development, including the work of W. Fairbairn, Melanie Klein, and D. W. Winnicott, has used a mechanistic terminology to describe the psychodynamics of infancy, employing terms like "object" "part object" and "good/bad breast." See W. Fairbairn, *Psychoanalytic Studies of the Personality* (London: Routledge, 1994); Melanie Klein, *Love, Guilt, and Reparation: And Other Works 1921–1945* (*The Writings of Melanie Klein*, Vol. 1, New York: Free Press, 2002); D. W. Winnicott, *Playing and Reality* (London: Routledge, 1982). This employment of specialized professional language, while perhaps useful from a clinical point of view, seems ill suited to giving a good account of a pre-verbal stage of life that combines emotion, perception, sensation, and other categories of human experience into holistic events. The mythological terminology of Jungian psychology, while limited (infants don't literally see Greek gods) comes closest, I believe, to capturing the spirit of this time of life. See, for example, Erich Neumann, *The Origins and History of Consciousness* (Princeton, NJ: Princeton University Press, 1995); and *The Great Mother: An Analysis of the Archetype* (Princeton, NJ: Princeton University Press, 1972).

26 Daniel Stern, *The Interpersonal World of the Infant*, pp. 37–182.

27 Daniel Stern, *The Interpersonal World of the Infant*, p. 176.

28 That the infant's amodal perception can resurface in language itself is observed time and again in the lives of highly gifted writers. Regarding color perception, writer Vladimir Nabokov wrote: "For me the shades, or rather colors, of, say, a fox, a ruby, a carrot, a pink rose, a dark cherry, a flushed

cheek, are as different as blue is from green or the royal purple of blood (Fr. *"pourpre"*) [is] from the English sense of violet blue. I think your students, your readers, should be taught to *see* things, to discriminate between visual shades as the author does, and not to lump them under such arbitrary labels as 'red.'" Quoted in the notes to Vladimir Nabokov, *The Annotated Lolita*, Alfred Appel, Jr. (transl.) (New York: Vintage, 1991), p. 364.

29 Joseph Campbell, *The Hero with a Thousand Faces: Commemorative Edition* (Princeton, NJ: Princeton University Press, 2004).

30 Carl Jung's essay "The Psychology of the Child Archetype" gives a particularly vivid symbolic account of the vulnerable infant or child confronting and overcoming almost insuperably in *The Archetypes and the Collective Unconscious, The Collected Works of C. G. Jung*, Vol. 9, Part 1 (New York: Pantheon, 1959).

31 Sandor Ferenczi, *Selected Papers: Vol. III. Final Contributions to the Problems and Methods of Psycho-Analysis* (New York: Basic Books, 1955), p. 136.

32 See David Sedgwick, *The Wounded Healer: Countertransference from a Jungian Perspective* (London: Routledge, 1995); and S. Luthar and E. Zigler, "Vulnerability and Competence: A Review of Research on Resilience in Childhood," *American Journal of Orthopsychiatry*, 1991, vol. 6, pp. 6–22.

33 Larry R. Vandervert, "The Evolution of Mandler's Conceptual Primitives (Image-Schemas) as Neural Mechanisms for Space-Time Simulation Structures," *New Ideas in Psychology*, 1997, vol. 15, no. 2, pp. 105–123. This agrees with Jung's belief that the archetype (or *primordial image*, as he originally called it) is fundamentally an instinct, or as he pointed out, the *instinct's perception of itself*: Carl Jung, "Instinct and the Unconscious," (1919), in R.F.C. Hull (trans.) *The Collected Works of C. G. Jung* (Vol. 8) (Princeton, NJ: Princeton University Press, 1981), p. 137.

34 Martin Buber, *I and Thou* (2nd ed). (New York: Charles Scribner's Sons, 1958), pp. 25–26.

Chapter 4
Early Childhood: The Magical Mystery Years

1 Quoted in Narayan Prasad, "Sparks of Psychic Fire," in *Education for a New Life* (Pondicherry, India: Sir Aurobindo Ashram Press, 1976), p. 10.

2 Lobsang Lhalungpa, "The Child Incarnate," *Parabola* 4, no. 3 (August 1979): 72–77. An account of the discovery of the Dalai Lama in early childhood is also given in the Dalai Lama's own autobiography, *Freedom in Exile* (San Francisco: HarperSan Francisco, 1991), and in *Kundun*, a screen adaptation of the Dalai Lama's life, directed by Martin Scorsese (1997).

3 Quoted in Ian Stevenson, "The Explanatory Value of the Idea of Reincarnation," *Journal of Nervous and Mental Disease* 164 (1977): 307–308.

4 See for example, Ian Stevenson, *Twenty Cases Suggestive of Reincarnation*, 2nd ed. (Charlottesville, VA: University of Virginia Press, 1980); Ian Stevenson, *Cases of the Reincarnation Type*, vol 1., *Ten Cases in India* (Charlottesville, VA: University of Virginia Press, 1975); and Ian Stevenson, *European Cases of the Reincarnation Type* (Jefferson, NC: McFarland, 2003). See also a popular trade book by Tom Shroder, a *Washington Post* columnist who followed Dr. Stevenson on some of his research travels: *Old Souls: The Scientific Evidence for Past Lives* (New York: Fireside, 1999); and a book written by Jim Tucker, the current director of the program at the University of Virginia founded by Ian Stevenson: *Life Before Life: A Scientific Investigation of Children's Memories of Previous Lives* (New York: St. Martin's Press, 2005).

5 For a voluminous compilation of similar cases, see Ian Stevenson, *Reincarnation and Biology: A Contribution to the Etiology of Birthmarks and Birth Defects*, 2 vols. (Westport, CT: Praeger Scientific Publishers, 1997).

6 Ian Stevenson, "American Children Who Claim to Remember Previous Lives," *Journal of Nervous and Mental Disease* 17, no. 1 (1983): 742.

7 Integral theorist Ken Wilber has argued that what may appear to be spiritual or transpersonal experiences in childhood are really "prepersonal" since children haven't yet developed the ego structures (the "personal" part of "transpersonal") that would enable them to transcend that ego. See Ken Wilber, "The Pre/Trans Fallacy," *Re-Vision* 3 (1980): 51–72. In building his theory of consciousness, Wilber has consistently relied upon the *body up* developmental models of Jean Piaget, Lawrence Kohlberg, Erik Erikson, and others to support his argument that early childhood belongs on a lower developmental rung in his "great chain of being" theory of consciousness (see Ken Wilber, *A Brief History of Everything*, Boston: Shambhala, 2000). This highly Western and reductionistic view of childhood contrasts starkly with the statements of mystics and religious figures in virtually every cultural tradition, who view childhood as imbued with spiritual or transpersonal dimensions. For a further discussion of my argument against Wilber's "Pre-Trans Fallacy," see Thomas Armstrong, "Transpersonal Experience in Childhood," *Journal of Transpersonal Psychology* 16 (1984): 207–30, and Thomas Armstrong, *The Radiant Child* (Wheaton, IL: Quest Books, 1988), pp. 102–11, 145–52.

8 See also Mark 10:14–15, Luke 9:47–48, Luke 10:21, and Luke 18:16–17.

9 Geoffrey Parrinder, "Charisma," in Mircea Eliade, ed., *Encyclopedia of Religion*, vol. 3 (New York: Collier Macmillan Publishers, 1987), p. 220.

10 James Legge, trans., *The Works of Mencius in the Chinese Classics*, vol. 2 (Oxford: Clarendon Press, 1895). See Book IV, Part II, Chapter XII.

11 Edward Hoffman, *Visions of Innocence: Spiritual and Inspirational Experiences in Childhood* (Boston: Shambhala, 1992), p. 4.

12 Joan Halifax, *Shaman: The Wounded Healer* (New York: Crossroads, 1982), p. 11.

13 Carl Jung, "The Psychology of the Child Archetype," in R. F. C. Hull (trans.), *The Collected Works of C. G. Jung*, vol. 9, part 1, *The Archetypes and the Collective Unconscious* (Princeton, NJ: Princeton Uiniversity Press, 1968), p. 179. See also C. Kerényi, "The Primordial Child in Primordial Times," in *Essays on a Science of Mythology* (New York: Harper and Row, 1963), pp. 25–69.

14 Heinz Werner, *Comparative Psychology of Mental Development* (New York: International Universities Press, Inc., 1980), pp. 72–74. Originally written in the 1940s, this book still stands as one of the truly great achievements of developmental psychology, despite its being largely forgotten by the mainstream psychological community. What makes it remarkable is that it portrays early childhood development as alive and dynamic, and provides numerous examples of child reports that give a sense of life from the child's point of view. Most current research in child development, on the other hand, fails to capture the inner life of early childhood, providing instead a scientific analysis that dissects the world of childhood into empty categories and lifeless models seen from the vantage point of rational adults.

15 This experience of synaesthesia can persist into adulthood. See, for example: Richard E. Cytowic, *The Man Who Tasted Shapes* (Cambridge, MA: MIT Press, 1998).

16 Patricia A. Paine, "Eidetic Imagery and Recall Accuracy in Preschool Children," *Journal of Psychology* 105, no. 2 (1980): 253–58.

17 Quoted in Thomas De Quincey, *Confessions of an English Opium-Eater* (New York: Dover, 1995), p. 60.

18 See, for example, Erol F. Giray et al., "The Incidence of Eidetic Imagery as a Function of Age," *Child Development* 47, no. 4 (1976): 1207–10.

19 Ben Johnson, ed., *My Inventions: The Autobiography of Nikola Tesla* (Williston, VT: Hart Brothers, 1982). The full text of Tesla's biography is available at several sources on the Internet.

20 Quoted in Virginia Haggard, "Life with Chagall," *The New York Times*, March 29, 1996.

21 Quoted in Dore Ashton, ed., *Picasso on Art: A Selection of Views* (New York: Viking, 1972), p. 104.

22 It should be noted here that Piaget in his early years was quite interested in psychoanalysis (and thus, the phenomenology of the unconscious), and even spent some time in therapy with one of Carl Jung's female disciples, Sabina Spielrein. See Fernando Vidal, "Sabina Speilrein—Jean Piaget—Going Their Own Ways," *Journal of Analytical Psychology* 46, no. 1 (2001): 139–53. Over time, however, his interests increasingly focused on matters of mathematics and logic, to the detriment of these researches into the rich inner life of the child.

23 Jean Piaget, *The Child's Conception of the World* (Totowa, NJ: Littlefield, Adams & Co., 1975), p. 212.

24 Ibid., p. 210.

25 Translated and interpreted by William Buck, *Mahabharata* (Berkeley, CA: University of California Press, 1973), p. 204.

26 See, for example, David Watkins, *Morality and Architecture* (Oxford: Clarendon Press, 1977).

27 Edward Robinson, *The Original Vision: A Study of the Religious Experience of Childhood* (Oxford: The Religious Experience Research Unit, Manchester College, 1977), pp. 32–33.

28 Quoted in Frances Wickes, *The Inner World of Choice* (New York: Harper and Row, 1963), p. 83.

29 Patricia L. Ryan, "Spirituality Among Adult Survivors of Childhood Violence: A Literature Review," *Journal of Transpersonal Psychology* 30, no. 1 (1998): 39–51.

30 See, for example, Jerome L. Singer, "Imaginative Play in Early Childhood: A Foundation for Adaptive Emotional and Cognitive Development," *International Medical Journal* 5, no. (1998): 93–100.

31 D. W. Winnicott, *Playing and Reality* (London: Routledge, 1982), p. 14.

32 Mihaly Csikszentmihalyi, *Flow: The Psychology of Optimal Experience* (New York: HarperCollins, 1991).

33 John M. Chernoff, "Music-making Children of Africa," *Natural History* 88 (1979): 75.

34 Derek Bickerton, "Creole Languages," *Scientific American*, July 1982, p. 116.

35 Johan Huizinga, *Homo Ludens* (Boston: Beacon Press, 1986), p. 173.

36 Quoted in Sir David Brewster, *Memoirs of the Life, Writings, and Discoveries of Sir Isaac Newton*, vol. 2 (Chestnut Hill, MA: Adamant Media Corporation, 2001), p. 407.

37 Quoted in Marshall McLuhan and Quentin Fiore, *The Medium Is the Massage* (New York: Bantam, 1967), p. 93.

38 See J. S. Rubin, "The Froebel-Wright Kindergarten Connection: A New Perspective," *Journal of the Society of Architectural Historians* 48, no. 1 (March 1989): 24–37.

39 Quoted in K. C. Cole, "Play, by Definition, Suspends the Rules," *The New York Times*, November 30, 1988, p. C16.

40 The phenomenon of adults retaining childhood playfulness (as well as children's synaesthesia, eidetic imagery, physiognomic perception, etc.) is called *neoteny* (Latin for "holding youth"), a term that is used in referring to physical characteristics in the field of developmental biology. For the importance of this process in the evolution of species, see Ashley Montagu, *Growing Young* (New York: McGraw-Hill, 1983).

41 Brian Sutton-Smith, *Toys as Culture* (New York: Gardner Press, 1986).

42 There is growing evidence that the demise of play may be related to an increase in hyperactivity and ADD/ADHD-related symptoms in our culture. One neuroscientist, Jaak Panksepp, has suggested, for example, that the absence of rough-and-tumble play among boys may play a key role in the frontal lobe/limbic system dysfunctions seen in ADD/ADHD behaviors. See, for example, Jaak Panksep, "Attention Deficit Hyperactivity Disorders, Psychostimulants, and Intolerance of Childhood Playfulness: A Tragedy in the Making?" *Current Directions in Psychological Science* 7 (1998): 91–98; Thomas Armstrong, "Attention Deficit Hyperactivity Disorder in Children: One Consequence of the Rise of Technologies and Demise of Play?" in Sharna Olfman, ed., *All Work and No Play: How Educational Reforms Are Harming Our Preschoolers* (Westport, CT: Praeger Publishers, 2003), pp. 161–75; and Thomas Armstrong, "Canaries in the Coal Mine: The Symptoms of Children Labeled 'ADHD' As Biocultural Feedback," in Gwynedd Lloyd, David Cohen, and Joan Stead, eds., *Critical New Perspectives on ADHD* (London: Routledge Falmer, 2006).

43 Marian Diamond and Janet Hopson, *Magic Trees of the Mind* (New York: Dutton, 1998), p. 54.

44 H. T. Chugani, "Critical Importance of Emotional Development: Biological Basis of Emotions: Brain Systems and Brain Development," *Pediatrics* 102, no. 5 (November 1998): 1225–29.

45 See Paul Thompson et al., "Growth Patterns in the Developing Human Brain Detected Using Continuum-Mechanical Tensor Mapping," *Nature* 404, no. 6774 (March 9, 2000): 190–93.

46 Psychoanalyst Ernest Schachtel writes that human beings have developed a special amnesia for early childhood experiences in part to protect the culture from these possibilities: "Childhood amnesia covers those aspects and experiences of the former personality which are incompatible with the culture. If they were remembered, man would demand that society affirm and accept the total personality with all its potentialities. In a society based on partial suppression of the personality such a demand, even the mere existence of a really free personality, would constitute a threat to the society. Hence it becomes necessary for the society that the remembrance of a time in which the potentialities of a fuller, freer, and more spontaneous life were strongly present and alive be extinguished." See Ernest G. Schachtel, "On Memory and Childhood Amnesia," in *Metamorphosis: On the Development of Affect, Perception, Attention and Memory* (New York: Basic Books, 1959) p. 320.

47 Maria Montessori, *The Secret of Childhood* (New York: Ballantine, 1992).

48 U.S. Department of Health and Human Services, Administration on Children, Youth and Families. *Child Maltreatment 2004* (Washington, DC: U.S. Government Printing Office, 2006).

49 Quoted in Fyodor Dostoevsky, *The Brothers Karamazov*, Constance Garnett (translator), Christian Classics Ethereal Library. http://www.ccel.org/d/dostoevsky/karamozov/karamozov.html.

50 Alice Miller, *The Drama of the Gifted Child* (New York: Basic Books, 1981), p. 67.

51 Frances G. Wickes, *The Inner World of Childhood* (New York: Mentor, 1968), p. 39.

52 For a discussion of past and current trends in thinking regarding homosexuality and psychoanalysis, see Ralph E. Roughton, "Rethinking Homosexuality: What it Teaches Us About Psychoanalysis," *Journal of the American Psychoanalytic Association* 50, no. 3 (2002): 733–63.

53 Peter Gay, *Freud: A Life for Our Time* (New York: W. W. Norton, 1988), p. 7.

54 Paul Okami, Richard Olmstead, Paul R. Abrahamson, "Sexual Experiences in Early Childhood: 18-Year Longitudinal Data from the UCLA Family Lifestyles Project," *Journal of Sex Research* 34, no. 4 (1997): 339–47.

55 Elaine Hatfield et al., "Passionate Love: How Early Does It Begin?" *Journal of Psychology & Human Sexuality* 1, no. 1 (1988): 35–51.

56 Alison Gopnik, Andrew N. Meltzoff, Patricia K. Kuhl, *The Scientist in the Crib: What Early Learning Tells Us About the Mind* (New York: Harper Paperbacks, 2000), p. 49.

57 One can see a good example of this inner psychic phenomenon in Günter Grass's Nobel Prize–winning novel *The Tin Drum*. In this novel, little Oskar uses his drumming and his glass-piercing scream to express his ultra sensitivity to the people and events around him during the Nazi era in Germany. See Günter Grass, *The Tin Drum* (New York: Vintage, 1990).

58 Wilhelm Reich, *The Children of the Future: On the Prevention of Sexual Pathology* (New York: Noonday Press, 1984).

59 Heinz Werner, *Comparative Psychology of Mental Development*, p. 360.

60 Bryant Furlow, "Play's the Thing," *New Scientist*, no. 2294 (June 9, 2001).

Chapter 5
Middle Childhood: Entering the Civilized World

1 Joseph Chilton Pearce, *Magical Child Matures* (New York: Dutton, 1985), p. xiii.

2 Rebecca Fraser, *The Brontës: Charlotte Brontë and Her Family* (New York: Fawcett Columbine, 1988), pp. 49–61.

3 Sadly, Branwell's adult life was marked by unstable employment, alcoholism, drug addiction, and an early death from tuberculosis at the age of thirty-one. Tuberculosis would also kill Emily two months later (after having caught a cold at her brother's funeral), and Anne the following year.

4 Robert Silvey and Stephen MacKeith, "The Paracosm: A Special Form of Fantasy," in Delmont C. Morrison, ed., *Organizing Early Experience: Imagination and Cognition in Childhood* (Amityville, NY: Baywood, 1988). See also David Cohen and Stephen A. MacKeith, *The Development of Imagination: The Private Worlds of Childhood* (London: Routledge, 1992).

5 It is true, of course, that some cultures decide that such entities should remain part of the objective world as the child grows up. These *rememberer* cultures are usually branded as "primitive" by an *adapter* culture such as ours.

6 Thomas Buckley, "Doing Your Thinking," *Parabola* 4, no. 4 (Winter 1979): 31.

7 Jean Piaget, *The Psychology of the Child* (New York: Basic, 2000).

Piaget's research has undergone substantial criticism over the past three decades, questioning both his methodology and his conclusions. Critics suggest, for example, that children often respond differently to a Piagetian activity when a question or situation is put in a slightly different way. They also claim that Piaget underestimated young children's cognitive abilities and envisioned the processes of cognitive growth as occurring much more smoothly and consistently than is actually the case. See, for example, D. F. Bjorklund, *Children's Thinking: Developmental Function and Individual Differences*, 2nd ed. (Pacific Grove, CA: Brooks/Cole, 1995). Others have argued that Piaget's work has a clear male bias and underplays the importance of early empathy and cooperation in young children's behaviors. See, for example, Carol Gilligan, *In a Different Voice: Psychological Theory and Women's Development* (Cambridge, MA: Harvard University Press, 1993). Having said this, however, it still remains true that many of Piaget's conclusions about the general processes of cognitive growth from early childhood to middle childhood are still regarded as foundational in contemporary education and cognitive psychology.

8 Jean Piaget, "Development and Learning," in R. E. Ripple and V. N. Rockcastle, eds., *Piaget Rediscovered* (Ithaca, NY: Cornell University, 1964), p. 12.

9 The experience of remembering mathematical operations recalls Plato's Meno dialogue, where he takes a boy (probably of adolescent age) through the steps of the Pythagorean theorem, demonstrating that the boy has within him all the knowledge needed to understand the concept. As Plato points out to his interlocater Meno, "his soul must have always possessed this knowledge." *The Dialogues of Plato* (New York: Bantam, 1986), p. 213.

10 Edward Robinson, *The Original Vision: A Study of the Religious Experience of Childhood* (New York: Seabury Press, 1983), pp. 27–28.

11 Edward Robinson, *The Original Vision*, p. 115.

12 Adapted from Edvard Grieg: "My first success". Original manuscript in Bergen Public Library. http://www.troldhaugen.com/default.asp?kat=19&sp=2. This type of experience, signalling an opening to a newly found ability, has been termed a "crystallizing experience," by psychologist David Feldman. See Joseph Walters and Howard Gardner, "The Crystallizing Experience: Discovering an Intellectual Gift," in R. J. Sternberg and J. E. Davidson, eds., *Conceptions of Giftedness* (Cambridge, England: Cambridge University Press, 1986), pp. 306–31.

13 Gordon W. Allport, *The Nature of Prejudice* (Reading, MA: Addison-Wesley Publishing Co., Inc., 1997), p. 307.

14 Jules Henry, *Culture Against Man* (New York: Random House, 1963), p. 288.

15 J. Krishnamurti, *Education and the Significance of Life* (New York: Harper and Row, 1953), p. 12.

16 In David Shribman, *I Remember My Teacher: 365 Reminiscences of the Teachers Who Changed Our Lives* (Kansas City, KS: Andrews McMeel, 2001), p. 134.

17 "20th Anniversary Celebration: About Oprah," O, *the Oprah Magazine,* October 2005.

18 Henry Adams, *The Education of Henry Adams* (New York: Oxford University Press, 1999), p. 252.

19 Maria Montessori, *The Secret of Childhood,* p. 34.

20 Rudolf Steiner, *The Kingdom of Childhood* (London: Rudolf Steiner Press, 1982), p. 20.

21 Sigmund Freud, "Three Contributions to the Theory of Sex," in A. A. Brill, ed., *The Basic Writings of Sigmund Freud* (New York: Modern Library, 1966), pp. 582–85.

22 William N. Friedrich et al., "Normative Sexual Behavior in Children: A Contemporary Sample," *Pediatrics* 101, no. 4 (April 1998): 9.

23 Dorothy Corkille Briggs, *Your Child's Self-Esteem* (New York: Doubleday, 1975), p. 143.

24 Iona Opie, Peter Opie, and Marina Warner, *The Lore and Language of Schoolchildren* (New York: New York Review of Books, 2000), p. 1.

25 A. C. Harwood, *The Recovery of Man in Childhood* (London: Hodder and Stoughton, 1958), p. 75.

CHAPTER 6
LATE CHILDHOOD: BECOMING A PART OF THE CROWD

1 Frances G. Wickes, *The Inner World of Childhood,* p. 163.

2 The original story is "The Frog-King, or Iron Henry," in *The Complete Grimm's Fairy Tales* (New York: Random House, 1972), pp. 17–20.

3 This tale has some similarities with an incident that occurs in Homer's *Odyssey.* At one point in his journey, Odysseus lands on an unknown island after a shipwreck and, being totally exhausted, falls into a deep sleep. The next morning, a princess named Nausicaa and her maids come down to a river near the place where Odysseus is sleeping to wash the princess's clothing. After they have finished their work and hung the clothes up to dry, the girls relax and play a game that involves throwing and

catching a ball. Eventually, someone misses catching the ball and it lands in a swirling pool of water. Upset by the loss of the ball, the girls shriek loudly in distress. This wakes up Odysseus who proceeds to make the acquaintance of the princess. The princess, who is attracted to Odysseus and would like to be his wife, directs him to her father's castle. Once admitted into the kingdom, Odysseus is honored with a feast and proceeds to tell the king and his followers a great part of the story of his trying to get back home to Ithaca. See Homer, *The Odyssey* (New York: Penguin, 1997), pp. 168–78.

4 Cris Beam, "Encouraging Loyalty to Friends," *Parenting*, September, 2006, p. 202.

5 Naturally, the future poets, mystics, psychics, artists, and philosophers of the world likely will experience *remembering* during late childhood (and be classed as often as not as "misfits," "dreamers," or worse, as noted in this chapter). But this stage of life as a whole represents a time when the child's need to *adapt* to his surroundings reaches a peak, and it comes just before the turbulence of adolescence blasts a large hole in the psyche allowing cosmic concerns to reemerge.

6 Martha K. McClintock and Gilbert Herdt, "Rethinking Puberty: The Development of Sexual Attraction," *Current Directions in Psychological Science* 5, no. 6 (December 1996): 178–83.

7 Quoted in McClintock and Herdt, "Rethinking Puberty," p. 178.

8 Ryan MacMichael, "First Kiss," *The Daily Ping*, June 7, 2001, http://www.dailyping.com/archive/2001/06/07/.

9 Dante Alighieri, *La Vita Nuova* (New York: Penguin, 1969), pp. 29–30.

10 H. T. Chugani, "Critical Period of Brain Development: Studies of Cerebral Glucose Utilization with PET," *Preventive Medicine* 27, no. 2 (1998): 184–88.

11 Marian Diamond and Janet Hopson, *Magic Trees of the Mind*, pp. 55–56.

12 J. N. Giedd et al., "Brain Development During Childhood and Adolescence: A Longitudinal MRI Study," *Nature Neuroscience* 2 (1999); 861–63.

13 Quoted in Curt Suplee, "Key Brain Growth Goes on into Teens," *Washington Post*, March 9, 2000, p. A1.

14 Quoted in J. N. Giedd et al., "Brain Development During Childhood and Adolescence," p. 863.

15 Annie Dillard, *An American Childhood* (New York: HarperCollins, 1988) p. 11.

16 Benjamin Franklin, *The Autobiography of Benjamin Franklin* (New York: Dover, 1996), p. 7.

17 Carl Jung, *Memories, Dreams, Reflections* (New York: Vintage, 1989), p. 89.

18 Quoted in Janet Sayers, "Teenage Dreams: Feminism, Psychoanalysis, and Adolescence," *Signs* 25, no. 3 (Spring 2000).

19 Harry Stack Sullivan, *The Interpersonal Theory of Psychiatry* (New York: W. W. Norton, 1968), p. 262.

20 Jean-Paul Sartre, *The Words* (New York: Fawcett, 1964), p. 131.

21 Barbara Leaming, *Orson Welles: A Biography* (New York: Penguin, 1985), p. 16.

22 See Jeanne S. Chall and Vicki A. Jacobs, "Poor Children's Fourth-Grade Slump," *American Educator* (Spring 2003). http://www.aft.org/pubsreports /american_educator/spring2003/chall.html.

23 Anne Grosso de León, "Moving Beyond Storybooks: Teaching Our Children to Read to Learn," *Carnegie Reporter* 2, no. 1 (Fall 2002): 1.

24 See Howard Gardner, *Frames of Mind: The Theory of Multiple Intelligences* (New York: Basic Books, 1993).

25 For information on how to translate the theory of multiple intelligences into practical learning strategies that can meet the needs of different kinds of learners, see Thomas Armstrong, *7 Kinds of Smart: Identifying and Developing Your Multiple Intelligences* (New York: Plume, 1999); Thomas Armstrong, *In Their Own Way: Discovering and Encouraging Your Child's Multiple Intelligences* (New York: Penguin/Tarcher, 2000); Thomas Armstrong, *Multiple Intelligences in the Classroom* 2nd ed. (Alexandria, VA: Association for Supervision and Curriculum Development, 2000); Thomas Armstrong, *The Multiple Intelligences of Reading and Writing: Making the Words Come Alive* (Alexandria, VA: Association for Supervision and Curriculum Development, 2003); and Thomas Armstrong, *You're Smarter Than You Think: A Kid's Guide to Multiple Intelligences* (Minneapolis, MN: Free Spirit Publishing, 2003).

26 For my own criticisms of school labels, see Thomas Armstrong's *In Their Own Way*, and *The Myth of the A.D.D. Child: 50 Ways to Improve Your Child's Behavior and Attention Span without Drugs, Labels, or Coercion* (New York: Plume, 1997).

27 There have been a number of recent books that have discussed children who seem to fit this description of *rememberer* children in at least some ways. See, for example, Lee Carroll and Jan Tober, *The Indigo Children*

(Flagstaff, AZ: Light Technology Publishing, 1999); Doreen Virtue, *The Crystal Children* (Carlsbad, CA: Hay House, 2003); and Georg Kuhlewind, *Star Children: Understanding Children Who Set Us Special Tasks and Challenges* (Forest Row, England: Temple Lodge Publishing, 2004).

28 For a look at research that has examined the creative abilities of individuals with disability labels, see Bonnie Cramond, "Attention-deficit Hyperactivity Disorder and Creativity: What is the Connection?" *Journal of Creative Behavior* 28, no. 2 (1994): 193–210; Thomas West, *In the Mind's Eye: Visual Thinkers, Gifted People with Dyslexia and Other Learning Difficulties, Computer Images, and the Ironies of Creativity* (Amherst, New York: Prometheus Books, 1997); and Temple Grandin, *Thinking in Pictures: And Other Insights from My Life with Autism* (New York: Vintage, 1996). For an excellent Web site that provides links to numerous papers and articles on this topic, see: http://www.neurodiversity.com.

29 Victor Goertzel and Mildred George Goerzel, *Cradles of Eminence: A Provocative Study of the Childhoods of Over 400 Famous Twentieth-Century Men and Women* (Boston: Little, Brown, and Co., 1962), p. 249.

30 In Milton Cross and David Ewen, *Milton Cross' Encyclopedia of the Great Composers and Their Music*, vol. 1 (Garden City, NY: Doubleday, 1962), pp. 315–16. This "paralyzing experience" contrasts sharply with Greig's "crystallizing experience" described in Chapter 5. Fortunately, Grieg had mentors that encouraged him to develop his musical abilities into maturity so that this gift was not lost to humankind. One wonders, however, how many artistic works, scientific discoveries, intellectual contributions, or spiritual gifts have been lost to us because of a teacher's or parent's paralyzing words.

31 Goertzel and Goertzel, *Cradles of Eminence*, p. 257.

32 See Judith Rich Harris, *The Nurture Assumption: Why Children Turn Out the Way They Do* (New York: Touchstone, 1999).

33 Anu Varma, "The Lost Girls: Pity Sarasota's Preteen Girls, Who Too Often Know Everything About Sex and little About Happiness," *Sarasota Magazine*, Summer 2003, p. 60.

34 Press release: "Girls Can Internalize Negative Body Images Even in Pre-Adolescence," Center for the Advancement of Health, March 7, 2001. http://www.hbns.org/newsrelease/girls3-7-01.cfm. At the same time, fueled by the fast-food industry, the media, and other social factors, there is an obesity epidemic running rampant through the childhood and adolescent years that threatens to set the scene for serious health problems in later life.

See, for example, Cara B. Ebbeling, Dorota B. Pawlak, and David S. Ludwig, "Childhood Obesity: Public-health Crisis, Common Sense Cure," *The Lancet* 360, no. 9331 (August 10, 2002): 473–82.

35 In some cases, the symptoms of ADHD (hyperactivity, impulsivity, and distractibility), are nothing more than the gender-appropriate behaviors of healthy boys and would have been considered perfectly normal fifty years ago. See Thomas Armstrong, *The Myth of the A.D.D. Child*, pp. 31–32.

36 Philip C. Rodkin et al., "Heterogeneity of Popular Boys: Antisocial and Prosocial Configurations," *Developmental Psychology* 36, no. 1 (January 2000): 14–24.

37 George Jowett was one of the first men to popularize weightlifting in the early part of the twentieth century. The schoolyard bully from my past grew up to become an Emmy Award–winning soap opera star who played the role of an abusive lawyer on daytime television for over twenty-five years.) My parents did not buy me the weightlifting equipment. I currently work out with weights at my local fitness center.

38 Timothy Egan, "For Image-Conscious Boys, Steroids are a Powerful Lure, *The New York Times*, November 22, 2002, pp. A1, A22.

39 S. J. Young, S. Longstaffe, M. Tenenbein, "Inhalant Abuse and the Abuse of other Drugs," *American Journal of Drug and Alcohol Abuse* 25, no. 2 (1999): 371–75.

40 Task Force on Education of Young Adolescents, *Turning Points: Preparing American Youth for the 21st Century* (New York: Carnegie Council on Adolescent Development, June 1989), p. 8.

41 Mary Shelley, *Frankenstein* (New York: Dover, 1994), p. 157.

42 Harry Stack Sullivan, *The Interpersonal Theory of Psychiatry*, p. 245.

43 Michael Thompson, with Catherine O'Neill Grace and Lawrence J. Cohen, *Best Friends, Worst Friends: Understanding the Social Lives of Children* (New York: Ballantine, 2001), pp. 59–62.

44 Ibid, pp. 60–61.

45 Lyn Mikel Brown and Carol Gilligan, *Meeting at the Crossroads: Women's Psychology and Girls' Development* (New York: Ballantine, 1993), p. 2.

46 Sydney Ladensohn Stern, *Gloria Steinem: Her Passions, Politics, and Mystique* (New York: Birch Lane Press, 1997), p. 35.

47 Quoted in Janet Sayers, *Boy Crazy: Remembering Adolescence, Therapies, and Dreams* (London: Routledge, 1978), p. 67.

CHAPTER 7
ADOLESCENCE: ADVENTURES IN THE TWILIGHT ZONE

1 Robert Museil, *The Man Without Qualities*, vol. 1 (New York: Vintage, 1996), p. 444.

2 There has been some concern that girls are reaching puberty at an earlier age than in the past. It's been estimated, for example, that in the 1830s in England the average age for the onset of mencharche was 17. Today, the average age of menarche in the United States is around 12 years, six months, and it is common to hear of girls beginning to show signs of puberty as young as 6 or 7. Different theories have been advanced to explain this downward shift, from insecticides and hormones in food products, to better nutrition, obesity, and stress. See Daniel Goleman, "Theory Links Puberty to Childhood Stress," *The New York Times*, July 30, 1992, and Theo Colborn, Dianne Dumanoski, and John Peter Meyers, *Our Stolen Future: How We Are Threatening Our Fertility, Intelligence, and Survival* (New York: Plume, 1997).

3 Anne Frank, *The Diary of a Young Girl* (New York: Bantam, 1993).

4 Paula Weideger, *Menstruation and Menopause* (New York: Knopf, 1975).

5 See, for example, James H. Stein and Lynn Whisnant Reiser, "A Study of White Middle-Class Adolescent Boys' Responses to 'Semenarche' (the First Ejaculation)," *Journal of Youth and Adolescence* 23, no. 3 (June 1994): 373–384; and Loren Frankel, "'I've Never Thought About It,' Contradictions and Taboos Surrounding American Males' Experiences of First Ejaculation (Semenarche)," *Journal of Men's Studies* 11, no. 1 (Fall 2002): 37–54.

6 Janet Sayers, *Boy Crazy: Remembering Adolescence, Therapies, and Dreams*, p. 72.

7 S. Shipman, "The Psychodynamics of Sex Education," in R. E. Muuss, ed., *Adolescent Behavior and Society: A Book of Readings* (New York: Random House, 1971), pp. 333–34.

8 A. A. Adegoke, "The Experience of Spermarch (the Age of Onset of Sperm Emission) Among Selected Adolescent Boys in Nigeria," *Journal of Youth and Adolescence* 22 (1993): 201–209.

9 L. Berne and B. Huberman, *European Approaches to Adolescent Sexual Behavior & Responsibility: Executive Summary & Call to Action* (Washington, DC: Advocates for Youth, 1999).

10 Edward O. Laumann et al., *The Social Organization of Sexuality: Sexual Practices in the United States* (Chicago: University of Chicago Press, 1994), p. 328.

11 In Deborah L. Tolman, "Doing Desire: Adolescent Girls' Struggles for/with Sexuality," *Gender & Society* 8, no. 3 (September 1994): 329.

12 See, for example, P. M. Thompson et al., "Growth Patterns in the Developing Brain Detected by Using Continuum Mechanical Tensor Maps," *Nature* 404, no. 6774 (March 9, 2000): 190–93. Contrary to popular belief, it is not so much the direct influence of hormones on the body that is associated with the emotional turbulence of puberty, but the impact that these hormones have on the development of the brain. Surges of testosterone at puberty, for example, swell the amygdala, an almond-shaped part of the limbic system (emotional brain) that generates feelings of fear and anger. Similarly, estrogen seems to affect serotonin levels at puberty, accounting for higher rates of depression among teenage girls See C. L. Sisk and D. L. Foster, "The Neural Basis of Puberty and Adolescence," *Nature Neuroscience* 7 (September 27, 2004): 1040–47; J. N. Giedd et al., "Quantitative MRI of the Temporal Lobe, Amygdala, and Hippocampus in Normal Human Development: Ages 4–18 Years," *Journal of Comparative Neurology* 366, no. 2 (1996): 223–30; and L. Born, A. Shea, and M. Steiner, "The Roots of Depression in Adolescent Girls: Is Menarche the Key?" *Current Psychiatry Reports* 4 (2002): 449–60.

13 Research suggests that the lateral prefrontal cortex, which is important for controlling impulses, is among the latest brain regions to mature without reaching adult dimensions until the early twenties. J. N. Giedd, "Structural Magnetic Resonance Imaging of the Adolescent Brain," *Annals of the New York Academy of Science* 1021 (2004): 77–85.

14 Kaspar Kiepenheuer, *Crossing the Bridge: A Jungian Approach to Adolescence* (La Salle, IL: Open Court, 1990), p. 4.

15 While today's teens may appear to be going through a less turbulent adolescence than teens at other historical or cultural periods (e.g.. the Cultural Revolution in China and the antiwar generation in America in the late 1960s), this may be more artiface than reality, screened as it is by the veneer of a "perky" consumerist, market-based, *adaptive* culture. The many problems of adolescents in today's society (e.g., binge drinking, eating disorders, depression, vandalism, gang violence, addictions) may be better indicators of what's going on beneath the surface.

16 Frances G. Wickes, *The Inner World of Childhood* (New York: Mentor, 1968), p. 108.

17 Mircea Eliade, *Rites and Symbols of Initiation: The Mysteries of Birth and Rebirth* (Dallas, TX: Spring Publications, 1994).

18 In Joseph Campbell's *Historical Atlas of World Mythology*, there is a rather grim historical photo of a number of aboriginal youth from Arnhem Land in Australia lying together in a circle during a rite of passage ceremony. The photo's caption reads: "Having been exposed both to a broiling sun and to a torment of stinging insects sprinkled over them, those with short white sticks at their heads have expired." See Joseph Campbell, *Historical Atlas of World Mythology*, vol. 1, *The Way of the Animal Powers* (New York: Harper & Row, 1988), p. 144.

19 Mihaly Csikszentmihalyi, "Education for the 21st Century," *Education Week*, April 19, 2000, p. 46.

20 Mihaly Csikszentmihalyi, Kevin Rathunde, and Semual Whalen, *Talented Teenagers: The Roots of Success and Failure* (Cambridge, U.K. : Cambridge University Press, 1996), p. 196.

21 See, for example, Gini Sikes, *8 Ball Chicks: A Year in the Violent World of Girl Gangs* (New York: Anchor, 1998); and Sayika Shakur, *Monster: The Autobiography of an L.A. Gang Member* (New York: Grove/Atlantic, 2004).

22 LSD seems to be a drug of *remembering*. The research scientist Albert Hofmann, who discovered LSD in 1943, said that his first experience of the drug was identical to a childhood mystical experience that he had at the age of ten. See Craig S. Smith, "Nearly 100, LSD's Father Ponders His 'Problem Child,'" *The New York Times*, January 7, 2006. While I have not used illegal drugs since adolescence, nor do I advocate the use of any illegal drug today, it seems possible to argue that there are drugs of *remembering* (LSD, mescaline, peyote, psilocybin, ayahuasca, etc.), and drugs of *adapting* (Ritalin, Prozac, Ambien, Viagra, etc.). Our *adapter* culture permits (and even encourages through media ads) the use of *adapter* drugs, while prohibiting by law the use of *rememberer* drugs. In indigenous *rememberer* cultures, however, *rememberer* drugs are often an integral part of their sacred rituals, while *adapter* drugs are largely unknown. For a recent Johns Hopkins University study that compared an *adapter* drug (Ritalin) with a *rememberer* drug (psilocybin) in their ability to trigger a mystical experience, see R. R. Griffiths, W. A. Richards, U. McCann, and R. Jesse, "Psilocybin Can Occasion Mystical-Type Experiences Having Substantial and Sustained Personal Meaning and Spiritual Significance," *Psychopharmacology* 187, no. 3 (August 2006): 268–83.

23 In the past twenty years there have been a number of community efforts to create intentional rites-of-passage programs for adolescents to help them craft their own identities within their particular culture. See, for example,

Louise Carus Mahdi, Steven Foster, Meredith Little, eds., *Betwixt and Between: Patterns of Masculine and Feminine Initiation* (Chicago: Open Court, 1987); Louise Carus Mahdi, Nancy Geyer Christopher, and Michael Meade, eds., *Crossroads: The Quest for Contemporary Rites of Passage* (Chicago: Open Court, 1996); Mary C. Lewis, *Herstory: Black Female Rites of Passage* (Chicago: African American Images, 1988); Paul Hill, *Coming of Age: African-American Male Rites-of-Passage* (Chicago: African American Images, 1992).

24 Quoted in Janet Sayers, *Boy Crazy: Remembering Adolescence, Therapies, and Dreams* (London: Routledge, 1998), p. 117. It should be noted here that such charismatic individuals, when they are themselves undeveloped, may end up being simply another class of "omni-impotent" parental archetypes that must be confronted and overcome; and this is certainly the case with many popular cult leaders. See Margaret Thaler Singer, *Cults in Our Midst: The Hidden Menace in Our Everyday Lives* (New York: Jossey-Bass, 1995).

25 Mary Pipher, *Reviving Ophelia* (New York: Ballantine, 1995), p. 254.

26 I have not yet seen any credible authority link Piaget's stage of formal operations with the spike in brain growth that occurs at about this same time, but it seems to me that this would be a topic worthy of further investigation.

27 This is different from the exploration of possibility described in the chapter on early childhood. Adolescents do not need to incorporate fragments of reality from the external world into their possible worlds in the way that young children do when they play. They're capable of laying the foundations for their possible worlds entirely in abstract thought.

28 G. Stanley Hall, *Adolescence: Its Psychology and Its Relations to Physiology, Anthropology, Sociology, Sex, Crime, Religion, and Education*, vol. 2 (New York: Appleton, 1904), p. 337.

29 Billy Graham, *Just as I Am: The Autobiography of Billy Graham* (San Francisco: HarperSan Francisco, 1999), p. 30.

30 Quoted in Edward Lucie-Smith, *Joan of Arc* (New York: W. W. Norton, 1977), p. 15.

31 Quoted in Arthur Osborne, ed., *The Collected Works of Ramana Maharshi* (London: Rider & Company, 1969), pp. 7–8.

32 Edna St. Vincent Millay, *Renascence and Other Poems* (Whitefish, MT: Kessinger, 2005), pp. 2, 8.

CHAPTER 8
EARLY ADULTHOOD: BUILDING AN INDEPENDENT LIFE

1 Charlotte Brontë, *Jane Eyre* (New York: Signet, 1997), p. 95.

2 Charlotte Brontë, *Jane Eyre* (New York: Signet, 1997); Wolfgang von Goethe, "Wilhelm Meister's Apprenticeship," in Eric A. Blackall, ed., *Goethe: The Collected Works*, vol. 9 (Princeton, NJ: Princeton University Press, 1989); and Ralph Ellison, *Invisible Man* (New York: Random House, 1980).

3 This cheery assessment of early adulthood needs to be tempered, however, by the realization that in the gay community, AIDS and HIV have had a devastating effect on the well-being and longevity of young adults. One 1997 study suggested that nearly half of all Canadian twenty-year-old homosexual and bisexual men would not reach their sixty-fifth birthday: Robert S. Hogg et al., "Modeling the Impact of HIV Disease on Mortality in Gay and Bisexual Men," *International Journal of Epidemiology* 26, no. 3 (1997): 657–61.

4 Diane E. Papalia and Sally Wendkos Olds, *Human Development* (New York: McGraw-Hill, 2003), p. 369.

5 Noted in S. T. Hauser and W. M. Greens, "Passage from Late Adolescence to Early Adulthood," in George H. Pollock and Stanley I. Greenspan, *The Course of Life, Volume V: Early Adulthood* (New York: International Universities Press, 1993), p. 402.

6 Cited in John W. Santrock, Lifespan Development, 5th edition (Dubuque, IA: Brown & Benchmark, 1995), p. 426.

7 See, for example, Jeffrey G. Johnson et al., "Childhood Maltreatment Increases Risk for Personality Disorders During Early Adulthood," *Archives of Family Medicine*, 9, no. 9 (2000): 783; and Rob McGee, Sheila Williams, Shyamala Nada-Raja, "Low Self-Esteem and Hopelessness in Childhood and Suicidal Ideation in Early Adulthood," *Journal of Abnormal Child Psychology* 29, no. 4 (2001): 281–91.

8 See, for example, A. C. Gelber, "Weight in Young Adulthood May be Linked to Arthritis in Later Life," *American Family Physician* 51, no. 5 (April 1995): 1225.

9 Robyn Hartley, "Adulthood: The Time You Get Serious About the Rest of Your Life," *Family Matters*, no. 30 (December 1991): 51.

10 Daniel J. Levinson, *Seasons of a Man's Life* (New York: Ballantine, 1986), p. 241.

11 Quoted in Alexandra Robbins and Abby Wilner, *Quarterlife Crisis: The Unique Challenges of Life in Your Twenties* (New York: Tarcher/Putnam, 2001), p. 50.

12 From Richie Magallano, "Oblogitory: This Is What Happens When You Give An Aimless Young Gay Man in Chicago Access to the Internet," http://www.heyrichie.com/2006/05/migrating-fag-four-years-later.html.

13 Kenneth Kenniston, "Youth: A 'New' Stage of Life," *The American Scholar* 39 (1970): 631–54.

14 For biographical information, see Robert Coles, Erik H. Erikson, *The Growth of His Work* (Boston: Little, Brown, and Co., 1970), pp. 14–18. For Erikson's theory of the life span, see Erik Erikson, *The Life Cycle Completed* (New York: W. W. Norton, 1998).

15 Quoted in Bruce Narramore and Vern Lewis, "Boomerang Children," *Psychology for Living*, Narramore Christian Foundation, http://www.ncfliving.org/bk_108_boomerang1.htm.

16 Lynn White, "Coresidence and Leaving Home: Young Adults and Their Parents," *Annual Review of Sociology* 20, no. 20 (1994): 81.

17 Quoted in Elina Furman, *Boomerang Nation: How to Survive Living with Your Parents . . . the Second Time Around* (New York: Fireside, 2005), p. 18.

18 Levinson, *The Seasons of a Man's Life*, pp. 91–97.

19 Goethe, "Wilhelm Meister's Apprenticeship," p. 28.

20 Quoted in *Quarterlife Crisis*. p. 74.

21 Judy D. Levinson and Daniel J. Levinson, *The Seasons of a Women's Life* (New York: Alfred A. Knopf, 1996), p. 239.

22 Ibid.

23 Mike Tate, "You Gotta Believe!" posted on blog: "Fair Wisconsin: A Fair Wisconsin Votes No," March 13, 2006, http://noontheamendment.blogspot.com/2006/03/you-gotta-believe.html.

24 Quoted in *Quarterlife Crisis*, p. 54.

25 Y. Stern et al., "Influence of Education and Occupation on the Incidence of Alzheimer's Disease," *Journal of the American Medical Association (JAMA)* 271, no. 13 (April 6, 1994): 1004–10.

26 Lauren B. Resnick, "Learning in School and Out," *Educational Researcher*, December 1987, pp. 13–20.

27 Mark Twain, *The Wit and Wisdom of Mark Twain: A Book of Quotations* (New York: Dover, 1999), p. 28.

28 Erik H. Erikson, *Childhood and Society* (New York: W. W. Norton, 1963), p. 266.

29 In the first volume of his history of sexuality, philosopher Michel Foucault, who was gay, made a point of emphasizing the heterosexual genital bias in Western culture. He wrote: ". . . from childhood to old age, a norm of sexual development was defined and all the possible deviations were carefully described . . . Were these anything more than means employed to absorb, for the benefit of a genitally centered sexuality, all the fruitless pleasures? All this garrulous attention which has us in a stew over sexuality, is it not motivated by one basic concern: to ensure population, to reproduce labor capacity, to perpetuate the form of social relations: in short, to constitute a sexuality that is economically useful and politically conservative?" Michel Foucault, *The History of Sexuality: An Introduction—Volume 1* (New York: Vintage, 1990), pp. 36–37.

30 The factors that lead to date and mate selection are complex and involve biology (e.g., pheromones or "attraction odors"), anatomy (e.g., cute/child-like facial features seem to be desired in all cultures), psychology (e.g., males prefer women who are sexually faithful), sociology (e.g., females prefer men who possess wealth, power, and social position), and even spirituality (e.g., being attracted to someone based upon karmic ties from a previous incarnation). See, for example, Michael R. Kauth, *True Nature: A Theory of Sexual Attraction* (New York, NY: Kluwer Academic/Plenum Publishers, 2000); Doug Jones, *Physical Attraction and the Theory of Sexual Selection: Results from 5 Populations* (Ann Arbor, MI: University of Michigan Press, 1996); David M. Buss, *The Evolution of Desire: Strategies of Human Mating* (New York: Basic Books, 1994); and Gina Cerminara, *Many Mansions: The Edgar Cayce Story on Reincarnation* (New York: Signet, 1990).

31 Percentage of those married by age 35: U.S. Census Bureau, 2001. Mean age for marriage: U.S. Census Bureau, 1999.

32 Arnold van Gennep, "Territorial Passage and the Classification of Rites" in Ronald L. Grimes, ed, *Reading in Ritual Studies* (Englewood Cliffs, NJ: Prentice Hall, 1960), p. 532.

33 Harold P. Blum, "The Maternal Ego Ideal and the Regulation of Maternal Qualities," in George H. Pollock and Stanley I. Greenspan, eds., *The Course of Life,* vol. 5: *Early Adulthood* (Madison, CT: International Universities Press, 1993), p. 43.

34 Anthropologist David Gutmann uses the term "parental emergency" to describe the particular adaptations that nature ordains new parents must make in order to restrain narcissistic drives in the service of the survival of their children. See David Gutmann, *Reclaimed Lives: Men and Women in Later Life* (New York: Basic Books, 1987), pp. 194–98.

35 Rob Palkovitz, Marcella A. Copes, and Tara N. Woolfolk, "It's Like . . . You Discover a New Sense of Being," *Men and Masculinities* 4, no. 1 (July 2001): 49–69.

36 Quoted in Palkovitz, Copes and Woolfolk, pp. 62–63.

37 Daniel J. Levinson, *The Seasons of a Man's Life*, p. 83.

38 Levinson and Levinson, *The Seasons of a Woman's Life*, p. 301.

39 Nancy Cleeland, "Young Workers Quickly Grow Cynical, Poll Says," *The Los Angeles Times*, September 1, 1999, p. 1.

40 Lynn Olson, "Bridging the Gap," *Education Week*, January 26, 1994, p. 21.

41 National Center for Health Statistics, *Advance Report of Final Divorce Statistics, 1989 and 1990*, Monthly Vital Statistics Report, April 18, 1995, vol. 43, no. 9.

42 Levinson and Levinson, *The Seasons of a Woman's Life*, p. 302.

43 Meher Baba was a Parsi (a Zoroastrian who lived in India) who lived from 1894 to 1969 and claimed to be the reincarnation of Zoroaster, Rama, Krishna, the Buddha, Jesus, and Mohammed. He kept silence for the last fifty years of his life. For a biography about his life and work written by a disciple, see C. B. Purdom, *The God-Man: The Life, Journeys, and Works of Meher Baba with An Interpretation of His Silence and Spiritual Teachings* (New York: George Allen & Unwin, 1964). I was initially drawn to Meher Baba in December 1970 after listening to a record album dedicated to him by his most famous devotee, Peter Townshend of the rock group The Who ("Happy Birthday," London: University Spiritual League/Eel Pie, 1970).

44 Diane Wood Middlebrook, *Anne Sexton: A Biography* (Boston: Houghton Mifflin, 1991), p. 42.

45 William Wordsworth, "Lines: Composed a Few Miles Above Tintern Abbey, On Revisiting the Banks of the Wye During a Tour, July 13, 1798," in Wordsworth, William. *The Complete Poetical Works*. London: Macmillan and Co., 1888; Bartleby.com, 1999. www.bartleby.com/145/. [November 15, 2006].

46 Carol Zaleski, "The Dark Night of Mother Teresa," *First Things* 133 (May 2003): 24–27.

47 From Bertrand Russell, *The Autobiography of Bertrand Russell* (New York: Routledge, 2000), p. 149.

48 Levinson and Levinson, *The Seasons of a Woman's Life*, p. 270.

49 Daniel J. Levinson, *The Seasons of a Man's Life*, pp. 98–99; see also *The Seasons of a Woman's Life*, pp. 237–41.

CHAPTER 9
MIDLIFE: MOVING THROUGH MUDDY WATERS

1 Dante Alighieri, *The Divine Comedy: Hell* (Canto I), Henry Wadsworth Longfellow (transl.). Project Gutenberg, http://www.gutenberg.org/etext/1001.

2 Simon Leys, trans., *The Analects of Confucius* (New York: W. W. Norton, 1997), p. 203.

3 There are also other unlucky years in the Japanese tradition (including 25 and 61 for men, and 19 and 70 for women), but the midlife years are considered *taiyaku* or "most unlucky." For more information on *yakudoshi*, see Claire Z. Mamola, "Yakudoshi: A Critical Age for Japanese Women and Japan," *NWSA Journal* 13, no. 2 (July 31, 2001): 149.

4 One sociologist suggests that for much of human history, life expectancy was around twenty-five to thirty years. Riaz Hassan, "Social Consequences of Manufactured Longevity," *The Medical Journal of Australia* 173 (2000): 601. Another article suggests the average life expectancy was in the midthirties, Lucy Mangan, "So How Long Have We Got?" *The Guardian*, December 1, 2005. http://www.guardian.co.uk/g2/story/0,3604,1654529,00.html.

5 There is a caveat to this, however, in the "grandmother hypothesis" that we will explore in the next chapter.

6 Eliot Jacques, "Death and the Mid-Life Crisis," *International Journal of Psychoanalysis* 46 (1965): 502–14.

7 Quoted in R. J. Hollingdale, *Nietzsche: The Man and His Philosophy* (Cambridge, England: Cambridge University Press, 1999), p. 118.

8 Fyodor Dostoyevsky, *Notes from the Underground*. Project Gutenberg, http://www.gutenberg.org/etext/600.

9 Marie-Louise Von Franz, *Puer Aeternus: A Psychological Study of the Adult Struggle with the Paradise of Childhood* (Santa Monica, CA: Sigo Press, 1981), p. 73. Von Franz uses the life of Antoine de St. Exupéry, author of *The Little Prince*, as an example of this phenomenon. For a classic example of a *puer aeternus* from literature, see Charles Dickens, *Bleak House* (New York: Penguin, 1997) (the character of Harold Skimpole).

10 For an account of their growing friction, see William McGuire, ed., *The Freud/Jung Letters* (Princeton, NJ: Princeton University Press, 1994).

11 Carl Jung, *Memories, Dreams, and Reflections* (New York: Vintage, 1989), p. 199.

12 Some of these images can be seen in Aniela Jaffe, ed., *C. G. Jung: Word and Image* (Princeton, NJ: Princeton University Press, 1979), pp. 69–72.

13 Carl Jung, *Memories, Dreams, and Reflections*, p. 183.

14 Carl Jung, *Collected Works*, vol. 8: *The Structure and Dynamics of the Psyche*, 2nd ed. (Princeton, NJ: Princeton University Press, 1981), p. 397. Also referenced as: *Collected Works*: 8:778.

15 Octavio Paz, *The Labyrinth of Solitude* (New York: Grove Press, 1985), p. 94.

16 Quoted in Kathleen Teltsch, "'Midlife Crisis' Is Investigated by One Who Doubts It's There," *New York Times*, December 18, 1989, p. A16. MIDMAC researchers defined midlife in their study as extending from the age of twenty-four to seventy-four, or more narrowly, from forty to sixty. For a review of their findings, see Orville Gilbert Brim, Carol D. Ryff, and Ronald C. Kessler, *How Healthy Are We? A National Study of Well-Being at Midlife* (Chicago: University of Chicago Press, 2005).

17 William Shakespeare, Sonnet II.

18 Quoted in Bernice L. Neugarten, *The Awareness of Middle Age*, in Bernice L. Neugarten, ed., *Middle Age and Aging* (Chicago: University of Chicago Press, 1968), p. 96.

19 Elizabeth M. Banister, "Women's Midlife Experience of Their Changing Bodies," *Qualitative Health Research* 9, no. 4 (July 1999): 530.

20 Cited in Robert J. Sternberg, Elena L. Grigorenko, and Stella Oh, "The Development of Intelligence at Midlife," in Margie E. Lachman, ed., *Handbook of Midlife Development* (New York: John Wiley & Sons, 2001), p. 221.

21 Elizabeth Gudrais, "Modern Myelination: The Brain at Midlife," *Harvard Magazine* 103, no. 5 (2001): 9.

22 Banister, "Women's Midlife Experience of Their Changing Bodies," p. 530.

23 Quoted in John Kotre and Elizabeth Hall, *Seasons of Life* (Boston: Little, Brown, & Co., 1990), p. 266.

24 Margaret Lock, "Menopause: Lessons from Anthropology," *Psychosomatic Medicine* 60, no. 4 (July–August 1998): 410–19.

25 Quoted in U.S. Congress, Office of Technology Assessment, *The Menopause, Hormone Therapy, and Women's Health* (Washington, DC: U.S. Government Printing Office, May 1992), p. 12.

26 N. E. Avis et al., "A Longitudinal Analysis of the Association Between Menopause and Depression," *Annals of Epidemiology* 4 (1994): 214–20. See also Louise Nicol-Smith, "Causality, Menopause, and Depression: A Critical Review of the Literature," *British Medical Journal* 313 no. 7067 (November 16, 1996): 1229–32.

27 Abigail J. Stewart and Elizabeth A. Vandewater, "'If I Had It to Do Over Again': Midlife Review, Midcourse Corrections, and Women's Well-Being in Midlife," *Journal of Personality and Social Psychology* 76, no. 29 (1999): 270–283.

28 See Clenora Weems-Hudson and Wilfred Samuels, eds., *Toni Morrison* (Boston: Twayne Publishers, 1990), pp. 1–9.

29 The idea of a male climacteric appears to be more accepted among European physicians than among American doctors. For a pro and con discussion by British physicians, for example, see Duncan C. Gould, Richard Petty, and Howard S. Jacobs, "The Male Menopause: Does It Exist?" *British Medical Journal* (March 25, 2000).

30 Quoted in Daniel J. Levinson, *The Season's of a Man's Life*, p. 307.

31 Henrik Ibsen, *Rosmersholm*, Robert Farquharson (trans.), Project Gutenberg, http://www.gutenberg.org/etext/2289.

32 Leo Tolstoy, *Confession* in Christian Classics Ethereal Library, http://www.ccel.org/ccel/tolstoy/confession.html. Tolstoy's midlife crisis of meaning was prefigured almost two decades before in the principal male character of *War and Peace*, Pierre Bezukhov, as this passage illustrates: "... dark thoughts of the vanity of all things human came to him oftener than before ... everything seemed to him insignificant in comparison with eternity; again the question: for what? presented itself...."; Leo Tolstoy, *War and Peace*, Aylmer Maude (trans.), Project Gutenberg, http://www.gutenberg.org/etext/2600.

33 Cited in Allan B. Chinen, *Once Upon a Midlife: Classic Stories and Mythic Tales to Illuminate the Middle Years* (New York: Perigee/Tarcher, 1992), p. 81.

34 H. Perry Chapman, *Rembrandt's Self Portraits: A Study in Seventeenth Century Identity* (Princeton, NJ: Princeton University Press, 1990).

35 Allen B. Chinen, *Once Upon a Midlife*, p. 83.

CHAPTER 10
MATURE ADULTHOOD: SCALING THE PEAKS

1 From Carolyn Wells, "My Boon," quoted on ThinkExist.com

2 For a historical discussion of Catholic and Protestant representations of the life span, see Thomas R. Cole, *The Journey of Life: A Cultural History of Aging in America* (Cambridge: Cambridge University Press, 1992), pp. 3–31, and J. A. Burrow, *The Ages of Man: A Study in Medieval Writing and Thought* (Oxford: Oxford University Press, 1989).

3 *As You Like It*, Act II, Scene VII.

4 "Beyond 50: A Report to the Nation on Trends in Health Security," *AARP Bulletin*, June 2002.

5 Dudley Clendinen, "What to Call People Who Used to Be Old," *New York Times*, July 2, 2000, section 4, p. 10.

6 Carol Magai and Beth Halpern, "Emotional Development During the Middle Years," in Margie E. Lachman, ed., *Handbook of Midlife Development* (New York: Wiley, 2001), p. 323.

7 Orville Gilbert Brim, "MacArthur Foundation Study of Successful Midlife Development," Inter-University Consortium for Political and Social Research Bulletin, Summer 2000.

8 Quoted in Cathleen Rountree, *On Women Turning 50: Celebrating Mid-Life Discoveries* (San Francisco: HarperSan Francisco, 1993), p. 59.

9 Quoted from author's website: http://www.johnkotre.com. See also John Kotre, *Make it Count: How to Generate a Legacy that Gives Meaning to Your Life* (New York: Free Press, 1999).

10 Ursula M. Staudinger and Susan Bluck, "A View on Midlife Development from Life-Span Theory," in Margie E. Lachman, ed., *Handbook of Midlife Development*, p. 14.

11 Drew Leder, *Spiritual Passages: Embracing Life's Sacred Journey* (New York: Tarcher/Putnam, 1997), p. 109.

12 Theodore Roszak, "The Aging of Aquarius," *The Nation*, December 28, 1998, p. 11.

13 Al Gore, *An Inconvenient Truth* (Emmaus, PA: Rodale Books, 2006), p. 40.

14 *An Inconvenient Truth*, directed by Davis Guggenheim, Participant Productions, rated PG (100 min.). For further information, go to: http://www.climatecrisis.net.

15 Jane Goodall and Philip Berman, *Reason for Hope: A Spiritual Journey* (New York: Warner, 2000), p. 6.

16 For information about The Jane Goodall Institute, go to http://www.janegoodall.org/.

17 George E. Vaillant, *Aging Well: Surprising Guideposts to a Happier Life from the Landmark Harvard Study of Adult Development* (Boston: Little, Brown and Company, 2003), p. 49.

18 George E. Vaillant, *Aging Well*, p. 144.

19 Margie E. Lachman, *Handbook of Midlife Development*, p. xxi.

20 T. Rantanen et al. "Midlife Hand Grip Strength as a Predictor of Old Age Disability," JAMA, 1999, 281: 558–560.

21 Susan Brink, "The Do or Die Decade," *U.S. News & World Report*, March 11, 2002, p. 60.

22 See Robert L. Kahn and John Wallis Rowe, *Successful Aging* (New York: Dell, 1999).

23 Orville Gilbert Brim, ICPSR Bulletin, Summer 2000.

24 Perdix was rescued from his fall by the goddess Athena, who changed him into a partridge.

25 C. G. Jung, "The Structure and Dynamics of the Psyche," in R. F. C. Hull, trans., *The Collected Works of C. G. Jung*, vol. 8 (Princeton, NJ: Princeton University Press, 1981), p. 407.

26 The use of "the golden years" to describe late middle age was the innovation of real estate developer Del Webb, who used it as a marketing tool to promote his Sun City retirement communities beginning in the early 1960s. See Marc Freedman, "Coming of Age," *The American Prospect* 1, no. 1 (November 23, 1999).

27 Quoted in Scott Winokur, "The Human Condition," in *San Francisco Chronicle Image*, August 2, 1992, p. 13.

28 Orville Gilbert Brim, ICPSR Bulletin, Summer 2000.

29 For more examples, see David Gutmann, *Reclaimed Powers* (Evanston, IL: Northwestern University Press, 1994), pp. 155–84.

30 K. Hawkes, J. F. O'Connell, & N. G. Blurton Jones. "Hadza Women's Time Allocation, Offspring Provisioning, and the Evolution of Long Postmenopausal Life Spans," *Current Anthropology* 38, no. 4 (August-October 1997): 551–65.

31 Natalie Angier, "Theorists See Evolutionary Advantages in Menopause," *New York Times*, September 16, 1997, p. F1.

32 Gail Sheehy, *The Silent Passage: Revised and Updated Edition* (New York: Pocket, 1998), p. 268.

33 Quoted in Alex Kuczynski, "Boston Foes Together Again," *New York Times*, May 4, 1998, section 9, p. 1.

34 Savina J. Teubal, "Simchat Hochmah," in Ellen M. Umansky and Dianne Ashton, eds., *Four Centuries of Jewish Women's Spirituality* (Boston, MA: Beacon Press, 1992), pp. 257–64. The chapter includes the complete text of the ceremony. Also available online at http://www.ritualwell.org.

35 Quoted in Melinda Voss, "Croning Ceremony Celebrates the Wisdom of Age," *USA Today*, June 12, 1996, p. D6. For descriptions of croning rituals, see Edna Ward, *Celebrating Ourselves: A Crone Ritual Book* (Portland, ME: Astarte Shell Press, 1992); and Ruth Gardner, *Celebrating the Crone: Rituals and Stories* (St. Paul, MN: Llewellyn Publications, 1999).

36 Anthropologist Joel Savishinsky writes that the government of Otto von Bismarck originally set seventy as the age of retirement in 1889, figuring few people would live that long to collect government benefits. This figure was reduced to sixty-five just before World War I, and then incorporated into the first Social Security system by the United States in 1935. Joel S. Savishinsky, *Breaking the Watch: The Meaning of Retirement in America* (Ithaca, NY: Cornell University Press, 2002), p. 11.

37 Tim Smart et al., "Retirement Realities: Planning and Purpose Can Lead to a Whole New Life," *U.S. News & World Report*, June 3, 2002, pp. 68–70.

38 Larry Bumpass, MIDMAC Report, #2. 1994. http://midmac.med.harvard.edu/bullet2.html.

39 Tim Smart, "Retirement Realities."

40 Quoted in Lyric Wallwork Winik, "America's Great Retirement Crisis," *Parade* magazine, June 13, 2004.

41 Joel S. Savishinsky, *Breaking the Watch*, p. 241.

42 Lynn White, "Coresidence and Leaving Home: Young Adults and Their Parents," *Annual Review of Sociology* 20 (August 1994): 81.

43 Carol Magai and Beth Halpern, "Emotional Development During the Middle Years," in Margie E. Lachman, ed., *Handbook of Midlife Development*, p. 334.

44 Quoted in Barbara A. Mitchell and Ellen M. Gee, "'Boomerang Kids' and Midlife Parental Marital Satisfaction," *Family Relations* 45, no. 4 (October 1996): 446.

45 Quoted in Bernice L. Neugarten, "The Awareness of Middle Age," in Bernice L. Neugarten, ed., *Middle Age and Aging* (Chicago: University of Chicago Press, 1968), p. 98.

46 Michael Durham, "The Nutcracker Generation," *New Statesman*, January 12, 2004, pp. 26–27.

47 Steven M. Albert, "Caregiving as a Cultural System: Conceptions of Filial Obligation and Parental Dependency in Urban America," *American Anthropologist* 92, no. 2 (June 1990): 319–31.

48 Theodore Roszak, "The Aging of Aquarius," *The Nation*, December 28, 1998, volume 267, no. 22, p. 11.

49 Quoted in Steven M. Albert, *American Anthropologist*, p. 324.

50 Berit Ingersoll-Dayton, Margaret B. Neal, and Leslie B. Hammer, "Aging Parents Helping Adult Children: The Experience of the Sandwiched Generation," *Family Relations* 50, no. 3 (July 2001): p. 262.

51 Ibid.

52 H. Winsborough, L. Bumpass, and W. Aquilino, "The Death of Parents and the Transition to Old Age," NSFH Working Paper No. 39, 1991, National Survey of Families and Households, University of Wisconsin, Madison, Wisconsin.

53 Joan Delahanty Douglas, "Patterns of Change Following Parent Death in Midlife Adults," *Omega* 22, no. 2 (1990–91): 123–37.

54 Quoted in Sharon Begley with Erika Check, "When You're Nobody's Child," *Newsweek*, April 3, 2000.

55 Alexander Levy, *The Orphaned Adult* (Reading, MA: Perseus Books, 1999), pp. 30–31.

56 John C. Morris et al., "Mild Cognitive Impairment Represents Early-Stage Alzheimer Disease," *Archives of Neurology* 58, no. 3 (March 2001): 397–405.

57 Quoted in Beth Azar, "Use It Or Lose It," *American Psychological Association Monitor* 33, no. 5 (May 2002).

58 See, for example, David Snowdon, *Aging with Grace: What the Nun Study Teaches Us About Leading Longer, Healthier, and More Meaningful Lives* (New York: Bantam, 2002).

59 Gene D. Cohen, "Creativity with Aging: Four Phases of Potential in the Second Half of Life," *Geriatrics* 56, no. 4 (April 2001): 51–57.

60 H. Van Praag et al., "Functional Neurogenesis in the Adult Hippocampus," *Nature* 415 (February 28, 2002): 1030–34.

61 See Elkonon Goldberg, *The Wisdom Paradox: How Your Mind Can Grow Stronger as Your Brain Grows Older* (New York: Gotham, 2005).

62 See Arthur Schopenhauer, *The Wisdom of Life and Counsels and Maxims*, (Amherst, New York: Prometheus Books), 1995.

63 Quoted in Bernice L. Neugarten, "The Awareness of Middle Age," in Bernice L. Neugarten, ed., *Middle Age and Aging: A Reader in Social Psychology* (Chicago: University of Chicago Press, 1968), p. 97.

64 In Vaillant, *Aging Well*, p. 81.

65 Carol Magai and Beth Halpern, "Emotional Development during the Middle Years," in Lachman, *Handbook of Midlife Development*, p. 324.

66 George Vaillant, *Aging Well*, p. 96.

67 Heckhausen, in Lachman, *Handbook of Midlife Development*, p. 350.

68 J. M. Satinover and L. T. Bentz, "Aching in the Places Where We Used to Play: A Jungian Approach to Midlife," *Quadrant* 25, no. 1 (Spring 1992): 21–57.

69 Quoted in William Ross Woofenden, ed., *Swedenborg's Journal of Dreams 1743–1744* (New York: Swedenborg Foundation, Inc., 1977).

70 Quoted in Carl Jung, *Memories, Dreams, and Reflections*, p. 293. Note the resemblance of this narrative to a prebirth experience (see Chapter 1).

71 I remember watching a film of Carl Jung being interviewed in his eighties, where he was asked if he believed in God. "I could not say I believed," replied Jung, "I know." This interview, which occurred in 1959 and was a part of a BBC *Face to Face* television series, can be seen on the DVD entitled *Matter of Heart: The Extraordinary Journey of C. G. Jung*, Kino Video, 1985.

72 Quoted in Dorree Lynn and Jennifer Cohen, "Both Sides Now: Spirituality and Old Age," online article available at: http://www.fiftyandfurthermore.com.

CHAPTER 11
LATE ADULTHOOD: APPROACHING THE HORIZON

1 Henry Wadsworth Longfellow, Letter, March 13, 1877, *The Columbia World of Quotations* (New York: Columbia University Press, 1996).

2 Sarah Lamb, *White Saris and Sweet Mangoes: Aging, Gender, and the Body in North India* (Berkeley, CA: University of California Press, 2000).

3 "Great Expectations," *Harvard Health Letter* 25, no. 2 (December 1999): pp. 1–2.

4 Philip J. Hilts, "Life at Age 100 Is Surprisingly Healthy," *New York Times*, June 1, 1999, p. D7.

5 Michael Vitez, "New England Centenarian Study," Knight-Ridder release, October 28, 1995.

6 See, for example, John Blofield, *Taoism: The Road to Immortality* (Boston: Shambhala, 1978).

7 See the journal *Rejuvenation Research* (edited by de Grey) for further information on his work, online at http://www.liebertpub.com. See also Michael Murphy's *The Future of the Body* (New York: Jeremy Tarcher, 1993), which suggests that the universal application of extraordinary states of human consciousness may ultimately lead to the evolution of an extrasomatic body that survives physical death.

8 See Ray Kurzweil and Terry Grossman, *Fantastic Voyage: Live Long Enough to Live Forever.* New York: Plume, 2005.

9 S. Jay Olshansky, Leonard Hayflick, and Bruce A. Carnes, "No Truth to the Fountain of Youth," *Scientific American*, June 2002, p. 92.

10 Cited in Washington University School of Medicine Web site at http://wuphysicians.wustl.edu.

11 Cited in www.menshealthnetwork.org.

12 Cited by The President's Council on Bioethics, Washington, DC, September 2005. http://www.bioethics.gov.

13 Quoted in Barbara Meyerhoff et al., *Remembered Lives: The Work of Ritual, Storytelling, and Growing Older* (Ann Arbor, MI: University of Michigan Press, 1992), p. 237.

14 "Lest We Forget I: Remembering and Forgetting," *Harvard Men's Health Watch* 6, no. 10 (May 2002).

15 Elizabeth C. Ward, "Beyond the Thin Line: A Book Review," *Alzheimer Disease and Associated Disorders* 7, no. 2 (1993): 118.

16 *As You Like It*, Act 2, Scene 7, lines 164–167.

17 "Fear of Falling," *Harvard Women's Health Watch* 7, no. 10 (June 2000): 7.

18 Louis F. Sandock, "From Rites of Passage to Last Rights (A Piece of My Mind)," *The Journal of the American Medical Association* (JAMA) 284, no. 24 (December 27, 2000): 3100.

19 There are an increasing number of alternative living communities for the elderly that incorporate positive life values and psychospiritual growth. See for example, ElderSpirit Community (http://www.elderspirit.net). For an

example of life-enhancing reform in a nursing home, see the Green House Project at http://thegreenhouseproject.com.

20 Barbara Meyerhoff, *Remembered Lives.*

21 Anjetta McQueen, "Troubling Study on Nursing Homes," Associated Press, in the *San Francisco Chronicle*, July 31, 2001. For Representative Waxman's congressional reports on nursing homes from 2001 to 2006, go to http://www.house.gov/waxman.

22 *Timon of Athens*, Act 1, Scene 2, Line 154.

23 Bruce G. Pollock, Charles F. Reynolds III, "Depression Late in Life," *Harvard Mental Health Letter* 17, no. 3 (September 2000): 3.

24 Jane Brody, "Keeping Clinical Depression Out of the Aging Formula," *New York Times*, November 3, 1998.

25 Pollock and Reynolds, *Harvard Mental Health Letter*, p. 3.

26 B. W. Pennix et al. "Depressive Symptoms and Physical Decline in Community-dwelling Older Persons," *Journal of the American Medical Association* 279, no. 21 (June 3, 1998): 1720–26.

27 Jean Amery, *On Aging: Revolt and Resignation* (Bloomington, IN: Indiana University Press, 1994), p. 18.

28 Quoted in Studs Terkel, *Coming of Age: The Story of Our Century by Those Who've Lived It* (New York: New Press, 1995), p. 438.

29 John M. Rybash and Brynn E. Monaghan, "Episodic and Semantic Contributions to Older Adults' Autobiographical Recall," *Journal of General Psychology* 126, no. 1 (January 1999): 85.

30 Quoted in Marie A. Mills and Peter G. Coleman, "Nostalgic Memories in Dementia: A Case Study," *International Journal of Aging and Human Development* 38, no. 3 (1994): 208.

31 Becca Levy and Ellen Langer, "Aging Free from Negative Stereotypes: Successful Memory in China Among the American Deaf," *Journal of Personality and Social Psychology* 66, no. 6 (June 1994): 989–97. Note, however, that modernization around the world may be contributing to a lower valuation of the elderly in many places that traditionally valued elders. See, for example, Erik Eckhol, "Homes for Elderly Replacing Family Care as China Grays," *New York Times*, May 20, 1998; Nicholas D. Kristof, "Once-Prized, Japan's Elderly Feel Dishonored and Fearful," *New York Times*, August 4, 1997, p. A1; and Stephen Buckley, "Inheriting the Burdens of a Changing Continent" [Africa], *Washington Post National Weekly Edition*, May 27–June 2, 1996.

32 Cited in Paul C. Stern and Laura L. Carstensen, eds., *The Aging Mind* (Washington, DC: National Academy Press, 2000), p. 38.

33 Simon de Beauvoir, *The Coming of Age* (New York: W. W. Norton, 1996).

34 Quoted in Lars Tornstam, "Gerotranscendence: The Contemplative Dimension of Aging," *Journal of Aging Studies* 11, no. 2 (1997): 151.

35 Florida Scott-Maxwell, *The Measure of My Days* (New York: Penguin, 2000), pp. 32–33.

36 Joan M. Erikson "Gerotranscendence," in Erik H. Erikson, *The Life Cycle Completed, Extended Version* (New York: W. W. Norton & Co., 1997), p. 127.

37 Michelle Gilbert, "Fon and Ewe Religion," in Mircea Eliade, ed., *Encyclopedia of Religion*, vol. 5, p. 386.

38 Cited in Christie W. Kiefer, "Aging in Eastern Cultures: A Historical Overview," in Thomas R. Cole, David D. Van Tassel, and Robert Kastenbaum, eds., *Handbook of the Humanities and Aging* (New York: Spring, 1992), p. 103.

39 Allan B. Chinen, "Fairy Tales and Transpersonal Development in Later Life," *Journal of Transpersonal Psychology* 17, no. 2 (1985): 101–102.

40 John Bayley, *Elegy for Iris* (New York: Picador, 2000).

41 Quoted in Lars Tornstam, "Gerotranscendence: The Contemplative Dimension of Aging," *Journal of Aging Studies* 11, no. 2 (1996): 148.

42 Frances G. Wickes, *The Inner World of Childhood*, rev. ed. (New York: Signet, 1966), pp. 257–58.

43 Robert N. Butler, "The Life Review: An Interpretation of Reminiscence in the Aged," *Psychiatry* 26, no. 1 (February 1963): 65–76.

44 Erik Erikson, *Childhood and Society*, pp. 268–269.

45 Robert Kastenbaum, "The Creative Process: A Life Span Approach," in Thomas R. Cole, David D. Van Tassel, Robert Kastenbaum, eds., *Handbook of the Humanities and Aging* (New York: Springer, 1992), p. 303.

CHAPTER 12
DEATH AND DYING: CROSSING THE BRIDGE

1 Quoted in Kenneth V. Iserson, *Death to Dust: What Happens to Dead Bodies?* (Tucson, AZ: Galen Press Ltd., 1994), p. 3.

2 See, for example, Herbert Mason, trans., *Gilgamesh: A Verse Narrative* (New York: Mentor, 1972).

3 See Northwestern Mutual's "The Longevity Game" Web site at http://www.nmfn.com/tn/learnctr—lifeevents—longevity.

4 See http://www.deathclock.com. Note that this clock appears on a commercial Web site and does not tabulate enough vital information to provide an accurate statistical estimate of life expectancy.

5 From Max Beerbohm, *Zuleika Dobson* (New York: Modern Library, 1926), p. 208.

6 See *Bullfinch's Mythology* (New York: Harper & Row, 1970), p. 207. *Bullfinch's Mythology* refers to the Roman version of this myth, where Eos is Aurora and Zeus is Jupiter.

7 Alfred Tennyson, Prologue to *Becket* (1893). Project Gutenberg, http://www.gutenberg.org/etext/9162.

8 Philippe Aires, *Western Attitudes Toward Death* (Baltimore, MD: Johns Hopkins University Press, 1974), pp. 11–12.

9 Philippe Aires, *The Hour of Our Death* (New York: Knopf, 1981), p. 560.

10 Denise Grady, "At Life's End, Many Patients Are Denied Peaceful Passing," *New York Times*, May 29, 2000, p. A1.

11 Sherwin Nuland, *How We Die*, (New York: Vintage, 1995).

12 Jennifer Proctor, "Advancing Quality Care at the End of Life," *AAMC Reporter*, September 2001, http://www.aamd.org.

13 The SUPPORT Principal Investigators, "A Controlled Trial to Improve Care for Seriously Ill Hospitalized Patients. The Study to Understand Prognoses and Preferences for Outcomes and Risks of Treatment," *Journal of the American Medical Association (JAMA)* 274, no. 20 (November 22, 1995): 1591–98. See also John E. Wennberg et al., "Use of Hospitals, Physician Visits, and Hospice Care During Last Six Months of Life Among Cohorts Loyal to Highly Respected Hospitals in the United States," *British Medical Journal* 328 (March 13, 2004), vol. 328, p. 607.

14 Cited in Kathleen M. Foley and Hellen Gelband, eds., *Improving Palliative Care for Cancer* (Washington, DC: National Academies Press, 2001), p. 280.

15 Michael W. Rabow et al., "End-of-Life Care Content in 50 Textbooks from Multiple Specialties," *Journal of the American Medical Association* 283, no. 6 (2000): 771–78.

16 E. B. Lamont and N. A. Christakis, "Prognostic Disclosure to Patients with Cancer Near the End of Life," *Annals of Internal Medicine* 134, no. 12 (June 19, 2001): 1096–1105; and Judy L. Mallory, "The Impact of a Palliative Care Educational Component on Attitudes Toward Care of the Dying in Undergraduate Nursing Students," *Journal of Professional Nursing* 19, no. 5 (September–October 2003): 305–12.

17 James Sexton, "The Semantics of Death and Dying: Metaphor and Mortality," *ETC: A Review of General Semantics* 54, no. 3 (Fall 1997): 333.

18 Denise Grady, "At Life's End, Many Patients Are Denied Peaceful Passing," *New York Times*, May 29, 2000, p. A1.

19 Irene J. Higginson et al., "Is There Evidence That Palliative Care Teams Alter End-of-Life Experiences of Patients and their Caregivers?" *Journal of Pain and Symptom Management* 25, no. 2 (February 2003): 150–68.

20 Sheryl Gay Stolberg, "A Conversation with Dame Cicely Saunders: Reflecting on a Life of Treating the Dying," *New York Times*, May 11, 1999, p. F7.

21 Carl Jung, *Modern Man in Search of a Soul* (New York: Harvest/HBJ, 1955), p. 112.

22 Nuland, *How We Die*, p. xviii.

23 From John Webster, *The Duchess of Malfi*, 1612, Project Gutenberg, http://www.gutenberg.org/etext/2232.

24 Denise Grady, "At Life's End, Many Patients Are Denied Peaceful Passing," *New York Times*, May 29, 2000, p. A1.

25 Nuland, *How We Die*, pp. 121–122.

26 Ibid., p. 123.

27 Stephen Levine, *Who Dies?*, pp. 268–69.

28 Karlis Osis and Erlendur Haraldsson, *At the Hour of Death* (New York: Avon, 1977), p. 35. See also Carla Wills-Brandon, *One Last Hug Before I Go: The Mystery and Meaning of Deathbed Visions* (Deerfield Beach, FL: Health Communications Inc., 2000).

29 Ibid., p. 33.

30 Quoted in Stanislav Grof and Joan Halifax, *The Human Encounter with Death* (New York: Dutton, 1977), pp. 133–34 (originally in: *Jahrbuch des Schweitzer Alpenklub* 27 (1892):327).

31 Pim van Lommel, Ruud van Wees, Vincent Meyers, and Ingrid Elfferich, "Near-Death Experience in Survivors of Cardiac Arrest: A Prospective Study in the Netherlands." *The Lancet* 358, no. 9298 (December 15, 2001): 2039–44.

32 Olaf Blanke et al., "Stimulating Illusory Own-Body Perceptions," *Nature* 419 (September 19, 2002): 269–70.

33 Quoted in Jerry Libonati, "Studying Life After Near-Death," *South Florida Sun-Sentinel*, April 7, 2002.

34 For a good research-based analysis of near-death experiences, see Bruce Greyson, "Near-Death Experiences," in Etzel Cardena, Stephen J. Lynn, and Stanley Krippner, eds., *Varieties of Anomalous Experience: Examining the Scientific Evidence* (Washington, DC: American Psychological Association, 2000), pp. 315–52.

35 Information on the methods different religions use in disposing of the body was taken from: A.B.M.F. Karim et al., eds., *Death: Medical, Spiritual, and Social Care of the Dying* (Amsterdam, Netherlands: VU University Press, 1998); and Glennys Howarth and Oliver Leaman, eds., *Encyclopedia of Death and Dying* (London: Routledge, 2001), pp. 67–68.

36 See for example, Richard S. Ehrlich, "Years of 'Corpse Meditation' Now Serving Monks Well," *Washington Times*, January 3, 2005.

37 The details of the body's decomposition were taken from Kenneth V. Iserson, *Death to Dust: What Happens to Dead Bodies?* (Tucson, AZ: Galen Press Ltd., 1994).

38 Jane Hollister Wheelwright, "Old Age and Death," in Louise Carus Mahdi, Steven Foster, and Meredith Little, eds., *Betwixt and Between: Patterns of Masculine and Feminine Initiation* (La Salle, IL: Open Court, 1987), p. 408. Jane Hollister Wheelwright died on April 27, 2004, in a Santa Barbara, California, nursing home at the age of ninety-eight.

CHAPTER 13
BEYOND DEATH: TRAVEL TO OTHER LANDS

1 Socrates is quoted in Plato's *Apology*, Benjamin Jowett (transl.), Project Gutenberg, http://www.gutenberg.org/etext/1656.

2 William K. Powers, "Lakota Religion," in *Encyclopedia of Religion*, vol. 8, pp. 435–436.

3 Harris Interactive Inc., "The Religious and Other Beliefs of Americans, 2005," Harris Poll, December 14, 2005, no. 90, http://www.harrisinteractive.com.

4 See Dennis Overbye, "The End of Everything," *New York Times*, January 1, 2002, p. D1.

5 See Friedrich Nietzsche, *The Will to Power* (New York: Vintage, 1968), pp. 544–50.

6 Lewis Thomas, *Lives of a Cell* (New York: Bantam, 1971), p. 114.

7 See E. O. Wilson, *Sociobiology: The New Synthesis* (Cambridge, MA: Harvard University Press, 2000).

8 From Jalalu'l-Din Rumi, "The Ascending Soul," in The Masnavi, Book III, Project Gutenberg, http://www.sacred-texts.com/isl/masnavi/msn03.htm.

9 William Shakespeare, Sonnet XIX.

10 Th. P. Van Baaren, "Afterlife: Geographies of Death," in *Encyclopedia of Religion*, vol. 1, p. 117.

11 Anna Seidel, "Afterlife: Chinese Concepts," *Encyclopedia of Religion*, vol. 1, p. 125.

12 Jane I. Smith, "Afterlife: An Overview," *Encyclopedia of Religion*, vol. 1, p. 112.

13 Blaise Pascal, *Pensées* (New York: Penguin, 1995), pp. 121–25.

14 We might call these "peri-thanatal" experiences (from Thanatos, the Greek personification of death).

15 W. Y. Evans-Wentz, *The Tibetan Book of the Dead* (Oxford: Oxford University Press, 1960), pp. 95–96.

16 This idea is explored cinematically in the M. Night Shyamalan film *The Sixth Sense*, 1999. See Ram Dass, "Thoughts at the Moment of Death," in Gary Doore, ed., *What Survives?: Contemporary Explorations of Life After Death* (Los Angeles: Jeremy P. Tarcher, 1990), pp. 162–63.

17 E. J. Gold, *The American Book of the Dead* (San Francisco: HarperSan Francisco, 1993), pp. 67–68.

18 Brihad-aranyaka Upanishad, IV, 4, 1–2, in S. Radhakrishnana, ed. and trans., *The Principal Upanishads* (New York: Harper & Row, 1951), pp. 269–70.

19 Stanislav and Christina Grof, *Beyond Death* (London: Thames and Hudson, 1980), pp. 70–71.

20 Sukie Miller, *After Death: Mapping the Journey* (New York: Simon and Schuster, 1997), p. 69.

21 Patricia Grace, *Wahine Toa: Women of Maori Myth* (New York: Viking, 1984).

22 Elisabeth Kubler-Ross, *On Life After Death* (Berkeley, CA: Celestial Arts, 1991), p. 15.

23 Accounts of the Islamic and Egyptian afterlife can be found in Slanislav and Christina Grof, *Beyond Death*.

24 Th. P. Van Baaren, "Afterlife: Geographies of Death," *Encyclopedia of Religion*, vol. 1, pp. 117–18.

25 Sura 55 of the Qua'ran. See, Abdullah Yusuf 'Ali, *The Meaning of the Holy Qur'an* (Beltsville, MD: Amana Publications, 1989), pp. 1403–1406.

26 Quoted in A. L. Basham, *The Wonder That Was India,* (NY: Grove Press, 1954), p. 296.

27 Austin Lescarboura, "Edison's Views on Life after Death," in *Scientific American*, October 30, 1920.

28 See Milbourne Christopher, *Houdini: The Untold Story* (New York: Thomas Y. Crowell Co., 1969), pp. 245–60.

29 Gary Schwartz, *The Afterlife Experiments: Breakthrough Scientific Evidence of Life After Death* (New York: Simon and Schuster, 2003).

30 Stanislov Grof, *Psychology of the Future* (Albany, NY: SUNY Press, 2000), p. 232–33.

31 See R. K. Siegel, "Life After Death," in George O. Abell and Barry Singer, eds., *Science and the Paranormal: Probing the Existence of the Supernatural* (New York: Scribner's, 1986), pp. 159–84; and Gerd H. Hovelmann, "Evidence for Survival from Near-Death Experiences" in Paul Kurtz, ed., *A Skeptic's Handbook of Parapsychology* (Buffalo, NY: Prometheus Books, 1985), pp. 631–44.

32 In the field of consciousness studies in philosophy, this is called the "hard problem," as opposed to the easier problems of discovering the specific neural mechanisms that create conscious experience. See Susan Blackmore, *Consciousness: An Introduction* (Oxford: Oxford University Press, 2003), pp. 18–21. See also, Thomas Nagel, "What Is It Like to Be a Bat?" *Philosophical Review* (October 1974): 435–450.

33 This limitation of science in refusing to value the subjective ground of its own methodology became a primary focus of the philosophical school of phenomenology in the twentieth century. See, for example, Edmund Husserl, *The Crisis of European Sciences and Transcendental Phenomenology* (Evanston, IL: Northwestern University Press, 1970), pp. 75–85.

34 This attitude has been changing since the early twentieth century, however, at least in the field of physics. Einstein's theory of relativity factors in the standpoint of the observer in making conclusions about the nature of time and space. Similarly, in quantum physics, the act of observing a subatomic particle appears to change its fundamental nature. See John Gribben, *In Search of Schrodinger's Cat: Quantum Physics and Reality* (New York: Bantam, 1984).

35 Levine and Levine, *Who Dies?*

36 David Hume, *A Treatise of Human Nature* (New York: Penguin, 1969), pp. 299–311.

37 I say *ironically* because the physical object of the brain itself becomes suspect once we begin to radically critique science and the objective world it studies. Note, for example, this passage from the eighteenth-century philosopher George Berkeley, who reasoned that the objective world doesn't exist apart from our perceptions of it (except in the mind of God): "The brain therefore . . . being a sensible thing, exists only in the mind." George Berkeley, *A Treatise Concerning the Principles of Human Knowledge/Three Dialogues Between Hylas and Philonous* (La Salle, IL: Open Court, 1986), p. 194.

38 The best-known example of multiple personality disorder is probably the case of Shirley Ardell Mason, whose psychiatrist claimed she had sixteen distinct personalities. She was later fictionalized as "Sybil." See Flora Rheta Schreiber, *Sybil* (New York: Warner, 1989), and also the TV movie *Sybil*, 1976.

39 Andrew Newberg, Eugene D'Azuili, and Vince Rause, *Why God Won't Go Away: Brain Science & the Biology of Belief* (New York: Ballantine Books, 2001), pp. 4–10.

40 Quoted in Shankar Vedantam, "Near Proof for Near Death?" *Washington Post*, December 17, 2001, p. A11.

41 Henri Bergson, *Time and Free Will: An Essay on the Immediate Data of Consciousness* (London: G. Allen & Co., 1959).

42 Jean Houston, *The Possible Human* (Los Angeles: J. P. Tarcher, 1982), p. 149.

43 Jorge Luis Borges, "The Secret Miracle," in *Ficciones* (New York: Grove Press, 1962), pp. 143–50. There is a similar story by American author Ambrose Bierce that precedes it by several decades, which is about a man about to be hanged who goes through many adventures in the instant just before death. See "An Occurrence at Owl Creek Bridge," in Ambrose Bierce, *Civil War Stories* (New York: Dover, 1994), pp. 33–40. Bierce's story was made into a 1962 movie of the same name that won an Academy Award for Best Short Subject.

44 It is interesting in this regard to note Einstein's theory of special relativity, which asserts that as objects approach the speed of light, time slows down with respect to observers in other frames of reference, until at the speed of light, time itself is eradicated. For an explanation of Einstein's model, see Richard Wolfson, *Simply Einstein: Relativity Demystified* (New York: W. W. Norton, 2003). An analogy here between light and consciousness is not

entirely without precedent. Many schools of mysticism have used the metaphor of light as a way of speaking about consciousness. Note, for example, the earlier reference in this chapter to the Dharma-Kaya or The Primary Clear Light of Absolute Being, in Tibetan Buddhism as the ultimate ground of all existence. One medical researcher has speculated that neuromelanin, a light-sensitive chemical in the brain, may be the crucial connection between matter and consciousness, a link that has eluded philosophers and scientists for millennia. See Frank Barr, "Melanin: The Organizing Molecule," *Medical Hypotheses* 11 (1983): 11–140. It may be that as the dying person approaches The Primary Clear Light of Absolute Being at or shortly after death, his awareness of time slows down until, at the point of liberation (if this is achieved), he moves into the Light where all subjective time is annihilated forever. This compares with Einstein's theory, which states that when objects achieve the speed of light, time itself is destroyed. As physicist Brian Greene says: ". . . light does not get old: a photon that emerged from the big bang is the same age today as it was then. There is no passage of time at light speed." Brian Greene, *The Elegant Universe* (New York: Vintage, 1999), p. 51.

45   For a good discussion of the relationship between consciousness and quantum physics, see Amit Goswami, *The Self-Aware Universe: How Consciousness Creates the Material World* (New York: Tarcher/Putnam, 1993). There has also been a feature movie made on this topic entitled *What the Bleep Do We Know?* (2004, Captured Light Industries, 108 min.).

CONCLUSION

1   Quoted in Bernard Lievegoed, *Phases: Crisis and Development in the Individual* (London: Rudolf Steiner Press, 1979), p. 39.

2   Homer's *Odyssey*, Book XI, lines 148–151. Project Gutenberg, http://www.gutenberg.org/etext/1727.

Permissions

Permission has been granted by the following to quote from their work, which the author gratefully acknowledges. Full citations appear in the individual notes associated with the quoted text.

George Braziller of George Braziller Publishers for Jean-Paul Sartre's The Words, New York: Vintage, 1981.

Dorothy Corkille Briggs, *Your Child's Self-Esteem*, Random House.

William Buck, *Mahabharata*, The University of California Press.

Joan M. Erikson, "Gerotranscendence," in Erik H. Erikson's *The Life Cycle Completed*, W. W. Norton & Co.

Alison Gopnik, Ph.D., Patricia Kuhl, PhD, and Andrew Meltzoff, PhD, *The Scientist in the Crib*, HaperCollins Publishers, 1999.

Erlendur Haraldsson, *At the Hour of Death*, New York: Avon, 1977.

Laura Huxley, *The Child of Your Dreams*, Inner Traditions, Bear & Co.

Monica Jangaard of the Edvard Grieg Museum for Edvard Grieg's "My First Success," original manuscript in the Bergen Public Library.

Arthur Janov, *Imprints: The Lifelong Effects of the Birth Experience*, New York: Coward-McCann, Inc. 1983.

John Kotre, www.johnkotre.com.

Stephen Levine, *Who Dies?*, Random House.

Dr. Dorree Lynn, www.fiftyandfurthermore.com.

Ryan MacMichael, "First Kiss," www.dailyping.com.

Richie Magallano, "Oblogitory: This Is What Happens When You Give an Aimless Young Gay Man in Chicago Access to the Internet," http://www.heyrichie.com.

Bruce Narramore, *Boomerang Children*.

Joseph Chilton Pearce, *Magical Child*, New York: Bantam, 1980; and *Magical Child Matures*, New York: Dutton, 1985.

James W. Prescott, PhD, "Essential Brain Nutrients: Breastfeeding for the Development of Human Peace and Love," *Touch the Future*, Spring, 1997.

Edward Robinson, *The Original Vision: A Study of the Religious Experience of Childhood*, New York: The Seabury Press, 1983.

Janet Sayers, *Boy Crazy: Remembering Adolescence, Therapies, and Dreams*, London: Routledge, 1998.

Shambhala Publications for Garma C. C. Chang's "The Hundred Thousand Songs of Milarepa." copyright 1999, used with permission from Shambhala Publications Ltd., Boston, Mass., www.shambhala.com.

Rachel Strauch-Nelson of Fair Wisconsin for Mike Tate's "You Gotta Believe!", posted at http://noontheamendment.blogspot.com.

Michael Thompson, *Best Friends, Worst Friends: Understanding the Social Lives of Children*, New York: Ballantine, 2001.

Thomas Verny, *The Secret Life of the Unborn Child*, New York: Delta, 1981.

Index

Mothers, 51–54, 64. *See also* Labor;
  Parenting
Mount Rushmore, 185
Mozart, Wolfgang Amadeus, 83
Munker, 245
Murdoch, Iris, 214
"Mutuality of orgasm," 153
Myelination, 89
Mystics, 6–7, 178
The Mythic Image (Campbell), 19

Nakir, 245
National Child Abuse and Neglect
  Data System, 84
Native American cultures, 6
NDEs. *See* Near-death experiences
  (NDEs)
Near-death experiences (NDEs),
  230–231
 interpreting, 252
 time slowing in, 253
 visions during, 249
Neglect, 218
Neoteny, 309–40
"Netherworlds," 246
Neugarten, Bernice, 198
Newborns, 56
Newton, Isaac, 81
Nicholson, Jack, 192
Nietzsche, Friedrich, 165, 240
Nightmares, 74
Nijinsky, Vaslav, 57
No Exit, 46
"Noble death," 224
Notes from the Underground
  (Dostoyevsky), 165
Nuland, Sherwin, 225, 228–229
Numinous process, 17
Nursing homes, 208

OAA. *See* Orientation association
  area (OAA)
"Ode: On Intimations of Immortality
  in Childhood," 7
The Odyssey (Homer), 1–2, 7, 13, 26,
  60–61, 109, 131, 159, 167, 176,
  217, 256
Oedipus complex, 17, 85, 102
Older generation, 183
Opie, Iona, 104
Opie, Peter, 104
Oppenheimer, J. Robert, 81

Organizations
  adolescence, 289
  afterlife, 293
  birth, 284–285
  death/dying, 292–293
  early adulthood, 289–290
  early childhood, 286–287
  infancy, 285–286
  late adulthood, 291–292
  late childhood, 288
  mature adulthood, 290–291
  middle childhood, 287–288
  midlife, 290
  prebirth, 284
Orientation association area (OAA),
  251
Osiris, 246
Osis, Karlis, 230
Othello, 165
Outer necessity, 14
"Over-the-hill," 183
Oxytocin, 28, 34

Page, Satchel, 182
Paracosms, 93
Paradise, 247
"Paralyzing experiences," 117
Paraventricular nucleus (PVN), 35
"Parental emergency," 325–34
Parenting, 154–156. *See also*
  "Superparents"
Parker, Dorothy, 138
Pascal, Blaise, 6, 46, 137, 242
Passion, 4, 11–142
Past lives, 70. *See also* Previous life
  times
Paz, Octavio, 168
Peace Corps, 150
Pearce, Joseph Chilton, 7
Peers, 118–122
Peery, Carolyn, 211
Penicillin, 81
Perls, Thomas, 204
Philtrum, 15
Physiognomic perception, 72
Piaget, Jean, 9, 72, 75, 95, 137, 311–7
Picasso, Pablo, 75
Pipher, Mary, 136
Pitocin, 28
"The Pit and the Pendulum," 36
Placenta, 23, 41
Plasticity, 52

ALSO BY RICHARD RUSSO

Mohawk

The Risk Pool

Nobody's Fool

Straight Man

Empire Falls

The Whore's Child

Bridge of Sighs

That Old Cape Magic

Interventions

Elsewhere

Elsewhere

RICHARD RUSSO

ALFRED A. KNOPF   NEW YORK

2012

THIS IS A BORZOI BOOK
PUBLISHED BY ALFRED A. KNOPF

www.aaknopf.com

Knopf, Borzoi Books, and the colophon are registered trademarks of Random House, Inc.

Library of Congress Cataloging-in-Publication Data
Russo, Richard, date.
    Elsewhere / by Richard Russo. — 1st ed.
       p.   cm.
ISBN 978-0-307-95953-9
    "This is a Borzoi book."
    1. Russo, Richard, 1949—Family.   2. Russo, Richard, 1949—Childhood and youth.   3. Novelists, American—Biography.   4. Gloversville (N.Y.)—Biography.   I. Title.
PS3568.U812Z46 2012
813'.54—dc23
[B]   2012016354

Jacket photograph courtesy of the author
Jacket design by Jason Booher

Manufactured in the United States of America
First Edition

For Greg

Elsewhere

Prologue

A few years ago, passing the sign on the New York State Thruway for the Central Leatherstocking Region, a friend of mine misread it as saying *laughingstock* and thought, That must be where Russo's from. She was right. I'm from Gloversville, just a few miles north in the foothills of the Adirondacks, a place that's easy to joke about unless you live there, as some of my family still do.

The town wasn't always a joke. In its heyday, nine out of ten dress gloves in the United States were manufactured there. By the end of the nineteenth century, craftsmen from all over Europe had flocked in, for decades producing gloves on a par with the finest made anywhere in the world. Back then glove-cutting was governed by a guild, and you typically apprenticed, as my maternal grandfather did, for two or three years. The primary tools of a trained glove-cutter's trade were his eye, his experience of animal skins, and his imagination. It was my grandfather who gave me my first lessons in art—though I doubt he would've worded it like that—when he explained the challenge of making something truly fine and beautiful from an imperfect hide. After they're tanned but before they go to the cutter, skins are rolled and brushed and finished to ensure smooth uniformity, but inevitably they retain some of nature's imperfections. The true craftsman, he gave me to understand, works around these flaws or figures out how to incorporate them into the glove's natural folds or stitching. Each skin posed problems whose resolution required creativity. The glove-cutter's job wasn't just to get as many gloves as possible out of a hide but to do so while minimizing its flaws.

Leather had been tanned in Fulton County, using the bark of hemlock trees, since before the American Revolution. Gloversville and neighboring Johnstown were home not only to gloves but to all things leather: shoes and coats and handbags and upholstery. My paternal grandfather, from Salerno, Italy, having heard about this place where so many artisans had gathered, journeyed to upstate New York in hopes of making a living there as a shoemaker. From New York City he took the train north to Albany, then west as far as the Barge Canal hamlet of Fonda, where he followed the freight tracks north up to Johnstown, where I was born decades later. Did he have any real idea of where he was headed, or what his new life would be like? You tell me. Among the few material possessions he brought with him from the old country was an opera cape.

Both men had wretched timing. My father's father soon learned that Fulton County wasn't Manhattan or even Salerno, and that few men in his new home would buy expensive custom-made shoes instead of cheaper machine-made ones, so he had little choice but to become a shoe repairman. And by the time my mother's father arrived in Gloversville from Vermont, the real craft of glove-cutting was already under assault. By the end of World War I, many gloves were being "pattern cut." (For a size 6 glove, a size 6 pattern was affixed to the skin and cut around with shears.) Once he returned from World War II, the process was largely mechanized by "clicker-cutting" machines that quickly stamped out presized gloves, requiring the operator only to position the tanned skin under the machine's lethal blades and pull down on its mechanical arm. I was born in 1949, by which time there wasn't much demand for handmade gloves or shoes, but both my grandfathers had long since made their big moves to Fulton County and staked their dubious claims. By then they had families, and so there they remained. It was also during the first half of the twentieth century that chrome tanning, a chemical procedure that made leather more supple and water resistant, and dramatically sped up the whole process, became the industry standard, replacing traditional vegetable tanning and making tanneries even more hazardous, not just for workers but also for those who lived nearby and, especially, downstream. Speed, efficiency, and technology had trumped art and craft, not to mention public safety.

That said, between 1890 and 1950 people in Gloversville made good money, some of them a lot of it. Drive along Kingsboro Avenue, which parallels Main Street, and have a gander at the fine old houses set back from the street and well apart from one another, and you'll get a sense of the prosperity that at least the fortunate ones enjoyed until World War II. Even downtown Gloversville, which by the 1970s had become a Dresden-like ruin, still shows signs of that wealth. The Andrew Carnegie Gloversville Free Library is as lovely as can be, and the old high school, which sits atop a gentle hill, bespeaks a community that believed both in itself and that good times would not be fleeting. On its sloping lawn stands a statue of Lucius Nathan Littauer, one of the richest men in the county, whose extended arm appears to point at the grand marble edifice of the nearby Eccentric Club, which refused him membership because he was a Jew. Down the street is the recently restored Glove Theatre, where I spent just about every Saturday afternoon of my adolescence. There was also a charming old hotel, the Kingsboro, in whose elegant dining room Monsignor Kreugler, whom I'd served as an altar boy at Sacred Heart Church, held weekly court after his last Sunday Mass. Once it was razed, visitors had to stay in nearby Johnstown, out on the arterial highway that was supposed to breathe new life into Gloversville but instead, all too predictably, allowed people to race by, without stopping or even slowing down, en route to Saratoga, Lake George, or Montreal.

How quickly it all happened. In the Fifties, on a Saturday afternoon, the streets downtown would be gridlocked with cars honking hellos at pedestrians. The sidewalks were so jammed with shoppers that, as a boy trapped among taller adults, I had to depend on my mother, herself no giant, to navigate us from one store to the next or, more harrowingly, across Main Street. Often, when we finished what we called our weekly "errands," my mother and I would stop in at Pedrick's. Located next to city hall, it was a dark, cool place, the only establishment of my youth that was air-conditioned, with a long, thin wall whose service window allowed sodas and cocktails to be passed from the often raucous bar into the more respectable restaurant. Back then Pedrick's was always mobbed, even in the middle of a Saturday afternoon. Mounted on the wall of each booth was a minijukebox whose movable mechanical pages were full of song listings. Selections made here—five for a quarter, if memory serves—were played on the real jukebox on the far wall. We always played a whole quarter's worth while nursing sodas served so cold they made my teeth hurt. Sometimes, though, the music was drowned out by rowdy male laughter from the bar, where the wall-mounted television was tuned to a Yankees ball game, and if anybody hit a home run everyone in the restaurant knew it immediately. I remember listening intently to all the men's voices, trying to pick out my father's. He and my mother had separated when I was little, but he was still around town, and I always imagined him on the other side of that wall in Pedrick's.

I also suspected that my mother, if she hadn't been saddled with me, would have preferred to be over there herself. She liked men, liked being among them, and on the restaurant side it was mostly women and kids and older people. Though I couldn't have put it into words, I had the distinct impression that the wall separating respectability from fun was very thin indeed. There was another jukebox in the bar, and sometimes it got cranked up loud enough to compete with whatever was playing on ours, and then my mother would say it was time to go, as if she feared the wall itself might come crashing down. To her, music getting pumped up like that could only mean one thing: that people were dancing, middle of the afternoon or not, and if she'd been over there, she would've been as well. A good decade after the end of World War II, Gloversville was still in a party mode, and regular Saturday festivities routinely continued right up to last call and often beyond, the town's prosperous citizens dancing and drinking at the Eccentric Club, the more middle-class folk in the blue-collar taverns along upper Main Street or, in summer, at the pavilion at nearby Caroga Lake, the poor (often the most recent immigrants with the lowest-paying tannery jobs) in the gin mills bordering South Main in the section of town referred to as "the Gut," where arrests for drunkenness or indecency or belligerence were much more likely to be recorded in the local newspaper on Monday than comparable exploits at the Eccentric Club.

By the time I graduated from high school in 1967, you could have strafed Main Street with an automatic weapon without endangering a soul. On Saturday afternoons the sidewalks were deserted, people in newly reduced circumstances shopping for bargains at the cheap, off-brand stores that had sprung up along the arterial. The marquee at the Glove Theatre bore the title of the last film to play there, though enough of the letters were missing that you couldn't guess what it was. Jobless men emerged from the pool hall or one of the seedy gin mills that sold cheap draft beer and rotgut rye, blinking into the afternoon light and flexing at the knees. Lighting up a smoke, they'd peer up Main Street in one direction, then down the other, as if wondering where the hell everybody went. By then the restaurant side of Pedrick's had closed, but since I turned eighteen that summer, now of legal drinking age, the other side was no longer off-limits. Now, though, it was quiet as a library. The Yankees were still playing on the television, but Mantle and Maris and Yogi and Whitey Ford had all retired, and their glory days, like Gloversville's, were over. The half-dozen grizzled, solitary drinkers rotated on their stools when the door opened, like the past might saunter in out of the bright glare trailing ten-dollar bills in its wake. Every now and then that summer of '67, I'd poke my head into Pedrick's to see if my father was among those drinking Utica Club drafts at the bar. But, like time itself, he, too, had moved on.

WHAT HAPPENED? Lots of things. After World War II, about when men stopped wearing hats, women stopped wearing gloves. Jackie Kennedy did wear a pair at her husband's inauguration, and that turned the clock back for a while, but the trend proved irreversible. More important, glove making started going overseas where labor was cheap. Gloversville went bust the way Mike Campbell declares his bankruptcy in Hemingway's *The Sun Also Rises*, "gradually and then suddenly." The "giant sucking sound" of globalism arrived decades early and with a vengeance. My maternal grandfather, who, despite being a veteran of two world wars, had been branded a Communist from the pulpit of Sacred Heart Church for being a union man, saw it coming even before crappy Asian-made gloves showed up in the shops, where a few buttons could be sewn on and the gloves stamped MADE IN GLOVERSVILLE. Around Thanksgiving, the trade's off-season, workers in the skin mills got laid off, and every year it took a little longer for them to be called back. Worse, they weren't all rehired at once, which practice allowed the shop owners to remind their employees that things were different now. What mattered was moving inventory down the line, not quality. After all, Asians and Indians were doing what the local stiffs did for a quarter of the cost.

My grandfather, who came home from the Pacific with malaria and soon afterward developed emphysema, was by then too sick to fight. He continued to work as always, refusing to cut corners and, as a result, making considerably less money than men for whom slapdash was good enough. The bosses could exploit him, give him the most flawed skins, and treat him like a robot instead of the craftsman he was, but he claimed the one thing they couldn't order him to do was a bad job. But of course they didn't need to. You only had to look at how his narrow, concave chest heaved as he struggled to draw oxygen into his failing lungs to know he wouldn't be anybody's problem much longer. His wife, who'd also survived the Depression, foresaw a diminished future. She began stocking the pantry with cans of wax beans and tuna fish earlier every year, aware that the layoffs would run even longer, and her husband, growing sicker by the day, would be among the last called back. Jesus on his best day could do no more with loaves and fishes than my grandmother did with a pound of bacon. Still, it was just a matter of time.

None of which had much effect on me. As a boy I was happy as a clam in Gloversville. My mother and I shared a modest two-family house on Helwig Street with her parents. They lived in the two-bedroom, single-bath downstairs flat, my mother and I in the identically configured one above. My grandfather, who'd never before purchased anything he couldn't pay for with cash out of his wallet, bought the house, I suspect, because he knew his daughter's marriage was on the rocks and that she and I would need a place to live. Our block of Helwig Street was neighborly, with a corner grocery store situated diagonally across the street. My mother's sister and her family lived around the corner on Sixth Avenue, which meant I grew up surrounded by cousins. In kindergarten and first grade, my grandmother walked me to school in the morning and was there to meet me in the afternoon, and in the summer we took walks to a lovely little park a few blocks away. On weekends it was often my grandfather who'd take my hand, and together we'd head downtown for a bag of "peatles," his peculiar word for red-skinned peanuts, stopping on the way back to visit with friends sitting out on their porches. By the time I was old enough to get my first bike and explore beyond Helwig Street, I'd discovered the magic of baseball, and so, wooden bat over my shoulder, mitt dangling from my handlebars, I disappeared with friends for whole mornings or after-noons or both. At my aunt's there was a hoop over the garage, and during the long winters my cousin Greg and I kept the driveway shoveled meticulously so we could shoot baskets, even when it was so cold the net froze and you couldn't dribble the ball. Come autumn I raked leaves, stealing this job from my grandfather, who loved to do it, though he didn't always have sufficient breath. Sometimes he'd start the job, and I'd finish while he snuck a cigarette around back of the house where my grandmother couldn't see him. Summers I mowed lawns, and winters I shoveled sidewalks. An American childhood, as lived in the Fifties by a lower-middle class that seems barely to exist anymore, in a town that seemed unexceptional then, and not, as it seems to me now, the canary in the mine shaft.

WHAT FOLLOWS in this memoir—I don't know what else to call it—is a story of intersections: of place and time, of pri-vate and public, of linked destinies and flawed devotion. It's more my mother's story than mine, but it's mine, too, because until just a few years ago she was seldom absent from my life. It's about her character but also about where she grew up, fled from, and returned to again and again, about contradictions she couldn't resolve and so passed on to me, knowing full well I'd worry them much like a dog worries a bone, gnawing, bury-ing, unearthing, gnawing again, until there's nothing left but sharp splinters and bleeding gums.

I keep returning to that wall in Pedrick's, the one separating the restaurant from the bar. How close she was to where she wanted to be. How flimsy that wall must've seemed, the music and laughter leaking through so easily. But then my mother was forever misjudging—not just distance and direction but the sturdiness of the barriers erected between her and what she so desperately desired. I should know. I was one of them.

Independence

THE NIGHT BEFORE we scattered my mother's ashes in Menemsha Pond on Martha's Vineyard, I had a dream in which she featured vividly. She'd been visiting my sleep regularly since her death in July, and it was now the last week of December. Was there some duty other than the scattering of her ashes that I'd left undone? Some other subconscious reason for her to pay me a visit? A lot had happened since July. I'd gone on a long book tour, our daughter Kate had been married in London over Thanksgiving, and we'd returned home just in time for the hustle and bustle of Christmas. Was she feeling abandoned? That, of course, was another way of asking whether I was feeling guilty about neglecting her in death as I sometimes worried I'd done in life.

We'd delayed scattering her ashes for so long because both my daughters wanted to be present. Emily had recently started a new job at a bookstore near Amherst and didn't feel she could request time off until after the holiday rush. And Kate and her husband, Tom, still very much newlyweds, couldn't get a flight to the States until after Christmas. Thus we convened on the island during the week between Christmas and New Year's to make good on what I'd come to think of as my final promise to my mother, the last in a long, unbroken string of obligations that extended back almost as far as I could remember.

In the dream my mother and I were on foot, heading toward some vague destination we'd apparently agreed on. That we were going at all must have been my idea, because I was feeling particularly guilty about how long it was taking, and for not knowing the way and taking several wrong turns. Of course, getting my mother, who didn't drive, to wherever she needed to be—the grocery store, the doctor's office, the hairdresser's—had been my responsibility, off and on, since I got my driver's license in 1967, so in that sense my dream was cribbing from reality. That I was lost was a more unusual and troubling aspect of the narrative, since I'd always been the one responsible for knowing the way. My mother's poor sense of direction was legendary, and it long had been a joke between us that she was a compass whose needle pointed due south. No doubt my feeling lost and helpless in the dream had to do with her real-life condition during the long months before her death. Diagnosed with congestive heart disease, she'd been given two years at the outside, which meant that for the first time in decades she was going somewhere on her own.

In the dream she wasn't dying, just weak and fatigued as we

soldiered on through the darkening streets, looking for signs or landmarks where there weren't any. Finally, she was unable to go on, and I had to carry her. Initially, this wasn't a problem. My mother had always been petite, and now she was frail, while I was strong from tennis and running. But gradually I began to feel her exhaustion, as well as her frustration with me for landing us in this predicament. There were just the two of us in empty streets that stretched on forever, with no option but to slog ahead.

That was the dream. My mother and I going on and on, forever and ever, until finally I awoke to the old knowledge that she'd been dead since the summer, that in reality the burden of her long illness and longer unhappiness had at last been lifted from her shoulders. And from my own.

Some dreams require no interpretation, and this was one of them.

FROM THE TIME I was a boy, my mother valued few things more than her perceived independence. The legal separation she'd negotiated with my father stipulated that he contribute to my maintenance, though he seldom did. For a while she tried to compel him but quickly gave up, probably figuring that in the long run she was better off. Even if he wasn't helping out, at least she wasn't saddled with his gambling debts. She paid rent to my grandparents—at market price, she always proudly claimed—for our flat in their house on Helwig Street. Her job at GE in Schenectady paid well; before taxes she made just over a hundred dollars a week, more than many of the men who worked in the skin mills. Most women in Gloversville who worked were sewing gloves in the shops or at home, underpaid piecework that complemented the earnings of husbands who got laid off every winter and whose wages otherwise were kept artificially low through the collusion of the mill owners and the local government they held sway over. She was much better off working for a big company in Schenectady, though there were attendant expenses. For one thing she was a professional woman and had to dress like one. That suited her fine, because she loved nice clothes, but of course they weren't cheap. Also, because she got home from work too late and too exhausted to cook, she had to pay my grandparents for my board. Then there was the cost of her ride to and from GE with coworkers; when we went places with my aunt and uncle and cousins, she always made a point of chipping in for gas.

She ferociously defended her hard-earned independence against all comers, even (and especially) my grandparents, who were in many respects its true source. In particular she didn't appreciate unsolicited advice about my upbringing, and when they crossed that line she reminded them that theirs was primarily a financial arrangement. She paid her rent, promptly, the first of each month, which to her way of thinking meant they had no more right to intrude into our lives than any other landlord. If her parents were ever angered or hurt by the curtness of this, they never said so, at least not in front of me, but who could have blamed them? After all, my grandfather had bought the house, at least in part, so my mother and I would have someplace to live. To my knowledge they never reminded her of this, and she clearly saw it differently. She let it be known there were lots of places for rent in both Gloversville and Schenectady, and if her parents couldn't mind their own business, she'd move into one and take me with her. I don't doubt my mother's threat was sincere—when angry she was always sincere—but there wasn't much danger of her following through, and my grandparents must have known that, too. *"Jean,"* one of them would say when she got on her high horse, and I'd think that this time they were going to have it out with her for sure, but then they'd look at me and let their voices fall.

Gradually I came to understand that my mother's seeming ingratitude was simply self-preservation. Her view of herself as a woman who could get things done on her own required constant tending and bolstering. She had to assert her independence, to say the words out loud, at every opportunity, if she herself was to believe it. She had to remind herself constantly that she had a *good* job at a *great* company in a *real* city. Not just a job, but a better, more responsible *position* than just about any other woman in Gloversville. She not only paid her own way in the world but also fed, clothed, and raised me. Moreover, she was broadening my horizons beyond the smug, complacent, self-satisfied, dimwitted ethos of the ugly little mill town we lived in. Tired as she was at the end of her long day, she made sure I'd finished my homework and done it well. If I brought home a form, she filled it out, never needing to be reminded, and if a check was to be attached for the rental of a uniform or a musical instrument, somehow she managed. I had clean, crisply ironed clothing to wear every day, even if it meant she had to stay up until midnight doing laundry. She would skip dinners to meet with my teachers to make sure I wasn't just learning in school but flourishing, that I wasn't being dismissed as an irrelevant, fatherless boy. These were real accomplishments. No other woman my mother knew struggled under such burdens or challenges, and she was doing it, she told herself, all by herself.

Except she wasn't, not really, and sometimes that terrible truth would punch through the defenses she'd erected and fortified at such a high personal cost. To her credit, she almost never shared her doubts, her temporary losses of faith, with me, her principal audience. She kept the narrative of our lives consistent and intact. We, the two of us, were all we needed. As long as we had each other, we'd be fine. For my part I never let on that I suspected the truth: that, yes, she had a good job, but that as a woman she was still paid less than men with the same duties. They had families to support, she was told, as if she didn't. By the time she paid for her ride to and from work and the clothes she needed to look the part there, she could have done almost as well working in Gloversville. Yes, she paid her rent faithfully, but at Gloversville, not Schenectady, prices, and my grandparents, though they never said so, could have charged anybody else more. And what would it have cost if she'd had to pay someone to look after me while she worked, a job my grandmother did, lovingly, for free?

Even so, most of the time she was able to make ends meet,

and our lives proceeded smoothly enough to maintain the necessary façade of independence. Every month my mother budgeted our expenses to the last penny, which meant that our cash flow was a frayed shoestring that occasionally snapped. Any surprise could push us into the red, and then she'd have to borrow from her parents, the very people she was forever claiming our independence from. Sometimes I grew too fast and needed new clothes sooner than she'd projected, or I'd tear a hole in a brand-new pair of pants climbing over the neighbors' fences on the way to school. Other times I'd *want* things. Big things. One Christmas my cousins got a *Book of Knowledge* encyclopedia, and she had to explain why we couldn't have one, how expensive it was, how long she'd have to work to pay for it, how many other things we needed more. And besides, I could use my cousins' whenever I needed to. Though I was just a boy, I knew that she was holding things together, holding herself together, by sheer force of will, that the cold facts bore down on her relentlessly. She always paid back the small loans my grandparents floated us, but their necessity undermined the cherished myth of independence. Our well-being, at least on occasion, was being subsidized. Not that any of this was her fault. My mother seldom mentioned my father, but in crisis she'd sometimes lament that the money we were short was exactly the sum he refused to pay.

Indeed, my father was a tricky subject. They'd separated not long after we moved to Helwig Street, and what little I knew about him was so contradictory I couldn't make sense of it. On the one hand he was a war hero. I knew what D-day was and that my father was there, at Utah Beach, and had fought his way through France and Germany all the way to Berlin. I knew he'd won a Bronze Star. My mother never minimized any of this. She said I should be proud of what he'd done in the war. But now he was a gambler, a man who couldn't be trusted to bring home his paycheck. He was the reason we sometimes got angry phone calls in the middle of the night. I wasn't to think badly of my father, though. His gambling was a sickness, and he couldn't help himself. He was trying to stop, but so far he couldn't.

What I knew about him paled by comparison to what I didn't. For instance, where did he live? I knew he was still in Gloversville because my mother said so, and my grandparents and my aunt Phyllis confirmed it. I associated him with the pool hall so strongly that for a while I imagined him living above it. When I asked my mother where he lived and who with, she said there was no telling. He wasn't like us. We lived in the same place and with the same people all the time. My father could be anywhere, with anybody. I assumed this must be tied somehow to his gambling. If there were always people looking for him, wanting their money back, then not having a regular address or a consistent group of friends meant he'd be harder to find. Still, it was difficult to square all this with his being a war hero. I wondered if one or the other might be a lie.

Of all the known facts about him, the one that was most significant to my mother was this: if he'd paid his due, his fair share, we'd be sitting pretty. That bitter logic seemed a comfort to her, as did the fact that she seldom needed help from him or anyone, and never needed much. She was making things work, almost.

HALF A CENTURY LATER, prior to her final illness, she was in much the same boat. In her eighties by then, she was living in Camden, Maine, a few short blocks from our house. When people asked if this Megunticook House was an assisted-living facility, she always replied, "Oh, *no*. I live independently."

Though she hasn't a mean-spirited bone in her body, this characterization always made my wife swallow hard. "What do you suppose she *means* when she says that?" Doing my best Wallace Shawn, I'd reply, "Inconceivable." *The Princess Bride* was one of our daughters' favorite movies growing up, and in it André the Giant says, referring to Shawn's character, "He uses that word a lot. I don't think it means what he thinks it does." Which was precisely my wife's point about my mother's claim of independence. After all, for the last thirty-five years we'd joked that we never went anywhere for longer than it took for her milk to spoil. Part of what my mother meant, of course, was that she wasn't living *with* us, in our house, but she also was proud that, for a woman her age, she was still spry and active. She took care of herself: made her grocery list and filled her basket only with what was on it; kept her own checkbook, paid her bills, and ordered clothes from catalogs over the phone, there being no place for an elderly woman who didn't want to look frumpy to shop along our stretch of the Maine coast. In fact, she had briefly tried assisted living but hated every minute of it—the phony cheer of group activities, the dining room's mushy, overcooked food and overheated conversation, the periodic, obligatory inspections of her apartment (*her* apartment!) to make sure she wasn't creating, as even she had to admit some of the other ladies did, some kind of fire hazard. My mother wanted none of that, and she was especially disdainful of the facility's other services: transportation to the grocery store ("My son does that"), to the doctor (ditto), the dentist (ditto again), and the hairdresser (and again). She didn't require a scooter and didn't need to hang on to anyone's arm or on to the ugly ubiquitous railings bolted to the corridor walls. She certainly didn't need to be wheeled anywhere. Despite chronic lower-back problems, she still cleaned her own bathtub and did her own ironing. Nor did she want me paying for it. We never showed her the bills, but she somehow found out that it cost about the same as a year's college tuition, and that was that.

So when she said she lived independently, she also meant— and this was another point of pride—that she received little financial help from us. And she had good reason to be proud. Having never in her life been well paid, her monthly Social Security check was meager in the extreme; and having divorced my father, she could lay no claim to his veteran's pension. She had no inheritance beyond her mother's Depression-era ability to stretch a budget, which owed much to a stubborn willingness to do without a lot of what other people considered necessities. She qualified for rent and heat assistance from the state, as well as food stamps, though she was too vain to accept these. Okay, there was a shortfall most months, just as there'd often been on Helwig Street, a shortfall that I, like any decent son who had the wherewithal, was happy to make up. And of course there was the occasional emergency. That said, the only times she and I ever argued about money was when I tried to give her more than she asked for, hoping to make her life a little easier. But she didn't *need* any more than I was giving her, she insisted. She took great pride, she explained, just as she had always done, in taking care of herself.

In the end, of course, after her health began to seriously fail and her needs grew exponentially, month to month, she'd take my hand and say, "What would I do without you?" I tried to reassure her by saying, "That's what I'm here for," and reminding her that, unlike far too many writers, I made an excellent living. To which she'd reply that, yes, of course she knew. She guessed it was still pretty much like the old days on Helwig Street. As long as we had each other, things would be fine. But then, anxious, she'd look around her apartment, at her increasingly constricting world, and say, "But if anything ever happened to you, I'd have to say good-bye to my independence."

AS A YOUNGER WOMAN my mother didn't see her inability to drive as inconsistent with her desire to be, and to be seen as, a bold and independent woman. Gloversville was a walkable town with small markets on every other corner, and in the postwar years lots of people still viewed cars as extravagances, though that was rapidly changing. My grandparents didn't own one, and neither did other people in the neighborhood. But there was also the gender issue. My aunt and uncle had a car, but she didn't drive, and of course my grandmother didn't either, though as married women independence wasn't a hook they were hanging their hats on. Driving was something men did. The fact that after separating from my father my mother didn't *have* a man anymore was to her irrelevant. All over America, men returning from the war were moving with their families into the suburbs, where their wives discovered they had to learn to drive or be trapped in their dream houses, but in Gloversville there was no such necessity. More to the point, my mother possessed another skill that was even more valuable than the ability to drive a car, and that was her ability to convince other people to take us where we needed to go.

That's how it had been when we visited Martha's Vineyard when I was ten, perhaps the most astonishing and luxurious occasion of my childhood. My mother thought the resort she'd chosen provided everything we'd need—food, drink, plenty of activities for a boy my age, even a small private beach of its own. But the beach was on the sound, where the water lapped gently against the shore, and my mother could see my crushing disappointment that first day. I'd been imagining huge waves that would toss me ass-over-teakettle in the surf. Whereas *this* would be like swimming in nearby Caroga Lake—the kiddie pool when I was desperate for the deep end. Though we'd already investigated the matter thoroughly at the front desk, that night my mother inquired, in a voice loud enough for people at adjacent tables to hear, what our waitress could tell us about public transportation to the other side of the island, where some real waves might be waiting for me. "Really?" she said, mock incredulous, when informed that there were neither buses nor trolleys. "None?" Next she inquired about taxis and was told that, yes, there were taxis, but to have one come all the way out-island from Vineyard Haven or Edgartown would be expensive, and then of course we'd have to prearrange for another to pick us up and bring us back to the resort. Bicycles, then? Yes, the resort did have bicycles we were welcome to use, but the nearest public surf beach was several miles away, and we'd be loaded down with beach stuff. Each revelation elicited in my mother an even deeper incredulity. "But what do people *do*?" she asked, the picture of innocence. Well, people who stayed out here generally brought their cars over on the ferry. "Oh," she said, crestfallen. "I wish we'd known." As if we owned a car.

It was at this point that a couple seated nearby introduced themselves and offered to take us to a surf beach the next day, just as my mother had been hoping all along. I could tell she'd been prepared to keep the uncomfortable conversation with the waitress going as long as need be, until someone came to our aid, but now someone had. "Of course we'll pay you," she told the couple. We wouldn't dream of imposing, and we weren't the kind of people who expected favors from complete strangers. But they said no, that was okay, they were going anyway. Before long, once it was common knowledge that we were stranded there, offers of assistance began to pour in. One rainy afternoon we were taken into Edgartown for shopping and a break from the resort's dining room, and midweek we rode along with a family to a makeshift theater in Chilmark, where an old western was projected onto a plain white wall by a projector that chewed up chunks of film, causing not just delays but gaps in the narrative, the last occurring in the final reel where, after the film was spliced, half the cast lay wounded or dead in the dirt at the O.K. Corral. By the end of the week we'd become the shared responsibility of the resort's other guests, who must have been thrilled to see us leave. "Weren't people *nice* there?" my mother said dreamily when we were back on the ferry, watching the island recede behind us like an illusion. "And punctual," she added, because everybody who promised to take us somewhere not only did so but even showed up at the agreed-upon time. "Some different, huh?"

At home we generally relied on my aunt and uncle to take us places, like the lake on weekends for picnics or special trips to Frontier Town or Fort Ticonderoga. Unlike the people who'd chauffeured us on Martha's Vineyard, they showed up when it suited them. "Why tell us ten?" my mother would say, pacing like a tiger in my grandparents' living room at 10:45, our beach stuff piled up outside on the front porch. "If you mean eleven, why not *say* eleven?"

"I'm sure they meant ten," my grandmother would say. "It's just taking them a little longer."

My aunt, of course, had to rustle all my cousins, as well as prepare the food and together with my uncle load everything into the back of the big wood-trimmed station wagons he favored. Absolved of cooking because she worked all week, my mother usually contributed Cokes and chips, which worked out to her advantage, because she disapproved of the off-brand sodas and snacks my uncle would buy if left to his own miserly devices. The longer we waited, the worse it got, until my grandfather left the room, refusing to listen. "I swear to God," she'd exclaim, "if we go to Green's after all this, I'm going to scream." Which beach we went to was always another bone of contention. My uncle preferred Green's, which was closer to town and had dozens of picnic tables interspersed on the grassy field that ran down to within a few feet of the water. There was no quick drop-off, which meant that we kids could play safely. "At Green's we ain't got to watch 'em every damn minute, Jean," he would explain when my mother complained about the little patch of sand that was always so wet you couldn't even put a blanket down. "Lay your blanket on the grass like everybody else," her brother-in-law told her. "Y'ain't gotta have sand to lie down."

My mother maintained that indeed you did need sand for a real picnic, that it was no day at the beach without a beach, that if you wanted to lie on grass you could throw a blanket down on your own backyard. "So, do that next time," my uncle, finally fed up, would tell her, winking at us kids and causing a fit of giggles. It was my aunt, I was pretty sure, who always insisted we be invited along. To her husband's way of thinking, *his* family was going in *his* car to the beach of *his* choice, and my mother and I were simply hitching a ride. My mother's logic was different. If you contributed gas money, you had certain rights, and hers were being violated every single Sunday. At the end of the day when we were dropped off on Helwig Street, she'd still be on the warpath. "Green's again," she'd tell my grandparents, clearly hoping they'd share her indignation. Instead they'd turn to me and ask if I had a good time, and I'd make the mistake of saying I had, because I loved Green's and its great expanse of grass where you could play Wiffle ball or badminton with the other kids. Better yet, there was no lifeguard, so my uncle, whose specialty was horseplay, could toss my cousin Greg and me, squealing, high into the air, somersaulting into the warm lake. I knew I wasn't supposed to like Green's, but I could never contain my enthusiasm when I described what fun we'd had, and my mother, disgusted, would clomp up the back stairs to our flat, betrayed yet again by everyone from whom she deserved some sympathy. "Whoever said beggars can't be choosers," my grandfather would remark when she was out of earshot, "never met your mother."

I HAVE TO remind myself of how young she still was back then. Not long after her death, when we were going through her things, my wife and I came across a full-page photo of her in a glossy magazine published by GE. Actually, it's a picture of their vaunted mainframe computer, but my mother's standing in front of it, looking a bit like a Fifties version of a TV game-show hostess about to tell the contestants what they'll win. Still in her thirties, she was slender and graceful, balanced expertly on high heels, her hair styled, her skirt flatteringly tailored. We showed the photo to Emily and Kate when they came home for the holidays. "Now *that*," Kate said, showing it to her new husband, "is one stylish woman."

And she was. My mother took great pains and great pride in her appearance and the contrast she offered to the slatternly, dumpy women who did shift work in Gloversville sweatshops. They dressed in cheap slacks and garish, mismatched blouses pulled from tangles of clothing mounded in the huge bins of discount stores. For them my mother felt pity that sometimes manifested itself as condescension, though she at least gave such women points for getting out of the house. She saved her real contempt for "homemakers" like the ones so popular on TV, perky, vapid wives with dull, reliable husbands and not a worry in the world. Sometimes, when my grandmother attempted to "interfere," she also got lumped into this reviled category, though God knows she was no stranger to money worries and would have looked for a job herself if she hadn't been married to a man who would've considered this an indictment of his abilities as a provider. Back then my aunt was also a homemaker, but she was raising five kids, and even my mother had to give her a pass for not having a real job. Still, she thought her sister's good fortune in having a hardworking husband who didn't drink or gamble made her one of the world's innocents, because she didn't have to face things alone, the inescapable consequence of which, of course, was dependence. And when these women's husbands brought home their paychecks and decided how the money would be spent, they had little choice but to accept their lot. They had nothing that the world needed, or nothing, at least, that it was willing to pay a living wage for. If you were a woman who'd never held a responsible job, if you didn't bring home your own paycheck at the end of the week and deposit it into an account with your own name on it, you had no right to criticize or interfere in the lives of those who did. Indeed, you had no opinions worth listening to. In the GE photograph my mother looks both old-fashioned and modern, both of her time and oddly outside of it, a strange mix of stubborn confidence and acute anxiety.

But there was another reason my mother took such ferocious pride in her personal appearance. Her marriage had failed, and having a kid in tow made things even more challenging, but she was still hopeful of finding romance. She'd always loved men and knew they found her not only attractive but likable as all get-out. She could tell a joke and take one, and she liked sports and had a good head for booze. She didn't giggle demurely like girls who were stupid or pretending to be. She presented herself as a woman seeking a mate more than a husband, as a Nora Charles searching for her Nick, except instead of having a yippy little dog for a companion, she had me. There must surely have been times she'd have liked to trade me in for a dog, because I could be as nervous and demanding as Asta and far less faithful. Worse, if allowed, I was just as willing to steal a scene.

Of course she had exactly zero interest in Gloversville men. The ones her own age she knew from high school, and there wasn't a Nick Charles in the lot. More to her taste were the guys who passed through the computer room at GE, or the kind of men who'd stopped by our table on Martha's Vineyard, men of the world who had manners and, even if they didn't major in repartee like William Powell, at least knew enough to hold the door for a lady instead of barging right on through. Many of the "fellas" who interested her had been in the service, and she was at ease with them, having been a camp follower until my father shipped overseas. After the war they'd taken full advantage of the GI Bill, as her husband had not, and now they were starting to get ahead. They dressed well and drove T-Birds and Caddies. Some took her out for lunch in Schenectady; others who were stuck there over the weekend were willing to hop on the Thruway and drive to Gloversville on a Saturday night. At this point she was legally separated but not yet divorced, and dating was one of many sources of discord between her and my grandparents, who might have suspected, despite my mother's protestations to the contrary, that some of her dates had wedding rings in their pockets. They thought she should think of me first, because Gloversville was a small town where people loved to gossip. Also, my father would cause a scene if he found out.

Which he invariably did. It was like he had a mole in the house. My mother didn't go out on dates all that often, but every time she did he'd telephone, wanting to know if this new guy understood she was a married woman. He'd ask where they were going to dinner. Maybe he'd stop by and buy them a drink. Introduce himself. Maybe he and this new guy would hit it off.

"We're separated," my mother would remind him.

"You're still my wife," he'd remind her back. "And I'm still our son's father, too."

"What's the matter? Forget his name?"

Often I'd awake the morning after one of my mother's dates vaguely aware that there'd been trouble in the night, shouting out in the street, maybe, or my mother calling downstairs, telling my grandparents that he was gone and for them to go back to sleep. Such confrontations were pretty rare, though, because they required focus and steadfast purpose on my father's part, and he famously lacked both. He'd have liked nothing better than to ambush my mother and her date at the restaurant, but apparently whoever tipped him off that his wife was stepping out didn't know where. There were no good restaurants in Gloversville itself, but too many in the surrounding area to stake out. Better to catch them later when the guy brought her home. Here this dumb bastard would be thinking maybe she'd invite him in, and instead—surprise!—there he'd be, waiting. Meanwhile, to pass the time, he'd find a card game. That was where things would invariably get away from him. He'd remember to check his watch at first, but then would get involved in the game and forget about it. Either the cards would be falling right at about the time my mother and her date would be returning, and he wouldn't want to kill his luck by cashing out, or he'd be a couple hundred bucks down and unwilling to leave until he won at least some of it back. Nor did it fail to occur to him that if he left he'd have to sit in a borrowed car up the block from my grandparents' house for who knew how long. What the hell, maybe he'd play one more hand and let the cards decide. If he won, he'd stay; if he lost, he'd drive over to Helwig Street and see what was what and what could be done about it. Except by then it would register that he'd probably waited too long: if she was already home, he'd be waiting in the dark, cold street for nothing. The next time he looked at his watch, when the game was breaking up, it was four in the morning, and the man who'd taken my mother out was back in Schenectady asleep in his hotel. My mother would be asleep, too, but sometimes he'd visit Helwig Street anyway before going home. There he'd stand beneath her bedroom window, hollering up to inquire if she'd had a good time.

Such was my mother's independence at age thirty. She was free, but couldn't do as she pleased. Though she could go wherever she liked, she had no way of getting there. She had her own money, but it ran out before she could spend it on anything she really wanted. Men liked her—how she looked and danced and laughed—and under different circumstances she would've had no great difficulty finding someone. But the circumstances weren't different; they were always the same. The men she liked were mostly passing through and often lost interest once they were introduced to me or to my tight-lipped grandparents or to Gloversville itself. Some of them probably came from places that were pretty similar, but after the war they were done with these backwater burgs.

Even to my mother, her hard-won autonomy must at times have resembled a cage. Still, it was a cage of her own design, different from and superior to the one my father and her parents and Gloversville itself would have put her in if she'd allowed them to. In retrospect what astonishes me is the courage she must have summoned in order to imagine—by working in Schenectady, by having her own checking account, by going out on the occasional date—that she was outside the cage she so clearly was trapped in. She had to muster that tough imagining day after day, year after year, with all of life's realities bearing down on her relentlessly, insinuating, as self-doubts always do, that the sensible thing would be to give up. And with no one to talk to about any of this but a boy.

What kept her going? Stubbornness? Vanity? My mother did love mirrors, often practicing in front of them. But I came to understand that this vanity had its origins in fear and, counterintuitively, intense empathy. One of her favorite family stories was of a particular Easter during the Depression. My grandfather had somehow managed to scrape together enough money to buy her and her sister new outfits, and he made a great fuss about how beautiful they were, picking each of them up and twirling them in the air above his head, assuring them they'd be the prettiest girls at Easter Mass. When he finally set them down, he took his wife in his arms and said, "And you look beautiful, too," though that spring there wasn't enough money to buy her anything new. My mother was on morphine the last time she shared this story with me. It was clear that the memory still haunted her, in part, I suspect, because it effortlessly yielded two irreconcilable morals. I don't think she ever doubted how much her father loved her mother, or that he thought she was beautiful, no matter how threadbare the dress she was wearing. Seen as a parable of love versus material goods, love wins hands-down. But I think to my mother the story also suggested, as it would to so many who'd weathered the Dirty Thirties, that in this world there's never enough to go around. Love couldn't stretch two new outfits into three, or fill three hungry bellies with food for two. If you depended on a man, even one who loved you, you could end up in church with people staring with pity at your moth-eaten clothes. And who knew? Maybe love followed the same laws, and there wasn't enough of that to go around either.

For whatever reason, or combination of reasons, I think my mother made up her mind never to be that woman without something pretty to wear. There was no character in literature or film with whom she identified more completely than Scarlett O'Hara (speaking of brave, ferocious, stubborn vanity), and her favorite scene in *Gone With the Wind* was when Scarlett, penniless and hungry, makes a gown out of Tara's velvet drapes. In the last few months of my mother's life, her Easter story seemed to morph on her, as if after so many tellings its true meaning was only now coming clear to her. She kept trying and failing to describe the exact expression on her mother's face when her father told her that she, too, was beautiful. I wasn't there, of course. I didn't see it. But I knew my grandmother, and I know her expression would have contained both love and understanding. But having seen photographs of her as a young mother, I also know what those Depression years, so full of want and fear, had done to her handsome features.

And so I wouldn't be surprised if what my mother saw on her face was defeat.

AND THERE WAS one more reason—this one less personal— my mother kept soldiering forward when reason dictated simply giving up: those were optimistic times. Like the men she occasionally dated, the postwar nation was thriving. Ser- vicemen had returned triumphant, and when the partying stopped they parlayed their brand-new GI Bill degrees, their new skills, their hard-earned worldly experience and brimming confidence into houses in the suburbs and two-car garages. When JFK became president, it seemed to many, including my mother, that the country had turned a corner, that barriers excluding people like her were finally coming down. Opportu- nities seemed to be everywhere. To be left behind when every- one around you was getting ahead, she thought, you'd have to be stupid or lazy—or married to Jimmy Russo and living in Fulton County (which JFK had not carried). My mother wasn't stupid, and she wasn't lazy, and she'd separated from my father, so . . .

So. "You," she told me throughout high school, "are get- ting out of Gloversville."

I was a decent student, but uneven and undisciplined, far too interested in girls and having a good time to really excel. I got excited about all sorts of things, then invariably lost inter- est when I discovered they were difficult and there was no one to help guide me through their intricacies. My mother had told me for as long as I could remember that I could be anything I wanted to be, and I took this to mean, despite a complete lack of evidence, that I was gifted. While my teachers tried their best to offer a counterbalancing view, I was having none of it. Senior year, though, I did well enough on my Regents Exams to qualify for significant financial assistance to any college in New York. But I'd also found out that the universities out west were much cheaper. If I lit out for the territories, the first year would be rough because I'd have to pay out-of-state tuition, but by the second I'd have established residency, and it would cost less to go to the University of Arizona without financial aid than to SUNY with a scholarship. I expected my mother to put up stiff resistance to this plan; after all, I'd be twenty-five hundred miles away and her mantra had always been that we were a team, that as long as we had each other, we'd be able to manage. So I should have been suspicious when she didn't object to my heading west. But even if I'd twigged to the possibility that she was up to something, I never would've grasped the obvious inference, and it was years before it occurred to me that maybe the westward-ho notion hadn't been mine at all, that she'd steadily been dropping hints—for example, that the best place to study archaeology, my current interest, was the Desert Southwest—and that I'd dutifully been lapping them up. Nor did she object when, in spring of my senior year, I announced I wanted to buy a car.

The reason she didn't, of course, was that we'd need one. Because she was coming with me.

A Good Talking-To

IN THE SPRING of 1967 I bought a big, hulking 1960 Ford Galaxie, the first car ever to sit at the curb of 36 Helwig Street. Everything about it—exterior, dashboard, vinyl upholstery—was a dull, battleship gray, so my friends immediately christened it the Gray Death. It's hard to imagine the car had ever been shiny, even in the showroom, but there was no rust on it, which in upstate New York was remarkable. Still, cars didn't get much more uncool, and to make matters worse the Death, with its small V-6 engine, was seriously underpowered. I would own worse cars, but never another in which you could slam the accelerator to the floor and nothing, absolutely nothing, would happen. You simply couldn't express urgency to the fucking thing. Getting on the Thruway at Fultonville, you wouldn't get up to the speed limit until Amsterdam, seven miles down the road.

For our trip across country I hitched a U-Haul to the rear bumper, and into this we crammed my mother's books, our clothes, television, kitchen stuff, and other miscellaneous items she couldn't bear to part with. Her plan was to find a furnished apartment in Phoenix, where General Electric had a branch office. She admitted to being a little worried she might not make quite as much money there as she did in Schenectady, but we had distant relatives who lived in Scottsdale, and they claimed that the cost of living was much lower, so hopefully the two would cancel each other out. Later, after she got established, my mother could move into an unfurnished place and have the bulk of our furniture shipped out from Gloversville. She kept this scheme hidden from her parents as long as possible, knowing they'd consider it rash and do everything in their power to dissuade her, as indeed they did. Phoenix was a big city, they pointed out, in which she didn't know a soul. Did she have any idea what rents there were like? Where was that kind of money going to come from? In nine months, tops, she'd be broke, and then what would she do? How would she even get back home? My grandfather's emphysema had progressed to the point where he couldn't work anymore, and his meager pension and retirement barely covered their monthly needs. Eventually my mother would discover her mistake and rely on them to rescue her, like she always did. Did she understand that now they simply couldn't manage to?

But all of this was assuming we'd make it there in the first place. Our whole trip, according to my grandfather, was underfunded, my mother's calculations based on wishful thinking.

Gas. Motels. Food. Auto repairs. At the wheel of our unsafe car was someone who'd had his license only a few months, and my mother couldn't even spell me at the wheel. Did she understand that what she was proposing wasn't just financial folly but also dangerous, potentially even tragic? To all this, my mother responded that she wasn't a child and didn't appreciate being treated like one, adding for good measure that their refusal to treat her like an adult was one of the reasons she was leaving. She'd carefully budgeted the trip according to the recommendations of AAA, which had even mapped out our route. And she *had* planned for the unexpected, laying aside an emergency fund we could dip into if we needed to. She had every confidence in my driving ability. We would go slow. We would be safe as houses.

In the weeks before our departure 36 Helwig Street, the sanctuary of my childhood, became a battleground, a place of bitter recrimination and slamming doors. The only thing that kept the arguments from escalating was that my grandfather didn't have the breath, and after a few minutes he'd have to get up from the kitchen table, go into the living room, and hook himself up to the oxygen tank standing sentry behind his armchair. Even my mother could see what the strife was doing to him, and so a terrible silence descended that was even worse. No matter where I happened to be, upstairs or down, I was behind enemy lines and chose, coward that I was, to stay away as much as possible. It was a summer of farewell parties, of the Doors advising us to break on through to the other side, of freedom. One day, though, I came home and found my grandfather sleeping in his chair, his chest heaving violently up and down, as it often did now, awake or asleep. I thought my mother was up in our apartment, but went into the kitchen and she was sitting there with my grandmother, who reached across the table and took her hand. The gesture surprised me, because they seldom touched or talked intimately. "Jean," she said, and waited until my mother met her eye. "This trip. You're in no *condition*."

I could have been wrong, but I got the distinct impression that my mother might be about to concede something important, perhaps a fear, or a misgiving, but she looked up, saw me, and quickly withdrew her hand, leaving me to wonder how that moment would have played out if I'd come home a few minutes later. It might have been my first intimation of how whole lives—maybe even my own—could pivot on such perfectly poised moments of stillness.

MY MOTHER'S "CONDITION." This was something the whole family seemed aware of, but no one talked about it. One word, *nerves,* was evidently deemed sufficient to describe, categorize, stigmatize, and dismiss it. As a child I remember being frightened of whatever was wrong with my mother because it seemed at once serious and, for the most part, without visible symptoms. Nor, apparently, was there anything to be done about it. I wondered anxiously if I might one day come down with nerves, but from what I could gather men didn't get them. Certain women, my mother among them, seemingly had more than their share, and if they became too nervous they could even have something called a breakdown. This had happened to other women in my grandmother's family and more recently to my uncle's mother, though she wasn't a blood relation. The idea of my own mother suffering one of these nervous break-downs was terrifying to me, because then she wouldn't be living with us on Helwig Street but rather in some kind of hospital. Some suffering women were given electroshock treatments, after which they weren't nervous anymore, or aware of their surroundings or that it was Tuesday. *Nervous Breakdown.* The phrase haunted my childhood, in part because it could happen to my mother, but also because I came to understand that I might be its cause. Her health was in *my* hands. Other kids were good because they didn't want to get punished if they misbehaved; I was good because I feared that if I misbehaved it was my mother who'd be punished.

But here's the thing about conditions, especially pervasive, largely asymptomatic ones: over time, when the worst doesn't happen, they gradually lose their power to terrify. They simply become part of the landscape—as real as anything else, but also as ordinary. I observed that my mother's nerves were cyclical, like the moon, waxing and waning, and by paying attention, I could tell where we were in the cycle. Which in turn suggested that maybe her health *wasn't* in my hands, at least not entirely. True, it was in my power to make things worse, a lot worse, if I chose to, but I couldn't make them much better. There were other forces at work, as powerful and inexorable and impersonal as gravity, as regular and predictable as the tides. And most of the time she seemed fine. At some previous low point she'd confessed to our family doctor that the stress of being a single mother and, in addition, working full-time sometimes made her awfully nervous, and he immediately prescribed a low dose of phenobarbital. Over the years these dosages incrementally increased, and in due course barbiturates gave way to newer drugs like Valium. Afraid of becoming addicted, she cut pills in half when she was doing well, but then upped the dosage when she "needed help." Eventually she developed a tremor in her hands, though it was never clear to me whether this was due to stress or the medication she was taking to alleviate it. Most of the time her condition was part and parcel of our lives, a subtext that under the right circumstances might become a text.

And, on occasion, a screeching ALL CAPS hypertext, a gale of fury and paranoia and accusation and heartbreaking despair. "I can't *take* it anymore!" she'd scream. "Doesn't anybody under*stand*? I can't *take* it!" Sometimes these episodes had specific triggers—a raise or bonus at work that she expected but that didn't come through, or I'd get into some kind of trouble at school, or a GE man she was dating would break things off, or she'd be blindsided by some unanticipated expense. But more often what she couldn't take anymore was vague, almost global. She felt it as a weight whose source might be too much responsibility or accumulated disappointment or mounting despair. Whatever was wrong or out of balance would grow slowly until suddenly everything in the world was wrong, and utter panic would ensue. Wild eyed, she'd often fix her gaze on me and ask unanswerable questions: "Don't I deserve a *life*? Am I so different from everyone else? Don't I deserve what other people have?" As a boy what scared me the most about such questions wasn't that I had none of the answers my mother so desperately sought. No, it was that it didn't seem possible for these questions to be asked without consequence. What would my mother *do* if I couldn't manage to console her? "Doesn't anyone understand that things have to *change*?" she'd wail. "That something will *happen* to me if they don't?"

By the time I was in high school, though, this much had become clear: in fact, nothing was going to happen. At least nothing as dramatic as her hysterical questions implied. Because the result was the same every time she had one of these meltdowns. The morning after she'd appear at the break-fast table, so exhausted by what she'd been through that she could barely lift the coffee cup, but her emotional equilibrium for the most part restored. "Ah, Ricko-Mio," she sighed, using her pet name for me. "Don't worry. Everything's going to be fine." She'd give my hand a reassuring pat. "Last night, after you went to bed, I gave myself a good talking-to."

That phrase always gave me the willies, because it squared with nothing in my experience. As a boy I'd had a condition of my own, a terrible temper, and knew firsthand what a near-total loss of control felt like. My mother's meltdowns could be scary, but at least they were analogous to something I myself had experienced. But I'd never given myself a good talking-to. For that to happen there would have to be two of me, and I was always one, even when unhinged. I understood that my mother's phrase could be interpreted as a figure of speech, though I also suspected that fundamentally it wasn't. She wasn't thinking things through more calmly or considering things from a new angle due to conscience, rituals I was conscious of and familiar with from a fairly young age. But I'd never given myself a dressing-down. There was simply no other me to assume the talked-to position. If I deserved a lecture, there was no me to give it; if I had one to impart, neither was there another me to receive it. Somehow, my mother was able to do that. More bizarrely still, it worked.

It just didn't last.

THE CONFLICT BETWEEN my mother and grandparents came to a head in the week before we were scheduled to leave. Given that our future well-being, if not our very lives, was being wagered on an ill-conceived cross-country journey, their final battle was over something relatively insignificant: my mother's furniture, the stuff we weren't taking with us in the U-Haul and that she couldn't afford to put in storage. She wanted to store it in Helwig Street's small, dark, dank basement, but my grandfather said there was too little space, that with all that furniture stacked down there, it would be hard to get at the furnace, should it need servicing. But more likely he hoped that when it came down to selling all her worldly goods for what little they'd bring, my mother would finally see the folly of the whole enterprise and come to her senses. Instead, she assured them that this was the last time she'd *ever* ask them for *anything* and promptly called a man who dealt in used furniture. He came to the house, looked everything over critically, and concluded that he'd be doing her a favor, really, just to haul it away. There wasn't much of a market for such old-fashioned stuff, he claimed, and a lot of the pieces sported dark cigarette burns, courtesy of my father, who couldn't be bothered to use an ashtray and who managed, despite his brief tenure on Helwig Street, to leave his mark on flat surfaces in every room.

By the time we got to Ohio, naturally, she'd decided the guy was a highway robber. She'd waited too long to get a second appraisal, and he'd known we didn't have time to haggle and would take whatever he offered, no matter how unfair it was. No doubt he'd spent a leisurely morning sanding the burns off the arms of our furniture, which was *not* old-fashioned but classic, timeless. By now he'd applied a coat of polyurethane and was selling it for three times what he paid us. Ten times, probably. And this was money we could use, she admitted, because of course by Ohio she knew that my grandfather had been right. Everything *was* costing more than she'd budgeted, and she now feared we might have to dip into the emergency fund, which she at last revealed was my college money. All because of a thief. "Gloversville," she muttered, shaking her head in disgust. How lucky we were to finally be shut of such an awful, awful place.

WE WERE SCARED, if not nearly as scared as we should have been. It was beyond lunatic to set out in a vehicle as dubious as the Gray Death with a novice at the wheel, on a twenty-five-hundred-mile journey. In the weeks before our departure, I'd gotten on the Thruway a few times to get used to interstate driving, but usually got off again at the next exit and returned home. I knew we were budgeted, as indeed we always were, right down to the last nickel, and it seemed a waste of time and gas to drive to Amsterdam, pay my toll, and then turn around and drive back. Those short trial runs weren't a waste, though. I at least got a sense of how much faster everybody else would be going, that even eighteen-wheelers were going to blow by me like I was standing still, and that even a vehicle as sluggish and heavy as the Galaxie could be tugged into their wake. I also learned to stay in the right-hand lane and to disregard the pissed-off expressions of impatient drivers who'd get trapped behind me, then roar past with horns blaring and middle fingers erect. What that relatively benign stretch of Thruway could not prepare me for, of course, was the white-knuckle traffic in and around major cities, nor for the trailer I'd be towing.

Nor could I imagine that while my plan to poke along in the right lane would work well enough most of the time, I'd eventually have to change lanes and learn on the fly how much space between cars to allow for both the Death and the trailer. Our first day on the road I must've nearly caused a half-dozen accidents, and the drivers I imperiled by unsafe lane changes, their red faces contorted with rage in my side-view mirrors, retaliated by laying on their horns before swerving in front of me to see how I liked it. One man I cut off pulled alongside and powered down his window to yell at me, but then didn't. I don't know if it was my age and obvious inexperience or my bewildered-looking passenger, but the righteous fury instantly drained out of his face, and I could read his thoughts clearly. Whoever we were and wherever we were going, we weren't going to make it. "What's wrong with all these people?" my mother kept wondering. "Why's everybody so *mad* at us?" I didn't have the heart to explain what I was only just coming to understand myself: we were a genuine menace.

On the morning of the second day, studying the course AAA had charted for us, she said, "I don't know why they want us to go around all these cities. The road we're on goes straight through. Why burn all that extra gas?" Her question got answered that afternoon in Indiana when we decided to ignore AAA's advice to loop around Indianapolis. Immediately we found ourselves locked in a sea of angry city commuters, and to my complete surprise the right-hand lane was no longer ideal, because it would end abruptly, forcing us to exit—or, rather, another driver would have. I, however, had no intention of getting off for the simple reason that we didn't want to. Putting on my left-turn blinker, I simply held my course, in effect creating my own lane, until one of the drivers in the lane I was determined to merge with, fearing death or dismemberment, let me in. "What a *good* driver you're becoming," my mother said every time we didn't have a wreck, and I couldn't tell if she was trying to bolster my confidence or actually meant it.

What we worried about even more than accidents were the interstate on-ramps. The Death, underpowered to begin with and further slowed by the U-Haul, simply wasn't up to them. I'd get up the best head of steam I could and keep the accelerator pressed to the floor as I entered the ramp, but then there was nothing to do but watch the speedometer inch backward—20, 18, 15, 11—until finally our forward momentum wouldn't even register at all and the car would begin to shudder violently. "Come on, Bess," my mother would whisper, patting the metal dashboard encouragingly, terrified that we'd come to a complete halt and block the long line of cars behind us, "you can do it." (She refused to call our getaway car the Death and became irritated when I did.) All the way to Arizona, our lives were ruled by ramps. We had to get on and off the interstate several times a day, but no matter how low we were on gas, or how hungry we were, or how badly my mother needed to pee, if the exit's ramps, whether off or back on, looked too severe we kept on driving until we found one with a gentler incline. At day's end we avoided the busy exits where we'd have a choice of places to stay and eat, opting instead for more remote ones where there'd be a lone Holiday Inn that had an on-site restaurant, because once we were done for the day, there was no chance we'd be getting back in the car before morning. We parked in the farthest, darkest reaches of the motel's parking lot, taking up three or four spaces, because our one absolutely inviolable rule was to never, for any reason, put the Death in reverse. One morning early on I'd wasted a good hour trying to back out of the space we'd taken near the motel's front entrance. No one had told me that backing a trailer would be counterintuitive, and before I'd figured that out I'd jackknifed the U-Haul so completely that the two cars to my left were utterly hemmed in. We'd had to enlist the help of the desk clerk to locate and rouse from their slumbers the drivers of the two vehicles on my right so I could extricate us by means of a forward gear.

My other great concern was the temperature gauge, especially in the afternoon when the July heat was worst and the needle crept slowly up into the red danger range. Then we'd have to pull over at a rest stop and let the ticking engine cool down. When I couldn't find one in time and radiator steam began to billow from under the hood, the only solution was to pull onto the shoulder and wait for an hour in the broiling sun. What I didn't like thinking about was that we still hadn't crossed the Mississippi. What would happen when we hit the desert and the temperature soared into the hundreds? Standing there beside the interstate, wilting in the brutal heat, the steady stream of air-conditioned cars and professionally maintained trucks whizzing by and blowing angry gales of dust in our faces, we must have looked utterly forlorn. Surprisingly few people stopped to offer assistance, and those who did we quickly sent packing. Everything was fine, we told them. No, we didn't need a tow. We were just waiting a bit for the engine to cool down, and then we'd be on the road again. We didn't want complete strangers to know our true plight, or that we were losing heart with each passing mile.

I kept expecting my mother to throw in the towel. As soon as she did, I was prepared to pack it in and return home. I'd find a job and put off college until the following year. Or maybe I'd contact my father. You never could tell with him. Sometimes he'd just happen to have what you needed, and if he had the money he'd buy me a plane ticket to Arizona or help get me on a road-construction crew if he didn't. But my mother knew me as well as I knew her, so she had to know what was going through my brain, and the closest she ever came to calling it quits was to remark, at the end of one of those long, hot, dusty, scarifying days, "Ah, Ricko-Mio. *When* are we going to catch a break?" As if our problem were bad luck.

Not long after, though, our luck did change, in the Ozarks of all places, where a gas station attendant with the smallest head I'd ever seen on an adult sold us a brown canvas water bag shaped like a pancreas that he swore would solve our radiator problem. As near as I could tell from his toothless explanation, offered up as he attached the thing to the Galaxie's bug-splattered grille, the hot outside air would be cooled as it passed through the bag, the cooler air then blowing directly onto the radiator. I had my doubts, but the gadget seemed to reassure my mother, who now had only entrance and exit ramps, reverse gear, wrong turns, and running out of money before we got to Arizona to worry about. First thing each morning, and every time we stopped for gas, I refilled the bag with cool water as quickly and unobtrusively as I could, hoping no one would ask what on earth I was doing and oblige me to repeat, this time with added consonants, the pump jockey's rationale. But guess what? *The car stopped overheating.* Then, a couple days later in the Texas Panhandle, somebody actually stole the bag when we stopped for lunch. This was a blow to my mother, whose excellent opinion of people outside of Fulton County was being rubbed raw by actual experience of them, but the theft cheered me considerably, suggesting as it did that there were apparently other idiots in the world. They weren't all in our car. Over the next several days, though, every time we stopped for gas in the parched southwestern desert, my mother inquired of the attendant whether they sold those great water bags, the ones you attached to the grille to keep car radiators cool. Even after she patiently described the bag's size and shape and color, nobody seemed to know what she was talking about. Apparently you could buy them only in Missouri from congenital nitwits.

MY MOTHER'S NEW JOB at the General Electric plant in Phoenix had always sounded a little vague to me. When I asked what she'd be doing there, if there'd be any correlation between her new duties and the work she'd done in the computer room in Schenectady, or how much of a pay cut she was taking, she said she'd find out all that when we arrived. The main thing, she added, was that the people were nice. Her new boss was somebody she knew, sort of, having talked with him on the phone, off and on, for years, and he was always saying how great it would be if she came out west. She spoke of him in the same tone of voice she used to describe the men she occasionally dated at GE, which might be why I never pressed her for details. Maybe they'd met in Schenectady. Maybe this was one of the guys who'd taken her out for lunch. I didn't want to know, that's for sure. Whatever her reasoning, she seemed confident that any salary or tenure she lost as a result of the move, she would quickly be able to make up. After all, the Schenectady plant was GE's flagship, and in lowly Phoenix she'd surely be recognized as someone who knew how things were done in the big leagues. She just hoped she could start work immediately because, well, the trip *had* cost more than she'd planned, and she didn't want to tap the emergency fund any more than she absolutely had to. Right around the corner there'd be first and last month's rent on her new apartment, and when you went grocery shopping that first time it was always extra expensive because you needed to get everything: salt, pepper, a two-pound bag of flour, wax paper, you name it. And she'd have to pay for her ride to work, just as she'd always done.

Nor was it just money that was in short supply. Time was also of our particular essence. In a couple weeks I'd be heading to Tucson to register for my fall semester classes and check into my dorm. My mother was a list maker, and the to-do items on the list she'd started back in Gloversville and updated periodically during our journey—find an apartment she could afford, move in, return the U-Haul and collect the deposit, open a bank account, set up phone and utilities, locate a grocery store within walking distance, find a new doctor—all had to be checked off before I headed south in the car.

As my mother obsessed about all these tasks, I became increasingly apprehensive, not so much because the list was long and time was short, but because she herself seemed so keyed up. After all, our harrowing journey was behind us.

Against all odds—we didn't even know enough to calculate them when we left Helwig Street—we'd somehow made it. The Gray Death hadn't killed us, and neither, miraculously, had I. We'd done the hard part, hadn't we? Once we got close to Phoenix, my mother had contacted our relatives, and they'd offered to let us stay with them for a few days until we settled in, and they proved a wealth of information about the area. Sure, there was a lot left to do, but unlike the journey itself none of it was likely to kill us. So, why was my mother behaving as if the tough part was only now beginning? The reason was that she hadn't written down on any list the most important thing she had to do: *Find A Job.*

In fairness, some part of her thought she had one. Not in the sense that an actual job had been offered and she'd accepted it, or that there'd been any discussion of things like salary or hours or a start date, and certainly not in the sense that there were any supporting documents. More like, *If you're ever out this way, look us up.* Or, *We could sure use somebody like you out here.* Her having a job there was essentially a reasonable conjecture, a deduction based on available data. Telling my grandparents that she had a job in Arizona wasn't a lie, exactly. It wasn't that she didn't have a job, only that she didn't have one *yet.* A matter of semantics, surely. She was confident about both her marketable skills and her considerable experience, and that when she presented herself to the man with whom she'd chatted so pleasantly on the phone, he'd recognize her value and find something for her. Having spent his entire working life in Gloversville's skin mills, my grandfather couldn't be expected to understand how things worked out in the wider world, in a big company like General Electric. GE people looked out for one another.

But mostly I think my mother believed she had that job in Phoenix because she needed it so badly. Because if she didn't have it, then doing what we'd just done was beyond folly. Because without a job waiting for her out west, when I went off to college she'd be left behind on Helwig Street. Because she was in her mid-forties now and still an attractive woman, but for how much longer? And more to the point, how long was any person with hopes and dreams expected to remain in a cage, without hope, without a life to call her own? She had the job in Phoenix because without it she was finished. Because for my sake she'd stuck it out in Gloversville as long as she could, and she couldn't stand it a moment longer. She just couldn't. And so she had a job.

THE GE FACILITY WAS located on the other side of Phoenix, even then, in 1967, an obscenity of urban sprawl. It was more of an outpost than anything, and I could see my mother's face fall when she saw how small it was, about the size of an automobile dealership. She'd dressed with great care that morning, but it was already close to a hundred degrees out, and in the hour it had taken us to drive there her hair and clothes were limp. Even more discouraging were the people emerging from and entering the facility, the women dressed in slacks and casual tops and sneakers, the men in jeans and shirts with snaps instead of buttons. A few even wore cowboy hats. One of these pointed my mother to an office door into which she disappeared on her high heels. I found a shady spot, expecting to roast there awhile in the punishing heat, but less than five minutes later she returned. The man who'd encouraged her to come by if she was ever in the area hadn't worked there for a year. In his place was a woman who informed my mother that not only were there no openings but also none were anticipated. Theirs was a very small operation, and almost everyone who worked there had done so forever. If she'd had such a good job in Schenectady, why did she leave it?

For a few minutes we just sat in the car and let the blazing desert sun bake us. I saw my mother's hands were shaking. I was about to ask what she meant to do now, when she said, "How can anyone even *think* in heat like this?"

We went to an air-conditioned coffee shop and sat in a window booth, our wet clothes sticking to the vinyl cushions. Outside, the heat shimmered in waves off the pavement. Everything was singed brown, even the weeds pushing up through cracks in the sidewalks. "What an awful, awful place," my mother remarked, more to herself than me. "All that way we came."

I was inclined to agree, but pointed out that we'd been in Phoenix less than twenty-four hours, perhaps not long enough to pass judgment.

"I can tell you one thing," she said, finally turning to face me, and there was something wild in her eyes, something so desperate it bordered on rabid. I'd seen it, or something like it, a few times before, usually when she was at wit's end and instead of helping I, her only ally, did or said something to make things even worse. At such times it seemed to occur to her that maybe I'd been enlisted in the swelling ranks of those determined to thwart her. Who knew? Maybe I'd always been against her. "I can tell you one thing," she repeated, challenging me to disagree. "I'm not going back."

EVENTUALLY SHE DID, of course, just as my grandparents had foretold, but by then a lot had happened, some of it predictable but mostly not, at least not by me. Sitting across from my mother in that Phoenix coffee shop, I couldn't even have predicted the next two weeks, at the end of which she and I would once again put the Gray Death on the road, minus the U-Haul this time, for the relatively short trip down to Tucson, where over the next decade, I would complete both an undergraduate and several graduate degrees, and where I would meet a girl named Barbara whom I had the good sense to fall in love with and, once I'd overruled her better judgment, marry. In Tucson I would become a man, a husband, a scholar, a father, and a writer.

In the summer of 1967, however, I was still a boy and my mother's son, and the University of Arizona larger and more populous than my hometown. I wasn't the boy who'd left Gloversville a month earlier, though. Nor, I think, was my mother the same woman. We'd become seasoned, fearless travelers and found first the U of A and then the dorm to which I'd been assigned (Apache Hall, I still remember), without difficulty or incident. There I met my roommate, an Arizonan who'd grown up in a small, godforsaken mining town he seemed proud of as only a small-town boy can be. To me, it sounded like the local equivalent of an upstate New York mill town. My mother garrulously told him all about where we were from, and from her description you never would've guessed that for her Gloversville held anything but the fondest of memories. Later, the kid told me he thought she was cool. In fact, motherwise, I'd lucked out. Definitely. He'd have continued in this vein, I suspect, if I hadn't cut him off.

We were broke, of course, so that night my mother and I ate dinner at a chain coffee shop near the interstate, a dead ringer for the one in Phoenix we'd retreated to after she learned she wouldn't be working for GE anymore. There was a pay phone outside, so we called my grandparents to let them know that this final leg of our journey had been successfully completed and I was registered for all my classes, which would begin next week. I gave them the number of the phone at the end of the hall in my dorm so they could reach me if they needed to. And of course they had my mother's new number in Phoenix. "How *good* they were to us," she said over dinner, and I understood from this that she'd begun the process of forgetting those last terrible weeks on Helwig Street. Hearing my grandfather struggle for breath on the telephone brought home to her not just how much she loved him but how much she'd depended on him, and her remark about how good they'd been to us was really about the whole of the last eighteen years.

"I don't know what we would've done without them," she said, as close as she'd ever come to admitting that we hadn't been wholly self-sufficient living under their roof and how secretly worried she was about losing the safety net they'd provided. "He was always my rock," she continued, her eyes brimming, "from the time I was a little girl," letting her voice fall, but not completely. "*You're* that rock now."

If it had occurred to me that she actually meant this, I'd have protested, because I didn't feel like anybody's rock, including my own. I was also acutely aware that for the last eighteen years the only rock I'd been was the one around her neck, threatening to pull her under. And if she was worried about the future, she had me for company. That afternoon I'd opened a checking account with a couple hundred dollars, money that would have to last me through the first semester, and in my pocket was a cafeteria meal ticket that would keep me from starving. I couldn't think of a single thing I had that would be of the slightest use if my mother ran into trouble. My two suitcases were full of clothes that were stylish back home but would brand me as a hated easterner out here in the desert, where the frat-boy uniform was cowboy boots, button-down oxford shirts, and jeans with button flies. I'd have all I could do not to become a figure of fun. My numerous misgivings about coming this far to study in what amounted to a foreign country must have been obvious to my mother. She might even have suspected I'd have done a straight-up swap to be enrolling back at SUNY Albany, where I'd know people and could hop on a bus and be home in Gloversville in an hour. So when my mother said that I was now her rock I assumed she was just expressing some kindly sunrise-sunset, swiftly-flow-the-years sentiment meant to buck me up in the face of new challenges.

She wasn't.

THE COFFEE-SHOP MELTDOWN in Phoenix turned out to be the nadir. Somehow my mother gathered herself, and we returned to Scottsdale, to the home of the people who were putting us up and in whose yard our detached U-Haul now sat, its ball hitch burrowing into their desert landscaping like an anteater's snout. My mother found an excuse to go straight to bed, where she slept around the clock. Bright and early the next morning, though, we set about crossing items off her revised to-do list, at the top of which she'd now written *JOB*.

The first major piece of the puzzle to fall into place was an apartment. Phoenix, a stunningly horizontal city, was even then deeply committed to both unplanned sprawl and the primacy of automobiles, policies that remain unquestioned to this day as far as I know. New apartment houses with acres of parking were springing up everywhere in an attempt to keep up with the influx of midwestern snowbirds. Their construction was shabby, but to easterners used to the grit and grime born of punishing winters they felt new and clean. Several complexes that were only half built offered a free month or two to anyone willing to sign a year's lease, and that put pressure on older, established properties to cut similar deals. My mother picked a place on Indian School Road that was reasonably close to most of what she'd need, though of course nothing was walking distance, a moot point since there were no sidewalks. Perhaps because it was so hot and gas was nineteen cents a gallon, people preferred to get in their cars even when their destination was just a block or two away.

She could've gotten by with a studio apartment, but my mother rented a one bedroom so I'd have at least a couch to crash on when I visited. She had to come up with the usual first and last month's rent, but after that her next check wasn't due until November, which seemed a long way off. To her surprise and delight, almost everybody in the complex was newly divorced and recently arrived from somewhere else, men seeming to outnumber women three to one. All of which made sense when you thought about it. In most divorces it would be the man who found himself without a roof over his head, and most of these guys wanted to put at least a few miles between themselves and the wives who'd told them to hit the bricks. Nobody seemed to have much money or to care much about it. There were a few flashy sports cars in the parking lot, but just as many beaters. In the interior courtyard was a large swimming pool with a communal grill where people congregated in the evenings after changing into bathing suits and grabbing a cold beer. On Saturdays, around midday, somebody would appear on the pool deck with a pitcher of margaritas and give a rebel yell. People would then spill out of their apartments, blinking in the bright sun like prisoners released from their cells by an invisible warden. Then the weekend festivities would begin.

It must've been pretty close to the kind of life my mother had been imagining back in Gloversville. She also must've felt like she'd arrived in the nick of time, because most of her neighbors were younger, in their thirties, but they welcomed her like the bunch of good-natured drunks they were. "New blood!" one bare-chested young fellow called up to us from the barbecue pit, his gleaming spatula raised in triumph, when we moved my mother's stuff into her second-floor apartment within hours of signing the lease. "Where you from?"

"Upstate New York," my mother called over the railing. She hadn't caught on yet that here in Arizona, hailing from back east was more likely to elicit derision than admiration.

"Well, Jean," he said, after they'd exchanged first names, "you're better off here. How do you like your burgers?" When she told him, he said to come down when we finished lugging boxes, then pointed his greasy spatula at me. "Bring your husband with you."

The next morning we dropped the trailer off at the nearest U-Haul facility where a HELP WANTED sign was taped to the cash register. "Not for here," the man behind the counter said, as if he feared my mother had designs on his job. "At the headquarters."

These were again located all the way across town, so we drove directly there, my mother having learned her lesson about dressing up for job interviews, and when she disappeared inside I again found a shady spot where I could plan, with the aid of a map of Phoenix, the rest of our day. My mother wasn't very good at sequencing the items on her to-do list. She always wanted to attend to things in the order of their importance, without taking geographical proximity and other natural progressions into account. I'd only just begun when she reappeared. "Where's that list?" she said. When I handed it to her, she crossed out *JOB*. "No kidding?" I said. No kidding. She'd been hired on the spot as a bookkeeper. The pay was shitty, but Arizona was a virulently antiunion, right-to-work state where the idea of a living wage had yet to be introduced. There were lots and lots of crappy, low-paying jobs, however, and the possibility of rapid advancement. I think what really sold her on this one, though, was that it was located straight down Indian School Road, so that even with her lousy sense of direction she wouldn't get lost. Turn right to go to work, turn left and return home. Easy as pie.

That was the other complication, naturally. My car wasn't mine anymore. "I wish there was some other way," she'd said the morning after her coffee-shop meltdown. But of course I'd seen it coming. The people we'd been staying with had explained when my mother mentioned I'd be taking the car down to Tucson that people in Phoenix didn't carpool. Or ride the bus, or take a train. If you needed to go anywhere, you climbed in your own car and you took off. If your wife needed to go somewhere, she got into *her* own car and *she* took off. You'd no more go two to a car than two to a horse. "But isn't that kind of, well . . . stupid?" I remember asking. "Welcome to Arizona," I was told.

So, since I didn't really need a car at the university anyway, we located the nearest branch of the Department of Motor

Vehicles, got my mother a learner's permit, and scheduled the written and driving exams for a week later. What we'd do if she failed either one we tried our best not to think about. With nothing but Camelback Mountain to go around and a few dry arroyos to go over, Phoenix wasn't a bad place to learn to drive. It was laid out on a grid, and its streets were wide and flat. To us, every intersection looked like every other intersection, but you could see for long distances, so it was possible to use the few landmarks that stood out to orient yourself. There was the heat, of course. Since the Death had neither air-conditioning nor power steering, we waited until late in the day for her driving lessons. For the first few evenings we practiced on quiet, residential streets and abandoned strip-mall parking lots. My mother was not a gifted student, but in her defense it must've been hard to learn such a basic skill so late in life and to be taught by someone who, in the normal scheme of things, you'd be teaching. Nor was I the most patient instructor. The fact that she'd never driven was one thing, but her ignorance of fundamental principles was so profound it seemed willful. She didn't notice street signs until I pointed them out to her. Worse, she was prone to panic. Once, when we were working on parallel parking, she forgot she was in reverse and accelerated when she felt the car moving backward, thinking that more gas was called for—despite my screaming, "Brake! Brake!"—and remained fully committed to this misconception until we plowed backward through somebody's front yard and totaled a saguaro cactus. The next day I couldn't coax her back behind the wheel without making two promises—that we'd give parallel parking a pass for a day or two and that, no matter what she did, I wouldn't yell at her.

Gradually, we moved from the relative safety of residential neighborhoods out onto busy Indian School Road. As time grew short we embarked on real-life outings with genuine purposes, to the supermarket or the drugstore. She always parked in the most remote reaches of the lot, where she was unlikely to encounter other cars or need to use reverse gear. We made a couple practice runs to her new place of employment, first during off-hours, then under more realistic rush-hour conditions. She got better. Not good—that would never happen—but hardly the menace her son had been a month earlier, towing a trailer down the interstate. At once terrified and game, she gripped the wheel as if expecting a sudden impact at any moment, and I came to realize that fear was probably her best defense against catastrophe. To see my mother grabbing hold like that was to understand that her mind, unlike that of 99 percent of drivers who were far more skilled and experienced, would never wander, even for an instant, from the task at hand.

On the morning of her road test she took an extra half pill with her coffee so her hands wouldn't shake, and by the time we arrived at the Department of Motor Vehicles, she was wearing a smile so serene that I feared her examiner would take in at a glance that she was pharmaceutically impaired, but he didn't. While they were gone I mentally drafted a contingency plan to call the university registrar and say I'd be a week or two late and beg them please, *please,* not to give my dorm room away.

What I dreaded most was having to explain what was happening. No, I couldn't predict exactly when I'd be joining my classmates, as it kind of depended on when my mother passed her driver's test. What if I were asked to assess her chances? Or if the registrar wanted to know how it was that a woman in her forties in this day and age had never driven a car until two weeks ago? Would he have my file on his desk as we spoke? Would he say, *Oh, right—Russo. The one from Gloversville. No wonder.* I was still working on my side of this imaginary conversation when I heard my mother's laughter from all the way across the room. She tossed her head girlishly as she approached, with her examiner, a small man a good fifteen years her junior, as firmly in tow as a dog on a leash. "And this is my son," she was saying, "the one I've been telling you about."

"Your mom did fine," the man said as we shook hands. "She didn't run over a single cactus."

Then he wished her luck on her new job, and they shook hands, and he and I shook hands again, one big happy, complicit family. "What a *nice* man," my mother said when we parted, loud enough for him to hear.

To celebrate, we went to a restaurant for lunch, and my mother ordered a Bloody Mary.

"You actually told him about backing over that saguaro?" I said.

"He thought that was the funniest thing he'd ever heard. They're apparently quite expensive."

I'd suspected as much, which was why, after quickly swapping seats, we'd hightailed it out of there and I'd chosen an entirely new neighborhood to practice in when we resumed parallel parking.

She showed me the temporary license she'd been given. "Hey, you know what this means?" I said. "You're free." Because every fifteen-year-old knows that a driver's license is really about freedom, and I figured my mother, given how desperately she longed for true independence, would register the symbolism. But she just looked at me strangely. After all, she wasn't fifteen; she was forty-five, and failing to learn would've sent her straight back to Helwig Street.

She wasn't blind to the magnitude of the moment, though, and when her drink came she reached across the booth and patted my hand. "Ricko-Mio," she said, her smile less serene now, more loopy, "we did it."

Which was true. There were a few small things left on the to-do list, but nothing important or difficult. "*You* did it," I said. Aware of how much all this had cost her, I was suddenly and unexpectedly proud of her, so proud it didn't seem to matter that what we'd done was in fact borderline moronic. And part of me understood, too, what this unforeseen pride meant—that like my grandfather, I hadn't believed she was capable of much of anything, really. I was proud she'd proved us both wrong, but also surprised. "In fact," I said, "seeing where we were a couple weeks ago, I'm not sure how you managed to pull it off."

"Well," she said, looking so deeply inward now that I knew what she'd say next before she said it. "I just gave myself a good talking-to."

———

ALL THESE YEARS later it seems incredible to me that after helping me get settled at the university she drove back to Phoenix on her own. Not that it was terribly difficult. We could see the I-10 freeway ramp from the restaurant where we ate that last dinner together. She'd get on the interstate and not get off until she came to the Indian School Road exit, and she'd stay on that until she reached her apartment. It was late August, so it was still light out when she left. It would be dark by the time she got to Phoenix, but the traffic wouldn't be bad. Of course if the Gray Death broke down in the desert she'd be all alone, and even if she could find a pay phone, what possible good would it do to call me? I don't think I worried about any of that. I'd badly underestimated her, as well as our escape vehicle in recent weeks, and they'd both taught me not to. They'd make it fine.

Indeed, as I walked back to campus along busy Speedway Boulevard, I had a profound sense that my mother's life and my own had just diverged, probably for good. I'd be with her for Thanksgiving, and again over the Christmas holidays between semesters. But I'd seen my father before leaving Gloversville, and he'd offered to pay my union dues while I was away at school. That way, if I wanted to come home for the summer, I could get a well-paid construction job, and I'd already decided to do just that. Eighteen was legal drinking age in New York, and he'd begun to show more interest in me since my birthday. By next summer my grandparents would have rented the upstairs flat on Helwig Street, but they had a spare bedroom and would be happy to see me. I could paint the house on weekends to save them some money. I already missed both of them terribly, and for the first time felt the full guilt of having abandoned them. Somehow I'd try to set this right.

My mother didn't factor into any of these plans. Hey, she had the new life she'd wanted for so long. She had people her own age and a nice apartment and parties on weekends and nobody looking over her shoulder, second-guessing her every decision and criticizing her for having a little fun. If the Death didn't die and she got a couple raises, her new ends might just meet. Why shouldn't things work out for her? After all, Phoenix seemed to be the city of fresh starts, of rising from the ashes. There were lots of single men around. And with me finally out of her way, there'd be opportunities for the kind of romance I knew she craved, maybe even marriage, though I doubted she had much interest in that. She just wanted to dress up and go dancing or out to dinner someplace nice now and then. There was no longer any reason she shouldn't have her wish. Back in Gloversville, her mantra had always been that we'd be just fine as long as we had each other, but that pact— unsustainable between a mother who would grow old and a son who'd eventually marry and have children of his own— could now be honorably dissolved by both parties. That's what our long journey across America, all those scary on- and off-ramps, had been about. As she herself had put it, "Ricko-Mio, we did it."

And if we'd done it, it stood to reason that it must be finished, right?

A Diagnosis

D^{ON'T DO IT.} That was my father-in-law's advice in a nutshell. He was not an unkind man, but he'd met my mother at the wedding and, like everyone else, he'd witnessed her fragile condition and sensed how near she was to unraveling. It would also have been clear how dependent she was on me, that if I ever left the room she'd nervously watch the spot I'd disappeared from until I returned. So when his daughter told him that my mother wanted to move in with us until she could find a job and start a new life in Tucson, he warned her that it would be a terrible mistake. "If you let that woman in," he said, "you'll never be rid of her."

She'd telephoned that morning in the throes of a full-blown panic attack. There was a three-hour time difference between New York and Arizona, and she'd waited as long as she could, but it was still early and also a Saturday, so Barbara and I were asleep. I'd been expecting the call for days, actually. My mother and I talked pretty regularly, so I knew where she was in the never-ending cycle of her anxieties. Sometimes venting to me did the trick, releasing some stuck emotional valve, allowing some of the pressure a means of escape, after which she'd pull herself together, give herself a good talking-to, and thereby avert coming completely unglued. "Can't you understand?" she'd sobbed. "Doesn't it matter that I'm a *person*? Don't I have a right to a *life,* like anybody else? How long am I expected to live in a *cage*?"

The cage was once again 36 Helwig Street, where she'd been living for a couple years. Phoenix had gone well for a time, but ultimately badly. She'd fallen in love with a man who looked like Sam Shepard and was about as laconic. He wore jeans and cowboy boots and drove a pickup truck. Then suddenly he was gone, and she was devastated. The story she told me was that they'd gotten too serious, too quickly. He had no desire to get married, so he'd left the state in hopes of forgetting her. That last part didn't sound like the man in question, and a friend of hers later confided that he hadn't left Arizona, or even Phoenix, or, for that matter, the neighborhood. He'd bolted once he discovered how intense my mother was about *him,* moving to another apartment house a few blocks away, where he was now seeing someone else. When my mother spotted his truck in the lot, it sent her into a tailspin. Had she mentioned, her friend wondered, that she'd lost her job at U-Haul? Well, no, she hadn't, but she did the next time we spoke, saying that it was okay, that she'd hated the job from the start. The company wasn't well run, nothing like the old GE in Schenectady, which for her always represented the gold standard of employment. What had she been thinking to leave it? she wondered out loud. Just imagine if she'd stayed. How many promotions would she have fielded by now? Just imagine her salary.

It didn't take her long to find another job, though it was no better, and she had no safety net if something went wrong, which was making her nervous. Her doctor had agreed to up the dosage on her Valium, but she didn't like the way it made her feel. While she wanted to stop taking the pills entirely, she needed them to stay functional. Something was amiss at the apartment house, too. It had been so fun-loving and gay at the beginning, but the parties had turned dark, and there were drugs now. (By then it was the mid-Seventies, so maybe.) Worst of all was the driving—the traffic, the heat, the lack of air-conditioning. Something was going to have to change, or she'd suffer a nervous breakdown.

Then, to my surprise, on the heels of the fleeing cowboy, there was suddenly another man in her life. Several years younger and recently divorced, he was clearly crazy about her. I'd met the man and liked him, though something didn't seem right. She was always a sucker for style, and the men she was usually drawn to—like my father and the most recent fugitive—were invariably handsome and had a certain swagger, a boyish, self-destructive charm, a hint of danger. Russ had exactly none of that going for him, but he was good-natured and solid, the kind of man who might actually be good for my mother if she could learn to see past his unromantic virtues.

"Well, I think he loves you," I said when she asked my opinion about what she should do. "Do you love him?"

She didn't answer, so I said, "It sounds like you have a decision to make," and she agreed that she did. Neither of us needed to articulate the exact nature of the dilemma: she could marry a man she didn't love or return to Gloversville.

The marriage lasted a couple years, one in Phoenix and another in San Francisco, then crashed and burned. After the split she moved to nearby Pacifica, which sat under a permanent bank of dense, wet fog. Her apartment was situated on a cliff, and from it you could hear the waves pounding on the beach below, and there she went about the business of once again putting herself back together. She had no job, though, and no means of getting one. I'd inherited the Gray Death when she and Russ went to San Francisco and was willing to give it back, but she said no, she was through with driving.

So, when the money from the small divorce settlement ran out, there was nothing to do but return to upstate New York. It was midsemester, and I was now in grad school, but I stole a few days and flew to San Francisco, where I rented a truck, packed her books and other possessions, put them in storage, and promised to drive them to Gloversville that summer. My grandparents found money for a one-way plane ticket to Albany. My aunt and uncle picked her up and drove her to Helwig Street, where my grandparents had evicted their upstairs tenant to make room for her. She arrived in Gloversville with two suitcases and an official narrative. She had *not* failed to make a new life for herself out west. Moving to Arizona had *not* been a mistake. She was *not* returning home in defeat, but rather because her father was failing fast, on oxygen all the time and for the most part confined to his armchair. The burden of his declining health on her mother was too much, so she was returning to help out. As with so many of my mother's narratives, this one was designed for people who knew better—her parents, her sister and brother-in-law, me. She never cared whether people believed her, simply that her version of events was never publicly questioned.

Being back in Gloversville worked for a while. She found a job and bought some furniture on credit. My grandfather's condition was truly grave, and for a while her own problems paled by comparison. My mother had always adored him, and the rift caused by our departure for Arizona got mended. Further disputes were now out of the question; he had all he could do just to draw his next breath. For over a year she and my grandmother lived to the rhythm of his gasps until finally they stopped. Then they were alone in the Helwig Street house, two women who'd never seen eye to eye about anything. While my grandfather lived, they'd managed to coexist; neither had wanted to upset him, but with him gone the conflict resumed. To the old resentments—my grandmother questioning my mother's decisions and offering unsolicited advice—was added another, far more toxic dispute. They simply could not agree on who my grandfather had been. To my grandmother, he was a loving husband, a model of responsibility and duty, the kind of man who quietly endured what could not be cured; to my mother he'd been a rebel, trapped just as she was in a town he hated, in roles as husband and father he'd never wanted but from which he could never escape. On top of all this, a recession hit, and my mother was laid off, and there wasn't much to do with the day's long hours except to take stock: once again stuck in Gloversville with no friends, no money, no future, no life. All of which had led to that Saturday morning when she'd called to ask me how long any human being was expected to live in a cage. There was only one person in the whole world who really cared about her, who understood and could help her, and that was me. She needed to make a new beginning, but she could hardly do it by herself, with no one to call her own.

At the time my wife and I were living in a fourteen-foot-wide mobile home that we'd parked in a remote trailer park on the outskirts of Tucson, where rental spaces were cheapest. It had two bedrooms, one on each end, the architectural wisdom of which we didn't fully appreciate until my mother came to live with us. It cost twelve grand, probably more than my grandfather had paid for the house on Helwig Street, and to me a terrifying sum to owe. How could we ever pay back that kind of money? My grad school stipend paid less than two grand for teaching two sections of freshman composition per semester. Barbara was a secretary at a tiny, fast-failing electronics firm that her father had started up with another engineer from Hughes Aircraft. They'd called the company Iota, which by the time we got married seemed to summarize its chances of surviving another year. For those reasons I'd hoped, right up until we closed, that the finance company would take a good look at us, come to its senses, and refuse us the loan.

"She'd only be with us until she finds a job and can afford her own apartment," I assured my wife. "She doesn't want to live with us."

"There's a recession here, too," Barbara pointed out. "What will she do in this trailer all day when we're gone? How will she get to job interviews? If she gets a job, how will she get back and forth to work? Who's going to hire someone who can't hold her hands still?"

All good questions. With no answers anybody would want to offer.

I didn't even recognize her getting off the plane. Too poor to travel, we hadn't actually seen each other in the year and a half since the wedding, by far the longest we'd ever been apart. She had to say my name, and I had to connect the sound of her voice to the frail, elderly woman coming toward me. Her hair had gone mostly gray, but it wasn't that. She seemed about half the size of the woman who a few short years before had climbed behind the wheel of a car she only half knew how to drive and pointed it toward Phoenix and the new life she was betting everything on. Had she been like this at the wedding? Caught up in the event and my own happiness, had I failed to notice? When had she become so *tiny*? Or was it me, simply that I was looking at her with new eyes? After all, I was now married. At least symbolically my mother's place in my life had been diminished. But, no, it was more than that. The way she came toward me had less to do with how I saw her than how she saw herself. In her *own* eyes she was about half her former size. When I held out my arms, she stumbled, nearly falling into my embrace. "Ricko-Mio," she said. "Always there. Always my rock."

SHE WAS IN terrible shape, shattered and barely functional. Determined to get back on her feet as soon as possible, my mother immediately scoured the help-wanted ads but on most days didn't make a single call, unable to control her voice, barely able to hold on to the phone because her hands shook so badly. On better days she'd set up interviews around my teaching responsibilities, then cancel them as the time approached and she became too nervous. I'd seen her in bad shape before, but this was new. It was as if her world had gotten smaller, or the part of it she felt safe in had. For Barbara and me the trailer was suddenly too small, its common areas, especially the kitchen, too cramped. We were constantly in one another's way. That was what my mother seemed to like best about it. Back in Gloversville, after my grandfather's death, she'd been living by herself in our old flat with the few pieces of furniture she'd bought and could no longer make the payments on. Whole days had gone by, she told me, when she never heard the sound of another human voice. The fact that we were so crowded in our trailer was having a healing effect. She was no longer alone.

It also seemed to help that I was never gone for more than

a few hours. Barbara had a nine-to-five job and left for work early, but my mother and I began each day over coffee, mapping out what she'd try to get done in our absence, and in the evening we all ate dinner together. I gave her my teaching schedule, so she knew when my classes got out and roughly when to expect me back. I knew to call if something unexpected came up at the university, because each afternoon she positioned herself at the window and waited for the Gray Death (yes, still alive) to pull up beside the trailer. Normally I'd have graded my papers and prepared for classes on campus, but things ran more smoothly if I didn't leave her alone too long. Gradually, her condition did improve. She was able to cut back on the number of pills she was taking, and the tremor in her hands became less pronounced. She set up more interviews and actually made it to a couple of them.

The problem was that though my mother was doing better, my wife and I were doing worse. She was finding reasons to stay later at work, and I couldn't blame her. Each night there were three of us at the dinner table, but mostly my mother talked to me as if Barbara weren't there. It was almost as if she'd forgotten I was married, that this extra, unnecessary person was my wife and not some girlfriend I'd soon tire of, or vice versa. She certainly didn't dislike or resent Barbara and often remembered to thank her for opening up her home. It was my wife's *existence* she couldn't quite account for, as if she were a hologram, and when I asked Barbara a direct question, my mother often answered it. At the end of the evening, after we'd done the dishes, Barbara and I retreated to our bedroom as early as we decently could, and after turning out the lights we crawled into bed and whispered all the things we normally would've talked about over dinner. I think we both imagined my mother on the other side of the door, desperate to give us her input. We could no longer have friends over and felt guilty (or at least I did) if we went out someplace and didn't include her.

Not that we'd have gone out much. Iota Engineering was then in its death throes, sometimes unable to make its payroll. One month Barbara was paid in office furniture, and she had little choice but to start looking for another job. It was against this stark financial backdrop that we began to make weekend trips to places like FedMart to start furnishing the kitchen of the apartment my mother didn't yet have. It seemed like a smart idea to do it little by little. A new frying pan or a set of cheap cutlery cheered my mother by bringing into imaginative focus the day when she'd be officially back on her feet and living, as she liked to put it, independently. It wasn't just for her that we did this, of course. Buying the pan also allowed Barbara and me to believe that day was coming. One Saturday, though, I went too far and put too many things into the shopping cart, as if to hasten its arrival, and when I looked up Barbara was gone. I found her in the car, in tears. I'd spent money we simply didn't have. Nor could we borrow it. Her father hadn't drawn a salary in months, so her parents' situation, with most of her nine brothers and sisters still living at home, was as dire as ours. There was simply no one in either of our families who had two nickels to rub together. And of course I made the mistake of saying we'd been fools to ever buy the trailer, and the look on my wife's face conveyed clearly what she was too kind to say. We'd been fools, all right, but not about the trailer. Even if we assumed the day would finally come when my mother had recovered sufficiently to live on her own, what would be left of us?

But eventually, that day did come, along with a great many others, and somehow there was still an "us" for my wife and me to protect and cherish. Indeed, over time our trials would appear to illustrate the old saw that what doesn't kill you makes you stronger. The threads we were dangling by in Tucson, both financial and emotional, proved more sinewy than we'd imagined. They would need to be.

THE FURNISHED APARTMENT my mother finally rented in Tucson reminded her of the one she'd loved in Phoenix, and she found a job she could get to by bus. Weekends I took her to the grocery store and wherever else she needed to go. Otherwise, Barbara and I returned as best we could to the routines of our young married life and told ourselves that maybe it would all work out. But then summer was upon us with its pulverizing heat. My mother's apartment was several blocks from the bus stop, and the buses weren't necessarily air-conditioned, so she often arrived at work already wilted, with eight hours still to go. She ate lunch at her desk, there being no restaurants within walking distance, at least in the midday heat, and there were no sidewalks anyway. In July came the monsoon rains, the skies darkening ominously every afternoon right as she got off work, and the downpours, though brief, were apocalyptic. She must've felt like the physical world was mocking her, because by the time she got home, drenched to her skin, the skies would be blue again and steam rising from the asphalt, the air not just hot but humid. "What an awful, awful place," she lamented, exactly what she'd said that morning in Phoenix after learning she wouldn't be working for GE anymore.

Ironically, what ended up doing her in was neither Tucson, with its heat and monsoons, nor the job she hated (her new company poorly run, nothing like GE), nor the fact that she'd made no friends, but rather the return of her emotional equilibrium. One of the ironies of my mother's condition was that her periodic tranquillity was usually a mixed blessing. Panic might cause her to spin out of control, but once she got her bearings again, she could see beyond her own torment. Back in Gloversville, her desperation to make one last grab at a fulfilling life hadn't allowed her to imagine what that would be like in Tucson. It *had* to be better because it couldn't be any worse. In her mind's eye everything she saw was on a Gloversville scale, only better. She pictured me living nearby, down the street, maybe, or right around the corner. But Tucson was like Phoenix, a sprawling city of identically ugly intersections, where you were always half an hour away from anywhere else. It was a sea of cars, and she didn't have or want one. Being "close" in Tucson wasn't ten minutes by foot; it was twenty minutes by car—and much longer if you were living, say, in a remote trailer park.

Worse, her failure to accurately predict her own life in Tucson was compounded by her inability to understand *ours*. She had no idea how hard we were working, me on my Ph.D., Barbara on supporting us while I did. Even before my mother's arrival, we'd been stretched thin in virtually every respect. As short as we were on money, we had even less time. I needed my Sundays for grading papers, and on Friday and Saturday nights, for extra cash, I was a singer in a popular restaurant. Barbara's large family all lived in Tucson, which provided plenty of other obligations. But whenever something unexpectedly came up in my mother's life, I always did my best to accommodate her, and she could tell it wasn't easy. "You're always there when I need you," she'd said one day, gratefully patting my hand in the dentist's office after she'd chipped a tooth. The plan we'd developed back at the trailer was intended to restore her independence, and its major components were now in place. She had an apartment and a job. What was dawning on her, though, was that none of this was sustainable. The truth was that she needed me, at least emotionally, all the time. The only thing that could work in the long run would be a version of the old Helwig Street model in which each of us was central to the other's daily existence. But eventually, Barbara and I would have children, and as a father I'd have even less time to devote to her. And when I finished the Ph.D., my university career would begin, and who knew where that would take me? Back in Gloversville it might have seemed that we were separated only by geography, by all those miles, but now she understood that our separation was not only more profound than she'd imagined but was in fact only going to get worse.

By the time the holidays rolled around, she'd given herself a good talking-to. Coming to Tucson had been a mistake. It was time to admit that. And also, starting over in her midfifties was, well, too late. She hated Gloversville, God knew, but maybe it was the right place for her, maybe the only place. Her mother had welcomed her back before and would again. They would simply have to find a way to get along. Toward that end, she had a new, better idea. Instead of living upstairs in our old flat, she'd move into the spare bedroom downstairs, and they would share expenses. The upstairs flat could be rented, further bolstering their bottom line, taking financial stress completely out of the equation. And, to put my worries to rest, she pointed out that it wasn't like we'd never see each other again. There were far more colleges and universities east of the Mississippi than west of it, so I'd more likely end up teaching somewhere back east, and we could spend our holidays together. She'd worked it all out, just as she had that long-ago plan to come west with me in the first place, letting me in on the details only after her own mind was made up. I wasn't asked what I thought of the decision, simply informed of it, which was just as well.

Maybe coming to Tucson had been a bad decision, as she said, but returning to Gloversville would be another. What I couldn't give voice to was my growing certainty that my mother was lost in some labyrinth of her own thoughts and impulses, and that if she was ever going to escape the maze, she'd have done so already. Since leaving Gloversville myself, I'd come to understand that this had also been my grandfather's fear. I remembered that last day on Helwig Street when he'd watched from the front window, gulping air from his oxygen tank, as my friends and I loaded the U-Haul. Over the long months of bitter conflict, his anxiety had morphed into resignation in the face of his daughter's tidal determination, but when my eyes met his I didn't yet understand the true nature of his concern. He was worried about what would become of my mother, of course, but also what would become of me. Even if he'd had the desire, he lacked the breath to say all this, and anyway it would have been a terrible betrayal of the daughter he couldn't stop loving, regardless. Probably less harmful, he must have reasoned, to maintain the long-established family narrative. My mother suffered from nerves. So did lots of people.

Ironically, the one person who ever openly questioned that narrative was my father. He wasn't one to indulge regret or apologize, but the summer I turned twenty-one we were working road construction together in Albany, and he must've decided the time was right to explain his absence during my childhood. We'd stopped at half-a-dozen roadhouses on the way home, as was our dangerous habit, and were very drunk. "I should've thought about you more," he admitted, "but you were easy to forget. There was always something going on, a horse at the track that couldn't lose or some poker game. You seemed to be doing fine without me." When he paused, I figured he'd said his piece, but then he added one last thing. "And anyway, I couldn't be your father without being married to that crazy woman." The expression on my face then must have been strange, because he leaned back on his bar stool so he could really take me in. "You *do* know your mother's nuts, right?"

I don't know what I looked like, of course, but I recall being for a time unable to speak. I probably just sat there with my mouth open, a series of unwelcome emotions washing over me in waves. First anger at the seeming ease with which my father, who had no right to do so, had offered his judgment. After all, if my mother was crazy, at the very least he was a contributing factor. But even more powerful than anger was a totally unexpected surge of relief, because his verdict was no sooner rendered than I realized it was true, that I'd known this myself at least since the morning in Phoenix when she'd finally come clean about not really having a job at GE awaiting her there; and probably, truth be told, some part of me had known it for much longer. How many meltdowns, followed by good talking-tos, had I witnessed as a boy, too frightened to draw the necessary inference? Later on, as an adolescent, how many times had I suppressed the terrible possibility that something in my mother was off-kilter? Hadn't I also suspected all along that other family members—my grandparents and aunt at a minimum—also knew this but refused to say anything? Now, for the first time, I understood how lonely I'd been in my fears and suspicions, how alone I'd felt in the possession of adult knowledge to which I was hardly entitled.

And, finally, I felt guilty. That I'd come to the same heartless conclusion as my father was a terrible betrayal, surely. I don't recall whether that came right away or later. I only know there's been enough to last a lifetime. How else to explain my willingness to jeopardize my young marriage a decade later and, as the next three decades unspooled and my mother's condition worsened, the many times I'd repeat that same mistake, refusing to acknowledge the primacy of other loyalties subsequent to those forged on Helwig Street. Suffice to say that my mother wasn't the only one caught in a dangerous loop of repetitive behavior.

NOT LONG AFTER she returned to Gloversville from Tucson, I began a decade-long academic nomadship during which I jumped from job to job, trying to teach and be a writer at the same time. For a while, after our daughters came along, we were even poorer than we'd been as graduate students. And I was a bad boy. Caring not a whit about tenure and promotion, I thumbed my nose at the advice of department chairs about what I needed to do to succeed in the university. I left jobs for other jobs that paid less but offered more time out of the classroom. In the summer, when many of my colleagues taught extra classes, I wrote stories and spent money we didn't have on postage to submit them to magazines. I wrote manically, obsessively, but also, for a time, not very well. I wrote about crime and cities and women and other things I knew very little about in a language very different from my own natural voice, which explained why the editors weren't much interested.

My first full-time job was as an assistant professor at a branch campus of Penn State University. Altoona was a good day's drive from Gloversville, close enough for holiday visits but too far for my mother to expect much more. We continued to talk on the phone at least once a week, and these calls were for her a lifeline. I knew things weren't going well. She'd moved into the spare bedroom downstairs as planned, but she and my grandmother, who was by then in her eighties and crippled by arthritis, still weren't getting along. They liked different TV shows and different food, and rather than come to an accommodation my mother insisted on cordoning off their existences. Since the dining and living rooms were roughly the same size, they set up their own camps. They had no choice but to share the kitchen, though my mother refused to cook or to allow my grandmother to, arguing she was the one who'd have to clean up. So at lunchtime each made her own sandwich using her own personal ingredients, and for dinner each warmed her own frozen dinner in the oven. Afterward, they watched their favorite shows on their competing televisions, bickering endlessly about whose volume was turned up too high. My grandmother seemed to understand that this was lunatic behavior, but confronting her daughter would only have made matters worse. With her husband gone, the balance of power had shifted. Short of threatening to toss her out, something my grandmother never would've done, she had little leverage, so gradually my mother's will became law. When we visited, usually during the holidays, they strove for a truce, but you could tell they were unused to speaking to each other beyond demanding that the rival television be turned down. One day my father stopped by to say hello, took in the arrangement at a glance—my grandmother's furniture crammed into one room, my mother's into the other, the two TVs a few feet apart blaring different shows—and regarded my mother for a long moment, then said, "Jean. What the hell's *wrong* with you?"

Not long afterward he was diagnosed with lung cancer, and this more or less coincided with my taking a new job in New Haven, which meant I'd be only four hours from Gloversville instead of eight; given the deteriorating situation there, closer seemed to me, if not better, at least more advantageous. My father did his chemotherapy and radiation, and his cancer went into remission before it ultimately returned even more aggressively. Finally, too sick to care for himself, he was admitted into the VA hospital in Albany, where I visited him every other week-end. He seemed less concerned about his own mortality than not having anybody to bet his daily doubles at the OTB. "You going over to Helwig Street when you leave here?" he'd ask, incredulous, like a man who'd dodged a bullet even more dangerous than death. "*That's* some crazy shit going on over there."

In the spring of our second year in New Haven I sold my first novel, as a result of which I was offered my first real job as a writer. Until then I'd been a teacher with a writing habit that was tolerated but not necessarily encouraged. The new job, in Carbondale, Illinois, offered everything I'd wanted for the last decade—a real writing program, good colleagues, time to do my own work. But it was too far away, I knew. Instead of being four hours from Gloversville, I'd now be three days. My mother needed me closer, not farther away. I explained why I had to take the job, and she agreed I'd be a fool not to, but not long after we were settled in Carbondale, I got what would be the last of those frantic Helwig Street phone calls from my mother demanding to know why she didn't deserve a life the same as anybody else and how long she was expected to remain locked in a cage. I called my aunt to see if things were as bad as they seemed and learned they were actually worse, much worse. There was a lot going on, most of it old: conflicts not only unresolved but also unresolvable. But one new thing my aunt mentioned scared me. My grandmother had been pre-scribed a new medication in capsule form, to be taken with food, and my mother had somehow gotten it into her head that this meant the capsules needed to be ground up in her food, which she then proceeded to do over my grandmother's tearful objections. When my aunt discovered what was going on and confronted her sister, explaining that the medication simply should be taken *with* meals, she became unhinged, scream-ing that if anything happened to their mother, it would be my aunt's fault. She had shouldered the entire burden of my grand-mother's deteriorating health for years, she claimed, expected to make every single decision, but if her judgment was going to be questioned, now or ever, then she wanted nothing more to do with it. My aunt could take over all those duties and see how well she liked them. Apparently this fracas had precipitated the call to Carbondale. My aunt knew and was very fond of my wife, and knew we had our hands full with new jobs and two small daughters, but I could tell she was also worried sick for my grandmother, and when I asked if I should come get my mother, she reluctantly agreed it might be for the best.

By the time I got to Gloversville, she'd calmed down some. The knowledge that I was coming, that I'd be there by week's end, allowed her to step back from the precipice, but she was clearly in terrible shape, far worse than when she'd come to live with us in Tucson. At the time I owned a pickup truck into which we loaded her things, mostly books. What didn't fit was left behind. I'd borrowed a camper shell so we could lock everything up at night when we checked into motels. Together, we drove back across the country on the same route we'd taken twenty years before. The truck had air-conditioning, but my mother suffered one panic attack after another, and she swore she couldn't breathe, so we had to drive with the windows open to the August heat. Between these fits she regaled me with stories about how awful the last few years had been, detailing every single responsibility that was hers and hers alone, how abusive her sister and mother had been. "You have no idea how cruel they were," she said, over and over. "I kept it all a secret."

As we made our slow journey west, my wife was busy trying to find a place for her to live. Before I headed to Gloversville, we'd negotiated as best we could the terms for how all this would go. Assuming she wasn't a danger, my mother would stay with us until September. She was retired now, on Social Security, so she didn't need to work, and she qualified for elderly housing, if we could find it. Halfway to Illinois I called Barbara, who said there was an opening at the senior-citizen tower, exactly the sort of place I knew my mother would veto.

The next day I explained patiently that the apartment would only be temporary until we could find something better, that it was five minutes from our house, and she'd have the rest of August with us to get back on her feet and orient herself to her new environment before moving in. Since her only other option was returning to Gloversville, she had to go along with this, though she had a stipulation. The tower had to be only for the elderly, with no Section 8 residents. She refused to live with crazy people.

She also wanted to know if my driver's-side window was rolled down all the way, because she couldn't breathe. I knew how she felt. I couldn't either.

FIVE YEARS LATER, in 1991, I was offered a teaching position at Colby College in Maine. What made the position especially attractive was that it was part-time, a relative rarity in academia. At long last I was earning some money from my writing, almost enough—maybe, if nothing went wrong—to live on. At Colby I'd have more time to write and health insurance despite my part-time status, as well as a tuition subsidy for our daughters. If things went well, I could imagine writing full-time in a few years. We were also anxious to put southern Illinois's buggy, humid, tornado-ripe summers behind us, not to mention its passive-aggressive religious fundamentalists. I was tired of answering the door on Sunday morning to find strangers wanting to talk about Jesus. When we politely (for the most part) declined, they'd peer inside and see all the books, then shake their heads and advise us to put away our pride. "All them books don't amount to nothin'," they'd tell me, "not if you don't know the *Good* Book."

There were, however, compelling reasons to stay put. Barbara liked her job, and our daughters had their friends, and I was pretty sure the university would match whatever Colby offered. And of course there was my mother. She'd changed apartments twice since I brought her to Carbondale, and while she hated it there, she at least was settled. Like she always did after leaving Gloversville, she now remembered it fondly as the home from which she'd been exiled. She called every week to talk to her sister and mother and ended all these conversations by saying how much she loved and missed them, how lucky they were not to live in the Midwest. During the long spring and summer months, when the tornado watches beeped and inched incessantly along the bottom of television screens, she phoned with a familiar lament: "What an awful, awful place."

She was anxious to go to Maine, of course, because she'd be closer to home, but could she make the trip? It would be, no matter how we handled it, a logistical nightmare. Say we went to Maine, found a place, moved in, and then returned for my mother. Well, she couldn't be left alone for longer than it took milk to spoil because it would, literally, spoil. Even more important, her emotional well-being was tied to our proximity. On any occasion when we'd be gone for just a week—taking the girls to Disney World, for example—it was necessary to let her know well in advance so she could accustom herself to the idea, and then she required telephone numbers not only for every place we'd be staying but also for various friends in case she needed backup. Still her anxiety level always rose to fever pitch in the days before we left, and afterward we were pretty sure she upped the dosage of her meds on her own authority. Since it might take us a month to get settled in Maine, leaving her behind was simply out of the question. The opposite scenario—setting her up in an apartment in a strange new place, then returning to Illinois to go through our own move—would be, if anything, worse. Therefore, we'd have to make the move together, putting everything in storage until we found accommodations.

Actually, after I accepted Colby's offer, we discovered all this was going to be even more difficult. What few decent apartments were available in the Waterville area got snapped up seasonally by faculty and staff, so finding a place for my mother was going to be a challenge. On top of that, the housing market there was tight and expensive. Barbara made two exploratory trips that spring, saw numerous listings, and came back dejected both times. There was nothing even remotely as nice as the house we were selling in Carbondale. Worse, it *wasn't* selling. After two months, no one had even insulted us with a lowball offer, whereas in Waterville, where we wanted to live because of the schools, anything good got snapped up before we could see it. Since we'd be moving over the summer, we were advised to rent a camp on one of the nearby lakes and look at our leisure. If we saw something we liked we could make an offer within twenty-four hours.

As our departure date approached, my mother again

showed signs of coming unglued. There was just so much to be done, she kept saying, and she had to do it all herself. Actually, I kept reminding her, there was nothing for her to do. I'd hired a mover, scheduling her things to be loaded onto the truck the day before the same mover added our own. I would pack up her books and anything that wasn't going on the truck myself. The night before the move, she'd stay with us. Yes, she said, but that still left hundreds of other tasks she'd have to do, though when I asked what they were, she'd collapse into the nearest armchair and claim she was too exhausted to think. Nor could we agree on how to handle the simplest details. It was June, and the temperatures already in triple digits, but she was adamant that we drive to the phone company to terminate her service, then to the cable company, and so forth. We could do that by phone, I pointed out. No, she said, she'd never had much *luck* with the phone. She was afraid the utility companies wouldn't refund her deposits, and that was money she couldn't afford to lose. I promised to make good on any losses, but she didn't want my money; she wanted *her* money. The day her stuff was to be loaded on the truck, it was more than a hundred degrees by nine in the morning, and when the truck pulled up and two skinny black kids got out, I knew we were in trouble. The driver couldn't have been more than eighteen, and the other looked about fifteen and weighed a hundred and ten pounds tops. "Stay here," I told her, then went outside to talk to the driver and sign the paperwork. "My mother's in a bit of a state," I warned him. "I'll try to keep her out of your way." I'd hoped to convey this vital information to the other kid, too, but he'd gone directly inside. He was in there for about ten seconds when I heard my mother wail, "Oooh! Oooh! *Oooh!*" as if he were jabbing her with a hat pin. Arriving on the scene, I saw that he'd picked up my mother's credenza by one end and was intent on taking it outside. It wasn't a heavy piece of furniture. He'd taken one look at it, sussed out that it was made of pressed sawdust, not wood, and hoisted it into the air. "You'll break it!" my mother was screaming at him, her hands over her mouth. "You'll *break* it!"

In the car, she sat there, her face in her hands, still picturing the kid with the credenza. "You need to calm down," I told her. "If it gets broken, I'll replace it."

"But I *love* it," she said.

"Mom," I said. "It's from Kmart."

It took a good minute for her to respond to this unwelcome fact. "Don't you have things that *you* love?" I didn't answer, and she was quiet until we pulled into the driveway of the house we'd be leaving the next morning. "Do you really think I'm not trying?" she said, her hands shaking and bottom lip quivering. "Because I am. I hope you never know how hard."

There wasn't much to say to that. She was trying. As hard as she could. As was often the case with my mother, it was her utter lack of success that strained credulity.

AND SO WHATEVER didn't fit into our two small cars went into storage, to be delivered we knew not when to we knew not where. For my mother, who always preferred to settle things wrongly than to leave them unsettled, a nightmare. For all concerned, the next five days turned out to be another. Barbara drove one car, with Emily and Kate listening to music on their headphones in the backseat, my mother riding with me in the other. Officially unraveled now, she suffered one anxiety attack after another, unable to breathe unless all the windows were down, muttering all the while, "Dear God, how much longer?" Our progress was slow, torturous. In the morning it took her a good hour and a half to get ready, and by late afternoon she'd had all she could endure, and we'd have to pull off. She needed a hotel room to herself, which was fine, because by then so did we. She needed another hour or more to shower and dress for dinner, and then we had to scout out the possibilities. "I'm sorry, but really I can't bear it," she'd say if the place was too loud or she could smell grease when we walked in. When we finally found a restaurant she *could* bear, the first thing she did was ask our waiter to turn down the air-conditioning because it was freezing, and often there was something wrong with the table we'd been seated at. What she was hoping for, of course, was never on the menu. "If only they just had a grilled cheese sandwich," she'd lament. "Could you ask if they'd make me one?" My mother never ordered for herself in restaurants. She explained what she wanted and expected me, as the man at the table, to communicate her desires. If a waiter addressed her directly, she'd say, "My son will order for me." Sometimes, depending on just how disappointed she was with the overall proceedings, she'd add, audibly, "If they were professionals, they'd know it's the man who orders." Emily, ever the peacemaker where her grandmother was concerned, would try to appease her. "I don't think that's the way things work anymore, Grandma," she'd say. "Certainly not in T.G.I. Friday's," her sister would add. Most days, I'd about had it by that time. "There are two hundred people in here, Mom. You have to order from the menu." Sometimes Barbara would note that there actually *was* a grilled cheese sandwich on the kiddie menu, which it would then fall to me to order. "That was perfect," my mother would say when she was finished, now in a better mood. "It was all I wanted." By then I'd usually had a couple bottles of beer or a margarita. *Would you please, for the love of God, just shut the fuck up and eat your Jell-O?* That was what I'd have liked to say. Items on the children's menu always came with Jell-O.

Our second day on the road, around dawn, we were awakened by a call from the motel's front desk. During the night somebody had broken into my car, smashing in the windshield with a tire iron. Nothing was stolen, but we couldn't get back on the road until we spent the morning getting the windshield replaced. The front seat and floor were vacuumed, but tiny glass shards had worked their way into the fabric of the seat cushions, and by the time I drove back to the motel where my family anxiously awaited, my undershorts were pink. My mother would now have to ride in the other vehicle. "Which car do you want to drive?" I asked Barbara. That is, would you rather have my mother in your car for the next seven hours or bleed from the ass in mine? After twenty-five years, she was used to such choices. Still, she seemed to debate this one for a long time.

We took a bath towel from the motel and put it down on the seat, and then I slid in gingerly behind the wheel. "Try not to squirm," my wife advised.

I gave her what I hoped was my most appreciative smile. "You too."

WE'D RENTED A large camp on Great Pond for this summer of house and apartment hunting, and the girls immediately claimed its loft for their own. They could listen to music on their headphones without disturbing the adults, and with the lake only a few feet from the back deck, they could swim whenever they wanted, which was always. Late afternoons Kate and I fished, though we never caught anything, and weather permitting I cooked outdoors on the grill. The nights were so perfectly black and quiet we could hear the water lapping gently against the dock, and we fell asleep more often than not to the singing of loons.

Barbara and I divided our two major tasks. Working with a local realtor, she scoured the market. Most of the nicer houses, at least the ones we could afford, were in developments outside town, whereas we wanted to be *in* town, near the college if possible, in the Waterville school district, but the few decent neighborhoods seemed to be out of our price range. One of the good things about moving to a grungy mill town, we'd thought, was that we'd be able to afford a nice house. Apparently we'd thought wrong. Every time Barbara returned from one of these expeditions she seemed more dispirited.

She had company. My job—finding a place for my mother—wasn't any easier. She was better now that we'd gotten off the road but was still a bundle of nerves, and I knew she wasn't going to calm down until things were, as she put it, "settled." That is, until she had an apartment and her belongings were installed and she could get back into her routines. A nice, cozy little one bedroom, bright and airy, carpeted, nothing extravagant. It was fine if this was in an apartment complex, but it had to be for elderly residents only (no families with children). She wanted nothing to do with "assisted living." Because she refused to take money from us—or at least no more than necessary, as on Helwig Street—we quickly determined that she couldn't afford market prices. That meant something subsidized, where her rent would be keyed to her monthly Social Security stipend. Unfortunately, these federal and state subsidies were tied to onerous regulations, the most objectionable of which was that Section 8 "crazies" could not be turned away, and she refused to live with people like that. In theory she didn't object to renting a flat in a private home, but she couldn't abide old plumbing, so the kitchen and bathroom would have to be modern. Unable to climb steep stairs anymore, she would need to be on the first floor, a preference shared by those who owned most of these homes. But finding a downstairs flat was no guarantee, because she hated to hear people walking overhead, so the upstairs floors had to be carpeted. After a week of poring over the ads in the local paper, of pulling up in front of apartments only to drive away immediately if a car was up on blocks at the curb (a Maine specialty) or the yard was infested with weeds or the house itself looked ramshackle, we quickly discovered that the place my mother was looking for simply didn't exist, at least not in Waterville. Once we knew where the clean neighborhoods were, we drove them street by street, hoping a FOR RENT sign might've magically appeared in a window since yesterday, but none ever did, and with each passing day my mother became more and more deflated. Eventually I decided to visit Colby College, ostensibly to introduce myself to my new colleagues, but also hoping to tap some local insider knowledge. Everyone agreed that we'd have to expand our search. The few good apartments in town were quickly rented by college faculty and staff. The time to look was late May, at the end of the school year, not mid-July. Under the circumstances our best bet would be to consider nearby Winslow or Oakland. Several people recommended we try Farmingdale.

Farmingdale, however, was a good half hour away, and given my mother's increasingly fragile condition, that would be stretching it. The apartment she'd envisioned wasn't just bright and clean and airy and carpeted and on the first floor, with updated plumbing, it was right around the corner from our house, the one we hadn't found yet and probably couldn't afford when we did. Even if we could find the perfect house, it wouldn't be perfect if it was so distant. That evening one of my new colleagues called to say that she remembered an apartment complex in Farmingdale on a hill overlooking the Kennebec River, so over dinner, I suggested we drive out there the next day, when it was supposed to be warm and sunny. We could have lunch on the river, then take a peek at the complex. What harm could it do? I didn't expect this weak pitch to succeed, but it did.

The apartments did indeed sit on a hill overlooking the river. They were tidy and clean, the grounds well kept. Better yet, to judge by the sign, an apartment was actually available. "It's an awfully long way from you," my mother said as we pulled into the lot. "It's a good distance from Waterville," I agreed. "The problem is we don't yet know where we're going to end up." Which was true. Just as she and I were expanding our apartment search, so was Barbara expanding hers. One of the nicer houses we'd seen was in Winthrop, a suburb of Augusta, about ten minutes from where we now sat.

In fact the vacancy, a one bedroom on the ground floor, was carpeted, if not as bright or airy as one might have hoped. But the complex looked to be about a decade old, so the plumbing was modern, and I pointed out the cable TV hookup. It was by far the best apartment we'd seen, and I could tell my mother was balancing this with the fact that it wasn't exactly what she'd pictured. She wasn't asking for a lot. Couldn't she, just this once, have what she wanted? In the kitchen, with the apartment manager looking on, she paused to draw her index finger along the surface of the stove.

Outside, noticing another complex farther up the hill, my mother asked about it, because it looked nice.

"That's for families," the woman said. "You said you didn't want that, right?"

"It's awfully close," my mother said. "Do the children come down here?"

"Never," the woman assured her. "The two complexes are completely separate."

"I think we'll keep looking," my mother told her, nodding at me. "My son and his family are going to be in Waterville, and he wouldn't want me to be that far away."

Back in the car, she took a tissue out of her purse and wiped her index finger over and over. "Did you notice how *filthy* it was?" she said. "And don't tell me the children don't come down that hill. And she admitted they took Section Eight."

"That's a federal law," I reminded her. "If it's subsidized, they can't turn away people who are eligible. It was the same back in Illinois, if you recall."

Of course she did. "Remember that first place I lived? Where that disgusting woman who lived across the hall refused to take her medications?"

But not being "settled," or even close to it, was wearing on her, I could tell, and when we pulled in back at the camp, she said, "Why isn't there something like that in Waterville?"

"I don't know, Mom," I said, "but you have to order from the menu."

Her mouth tightened at this. I'd been saying it a lot lately.

THEN WE CAUGHT a break. Two of them, actually. During one of her trips that spring, Barbara had seen a house she loved, though it was too expensive. It was still available, and the price had come down a bit, but what really made it worth reconsidering was something we hadn't considered: taxes. We'd been warned by my Colby colleagues and just about everyone else, including realtors, that real-estate taxes here were brutally high. It hadn't occurred to us that people almost everywhere believe they're overtaxed—a belief particularly virulent in Maine. One afternoon, as an exercise, Barbara sat down with our realtor for the first time and actually ran the numbers on that house, only to discover that it wasn't completely out of our range and that, compared with Illinois, taxes in Maine were a bargain. True, you got less house for your dollar, but a smaller percentage of that dollar went to the state. The result was a push. Better still, now that the house had been on the market for almost two years, the sellers were thought to be motivated. What could it hurt to look? Given that love invariably enters through the eye, that was a dumb question. We looked, and of course it was the ideal house. Back at the realtor's we ran the numbers again with the same result. It would be a stretch, but not impossible. I called my literary agent to ask what kind of money we could reasonably anticipate in the coming year, then told the realtor we'd sleep on it and decide in the morning whether to make an offer or not. But by the time we got back to the lake, we'd changed our minds and called our realtor and instructed her to make an offer that would reveal if *motivated* meant the same thing to these sellers that it did to us a few months earlier in southern Illinois, when it had been synonymous with *desperate,* or *about to pray for the first time in twenty-five years.*

We might have guessed what effect our finally finding *the* house would have on my mother, but we didn't. My mantra—that come the end of the day, she was going to have to order off the menu—was an idea she'd always resisted. Usually she stood her ground, maintaining that we just had to keep looking, that there had to be something we simply hadn't found yet. And of course by *we* she meant me. But the journey from Illinois had taken more out of her than we knew, as had the repeated rental disappointments. Maine itself—the deep stillness of the woods, the piney dampness of the camp, the lonely sound of the loons out on the pond in the middle of the night—seemed to unmoor her; these rustic routines were ours, not hers, and she was increasingly desperate for control over some little corner of our present existence. One evening Barbara and I met a new colleague and his wife for dinner in nearby Belgrade Lakes, leaving her and the girls alone at the camp for a couple hours. Emily and Kate were up in their beloved loft, headphones on as usual, listening to music and dancing. Their youthful exuberance must've been too much for my mother. Eventually, even with their headphones on, they heard her calling up to them from the bottom of the stairs, asking them to please keep the noise down. She was trying, she explained, to count her change.

The next day things came to a head. We'd been in negotiation all week with suddenly *un*motivated sellers who were playing things as if they had the stronger hand, which meant they did. They'd apparently heard that the bidder was a Colby College professor, and in a mill town like Waterville that was their dream come true. Worse, it was now early August, and classes would start in a few weeks. The sellers had no doubt also heard that we were out on Great Pond in an unheated camp that would be impossible to stay warm in past the end of September. To their way of thinking, we were like Napoléon. On impulse we'd invaded Russia, and winter was coming.

On the night in question, all five of us gathered around the camp's television with the sound down low so we could hear the phone if it rang. The patio door was open just a crack, because the nights were already chilly. Through the opening came a sound like paper being wadded into balls—but loud, as if played through a bullhorn. Orange light, for some reason, was dancing on the smooth surface of the lake. The camp two doors down from ours was ablaze, huge columns of fire soaring into the sky. All around the cove people had come out onto their decks to watch. When the fire leaped from the camp itself to the two nearest pine trees, I said, "Uh, I don't mean to be an alarmist, but let's get in the car and drive up to the main road." On foot, it would be an uphill climb along the dirt road, and my mother didn't do uphill anymore, even in broad daylight. There wasn't much of a breeze, but if it shifted in our direction, I'd have to carry her, leaving Barbara to attend to the girls. We'd all just piled into our cars when the fire trucks careened down the road, effectively trapping us in our drive. Along with the neighbors, we watched the building burn down to its foundation, the firefighters seemingly content to keep the flames from leaping from tree to tree and camp to camp. As often was the case with my mother, when faced with a real worry, some clear and present danger, she was remarkably calm, reassuring Kate and Emily that everything would be fine, that the firemen knew what they were doing.

The episode did, however, provide her with a valuable new context. "I've changed my mind about the Farmingdale apartment," she said the next morning over breakfast. "Let's take it."

I nodded, not wanting to queer the deal with excess enthusiasm. "Do you want to go look at it again?"

"No, I've decided."

"Are you sure?"

"Let's call her now," she said. "Then it'll be all settled." And after that, we could call the movers and set a date for the delivery of her things. She could start making out a grocery list.

"It looks like we might be getting the house we want," I told her (as we did, the day after). "You can stay with us for a while if you aren't sure," I said, feeling Barbara stiffen next to me. "We can keep looking."

"I'm sure," she said. "Let's call now."

Right now, she meant, right this *second*. Which was fine. I'd just needed to hear her say the words. Otherwise, when the Farmingdale apartment didn't work out (as it wouldn't), she'd remember it as being all my fault, and at the very least I had to make her complicit.

So we made the call. The apartment was still available. Yes, we could drive to Farmingdale later that morning with a deposit. And when we returned, we could start calling the telephone, cable, and utilities. That afternoon, when Barb and the girls were out, she called her sister in Gloversville to celebrate, describing the apartment in detail and how quiet the complex was—all elderly, no Section 8s—and how it sat on a hill overlooking the river. My aunt must have said it sounded perfect because I heard my mother agree, and of course she'd convinced herself that it was. "And the best part?" she added. "It's not just a new apartment. It's a new life."

By the time she hung up, she was aglow. "Oh, Ricko-Mio," she said, giving me a hug. "It feels so *good*. I don't know why it took me so long to decide."

That evening, though, she began to come down from her manic high. The movers had called, and it would be at least two weeks before they could deliver her things from Illinois. No, they couldn't give her a specific delivery date; the problem was she had so little that it would have to go on the back of a truck bound for New England with a larger load. And, of course, she'd begun to remember her original misgivings about the apartment. "Before we move in so much as a stick of furniture, the whole place will have to be professionally cleaned," she said. "Remember the layer of *grease* on that stove top?"

I considered saying no, since I didn't, then decided to agree that, yes, it had been greasy.

"It'll be worth the money," she continued, her conviction on this point unshakable. To the uninitiated, it no doubt would have appeared that it was her own she meant to spend.

Again I agreed, this time really meaning it. For the bargain price of a good cleaning, we'd be purchasing peace of mind. Temporary, yes, but no less necessary for that.

Unsettled

THAT'S YOURS, you know," my mother said, startling me. She'd drifted off to sleep in her chair, and for the last hour I'd worked quietly, packing her books in preparation for yet another move. She was now living in Winslow, in her third apartment since we moved to Maine a decade earlier. How long had she been awake, observing me? I'd been listening to her low, regular breathing as I worked and hadn't noticed any change. I made a point of not watching my mother when she slept. Whereas other people relaxed in sleep, my mother's face always became rigid, a rictuslike mask, as if even in sleep she was doing battle with demons that would advance whenever her conscious guard was down. A month earlier she'd had another major meltdown, after which she'd slipped into one of the listless fugue states that so often followed a manic event. Coming out the other side, there was always a return to sanity, and at least for a time she'd rediscover her ability to see things as they were, her thoughts no longer barbed and dangerous. But this most recent meltdown seemed to have taken a greater toll than any of the others, and things we'd fought pitched battles over in the past seemed not to matter now. All of which was both welcome and a little unnerving, and all afternoon as I'd packed her books, my mother drifting in and out of sleep in her reading chair, I couldn't help wondering if something had finally broken inside her. I feared it might be her spirit. What made me almost physically ill to contemplate was that there'd been times when I'd secretly wished for precisely this, because it was her indomitable will that fueled this costly, unwinnable war, her intractable determination that was responsible for her seemingly endless suffering. Now, though, seeing her as listless and malleable as she'd been these last few weeks, I understood that this had been a mistake to hope for.

"I do wish you'd take it home with you," she sighed, referring to the copy of Anita Brookner's *Hotel du Lac* I'd just run across. I'd loaned her the book the year before, and at the time she'd claimed to like it, though when I offered other Brookners, she'd quickly said no, she didn't think so, there was so little room on her shelves.

Which was true enough, I thought, setting the novel aside. Her bookcases were crammed, many of the shelves double stacked. But of course there was more to it than that. I was forever buying or loaning her books I thought she might like, something at least entertaining enough to distract her from her growing list of physical ailments. She suffered crippling arthritis in her fingers, toes, and lower back. For this she took Aleve, which made her stomach feel like someone was clawing at it from the inside with a garden tool. She had acid reflux and high blood pressure and a thyroid condition, all three of which required medication, and she complained of her legs "locking up" when she had to walk uphill or for any distance. She was also suffering periodic TIAs, or ministrokes, that left her exhausted and afraid, the fear making another such event all the more likely. And even if there'd been a cure for these problems, it wouldn't address the relentless cycle of her anxieties, the feeling that the walls of her world were closing in.

Occasionally I'd pick a winner, something "in the tradition of" Agatha Christie or Margery Allingham or Mary Stewart or one of her other favorite authors, but mostly she'd read a few pages and declare that they were in the tradition of trash, of rip-offs, of a fast buck. The next time I visited they'd be sitting on the table by the front door, usually in a ziplock Baggie, to be donated to the next library book sale. As the Baggie suggested, the issue was contamination. My mother loved every single book on her sagging shelves, as they'd allowed her countless hours of escape. She didn't want them rubbing spines with books she deemed unworthy.

Which I kind of understood, and was why, despite having had to do it a dozen times or more, I never minded packing up her books for each subsequent move. My mother had what you could call a library. While there were fewer than five hundred books, almost all of them inexpensive paperbacks, some with printed prices as low as a quarter on them, they revealed her taste and personality. I had ten times as many but nothing like a library. My wife and I had combined our books long ago—our tastes mostly compatible if not identical—and many on our shelves were written by former students or colleagues. An astonishing number were advance readers' editions sent by publishers hoping for endorsements, and of course there were others that for one reason or another I felt obliged to read. Barbara and I both have a hard time disposing of books, even those we don't like, aware that behind even the most wretched failures there's an author who slaved lovingly, for who knows how long. That's a sentimental attitude, of course, and if you indulge it, you'll never have a real library, certainly not one like my mother's. If a stranger came into her apartment, a quick scan of her books would give him a pretty good idea of who she was, whereas all he could say about ours was, *Boy, these people sure have a lot of books.*

"Why don't you let me buy you another bookcase," I said, going back to work. "Your new apartment's bigger. I'm pretty sure there'd be room."

What I was really hoping to elicit was some kind of enthusiasm for her new place, though I was pretty sure no such remarks would be forthcoming. Her next apartment, in an assisted-living facility, was very expensive (though we'd concealed the cost from her) and upscale, and she hated everything about it: the cheery regimented activities, the noonday meal in the large dining room, the railings along every hallway (implying that everyone not on a walker would need to clutch onto these in order to keep upright), the van used to ferry residents to the supermarket and the doctor and the hairdresser (which she'd never take because "my son does all that"). We'd put her name on the list at several other housing complexes, but it wasn't moving up those lists fast enough, and she grew frustrated with me for not calling every few days to check. I explained this in effect meant I was asking if anyone had died or had been hospitalized or was feeling poorly, because illness and death were what created vacancies. So rather than wait, she'd decided on the assisted living she knew she'd hate, since at least she'd be settled.

"I don't want a new bookcase," she sighed. "I just want all this to be over."

The move, she meant, but maybe more than that.

"You don't have to go anywhere, Mom," I reminded her. "If it's too much, you can stay right here."

"We signed a lease."

"Those can be broken."

"You've hired movers. We've canceled the cable, the phone . . . everything."

"Yes, but we can undo all that."

She rubbed her temples. "Can we please, *please,* just not talk about this?"

The apartment in Farmingdale had lasted only a year. It was too far from Waterville, as I'd known it would be, even before I saw it. We'd tried to mitigate the distance by inviting her to dinner every week or so and including her in school plays and other activities involving her granddaughters, as well as college events like the annual Carols and Lights holiday fes-

tival. Most important, we strove for continuity by reestablish-
ing our usual routines. Saturday was for grocery shopping, just
as it had been in southern Illinois, after which she and I went
out to lunch, something she always looked forward to. And of
course we talked on the phone during the week. Still, she made
no secret of how isolated she felt in Farmingdale, mostly from
me but also from Emily and Kate, who were growing up fast.
Though there were a lot of women her age in the Farmingdale
complex, she'd made no friends there, claiming women from
Maine were provincial and clannish and dull. They cared little
for politics, less for sports, nothing at all for fashion. They
liked their seafood fried and their pastries dense. They were
sluggish and self-satisfied. They gossiped incessantly about
people my mother didn't know, and they weren't interested in
her opinions.

So when an apartment not far from our house in Waterville
came on the market, Barbara and I immediately checked it out
on our own. That way, if it was a sty, there was no reason to get
her hopes up. But it was lovely, half of the downstairs of a large,
rambling old house, and the landlord and his wife lived just up
the street. About twice the size of the cramped Farmingdale
place, it had high ceilings and tall windows, a fireplace, and
a nice front porch for summer sitting. Naturally it was more
expensive, but we were happy to make up the difference—or
would have been if we thought she'd be happy there. Lovely,
you see, is in the eye of the beholder, and Barbara was shaking her head in dismay. Over the years she'd grown almost as
adept as I was at seeing things through my mother's eyes, and

that's what she was doing now. The fixtures in the kitchen and bath were of the same vintage as those on Helwig Street in Gloversville, and the fridge wasn't frost-free. There were outlets in the unheated utility room for a washer and dryer, which my mother, a confirmed apartment dweller, didn't own. The beautiful oak built-ins would have to be dusted. Ditto the hardwood floors. My mother much preferred wall-to-wall carpeting, since you could run a vacuum over it.

"You think she'll hate it?" I asked.

"Not immediately. Not until after we sign the lease."

Which is pretty much how it had happened. A few days later, standing in the kitchen, the landlord and his wife awaiting our decision in the living room, she'd raised all the pertinent, predictable objections. Her back wouldn't allow her to defrost a refrigerator. (That was fine, we'd get her a new one.) And she had no way to get to a laundromat. (No problem, we'd scout out a nice used washer/dryer unit.) And she hated wood floors. (A few area rugs would do the trick.) Knowing what would come next, Barbara left the room. "And of course the whole place will need a *professional* cleaning," she said, sotto voce, drawing her index finger across the surface of the stove. "There's a layer of grease over everything." (From the next room came the voice of the landlord's wife, "*What* did she say?")

So we signed a lease and later, back at our house, my mother called Gloversville to tell my aunt about her lovely new place, how much it reminded her of the Helwig Street house, and how close she'd be to us. To hear her tell it, this move was really for me. I'd grown weary of the half-hour drive to Farmingdale to take her grocery shopping. Now we could shop together in Waterville, and she'd really be part of Emily's and Kate's lives again. Her enthusiasm, I knew, was more for herself than her sister. She was giving herself one of her talkings-to, convincing herself that she was doing the right thing, that all would at last be well.

For a while things *were* better, but then ultimately worse. It was an old house, so the tall windows, while elegant, didn't glide up and down smoothly on their fraying ropes, and the glass panes rattled when the wind blew or a big truck rumbled by. Summers, the street was too hot and noisy to sit out on the porch, or so she claimed. Her neighbors weren't elderly, which meant they made noise. The woman in the upstairs apartment was heavy-footed and played music, and on the other side of her bedroom wall my mother could hear the tenant in the adjacent apartment—a sad young woman—weeping inconsolably over a long-lost boyfriend. I visited regularly and never heard any of this, but the house *was* old and full of sounds.

There were other disappointments, too, unavoidable but real. Though she was closer to us now and saw her granddaughters more regularly, they were in middle and high school and had full lives with their friends. Barbara was by then working full-time at Colby College, and I was both writing and teaching, so even though she was now three minutes away instead of thirty, she didn't see ten times as much of us; the imagined arithmetic was false, as it always seemed to be where she was concerned. And now that she wasn't in a seniors' complex anymore, when she went to the mailbox there were no other women her age to talk to, even in passing, about the weather and who'd come down with a cold or had visitors over the weekend. When I called to check on her at the end of the day, she'd say, before hello, "Do you realize that yours is the first voice I've heard today that didn't come from the television?"

Then one day a bat came down the chimney, and that was that; we were off to Winslow, ten minutes away, on the other side of the Kennebec River, where I'd been tracking a small elderly housing complex, and finally our timing was right. Truthfully, we hadn't expected this apartment to work out either, but it did, largely because my mother, against all odds, had made a friend there, a woman her age, also "from away" and therefore unattached. Dot was kind and had a terrific sense of humor and also seemed to have the great reserves of patience this friendship would require. She had family down-state, though, and sometimes spoke about moving to be closer to them, talk that always sent my mother into a tizzy.

Dot was one of my many reasons for feeling particularly dubious about this upcoming move. I was more than willing to make the weekly drive from the coast to take my mother gro-cery shopping and out to lunch and wherever else she needed to go. Some weeks, if she had a doctor's appointment, I might have to make the trip twice, a strain, sure, but doable. And of course we could talk on the phone as needed. There was no guarantee she would find somebody she liked as well as Dot in her new place. But my mother believed she could read the future. If she remained in Winslow, Dot would leave, and then she'd be alone. Okay, I said, but wouldn't *that* be the time to move? Why not enjoy her friend for as long as she could? Because, I was given to understand, if there was the possibility of moving in the future, that would mean she was unsettled in the present. No, she'd just go. If she didn't find another friend, well, she'd do without.

"There," I said, taping the last of the boxes shut. "Done."

"You should go home," she said, offering up one of her despondent smiles. "You have responsibilities there."

"Mom. We're going to walk away from this," I reminded her. "I'll be here an hour before the movers. We let them in, and then we drive away. They're going to pack everything here and unpack it at the other end."

This new moving strategy was one I'd expected her to challenge me on. In the past she'd insisted on being present for both the loading and unloading, as if her physical presence and attention to the smallest details would prevent damage to objects that, once put in their proper and accustomed place, would reconstitute her small interior world. The resulting spike in her anxiety levels in the weeks prior to a move made her impossible to live with, and naturally she'd be wiped out for weeks afterward, too tired and worn out even to eat. Over the last few years she'd become wobbly, unsteady on her feet (in need, actually, of the wall railings her new place boasted). Always managing to position herself in doorways when the movers, carrying something heavy or fragile, were trying to get through, she was a danger to both herself and them. And if anything got dirty or scuffed on the truck, she'd squeal in horror at the smudge and demand that it be cleaned then and there, before it entered the apartment, so everything came to a screeching halt. The placement of every stick of furniture was a battle in itself, and common sense was not allowed onto the battlefield. If the cable plug was on one wall, she'd invariably want her television by the opposite one, requiring the cable company to send out a technician to provide a second outlet. No feng shui enthusiast could take more seriously the arrangement of a bedroom, which had to "feel" right to her, irrespective of function. If there were only two electrical outlets in the room, you could rest assured of my mother's intention to cover them, after which another electrician would have to be hired.

I was determined to avoid all of this unnecessary angst by getting her out of the Winslow apartment the moment the movers arrived, establishing her at our Camden house for the day until her things were off-loaded at the new apartment. Toward that end I'd drawn a schematic of her new place and asked her to decide where the major pieces of furniture should go, promising she wouldn't be held to any decisions and that anything could be repositioned later if need be.

"Really," I reassured her. "There's nothing for you to do. Nothing for you to worry about. Call me if anything comes up."

But I only had to look at her to know that her imagination was already running wild. What if they cut off her utilities too early? What if she couldn't reach me? What if, what if, what if?

"Would you rather come to Camden with me now?"

"Dot and I are going to the Lobster Trap. Did you forget?"

"No, I didn't forget," I assured her. "I know you've been looking forward to it. I was just offering. I'll call you tomorrow. We can talk everything through again if you'd like to. Absolutely nothing's going to go wrong."

I was halfway to the car when her door opened behind me, and I heard her calling out. "What?" I said, turning back. She was holding up the Anita Brookner. See? I forgot things. I'd forgotten that, at least. Things *could* go wrong.

In fact, though she didn't say so, everything *was* going wrong.

HER MOST RECENT MELTDOWN had been occasioned by a number of related factors that could be reduced to this: our lives were changing. Buoyed by the success of the movie Robert Benton made of my novel *Nobody's Fool* and some screenplay opportunities, I'd resigned my position at Colby College to write full-time, a decision that struck my mother as both rash and dangerous. Two decades earlier she'd felt much the same way about my out-of-the-blue determination to become a novelist, an act of hubris, she thought, that threatened my stable career as an English professor. My recent successes as a writer were tangible, but to her they remained utterly baffling. She read each glowing review with genuine pride, often tearing up, and reveled in the modest regional prizes my books garnered. If she'd had the money, she no doubt would've hired contract killers to settle the score with critics who had the temerity to doubt my brilliance. After the *Nobody's Fool* movie, the novel itself made a cameo appearance on the *New York Times* best-seller list, which threw her for a loop. "It's like it's all happening to someone else" was how she put it, and I sympathized because it mostly felt that way to me, too.

From various comments she let drop, I knew she was deeply mystified by how many people apparently wanted to read stories set in the kind of industrial backwaters from which she'd worked so hard to escape. Even more perplexing was the fact that I not only wrote about such places but returned to them again and again. After all, I had a Ph.D. and a valid passport and made a good living among distinguished colleagues. Why was I slumming (imaginatively) back in Gloversville? She probably felt quite certain that in short order people would decide they'd had enough of stories set in dirty mill towns, and if I quit my job, where would I be?

The success of my fiction gravely conflicted with her own experience of life, as well as her profound sense of how the world went round. After all, she'd grown up during the Depression. My teaching position to her felt every bit as solid as the college that employed me. If Colby wasn't going anywhere and my tenure couldn't be revoked, then I was set for life or, to use her word, *settled*. Why court disaster by exposing myself to unnecessary risk? Why *choose* to be unsettled? As things stood I got a good paycheck every two weeks, whereas an author's life would be one of feast or famine. Its feasts not only were unpredictable but came intertwined with all kinds of whens and ifs—like, *if* you can finish the book you're working on, *when* you can deliver it—and such uncertainties were dry tinder, lacking only a spark to ignite a conflagration. We already had one daughter in college, and the other would soon follow. Could we cover those heart-stopping expenses by means of my writing alone? I assured her that we could and tried to explain that at least for the moment my being a teacher was actually counterproductive, that the time I spent in the classroom diminished rather than increased my earning power, but that didn't register. To her, resigning my teaching position wasn't just folly but a particular kind of folly of which she had personal knowledge. Forty years before, on a whim, she'd quit a good job, and look what that had gotten her.

And it went even deeper than this. One of my mother's most cherished convictions was that back on Helwig Street she and I had pledged an oath, each to the other. She and I would stand together against whatever configuration the world's opposition took—her parents, my father, Gloversville, monetary setbacks. Now, forty-some years later, I was a grown man with a wife and kids, but this original bond, she believed, was still in force. However fond she was of Barbara, however much she loved her granddaughters, none of that altered our original contract, which to her way of thinking made us indivisible. She'd never really considered us two separate people but rather one entity, oddly cleaved by time and gender, like fraternal twins somehow born twenty-five years apart, destined in some strange way to share a common destiny. If I was about to make a colossal blunder, then it was her duty, her moral obligation, to prevent it. Having been prideful herself, she knew what pride goeth before. What's more, my pride was risking not just my own future but my family's, putting them and, yes, herself in unnecessary danger. Because when things came unraveled, a son who at times failed to acknowledge the primacy of the Helwig Street contract might, if there weren't enough resources to go around, put his wife and children before her. I don't think these were conclusions my mother arrived at in the front of her brain; instead they were constant, ambient whisperings that originated in the shadowy recesses, as undeniably real as anything in the world for the simple reason that they never, even in jaw-clenched sleep, went away.

STILL, MY MOTHER MIGHT have been able to give herself a good talking-to and keep the worst of these anxieties at bay had I not compounded matters by announcing, not long after quitting my teaching job, our plan to move to the coast. Not that she didn't understand the logic. Now that I was untethered to the college, there was nothing holding us in Waterville. A few years earlier, we'd purchased a condo in Camden that we used as a weekend and summer retreat. It was three stories tall, one full quarter of a former Methodist church. Our unit was beneath the smaller of the two steeples, a place full of light and air, especially the master bedroom on the top floor, from which we had a view of the harbor. Barbara and I both loved it there but finally had to admit that it just wasn't working out. For one thing, our girls were then in high school and hated being yanked away from their Waterville friends and activities. For another, though she never said so in so many words, our having the place in Camden put my mother out of sorts. If we spent the weekend there, I'd have to take her grocery shopping on Friday instead of Saturday, our long-established grocery day. And in the summer, though we frequently invited her to come along, she felt abandoned. She liked Camden itself, its shops and restaurants a vivid contrast to dark, moribund Waterville, but the hills, so beautiful to look at, frustrated and defeated her. All the places she wanted to go were within a hundred yards of our front door, but at the bottom of the slope. She had no trouble going down it, but once there she couldn't make her legs carry her back up again, which meant that whoever she was with would have to return home for the car. With the part of her brain that was rational and reasonable, she understood our preference for bright, vibrant Camden; the irrational, fearful part, however, harbored a suspicion that we'd purposely selected a place where she couldn't follow or, if she did, couldn't function. This was precisely the sort of paradox she was forever trying and failing to reconcile. On the one hand, we'd never once in thirty-five years abandoned her. On the other, we always appeared to be on the verge of doing so.

Moreover, the worst of her personal demons was the one who dwelt in the details, and this was especially true of our plan to move to the coast. Had we been able to give her a series of dates etched in stone—for selling the Waterville house, finding a new house in Camden, locating her new apartment, and the actual physical moves themselves—she could have written them on her calendar and checked them off, one by one, the way her mother had always done with Holy Days on the liturgical calendar. But we could offer nothing that was "for sure." Because property was more expensive on the coast, there was a real possibility we wouldn't be able to find or afford what we were looking for—but then again maybe we'd get lucky! To further complicate matters, after a couple of mills around Waterville closed, half the town was for sale, which guaranteed that unloading our house—something we needed to do in order to buy in Camden—was going to be tricky.

And these were just the surface complexities. Supposing we found a new place and managed to sell the old one, what would happen next? We couldn't say with any certainty. Normally her need to be settled, to reestablish her old routines in a fresh environment, would have been trump, but there were simply too many moving parts to accurately predict how things would go. If we rented an apartment on the coast and moved her in, it might be six months or a year before we could follow, and there was no chance she'd make it that long in a strange place, with us a good hour away. If *we* went first, there was the possibility of a similar gap before she could follow, because senior housing here was as problematic as it had been in Waterville. And while there were more options, they were all more expensive, so she'd be more financially dependent on us. And every place we looked into had a waiting list. How long would you have to wait for an apartment in a complex of twelve units if there were three people ahead of you? Or eight people in one of twenty-five? The answer to both questions was the same: as long as it took. If she put her name on the list too soon and an apartment came available before she was ready, what then?

We'd presented her with a Rubik's Cube of possibility, the very thing we should have known she couldn't handle. The best we could do was to assure her that we'd take care of everything when the time came. Meanwhile she only needed to be patient. It was a doomed strategy, but it was the only one we had. It was either that or . . .

Over the last thirty-five years, my wife and I had taken turns bringing up the inevitable *or*. This time it was Barbara's. We *did* have a choice, she reminded me. Either we asked my mother to live with things being unsettled until we could settle them, *or* we could just put our own lives on hold. We didn't *have* to move to the coast to be happy. I'd quit my job at Colby, but Barbara was still employed there and liked her job. We didn't *need* to move; we just wanted to. The question we had to articulate correctly and then answer carefully was the same one we'd confronted so often before. In the end, was doing what we wanted to do—what other people like us seemed to do without having to think about it—really worth it? Was the reward equal to the risk? My mother was no longer a young woman, and her health was clearly in decline. Even though we'd managed her last two moves—both of which she'd instigated—as much as she'd allowed us, it had taken her long months to recover from them. Another move—this one played under protest—might just do her in. Why not put everything on hold?

To this persuasive argument I had a one-word answer: genetics. Yes, my mother's health was in decline, but my grandmother had also suffered from high blood pressure, a thyroid condition, crippling arthritis, and ministrokes, and she lived into her nineties, as had her sisters. By contrast, my father hadn't made it to his sixty-fifth birthday, and neither had a couple of his brothers, nor had Barbara's parents. If my mother lived to be ninety, we'd be in our early sixties before we were allowed to make unencumbered decisions about our own lives. I was a Russo male, a bloodline ripe with its own genetic challenges, cancer primary among them. Add to this the environmental issue: I'd grown up in Gloversville, where cancer statistics soared off the actuarial charts. If my mother lived to be ninety, odds were good she'd outlive me. When I spoke with my cousin Greg on the phone and inquired after my aunt's health, he always joked that these old women—his mother and mine—were going to bury us both. Except it wasn't a joke. When in the last thirty-five years, I asked my wife, had we ever had the luxury of making a major decision purely on its merits? Of necessity we'd always had to consider my mother's needs before our own. Surely by now we'd earned a reprieve. Didn't we deserve the right to think about ourselves first for once? It wasn't as if we were planning to abandon her. We would find her a nice place to live, just as we'd always done. We'd pay for what she couldn't afford and make the move as stress-free as possible.

I was right, of course, and Barbara admitted as much. After all, she'd been throwing the same argument at me for more than thirty years, every time it was my turn to raise the dreaded *or*. The problem was that I was also wrong, and we both knew that, too. Nor was I surprised when she remembered my grandfather. "What was that saying of his?" she asked. He'd always been full of aphorisms, but I knew all too well the one she was referring to. "With your grandmother, you always have a choice," he was fond of remarking when I was a boy. "You can do things her way or you can wish you had." He was speaking about his wife, of course, but he might have been talking about his strong-willed daughter. By the end, he was.

THE HOUSE WE ENDED UP buying in Camden was old and elegant. Also, a potential money pit. In its most recent incarnation it had devolved into a three-family dwelling. The principal renters had lived on the ground floor in the main house, where there was a master suite with a lovely bathroom. On the second floor were two more small bedrooms, as well as a tiny apartment with its own entrance. At some point a large garage had been added at the back of the house and, above it, a second, larger apartment with a third-story loft. It wasn't a house we were originally interested in, but Chris, our realtor, knew I was a writer and thought the loft apartment over the garage would be a perfect workspace for me. "And if you fix up the little apartment," he added, "it might work for your mom." Early on we'd told him what we were up against, that in addition to selling our Waterville house and finding something we could afford in Camden, we'd also need to find a place for my mother, and he'd promised to keep an eye out for a one-bedroom apartment.

"Or not," he said with a smile, seeing that his helpful suggestion had caused all the blood to drain from Barbara's face. An observant breed, realtors. My wife would later become one.

Chris was right about the loft workspace, though, and while the main house needed a lot of work, it was pretty much what we were looking for. The wiring wasn't up to code, a costly fix, and the kitchen was mired in the Sixties. Many of the windows needed to be replaced. The real problem, however, was the tiny run-down apartment. We had no interest in renting it, so what on earth would we do, pretend it didn't exist? On the other hand, it was one of the reasons the house was in our price range. The property had been on the market for years and, according to the seller's agent, most prospective buyers were put off by the three-family arrangement. Eventually, he thought, it would sell to an investor who'd fix up and rent all three spaces. Because of the apartment the house was definitely wrong for us, but there was something right about it, too, something that made me not want to dismiss it out of hand. Maybe it was just that we'd been looking for months and coming up empty. At any rate, I suggested we go up and look at that apartment one more time on the theory that if we considered the house at its worst, we'd feel better about turning our backs on what we liked.

You entered the apartment through the kitchen, and right away you thought, *No, no,* and again, *no.* The appliances were old and so grungy I immediately imagined my mother running her index finger along the surface of the stove. The stained, cracking linoleum was coming up from the floor. The living room was low ceilinged and so small it would hold little more than a sofa and coffee table, maybe a small TV in the corner. The bedroom was the size of a walk-in closet, with room for a single bed with one bedside table or a double bed without. In the bathroom, when you sat on the toilet your knees would touch the shower on one side, the wall on the other. The only good feature was the large and lovely screened-in porch that overlooked the back patio. I went out and just stood there. In winter, you'd glimpse the ocean through the bare trees. In summers I could imagine us sitting out there reading, cooled by breezes off the water. Sweet.

Barbara and Chris were in the hot little apartment waiting for me to come to my senses so we could leave. When I stepped inside, I got a flash. "What you're standing in," I said to Barbara, "is our master bedroom."

Chris blinked. My wife frowned. Whose master bedroom? Not hers. Not by a long shot.

But in a heartbeat I saw she was with me, seeing in her mind's eye what I was seeing in mine, and before I was half finished explaining, she was already ahead of me. You'd tear out the kitchen, knock down the wall that separated it from the living room, as well as the one between the bedroom and the bath. With its four tiny rooms reduced to two, the apartment could become a reasonably luxurious suite with its own private porch. Chris was grinning at us. "Moments like this," he said, "are why I'm a realtor."

Instead of returning to Waterville as planned, we booked a room at a B&B, and over dinner and a bottle of wine at the local chowder house we ran the numbers, trying to contain our mounting, irrational excitement, then ran them again. It was impossible. We could afford either the property or the work needed to transform it, but not both. Not unless we did all these things over a period of years. Not unless we moved into the loft apartment over the garage while the work was being done on the main house. Not unless I sold another screen-play. Not unless we sold the Waterville house, which after a month on the market still hadn't generated a single showing. Not unless we could find an apartment nearby for my mother. We'd have to hire a structural engineer to make sure the walls we meant to tear down weren't load bearing, and we'd have to bring the girls to see if this was a house they could see them-selves returning to in the future with children of their own. Yet somehow, in the moment when we'd seen how it might be done, how the house's many drawbacks could be trans-formed into a real asset, we'd already bought it in our imagi-nations. Impossible had become something we'd just have to deal with.

And my mother? Well, she hadn't come into our thinking at all, not until we came home late one evening not long after-ward to find a message from her on the answering machine, telling me to call the minute I got back, no matter what time. Okay, I thought, this is it. Now we pay. I dialed her number.

She answered on the first ring. She'd been thinking about it for a long time, she told me, her voice rich with both challenge and mania, and had come to an important decision. She was going home.

————

RETURNING TO GLOVERSVILLE yet again might have been a lunatic notion, but it was hardly a new one. The idea began to take form, as near as I could tell, in the camp we rented when we first came to Maine, after which it advanced and receded according to the cycles of her mind. The problem (and I'd been aware of this since she and I made that first journey to Arizona) was that to my mother there were two Gloversvilles—the one she was always trying to escape from when she lived there, and the other she nostalgically considered, every time she fled, as home. When she was actually in residence, it was a small, insular, uncouth, narrow-minded place that prevented her from being her truest self—free spirited, unconventional, and unfettered. Once she'd flown the coop, though, the very qualities she detested became more attractive. The smallness she so despised became cozy; it meant you didn't need a car to live there. Your loved ones, the very people who intruded upon your privacy and always spouted unwanted advice, were a convenient block away. Seen from a distance, they weren't so much nosy as thoughtful and caring, their concern now a safety net.

What took me longer to understand was that just as there were two Gloversvilles, my mother also had two sisters. In reality, she and Phyllis couldn't have been more temperamentally different, and when my mother was living there it was always their differences that defined their relationship. She saw my aunt as conventional and interfering and judgmental, qualities Phyllis inherited, she thought, from their mother. There were many bones of contention, but it particularly infuriated my mother that neither her sister nor the local man she married, my uncle Mick, seemed to have any aspirations beyond the town line. To my uncle, who'd grown up on a farm and been too young to serve in World War II, Gloversville was the big city, and he made no secret of his affection for it. Their oldest son, Greg, my cousin and boyhood friend, had gone away to college but returned to marry a local girl and settled down to a life of deflated Fulton county wages. He and his wife lived next door to my aunt and uncle, and next door to them lived Mick's mother, Beatrice, for whom my mother had even less use than her son. That three generations were all living in the same block struck my mother, back when she'd returned to live on Helwig Street with my grandmother, as beyond perverse. They all walked into one another's homes without knocking, freely investigating the contents of the refrigerators and helping themselves without permission. Lacking even the most rudimentary notion of privacy, they saw no reason not to comment on everyone else's lives and day-to-day decisions. Who could bear to live like this?

Once away from Gloversville, however, my mother immediately saw things differently, and as she grew older, her nostalgia for the very proximity that had always stifled her so became more pronounced. "How *happy* we were on Helwig Street," she'd recall, her eyes misty with memory, as if we'd been cruelly banished from this Eden. "We didn't have much money," she'd concede, somehow imagining this had been the only impediment to our contentment, "but everything seemed so *safe*. Remember how we used to rap on the floor?" I did indeed. When we wanted to parlay with my grandparents or they with us, we would rap on the kitchen floor (they on the ceiling) with a broom handle, and we'd convene invisibly, but close enough to whisper—in the back hallway. At the time I regarded the broom handle as one of the many advantages to our upstairs/downstairs circumstances and assumed everyone would be envious to know how easily and efficiently we communicated, with no need even to pick up a phone. Whereas my mother always cited this broom knocking as an example of how much better our lives would be when we finally escaped Helwig Street. We'd be independent, she explained, without people beneath us who at their every whim felt entitled to so rudely summon us.

When rational, she knew returning to Gloversville was a pipe dream, but desperation had a way of transforming every image projected in the theater of her mind, neither vague nor cloudy, as you might expect, but in brilliant high definition. Maine was all muted sepia tones, whereas Helwig Street—and Sixth Avenue, where her sister lived—seemed close enough to touch, everything painted in bright primary colors. Just as vivid in her imagination was the self she would become once she returned home. In Gloversville, she wouldn't be pushing eighty. She'd be the age she was during her last stint, when my grandmother was still alive. To be sure, she hadn't been in the best of health even then, but she'd managed well enough and would again.

She'd only been in that first Farmingdale apartment a few

months before she floated the idea of moving home again. It was a Saturday afternoon, after we'd done the grocery shopping, and we were watching a ball game before I headed back to Waterville. She'd been out of sorts the whole time.

"We might as well face facts," she finally said. "I hate Maine. I never should've come here." I had to smile, given how she made it sound like she'd done it all on her own. "It was a mistake. I should've gone straight to Gloversville from Illinois. I don't know what I was thinking."

"Okay," I said, "but while we're facing facts, here's another. You also hate Gloversville. You have your whole life. The last time you went back there, it was—in your own words—a terrible mistake."

There were few things my mother liked less than having such statements thrown back at her, so this put her into a dark funk. "It's true I've always hated Gloversville," she conceded half an hour later when the game ended and I rose to leave, "but things there have changed."

Which was true. They'd become even more problematic. In the past she'd always had the Helwig Street house, but that had been sold, in part to pay for the long-term care my grandmother required toward the end of her life. What my mother was referring to, however, was that my aunt and uncle had swapped houses with my cousin Greg and his wife, Carole, who had two kids and needed the extra room. Phyllis and Mick now occupied the downstairs flat of the house next door. My mother's idea, it finally came out, was for them to evict their upstairs renters so she could move in. "I'd have some kind of life there, at least," she concluded. "Aren't I entitled to that much?"

"Are you forgetting you can't do stairs anymore?" I couldn't help pointing out. After all, this consideration had governed every apartment search we'd made since Illinois. Indeed, when she visited our house these days, all activities had to take place on the ground floor because the pitch of the stairs up to the girls' bedroom was too steep. "I could *there,*" she said, her stony expression daring contradiction. "You forget. I always lived on the second floor in Gloversville."

In fact, she went on, nothing was really wrong except *Maine.* Once back in Gloversville she'd not only feel better, she'd *be* better. Why? Because there she'd at least be a person. Her family would be close by, along with other people who'd known her all her life, who knew she was a human being, who believed not only in her but also in her resilience and her ability to accomplish things. In Maine, none of the above.

I didn't see any point in debating whether she'd be more of a person in Gloversville than Camden, so I moved on to other problematic specifics, though I was pretty sure this tactic would prove equally futile. "How would you do your groceries? How would you get to the doctor or the hairdresser?"

"Greg would take me."

"Greg's juggling three jobs, and Carole works all week at the bank."

"Then I'd go with Mick and Phyl."

"Except you like to hold to your own schedule. Remember how you always complained, when you and Grandma lived together, that every week there'd be a different grocery day? They'd call and tell you to be ready in five minutes, and forty-five minutes later you'd still be waiting? How would that be different now? Have they changed? Have you?"

Her mouth had formed a thin line. "I'd *walk* to the store if I had to."

"In winter?"

Yes, she insisted, even in winter. Furthermore, if I was worried about money, there was no need. She'd get a job.

Of course I knew these wild assertions were trial balloons whose credibility she had to test by letting them float away, and that despite the brazenness of this last balloon—that she'd get a job—even she knew it would never gain altitude, no matter how much heated conviction she pumped into it.

"Mom," I said, "I'm not trying to make you feel bad, but we can't make real-world decisions based on magical thinking."

She was silent for a while, her face a dark thundercloud. "If only you wouldn't disagree with every single thing I say," she told me. "You take such pleasure in shooting down any idea I ever have. Why can't you be on *my* side for once?"

"What exactly would you like me to agree with?"

She thought for a moment. "That Greg would take me shopping. He's my nephew and he loves me."

"Yes, he would, and of course he does. That's why it would be so wrong to ask him to. He has too many other responsibilities and too few resources. The last thing he needs is another burden."

Now she threw me a triumphant look, as if this was the

concession she'd wanted from the start. "That's all I am, then? A burden? Is that what you're saying?"

"No, I'm saying that getting you to the hairdresser is my responsibility, not Greg's."

"Fine," she said. "Then I guess I'll just have to stay here in my cage."

The next day she called to apologize. After I left, she'd given herself a good talking-to. Her problem, she'd concluded, was always the same. She wanted to be independent, no one's burden or responsibility, not even mine. I had a career and a wife and two daughters to raise, and she hated that on top of all that I also had to think about her. She didn't know why her thoughts always returned to Gloversville, as if it were Briga-doon. She knew better. In the future, I was to simply ignore her when she "got like that."

The trouble, as she knew full well, was that when she got like that there *was* no ignoring her. Since then we'd been through the same bitter, futile exercise twice more, the volume turned up a notch or two each time. Now, on the eve of our move to the coast, we were back in familiar territory yet again, the only difference being that this time her fury was exagger-ated by further changes in the Gloversville landscape. Earlier that year my uncle Mick had died after a long, terrible illness, leaving my aunt hollowed out by grief and by the guilty relief that comes when a loved one's suffering finally ends. She and my mother had begun talking on the phone more regularly, usually once a week, usually reminiscing about their girlhoods on West Fulton Street, one of Gloversville's many immigrant neighborhoods. I think they both enjoyed these strolls down memory lane, and their nostalgia for simpler times made it easy to paper over their many ideological and temperamental differences. Lately, though, according to my aunt, with whom I also spoke regularly, my mother's mood had grown darker, as if she no longer had access even to the pleasures of the past, and the last time Phyllis asked her how things were going in the present, she said that there wasn't much point in talking about it, that she had no life, and there was no reason to pretend she did. Hearing this, my aunt called to warn me that another storm was approaching.

I, of course, needed no such warning. I'd seeded the clouds myself by ignoring my wife's *or* and sticking that FOR SALE sign in the yard in front of our Waterville house. Still, when the storm finally broke, even I was stunned by its ferocity. This time instead of telling me what she *wanted* to do, she was announcing what she *intended* to do, with or without my help. Having already been through the whole Gloversville scenario, she knew all my objections by heart and had no intention of listening to them again. She wasn't a child who needed to be told what she could and couldn't do. She was *going,* and that's all there was to it. There was nothing I could do to prevent it. If I didn't want to pay the movers, she'd leave every single thing she owned behind. If I wouldn't drive her there, she'd take a bus. If I wouldn't drive her to the bus, she'd take a taxi. Gloversville was where she belonged. She was going.

"Okay," I said, "but where specifically?" I knew, of course. My uncle's death meant that my aunt was now living alone in the two-bedroom downstairs flat, and it was that second bed-room my mother had in mind.

"Where do you think? With my sister."

The last thing I wanted was to ask the obvious question, but there was no avoiding it. "She's invited you?" I said.

This question was so cruel because I already knew the answer. My aunt had told me more than once that she was unsure whether she'd be staying in Gloversville much longer. Both of her daughters had asked her to come live with them, and she thought she might. I wondered now if she'd maybe mentioned this possibility to my mother, if perhaps that was what had precipitated the current meltdown. Because if Phyllis meant to move away, then my mother's final refuge, her last desperate hope for the independent life that existed nowhere except in her imagination, was disappearing before her eyes.

"What do you *mean,* has she invited me?" she demanded to know. "What are you *saying?*" But before I could explain that I wasn't *saying* anything, merely asking something, she continued, her voice now shaking with rage. "Are you actually imply-ing that my sister would refuse to take me in?"

I took a deep breath and lowered my voice, hoping to bal-ance her frenzy with calm and reason, though in truth I'd never known this strategy (or any other, for that matter) to work when she came totally unglued. "I'm saying your sister recently lost her husband. I'm saying she's raw with grief and unsure in her own mind what comes next."

"You know," my mother said, "it's all finally coming clear."

"What's that?"

"What you think of me. What you've always thought of me."

"Mom—"

"Did it ever occur to you," she wanted to know, "that maybe I could *help* my grieving sister? That there might be somebody in the world who actually likes me? As a person? Who might enjoy my company? That instead of being a burden—like I am to you—I might actually make someone's life better?"

"Mom—"

"Why don't you come right out and say it. You think I'm incapable of happiness. That I'm incapable of making anyone else happy."

To my surprise, I heard myself say, with a sinking heart, "All right, Mom. You win. Call Aunt Phyl. If Gloversville's what you want, I won't stand in your way."

The immediate and profound silence on the other end of the line suggested that I wasn't the only one surprised by this. She'd been prepared for several more rounds of verbal bludgeoning, but now she had to improvise. "As you say," I told her, "you're not a child."

After hanging up, I called my aunt and gave her the short version of what had just transpired. "Oh, poor Jean," she said.

"Yes," I said, immediately choked up that she could so perfectly sum up her sister's plight in three small words, and suddenly I felt both the weight and truth of the bitter questions my mother had just hurled at me. Had I considered even for an instant that she might be able to help her sister in her grief and loss? Had it occurred to me that my aunt might actually enjoy her company? That there actually might be someone, somewhere, who wouldn't see her as a burden? That there might be a place for her, a life? Because the honest answer to all those questions was a resounding no. No, nothing like that had crossed my mind. Worse, the real reason I was now calling my aunt was to apologize for the fact that my mother, who'd more than once accused me of trying to keep her in a cage, had broken out. Now Phyllis, whom I wanted to spare, was going to have a difficult morning.

"She keeps saying she wants to be with her family," I explained, "with people who love her."

"But *you* are her family," my aunt said. "You and Barbara and the girls."

"I know."

"It would cost you thousands to get her here, and two months later you'd have to bring her back again."

"I know," I repeated weakly.

"Oh, honey, I'm so sorry. And after all you've done . . . all these years. I wish I knew what to tell you."

"I wish you did, too."

We were silent for a time. "How's Barbara?"

"At the end of her tether," I admitted, grateful to have my wife, who'd borne all of this so patiently for three long decades, finally acknowledged. "Still here. Though, honestly, I can't imagine why."

"I feel so bad for her."

Suddenly I was anxious for the conversation to be over. You couldn't ask for a better confidante than my aunt, but I always felt like our shared understanding of my mother's condition, "her nerves," amounted to a shabby conspiracy against a sick woman, and I suspected Phyllis felt all too keenly that same sense of betrayal. And perhaps most unforgivable was that telephoning my aunt this evening, to prepare her for the call she'd be getting in the morning, constituted poisoning the well in advance of my mother's thirsty arrival.

That must've happened near the crack of dawn, because it was still very early when our telephone rang, waking us up. "Well, it's over," my mother said, not bothering with hello. "I guess I'm not going anywhere."

"I'm sorry, Mom," I told her, but she'd already hung up.

I lay there in bed for a long time, trying to imagine that terrible conversation with my aunt, who would've told her, as gently as possible, that what she was proposing simply wouldn't work, that most likely she wouldn't be staying in Gloversville that much longer herself, that by the end of the year she'd be putting the house on the market for what little it would bring, that after sorting things out she'd probably move in with one of her daughters. Knowing my aunt, I suspect she put in a good word on my behalf, reminding my mother that I loved her, that I'd always been there when she needed me, that she belonged close by so I could look after her, that she was lucky to have a son willing to do all that.

At some point another possibility occurred to me: that my mother hadn't called her sister at all, that all this was just between us, as it had always been. Locked in a two-person drama, we had no need for additional players.

BUILDING FLOOR-TO-CEILING SHELVES in the downstairs bedroom, which would double as a library and reading room when we didn't have guests, was the first order of business in the new Camden house. We'd hired a carpenter to begin work the day after the closing. "This whole wall?" he said dubiously, convinced we were nuts once we explained what we had in mind. After all, the living room already had ceiling-height bookcases, and the wall in question was very long indeed. Nobody had *that* many books. When we assured him we knew what we were doing, he reluctantly agreed, as if it were a bathroom he was remodeling and we'd instructed him to install three toilets, side by side. "As long as you won't get mad at me."

In a sense the carpenter had been right. We *had* badly misjudged—by underestimating what we needed. I'd forgotten that in addition to Barbara's and mine from the Waterville house there were all the books from my office at Colby College. We'd unpacked the books onto the new shelves hurriedly, almost helter-skelter, figuring that later we could rearrange them at our leisure and make sure Dickens and Trollope and Austen were comfortably rubbing spines and that Hammett and Chandler and James M. Cain and Ross Macdonald were in close enough proximity to swap soft-spoken, tough-guy lies after lights-out. Returning from Winslow after packing my mother's books, I collapsed, *Hotel du Lac* in hand, into a chair in the living room, too exhausted to do anything but stare at the wall of my own books, as well as the impressive pyramid of those that remained boxed and stacked right up to the ceiling in the corner. I counted these, trying to gauge how many additional bookcases would be required, where on the coast of Maine we'd find them, when there'd be time to look, and where we'd put them, but it had been a long day and I was far too tired to solve a problem with so many moving parts. I even was too worn out to roust myself from the chair and locate the shelf that contained the other Anita Brookners. Possibly they were still in one of those side boxes. Sitting there utterly drained, I wondered if maybe I was slipping into a funk of my own. Over the years I'd noticed that I was susceptible to my mother's moods, especially after spending a fair amount of time in her company. It was something I had to be careful of, because her periods of irrationality and dark depression had a tendency to infect both my writing and family life. I'd expected to feel better as soon as I got home, but instead, for some reason, I felt worse. Staring at all those books, shelved or not, I suddenly felt something akin to the anxiety—dread, really—that I knew my mother was prey to when her routines were in disarray.

One of her most cherished (and to my mind absurd) convictions had always been that she and I were essentially the same. If we didn't always see eye to eye, that was because I was twenty-five years younger; given time, I'd surely come around. Furthermore, at the heart of our most serious disagreements, she believed, was our fundamental similarity—our magnetic poles in effect repelling each other. I'd long imagined that she developed this ridiculous theory in order to explain to herself how she could have brought into the world a kid who couldn't have been more different from her if he'd been a foundling. But what if she was right? Was I really so different? In this respect her relationship to her own mother—a woman she considered conventional and moralistic and repressed—was illustrative. On the one hand there was no denying the two women agreed about virtually nothing, but there were some truly eerie temperamental similarities. One of my most vivid early memories of my grandmother had to do with her ongoing battles with milk. She preferred milk in bottles, but when home delivery ceased she had no choice but to switch to supermarket cartons, which she invariably tried to squeeze open at the wrong side, then attacked with a dull paring knife. Like my mother, once she embarked upon a particular course of action, however misguided, she was incapable of reversing it, and the consequences could be explosive, even bloody. Many times I'd found her in the kitchen, emitting a high, throaty moan, with a pool of milk dyed pink at her feet. When I asked what happened, she'd show me her punctured thumb or wrist and say, in the voice of a little girl, "I hurt me," as if the wound itself was the explanation I'd asked for.

In no time her ferocious, irrational attacks on these cartons became legend, the stuff of sidesplitting comedy when reenacted at family gatherings, but as a boy, though I couldn't have articulated why, they troubled me. That someone would remain so faithful to a misbegotten strategy made no sense to me, and like most children I wanted things to make sense, for the world to be a rational place. "Gram," I'd say, picking up the mutilated carton from the floor, "look." And then I'd squeeze at the correct end, which opened obligingly. I imagined I was showing her that the hurt and blood and mess were all unnecessary, but of course I had it exactly wrong. It was the mutilation of the carton and the wounding that were necessary. These satisfied some need I couldn't begin to fathom but that was, in any case, real.

Moreover, while I couldn't have explained this either, my grandmother's syntax, as well as the little-girl cadence she used only when she'd injured herself, creeped me out. She never said *I hurt myself* but rather *I hurt me,* as if *me* and *I* were different people entirely, and the one holding the paring knife had stabbed an innocent bystander. Showing me her angry gashes and puncture wounds, she always seemed to want sympathy and understanding, but these, though I loved her, I was never able to summon. It seemed to me that such irrational behavior needed to change, that warring with the milk cartons was simple lunacy. Perhaps in some remote sector of my kid's brain I'd also linked my otherwise sane grandmother's short-lived but recurring bouts of madness to whatever it was that possessed my mother from time to time. I'd be much older before I began to see the good talkings-to my mother was always giving herself as somehow related to my grandmother's "I hurt me"—both implying a divided or fractured self—but I might have sensed the correlation even then. Nor would the necessary inference have completely escaped me. If my mother was like my grandmother with her cartons, then she'd never truly learn. Like her own mother, she'd just keep hacking away and hurting herself in the process. Which, forty years later, seemed a pretty fair description of how things stood.

Still, did the fact that my mother was more like her mother than she cared to admit mean that I was more like mine than I cared to? Did the fact that I occasionally had more sympathy for and insight into my mother's behavior than, say, my wife, who was justifiably weary of it, suggest that I was like my mother, as she always so confidently claimed, or simply that I'd been observing her longer? The latter, surely. For compelling evidence I needed to look no farther than the book in my hand. I opened *Hotel du Lac* and read the first page:

> From the window all that could be seen was a receding area of grey. It was to be supposed that beyond the grey garden, which seemed to sprout nothing but the stiffish leaves of some unfamiliar plant, lay the vast grey lake, spreading like an anaesthetic towards the invisible further shore, and beyond that, in imagination only, yet verified by the brochure, the peak of the Dent d'Oche, on which snow might already be slightly and silently falling. For it was late September, out of season; the tourists had gone, the rates were reduced, and there were few inducements for visitors in this small town at the water's edge, whose inhabitants, uncommunicative to begin with, were frequently rendered taciturn by the dense cloud that descended for days at a time.

What in the world had possessed me to think my mother would enjoy a book that began like this? "Grey" was used three times in the first two sentences to describe the physical landscape, and my mother's interior landscape was gray already. Her purpose in reading was to flee that grayness into a brighter, more colorful world. She loved for books to take her to exciting new places, and she might well have enjoyed a novel set in a swank Swiss hotel on a lake, but she never would've wanted to go there out of season at reduced rates after all the interesting people had left. I'd taught the novel at Colby the year before, so its narrative details were still fresh in my mind. The protagonist was a middle-aged writer named Edith Hope, who, unlike Anita Brookner, wrote the kind of romance novels my mother might actually have liked to read. At the hotel Edith meets a man named Neville, who makes her an insulting proposal of marriage, not a love match but a union of convenience that will allow each of them societal "cover" as well as romantic freedom. Lest she reject the unflattering offer out of hand, Neville rather cruelly adds that given Edith's age and rather plain appearance (in her cardigan sweaters she resembles Virginia Woolf), she's unlikely to get a better one.

My Colby students, an otherwise pretty savvy bunch, had immediately identified Neville as the novel's villain, ignoring the more subtle, lifelong cruelty Edith had suffered at the hands of her mother and female friends, the very ones who'd packed her off to Switzerland after she fell in love and made a fool of herself back in London. My female students—all in their early twenties—were particularly unwilling to acknowledge the grim possibility that Neville's offer might in fact be the best Edith would ever get, and they were of one voice in proclaiming that she should reject his cynical proposal and wait for love. If their male classmates thought differently, they held their tongues, suggesting just how thorough the cultural training of the late Eighties had been for both genders.

That, I now recalled, was why I'd given the book to my mother in the first place, because she'd gotten her cultural training in an upstate New York mill town four decades earlier, and I was curious to see if she'd twig to what my female students had ignored. The results of this experiment had been both gratifying and dispiriting. My mother hadn't really enjoyed the book and certainly didn't want to read any more Brookner, but just as I suspected the novel's theme of women's cruelty to women had resonated deeply, and her identification with poor Edith Hope, while not wholehearted, had been sufficient to initiate one of her diatribes against her own mother and sister, who had done their level best, she reminded me, to undermine her at every turn and might ultimately have succeeded in destroying her self-confidence if she hadn't escaped Gloversville when she did. The choice Edith had to make didn't particularly interest her. The solution—as my mother saw it—was to return next year, in season, with a better wardrobe, so she'd likely meet a better class of man. She saw Neville as less of a villain than a nonentity.

All of which was, though I hadn't foreseen it, an entirely predictable response. In truth my mother had always been suspicious of women. If there were two lines at the bank or the post office, she'd invariably queue up in the man's, even if the woman's was shorter. The more important the circumstance—to purchase a money order, say, or pay a bill—the more determined she was to wait. If a new window opened and she was asked by a female clerk if she could be of service, my mother would smile and say, "Thank you, but I'll just wait for the man," as if this were perfectly reasonable, as if hers was the well-established and undeniable preference of both genders. Of course in those days the man *was* more likely to be senior, but it wasn't that so much as the fact that my mother always did better dealing with men. She was attractive, and men often fell all over themselves trying to help her out. If she made a mistake in filling out a form, they'd produce a new one and correct the error themselves, where a woman might've sent her away with fine-print instructions.

But it went deeper than that. The whole time I was growing up, I never knew my mother to have a female friend. There was one woman, a coworker at GE, whom she was close to for a time, until they had a falling-out over what my mother claimed was a betrayal—the other woman getting a promotion my mother had assumed would be hers. This was a pattern that would repeat itself again and again over the next several decades. She'd meet a woman her age, usually at a new job, and they'd discover they had interests in common; a tentative friendship would develop, one that seemed destined to evolve into emotional intimacy, but then something bad would happen. Whether it was friction on the job, or that they'd become interested in the same man, things always ended with my mother feeling backstabbed. She must've been as frequently disappointed by men as she was by women, but she treated these as individual, indeed isolated, cases. Often, when she looked back on a failed romantic relationship, she blamed herself, admitting that all the signs had been there and she'd just been too blind, too taken in, to see through his charm, whereas when a woman disappointed her, all women were to blame, and her resolution not to waste her time on female friendships grew much stronger. That was why I was reluctant for her to so easily surrender her friendship with Dot, her Winslow friend. Their camaraderie had lasted quite a while, and I'd begun to wonder if the relationship's longevity might represent a breakthrough.

But perhaps not. As her reaction to *Hotel du Lac* had demonstrated, her distrust of women was deep-seated. While she must have realized that Brookner, at least thematically, was a potential soul mate, that didn't matter. Though she'd understood the novel far better than anyone in my class, she'd disliked it every bit as much, if for the exact opposite reason. Because it had challenged a received feminist truth about female solidarity, my students had concluded that Brookner was lying to them about the world. Whereas my mother disliked the book precisely because she was being told the truth. That wasn't what she read fiction for.

Indeed, the books I'd spent the afternoon packing—so varied in genre, including historical romances, detective novels, romantic thrillers, travel books—had in common a reassuring conventionality that couldn't entirely be accounted for by the decades, the Thirties through the early Sixties, during which most of them had been written. My mother's large collection of murder mysteries was particularly instructive. She much preferred the English variety, with its emphasis on the restoration of order. In books by her favorite "Golden Age" British mystery writers—Josephine Tey, Margery Allingham, Dorothy Sayers, Ngaio Marsh, John Dickson Carr, and Agatha Christie—evil might lurk around every foggy corner, and murder most foul would throw everything into temporary flux, but in the end the detective, often a rogue aristocrat like Lord Peter Wimsey or Roderick Alleyn, ferreted out the culprit in a stunning display of logic, intuition and, often, an understanding of complex social realities for which aristocrats, in novels like these if nowhere else, are famous.

American murder mysteries left her cold. She thought they were less clever, which was true enough; Raymond Chandler famously couldn't follow his own plots. But they also operated on an entirely different set of premises. Here detectives didn't solve crimes by means of brilliant deductions or arcane knowledge. In American detective novels the hero's primary virtues are his honesty and his ability to take a punch. Sam Spade hasn't much interest in restoring order because, as he knows all too well, that order was corrupt to begin with. Villains are typically either rich men who made their money dishonestly or, worse yet, people of limited moral imagination who aspire only to what money and power can buy, who want to move up in class and don't care how. In this noir world, cops are on the take, lawyers and judges all have a price, as do doctors and newspapermen. In a sea of corruption your only hope is a lone man, someone *you* can hire but who can't be bought off by anybody who has more money. There probably is no figure in literature more romantic than Philip Marlowe, whose very name suggests knight-errantry, and my mother was herself a romantic of the first order, but she had no more use for Marlowe than she had for Anita Brookner. Men like Marlowe always ended up telling her what she didn't want to hear. Okay, he might find your missing child or husband, but often you'd end up wishing he hadn't, because he'd also find out something you didn't want to know about that child or husband or even yourself, something you'd been trying hard not to look at, or admit to. What kind of escape was that? Better to get good news from a fop like Lord Peter, whose sell-by date in the real world would have long since expired, had anyone like him ever existed in the first place.

The historical novels my mother favored were similarly revealing. They featured a brave, stalwart heroine who invariably would prove herself worthy of the dashing fellow she'd fallen in love with, often by testing her mettle in his world. If she fell in love with a pirate, she might for a time become a pirate herself. Their freedom from social mores, however, was understood to be a phase, like adolescence, and their adventures always culminated in marriage, an institution that would tame the heroine's wilder impulses and make the hero a responsible citizen. To facilitate these matters, the former rogue would be discovered to be actually an aristocrat who'd been cheated out of his estate, which in the final chapter is restored to him. It was a complicated fantasy, one that allowed my mother to think of herself as a rebel while actually being, in her heart of hearts, a conformist. Though she claimed not to be a prude, she preferred sex not to be explicit but rather relegated to the space breaks or implied by the coy nicknames ("my sugar wench") given the heroine by her paramour. Reality, especially of the grim sort, should at all costs be kept at bay, regardless of the genre. She claimed to love anything about Ireland or England or Spain, but in fact she needed books in these settings to be warm and comfy, more like Maeve Binchy than William Trevor. Not surprisingly, given that she'd felt trapped most of her life, she loved books about time travel, but only if the places the characters traveled to were ones she was interested in. She had exactly no interest in the future or in any past that didn't involve romantic adventure.

Still, illuminating though literary taste can be, the more I thought about it, neither my mother's library nor my own meant quite what I wanted it to. If my books were more serious and literary than hers, that was due more to nurture than nature. If I didn't read much escapist fiction, it was because I lived a blessed life from which I neither needed nor desired to escape. I wasn't a superior person, just an educated one, and for that in large measure I had my mother to thank. Maybe she'd tried to talk me out of becoming a writer, but she was more responsible than anyone for my being one. Back when we lived on Helwig Street, at the end of her long workdays at GE, after making her scant supper and cleaning up, after doing the laundry (without benefit of a washing machine) and ironing, after making sure

I was set for school the next day, she might've collapsed in front of the television, but she didn't. She read. Every night. Her taste, unformed as mine would later be by a score of literature professors, was equally dogmatic; she read her Daphne du Mauriers and Mary Stewarts until their covers fell off and had to be replaced. It was from my mother that I learned reading was not a duty but a reward, and from her that I intuited a vital truth: most people are trapped in a solitary existence, a life circumscribed by want and failures of imagination, limitations from which readers are exempt. You can't make a writer without first making a reader, and that's what my mother made me. Moreover, though I'd outgrown her books, they had a hand in shaping the kind of writer I'd eventually become—one who, unlike many university-trained writers, didn't consider *plot* a dirty word, who paid attention to audience and pacing, who had little tolerance for literary pretension.

No, in order to make the case that my mother and I weren't two peas in a genetic pod, I needed to identify something in my basic nature, some habit of mind or innate ability that I'd always possessed, traceable all the way back to who I'd been on Helwig Street, not who I'd become in the meantime. Was it possible I was literally staring at it? Could it be that our bookshelves—not the books themselves or what was in them but rather their current haphazard arrangement—provided the answer to why my mother and I were forever at loggerheads? Two weeks earlier, Barbara and I had hastily thrown onto the shelves as many books as would fit, then moved on to more pressing tasks. Indeed, since moving to Camden, we'd been in what I thought of as "this now, that later" mode. With dozens of tasks to complete each day (with everything, to borrow my mother's word, *unsettled*), they all were constantly being prioritized and reprioritized. *This now, that later* mode was all about making sound decisions on the fly about what had to be attended to now and what could wait. Logic and reason were important, but often you had to go on intuition and feel. What you saw in your peripheral vision could be as important as what you were looking at directly. On the basis of incomplete data, you had to make educated guesses and try to see three or four moves in advance, to anticipate the Law of Unintended Consequences before it kicked in. Just as vital, you had to accept that you were going to make mistakes from time to time. When you messed up, it was important not to mind and even more important to promptly reverse course. You also had to understand that at any given moment there were decisions you simply couldn't make yet and have faith that given time some problems would resolve themselves. What we were engaged in was a kind of domestic triage, and I'd always been pretty good at that, God only knew why, because this was something completely left out of my mother. I hadn't forgotten how, back in Phoenix, I'd had to reorder her daily to-do lists so they made at least a little sense and we didn't waste time retracing our steps. At eighteen I was already cringing at her due-south instincts and her inability, once she'd begun a task, to abandon it for a more important one. She couldn't possibly have lived with the chaos of our bookshelves for two days, much less two weeks. Even as a young man I could see how much her faulty decision making was costing her, that because of her inflexible adherence to poor sequencing she was forever discovering, too late, that her ship, which could easily have been turned around while out at sea, now had to be rotated in the cramped harbor.

It now occurred to me that I'd been trying to resequence my mother's to-do lists ever since, with decidedly mixed results. Sometimes she'd grasp my organizing principle and say, "Oh, aren't you clever!" But more often she'd insist on doing things her own way and become monumentally annoyed when I pointed out that *B* really had to follow *A,* that getting *A* right was the key to both *B* and *C,* that *A* was the necessary foundation upon which the remaining alphabet would rest. To this she'd respond that different people saw things differently, and that to her, *B* was more important than *A*. Worse, she was always so proud of her tortured logic. She loved to explicate, detail by wobbly detail, how she'd arrived at her dubious conclusions. She wasn't unlike the detectives in her locked-room mysteries, who would reveal in the final excruciating chapter how the villainous deed was done, that the murderer was legless, which was why, once he'd removed his prostheses, no one had observed him running away on his stumps on the far side of the shoulder-high hedge. Leaving the reader to say, "I'm sorry, *what?*"

When I was eighteen and my mother in her forties, our disagreements over process were seldom serious. She liked to say there was more than one way to skin a cat and that when I got to be her age I'd have odd habits, too. But over the years, as I became increasingly responsible for the outcomes of her insistence on doing things out of their natural and practical order, together with my growing impatience with her interminable, brain-scalding explanations, there were more serious disputes. At times, rather than argue, I'd just throw up my hands. "Do what you want," I'd tell her, halfway out the door. "Let me know how it turns out." And sometimes, the phone would ring an hour later, and she'd say, "*Now* I see what you meant." But just as often her voice would be triumphant, once she'd somehow succeeded in forcing the square peg into the round hole with a mallet and now was eager to explain the brilliance of her violent solution. This, then, was surely what I was looking for: the hardwired difference, probably genetic in origin, between my mother and me, the root of our ongoing conflict and the reason that I was seldom able, as she put it, "to take her side."

Except this didn't really wash either. For one thing, while it might be true that I was good at domestic triage and she sucked at it, a more significant truth was that my mother and grandmother weren't the only ones who wouldn't stop flying in the face of reason. It would've been nice to see myself as Sisyphus and my current exhaustion as existential, the result of three-plus decades of attempting to correctly sequence my mother's metaphorical to-do lists without her permission or assistance. But in fact I was worn out from dealing with the consequences of what I myself had set in motion back in the spring when I stubbornly ignored Barbara's *or*. Because surely some part of me had known it was folly to plant that FOR SALE sign in front of our Waterville home and even worse folly to imagine I could put my mother and her needs on the back burner for however long it took for us to get settled.

More specifically, the time had come to admit that none of my plan was working out. Since moving to Camden, we'd become a literally divided family. The girls' bedrooms were on the second floor of the main house; Barb and I occupied the apartment over the garage, so we were often not aware of their comings and goings. We'd planned on using money from the sale of the Waterville property to convert the upstairs apartment into our master bedroom suite, but it hadn't even been shown in more than a month, which meant we might be exiled from our house-in-progress for the foreseeable future while carrying *two* mortgages. In another six weeks Emily's college tuition would come due, as would Kate's to her new prep school. The upscale assisted-living apartment we'd eventually found for my mother would cost almost as much as a third tuition. We were keeping the rent a secret from her, but she was bound to find out soon. Barbara, having quit her job at Colby, was looking for work on the coast and not finding any, and my West Coast film agent was looking for screen projects for me and not finding any, and at long last it was becoming clear that the back-end money I'd been hoping for from the *Nobody's Fool* movie wasn't going to materialize for the simple reason that there wasn't any, at least not for writers, and only a fool would have believed otherwise. As if all this weren't enough, I was still a good year from delivering (and getting paid for) my next novel. The problem wasn't sequencing but rather my unwillingness to admit I'd been wrong. After realizing how the Camden house could be made to work for us and then imagining us in it, I'd become not only determined to see it through but also blind to reason. While there'd been numerous opportunities to turn this ship around, I'd stubbornly held to our dubious course, expertly navigating us into Camden's tiny, expensive harbor, where we were now trapped.

All of which was beginning to feel like a cosmic I-told-you-so. My mother's deep conviction had always been that she and I were cut from the same cloth. From the time I was a boy, whenever we disagreed, she'd tell me that later on, when I was her age, I'd think as she did, an assertion that never failed to infuriate me, suggesting as it did that I wasn't her offspring but her clone, and over the years nothing gave me more pleasure than to reflect on how wrong she was, that I most assuredly didn't think like she did, and that time had only widened this gap, not narrowed it. What I hadn't realized was that in addition to being dead wrong, she was also profoundly right, or would have been if her claim had been articulated just a little differently. She said I'd one day *think* as she did; what she probably meant was that one day I'd *be* like her—obsessive, dogged, and rigid.

How could I have failed to see in myself the very traits I'd so confidently assigned to her? The evidence was everywhere. Take, for instance, my freshman year at the university, when I'd become addicted to, of all things, pinball. For several months a particular machine in the basement of the student center took total possession of my mind. It had begun innocently enough. One evening, after dinner at the cafeteria, I'd visited the game room with some friends and wasted a couple of quarters, which back then got you three plays. The next night, though, I'd returned without my friends, and the night after that. Very quickly I began thinking of this machine as mine and during dinner would become panicky at the thought of somebody getting on it before I could. Once I'd claimed the machine, if I had a run of bad luck that necessitated my leaving it to get more quarters, and some other sallow, pathetic nerd was at its controls when I returned, I'd have to swallow a black, homicidal fury. In a matter of days there was simply no life outside the game room. I went to class, of course, but even there, as my professors spoke, I could hear my machine's distinctive clangs and clanks on the other side of campus, its score hurtling upward, registering bonus points from the bumpers and targets that were hardest to hit, then the lovely, sweet thunk of free games popping up in its tiny window, a sound that caused the other wretched denizens of the game room to suspend their own activities and crowd around. Soon, to ensure I'd have enough quarters to play for a couple of hours, I started selling my evening meal ticket, telling myself I wasn't hungry anyway, and playing late into the evening when I should have been studying, stopping only when my luck and skill ran out. Worse, since I always told my roommates I was going to the library, they regarded my late nights and my pale, drained appearance when I finally returned to the dorm as evidence of a virtuous dedication they themselves lacked. There were girls from my classes I wanted to ask out, but whatever money I set aside for the weekend would be gone by midweek. I lost weight, becoming as wraithlike as Gollum with his "Precious." For months that inexplicable and humiliating madness held me in its grip until one evening, on my very first quarter, I entered some kind of zone, winning so many free games that the thought of actually playing them made me ill. Suddenly both sated and sane, I simply walked away and never went back.

A couple years later, though, in graduate school, I was seized by my father's particular mania and found myself on a shuttle between the grungy dog track in South Tucson and any nickel-and-dime poker table I could find. The track was particularly depressing, a magnet for the city's poorest and most desperate souls. Friday nights were the worst because you could tell at a glance that some of the men had come directly from work, that instead of going home, they'd cashed their paychecks at the track and were betting the week's grocery money. I recognized them—the way they studied the racing form so furtively, their darting eyes mining the abstruse data for tips; they were Gloversville men, somehow magically transported to the desert, and here I was among them again. Being a literature student, I was of course susceptible to metaphor, and when the mechanical rabbit made the turn in front of the starting gate and the foolish greyhounds bolted after it, I remember wondering if I was the only one in the park who understood its terrible significance, and if that made me any smarter or dumber than these guys with low-wage, dead-end jobs. Poker? Well, betting nickels, dimes, and quarters you couldn't get hurt too bad. That's what I told myself, but you be the judge.

Even more horrifying than such ugly, stupid obsessions

was the fact that I couldn't even take credit for triumphing over them. The day I sold blood to buy my way into a poker game, I hadn't looked at myself in the mirror and said, *Enough*. Nor, to borrow my mother's phrase, had I given myself a good talking-to. That would have been pointless. I knew myself well enough to know I wasn't listening. No, I'd simply bided my time and waited for the current madness to run its course, after which it would likely be replaced by some new, as-yet-unimagined idiocy, no doubt every bit as humiliating and self-destructive as the last. Or perhaps worse. This was what really terrified me. If I could be seduced by a pinball machine, by the tacky allure of a dog track, what would I do if I was offered a real temptation? What if my next obsession took the form of a woman? Would I give myself a good talking-to then, reminding myself that I loved my wife, that I'd been preparing for a life of the mind, that I wanted to be a good man? Or would I become a character out of a Jim Thompson novel, pathetic and helpless in the grip of something strong and merciless and utterly relentless? It was possible.

The Camden house was empty and still. My daughters had taken summer jobs at a popular waterfront restaurant, and Barbara was off somewhere. I'd been looking forward to seeing them when I got home, a distraction from the guilt and fear and dread that had gnawed at me as I'd driven home from Winslow, to our chaotic, jumbled library, with its boxes waiting to be unpacked. But for some reason I now felt like unfit company and was grateful to be alone. Unless I was mistaken, something inside my mother had finally broken, and it was my fault. I thought about calling her and apologizing for everything, especially for asking her to do something I knew she was incapable of: to be patient for an unspecified period of time, to live with every last thing up in the air. But then I remembered that she was going out to dinner with Dot.

Across the room, on a high shelf, were copies of books I'd written and literary periodicals where I'd published stories and essays and reviews. Rising at last, I walked over and ran my fingers along their spines, smiling not so much with pleasure at the achievement as with the realization of its source. The biggest difference between my mother and me, I now saw clearly, had less to do with either nature or nurture than with blind dumb luck, the third and often lethal rail of human destiny. My next obsession might well have been a woman, or a narcotic, or a bottle of tequila. Instead I'd stumbled on storytelling and become infected. Halfway through my doctoral dissertation, I'd nearly quit so I could write full-time. Not because I imagined I was particularly gifted or that one day I'd be able to earn a living. I simply had to. It was the game room and the dog track all over again. An unreasoning fit of *must*. That, no doubt, was what my mother had recognized and abhorred, what had caused her to remind me about my responsibilities as a husband and father.

It didn't take long for me to learn that novel writing was a line of work that suited my temperament and played to my strengths, such as they were. Because—and don't let anybody tell you different—novel writing is mostly triage (*this now, that later*) and obstinacy. Feeling your way around in the dark, trying to anticipate the Law of Unintended Consequences. Living with and welcoming uncertainty. Trying something, and when that doesn't work, trying something else. Welcoming clutter. Surrendering a good idea for a better one. Knowing you won't find the finish line for a year or two, or five, or maybe never, without caring much. Putting one foot in front of the other. Taking small bites, chewing thoroughly. Grinding it out. Knowing that when you've finally settled everything that can be, you'll immediately seek out more chaos. Rinse and repeat. Somehow, without ever intending to, I'd discovered how to turn obsession and what my grandmother used to call sheer cussedness—character traits that had dogged both my parents, causing them no end of difficulty—to my advantage. The same qualities that over a lifetime had contracted my mother's world had somehow expanded mine. How and by what mechanism? Dumb luck? Grace? I honestly have no idea. Call it whatever you want—except virtue.

Real Time

WHEN SHE OPENED the door, I took an involuntary
step back at the sight. Her hair wild, her eyes wide and
frantic, she was still in her nightgown, the madwoman in the
attic, straight out of *Jane Eyre*. She grabbed my arm, pulling me
inside. "What time is it?"

Eight forty-five, I told her. I'd arrived, as I always did, at the
appointed moment. Being late, even by a minute or two, was
always a mistake. When I knocked, she'd often open the door
before my hand could fall to my side; in winter she'd already
have her coat on, her purse over her arm. "I saw you from the
kitchen window when you pulled in," she'd say, as if waiting at
the window was less nutty than waiting at the door. So what on
earth was this? Had she overslept? Given how lethargic she'd
been lately, it was possible.

But she wasn't lethargic now. Indeed, when I told her the

time, she flew across the room with alarming haste, especially given her claim that her legs always locked up whenever she had to hurry. On the pad of paper she kept next to her telephone, she scrawled *8:45* and, underneath that, *REAL TIME*. Then she stared at the pad, as if expecting the words or numbers to change before her eyes.

"Mom," I said. "Why did you write down the time?"

"So I'll know," she said, still studying what she'd just scribbled.

"Know what?"

"The time. Later, I'll want to know."

"But it won't be eight forty-five anymore."

When she stared at me blankly, I decided to try a different tack. "Mom, did you forget about the doctor?" We were due at his office in half an hour.

Abject terror now. "Did we miss the appointment?"

"No, there's plenty of time. But you need to get dressed."

"I can't."

"Why not?"

"I haven't showered. I didn't know what time it was."

"You can shower when you get home."

She blinked at me in incomprehension, then gazed aimlessly around her new apartment. Was *this* home?

"Do you think you can get dressed?" She followed me into the bedroom, where the clothes she'd planned to wear were hanging on the inside doorknob. I pointed out her dresser, where the day before she and Barbara had arranged her undergarments in the top drawers.

She sat down on the bed. "I need to think." She picked up her alarm clock and peered at it. For some reason it said 3:17.

"You need to get dressed, Mom. So we can go to the doctor."

Terror again. "Did we miss the appointment?"

"Just get dressed, okay?"

In the living room I called home, catching Barbara just as she was about to leave the house to run an errand. "I need you," I told her. "Right away, actually."

"What's wrong?"

"I wish I knew. Maybe another TIA." Somehow I didn't think so, though. Her ministrokes always left my mother exhausted, one side of her face tingling, her speech for a time impaired. But she always knew what they were and what had just happened to her. This was something new. Except for the fact that she wasn't making any sense, her speech seemed fine. "She's disoriented. Confused."

It would take Barbara twenty minutes to get here. I called the doctor's office to say we'd be a few minutes late. Setting the receiver back in its cradle, I noticed that the clock on the lamp table said 11:22. The one on top of the TV said 7:03; the one on the stove, 1:54. All these clocks had been set correctly the day before. "How you coming, Mom?" I called.

No answer.

The bedroom door was open. "Mom?" I said.

She was sitting on the bed, still in her nightgown, her back to me. Morning light was filtering in through the curtain, but the room was dark. In her hands was her favorite clock, the gold-plated one I'd bought her for Christmas years ago. At first I thought she was winding it, and started to tell her that while time was of the essence, the clock, ironically, wasn't. She wasn't winding it, though, just making the hands go around, minutes and then whole hours, passing in a few seconds.

I sat down next to her. "Mom," I said. "What's wrong? Can you tell me?"

"Why do the hands go this way?" she said.

When it was clear I didn't understand, she made the universal motion indicating clockwise. What she wanted me to explain was why the hands wouldn't go in the opposite direction. Still anxious that I understand, she demonstrated by twisting the stem counterclockwise, grunting with the effort.

"You're going to break it," I told her. "See, you've already bent the stem."

This didn't interest her. The mystery she was trying to fathom ran much deeper than that.

AMAZINGLY, EVERYTHING HAD gone off without a hitch. The movers had arrived in Winslow when they were supposed to and immediately went to work. I fully expected my mother to renege on our agreement and demand to stay behind and ramrod the whole job, but instead she got in the car with Barbara and off they went to Camden, leaving me to inventory her possessions as they were carried out the door. "This lady moves a lot," one of the men remarked. He had her dinette upside down on the floor (which, had my mother been there, would have elicited cries of *Oooh! Oooh! You're scratching it!*) and was unscrewing its legs. The table's underside sported several stickers in different colors applied from previous moves.

At one point Dot stopped by, and I learned they hadn't gone out to dinner after all, that my mother had phoned to say she was too tired. "I've never seen anybody so worked up," Dot said.

"It's like this with every move," I told her.

"I don't know if it's the move or the idea of a new doctor," Dot said.

Which was true, of course. Changing doctors always weighed heavily on my mother, because she had a good dozen prescriptions that would need to be filled; high on her list of anxieties was whether the new drugstore and the new doctor communicated effectively, otherwise giving her the wrong meds or leaving her totally without. A new doctor also meant unwelcome questions, about her unhealthy eating habits and lack of exercise and all manner of things she considered nobody else's business. It had taken her a long time, but she'd managed to train her Waterville doctor to accept what she told him as true and to write the scripts she believed she needed, including, for the past few years, Paxil, about which I was beginning to hear disturbing stories. The new doctor might express misgivings about the efficacy of all this.

"She says she's exhausted from having so much to do," Dot continued, "but when I ask her what I can help with, there doesn't seem to be anything."

"You can't help her worry."

"I also said I hoped we'd be able to keep in touch. Camden's not so far, but I got the impression she's not interested."

"Maybe after she's settled," I said hopefully, though I was pretty sure their friendship was over. My mother hated all maybes, ifs, and whens, preferring to resolve things badly than leave them up in the air with a good outcome a mere possibility. "Thanks for being such a good friend."

"I'll miss her," Dot said. Then she added, almost apologetically, "I really like your mom, it's just a shame she's so . . ." She struggled to find the right word but finally gave up. Either that or the word *impossible* suggested itself, and she was too kind to use it. "Maybe that's why I like her. Being your own worst enemy is something I understand."

Later, back on the coast and armed with my diagram of the new apartment, I told the movers where to put the furniture and stack the boxes of books. "Wow," said the guy who'd mentioned how often my mother moved, taking the place in. "I wouldn't mind living here myself."

I stifled the urge to tell him to check back in a few months when this very apartment would probably be available. Because my mother was clearly going to hate it here. We'd looked everywhere, coming up against the exact same obstacles that had plagued us inland. She preferred not to live among old people, because all they ever talked about was their illnesses and their new meds and which of their daughters was ignoring them this week and which would be visiting next. She wanted someplace lively, like where she'd first lived in Phoenix. She wanted to feel alive, and for that you needed young people. With young people, however, came music and noise and children, and she wanted none of that. She couldn't have anyone living over-head. Underfoot would be okay, except that she couldn't man-age stairs, which pretty much ruled that out. She preferred apartment complexes but hated subsidized places, because the law didn't allow them to discriminate, and you might end up living next door to some Section 8 nutjob. Unsubsidized places she couldn't afford, and she didn't want us making up the dif-ference, especially if it was considerable. And we knew from experience that whatever she settled on had to be within half an hour from Camden. Nothing we'd seen was suitable and, to complete the Woody Allen joke, they all had long waiting lists.

The place I thought would be best for her, Megunticook House, was actually in Camden. The rents were subsidized, and she clearly qualified. The residents were all elderly, and the complex provided no services, so by and large they weren't terribly infirm. The apartments themselves were nice, the grounds clean and neat, but when we pulled in she took one look and said, "Oh, Rick . . . really, I don't think so, do you?"

"Could we look, at least?"

She grudgingly agreed, but it was clearly a no-go. "Shabby," she explained later, when we were back in the car. "Did you see how run-down the whole place was? And did you see all the walkers there in the foyer? People who need those should keep them in their rooms. Didn't you notice how the paint was peeling outside?"

I explained that we were now on the coast and the complex

was a quarter mile from the ocean, with harsh winters and salt air, well, paint peeled.

"I couldn't live there," she said. "The other place was better."

By this she meant Woodland Hills, an assisted-living facility in Rockland, twenty minutes away. Its long drive and carefully manicured grounds made it resemble a country club, but this, too, had put her off. "I don't need anything *this* posh," she said. Inside, the corridors were wide enough that two wheelchairs could pass each other going in opposite directions, and handrails were affixed to all the walls. There were endless activities—from wheelchair aerobics to computer classes—and she wasn't interested in any of them. "I'm used to living independently," she explained to the lady who showed us around. She naturally didn't care about the van that took residents to the supermarket and doctors' offices: "My son does all that." The meals were served in a large dining room, though the schedule instantly offended her. "Who eats their main meal at noon?" she said once we were back in the car.

"Well . . . ," I began.

"Assisted living, my foot," she said. "That's a nursing home. There wasn't anyone there who walked without a cane."

"The apartment itself was nice," I pointed out for the sake of argument. "Light and airy." Better yet, she'd run her index finger over the surface of the stove, and I could tell it had come away clean. "Plus there's no waiting list."

"Let's keep looking," she said.

And so we had, until there was nothing left to look at.

MARK, MY MOTHER'S NEW DOCTOR, was less than half her age. Having recently taken on Barbara and me and the girls, he'd agreed to see her as well. He was new in town but already had a reputation as an excellent diagnostician. His manner was no nonsense to the point of being brusque, so I was surprised when he tenderly took my mother's hand. "Okay, Jean," he said, "I'm going to give you four words and ask you to remember them. Then we're going to chat for a while, and then I'm going to ask you to tell me what the four words were. Do you understand?"

My mother nodded, before glancing over at me for confirmation, as if her understanding were an issue I could speak to.

"Here are the four words: *bird, window, car, book*."

Good, I thought. She'll get *book*, at least.

Barbara had somehow managed to get her dressed, and we'd only been half an hour late. I'd quietly informed the admitting nurse of the basics, that this was supposed to be a get-acquainted appointment but that my mother had been disoriented when I arrived to pick her up, that for some reason she was obsessing about clocks and time, and that I'd never seen her like this before. We were now—Barbara and the doctor and my mother and me—in one of his small consulting rooms.

"How are you feeling today?" the doctor asked her.

She turned to me. "What time is it?"

I told her (three minutes later than the last time she asked, just before we left the waiting room).

"Jean. Can you look at me?"

Good, I thought again. A strong male voice. She responds well to those. My own the obvious exception.

"How are you feeling?"

"I'm a little worried," she confessed.

"About what?"

"The time."

"Why are you worried about the time?"

"I have a very important doctor's appointment."

"You're at your appointment now. I'm your doctor. You don't have to worry about that anymore, okay?"

My mother looked greatly relieved to learn it and smiled over at me.

"Do you know what time of year it is?"

She thought about it, then admitted she wasn't sure.

"Can you tell me where you live?"

She again looked over at me. "Woodland Hills," I told him, immediately flushing, because of course he didn't care where she lived. He just wanted to know if she knew. "She just moved in," I explained.

"And who's the president?"

She smiled. Here was an answer she knew. She started to answer, then suddenly couldn't remember. She turned to me. After all, I'd supplied the last answer, so maybe I knew this, too. "Oh," she said, nudging me, "*you* know."

I tried to send her a telepathic message. *George W. Bush. You hate the little twerp. You're hoping to live long enough to see him indicted for crimes against humanity. Remember?*

But she didn't. She remembered neither the man nor how much she loathed him. My heart sank then, because the look on her face suggested in addition to being stumped by the question, she was beginning to grasp that something was terribly wrong. Or maybe she was just mimicking the look on my own face.

"How about those words?" the doctor asked. "Can you tell me what the four words were?"

My mother shook her head and then let it hang, completely out of answers.

WHEN HE FINISHED his examination, Mark took me aside. "Your mother is suffering from dementia," he said.

I nodded, not terribly surprised, given what had transpired in the consulting room. Still, something seemed wrong. "But why?"

"We don't know the cause, exactly, but it's not unusual in people your mother's age."

"Yeah," I said, "but overnight?"

"The onset of symptoms can appear rapid."

Something about his use of *appear* made me wonder if we were talking at cross-purposes. "Yesterday, she was fine."

At this he knitted his brow, clearly dubious.

"She's been very anxious about the move. She's been having TIAs over the last couple years. Is it possible she had one during the night?"

"Where was she living before Woodland Hills?"

"She had an apartment in Winslow."

He looked like I'd just given him a stiff left jab. "An apartment."

"Yes."

"Are you telling me that your mother's been living alone?"

"Yes. The only reason she's in Woodland is that they had a vacancy."

"Yesterday she could have remembered all four words? She'd have known who the president was?"

"Absolutely. She'd have shared her opinion of him, which is low. And she certainly wouldn't have forgotten the word *book*." When he still appeared doubtful, I added, "She's been living independently," realizing as soon as I said it that she would've been thrilled by this representation.

"She isn't normally confused?"

This question was more difficult. "She likes to rearrange facts," I admitted. "She prefers her own version of things. But nothing like what you saw in there."

"Tell me about her medications."

I did, at least the ones I could remember—for high blood pressure, the thyroid, the anxiety, the acid reflux, the arthritis, a couple other things.

"Let me do some research," he told me. "If she's been upset about the move, it's possible the veil will lift. Can you bring her home with you for a few days?"

I thought of Barbara, who'd bear the brunt of this—the dressing and undressing and bathing. And I thought of what it would look like if I said no.

Noting my reluctance, he said, "She really shouldn't be left alone in this condition."

"Of course not," I said as we emerged into the outer office, where Barbara and my mother were waiting. My wife had heard the last part, and our eyes met. "I'm just not sure we can handle her."

"It doesn't look like she'll be much trouble," he said, and I really couldn't blame him for not understanding. My mother had been docile as a lamb during the examination, and she weighed all of ninety pounds. What the hell kind of son would hesitate to take his *mother,* a sick and confused and lost old woman, into his home for a few days? Of course, I wasn't worried about my mother in her present condition, but of what might occur if, as he put it, the veil lifted.

"How about you bring her back tomorrow," he suggested, "and we'll see how things are progressing?"

I took a deep breath. "Okay," I said. "Sure."

ON THE RIDE BACK to Camden she continued to ask what time it was every few minutes, apparently still worried about missing the doctor's appointment that was now safely consigned to the past. At home we installed her in the guest room with all the books, but nothing in the real, physical world seemed to interest her but the gold-plated clock, which she refused to set down. She continued to spin the hands round and around, as if she feared time itself would stop if she quit.

Hoping to distract her, we turned on the TV in the family room and found an old movie we thought might interest her. It was only a matter of, well, time before she broke her clock, so I suggested we put it on top of the television where she could see it from the sofa. She reluctantly agreed, but then sat there staring at it as if the movie weren't playing. Every time I got up to answer the phone or get something from the kitchen, she'd have the clock in her lap again by the time I returned, still fast-forwarding its hands. Emily, our older daughter, was working the lunch shift and missing all this, but at one point I went into the living room and found her sister, Kate, sobbing in front of the fireplace. "It's just so terrible" was all she could say. Midafternoon, Emily called to say she'd been asked to stay on for the evening shift as well, and I encouraged her to. After all, there was nothing she could do, and seeing her grandmother in her present state would have torn her up. Kate went to work that evening herself, which left Barbara and me alone with my mother, whose interest continued to be strictly chronographic.

Instead of lifting, the veil that had lowered over her rationality seemed to descend even further. As the hours passed she became increasingly anxious, though she couldn't explain why. We tried to get her to eat something, but that would have involved putting down her clock. By early evening it was becoming apparent that bringing her home had been a mistake. I called the doctor's office, which by then was closed, and left a message with Mark's service. When he returned the call half an hour later, I described our dilemma. Far from calming down, my mother was becoming more and more agitated. She was still obsessing about time and trying to understand how it worked and how to make it stay put or, better yet, reverse course. What worried us the most was what might happen that night. Barbara and I couldn't sleep in our apartment over the garage—that was too far away. We'd either have to take turns outside her bedroom door or risk finding my mother out walking the streets of Camden in her nightgown. This last fear seemed to convince him. "Do you think you can get her to come to the emergency room?"

Normally, getting my mother to do anything she was disinclined to would have been a struggle, but not now. I'd simply ask to see her clock, then tell her I'd give it back to her as soon as we were in the car. She'd follow that clock anywhere.

"THE *FIRST* THING I'm going to do," my mother announced from the backseat, "is get a new doctor."

We weren't even out of the hospital parking lot when she dropped this bombshell. Clearly she'd been saving it for some time and was anxious to see just how large a crater its impact would create. After four days in the hospital things had returned to the old normal, her new obsession and recent lethargy now past. Concerned about the number of medications she was taking and their possible negative interactions, and needing to establish some sort of baseline, Mark took her off everything but her blood pressure pills. When her blood work came back, it revealed a massive sodium imbalance, caused in large part by the heavily salted, overly processed frozen foods that represented her entire diet. It was also possible that her worries about moving yet again had gotten the upper hand, and she'd been overmedicating. At any rate, within hours her rationality began to return—along with a tremendous fury. For the hospital staff it was unnerving to see an almost-eighty-year-old woman "wake up" from her sleepy doldrums so monumentally pissed off.

For my mother, of course, being rational didn't guarantee that she'd now arrive at valid conclusions. *"Bird, window, car, book,"* she continued. "Does he think I'm crazy? That I can't remember four simple words?"

Before releasing her from the hospital, Mark had given her the same examination that had been such a disaster earlier, including the memory test, and this time she'd rattled off the four words effortlessly. I was impressed, since on neither occasion had I been able to recall them all myself. She'd also given him her thoughts on Bush, which seemed to please him, though perhaps he was merely heartened by her lucidity.

Barbara was at the wheel, so I could turn around to look at my mother. "The last time he asked you about those same four words, you couldn't recall even one," I told her, not without misgiving. She had little memory of the days leading up to her hospitalization, and I knew this troubled her greatly. As her world had begun shrinking over the last decade, her need to control whatever remained became paramount, and the idea of losing time, of having to ask for help to fill in the blanks, left her both frightened and unmoored. She'd grilled both her granddaughters about the event she couldn't remember, as if Emily and Kate could be trusted more than their parents, who for all she knew might be in league with the doctor she now pledged to shitcan.

"You've been very sick."

"And who does he think he is, saying I can't have my Paxil?" she continued, impossible, as always, to corner when she'd built up a head of steam and was determined to let it off.

"He thinks he's your doctor."

"Then I'll call my old doctor. He'll prescribe it."

"Actually, no, Mom, he won't."

"Plus," she noted, "I've got a good two-month supply at home."

At this Barbara and I exchanged glances. One of our first duties after she was admitted to the hospital had been to gather all her meds from the Woodland Hills apartment and bring them in. The stash she was counting on was gone, and I felt like a parent who'd disposed of the weed he discovered in the back of his kid's closet.

My mother's real beef with Mark was his quiet, calm refusal to be bamboozled. It was as if he wasn't treating *my* mother but his own. He was onto all of her tricks in a heartbeat. When she evaded his questions, he simply repeated them. When she pointed this out to him, he assured her that as soon as she gave him a clear, honest answer he'd be happy to move on to a new topic.

"Telling me what I can and can't eat," she continued, "like I'm a child."

"I'm sorry you aren't fond of him, but he's a good doctor, and he did save your life."

"Piffle," she said, but then she fell silent, examining the ugly blood blister on her right thumb that had resulted from her twisting the stem of that damn clock for hours on end. Was she considering the larger implications of harming herself without meaning to? Her bedrock conviction in life had always been: *I know what's best for me.* Had enough evidence to the contrary finally caused her to reconsider? Might she be entering a new phase of trusting the wisdom of others and doubting her own? Was it possible at eighty to shift gears so fundamentally?

"How long will I be staying with you, then?" she wanted to know.

"As long as you need to." We'd been over this before, of course. She was in withdrawal, and the next few days were bound to be so ugly that she'd need companionship and support to survive them.

"Is there a lot to do at the apartment?"

"Very little," I assured her, which was true. I told her again how, in addition to Barb and me, the girls had pitched in to get everything ready for her, the clothes hung up in the closet, her dishes and glasses in the cupboards. She'd told us where she wanted things, and we'd followed these instructions she now couldn't remember giving. The aluminum foil and plastic wrap and wax paper rolls were safe in the oven, an appliance she had no other use for, relying on the microwave to warm her frozen dinners. She and Barbara had already arranged her bedroom, and we'd hung her pictures and mirrors on the walls. The television was hooked up, the cable turned on, the phone service activated. She and I would need to go grocery shopping soon, and she'd no doubt want to make a few cosmetic changes, but otherwise she was good to go. "And of course we'll have to reset all the clocks," I added.

For her, that had been the scariest detail of all. In the hospital, after the fog had lifted, I told her about how we sat on the edge of the bed the morning of her first doctor's appointment and she asked why the hands of the clock only went forward when she wanted to make them go back. "I must've been in la-la land," she said, shaking her head in disbelief.

Now, at my mention of the clocks, she grew pale again, so I said, "The worst is behind you, Mom."

She took a deep breath, hoping, I could tell, that I was right. As a general rule, I wasn't.

THE NEXT FEW DAYS proved every bit as rough as predicted. "I feel like I'm coming out of my skin" was how my mother put it. Clothes were insupportable, so she stayed in her nightgown and robe all day long. Unable to get comfortable, she moved between rooms like the ghost of someone who'd died a sudden, violent death. The girls, though glad their grandmother was recovering, were also grateful that their restaurant jobs got them out of the house. Barbara and I had no such refuge, and at the end of each day we huddled in our bed in the apartment above the garage, out of earshot for a few hours and thankful she couldn't possibly negotiate the stairs. By the end of the week, though, her appetite returned, and she was clearly feeling better. She thought maybe the time had come to return to Woodland Hills. Her doctor agreed. So did Barbara. So did I.

The first thing she saw when she entered the apartment, as if for the first time, was the piece of paper on which she'd scratched *8:45* and then *REAL TIME*. I couldn't tell what scared her more, the message itself or that her beautiful Palmer Method handwriting was a barely legible scrawl. She pulled one of the chairs out from the dinette and sat down in it heavily, suddenly drained. The plan had been to take inventory of her kitchen, make a list of everything she'd need, and hit the supermarket, but I could tell she was done for the day.

"Is it too soon?" I said, trying to imagine what it must be like to return to a "home" she hadn't yet lived in and couldn't remember.

She shook her head. "I have to do it sometime."

"How about we make out a small list of stuff for the next day or two, and I'll go to the store? We can save the big order for later in the week."

"Whatever," she said, and paused. "Do you honestly think Mark saved my life?"

"I'm certain of it."

She was staring at the refrigerator now. "What am I supposed to do with all those frozen dinners?" A true child of the Depression, she hated few things more than wasting food.

"It's not that you can't have frozen dinners anymore," I reminded her. "Just that you have to eat some other things, too."

"No," she said, never one for half measures. "We'll toss them out." Next she turned her attention to the living room. "You did such a nice job with my books. You know just where everything goes. It's perfect."

We both knew it wasn't, of course. Over the next days and weeks, she'd find things that were out of place and rearrange them, making them, as she liked to put it, "just right." But she wanted to pay me a compliment, and I was pleased to accept it.

What she said then surprised me. "Do you think I'll ever be able to read again?"

She hadn't read anything at our house, which was predictable if you thought about it at all. How can you read when you can't sit still? Worse, there wasn't much inducement, our shelves sagging under the weight of Anita Brookner and her truth-telling ilk. What my mother really wanted to know wasn't whether she'd be able to read again but if that could ever again be a reliable means of escape. At the possibility that it might not, I felt my own spirits plummet in sympathetic dread.

She looked around aimlessly once again, though in a new way. "I hate it here," she said sadly. "I'm sorry. I wish I didn't, but I do."

Though normally I'd have pointed out that she hadn't been there long enough to render such a judgment, I was weary of such futile nonsense. She *was* going to hate it, and we both knew it. "We'll keep your name on the other lists," I assured her.

Actually, I'd driven by Megunticook House when she was in the hospital and noticed the exterior was being painted, so

I stopped by and added her name to their list as well. (Later in the year a vacancy would come up, and this time my mother loved the place. In fact, the painting had transformed it so completely that she insisted I'd never taken her there before. She would've remembered, she said, because it was perfect, *just* what we'd been looking for, *so* much better than Woodland Hills.)

"You look exhausted," she said now, taking my hand. "What a long haul this has been for you."

I started to say that it'd been a tough few days, all right, but then realized she was going all the way back to Arizona, maybe even to Helwig Street. "I just wish you could be happy, Mom."

"I *used* to be," she sighed, and in her inflection was the same profound mystification I'd heard the week before when she asked me to explain why, despite her formidable will, the hands of the clock would only go in one direction. "I know you don't believe that, but I was."

Here and There

IT WOULD'VE TAKEN about forty minutes to drive out-island from Edgartown in the summer, but in late December, with so few tourists on the island and no mopeds or cyclists clogging the narrow, two-lane roads, it took about half that long. To me, the winter landscape was starkly beautiful, but I found myself wondering if my mother would agree. Given that the alternatives were Gloversville and coastal Maine, she'd wholeheartedly embraced the idea of scattering her ashes in Menemsha Pond, a place the rest of us would regularly visit, but today it wasn't hard to imagine her taking one look at the frigid, windswept, gunmetal-gray landscape and saying, *What an awful, awful place.* Was the island simply the last in a series of wrong places for her? Is that what the previous night's dream, in which I'd carried her through the streets of that nameless town in search of an unknown destination, was trying to tell me?

Emily and Kate both planned to speak at this interment, and driving out there I found myself wondering what they'd say. Their approaches to dealing with my mother had always been different, Emily infinitely patient and loving and accommodating, Kate deeply sympathetic to her isolation and loneliness but far less able to surrender to her unreason. In Illinois, when they were still young and Barbara and I had obligations at the university or just needed a night out, my mother had been their occasional babysitter. Once we were out the door, the three of them would caucus in the living room and decide on a theme for the evening's entertainment, after which, while my mother watched TV or read, the girls would raid my wife's closet for costumes, practice their lines in their bedrooms, then stage a play or musical for my mother's edification and critical evaluation. Both girls had fond memories of such evenings, of having the undivided attention of an appreciative adult, though things had changed by the time we moved to Maine. As teenagers, they weren't so malleable or as easily delighted. More important, by then the roles were reversed. On those rare occasions when Barbara and I both had to be absent for a few days, my mother would come over to the Waterville house to look after them, but they both understood without having to be told that it was their responsibility to keep an eye on her. We'd tried hard not to undermine their affection for their grandmother, but of course they'd borne witness to her mood swings and meltdowns, not to mention our difficulties in keeping her relatively calm and stable.

Though they'd been told a good deal about my mother as

a young woman, her yearning for a life of dancing and clever repartee and nice clothes and personal freedom, the old GE photo we found after her death had knocked both girls for a loop, and I knew they were still trying to reconcile it with the grandmother who later in life made them sit still when they visited her apartment and instructed them not to touch anything; whose shirts and slacks and sweaters hung in the closet sheathed in plastic, nothing allowed to touch anything else for fear of wrinkles; whose refrigerator reflected the same obsessive distance, the milk carton always a respectful three inches from the orange juice. As a young woman, my mother had in many ways been ahead of her time, determined to make it on her own in a man's world. Back then, GE was almost exclusively male, and the men she'd worked for and with had both accepted and admired her. In this respect she wasn't so different from the brave, trailblazing women our daughters had studied in their college courses, who helped to institute workplace reform and equal-pay-for-equal-work legislation. How could this woman in the photo be the same person who'd lectured them so tirelessly, and often inappropriately, on highly conservative gender roles (*This is what the man does* and *That is what the woman does*). To prepare them for marriage, my mother had given them to understand that in every relationship, one partner or the other had to rule the roost, and that in good marriages the roost was ruled by the rooster. As the girls grew older, it became clear to her that these lectures were falling on deaf ears. Kate in particular worried her, and my mother had warned us throughout her adolescence that we were allowing her to grow up headstrong, that her unflinching independence was decidedly unfeminine. In the end, despite having fewer sharp temperamental edges and always lavishing on her grandmother such generous forbearance, Emily fared little better. When she fell in love with Steve, our shy, brilliant son-in-law-to-be, my mother wondered out loud if he'd be man enough to tame and rule her. ("I suppose I could slap you around a little," he'd offered, when Emily reported this concern to him, "if that would make her feel any better.")

We'd timed our arrival for sunset. Tom, Kate's husband, a talented photographer, had brought along a camera to document an occasion whose exact nature we'd not discussed, preferring spontaneity. Menemsha, a hive of activity in season, was deserted now, which suited us fine given that what we intended, though unscripted and benign, was quite possibly illegal. A few fishing vessels bobbed in the swell against a nearby dock, and every now and then a voice or two would be borne in on the wind. Somewhere out in the harbor a buoy clanged, surely the loneliest sound in the world. A pickup truck rumbled by, its driver leaning forward for a better view of six well-dressed out-of-towners congregated at the water's edge. It wouldn't have required much imagination for the fellow to guess our purpose, though I suspect he'd have been surprised to learn that the person whose ashes we meant to scatter had been to the island only once, for a single week some fifty years before, determined to show the little boy she had in tow that beauty existed in the world.

With the sun hovering a few inches above the western horizon, I clambered down, urn in hand, over jagged rocks that were wet and slippery with moss to where the water was lapping the shore, thinking to myself that it would be about right if I broke my ass trying to accomplish one last foolish thing on my mother's behalf. Not much is left of a human professionally reduced by heat and flame, and it took me just a few seconds to scatter that biblical dust in the churning waves, where it swiftly mingled with sand and silt and tiny pebbles. By the time I scrambled back up the embankment, the sun was sitting on the western waves, large and red but without the power to warm. Emily spoke first, thanking her grandmother for the gift of this island that over the years had played such a magical role in the lives of our whole family; then Kate recalled with bittersweet affection her grandmother's ability to imagine vividly a happier, better future, even if she couldn't quite see herself in it. When they were done, I read the Shakespeare sonnet that begins "Fear no more the heat o' the Sun," partly because it was appropriate to the occasion and one of the most beautiful poems in the language, but also because I hoped it might hide from my loved ones the fact that I myself had nothing to say, that while part of me was here with them on this beloved shore, another part was wandering, as it had been for months, in a barren, uninhabited landscape not unlike the one in my dream. I realized I'd felt like this for a while. Though life had gone on since my mother's death—Kate had gotten married, I'd finally published another book and gone on tour with it— some sort of internal-pause button had been pushed, allowing another part of me, one I'd specifically kept sequestered to deal with my mother, to fall silent. Since her death, Barbara and I had gone through all her things and settled her affairs, but we'd barely spoken of her. After thirty-five years, for the first time, we were alone in our marriage, and neither of us seemed to have the heart to discuss what that meant. There might have been more to say if the girls had been around, but Emily was living in Amherst and Kate in London, and the rest of my family still in upstate New York.

We therefore scheduled a family memorial service for the following summer in Gloversville, the sort of gathering my mother would've liked—just family and friends and food and swapping stories, like the one about the Christmas when she, all dressed up, was trapped astraddle a snowbank, everybody laughing too hard to help her get unstuck. But in the meantime, not much had been said; and when you say nothing, it speaks volumes.

The last year of my mother's life had been particularly grueling. The specialist who'd diagnosed her congestive heart failure had explained how things would likely go over the year or possibly two that remained to her. Given how hard her heart was now working, she might suffer a major heart attack, but it was far more likely that her decline would be gradual. For a while, at least, she'd continue to feel sluggish and tired, nothing more. Over time, though, she'd be increasingly short of breath, especially when she exerted herself. Every now and then there'd be days when she'd feel better, even energetic, her breathing less labored, and he advised her to stick with her normal routines for as long as she could, to continue her weekly trips to the supermarket and to the hairdresser. Eventually, however, her good days would be fewer and farther between; she'd become housebound, then bedridden. Toward the end she'd require morphine, not for pain, but to make her breathing easier. I was the one choking back sobs as the doctor delivered this grim prognosis. My mother accepted it with near-perfect equanimity. She was being told what would happen, not what might, and certainty never frightened her, even certain catastrophe. She wasn't scared to die. As we drove home, she actually comforted me.

Living, on the other hand, in the greater scheme of things a relentless march of inconsequential minutiae, continued over the ensuing weeks and months to generate crises. Appearances, as always, weighed far more heavily on her decisions than they should have. No doubt recalling the enormous oxygen tank that stood sentry behind my grandfather's chair on Helwig Street, the one my grandmother used to glare at homicidally every time he got up to leave the room, muttering "Ugly" beneath her breath, my mother wasn't anxious to start on oxygen. Her living room was arranged just so, to accentuate her "pretties," the menagerie of small, ornate objects (a ballerina, a cut-glass bowl, etc.) she'd been collecting down through the years, and a few were given pride of place on the sill, where they made it difficult to open or close the windows. As the perimeter of her world continued to contract, it was imperative for her to keep control over what remained, and an oxygen tank, unsightly and utilitarian, represented a serious breach of taste. Of course the technology had come a long way, and the small, boxlike oxygen machine we eventually rented could be tucked away behind an end table, but that didn't matter; she knew it was there, unwanted, a violation. We also got her a small, portable tank for when she needed to leave the house, but she'd seen people out in public with such unwieldy contraptions, and she didn't want to be one of them. She would use it when she came to our house, but refused to be seen in stores or restaurants with a breathing apparatus. The plastic tubing, once inserted, made her nose look like a pig's snout, or so she claimed, and she couldn't bear to be seen looking like that. Hearing she was ill, people at Megunticook House were concerned, but after going on oxygen, she let it be known that she didn't want visitors, even people she liked. And so, in short order, her world shrank to her own two rooms, the apartment of her one good friend across the hall and, when she was feeling up to it, our house across town.

For what seemed like a very long time, my own world wasn't much larger. With few exceptions, I declined speaking engagements and canceled personal appearances. Except for visiting our daughters in London and Amherst, we stuck close to home. Faced with an undefined period of staggering health-care expenses, I hunkered down with the novel I was working on, while Barbara, who'd recently gotten her real-estate license, kept busy learning the ropes of a new profession. For a while I did most of what needed doing—shopping for my mother's groceries, making small repairs in the apartment, taking care of trash and recycling—but before long it became necessary to hire professionals to help with more intimate duties.

Moving her in with us was something I refused to even consider because it would have made a nurse of my wife, and besides, what my mother seemed most adamant about was keeping things just as they were for as long as possible, especially her apartment, so I promised to make that happen.

Even in terminal illness, her emotional cycles continued, exacerbated now by physical ones that proceeded as expected and predicted. There were good days and bad days, and it was the good ones we all came to fear. On bad days, when her energy level was low, her breathing difficult, my mother fussed and found fault less. On bad days her Meals on Wheels were a godsend, the people who delivered them saints. When listless, she understood she was too ill to be left alone, that she needed help with almost everything, even getting up from the sofa to go to the bathroom. On days when she woke up feeling better, though, watch out. Then the Meals on Wheels were inedible, and (again, shades of Woody Allen) the portions inadequate. When a delivery was running late, she'd call and tell them not to bother; when it came anyway, she wouldn't ring whoever was bringing it into the building. The health-care workers, who'd all been warned, bore the brunt of it when she went on the warpath. Some quit. Others—several of whom she'd taken an aversion to at first sight—she refused to let in the door. She knew as her condition deteriorated that she was becoming increasingly dependent on them, but on good days she couldn't see why people who most of the time just sat and watched television with her were paid so much. We'd never discussed what these costs amounted to, but she knew it was expensive and not covered by Medicare, which was partly why she was so unreasonable on this subject. To her way of thinking, to justify such expense, the people we hired should always be working, vacuuming or scrubbing the bathtub, as if they were maids with medical training. Did they have to be in the apartment with her when they weren't needed? Couldn't they wait out in the hall? Couldn't she ring for them? "Maybe you don't care if you're getting ripped off," she said whenever I tried to explain what their duties were and weren't, "but I do."

That spring, before we went to London for a few days to visit Kate, we planned our absence, hour by hour, with Vickie, who ran the health-care service, making sure my mother's days and evenings were all covered. Night had become a particular bone of contention. Not long after she was diagnosed, she'd gotten a push-button necklace that would summon help in case of an accident, but she didn't want anybody in her apartment overnight. Only after intense negotiation did she reluctantly agree to have someone stay for the duration of our London trip. I was still worried, so we came up with a contingency plan. If she took a turn for the worse in the run-up to our departure, I'd remain behind. For a while it looked like that's what was going to happen, but after a string of bad days she rallied, and her doctor assured us that she'd be stable until we returned. I called one last time from the airport to make sure, but she swore everything was fine. The night person had just arrived, and they were watching TV. I should go and have a good time. Something in her voice gave me pause, though, and when we landed at Heathrow seven hours later, I wasn't surprised to find there was a message on my cell from Vickie. My mother had waited until we were safely onboard our plane, then fired everybody.

A month later she had a minor heart attack that put her in the hospital, and things got even worse. She claimed the recommended regimen of physical therapy was simply too difficult to do, though the nurses said she'd never so much as tried. They'd also recommended what they made the mistake of referring to as "psychological therapy." I explained that this was all about rethinking how, after you'd suffered a heart attack, you rose from a chair and got out of bed in the morning, but my mother was having none of it. There was nothing wrong with her head, and she knew perfectly well how to get out of a chair. Which left the hospital staff little choice but to return her to Megunticook House, where it soon became apparent she was going to need a lot more care. Whether she liked it or not, somebody had to be there at night to help her get to the bathroom. The problem was that of all the workers sent from the agency to help her, she liked only a couple. They of course had families and lives of their own, and there were more hours in the week than any two people could cover. Shift changes were especially problematic. My mother particularly hated falling asleep with one caregiver in the next room, then waking up to another the next morning. Moreover, she didn't want the night attendant to stretch out on her sofa, fearing for its springs. "It wasn't *made* for people to sleep on," she complained, "especially not obese Mainers." I tried to catch her caregivers near the end of their shifts, in part so they could bring me up to speed on what had transpired but also to find out how badly they'd been abused and insulted and to apologize. They were no sooner out the door than my mother would use what little remained of her failing heart and lungs to berate those she considered lazy or stupid and to bemoan the fact that her favorites weren't always available. Vickie, she believed, was saving all the good ones for her favored clients, whose families insisted on top-quality care.

There were times when I seriously considered wringing her neck, but then the cycle would end, and there she'd be again, my mother, lost and frail and afraid, with barely enough energy to draw her next breath, her heart a sledgehammer in her chest—anxious, it seemed, for this terrible struggle to be over. In the weeks before she entered the hospital for the last time, she couldn't get comfortable. In the living room she'd struggle to her feet and announce that she couldn't stand it there any longer and was going to bed early. I should go home. (By this time I was visiting, literally, morning, noon, and night.) But twenty minutes later she'd emerge from the bedroom saying she couldn't bear lying down, that sitting up was better. In addition to sapping what little strength remained, these short journeys were also treacherous. Forgetting she was tethered to the oxygen machine, she often managed to tangle her long lead of plastic tubing when she went around corners, pulling it free of her nose, which she sometimes didn't notice or immediately realize was why she suddenly couldn't fill her lungs. Back and forth she went, ninety pounds of pure will and desperation, life reduced to purposeless, exhausting motion, until another heart attack, after which even that tortured, senseless motion became impossible.

MORPHINE. A BLESSING. During the last month of my mother's life in the hospice wing at the hospital, the drug did its almost-mystical business of protecting the self from itself, of relaxing her so that she could "breathe easier" both literally and metaphorically. Under its influence her features sometimes unclenched, allowing me to glimpse in the tiny, mummified figure in her hospital bed the confident, lovely, brave young woman I'd known as a boy. When a new dose was administered, she'd smile and slip under the wave, and often, exhausted, I'd follow her down, falling asleep in my chair as if I, too, were connected to the drip. At other times, powerful though it was, even morphine failed to vanquish the anxiety that had come to rule her life, and then her eyes would grow small and hard with concentrated terror and defiance, the old, unwinnable battle still raging on. I tried to calm her by saying I was right there at the foot of the bed and promising I wouldn't go anywhere. But knowing she wasn't afraid of death, I was curious, as well, and asked more than once what was scaring her so. "That things, you know . . . ," she'd begin, but having gotten that far, she'd grow confused and frustrated.

"Can you explain?" I persisted, hoping that, even at this late date, if she could just articulate her fear, I might be able to help her dispel it.

"You know," she said, as if she suspected I'd somehow forgotten something I knew perfectly well, that I could summon the memory if I just concentrated hard enough. "That things . . . you know . . . won't . . ."

"Won't *what*, Mom?"

"You know," she insisted, smiling weakly now, "won't turn out right."

MY MOTHER WASN'T the only one confused and disoriented those final weeks. Meaning to visit her, I'd often drive over to Megunticook House, realizing only after I'd pulled in to the parking lot and turned off the ignition that she wasn't there anymore.

One night not long after she moved into the hospital's hospice wing, I went home early and fell into a deep, dreamless slumber from which I was awakened, bewildered and panicked, when the telephone rang a few minutes before midnight.

"Rick?" she said, perhaps not recognizing my sleep-thick voice.

Had I forgotten, I wondered, to go over to her apartment after dinner?

"Rick?"

"Mom?" I said. "What is it?"

"I need you to come."

"Mom, it's midnight," I said, staring stupidly at the clock on the nightstand. Had five whole hours passed? How was that possible?

"I pressed the button."

"What button, Mom?"

"For the nurse. Ten minutes ago. She never came."

"She will," I told her. Barbara put a hand on my shoulder and rested her forehead on the back of my neck. "Be patient."

"It's you I need."

"I'll see you in the morning. I promise."

Silence on the line, then. Had she hung up? No, she was back, needing me to understand. "It's terrible here," she said. "You have no idea."

IT'S YOU I NEED . . . *it's terrible here.*

Seven small words, but embedded in them, somewhere, is the reason that a man who makes his living with words isn't able to offer any when Emily and Kate finish speaking. The closure that death is supposed to bring has somehow eluded me, which must be why in last night's dream I was carrying my mother toward that unknown destination and why it felt like I'd be doing so forever. Although it's been several months since her death, when the phone rings in the middle of the night, I still expect to hear her voice on the other end of the line, wanting to know where I am, why I've abandoned her.

It's terrible here. I've belatedly come to understand that for my mother *here* was really the place inside her head where everything played on an endless loop. *There* was the place she never stopped trying to get to, where she'd be happy. *Don't I deserve a life?* She must have asked my grandfather this before me, the question serving as explanation for why she was leaving Helwig Street for Arizona. How had he answered it? He'd served in two world wars and was exhausted and slowly strangling, his lungs full of leather dust. I can imagine him telling her that nobody, including her, was entitled to anything, but of course I wasn't there and he might well have said nothing of the sort. She never asked me if I minded her tagging along. She just told me about the job awaiting her in Phoenix and painted a vivid picture for me of the new, free life she'd have when we arrived, leaving me to challenge her right to it.

Or am I misremembering? Did she ask me, and I just forgot? It's possible. That I honestly can't recall something so important seems right, somehow. The mechanism of human destiny—that intricate weave of chance and fate and free will, as distinctly individual as a fingerprint—is surely meant to remain life's central mystery, to resist transparency, to make blame a dangerous and unsatisfactory exercise. I don't blame my mother for anything, certainly not for her ongoing unhappiness, any more than I take pride in having managed to parlay the same genetic character traits that bedeviled her—stubbornness, defiance, an inclination to obsess, an excess of will, a potentially dangerous need to see things my own way—into a rich and satisfying career.

It's you I need. From the time I was a boy I understood that my mother's health, her well-being, was in my hands. How often over the years did she credit me, or my proximity, with restoring her to health? *My rock,* as she was so fond of saying, always there when she needed me most. My own experience, however, had yielded a different truth—that I could easily make things worse, but never better. Or at least not better enough. I was, just as she said, always there, but to me that meant always failing, never being able to cure what ailed her. I could help her step back from the precipice and restore the status quo, but the status quo was neither health nor happiness.

Now, standing with my family in the deepening dark, I feel profoundly what a terrible mistake she made in trusting me, in believing that we were cut from the same cloth, that one day I'd see things as she did, that given time I'd grow into the soul-mate role that she'd planned for me. She seemed not to grasp that I'm by nature a problem solver, that I'm fundamentally optimistic and believe most problems have solutions. When she asked me if she didn't deserve a life like anybody else, she probably thought of it as a rhetorical question. Who would deny another human being the right to a life? She couldn't have known that I'd take it as a riddle I was supposed to figure out, a problem that had a solution I'd eventually discover if I just kept looking, that I'd never give up.

But of course I now realize that isn't quite true. At some point along the spectrum of what we like to think of as "real time," I simply flatlined and, without admitting it to myself, conceded defeat and started just going through the motions. This was why my dreams were haunted. Because I'd given up on someone I loved, someone who'd never, ever, given up on me. I couldn't speak because the only thing left to say was *I'm sorry,* and the person I needed to say it to was gone.

High and Dry

Aftera the vineyard, Barbara and I could feel the pendulum begin to swing, tragedy waning and comedy, at least in the Shakespearean sense, waxing. Kate and Tom had gotten married in London back in November, and we were now again in the nuptial mode, preparing for Emily's in September. Caught up in the spirit of these proceedings, I started work on a wedding story. At least I thought it was a story. It turned out to be a novel, though, one that was cleaved right down the center, a wedding anchoring each half. Compared with the book that preceded it—my darkest, written and revised during my mother's long, final descent—this new novel was a breezy tale that seemed to suggest I was finding my way back to the cautious, hard-won optimism that characterizes my fiction. Back on the Vineyard I'd feared that my nightmare—about carrying my mother through unfamiliar streets toward an unknown destination—might be a recurring one, but I hadn't had it since, and I took this to mean that my mother was finally at rest, or perhaps that I was. It seems strange to admit it now, but just being alive was at some level surprising. In contrast to the remarkable longevity of the women on my mother's side of the family, Russo males had a piss-poor track record, and somewhere in the back of my mind I must've linked my mother's chronological destiny with my own. Yet here I was, not only alive but, according to my doctor, in excellent health.

So Barbara and I started making plans. After all, our circumstances had changed dramatically. Suddenly we had neither ailing parents nor heart-stopping medical bills. Our daughters' educations were paid for. By autumn both girls would be married to the kind of young men we'd hardly dared to hope for, and all four young people were embarking on careers they were passionate about. Which begged an obvious question: what in the world were Barbara and I going to do with ourselves? At long last we'd been left to our own devices, only to discover we couldn't recollect precisely what those devices were. Perhaps we'd need all new ones.

One of the things we'd been unable to do while my mother was alive was to travel, at least not together. I could go off on a book tour, or to L.A. or New York for a script meeting, as long as Barbara remained behind to hold down the fort, and of course she could visit her family in Arizona if I stayed put. Now we could actually go places together. For years we'd longed for an apartment in Boston so we wouldn't have to fly out of Portland, Maine, the preferred airport of hijackers and no one else. A place in the city would also give us somewhere to spend the darkest months of Maine's interminable winters. All this was down the road, though. Meanwhile, the theme would be weddings, fictional and real. That felt both right and appropriate. Weddings are all about our hopes for and faith in the future, right? Right.

Except not entirely. As I knew all too well from recent experience, and was learning more about with every new page of my novel-in-progress, weddings are also about the past.

KATE'S WEDDING HAD BEEN HELD at the Royal Society for the Arts, a series of underground vaults, formerly wine cellars, just off the Strand. She and Tom, who's English, would be living in London, so there'd been no question of having the ceremony in the States. The wedding was relatively small: Tom's family; some friends from the Slade Art School, where they'd met; a few of Kate's college friends. Understandably, given the distance and expense, not many family members from our side of the Atlantic made the trip. The exception was my cousin Greg and his wife, Carole, both of whom have always lived in Gloversville. "Quite a ways from Helwig Street," Greg said, taking in the venue. It wasn't as grand as "Royal Society" might suggest, but the arching brick vaults, candlelit for the occasion, were impressive. There's nothing remotely like it in an upstate mill town. The person who would've appreciated it the most, of course, was my mother.

While we waited for the bride and groom to finish having

their photos taken, the how-far-we'd-all-come theme occupied the American contingent. Nat Sobel, my friend and literary agent, immediately took to my cousin, telling Greg that as a boy he, too, lived near a tannery that released its toxins into the local stream, the water running a different color each day depending on the dye batch. And so, flutes of Prosecco in hand, we began swapping stories about the worst jobs we'd ever had.

I recalled my brief nonunion construction job in Johns-town. Other summers I'd been able to get union work at an hourly rate nearly twice what men were making at the skin mills. That year, though, jobs were scarce, and I hadn't gotten one. Nonunion construction was a different world. The first week we had to drill holes in a concrete abutment, not a dif-ficult task if you have a drill. We didn't. What we did have was a jackhammer and a foreman who was unconstrained by con-ventional thinking. The jackhammer guy and I formed a team that afternoon. Balancing his weapon on my shoulder, I held on for dear life as we jacked horizontally into the wall, sharp shards of concrete blasting back into our faces. Another thing we didn't have was a spare set of goggles.

This story will win a lot of bad-job contests unless your competitor has worked in the beam house of a skin mill doing the wettest, foulest, lowest-paid, and most dangerous work in the whole tannery. Greg had worked in one for a couple months one summer, and his younger brother, Jim, for much longer. The first and probably nastiest job in the beaming operation was unloading the skins, which arrived at the load-ing dock on railroad cars, still reeking of the slaughterhouse.

The word *skin* probably gives the wrong impression. Most people have never seen a hide—sheep, pig, calf, cow—unattached from its living owner. Stretched out flat it's big and, especially with cows, surprisingly heavy. (Our grandfather gave himself a hernia tugging hides from one position to another over his cutting table.) When the skin arrived in the beam house, the top side was still covered with coarse hair, the underside with patches of maggot-infested flesh and gristle. The stench? You don't want to know, but imagine—if you can—what it must be like to spend an eight-hour shift unloading a railcar full of them in extreme temperatures.

Later, inside the beam house, Greg assured us, things got even worse. Here the skins were submerged in huge vats and soaked for days in a chemical bath that stripped off most of the hair and the last of the clinging flesh. Naturally, these chemicals could easily do the same to hair on the hands and forearms of men who hoisted the soaked skins out of the vats, so long rubber gloves were issued. You'd think the skins would be lighter minus the hair and flesh, but you'd be wrong, because untanned skins reabsorb the moisture lost during transport and this cleansing. The soaking also turns the heavy skins slippery. The rubber gloves make the slick skins harder to grab hold of, as does the fact that you're bent over the vat and standing on a wet concrete floor.

At some point, like the men farther down the line who prod the tanned skins into staking machines and roller presses, you'll do what you know you shouldn't: you will take off the rubber gloves, because that immediately makes the job easier.

At the end of your shift you'll wash your hands and arms vigorously with the coarsest soap you can find, and when you get home you'll do it again. You'll gradually lose the hair on your hands and forearms, but otherwise, for a while, everything seems fine. Okay, sometimes your fingers itch. A little at first, then a lot. Your skin begins to feel odd, almost loose, as if moisture has somehow gotten beneath it and what you're trying to scratch isn't on the surface. Finally it itches so bad you can't stand it anymore, and you grab your thumb or forefinger and give the skin a twist, then a pull. The skin, several layers of it, comes away in one piece, like the finger of a latex glove. (On the other side of the Atlantic, at the Royal Society for the Arts, my cousin demonstrated with his thumb, everybody wincing as he pulled off the imaginary prophylactic of skin.) Instantly, the itching becomes stinging pain as the air impinges on your raw flesh. Later, someone comes around with a jar of black goop and you plunge your raw thumb into it, the coolness offering at least some relief, and for a while you go back to wearing the rubber gloves.

This is only the beginning, though, just the beam house's way of saying hello when all you want to say is good-bye—to the skins, the foul chemical air, even your coworkers, because let's face it, the ones who've been at it for a while, many of them with fifth-grade educations, aren't quite right. You all make the same shitty pay, but at the end of the summer you get to go back to college, and for that the others hate you. Meanwhile, you can't imagine getting used to work like this, or that the day will ever come when the lunch whistle sounds and instead of going outside into the fresh air you'll decide it's easier to just stay where you are, take a seat on a pallet of decomposing hides, wipe your hands on your pants, and eat your sandwich right there—because what the hell, it's been forever since you could really smell or taste anything anyway. Plus, in the beam house there's entertainment. You can watch the rats chase the terrified cats that have been introduced to hunt them.

As my cousin related this story, which I was hearing for the first time, I became conscious of being in two places at once. I had one dry, wing-tipped foot in the candlelit world of a fancy arts society in London in 2007; the other work-booted foot was sloshing through the wet, slippery beam-house floor in Gloversville, New York, circa 1970. That younger me wasn't a novelist, or even a husband or a father. He was just a twenty-year-old whose future could be stolen from him, who might indeed be complicit in the theft, because I remembered vividly how sometimes, late in August, working road construction with my father, my body lean and hard from the summer's labor, I'd think about not going back to school. I could live with my grandparents on Helwig Street and do that hard, honest work my father and his friends did all year-round. The wing-tipped me, now holding an empty champagne flute, felt a sudden crushing guilt, as if to be where I was I must've cheated destiny or, worse, swapped destinies with some other poor sod. I felt my throat constrict dangerously, though I couldn't tell if that was due to my cousin's story or because the wedding party—with Kate absolutely radiant in the first hour of her marriage, and Emily laughing her throaty laugh and looping her arm through her fiancé's—had at this moment returned. Two smart, confident, beautiful young women, their feet planted squarely in the candlelit world before them, on *this* day—for them, at least—the only one that existed. The time might come when they, too, would feel haunted, guilty about what they'd been spared in life, keenly aware of how things, but for the grace of God, might have gone otherwise. But that day seemed a long way off.

"More Prosecco?" one of the waiters inquired.

"Yes, please," I told her, holding out my glass. Gloversville, I reminded myself, was on the other side of the world. "Absolutely. Lay it on me. Right to the brim."

UNTIL WE BEGAN PLANNING Emily's wedding we didn't fully comprehend how easily we'd gotten off with Kate's. We'd feared a London wedding would be a logistical nightmare, but being on the other side of the Atlantic had the unintended consequence of lowering everyone's expectations, at least of us. Nobody assumed we would deal with day-to-day details and crises. Tom's parents stepped up. Decisions got made without us. We showed up. We wrote the check.

By contrast, Emily's wedding was larger and would take place in Camden, where a matrimonial clusterfuck like the one I was gleefully imagining in my new novel would long be remembered. With no ocean to protect us, our very different families showed up en masse. Barbara's Arizona contingent, none of them seasoned travelers, needed assistance at every juncture. My own Gloversville squad wasn't much better, but at least they'd be arriving by car. And of course there was our future son-in-law's family and friends to consider. Add to all this the normal wedding anxieties about who, for personal reasons, should be kept well clear of whom, and what would happen if the Red Staters were allowed too close proximity to the Blue. When the whole thing threatened to overwhelm us, we reminded ourselves that our tribulations would have been multiplied exponentially if my mother had been alive.

Truth be told, Barbara and Emily handled most of the wedding arrangements while I forged ahead with the book I hoped would pay for them. About this time I had a few odd dreams about my mother in which she telephoned from Europe, wanting to know why I'd abandoned her there and when I was coming to get her. These made me wary, but they were too comic—Europe? my dead mother was calling from Europe?—to be truly unsettling. Otherwise, I thought I was doing pretty well, certainly better than my novel's protagonist, Jack Griffin. At the book's outset he'd been heading to the first wedding on Cape Cod with an urn containing his father's ashes in the right wheel well of his trunk; now, driving to the second wedding, this one in Maine, he'd added his mother's urn to the left. Poor Jack, I thought. Scattering my own mother's ashes hadn't been easy, but my character seemed utterly unequal to this fairly straightforward task. Death had made his mother even more loquacious than she'd been in life, even more determined to insinuate herself into his life and marriage, both of which were coming apart. A terrible snob of an English professor, she was (to me, if not to him) wonderfully entertaining, in part because she was about as different as anyone could be from my own mother. Nor was Jack, despite superficial similarities of age and profession, all that temperamentally similar to me. And so far as I knew, my own marriage wasn't failing. All of which allowed me to believe, as a writer must, that I was writing fiction, not thinly veiled autobiography.

IT WAS AROUND this time that a large padded envelope arrived in my mailbox bearing a Gloversville postmark, never a welcome sign. Inside were two books, the first a copy of my novel *Bridge of Sighs*. The man who sent it in hopes of an autograph was a judge named Vincent DeSantis, who, except for college and law school, had spent his life in Gloversville, and who, as he explained in the accompanying letter, had strongly identified with Lucy Lynch, the book's protagonist, who'd done the same thing. Clearly he thought he was writing to Lucy's friend Robert Noonan, an artist who in the novel flees their boyhood town, never to return. I couldn't really blame him, given how infrequently I go back to Gloversville.

The other book in the padded envelope was *Toward Civic Integrity: Re-establishing the Micropolis,* written by, well, Vincent DeSantis, and seeing this my heart sank, as it always does when I'm sent books I haven't asked for with a view toward my endorsement. But Mr. DeSantis wasn't looking for a blurb, and his book, despite its rather scholarly title, wasn't an esoteric work of nonfiction. It was about Gloversville, and the question he posed was whether it and similar communities had a future in the global twenty-first century or were in inevitable and irreversible decline. "All is not lost in your hometown," the author assured me. "A network of dedicated and talented individuals has lately been working to reassemble the pieces of this fractured micropolis." My knee-jerk reaction to this Humpty Dumpty sentiment was *Yeah, right. All the king's horses and all the king's men . . .* I tossed the book on a tall stack of volumes whose common denominator was that I was unlikely to read them in this or any other lifetime. Not interested.

Yet that wasn't quite true. Since Kate's wedding my cousin's beam-house stories had been in my thoughts. I was also worried about Greg himself. A few years earlier he'd had open-heart surgery to replace a malfunctioning valve, but he still couldn't sleep very well lying down and was getting by on a couple hours a night. Though I'd tried to keep in touch, when I inquired about his health he always put me off with his standard line, "Nah, I'm doing great for an old guy." Then we'd talk about what our kids were up to and what movies we'd seen and whether I was working on something new. And eventually the talk would turn to Gloversville: who'd been jailed or diagnosed, who'd gone into a nursing home or died. When I mentioned I couldn't get his beam-house experiences out of my head, he launched into a litany of Gloversville woe with which I was all too familiar: men mangled by machines or slowly poisoned or killed in accidents. The three guys who worked the spray line in one mill all dying of the same exotic testicular cancer, a case so outrageous it made the *New York Times*. Then there was the retarded boy hired to clean out the blues room, so named because the chrome used to tan the skins turned them blue. The world of leather is full of scraps—strips of worthless skin and hoof and tail—and every now and then these have to be disposed of and the whole lethal place, including its giant vats, swamped out. One evening, when this kid didn't come home, his mother called the shop to see if he was still around. No, she was told, everybody from the day shift had left. The following morning her son was found lying on the blues room's floor, asphyxiated by fumes. Another man, nearing retirement age, was working a press when his partner inadvertently stepped on the pedal that starts the rollers, catching the man's hand—more like a fin, now—in the mechanism. Yet another day, when it was unseasonably cold on the floor, the foreman sent a man to fire up a boiler that hadn't been inspected in twenty years, and it promptly blew up, killing him. Stories upon stories, each reminding my cousin of other men who died, their families uncompensated. Some dated back to my grandfather's days, ones I'd heard so many times I knew them as well as Greg did, but I understood why he needed to repeat them. The guys who lived this life in this world are, like World War II veterans, mostly gone. Somebody *should* give a shit.

But why me? Hanging up after such conversations with my cousin, I'd find I was roiling with rage I wasn't at all sure I was entitled to. Obviously, I'd never spent a minute in the beam house. Unlike my cousin Jim, on hot summer days I don't have to lance with a needle the hard pustules that still form on my hands, thirty years after the fact. What right does one who'd fled at the earliest opportunity have to speak for those who remained behind? If Vincent DeSantis isn't pissed, why should I be?

NOT LONG AFTER Emily was married, I finished my wedding novel, at the last minute pulling poor Jack Griffin back from the drain he'd been circling. His parents' ashes finally scattered, he was able to make a grudging peace with his past and live again in the present. The book came out and sold well enough for Barbara and me to consider getting that apartment in Boston, so when my book tour concluded we started scouting neighborhoods—the North End, which we both loved though it seemed not to offer what we were looking for; the South End, which was wonderful but not well served by the T; the Back Bay, which had little, at least in our view, to recommend it; and a small rectangle of blocks near South Station called the Leather District, which was convenient to both the train station and the Silver Line T that provided a straight shot out to Logan Airport. Emily and Steve were living in Amherst, Kate and Tom in London, and a place in Boston would make visiting both couples easier. Because, alas, we were entering a new world, one where we had to share our newly married daughters. Holidays would now have to be rotated—Christmas at one set of in-laws, Thanksgiving at the other.

That first year Christmas was ours, and we celebrated in Camden. Ten glorious days' worth of long dinners fueled by red wine, followed by card and board games that lasted into the wee hours and made zombies of us the following morning. Such festivities would have been impossible if my mother had been alive, which made for an odd mix of emotions, guilt chief among them. There were times when, to me, at least, she felt oddly present. *Why,* she seemed to be asking, *had we never had such good times when I was alive to enjoy them?* Had she ever had any idea that she was the one who'd been putting a damper on things? I doubted it. As a young woman she'd always been the life of the party, and she continued to think of herself in that role, even forty years after she could no longer play it. "Remember what *fun* we used to have at Christmas back on Helwig Street?" she liked to ask, genuinely bewildered that fun should elude us so completely now.

At the end of the holidays, though, came a surprise. Just before she and Tom were to return to England, Kate, partly at his insistence, confessed that she hadn't been doing so well in London. When she began to explain what was troubling her, the symptoms she needed to confront, some things came into focus. At times during their visit she'd seemed strangely on edge, borderline manic. We'd noticed that when anyone used the small, communal laptop computer we kept in the kitchen, she'd leave the room and return only when it was unoccupied. Over the last nine months, she told us now, certain sounds— the clacking of a keyboard, for instance—had begun to inspire in her not just annoyance but also genuine terror. Boarding the Tube or a London bus, she had to scan the compartment for laptop users and stay as far away from them as possible. If somebody pulled out a computer after she was settled, she had to move. She'd hoped that being home, away from the cacophony of urban sounds that were driving her nuts, would help, but in Camden the problem actually seemed exacerbated. Having done some online research, she thought she'd identified the problem, and she meant to see somebody as soon as she returned to London. For Barbara and me that wasn't soon enough, so with her permission we arranged for Kate to see a well-regarded anxiety specialist in Portland, and it took him about twenty minutes to confirm her self-diagnosis. She suffered from obsessive-compulsive disorder. With appropriate treatment, she would be fine. Without it, he warned, it would eat her alive.

The next day she and Tom left for London with the names of several good therapists there, and we returned to Camden with a newly purchased book on the subject, which I began to read with foreboding that quickly escalated into full-blown horror and roiling nausea. Because right there in the introduction was the long parade of bizarre behaviors I'd been witnessing in my mother since I was a boy: how she always had to keep her possessions arranged "just so," her love of arbitrary rules for their own sake, her need to "even things up" (the same number of folds to the right and left of the middle on her curtain rods), her constant checking on things she'd already checked in order to "be sure," but then continuing to worry anyway. Worse, all this was here defined as mental illness. That, of course, had been my father's amateur diagnosis: "You *do* know your mother's nuts, right?"

But surely his observation wasn't intended to be clinical.

He'd only meant that for the sake of my own sanity I'd do well to accept that my mother was "batty," half a bubble off of plumb, one card shy of a deck, a few rungs short of a ladder. Supply your own comic metaphor. But the language of this book was neither comic nor euphemistic. Here my mother's "nerves" were anxieties and panic attacks. Nor were such distinctions merely semantic. Crippling anxieties and incapacitating panics (unlike nerves) were serious conditions that demanded treatment. Mental illness, like physical illness, first required diagnosis, then appropriate therapy. Kate had already gotten the first and was embarking on the second. My mother had received neither, and the result had been precisely what the Portland anxiety specialist predicted. She'd gradually been eaten alive.

It wasn't a long book, but I found I could read no more than a short chapter at a sitting. Even then I sometimes had to put the book aside for days or weeks before I returned to it. Description after description, case study after case study, and every single one pertinent. How many times, going as far back as Phoenix, had I asked her why she was obsessing over little things when important matters demanded our attention? *Obsessing* was the word I'd actually used, but I was still astonished to encounter it in a medical book about a condition my mother apparently suffered from. And of course it was beyond demoralizing to see that so many of her "idiosyncrasies" were in fact quite common in the literature of obsession, that they were linked in some fashion to a general, irrational fear of contamination, the same broad anxiety that led so many OCD sufferers to indulge in ritual, repetitive hand washing. When

I'd confronted my mother about obsessing over minutiae, I was merely recommending that she act rationally. It never occurred to me that, as this book suggested, she *couldn't,* that something was preventing her and actually holding her reason hostage. In those afflicted by OCD, the book explained, the part of the brain responsible for decision making is thought to be impaired, which is why they have trouble with rational sequencing or, as I referred to it earlier, triage—*this now, that later.*

Also under constant attack is the obsessive's sense of proportion. All her life my mother had a profound aversion to anything yellow, even to flowers that came in that color. Daffodils in particular provoked in her a visceral disgust. Of course healthy people have favorite and least favorite colors. M&M'S all taste the same, but many people irrationally prefer the red ones. Normal people, however, don't *fear* the red ones. They wouldn't cull the red ones or become ill if forced to eat some. Nor would a healthy person come totally unglued if one day her favorite brand of tissue was available only in yellow, as my mother once had in a supermarket. A normal person wouldn't stand paralyzed in the middle of the aisle, quivering with rage and frustration. Yellow made my mother sick to her stomach. She knew it shouldn't and that it didn't do that to other people. But that's what yellow did to her, and how do you argue with a sensation?

Indeed, it's at the level of sensation that an obsessive's anxieties often rule. From the time she was a girl, my mother claimed, she'd had an extraordinarily acute sense of smell. She regarded this as an asset, like twenty-twenty vision, though its consequences were uniformly unpleasant. She considered olive oil a foul, corrupt substance, and no amount of evidence regarding its health benefits could shake that conviction. Back on Helwig Street, when we sat on the front porch on summer evenings, she'd be driven indoors by "vile" smells that only she could detect emanating from a house across the street, where an Italian American family lived. They cooked in *oil,* she explained, her face contorting in revulsion, not butter, like we did. Her obsession with food odors intensified after she left Helwig Street and started living in apartments, where her neighbors were closer to hand, their kitchens on the opposite side of a thin wall. "What's with your mother and all the Air Wicks?" my wife wanted to know the first time we visited her in Phoenix. Even then there'd been air fresheners in every room, two in the bathroom, all opened to the max. Every apartment my mother ever lived in smelled like the inside of a can of Glade.

She was still relatively young when I first began wondering if the smells that tormented her might not have any basis in objective reality. Often the same odor that made her gag seemed to me quite pleasant, if sometimes redolent of spices and herbs she herself never used, such as cumin, coriander, tarragon, and cilantro. More tellingly, the offending aromas always emanated from the apartments of people she didn't like anyway, as was the case with the Helwig Street Italians. In my own house garlic and olive oil came together in the early stages of a great many meals, and for a long time I thought only politeness had prevented my mother from remarking on the same smells there that elsewhere made her ill. Each time she recounted some new tale of oil or garlic wafting across the hall into her apartment, I wondered if this was a hint that I should refrain from using these ingredients whenever she came to dinner. Except in truth it was the exact opposite. Many of her favorite meals, the ones she most often asked for, were heavy with the very ingredients she claimed to loathe.

It also occurred to me that there might be a link between these odor aversions and her lifelong devotion to frozen dinners. Back in Gloversville they'd made sense. At the end of a long workday, why would she want to take the time and trouble to prepare a meal for just herself? Furthermore, as she was always quick to point out, cooking for one was expensive. American food manufacturers packaged their products for families, not single people. But at some point I began to suspect it was really all about the odors, which she maintained were magnified in the small kitchens that were part and parcel of apartment living. Residing as I did in a big house, she gave me to understand (as if I'd never lived in confined quarters), I'd have no way of knowing that. By the time she was middle-aged, though, even her frozen dinners had become problematic, and she often confessed to dreading meals, almost as if the necessity of eating were itself somehow shameful. In her apartment she ate quickly, then immediately rinsed the aluminum container the food came in before crushing it and putting it in the trash. Next she tied off the garbage bag, even if it was only a quarter full, and hurried it out to the Dumpster or the garbage room, because otherwise, she explained, by morning the *stench* would be unbearable. Where other obsessives feared contaminated fluids or dirt, my mother seemed particularly focused on airborne contagion. She lived in terror of common colds, and when she caught one she always claimed to know exactly who'd given it to her. Invariably, the culprit was someone she didn't like.

As dispiriting as it was to recognize my mother on virtually every page of the OCD book, it was even more painful to recognize myself as her principal enabler. Because, like alcoholics and other addicts, obsessives can't do it on their own. As they gradually lose the control they so desperately seek, they have little choice but to ensnare loved ones. My mother had begun that process back in Gloversville, by threatening on one hand that she might suffer a nervous breakdown if I wasn't a good boy and on the other crediting me with helping to pull her back from the brink each time she melted down. As a kid, though, my enabling duties had been shared with my grandparents, who lived right downstairs, as well as, to a lesser extent, her sister, my aunt Phyllis. Moving to Arizona, of course, got me promoted to Chief Emotional Guardian.

One of the sadder truths of childhood is that children, lacking the necessary experience by which to gauge, are unlikely to know if something is abnormal or unnatural unless an adult tells them. Worse, once anything of the sort has been established as normal, it will likely be perceived as such well into adulthood, and this is particularly true for the only child, who has no one to compare notes with. As a boy—and later a young man—I'd often wished my mother wouldn't enlist me in her personal, highly private struggles, but I never saw anything really wrong with her doing so. To me, this seemed a natural extension of our old Helwig Street accord, our mutually acknowledged special relationship—that I would always be able to depend on her and she on me. In one respect she and I were fortunate. Compared with others suffering from OCD, she exhibited relatively few time-consuming rituals (like hand washing). What she did require was lots of bolstering ("bucking up," she called it), especially when she suffered an actual or imagined setback. She constantly needed to be assured that everything was okay, that *she* was okay or at least would be once this or that obstacle to her emotional equilibrium had been removed. It never occurred to me, even as an adult, that such assurances could be damaging, that in offering them over and over I was making her situation worse, not better. My failure, or so I concluded, was that I didn't offer even more of them; imagining this lack of generosity, born of exasperation, was my biggest shortcoming.

What *I* couldn't see was, however, clear to others. My father-in-law had immediately recognized that something was wrong, which was why he'd warned Barbara not to let my mother move in with us that first time. Over the years, as she wove herself more deeply into the fabric of our married lives, my wife also came to understand that I was aiding and abetting her demons. In fact, she warned me of this repeatedly, for all the good it did her. She and her father came by their wisdom rightly. Barbara's mother was an alcoholic, and it was her father who, through willful ignorance and disregard of mounting evidence, had enabled her to appear normal to both outsiders and Barbara's younger siblings. Of course Barbara had no more idea than I did that my mother had OCD. Even now she's less certain of it than I am. But she'd witnessed firsthand what came of trying to reason with someone whose reason was compromised. And it was clear to her that by covering up for my mother when she came unglued, by giving her to understand that no matter what she said or did I'd never abandon her, by not insisting that she seek help, I was giving her what she wanted but not what she needed. She also understood that if my mother was trapped in repetitive behaviors, so was I. Indeed, I must have reminded her of her father, whose inability to intervene when his wife's drinking spiraled out of control had been rooted in love, yes, but also in fear, not just that something terrible could happen if he interfered, but that it would be his fault. He wasn't going to confront his wife because he couldn't, and I wasn't going to challenge my mother for the same reason. Which meant that Barbara's choice was simple and stark and diabolically unfair: she could stay or leave. What she couldn't do was alter in the slightest our doomed trajectory.

NOT LONG AFTER Kate and Tom returned to London I got a letter from John Freeman, the editor of *Granta,* asking if I had any interest in writing about Gloversville—the real place, not one of my many fictional avatars. The magazine was planning a special "going home" issue, and a couple days earlier,

on the New York State Thruway, he'd passed the Gloversville
exit and thought of me. If I were to take on the assignment,
Freeman reminded me, the article itself would be a kind of
homecoming, as *Granta* had published an excerpt from one of
my early novels back in the mid-Eighties. I hadn't been in the
magazine since, so the idea was appealing. I hesitated, though.
Would I actually have to go to Gloversville? If so, what would
I do there, exactly? Write about how things seemed there now
compared with when I was a kid? See if Pedrick's still existed
and who was drinking there these days? Knock on the door at
36 Helwig Street and introduce myself to whoever lived there
now? Because I emphatically wanted no part of any of this. For
the family memorial service we'd held that summer, Barbara
and I had gotten a motel room out on the arterial highway and
reserved a private room at an old-line Johnstown inn, a favorite
of my mother's, for the dinner in her honor. I didn't go into
Gloversville at all. Had I read the OCD book at the time, I
might have recognized that my sneaking in and out like a bur-
glar fell quite comfortably within the spectrum of unnatural
and unhealthy behaviors, but that would come later. The way I
saw it then, I was like Bartleby. I *could* go to Gloversville; I just
"preferred not to."

Now, a year later, I was even more adamant, so when I
called John I told him that yes, I'd like to write for the special
issue, perhaps using some of my cousin's beam-house stories as
a jumping-off point, my only stipulation being that my "going
home" was strictly metaphorical. He quickly agreed, since, if
I had everything I needed to write the piece, why make the

physical journey? Perhaps, sensing just how strong my aversion was, he'd intuited that I had become the literal embodiment of Thomas Wolfe's famous maxim and that maybe *this* was where the real story was. With a little luck, my inability to actually go home again might bring to the theme something interesting, off-kilter, and possibly insane.

Not long after our conversation, as I worked at putting some of my cousin's experiences onto the page, my wandering eye happened to fall on *Toward Civic Integrity: Re-establishing the Micropolis,* that Gloversville book. It sat right where I'd tossed it so contemptuously months earlier, half buried now by a dozen other unwanted volumes on my personal literary slag heap. Recalling the vague boosterism of the accompanying letter and guessing the book probably had a shaky foundation of sentimentality and unguarded optimism, I doubted yet again whether there could be anything in it for me, though of course that was hardly fair. After all, I hadn't read a word of it. Was it possible that beneath my mean-spirited, semieducated assumptions there lurked a revealing prejudice? *How good could the book be?* had been my unconscious logic. *The author's from Gloversville!* And so, in a spirit of grudging fair play, I picked up the book and began to read.

To my surprise I discovered that Vincent DeSantis and I shared quite a few political and cultural convictions. It was clear to both of us, for instance, that the old manufacturing jobs that provided the economic lifeblood of towns like Gloversville were gone for good, no matter how much we might wish otherwise. We also agreed that an America that makes less *is* less. He was as profoundly interested in the new urban movement as I, and just as convinced that the time has come to start planning communities for people instead of their cars because the days of cheap energy are dwindling down to a precious few. A micropolis, as DeSantis defined it, had, like Gloversville, a population of ten to fifty thousand, and he argued persuasively that such communities might be well positioned to prosper in a less autocentric future. They had the kind of infrastructure—a downtown—that would be essential, assuming it hadn't been razed back in the Sixties. Ironically, the abandoned mills, rather than being a blight on the landscape, could become part of the solution once they'd been retrofitted to new purposes. What's more, Mr. DeSantis argued, while their next incarnation was unlikely to have much in common with the original one, that didn't mean it wouldn't be just as valid. What he and I saw eye to eye on, strangely enough, was the future, or at least a possible future.

But what a nest of thorns the past can be. "The glove industry sustained Gloversville in fine style," he enthused. "Factories were full of glove cutters and glove makers, and the sound of sewing machines and the smell of finished leather . . . were a part of everyday life in Gloversville." I, too, happen to love the smell of finished leather, but I'm able to appreciate it only because I never worked in a beam house (and my guess was that DeSantis hadn't either). But weren't there women in his family, as there were in mine, who'd sewn gloves for fifty years and, after they finally retired, earned pensions of less than fifty dollars a month? While his view of the Gloversville of our youth—it turned out he was just a year older than I—wasn't false, it rested on a foundation of carefully selected facts and memories. For him, the old days when the skin mills were in full swing were good because of the wealth and prosperity they generated. He recalled his aunts and uncles lamenting the loss of jobs overseas, then generously concluded that "in fairness to the glove companies . . . failure to take advantage . . . of cheap labor would have been tantamount to corporate suicide." Well, okay, but if a dramatic phrase like "corporate suicide" fairly describes the tanneries' untenable options in 1950, by the same token didn't their disregard for the health and welfare of the workers who created their fortunes qualify as "corporate murder"? Or, coupled with a bottom line mentality that led so many to flee the scene of the crime, "corporate rape"? Chrome tanning had never been anything but lethal, its byproducts including lime, chlorine, formaldehyde, sulfuric acid, chromium (III), glycol ether EB, toluene, xylol, magnesium sulfate, lead, copper, and zinc, to name just a few. Anyone who thinks the tanneries didn't know they were releasing carcinogens into Gloversville's air, water, and landfills probably also believes that tobacco companies had no idea their cigarettes might be hazardous to the health of smokers. In addition to chasing cheap labor overseas, the big glove shops had tried to escape— successfully, for the most part—their own day of reckoning. New environmental restrictions imposed by the Department of Labor, and later by the Occupational Safety and Health Administration, had made the industry unprofitable, whereas on the other side of the world there were no such restrictions (and wouldn't be for decades). When it became clear that Fulton County tanneries wouldn't be allowed to keep dumping into the Cayadutta Creek, they up and left rather than pay the sewer taxes levied to support a new facility specifically designed and built to safely dispose of their waste. Off they blithely went to pollute rivers in India and the Philippines, leaving behind a veritable Love Canal of carcinogens, the cleanup bill to be paid by the poisoned.

Of course in its heyday, as DeSantis rightly pointed out, Gloversville was more than glove shops and tanneries. A community, even one dominated by a single industry that hated and feared competition, still needed grocery stores, bakeries, restaurants, insurance agencies, clothing stores, and car dealerships, schools and teachers and libraries and a movie theater, but when that industry vanishes these other enterprises inevitably become endangered. It wasn't just the mills that were abandoned when the good times—if that's what they were—stopped rolling. What's also lost, as he noted, is part of your identity, your reason for being, a shared sense of purpose that's hard to quantify. People who make things are often proud of what they produce, especially if it endures. One summer my father and I worked on exit 23 on the New York State Thruway, and thereafter we were never able to get on that cloverleaf without sharing a knowing look. But sometimes people are so proud of what they make that they willingly overlook its true cost. That Gloversville once had an identity based on a common sense of purpose is a potent argument. It's been used, for instance, to explain the construction of the great cathedrals of Europe, and what were they if not symbols of communal wealth and belief? Given the technology of the day, the Pyramids are even more awe inspiring, at least until one remembers they were built with slave labor. Closer to home, the Confederacy was a case study in shared values and cultural identity, whose foundation, of course, was slavery; decades after the war that freed its victims, Margaret Mitchell did precisely what Vincent DeSantis was now doing by inviting her readers to lament the passing of those halcyon days that in her beloved South were now *Gone With the Wind*.

My mother's favorite book.

WORKING ON the *Granta* piece, I once again began dreaming about her. Not nightmares like before—no more carrying her through Kafkaesque dreamscapes, no more crazy, middle-of-the-night phone calls wanting to know when I was going to come fetch her home from Europe. In this round she and I are back in Gloversville, in my grandfather's house. I'm not visiting; I live there, and in fact have never lived anywhere except on Helwig Street. I'm a younger man, but not a kid. I'm neither married nor a parent. My life as a teacher and later as a writer never happened.

There's something oddly sweet and comforting about all this, probably because, except for my grandfather, we're all together again in a familiar and well-loved place. But it's unsettling, too, since in these dreams the house is always in terrible decay, something my grandfather would never have allowed to happen. Gaping holes in the roof allow the weather to come in, and the walls have been invaded by rot. The porches slope, and the railings have detached from their posts. Sometimes all this is something we're aware of, part of the dream's dramatic structure and plot. More often, though, I alone discover it and then have to conceal this terrible knowledge from my mother and grandmother, because we have no money for repairs. Finally I have no choice but to take my mother up into the attic to show her the holes in the roof, then down into the cellar where a black lake has formed, and she shrieks with horror. She wants to know what we're going to do. It's the only home we've got.

Though she invariably appears in them and has a dramatic role, I realize these dreams aren't really about her at all. They're about Gloversville, about a ruined house that in the slightly out-of-plumb language of dreams stands in for the town Vincent DeSantis believes can be saved and I do not. Their inspiration wasn't my mother's illness and death so much as my grandfather's. The central drama is located in the years immediately after his passing, when my mother and my grandmother lived together and didn't have enough money to keep the house in good repair. Not long afterward, once I'd brought her to southern Illinois to live near us, the house had to be sold. Later, after my grandmother's death, when I visited my aunt and uncle and cousins, I always drove by 36 Helwig Street and saw all-too-evident signs of neglect—the peeling paint, the unmowed lawn—and felt at once the betrayed and the betrayer. One year the hazardously sloping back porches, up and down, had been amputated, and nobody had even bothered to paint over the scars. The back door I was in and out of a hundred times a day as a boy now opened into thin air, a four-foot drop to a rectangle of hard brown earth that the house's new owner couldn't be bothered to seed. After that I no longer had the heart, or maybe the stomach, to bear witness, so strong was my sense of personal failure. Now, more than a decade later, I couldn't bear to return to Gloversville at all.

Maybe these new Helwig Street dreams didn't originate in my mother's death, but that didn't mean her powerfully ambivalent feelings about Fulton County weren't their ultimate source. From my childhood, her hatred of Gloversville was like the North Star, the one you navigate by, because otherwise you're lost, completely untethered. That was precisely what happened to her every single time she left. No sooner was she elsewhere—*anywhere* else—than her loathing morphed seamlessly into loss. Once she was free of it, the house on Helwig Street, the cage she was forever trying to escape, became the central object of her longing. She wasn't well, of course, but I don't think paradoxes of this sort are unknown to healthy people, and I don't blame her for being unable to resolve it. After all, I haven't been able to either.

Rather than confront my own love-hate relationship with my hometown, I simply created other Gloversvilles in my imagination. Since they don't exist outside my head, I'm free to love Mohawk and Empire Falls and Thomaston without inviting the sense of betrayal I felt when my mother and I returned from Martha's Vineyard and I made the mistake of telling her I was glad to be home, an innocent remark that for all I know set in motion our foolhardy journey to Arizona years later, as well as everything else that was to follow. My fictional towns never trailed real-world consequences. Better yet, there's no question of going back because, like the "me" of the new Helwig Street dreams, I never left. I click the heels of my ruby slippers and there I am with Sully and Miss Beryl and Sam Hall and Mather Grouse. Tessa and Big Lou Lynch are right around the corner, as are Miles Roby and his daughter, Tick. Ikey Lubin's corner store is nearby, and a few blocks farther along, on lower Main Street, there's Hattie's Lunch. They're not Mayberry, my stand-in Gloversvilles. Bad things happen there. Out behind the old Bijou, Three Mock, a black boy, gets beaten half to death for sitting next to a white girl in the theater; young, horrifically abused John Voss furnishes his wardrobe out of the Dumpster behind the Empire Grill and plots revenge; and on the outskirts of town another unfortunate boy hangs impaled atop a fence, an iron spike protruding from his open mouth like a black tongue. And the toxic stream, running blue one day, red the next, always meanders through town, touching everyone, linking everyone, poisoning everyone.

My fictional hometowns are no better or worse than the real one. They're just mine, mostly because I'm free to see them with my own eyes, whereas the real Gloversville (as I'm coming to understand, thanks to Vincent DeSantis's book) I still see with my mother's. The paralyzing anxiety I feel at the thought of returning home is her legacy. She always maintained that her one claim to fame was getting me out of there, away from the shambling, self-satisfied, uncouth, monumentally stupid people who believed they were lucky to live where they did, lucky to have low-paying jobs in the skin mills that starved them and chopped off their fingers and gave them cancer before moving shop to the Third World. When I listen to my cousin's stories about men diagnosed and maimed and poisoned and killed, part of what I feel is grim satisfaction that so little has in fact changed since he and I were boys. We share a profound sense of moral outrage that Mr. DeSantis has somehow escaped, but Greg, because he's not only lived his whole life in the real Gloversville but also raised a fine family there, has resolved the paradox that eluded my mother and still eludes me. Gloversville is his home. It breaks his heart on a daily basis, but that doesn't change the fact. His father's buried in the cemetery there, along with both his paternal and maternal grandparents, their lives and deaths tied, directly or indirectly, to the skin mills. If there were a magic wand that could make the place all better, he'd wave it until his arm fell off, and that, I suspect, is the biggest difference between us. The shameful truth is that part of me doesn't *want* Humpty Dumpty to be put back together again. I readily admit that's neither fair nor just. Though I can't justify doing so, it appears that on this topic I've taken my mother's part. Gloversville got what it deserved. So what if this opinion isn't really even mine? So what if it's contradicted by all my novels? It's still the oldest opinion I know. Surrender that one, and it would be like she was never here.

IT WILL PROBABLY COME as no surprise that the apartment my wife and I eventually settled on in Boston is located in the old Leather District. Just about every building there sports a plaque identifying the business that originally was plied there. We're on the seventh floor of an eight-story building, high and dry, as the saying goes, which I think would have made my grandfather smile. Leather was always a vertical industry. It went from low and wet in the beam house to high and dry in the sewing and cutting rooms, where the work was slightly better paid and less hazardous. As a small boy I remember standing on the sidewalk below and sighting along my mother's index finger up to the top floor of the glove shop where my grandfather worked and sensing her pride in him. Perhaps I understood the principle of verticality even then.

Though I'm sure he was grateful not to work in the beam house, I doubt my grandfather really thought of himself as privileged. His pay was never commensurate with his craft. The efficient new machines, together with the relentless drumbeat of piecework and the ever-shorter work season, ensured that he'd die poor. And he surely knew the work, even on the top floors, was far from safe. Sure, the tanned skins were dry by the time they got up there, but they were also full of hide dust that, breathed over a lifetime, could kill you. For years he didn't worry about his shortness of breath. He'd come home from the Pacific with malaria, and maybe that explained it. But by the time he bought the house on Helwig Street he must've known his luck had run out. A decade later, when it was no longer possible to ignore his worsening symptoms, he was finally diagnosed with emphysema by doctors who had little doubt that his occupation was a contributing factor. But he was also an occasional smoker, and he never stopped, not entirely, even when he knew that each new cigarette reduced the time he had left. Even if he thought he could win, I doubt he would've sued his employers because, as he would've been the first to point out, the glove shops had put bread on his family's table for all those years, and without them what would he have done? How would he have made a living otherwise? Bitterness and recrimination weren't worth the little breath he still had. In his way my grandfather was a philosopher, and he would've wanted me to be suspicious of any bitterness I harbored on his behalf, just as he would've reminded me of the terrible possibility that what nourishes us in this life might be the very thing that steals that life away from us.

I sometimes wonder what he would have made of the fact that the house and town my mother and I fled back in 1967 would nourish my creative life for more than three decades. I have no idea what he'd make of my reflex anxiety at the thought of ever returning home. The part of me that's rational knows perfectly well that I have nothing to fear there. I'm often reminded that many people in Gloversville have embraced my stories and think of me as a favored son. There's no reason that the mere thought of returning should make a frightened boy of me, a boy who, as the Helwig Street dreams suggest, will be overwhelmed by adult responsibilities he's helpless to meet. I loved that house and everyone in it. I still do. Just how much was revealed one night not long after we closed on the Boston apartment. Barbara was away, and after dinner I found myself navigating through the unfamiliar television channels, stopping on one called American Life. It was playing an episode of *77 Sunset Strip,* which was followed by *Bourbon Street Beat, Hawaiian Eye,* and *Surfside 6,* all shows we watched when I was a boy. At some point I became aware of the tears streaming down my face, realizing that I wasn't in Boston anymore, not really, but rather back home, stretched out on my grandparents' living room floor, with a pillow wadded up under my chin and—I have to say—happy.

But I don't want to be a boy again, not ever.

I wonder, too, what my grandfather would've thought about my mother's life had he been able to see it all the way to the end. Would he have blamed himself as a father, as I've sometimes blamed myself as a son? I have little desire to speculate on what his specific regrets might have been, but he wouldn't have let himself off easy, which maybe is why I can't. My own regrets, as these pages attest, are full and sufficient. It's worth saying, I think, that my own feelings of guilt and remorse have little to do with my failure to comprehend what was medically wrong with my mother, if indeed I understand it now. After all, it's only recently that OCD has been recognized for what it is, much less treated effectively. What distresses me most is that I made an exception for my mother in how I normally go about things. For almost as long as I can remember, my personal mantra has been: *When you don't know what to do, try something; if that doesn't work, try something else.* Perhaps I came to this philosophy as a natural consequence of living with an obsessive. One thing obsessives have in common is they seldom try something else. By nature ritualistic, they try the same thing over and over, always hoping against hope that this time the results will be different, possibly even good. Their cycles have to be interrupted or they're doomed. Perhaps because my mother's were so clearly established when I was a boy and I'd been drawn into them so early, I never had much faith that they *could* be altered. To me they seemed like the tides: necessary, inevitable, much more powerful than I.

I now know that I should have tried something else. Not as a boy, of course, but later as a man. Because even if I couldn't comprehend what I was dealing with, I was not ill equipped to at least try something and, if that didn't work, to try something else. For the last two decades of my mother's life, I was a working novelist, and novelists, if they know anything, should know how important stories are, that narratives often provide the key to things that run deeper in us, in our basic humanity, than can be diagnosed by even the most skilled physician. Given how often I'd heard it, I should have recognized the importance and meaning of my mother's Easter story, the one where she and her sister got new dresses and my grandmother did not.

One of the heartbreaking ironies of OCD is that the myriad anxieties of those afflicted invariably have a common denominator if not a single source. A person terrified of being abandoned and ending up alone will inevitably develop a series of obsessions and rituals that virtually guarantee this precise result. What my mother, a child of the Great Depression, dreaded most was poverty, a fear rooted in her not-at-all-insane conviction that in America, poor people might make the nation's clothes, build its highways and bridges, and win its wars, but in the end they don't matter. Her need to be free and live independently was real, but that wasn't the point. What independence meant to her was that she wouldn't be poor like her parents were, like the people she grew up around had always been, like the nation itself was during her formative years. What must have terrified her after I came along and her marriage to my father failed was the possibility that no matter how hard she tried, she'd always come up a little short. That fear wafted across Helwig Street from the house where the poorest family on the block lived. To her, fear smelled like the olive oil they cooked with because—or so she imagined—they couldn't afford butter.

Poverty. *That* was the odor that turned her stomach and made her sick with yellow panic and suggested that "things . . . you know . . . won't turn out right," a thought that scared her worse than death itself. Had I understood this in time, had my moral imagination—any writer's most valuable gift, perhaps everyone's—not failed me, I could at least have . . .

Could have what? The story ends here because I don't know how to complete that sentence. My family assures me I did everything that could've been done, and I don't know why it should seem so important that I resist the very conclusion that would let me off the hook. Maybe it's because I've never been a fan of grim, scientific determinism, or perhaps it's a writer's nature (or at least mine) to gnaw and worry and bury and unearth anything that resists comprehension. But who knows? Maybe it's just hubris, a stubborn insistence that if we keep trying one thing after another, we can coerce the ineffable into finally expressing itself. How tantalizingly close it seems even now, right there on the tip of my tongue before slipping away. But no doubt I'm misjudging the distance, being my mother's son.

Acknowledgments

No memoirist likes to admit to a poor memory, but that, alas, is what I'm saddled with. For this reason I'm particularly grateful to my wife and daughters for correcting me on details I got wrong or out of sequence. I'm also deeply indebted to my aunt Phyllis Gottung, who set me straight about some events from the early years. She fiercely loved and was loyal to her big sister, and if she'd known at the time to what use I meant to put our conversations about my mother's life and struggles, she might not have been so forthcoming. At the beginning, of course, I myself didn't know where my curiosity was leading. I'm also much indebted to my cousins, Greg and Jim Gottung, for all the Gloversville skin-mill stories they shared with me over the years. Whatever I managed to get wrong despite the best efforts of my family is my fault, not theirs.

Acknowledgments

Despite my initial treatment of it, I'm also grateful to Judge Vincent DeSantis for sending me his book about Gloversville. I suspect we each love our hometown, if for very different reasons. And special thanks to John Freeman at *Granta* for nudging me at just the right moment.

To my mother I owe, well, just about everything, and to some readers these pages may seem like a strange way to repay such an enormous debt. All I can say is, this isn't a story I tried to remember; it's one I'd have given a good deal to forget. But despite my impressive amnesiac gifts, it refused to be forgotten, and I hope that that's because it's true in the ways that matter most.

A NOTE ON THE TYPE

This book was set in Garamond, a type named for the famous Parisian type cutter Claude Garamond (ca. 1480–1561). Garamond, a pupil of Geoffroy Tory, based his letter on the types of the Aldine Press in Venice, but he introduced a number of important differences, and it is to him that we owe the letter now known as "old style."

The version of Garamond used for this book was first introduced by the Monotype Corporation of London in 1922. It is not a true copy of any of the designs of Claude Garamond, but can be attributed to Jean Jannon, a Protestant printer working in Sedan in the early seventeenth century, who had worked with Garamond's romans earlier but who was denied their use because of Catholic censorship. Jannon's matrices came into the possession of the Imprimerie Nationale, where they were thought to be by Garamond himself, and were so described when the Imprimerie revived the type in 1900. The italic is based on the types of Robert Granjon, a type cutter and printer active in Antwerp, Lyons, Paris, and Rome from 1523 to 1590.

Typeset by Scribe, Philadelphia, Pennsylvania

Printed and bound by R. R. Donnelley, Harrisonburg, Virginia

Designed by Cassandra J. Pappas